Defining Identity and the Changing Scope of Culture in the Digital Age

Alison Novak
Rowan University, USA

Imaani Jamillah El-Burki
Lehigh University, USA

A volume in the Advances in Human and Social
Aspects of Technology (AHSAT) Book Series

Information Science
REFERENCE
An Imprint of IGI Global

Published in the United States of America by
    Information Science Reference (an imprint of IGI Global)
    701 E. Chocolate Avenue
    Hershey PA, USA 17033
    Tel: 717-533-8845
    Fax: 717-533-8661
    E-mail: cust@igi-global.com
    Web site: http://www.igi-global.com

Library of Congress Cataloging-in-Publication Data

Names: Novak, Alison, editor. | El-Burki, Imaani Jamillah, 1981- editor.
Title: Defining identity and the changing scope of culture in the digital age
  / Alison Novak and Imaani Jamillah El-Burki, editors.
Description: Hershey, PA : Information Science Reference, [2016] | Includes
  bibliographical references and index.
Identifiers: LCCN 2016003146| ISBN 9781522502128 (hardcover) | ISBN
  9781522502135 (ebook)
Subjects: LCSH: Information technology--Social aspects. | Technological
  innovations--Social aspects. | Identity (Psychology) | Social change.
Classification: LCC HM851 .D4346 2016 | DDC 303.48/33--dc23 LC record available at http://lccn.loc.gov/2016003146

This book is published in the IGI Global book series Advances in Human and Social Aspects of Technology (AHSAT) (ISSN: 2328-1316; eISSN: 2328-1324)

British Cataloguing in Publication Data
A Cataloguing in Publication record for this book is available from the British Library.

All work contributed to this book is new, previously-unpublished material. The views expressed in this book are those of the authors, but not necessarily of the publisher.

For electronic access to this publication, please contact: eresources@igi-global.com.

Advances in Human and Social Aspects of Technology (AHSAT) Book Series

Ashish Dwivedi
The University of Hull, UK

ISSN: 2328-1316
EISSN: 2328-1324

Mission

In recent years, the societal impact of technology has been noted as we become increasingly more connected and are presented with more digital tools and devices. With the popularity of digital devices such as cell phones and tablets, it is crucial to consider the implications of our digital dependence and the presence of technology in our everyday lives.

The **Advances in Human and Social Aspects of Technology (AHSAT) Book Series** seeks to explore the ways in which society and human beings have been affected by technology and how the technological revolution has changed the way we conduct our lives as well as our behavior. The AHSAT book series aims to publish the most cutting-edge research on human behavior and interaction with technology and the ways in which the digital age is changing society.

Coverage

- Information ethics
- Philosophy of technology
- Technology Dependence
- Technology Adoption
- Human-Computer Interaction
- ICTs and human empowerment
- Computer-Mediated Communication
- Technology and Freedom of Speech
- End-User Computing
- Cultural Influence of ICTs

IGI Global is currently accepting manuscripts for publication within this series. To submit a proposal for a volume in this series, please contact our Acquisition Editors at Acquisitions@igi-global.com or visit: http://www.igi-global.com/publish/.

Titles in this Series

For a list of additional titles in this series, please visit: www.igi-global.com

Gender Considerations in Online Consumption Behavior and Internet Use
Rebecca English (Queensland University of Technology, Australia) and Raechel Johns (University of Canberra, Australia)
Information Science Reference • copyright 2016 • 297pp • H/C (ISBN: 9781522500100) • US $165.00 (our price)

Analyzing Digital Discourse and Human Behavior in Modern Virtual Environments
Bobbe Gaines Baggio (American University, USA)
Information Science Reference • copyright 2016 • 320pp • H/C (ISBN: 9781466698994) • US $175.00 (our price)

Overcoming Gender Inequalities through Technology Integration
Joseph Wilson (University of Maiduguri, Nigeria) and Nuhu Diraso Gapsiso (University of Maiduguri, Nigeria)
Information Science Reference • copyright 2016 • 324pp • H/C (ISBN: 9781466697737) • US $185.00 (our price)

Cultural, Behavioral, and Social Considerations in Electronic Collaboration
Ayse Kok (Bogazici University, Turkey) and Hyunkyung Lee (Yonsei University, South Korea)
Business Science Reference • copyright 2016 • 374pp • H/C (ISBN: 9781466695566) • US $205.00 (our price)

Handbook of Research on Cultural and Economic Impacts of the Information Society
P.E. Thomas (Bharathiar University, India) M. Srihari (Bharathiar University, India) and Sandeep Kaur (Bharathiar University, India)
Information Science Reference • copyright 2015 • 618pp • H/C (ISBN: 9781466685987) • US $325.00 (our price)

Human Behavior, Psychology, and Social Interaction in the Digital Era
Anabela Mesquita (CICE – ISCAP/Polytechnic of Porto, Portugal & Algoritmi Centre, Minho University, Portugal) and Chia-Wen Tsai (Ming Chuan University, Taiwan)
Information Science Reference • copyright 2015 • 372pp • H/C (ISBN: 9781466684508) • US $200.00 (our price)

Rethinking Machine Ethics in the Age of Ubiquitous Technology
Jeffrey White (Korean Advanced Institute of Science and Technology, KAIST, South Korea) and Rick Searle (IEET, USA)
Information Science Reference • copyright 2015 • 331pp • H/C (ISBN: 9781466685925) • US $205.00 (our price)

Contemporary Approaches to Activity Theory Interdisciplinary Perspectives on Human Behavior
Thomas Hansson (Blekinge Institute of Technology, School of Management (MAM), Sweden)
Information Science Reference • copyright 2015 • 404pp • H/C (ISBN: 9781466666030) • US $195.00 (our price)

www.igi-global.com

701 E. Chocolate Ave., Hershey, PA 17033
Order online at www.igi-global.com or call 717-533-8845 x100
To place a standing order for titles released in this series, contact: cust@igi-global.com
Mon-Fri 8:00 am - 5:00 pm (est) or fax 24 hours a day 717-533-8661

Editorial Advisory Board

Table of Contents

Section 1
Race/Ethnicity

Section 2
Gender

Section 3
Age

Section 4
Intersectionality

Detailed Table of Contents

Section 1
Race/Ethnicity

Chapter 1

This chapter analyzes the content and responses of a popular video, "Shit Asian Dads Say," produced by YouTube production company JustKiddingFilms. In analyzing video content in conjunction with themes emerging from comments left in response to the video, the chapter discusses the ways in which comedic/ satirical, citizen-produced content on YouTube helps to shape, construct, and reflect the boundaries of group membership. As the video hinges on second-generation performances of immigrant parenthood, its content provides a prime site to investigate how age, gender and race are performed and become contested or reified in digital space. An analysis of the YouTube videos grounded in the responses, commentary and discussion that accompany the videos in the user comments, ultimately empowers viewers' interpretations of digital creative expression.

Chapter 2

Research shows that media representations of race, gender and social class designed for consumption by the millennial generation create a world of symbolic equality via narratives of racial harmony, female empowerment and forms of exaggeration where everyone seems to have a middle and or upper middle class quality of life. In general, the changing face of diversity as represented in media has been cast as a neoliberal politic, where ideologies of free markets are extended into representing a sense of equality among individuals and their respective social groups. While scholars have investigated exaggerated representations of inclusivity in a variety of media genres, there is limited scholarship investigating the ways in which comedy serves the neoliberalist agenda. Comedy Central's Roast of Justin Bieber aired March 2015 and has been replicated in multiple forms. The current study is an in depth discourse and content analysis of the racial and gender jokes appearing in this program. It concludes that what appears to be a move beyond race is instead working against a post-race reality.

Chapter 3

China's two major social media, the microblog Weibo and the messaging service WeChat have played important roles in representing citizens' voices and bringing about social changes. They often grow an ordinary event into a national debate as in the case of the Bi Fujian incident. They have also turned ordinary Chinese citizens into amateur reporters, empowering them to influence on issues that matter to them. An equalizer of power and discourse opportunity, the personalized and personal social media "weapons" are delivering the much needed social justice and consolation to the Chinese citizens amid widespread injustice, inequality, hypocrisy, indifference and corruption in the Chinese society.

Chapter 4

In our digital age, "Is there an app for that?" gets asked and answered for books, but not the canon, until the invention of an online, tessellating medium of personal choice expansion called TasteKid. Its voter-influenced algorithm continuously updates users' personalized canons seeded from whatever writer or title they choose. This atypical engendering of literacy challenges—perhaps inadvertently—what the canon is and how it can be experienced for readers new to critical or cultural literacy and Toni Morrison fans alike. In fact, her works get linked to other media by the thumbs up or down responses of site visitors. In this way, technology eclipses the canon's previous assumption of "the center" because only a reader's choice can occupy it. Likewise, with the distance between authors decreasing, (at the pace of the site visitors' unpredictable orders), the obsolescence of "margins" effects a power shift.

Chapter 5

In 2011, while the causes of Greek "crisis" started becoming the subject of public controversy, a documentary series aired on Skai channel vowing to challenge nationalist and populist accounts of the 1821 Revolution. By popularizing the main arguments of modernization theory, the "1821" documentary approached the past through the lens of "Cultural dualism" – the clash between a 'reformist' and an 'underdog' culture – and operated as a metaphor for contemporary Greece. Via the study of the media spectacle and the ways the history of 1821 goes public, historical inquiry can reflect on the normative/descriptive complex of rival historical narratives, exercise itself in perspectival seeing and self-reflexivity and move towards a history of the present.

Section 2
Gender

Chapter 6

Bryan McLaughlin, Texas Tech University, USA
Shawnika Hull, George Washington University, USA
Kang Namkoong, University of Kentucky – Lexington, USA
Dhavan Shah, University of Wisconsin – Madison, USA
David H. Gustafson, University of Wisconsin - Madison, USA

In the United States, women with breast cancer often find their identity confined by a sociocultural context that encourages them to adopt an overly optimistic outlook while hiding signs of their physical illness. Online social support groups offer a promising venue for breast cancer patients to take control of their self-definition and connect with individuals going through similar experiences. During the analysis of discussion board posts for an online breast cancer support group, ice cream unexpectedly emerged as a central component of group discussions. This included frequent sexual jokes about the deliverymen that brought the women ice cream. A grounded theory analysis revealed that ice cream symbolized the pursuit of everyday, physical desires, which allowed group members to construct a joyful, but forthright, shared identity. This paper demonstrates how online support groups can enable individuals facing a health crisis to use seemingly trivial symbols to take control over their self-definition.

Chapter 7

Greg Niedt, Drexel University, USA

This chapter presents an overview of the September 2014 controversy surrounding Facebook's enforcement of their "real name policy," the disproportionate targeting of drag performers for profile suspension, and the queer community's brief exodus to the network Ello. By drawing on research about identity in the online age, queer and subcultural theory, and the concept of affordances in social media, the author seeks to illuminate some of the causes of this incident, and the motivations of the actors involved. The online profile is framed as a locus for the construction of alternative identities—particularly those which challenge gender norms—as well as tension when that process is restricted. The author attempts to locate this concept of profiles, and the networked communities built from them, within a larger web of capital relations, exploring how the online and offline intersect therein.

Chapter 8

Dustin Kidd, Temple University, USA
Amanda J. Turner, Temple University, USA

The GamerGate controversy exploded in late 2014 and seemed to pit feminist game critics against misogynistic male gamers who were defending their territory. GamerGate has been filled with intense anger on all sides, and has even resulted in threats of murder and rape. This chapter attempts to explain why so much hostility erupted over what appears to some to be a feminist critique of gaming and to others to be a misogynist-gamer critique of feminism. At heart is a surprising debate about mainstream gaming vs. indie gaming, and discomfort over changes to the notion of what counts as gaming and who counts as a gamer. The authors use online ethnographic methods to piece together the various elements of this cultural narrative from the online and social media contexts where it unfolded.

Chapter 9

Charting connections between consumer protest, feminist activism and affordances of digital media, this chapter argues that social media and blogging platforms are becoming instrumental in creating new spaces for feminist action. Women's blog Jezebel (www.jezebel.com) has been chosen as a case study to examine how feminist bloggers use the dialogical environments of digital media to construct narratives of involvement in consumer culture. The chapter provides a critical overview of the major thematic categories identified on Jezebel. Such an analysis is particularly important for situating the blogosphere as a site of ongoing cultural negotiations while marking the limits of feminist consumer mobilization under the conditions of neoliberalism. The chapter concludes with the discussion of how Jezebel.com establishes a feminist networked space where bloggers construct diverse narratives of consumer activism.

Section 3
Age

Chapter 10

Previous scholarship has identified that as digital media platforms evolve, the potential of intercultural and cross generational communication continues to grow. Digital social media, in particular, has proven to be a valuable channel for users of different backgrounds (and ages) to communicate and speak with each other, often articulating and discussing cultural tensions. Previous research has identified the ubiquitous nature of digital social media as benefiting cross generational communication, as generational groups are often isolated from each other in the physical world, but connected in the digital field. This connection, therefore, provides an opportunity for intergenerational communication to take place, giving a platform for users of different age backgrounds to discuss topics previously quiet in the limited physical interactions.

Chapter 11

This chapter aims to focus on the impacts of some particular fashion adverts which are breaking the prevalent ideas regarding 'the representation of men' on Bangladeshi youths of different ages and areas by making a survey on the youths studying at different Bangladeshi universities. The media of the western countries are acquainted with these types of representation of men while the Bangladeshi media has let its viewers know about this lately through different advertisements specially fashion adverts. This new type of representation of men and "masculinity" or the emergence of "Metrosexual men" in the Bangladeshi media has its own impacts on the youths of Bangladesh whether it is about creating a new concept or it is only about dealing with the consumer culture. However, this chapter points to highlight on the fact that to what extent the concepts of the urban Bangladeshi youths (both male and female of different ages and areas) are molded by the emergence of this type of adverts in Bangladeshi media.

Chapter 12

Children and adolescents have become active users of electronic technologies, with many of them blogging, watching videos, and chatting via instant messenger and social networking sites. Many of these activities have become a typical part of their lives. Electronic technologies have brought many conveniences to the lives of children and adolescents. Along with the opportunities associated with these technologies, children and adolescents are also susceptible to risks, including cyberbullying. Therefore, many researchers have become concerned with identifying which factors might predict children's and adolescents' involvement in these behaviors. Some predictors that researchers have focused on include age, gender, and ethnicity, but the findings were mixed. This chapter draws on research to review studies on the relationship of age, gender, and ethnicity to children's and adolescents' cyberbullying involvement and concludes with solutions and recommendations as well as future directions for research focused on these predictors and cyberbullying.

Section 4
Intersectionality

Chapter 13

The internet has clearly become crucial for feminist organizing, enabling feminist associations to undertake both campaigns and counter-campaigns. Feminist groups and individuals are using social media to advocate policy, fight policy, promote discussions of problems, and argue against anti-feminist, misogynist and anti-progressive ideologies. This textual analysis of feminist accounts on Facebook, Twitter, Instagram, Tumblr and Pinterest demonstrates that feminist individuals and groups used these platforms to discuss structural gender issues, aspects of identity, daily practices, provide motivational material, and both justify and defend intersectional feminisms. Few groups on and site were anti-feminist. Using the theory of fluid public clusters, this chapter argues that social media are especially significant for minority feminists and feminists of color; they enable White and majority feminists to go beyond rhetorical proclamations of intersectionality and to enact alliances.

Chapter 14

Jannatul Akmam, Chittagong Government Women's College, Bangladesh
Nafisa Huq, Eastern University, Bangladesh

With the marking of the digital age, all forms of digital technologies become a part of the existence of human life, thereby, an extension of self. The ever-increasing influence of the virtual world or Internet cultures demands to read its complex relationship with human existence in a digital world. Theory of psychoanalysis, specifically object-relation theory can be called forth to analyze this multifaceted relationship. Within the light of this theory, Internet cultures are acting as "objects" like games, memes, chat rooms, social net etc. and the virtual world can be interpreted as the "object world". The chapter is interested in reading the deep psychoanalytic experience of people (with a special focus on the youth) in reference to their relationship with the virtual arena. The experience can be associated with religion, spirituality, perception of beauty, sexuality, Identity formation and so on. Their behavior and responses to the virtual world will be framed within the psychoanalytic paradigm in the light of "object relation theory" in a digital age.

Chapter 15

Gilbert Ndi Shang, University of Bayreuth, Germany

This chapter examines the revolution in self-representation across the cyber-space engendered by the advent of new interactive social medias. It argues that in the attempt to face the challenges of self-imaging in everyday life and in an era where discourses of "identities in flux" have become the norm, photographic trends on Facebook usage seek to portray a sense of coherence of the self through popular media practices. In this dimension, the new media spaces have provided a propitious space of autobiographic self-showing-narrating through a mixture of photos/texts in a way that deconstructs the privileges of self-narration hitherto available only to a privileged class of people. The self (and primarily the face) has thus become subject to a dynamic of personal and amateurish artistic practices that represent, from an existentialist perspective, the daily practices of self-making, un-making and re-making in articulating one's (social) being.

Chapter 16

Benjamin J. Cline, Western New Mexico University, USA

This chapter will use media ecology, and rhetorical theories of ideology construction and social intervention to look at the ways that contemporary digital media interact with religious and spiritual practices in order to inform and create identities. This chapter will examine the ideology construction that occurs in the Crosswire.org applications, specifically PocketSword designed for the iPhone/iPad and AndBible designed for Android devices. This chapter will also look at the ideology construction and identity creation in the English language section of onislam.net, a website designed to help English-speaking Muslims live out their faith. Finally the chapter will consider Osel Shen Phen Ling, a website designed for "Practicing Buddhadharma in the Tibetan Gelugpa Tradition".

Foreword

The present volume heeds a powerful call to address questions around identity formation and cultural shifts in the global digital world. As digital media continue to shape our reality in unprecedented ways, the selected contributions of *Defining Identity and the Changing Scope of Culture in the Digital Age* highlight the increasingly multi-layered and multidimensional relationships between life, media, and identity. Anchored in the rich discourses of intersectionality, the contributions to this volume shape the expanding academic work on globalization and changing understandings of policy, identity, culture and the public sphere.

The selections included in this collection provide important insights for scholars, activists, students and global citizens by creating an awareness of how the intersection of identity politics and digital media has collectively reconfigured our understanding of others and of ourselves. As social scientists and media specialists, the editors have done the heavy lifting of culling and organizing the most relevant and innovative, research in the field. In a contemporary moment where increasing social tensions along gendered, racial and generational coordinates continue to cast their corresponding publics into uncertainty and turmoil, *Defining Identity and the Changing Scope of Culture in the Digital Age* reflects and recognizes the layers of intersectionality required for engaging these critical issues. In a global digital world, the politics of identity and representation produce multiple points of contention in academe and in our broader society. The chapters in this volume deftly navigate the complexities of race, gender, and generational shifts within contemporary culture, directing attention to the way digital media narrate, incubate, and at times directly confront some of the most sensitive topics in the ever-expanding public sphere.

Moreover, the collected works of this volume acknowledge and respond to shifts in political discourse that prioritize an assumption of neoliberalism and hyper-individualism resulting from the illusion of a post-race, post-feminism, and post-age world. At the thematic heart of the volume is a progressive reflection upon the relationship between new media platforms and globalization. The volume includes authors from within the United States and from outside of the US and "the West". The diverse perspectives reflected in this project facilitate and promote intercultural exchange and understanding and in turn they reflect the editors' investment in global approaches to the complexities of identity in the digital age. No forward or preface can properly estimate the important work collected here but I am humbled by this brief opportunity to support the work of these astute editors and insightful contributors who remain on the cutting edge of their fields and committed to the requisite critical attention necessary for progressive media research in the 21st Century.

James Braxton Peterson
Lehigh University, USA

Preface

Since the popularization of Internet technologies in the mid-1990s, human identity and collective culture has been dramatically shaped by our continued use and engagement with the digital world. Despite a plethora of scholarship on digital technology, questions remain regarding how these technologies impact personal identity and perceptions of global culture. How does the use of social media, mobile devices, and digital technologies affect our understanding of race/ethnicity, gender, or age? How do these seemingly separate demographic indicators intersect in the digital age to produce culture? And, how do digital technologies impact our ability to learn from, communicate to, and engage with others? This edited volume seeks to address these lingering questions by showcasing scholarship from around the world investigating the intersections of culture and identity in the digital age.

This examination of digital culture and identity begins by adopting the lens of intersectionality. Intersectionality refers to an examination of multiple points of identity and difference working together to produce a lived experience and position in culture. First introduced as a theoretical foundation in the early 1990s, intersectionality has proliferated alongside the development of digital technologies such as the Internet, mobile media, and social networks. This relationship is purposeful and fluid to account for the introduction and proliferation of new technologies and facets of identity. For example, Facebook's 2014 decision to monitor the gender identity of users was complicated by shifting definitions of gender, sex, and sex category. Alongside supporters, digital Drag Queens protested Facebook's new rules on the basis that they did not reflect contemporary notions of identity and culture. This phenomenon is further reflective of neoliberalism's priority of hyper-individuality, a framework manifested through race/ethnicity and age. Scholarship notes that our current notions of neoliberalism are supported by the aging of the Millennial Generation, the same group responsible for the popularization of Facebook in the first place. In cases like this it is impossible to ignore the complex intersections of race/ethnicity, age, and gender in the digital age.

THEORETICAL BACKGROUND

Cultural studies asks the question of what is media's role in a changing society. Generating from Stuart Hall's work on hierarchy, social discourses, and media narratives, cultural studies integrates primarily qualitative research with larger questions on how culture is depicted, transformed, or presented through technology and media. Books written through the cultural studies perspectives provide case studies of historical roles and forms of culture, such as gender, age, and race/ethnicity. This volume expands upon this vein of research by exploring how these cultures appear in digital technologies.

Previous publications on digital media technologies focus of blogs, social networks, message forums, and digital discussion spaces. Through digital communication in these spaces, users communicate identity information revolving around age, gender, and race/ethnicity. Digital identity literature argues that users have the ability to control how facets of their identity are displayed in these spaces, as well as make decisions to change, modify, or hide other parts. In this way, digital platforms provide an entry into investigating how identity is constructed around technology.

Globalization, advances in media technology, and changes in social policy have called into question traditional definitions and expressions of culture, individual and group identity, and social categorization. Most prevalent is the shift in popular understandings of race/ethnicity, gender, and age as cultural categories for constructing identity and shaping social policy. In a post-race, post-feminist, youth-centered world, this edited volume incorporates timely research investigating the ways in which digital technology has become a new space for forming, shifting, (re)defining, and marking race/ethnicity, gender, and age.

Digital media spaces are actively transitioning individual and collective definitions of identity. By blurring lines between the public and private sphere, and producer and consumer, digital technology has had unprecedented impacts upon society. This research acts as the next phase in the academic investigation of the relationship between culture, identity, and media. The volume builds upon the strides of cultural theorists such as Stuart Hall, Michele Foucault, and Edward Said as well as those who investigate contemporary shifts in human behavior that result from changes in media technology including Marshal McLuhan, George Ritzer, and Nathan Jurgenson. The pieces collected herein serve as intellectual resources to an academic audience.

Many scholars have noted the changing cultural landscape as a result of digital technologies such as blogs, social networks, forums, and online games. Traditionally, race/ethnicity, gender, and age are considered the three largest breakdowns of culture, considering most people identify as a type or category of each. While far from the only cultural categories worth studying (social class is easily another dominant and critical lens), these three categories are identified as being the most complicated in the digital age. These categories are complicated by the evolving norms of online spaces which frequently produce textual representations of users. As a result, these largely visual cultural divisions have evolved and changed to keep up with new channels of communication. Traditionally, these three cultural categories manifest independent of the individual's control through visual cues and social standards or constructs. However, digital technologies give users unprecedented control over their appearance and the way they communicate their identity. At the same time these shifts occur, there is competing evidence that traditional hierarchies are reproducing and re-appearing online. This calls into question the democratic potential of digital media. Thus, more research is necessary about the way these three cultural divisions manifest in digital spaces.

Finally, this volume addresses the dissipation of traditional notions of nation-state sovereignty that result from rapid globalization. Ultimately, the pieces consider competing and shifting notions of access and freedom of information, the realigning of one's political identity with those who live in other countries/societies (either/or for living in other countries or digital access) and that we only have digital access to, shifts in both micro and macro level social norms that come from unprecedented interconnectivity, and the necessity of sustained intercultural dialogue, communication, and understanding. As the world becomes increasingly smaller and interrelated, understandings of the self are drastically reconfigured and various understandings of reality work collectively to reshape culture across the globe.

This book is ideally suited for scholars interested in the fluid and rapidly evolving norms of identity and culture through digital media. The case studies presented herein provide global reflections on the notions of gender, age, and race/ethnicity. The book also serves as a template of how the theoretical framework of cultural studies and intersectionality can be applied to a variety of methodologies, onto-logical, and epistemological investigations. The language and concepts make it well suited for graduate students beginning their critical investigations of the digital world and scholars who are looking for resources or information about contemporary culture.

OVERVIEW

The first section of this volume explores expressions and impacts of race and ethnicity in digital culture. Race and ethnicity is considered a primary postcolonial cultural categorization due to its socio-historical and contemporary dominance and presence in everyday interpersonal, mediated, and digital communi-cation. Many scholars argue that contemporary society has shifted to a post-racial landscape. However, far from consensus on this issue, the pieces in this volume investigate the continued relevance of race in digital identity and communication. For example, Ho's, piece on Asian American's use of YouTube takes a thorough look at the complex descriptions and humor used, they describe Asian immigrants by their first-generation American children. In this context she provides evidence that supports notions of the perpetual foreigner, dual cultural experiences of Asian families, and issues around assimilation, clearly problematizing narratives of a post-race society.

El-Burki and Reynolds explore the use of humor to engage neoliberalist notions of race. A look at pop cultural icon Justin Bieber's Comedy Central Roast investigates how race becomes fluid and non-consequential space of entertainment among both Bieber and roast participants. In this sense, Justin Bieber and those engaged in the comedic rendition of his career represent contemporary examples of the commodification of blackness and black masculinity by young, attractive white males in popular culture, major media outlets and media content targeted to millennial consumers. Justin Bieber as a brand be-comes a consumable package for millennials and an indication that issues of difference are not reflective of persistent inequality but rather simple diversity that normalizes and celebrates cultural appropriation

Zhang's analysis of Wiebo and WeChat investigates the increasingly important role of social media in engaging a public dialogue around politics and political gatekeepers. With a focus upon the paradoxes produced by the changing relationship between media use and the expression of political dissent in China, Zhang calls attention to the influence of online citizen journalism upon the role of government.

Wigfall's piece, *Nothing Random About Taste: Toni Morrison and the Algorithmic Canon*, consid-ers the implications of shifts in media technology for the canonization of authors via the digitization of knowledge. Her piece looks at how new media spaces, such as Tastekid, reconstruct the processes of selecting works, create authoritative lists, and collaborating to canonize the work of American author Toni Morrison.

The final piece in our section on race/ethnicity, Andriakaina's Public History and Cultural Identity: The 1821 Revolution as Metaphor for the "Greek Crisis" investigates the mass distribution of historical nostalgia during times of financial and social change and uncertainty. Her look at a documentary series, "1821" appearing on *Skai* channel analyzes media framing of key patriotic events that shape collective consciousness as well as the ways that the *Skai* channel challenges collective identity through its render-ing of key historical events.

The contributions on race and ethnicity address disconnects between the ideals of post-racial world and continued relevance of racial and ethnic identities in the digital age. Collectively these chapters take multifaceted approach to exploring the impact of such identities upon our continued lived and digital experiences.

The second section of the volume explores gender identity as it manifests through digital technologies. Instances such as Facebook's policy on gender identification present a challenge for those who both conform to traditional male/female norms, as well as those who prefer to self-identify through alternative vocabulary. This section of the volume presents research on the ways in which gender is implicated in digital culture. McLaughlin et al.'s work on women with breast cancer and online support groups confirms that these digital spaces help women process, articulate, and reflect upon their own identity, particularly in the face of a medical crisis. They conclude, that although having a positive or optimistic outlook regarding diagnosis was important, using digital technologies to reflect on changes to their physical bodies also produced a means for the users to cope and re-establish themselves as women.

Neidt's chapter explores Facebook's controversial decision to require users to use their real, birth name, as their profile name. As the world's largest social network, Facebook's policy to punish or ban anyone using a pseudonym was quickly adopted by other platforms, leaving users who used performer-names (particularly Drag Queens) desperate to find another platform that would embrace their approach to identity. Neidt's chapter examines the affordances of social network, Ello, as a means to understand how gender identity is conveyed and shaped online. Studying this incident is important to understanding how identity can lead to protest or advocacy in digital spaces, particularly as it relates to controversial issues such as sexual orientation and gender norms.

Kidd and Turner's piece on #GamerGate presents the complicated scope and intersections of gender in video games and digital gaming. Over the course of summer 2014, #GameGate became one of the most frequently used hashtags on social media as the public engaged in a debate over the role of women in gaming culture. As the masculine norms of gaming and growth of women participating in international competitions coincide, feminist critiques of video games (particularly violent ones) and their inferior treatment of women upset traditional users. While no definitive conclusion regarding the role of women in gaming were reached, Kidd and Turner's chapter describes the controversy and how gender is articulated and debated within the scope of digital games.

Novoselova's last chapter in the gender section describes consumer activism in digital and online spaces. Through a thematic analysis of Jezebel.com, Novoselova looks at how consumption and the protest of consumption engages gendered communication online and shapes gender identity. Jezebel.com is controversially labeled a feminist news magazine website, thus asking users to protest or advocate for a particular view engages feminist readers and shapes larger socio-political norms.

Together, the four chapters in the gender section explore the controversies of gender and identity in online spaces. While far from a census of all digital media, the focus on social networks, online journalism, and gaming represents an effort to look at a variety of spaces and their intersections with other areas of culture.

The third section of the volume includes pieces that reflect on age as a component of digital culture and identity. Age, generation, and age cohort are vital categories of identity as they help individuals build collective identity surrounding their cultural associations. However, recent literature suggests that as digital media proliferates, the ability to conform to generational norms or seek out other members of an age cohort becomes challenged or shaped by the digital spaces this interaction exists within. This presents a very complicated task for researchers looking into how digital interactions may shape personal identity or larger generational patterns. Other research suggests that the variety of digital media available to today's youth has further isolated and perhaps limited the group's ability to interact physically or conform to traditional values and behaviors. Thus, the question remains, what effect does the proliferation of digital media have on age identity and generational groups? The three chapters in this section not only address this critical question, but provide unique insights into the myriad of ways that age is ever-present online.

Novak and Richmond's chapter on the role of intergenerational communication on Tumblr documents the ways that digital media serves as a vent or forum for age groups to criticize and address the perceived weakness of each other. Through a discussion of older feminists, hundreds of thousands users on Tumblr shared their frustration with other women and earlier feminist movements through visual and text-based posts. This analysis presents the discourses of intergenerational communication as facilitated through the Tumblr social network.

Second, Mou's work on how youth view widely-circulated male and female digital-fashion advertisements, demonstrates the ongoing importance of cultural studies to intersectionality studies. The chapter concludes by examining the effectiveness of advertising strategies on youth, especially as they regard sexual appeals, provocation, and the viral nature of advertising.

Finally, Wright's work on cyberbullying and its relationship to gender and age identities presents ongoing research into the more-harmful potential of digital communication. The implications of anonymity and the online disinhibition effect are tested within the study as the author draws conclusions regarding predictors of cyberbullying and its victims. The researcher concludes that there is a relationship between age and ethnicity when looking at who is likely to bully and who is likely to be a victim of bullying. Importantly, this chapter provides an in-depth look at an ongoing social-cultural problem, using intersectionality to examine how the complexities of digital identity may play a role.

The chapters of the age section primarily look at how youth groups use and engage with digital media. However, each chapter also delineates how these younger users interact or communicate with older populations, through social media, direct messaging, and viral advertising content. As we move forward explore how digital media impacts the maturation process and ageing, looking at these spaces of intergenerational communication are key.

Finally, the volume concludes with a section on intersectionality and the applications of the theory to specific digital case studies. Five chapters take on the challenge of presenting the intersections of all three cultural categories: race/ethnicity, gender, and age. As a true demonstration of intersectional research aims, Eckert and Steiner's chapter explores the many instances of feminism in digital spaces, especially looking for places of feminist critique and discourse on race/ethnicity and age. Their chapter look at how the label "feminist" is used in social media, as a way of looking into claims of participatory culture and democracy as they relate to the contemporary placement and hierarchy of genders in digital spaces. They conclude that contemporary feminism largely intersections with questions of race/ethnicity and age to help its practitioners form their own sense of self and group identity.

Akmam and Huq's chapter examines how digital technologies serve as an extension of the self, often bearing consequences and benefits for users. Thus, internet culture and digital media serve as an object world that can be learned and shared through communication. Selfies, or digital photos taken of oneself, serve as way to express and insert users into the object world, thus shaping and reflecting the norms and cultural values of the space. While selfies were once an adaptation of digital technologies to fit the needs of the users, today's digital technologies (such as forward facing cameras) are now designed with this use in mind. Akmam's work in this chapter looks at the appropriation of technologies, such as the digital camera, to inserts users into the digital world.

As a follow up, Ndi's chapter similarly looks at selfies, but this time how the actual photo may serve as a contemporary form of self-representation and how collections of selfies may help establish group or shared cultural norms. Through a historical look at the evolution of self-photography, Ndi proposes that selfies are emblematic of the primacy of visual signifiers in digital culture, further emphasizing a connection (or rather a fluidity) between the physical and virtual realms.

Finally, the volume concludes with Cline's theoretical investigation of faith, spirituality, and ontology in digital culture. After exploring websites and platforms that are committed to giving users a closer connection to religion (ex: Christianity, Islam, and Buddhism), Cline concludes that these digital spaces reify cultural and religious practices, further bridging the spiritual and virtual.

Throughout the case studies presented in this volume remains a commitment to explore the variety of platforms, media, and technologies that help shape and reflect 21st century identity and culture. While the digital world continues to expand, grow, and change, the theories and analyses presented within this volume reflect some of the most compelling and relevant ways that age, gender, and race/ethnicity intersect. As such the scholarship in this volume acts as an important contribution to the field of cultural studies, communication, and media studies as well as the development of inquiry, research and understanding of the subject of identity and culture in the digital age.

Acknowledgment

The completion of this book would not be possible without the contributions, support and encouragement of our colleagues, advisors, friends and family. While we are unable to individually name everyone who assisted us in reaching our goal, we feel compelled to express our deep appreciation and indebtedness to the following individuals, in particular:

Alison N. Novak personally thanks Drs. Ernest A. Hakanen, Ronald Bishop, Barbara Hoekje, Sean Goggins, and Kathleen E. Kendall.

Imaani J. El-Burki personally thanks Drs. Jack Lule, James B. Peterson, Monica Miller, Douglas V. Porpora, and Rachel R. Reynolds.

Finally, we would like to thank our entire Editorial Advisory Board, external reviewers, and anonymous peer reviewers. We also appreciate the support of the staff at our publishing company, IGI Global, for answering our questions, providing guidance, and believing in the relevance of our project.

Alison N. Novak dedicates this volume to her parents, Michael and Denise Novak; her colleagues and friends at Drexel University, Rowan University, and Temple University.

Imaani J. El-Burki dedicates the project to her daughter, Suraayah H. A. Greene; mother, Michelle D. Byng; sister, Aminah J. El-Burki; the memory of her father, Mustafa H. El-Burki and grandmothers Venetta E. Byng and Barbara J. Bryant.

Section 1
Race/Ethnicity

Chapter 1
Embodying Difference on YouTube:
Asian American Identity Work in "Shit Asian Dads Say"

Helen K. Ho
Saint Mary's College, USA

ABSTRACT

This chapter analyzes the content and responses of a popular video, "Shit Asian Dads Say," produced by YouTube production company JustKiddingFilms. In analyzing video content in conjunction with themes emerging from comments left in response to the video, the chapter discusses the ways in which comedic/ satirical, citizen-produced content on YouTube helps to shape, construct, and reflect the boundaries of group membership. As the video hinges on second-generation performances of immigrant parenthood, its content provides a prime site to investigate how age, gender and race are performed and become contested or reified in digital space. An analysis of the YouTube videos grounded in the responses, commentary and discussion that accompany the videos in the user comments, ultimately empowers viewers' interpretations of digital creative expression.

INTRODUCTION

While Asian American participation in film and television has been growing it remains relatively sparse, particularly given the demographic composition of the Hollywood entertainment industry. A 2015 Writers Guild of America brief reported that minorities are underrepresented as television writers by a factor of nearly 3 to 1, with whites making up over 85% of television writers and writers/producers in Hollywood (Writers Guild of America, 2015, pp. 2-3). The numbers of minorities on screen are similar: while minority leads in film have increased, minority actors make up just under 17% of the faces seen in movies despite making up 37% of the US general population; among lead roles in broadcast scripted television, minorities are underrepresented by a factor of nearly 6 to 1 (Hunt & Ramón, 2015, pp. 9, 13). Asian Americans, in particular, remain largely underrepresented: Asian Americans constituted only 4.4%

DOI: 10.4018/978-1-5225-0212-8.ch001

of the speaking roles across 100 of the top grossing films of 2013 (Smith, Choueiti, & Pieper, 2013, p. 1). The ratio was similar for broadcast TV shows in 2014-2015, with just 36 Asian-Pacific Islander characters out of a total of 813 (GLAAD, 2014, p. 5).

In addition to these numbers, diversity reports have consistently shown that minority writers are more likely to be found on television dramas rather than sitcoms (Writers Guild of America, 2015, pp. 4-5); this is partly due to the multiracial ensemble casting of major network dramas including *Lost* (ABC), *Heroes* (NBC), *Grey's Anatomy* (ABC), *Scandal* (ABC), and the like. Asian American representation on broadcast network comedies has been more limited, with few leading roles. In fact, 2015's *Fresh off the Boat* (ABC), centered on an Asian American family, is the first network primetime show to feature an Asian American family in 20 years – the first being Margaret Cho's short-lived venture, *All-American Girl* (PBS Newshour, 2015). Overall, commercially successful Asian Americans on mainstream screens have remained relatively invisible in comparison to their white counterparts.

To those habitually ignored or misrepresented in mainstream narratives, independently produced content can provide a voice and an outlet (Guo & Lee, 2013; Rhagavan, 2009). On the Internet sites like YouTube, Vimeo and blogging platforms afford minority producers/consumers the space to create and share narratives that resist stereotypes commonly found in the more generalized, mainstream content of network television and studio films. The medium of online video thus provides a rich site of analysis in regard to minority youth, how they articulate their sense of belonging and difference, and what narratives they find relevant to address, as they create content.

This chapter analyzes the content and responses of a popular video, "Shit Asian Dads Say," produced by YouTube production company JustKiddingFilms. In analyzing video content in conjunction with themes emerging from comments left in response to the video, the chapter discusses the ways in which comedic/satirical, citizen-produced content on YouTube helps to shape, construct, and reflect the boundaries of group membership. As the video hinges on second-generation performances of immigrant parenthood, its content provides a prime site of analysis to investigate how age, gender and race are performed and become contested or reified in digital space.

BACKGROUND

Using the Internet to produce and promote independent videos, racial and ethnic minorities have found a medium with which to portray themselves to audiences. A body of literature is growing regarding the role of Internet sites such as YouTube, Vimeo, Twitter and Facebook in minority self-representation. Kent Ono and Vincent Pham's (2009) work, for example, provides insight into Asian American blogs on the Internet that facilitate discussions on a variety of issues concerning Asian American experiences; these sites provide forums for consumers to interact with mainstream information in a critical context to discuss racial tensions, gender politics, and issues of ethnicity (Ono & Pham, 2009, p. 148).

Technology use trends show that Asian Americans understand race, culture and their bodies online more than ever. A Nielsen Media report on "The New Digital American Family" (2011) shows that Asian Americans view 1,000 more web pages than any other ethnic group, and watch YouTube more than any other demographic (Anderson & Subramanyam, 2011, p. 5). In fact, English-speaking Asian Americans led the way in Internet use and home broadband access in 2011, outpacing all other racial/ethnic demographics (Rainie, 2011). Viewership with television sets has declined amongst Asian Americans, but streaming online video is double the national average (Anderson & Subramanyam, 2011, p. 5). It is also possible that YouTube participation is becoming a norm for Asian American young adults, as evidenced by the wave of replies, parodies and rants that appeared in response to UCLA student Alexandra Wallace's infamous 2011 video complaining about "Asians in the Library." Indeed, Asian Americans – some with millions of followers, such as Ryan Higa ("NigaHiga"), Michelle Phan, and Freddie Wong—constitute some of the top personalities on YouTube (Tsukayama, 2012).

YouTube is a free, online video sharing service that has grown exponentially in popularity since its conception in 2005. Anyone with video content and Internet access can post public or private videos and start their own "channels;" essentially feeds that can garner followers who subscribe to the channel's content. Given the culture of re-posting – users who wish to respond to videos can post a comment underneath the video, as well as share the video on other sites like Facebook, Tumblr, Google+, Twitter, and the like – and YouTube's 2Gb file size limit, YouTube videos are often only a few minutes long. For "Shit Asian Dads Say" and other entertaining, comedic content produced by YouTube users, comment culture centers on being the first to comment on a video, sharing a quick "haha," "LOL" or smiley face emoticon; favorite lines or quotations from the video; or even just time stamps of key moments favored in the video.

While viral videos, memes and satirical content might be seen by some as frivolous or playful participation in Internet culture, this content also speaks to the larger capacity of YouTube as a digital site for racial expression and identity management. Whether through performance or viewer response on the site, Asian Americans engage with displays of age, gender and race, which can provide some control over how they and others understand Asian American identity and experiences within dominant social hierarchies. With the plethora of videos available on YouTube some producers and viewers have specifically taken on issues of racial and ethnic identity in their performances and responses. Even with some comedic, satirical or caricatured performances, narratives and responses can prompt serious racial identity management in the form of exchanges and comments among YouTube users.

Guo and Lee's (2013) analysis of Asian American YouTubers Kevin Wu and Ryan Higa, for example, points out that the comedic videos produced by these online celebrities challenged hegemonic views about Asians and Asian Americans "while simultaneously establishing their own vernacular rhetoric and thus (re)building a new YouTubed Asian community" (p. 404). In one video ("Asians Just Aren't Cool Enough," with 6 million views), KevJumba ranted in front of his computer camera on the Hollywood practice of replacing Asian/Asian American characters with white actors. Guo and Lee point to the importance of the racial identity management at work in the video despite its simple execution and comedic ranting; KevJumba's use of the words "we," and "our," to explain Asian American culture helped to "break down the boundaries between himself and his audience," with rhetoric "challeng[ing] mainstream discourse against Asians/Asian Americans" (p. 400). KevJumba's channel also featured a series entitled "My Dad is Asian," starring his own father in episodes that earned over 1 million views each, with some nearing 5 million views. These videos functioned similarly to "Shit Asian Dads Say," in that young adult Kevin noted a variety of awkward circumstances that pit him and his father against each other culturally, linguistically, and behaviorally. Guo and Lee suggest that the humor from these "My Dad is Asian" videos stems from KevJumba's stance as an 'ordinary' Asian American, strategically distancing himself from his own 'more Asian' father. From costuming and language it is apparent that "Papa Jumba" is a first-generation immigrant, and Papa Jumba stands in stark contrast against KevJumba's more Westernized, second-generation behaviors and attitudes. The overall determination of videos such as these is ambivalent, however. The premise of these videos implies assimilative anxieties that KevJumba feels the need to address as a minority in the United States; at the same time, Guo and

Lee argue, Papa Jumba's Asian character serves to essentialize a Euro-centric construct of "Asianness" that reproduces racism and discriminatory attitudes for the sake of entertainment (p. 404).

YouTube creators straddle the line between user and producer, just as their creations often blur the boundaries of mainstream/alternative, global/local, and entertainment/information. Previous research on YouTube videos suggests that the nature of the site itself requires videos to pander to entertainment and humor in order to generate views, limiting political dialogue or discussions of serious identity issues (Guo & Lee, 2013; Hess, 2009). While one cannot deny the entertainment role of YouTube content in the context of contemporary digital media, assuming that serious discussions fall to the wayside to make room for humor fails to address YouTube's many viewers and their reactions to the site's content. Videos may acquire popular status merely because they are funny, but also perhaps because communities systematically denied representation in mainstream media find online representations a refreshing change (Rhagavan, 2009). Additionally, while videos themselves may not directly address serious identity issues, they may serve as a prompt for viewers to engage in important discursive identity work in the comments section.

MAIN FOCUS OF THE CHAPTER

Asian American producers' presence on YouTube has worked to bring issues of Asian American experiences into the public eye; one such example is Wong Fu Productions' short film "Yellow Fever" (2006), chronicling the difficulties to get Asian women to date Asian men in the United States. "Shit Asian Dads Say" is part of a short-lived phenomenon of identity-focused YouTube videos depicting stereotypes of various groups. In December 2011 Toronto comedians Kyle Humphrey and Graydon Sheppard posted "Shit Girls Say," in which Sheppard acted out stereotypical "female moments." Earning 4 million views in just one week, the video prompted various spin-offs and the development of a larger "Shit People Say" meme. Videos included "Shit Black Girls Say," "Shit White Guys Say to Black Girls," and more. In January 2012, Bart Kwan and Joe Jo of JustKiddingFilms posted "Shit Asian Dads Say." Videos in the "Shit People Say" category follow similar structures: quick cuts, one-liners sometimes repeated in varying contexts or physical locations, and a minority actor presenting themselves as a member of an insulting out-group who "says shit." Often, this group-switching incongruity is the source of humor in these videos: for example, a black man dressed as a black woman for "Shit Black Girls Say," or an Asian American woman dressed in a blond wig and moustache for "Shit White Guys Say to Asian Girls."

In "Shit Asian Dads Say," Bart Kwan embodies "Asian Dad" by donning a graying comb-over wig, wire framed glasses, and a puffy vest and slippers. Asian Dad is often seen shouting to his children in accented, pidgin English, with questions like "Did you get good grade," or "Why you not a doctor?" Key punch lines also include, "Respect your elder," "Rap music is black," and "No boyfriend till you married." Scenes with Asian Dad show him with a remote control wrapped in plastic, tapping melons for ripeness at the supermarket, and trying to park his car with great difficulty; a series of quick cuts also show him cleaning his ears, blowing and picking his nose, coughing over food at the supermarket, and asleep and snoring in a variety of locations.

A digital performance of Asian/American identity, "Shit Asian Dads Say" is produced by comedic production company JustKiddingFilms. The popularity of "Shit Asian Dads Say" and its accompanying viewer comments are important cultural sites of self-representation and the (re)articulation of Asian/

American identity online. Looking at how viewers identify with and against the caricatures present in "Shit Asian Dads Say," it becomes evident that performing "Asianness" through the character of Asian Dad allows for a younger generation to articulate racial/ethnic, generational and assimilative anxieties -- most notably the stereotype of being inassimilable or "forever foreign" (Tuan, 1998). At face value, the portrayal of a "foreign" or "Fresh Off the Boat" (FOB) Asian Dad simultaneously helps Asian American youth make sense of a shared experience while maintaining existing hierarchies of assimilated minorities. However, the thousands of viewer comments left in response to the video points to the polysemy of online texts and the affordances of online space to deliberate and articulate boundaries of identification. An analysis of the YouTube videos grounded in the responses, commentary and discussion that accompany the videos in the user comments ultimately empowers viewers' interpretations of digital creative expression. The video and its reception provide a case study that may be applied to other contexts and minority performances, particularly those that use humor and caricature as tools for identity management.

Comments are continually posted in response to YouTube videos after they are shared. As a result archiving video reception online results in a mere snapshot. At time of writing, the "Shit Asian Dads Say" video had received 12,127 comments. Through the use of Netlytic, a social networks and text analyzer tool, all the comments were collected as a data set and analyzed thematically. Comments that simply stated "LOL", "haha", emoticons, or timestamps were not included in the analysis, which left 2,474 individual comments with substantial text. These comments were broken down into thematic categories pertaining to the video's reception. The first two categories encompassed emotional/valenced responses to the entertainment value of the video: *Positive* comments included the terms "comic," "funny," "hilarious," "humor," and "humorous;" *Negative* category comments included phrases and words like "don't like," "not funny," or "offensive." The third category was *Race,* which sought out comments specifically using phrases and words like "American," "Asian," "Ethnic," "Race," "Racial," "Racist," "Stereotype," and their iterations.

Broken down, comments concerning race (1,364) and positive emotions (1,091) constituted the majority of the responses left to "Shit Asian Dads Say." A negligible few (19) comments mentioned negative feelings. Overall, comments revealed YouTube viewers trying to make sense of their community/in-group boundaries in three major ways: locally (i.e., sharing geographic knowledge of the video's production), racially (i.e., trying to determine whether their ethnicity would constitute "being Asian"), and generationally (i.e., understanding Asian Dad as a stand-in for less assimilated, immigrant family members).

The easiest way some users found to identify with or relate to the video was geographically. This was evidenced by viewers attempting to recognize spaces and places shown in "Shit Asian Dads Say." There were 196 unique comments with viewers sharing delight over being able to identify filming locations, particularly the grocery store at which Asian Dad shops: "Omg, I go to that super market,"[1] wrote user Kalvin Loc; user kay len wrote, "I luv 99 ranch market!" Even if viewers realized they did not share the same geographical location as the scenes in the video, they mentioned the similarities of their grocery experiences wherever they were: user JoeyLuTV wrote, "that market looks like one 4rm LA," and another with the handle mellowandjello shared, "in my work as a stock boy at a grocery store, there are an untold amount of Asian people that do that at my store lol." At this most basic level, YouTube video viewers felt compelled to share their sense of community with other users and video creators.

Limiting analysis to the 1,364 comments regarding race and ethnicity, it becomes clear that viewers grappled with the concept of "Asian" in the context of "Asian Dad." The video's generalized caricature prompted users to critique the performance, finding indicators that "Asian" Dad was more specifically ethnic than the title suggested. The types of comments below were common:

negee3 : More like Shit Korean Dads say rather than Asian. -__-

yiperoo : Yea, this is more like Vietnamese or Southwestern Asia kind of dad. East Asian dad's are a little different.

rara15avis : Not applicable to ALL ASIAN DADS but is mostly accurate if you compare it to EAST asian dads

van jo : This thing is not Asian! This is VIETNAMESE!

Patrick Pan : lol this is not Asian Dad... this is just Cantonese dad.

While some of these users were adamant in labeling Asian Dad as a particular ethnic stereotype, these comments taken in totality point to Asian Dad's caricatured "Asianness" as breaking ethnic boundaries: so many users' claims of Asian Dad's different ethnicities solidified the performance as multi-ethnic. As an all-purpose Asian stand-in, Asian Dad was enough of a caricature to prompt viewers of different Asian ethnicities to identify cultural specificities from a very generalized performance.

Ethnic identification also prompted YouTube commenters to engage each other in conversations about the ethnic boundaries of being Asian. Some users commented that their ethnicity was not considered Asian, reflecting the common American racial framework that often only considers East Asian ethnicities as Asian American. User BillyBobthe8th wrote, "My dad says most of these things, but he's like southern asian lol," and V Reyes wrote, "Im asian and my dad is acuratly like that but um a different asian race im phillapeno." User lwst82 also wrote, "I like how non[e] of this applies to Filipino dads, namely because Filipinos aren't asian! They're only considered asians to other filipinos!" The claim that "Filipinos aren't Asian" is tied to the prominent American/Western belief that Asian Americans consist of mostly East Asian (Japanese, Korean, Chinese) ethnicities; what lwst82 points to is a specific contention that there are a myriad of Asian ethnicities left on the periphery of the Asian American community.

An exchange between a few users highlighted the difficulty of these ethnic definitions when user Hannahc02 asked, "I don't understand why it's 'Asian' There are just waaay too many countries and cultures to just say asian...?" In response, user HRentai wrote, "Saying Asian would also cover up indians, chinese, vietnamese, koreans, the Japanese, Filipinos, etc." User snotberg123 clarified, "when one says asian, it is generally understood that it means oriental Asians, specifically chinese and koreans, though filipinos, japanese, and vietnamese can also be included." Jagggy09 wrote that "Indian parents are like this too," to which others like SofaKingAwesome23 responded, "indian people ARE technically asian bro." As lived experience and histories of race relations in the United States might support, users like Jagggy09 and lwst82 felt excluded from the term "Asian." Exchanges about what it means to be Asian, Asian American, and a member of a particular ethnic group show that YouTube commenters do engage in quite nuanced discussions of racial and ethnic identity. One of the affordances of YouTube is that it allows users from around the world to help expand the boundaries of group inclusion beyond the cultural and racial frameworks of one's country.

While some users felt that it was dangerous to group multiple ethnicities together – user sp91106 wrote, "Chinese, Korean, Japanese, Vietnamese, Thailand, etc. are different. I don't think we should lump them all together. It's like lumping all white skinned people together as 'white people'," – it's important to note that the generalized caricature of Asian Dad in the video helped to promote pan-ethnic Asian identification. As user AngeSpitz wrote, "I love that Asian dad spans multiple nationalities." Indeed,

Kwan's performance of Asian Dad uses several catchphrases and curses from a variety of Asian languages, which did prompt users to try to decipher ethnicity. User Kaother wrote, "did he just say shiibal? That's korean? And he's speaking in a viet accent, and reading a Chinese newspaper ah so confusing." While perhaps confusing, the character of Asian Dad becomes an almagamation of multiple ethnicities to prompt discussion of what it means to be Asian. User pimasta314 appreciated the caricature: "i think he's just a mix of all general asian-ness doesn't matter I know viet/chinese/japanese/korean/cambodian parents who all say this." User William C also shared similar sentiments: "The exaggerated stereotypes are ridiculously funny! This dad was all Asian, mostly Canto, some Viet, and some Korean. Excellent."

This appreciation of caricature prompted most YouTube users to identify with experiences and memories rather than ethnic-specific characteristics. For many users, the video prompted identification as an Asian child, regardless of ethnicity and regardless of the parent involved: User ForTehNguyen wrote, "this should be renamed Shit Asian Parents Say, moms say the exact same things," and others also posted similarly:

louise988 : [t]his is both my asian parents.
Heartachetickles : Thumbs up if this applies to both your Asian parents at a ridiculously high level.
Athina Angeles : I think Asian Mum's Grandfathers and Granmothers do the same thing LOL

User HRentai, who provided a definition of "Asian" above, also wrote, "It's just common that Asian parents/grandparents do a few of these things." Users identified in-group boundaries on a generational level, moving beyond ethnic-specific identification toward generational experiences.

In fact, comments (238) shared that the video seemed to be representative of Asian grandparents. User Adsf wrote, "Shit REALLY OLD Asian Dads say," which was echoed throughout the comments. User JamesQiu16 exclaimed, "This is more like Asian grandpa!" and user Jonathan Truong wrote, "This is ALL asian parents/grandparents." From this perspective, the humor of the video stems from the fact that it features first-generation immigrants as an out-group, with users and producers sharing in-group status as the youth of successive generations. Using this distinction, the concept of "Asian" becomes even more generalized, transcending ethnicity and perhaps even race, as users focused on generational divide.

"I'm not even Asian, I'm an American," user Yanki Rio wrote, "But my parents are not American and threy act just like the parents in the vid." The users commenting on generational differences focused on their shared experiences of being children of immigrants:

MsMusiclover95 : This video does not discribe just asian dads but, foreign families in general.
Zazu Mali : I don't think this pertains to asian dads only. I think all immigrant dads are cut from the same cloth.
Shyariety A. : asian parents? Dude this is most foreign parents

In embodying Asian Dad, Kwan is able to define, articulate and present differences between ostensibly first- and second-generation immigrants, setting apart "FOB" behaviors from those of a younger, more assimilated cohort.

From the comments left in response to this video, it becomes evident that sites like YouTube can become an important site for critique and consumption, as the democratization of creation and dissemination provide "unprecedented opportunities for traditionally marginalized communities to express their voices" (Guo & Lee, 2013, p. 394). YouTube and videos like "Shit Asian Dads Say" allows participants to present and perform their cultural experiences (Burgess & Green, 2009, p. 48), which are then affirmed, discussed and debated in the comments section.

Issues, Controversies, Problems

While "Shit Asian Dads Say" provides an alternative space for Asian American performance and narrative, as well as a rich site for identity work and meaning making, there exists a deep ambivalence amongst literature and Internet users regarding the role of humor in performing minority identities. While YouTube has provided independent producers like JustKiddingFilms a venue for their creative endeavors, it is also a site where support for users, such as monetization from advertisements, still subscribes to the capitalist logic of mainstream entertainment (Burgess & Green, 2009; van Dijck, 2009; Guo & Harlow, 2014; Guo & Lee, 2013). When racial humor is involved, it becomes unclear as to whether or not the humor serves a mocking or self-reflective function. Boskin and Dorinson write that historically, black artists had to participate in self-caricature, perpetuating stereotypes in order to fit into an entertainment culture dominated by the racial tropes of a majority white audience and creative industry (1985, p. 112); similar arguments have been made over Yiddish and immigrant performances in America's vaudeville era (Butsch, 2000). Users across the Internet can often be found responding to affronts or criticisms with claims that content is "just a joke," or "just for fun," and the same is true for "Shit Asian Dads Say." Looking at comments discussing stereotypes and the comedic function of the video, it becomes clear that users reflected this ambivalence in their discourse.

To some, the caricature of Asian Dad perpetuated existing stereotypes from mainstream narratives. User PhunkieProdiG wrote, "This is funny and all, but let's get real here. Aint anybody tired of the asian stereotype?" Similarly, user minkyun park wrote, "I hate this video…even if this is just kidding film, this video makes more stereotypical negative asian image which was already bad image. asians are usually described as target of ridicule, monkery." What these users represent with their statements, in part, is the concern that the YouTube audience is wide and diverse; to an ostensibly mainstream YouTube viewership the stereotype of Asian Dad reflects mainstream ideologies regarding Asians' minority status. These types of comments, focused on racial identification rather than generational or assimilative characteristics, were more focused on policing in-group boundaries. Some viewers, for example, needed to identify themselves as Asian in order to be seen enjoying the video: for example, user Lucien Han wrote, "this is actually true, and Im asian," and user Omgqt92 shared, "I am asian and this makes me laugh so much hahahahahah." The qualifying statement of being Asian helps to identify a user's most basic in-group status: racial similarity with the performers. This in-group membership is based precisely on exaggerated representations of experiences (interactions with Asian parents) that may have, at various points in time, made users feel part of an out-group by dominant culture. User Msmotokosan wrote, "If other people made fun of asians, it would have been offending, but since there are asian people who made this, it's funny." User KcHawaii expressed this sentiment most succinctly: "this is funny cuz I'm asian, but I hate when White people comment saying its funny, then it's like…. you cannot talk."

A more nuanced problem that the above comments point to is the function of ethnic/racial humor for minorities: Juni and Katz (2001), for example, suggest that ethnic humor can be read as a defense mechanism, as performers "re-experience the trauma [of victimization] in an attempt to master failure and negate earlier deleterious effects" (p. 129). "Shit Asian Dads Say" allows Asian Americans to use visual and aural modes of representation to mark difference, with humor as an aid to present racial, ethnic, gendered and classed anxieties within the performance. Addressing and performing stereotypes is seen by some scholars of humor as masochistic; a cathartic performance of self-hate (Boskin & Dorinson, 1985; Juni & Katz, 2001). However, what underlies the comments made by users like Msmotokosan and KcHawaii is a sense of ownership over the narrative presented in "Shit Asian Dads Say;" other users, who identify with the video as children of immigrant parents, also imply the same ownership.

A number of users shared a sense of regret over the video's creation, calling it ignorant of immigrant heritage:

boloh88 : this is really disprespectful...our parents who immigrated to north america sacrificed everything to give their children a better life. It's shameful to be stereotyping asian parents in this crude manner.

Skyline4ever : I don't know why this video gets so many likes, I personally dislike it.... I hate to see Asian kids making fun of their parents because of the way their parents act. Asian parents are probably the most protective of all. They are strict. They don't usually act as your friends but they always feel responsible for you until they die.

JS Yip : i feel sad about this video it's not funny to make fun of parents. ...they came all the way to a different country for the whole family to have a better life..... but the old Asian habit and culture difference became jokes to their 'American-Asian' kids.

To these users and others like them, Asian Dad highlights the inassimilable nature of Asian parents, by marking difference based not only on appearance by on the language barriers between native and non-native English speakers. Asian Dad has a limited understanding and control of English and American/Westernized culture. Scenes featuring Asian Dad's awkward behaviors highlights the incongruity of a foreign body inserted in American space, and the disjuncture between the character's behaviors and American social norms creates the comedic value of the performance. This disjuncture was something that the original "Shit Girls Say" creator, Graydon Sheppard, touched upon in an interview about his video: "Coming from a gay man, it's a little less threatening than, say, a guy or even a woman acting the part.... We also have the advantage of being on the outside looking in" (Mudhar, 2011). Since Bart Kwan shares the same race as Asian Dad, the video's humor comes more from a generational disjuncture: it positions Asian American *youth*, to use Sheppard's words, "on the outside looking in."

SOLUTIONS AND RECOMMENDATIONS

While the content of "Shit Asian Dads Say" and similar videos may be seen as problematic, comments show users – despite how they feel about the video – negotiating with and implicitly assuming boundaries of inclusion. For example, the presumed negative effect of the Asian Dad stereotype expressed by some viewers reflects a Western/American racial framework which has long shaped portrayals of Asians as foreign threats, inassimilable outsiders or model minorities. Even when criticizing the negative effects of a racialized caricature, or claiming that the video disrespects Asian/immigrant parents and their sacrifices, users adopt a Westernized, assimilative stance in defense of Asian Dad. Bart Kwan affirms this identification at the end of the video when he talks to viewers:

If you can relate because you've got some crazy Asian parents, or if you've got a homie that's got crazy Asian parents, make sure you that you show them this video and see what they think about it.

The idea that one *can relate*, as Bart Kwan says, sets the boundaries of an in-group that can identify with or understand the behaviors and statements, however exaggerated, made by Asian Dad. In spite of criticisms against the character of Asian Dad, those condemnations are derived from a shared awareness of existing stereotypes he is thought to perpetuate. "Shit Asian Dads Say" serves to reinforce the viewpoint that there is an essential "Asian-ness" wholly different from the viewers of the video, who represent "Americanness" as much as Asian dad serves to represent its opposite.

By presenting themselves and members of their own culture, minorities can gain control over the discourse that shapes them. Humor can have benefits for disparaged groups, helping minorities both "absorb…the barbs and defuse…them by passing them along as of their own manufacture" (Boskin & Dorinson, 1985, p. 82). "Shit Asian Dads Say" acknowledges the existence of stereotypes and, despite its extreme exaggeration and generalized "Asianness," goes even further to suggest that there are *more* stereotypes in the viewers' community, identifiable by those who share similar experiences of their Asian Dads testing melons at the grocery store, wrapping remote controls in plastic, and the like. In playing up these stereotypes, "Shit Asian Dads Say" (re)creates boundaries of inclusion distinct from mainstream frameworks of race and ethnicity, and empowers viewers to claim their identity separate from these prevailing discourses.

Indeed, a select number of viewers went far enough in their comments to think seriously about how Asian Americans were using stereotypes in "Shit Asian Dads Say." User Warby Pepper mused, "I believe one way to eradicate any stereotype is for the people of that race's stereotype to perpetuate it through ridicule, and mockery until it becomes trite, clichéd, and, meaningless." While seemingly tongue-in-cheek, user Studio Revolt wrote, "This is a revolution!!! Asian America owns its own stereotype and [it's] actually funny!!" The overall sentiment in these types of responses was that viewers found the video entertaining and somewhat true *despite* its stereotyped portrayal. Perpetuating a stereotype, enjoying a stereotype, and agreeing with a stereotype were not seen as negative or shameful to these users. User Simplyblla wrote, "this is scary accurate..i would know. I have an asian dad. C: i love you daddy." Similarly, user Aden Wu wrote, "Although satirized, but now looking back at what my dad has done for me and my brothers. I'm proud to have a 'bad' Asian dad."

Ethnic humor can provide room to air grievances about stereotypes, but can also exploit that stereotype in order to reap the rewards – likes, shares, hits – of producing and performing entertaining content. Jones and Schieffelin (2009) argue that such humor is best read as ambivalent, with different constituencies understanding the text in their own ways. What the comment section for "Shit Asian Dads Say" reveals overall is the highly polysemic nature of cultural content as well as the importance of looking beyond digital texts to consider, seriously, digital reception. Humor work depends on the violation of expectations and creation of incongruities; on one level online humor can be seen as quick, easy entertainment but on another it can reveal in-group assumptions as to whose expectations are defied, and whose experiences are incongruous. Even if reception seems ambivalent, with likes, criticisms, and expressed ambivalence, comments can reveal decisive moments of identification that can be helpful in understanding how digital spaces build community.

FUTURE RESEARCH DIRECTIONS

Any study of a text is limited in its inability to decipher authorial intent, and this is the case not only for the creators of "Shit Asian Dads Say" but comment writers as well. JustKiddingFilms claims that it was "founded on the principle of promoting cultural unity using comedy as the vessel," and the company's motto is, "Teaching good things in a bad way." Yet, while these company statements suggest thoughtful consideration of video content, characters and narrative, interviews with JustKiddingFilms creators Jo and Kwan also reveal that content can be made solely because they find it funny. Regardless, textual analyses have long proven that authorial intent does not prevent rigorous research or discussions of narrative context.

Many Internet users may not often participate in the comments sections of online content, or may understand those spaces, particularly on large sites like YouTube, to be reserved for die-hard fans, critics, or trolls. Closer analysis, even textually, reveals that YouTube videos can prompt moments of intense reflection and solidarity between disparate users based on various points of identification, be they racial, ethnic, cultural, or generational. It also becomes clear that users commenting on the video show overwhelming support for its content, despite the exaggerated caricature and potential negative effects of stereotyping. Comments sections on YouTube are filled with musings from self-selected individuals who are prompted enough by the video to respond; it's highly possible that negative or truly ambivalent attitudes may not be as prevalent as these viewers may never view the video in its entirety. It is impossible to verify the ethnicity or race of commenters unless they declare it in their posts, and even then a profile picture and an exclamation of "I'm Asian," may not prove much. Regardless, looking closely at comments and user exchanges reveals the ways in which race and ethnicity are being discussed in day-to-day digital practice.

While a majority of written responses to YouTube entertainment can be dismissed as quick and easy expressions of enjoyment – a timestamp for a favored moment, an "LOL" or emoticon, the equivalent of a Facebook "like"—some users are spurred to think critically about identity issues, even to the point of engaging in conversation with each other. Scholars may find "Shit Asian Dads Say" looking similarly problematic to KevJumba's portrayal of his Asian dad; however, the comments from the user community suggest that even short, entertaining memes can prompt serious conversations of race, ethnicity, inclusion and exclusion. With a growing array of tools available for social media analysis of comments, networks, and online discourse, it is becoming ever more possible to take seriously the expressions of young minority users, consumers, and producers online as they take digital space to claim for themselves.

CONCLUSION

In recent years, Asian Americans have risen to popularity as comedians in particular, with production houses like Wong Fu Productions and JustKiddingFilms creating short online films and building a solid fan base. JustKiddingFilms, for example, claims an "international fanbase of over 706,000 subscribers" (JustKiddingFilms). Asian American digital presence continues to grow and more Asian Americans then ever are producing content for digital audiences, reshaping the boundaries of where they are seen as well as narrative constructs that have defined Asian American presences on screen.

With videos on YouTube like "Shit Asian Dads Say," young Asian Americans' performances of Asian identity on YouTube work to create a sense of community through the caricature of Asian difference. Ignoring the comments section of "Shit Asian Dads Say," it would be easy to critique the video for its racial caricature and argue that it perpetuates mainstream stereotypes; however, viewer responses suggest that Asian Dad – a character JustKiddingFilms later developed into an even more caricaturized character, "Crazy Asian Dad" – presents humorous and identifiable tropes as an homage to a less assimilated generation of parents. While some users focused on ethnic identification, more chose to focus on a pan-ethnic Asian identity, prompted by the generalized, multi-national caricature of Asian Dad; these comments indicate that such digital performances allow Asian American youth to weave stereotypes into their identity narratives and to adopt a stance of ownership rather than resistance. Even more enlightening is the fact that non-Asian viewers seemed to identify with Asian Dad alongside self-proclaimed Asian/American viewers; what their shared experience suggests is that, for a global site like YouTube, digital youth can converge on a text and recreate boundaries of inclusion. In this case, users identified Asian Dad as a first-generation immigrant, acknowledging their more assimilated in-group status alongside the makers of the video. This identification is further spurred by "Shit Asian Dads Say"'s inclusion of ostensibly FOB-specific behaviors, readily identifiable by viewers who grew up with less assimilated relatives or parents. In this sense, Asian Dad becomes a stand-in for Immigrant Dad; a stand-in for a community of young adults' home experiences; an homage, and insider wink, to globally conscious, culturally aware minorities who may not yet have a home in mainstream media spaces.

REFERENCES

Anderson, D., & Subramanyam, R. (2011, April 12). *The new digital American family: Understanding family dynamics, media and purchasing behavior trends.* Retrieved January 10, 2015, from Nielsen Media Research: http://www.nielsen.com/us/en/insights/reports/2011/new-digital-american-family.html

Boskin, J., & Dorinson, J. (1985). Ethnic humor: Subversion and survival. *American Quarterly, 1,* 81-97.

Burgess, J., & Green, J. (2009). The entrepeneurial vlogger: Participatory culture beyond the professional-amateur divide. In P. Snickars, & P. Vonderau (Eds.), The YouTube reader (pp. 89-107). Stockholm: Kungliga biblioteket.

Butsch, R. (2000). *The making of American audiences: From stage to television, 1750-1990.* Cambridge, UK: Cambridge University Press. doi:10.1017/CBO9780511619717

GLAAD. (2014). *2014 GLAAD TV reports.* Retrieved June 10, 2015, from http://www.glaad.org/files/GLAAD-2014-WWAT.pdf

Guo, L., & Harlow, S. (2014). User-generated racism: An analysis of stereotypes of African Americans, Latinos, and Asians in YouTube videos. *The Howard Journal of Communications, 25*(3), 281–302. doi:10.1080/10646175.2014.925413

Guo, L., & Lee, L. (2013). The critique of YouTube-based vernacular discourse: A case study of You-Tube's Asian community. *Critical Studies in Media Communication, 30*(5), 391–406. doi:10.1080/15295036.2012.755048

Hess, A. (2009). Resistance up in smoke: Analyzing the limitations of deliberation on YouTube. *Critical Studies in Media Communication, 26*(5), 411–434. doi:10.1080/15295030903325347

Hunt, D., & Ramón, A.-C. (2015, February 25). *2015 Hollywood diversity report: Flipping the script.* Retrieved June 10, 2015, from http://www.bunchecenter.ucla.edu/wp-content/uploads/2015/02/2015-Hollywood-Diversity-Report-2-25-15.pdf

Juni, S., & Katz, B. (2001). Self-effacing wit as a response to oppression: Dynamics in ethnic humor. *The Journal of General Psychology*, *128*(2), 119–142. doi:10.1080/00221300109598903 PMID:11506044

JustKiddingFilms. (2012, January 15). *Shit Asian dads say*. Retrieved from https://www.youtube.com/watch?v=o5MJbZ4l4J8

JustKiddingFilms. (n.d.). *About*. Retrieved from http://www.justkiddingfilms.net/about/

Mudhar, R. (2011, December 13). "Shit Girls Say" video a viral hit for Toronto duo. *The Toronto Star*. Retrieved from http://www.thestar.com

Ono, K. A., & Pham, V. N. (2009). *Asian Americans and the media*. Malden, MA: Polity Press.

PBS Newshour. (2015, February 14). *Will 'Fresh off the Boat' turn the tide for Asian Americans on TV?* Retrieved June 10, 2015, from http://www.pbs.org/newshour/bb/will-fresh-boat-turn-tide-asian-americans-tv/

Rainie, L. (2011, January 6). *Asian-Americans and technology*. Retrieved November 11, 2014, from http://www.pewinternet.org/2011/01/06/asian-americans-and-technology/

Rhagavan, R. (2009, July 22). *Digital activism on YouTube*. Retrieved February 12, 2015, from http://googleblog.blogspot.com/2009/07/digital-activism-on-youtube.html

Smith, S., Choueiti, M., & Pieper, K. (2013). *Previous research*. Retrieved June 10, 2015, from http://annenberg.usc.edu/pages/~/media/MDSCI/Racial%20Inequality%20in%20Film%202007-2013%20Final.ashx

Tsukayama, H. (2012, April 23). In online video, minorities find an audience. *The Washington Post*. Retrieved November 11, 2014, from http://www.washingtonpost.com/blogs/faster-forward/post/in-online-video-minorities-find-an-audience/2012/04/23/gIQAQneobT_blog.html

Tuan, M. (1998). *Forever foreigners or honorary whites?: The Asian ethnic experience*. New Brunswick, NJ: Rutgers University Press.

van Dijck, J. (2009). Users like you? Theorizing agency in user-generated content. *Media Culture & Society*, *31*(1), 41–58. doi:10.1177/0163443708098245

Writers Guild of America. (2015, March 3). *News and events*. Retrieved June 10, 2015, from http://www.wga.org/uploadedFiles/who_we_are/tvstaffingbrief2015.pdf

KEY TERMS AND DEFINITIONS

Asian American: An American of Asian descent. As a pan-ethnic category its criteria for inclusion have varied based on immigration policies, socioeconomic status, and more. In its definition of Asian America, the U.S. Census Bureau includes those from the Far East, Southeast Asia, and the Indian subcontinent as places of origin.

Caricature: A comically exaggerated representation.

"Fresh Off the Boat" (FOB): A slang term applied to immigrants who are "fresh off the boat" in a new host country. FOBs are understood to be unassimilated in behaviors, culture and language.

Meme: A cultural element passed along or copied rapidly by individuals in a network; online, this is usually a humorous piece of digital content that is imitated with slight variations.

Model Minority: A stereotype of Asian Americans as hard workers, academically inclined and helpful to others. While this is understood by some to be a more positive stereotype, it is also associated with being deferential or subservient (i.e. to white superiors or co-workers) and socially awkward.

ENDNOTE

[1]   Original user spellings, capitalizations and punctuations have been retained throughout.

Chapter 2
It's No Secret Justin Wants to Be Black:
Comedy Central's Justin Bieber Roast and Neoliberalism

Imaani Jamillah El-Burki
Lehigh University, USA

Rachel R. Reynolds
Drexel University, USA

ABSTRACT

Research shows that media representations of race, gender and social class designed for consumption by the millennial generation create a world of symbolic equality via narratives of racial harmony, female empowerment and forms of exaggeration where everyone seems to have a middle and or upper middle class quality of life. In general, the changing face of diversity as represented in media has been cast as a neoliberal politic, where ideologies of free markets are extended into representing a sense of equality among individuals and their respective social groups. While scholars have investigated exaggerated representations of inclusivity in a variety of media genres, there is limited scholarship investigating the ways in which comedy serves the neoliberalist agenda. Comedy Central's Roast of Justin Bieber aired March 2015 and has been replicated in multiple forms. The current study is an in depth discourse and content analysis of the racial and gender jokes appearing in this program. It concludes that what appears to be a move beyond race is instead working against a post-race reality.

INTRODUCTION

Research shows that media representations of race, gender and social class designed for consumption by the millennial generation create a world of symbolic equality via narratives of racial harmony, female empowerment and forms of exaggeration where everyone seems to have a middle and or upper middle class quality of life (Gill, 2011; Nakamura, 2008; Kendall, 2011). Often, representations of inclusiveness ideationally substitute for face-to-face interactions and give the impression of pluralism and diversity in our real social environments. Furthermore, such images and narratives have the potential to distract

DOI: 10.4018/978-1-5225-0212-8.ch002

media consumers from engaging in public sphere discussions on systemic inequality and the need for social change (Schiappa, et al, 2006; Winograd & Hais 2011, Gallagher 2003). In general, the changing face of diversity and equality as represented in media has been cast as a neoliberal politic, where ideologies of free markets are extended into representing a sense of equality and an even playing field among individuals and their respective social groups. And yet, neoliberal race politics directly mask growing inequalities among social groups in the USA since the 1970s (Goldberg 2008).

While scholars have investigated exaggerated representations of inclusivity in a variety of media genres, there is limited scholarship investigating the ways in which comedy serves the neoliberalist agenda (however, for a discussion of race comedy as critical project, see Rossing 2012). Our study investigates not only the ways in which dominant understandings of race, and gender identity are communicated in the contemporary mainstream comedic genre; we further seek to address the paradox of post-race norms in a comedy show where the majority of jokes are about race, bringing embedded race-gender identity stereotypes into the service of the present.

The *Comedy Central Roast of Justin Bieber* originally aired March 2015 and has since been partially replicated in multiple forms including Comedy Central website outtakes, officially and unofficially reproduced YouTube videos, twitter, and multiple celebrity news reports. The roast program serves well as a media element for analyzing the ways in which race continues to function as the elephant in the room best addressed via comedy, creating comic relief as the ideal space for processing continued racial anxiety in a post-racial world. After an extended discussion of racialized jokes, we also explore tentatively the complexities around gender and gender norms particular to the construction of Bieber as a racially and sexually controversial star, where ideas of aberrant masculinity are used comedically to marginalize the subject of the roast, Justin Bieber.

By way of conclusion, we address the social implications of racist humor within the neoliberal context. We argue that hegemonic and counter-hegemonic race and gender jokes within the international, multimedia context of the *Comedy Central Justin Bieber Roast* maintain dominant assumptions of a 'post-' world wherein continued marginalization is both laughable and inconsequential, e.g. 'we are over the race thing.' Lastly, we encourage future scholarship designed to specifically address comedy targeted to the post-generation as a means of maintaining illusions of progress and reconciliation.

The Justin Bieber Roast itself serves as a fitting subject in that we found that the large majority of jokes were about race. Watching the roast led us to ask: if Millenial audiences are indeed post-race or beyond race as a factor in how they reckon the world, then why is the Justin Bieber roast so saturated with both offensively stereotypical and critical jokes about race?

POST-RACE TELEVISION

To be clear, because mainstream popular culture has embraced a world of symbolic diversity and inclusion, we are now in a media world where white rappers receive accolades and awards for originality, and where reality shows with multicultural casts provide the impression of equal access and interaction among various racial groups and genders; and yet these reality shows nonetheless garner their ratings through social shaming of individual cast members whose looks, body types, and stereotypical race portrayals of pathological behavior fall outside the norm (Pozner, 2010). In such television content, post-race America means that race has a new kind of mutability in which white artists might win awards for "Black Music," a label which has recently been supplanted by the term "Urban." Ironically, the movement of white and other ethnicities into territories and genres of cultural production formerly understood to be exclusively black has also eased audiences into conceiving themselves as members of a post-race nation. Likewise, post-feminism allows for the expression of gender equality via the creation of a space for women's sexual self-ownership, even though that self-ownership might foreground sexual power over the ideals of power through educational or professional achievement and self-sufficiency that are considered the markers of success in a neoliberal environment. Finally, theories of the neoliberal media environment help to explain the popular media trope of merit, where having "the pipes" (*American Idol*), succeeding against nature and competitors to survive (*Survivor*), and surpassing others through cutthroat individualism (*The Apprentice*) all teach us that the best individual always wins and those who are not winners are losers because of their lack of talent, ability and cunning (Bell-Jordan, 2008).

While reality shows and music award shows are demonstrative of a neoliberalist agenda, comedy has yet to be fully investigated. In the sections that follow we first contextualize our discussion of how race appears within the Justin Bieber roast with brief mention of the process of normalizing a pop cultural obsessions with celebrities. Next we look at Justin Bieber as an artist turned brand. Here we specifically investigate how the "Bieber brand" exploits post-race notions or racial fluidity and cultural sharing via the branding of his celebrity identity through the use of race. This increasingly normalized process (for instance, the branding of Macklemore, Izzy Azalea and Justin Timberlake can be considered additional examples of the success of such a process) creates more space for celebrity manipulation of identity politics as well as increased influence upon how millennials understand the post-racial world.

BRANDING BIEBER: NEW MEDIA AND CELEBRITY OBSESSED CULTURE

The changing contemporary media environment continuously bombards consumers with media products that shape their understanding of the world (Hardy, 2011, 2015; Couldry, 2011 as cited in Hardy, 2011, 2015; Pozner 2010). Celebrity culture, fandom and the infotainment industry have taken on new life in the world of constant media streams (McDonald & Lawrence, 2004). Media has become the primary marketing tool in normalization of new forms of massive infatuation with celebrity practitioners and various products that are marketed via this collective obsession. And, as such, celebrity culture and fascination has in many ways blurred the lines between information, social engagement and entertainment. As branded commodities and with the aid of the continuous media, celebrities connect to the identity construction of fans in ways that have never happened before. Studies show that fan obsession has taken on a more personal form, moving beyond simple parasocial contact to a space of encounter and two-way communication (Marwick & boyd, 2011, 2015). Celebrities have created a following and a focus that means they become the sites for understanding other aspects of culture and society. Thus, this article explores how neoliberalist constructions of race and equality are normalized under media practices around celebrity culture; we also wish to suggest that these constructions have a higher probability of influencing dominant perspectives when embraced and practiced within the context of celebrity culture.

WHO IS JUSTIN BIEBER? THE CREATION OF A POST-RACIAL POP CULTURE ICON

Justin Bieber rose to stardom in part through the fandom of his young audiences on new media—by receiving likes on youtube.com and twitter buzz. His career was also helped considerably by relationships with popular older artists, including rapper and block-buster actor Ludacris, and through work with singer/songwriter turned producer, Usher Raymond. Justin Bieber embodies many of the attributes of former pop culture stars who borrow their styles and genres from African-American culture. Like Justin Timberlake, his career begins as a young, white male who is attractive and sings rhythm and blues, a traditionally African-American musical genre that is very marketable as mainstream entertainment. Justin Bieber's popularity grew more particularly out of a late 1980s and early 90s environment in which all white male boy bands would sings R&B popularized in the mid-1980s. Groups like *New Kids on the Block* for example, built a solid following via the commodification of black musical styles by very young, attractive white men.

Justin Bieber is particularly fascinating because of the successful incorporation of deviant, black masculinity into his celebrity persona (see also Authors 2015 on Bieber and sexuality as well). Recruited to Hollywood after posting YouTube videos, Bieber's first album went platinum when he was 15 years old. Turning 21 at the time of the Comedy Central Roast, Bieber has managed to maintain his maturing fan base by at least partially shifting his pretty boy persona to one of a bad boy who interacts with rappers and other black male celebrities, while violating the law and having transitory relationships with attractive, and often famous, women. Throughout his rise to stardom, Justin Bieber has strategically played off of the color line (for example, by using the n-word repeatedly, by recording R&B songs with black artists, and by dating a Latina celebrity) in a way that has made him millions and made his Comedy Central Roast an excellent site for understanding the complex moments when neoliberalist definitions of race and masculine identity intersect (Bucholtz, 2001).

COMEDY CENTRAL AND THE COMEDY CENTRAL ROAST

Owned by Viacom, Comedy Central is a cable television channel known for its cutting-edge and sometimes crass comedic programing. The channel is aired globally with international channels operated by Viacom International Media. In recent years Comedy Central has capitalized on the pseudo-news programming format and use of comedy to discuss social issues in a way that is attractive to Millennials, creating a clear presence of the channel, and its programming, in pop culture. Shows appearing on Comedy Central, including *The Daily Show with Jon Stewart, The Colbert Report, Chappelle's Show* and, more recently, *The Nightly Show with Larry Wilmore, Why? With Hannibal Buress* and *Key & Peele* are known for tackling contemporary social issues via humor (Rossing 2012; Bahm 2005).

The Comedy Central Roast brand is a combination of pop culture references designed to sell celebrities, and outright mocking of the looks and character of the featured guest. To date, Justin Bieber is the youngest person to be roasted on Comedy Central with other controversial pop culture icons including, Flavor Flav (2007), Donald Trump (2011), and Charlie Sheen (2011). A key pop culture roaster has been Seth McFarlane, a comedian, actor and producer whose comedic style is often filled with racist, classist, ableist and sexist jokes. The Comedy Central Roast format undeniably is one wherein roasters engage the audience with blatantly politically incorrect comedy that addresses issues that would otherwise be considered inappropriate for public discussion. In the Justin Bieber roast these jokes tend to be racist, lookist, and a bit misogynistic in nature while at the same time laughable and conceived of as harmless. In this sense, roasts are part of an age-old function of formal comedic events in which shared anxieties are released as the social order is inverted and mocked in a kind of group catharsis.

The particular roast analyzed below was two-hour television special, hosted by an EmCee, comedian and blockbuster actor Kevin Hart, and a roast master, Jeffrey Ross of the Friars Club. The cast members of the roast were sports legend Shaquille O'Neill; popular television actress Natasha Leggero; septuagenarian home-improvement celebrity and ex-con Martha Stewart; rapper Snoop Dogg; rapper/actor Ludacris; and several other comedians.

The comedians were Hannibal Buress who, although well-established on the comedy circuit, has only recently achieved widespread recognition through his comments about the rape accusations against Bill Cosby and a program launched three months after the Bieber roast on Comedy Central, *Why? With Hannibal Buress* (July 2015); comedian Chris D'Elia, billed as a close friend of Justin Bieber's; and Pete Davidson, a first year cast member of Saturday Night live famous for having a father who died in the attacks on the World Trade Center, and known for playing off his ethnic ambiguity in his comedy. Justin Bieber's role was to sit by the podium and look like a good sport, and at the end to finally take the microphone and fire back his own comedic insult at each guest.

The rhythm of the show involved each guest being invited to stand up at the microphone after either a kind or a mocking introduction by Kevin Hart. Each celebrity would deliver approximately 18 one-liners, although as roast master, Kevin Hart delivered considerably more in a staccato-like rapid fire delivery. Commercial breaks were presented between each celebrity segment at the podium. The audience included gala-dressed attendees who were shown frequently reacting to the jokes. There were many celebrities such as Jaden Smith and Kourtney Kardashian, including friends and former girlfriends of Justin Bieber like Kendall Jenner and Scooter Braun, and a few mass appeal or superstar comedians like Dave Chappelle, whose presence was acknowledged by multiple roast participants. Finally, near the end of the roast, a special guest put in an appearance when comedian and blockbuster actor Will Farrell appeared on stage in the character and costume of Ron Burgundy, a character one of his movies, *Anchorman* (2004). Farrell also presented a series of 18 one-liners about Justin Bieber and then walked off stage. The roast was written by a head writer, Chris McGuire, and nine additional writers. Three writers were billed as providing additional special material.

In general, stand up forms of comedy are reliant upon smoothness of timing, where gaps between jokes and audience laughter must be carefully managed so as to not lose momentum. The roast participants carefully adhered to a schedule and to a proscribed rhythm to keep the roast moving apace, and the audience buzzing with laughter. Additionally, each roaster would begin his or her time at the podium generally with an indecent or extremely insulting joke as a way to refocus audience attention on the matter at hand – laughter and the overturning of social norms. This pattern can be seen in other roasts, and its structure is even overtly referred to by the comedians in metacomedic statements, such as in the second line of the entire roast, where Kevin Hart's metacommentary joke on his first joke of the roast was, "Yeah, that's a dick-sucking joke."

METHODOLOGY AND THE DATA

The current study is discursive and descriptive content analysis of the entire roast. It is concerned with the ways that comedy programming within a 'post' context, and targeted to the millennial generation, works to shape and maintain dominant perspectives on race and gender. More importantly we use the data to interrogate the neoliberal nature of the humor both on part of the comedic cast and the media consumers. To this end, we analyze especially jokes on race and at least a few on gender. Such features are analyzed as a means of assessing comedy as a neoliberalist ideological tool wherein assumptions of equality and inclusion are normalized via the creation of an atmosphere where stereotypes, slurs and epithets, inequality, and social positioning can be laughed at and ultimately marginalized and disregarded.

We transcribed the 300 individual lines delivered by the ten participants in a program that lasted just under one hour and 40 minutes, commercials not included. It should be noted that all but eight lines of the 300 spoken lines at the roast contained jokes. Next, we tabulated the lines that were jokes by topic and/or type. Over half the jokes were multivalent, which is common with humor, so several were categorized under at least two topics or types. An example of a multivalent joke would be the following joke which is both classic form embodied in *you're so ugly jokes* and a joke that impugns the *masculinity* of the addressee. "Snoop, you look like a retired WNBA player." This, the joke was categories as an "ugly" joke as well as a "masculinity" joke.

A very large number of the jokes were of the formulae or topics widely used in well-recognized forms of comedy and even daily forms of humor – *gay jokes*, *has been jokes*, jokes about *age*, and jokes about *abnormal size,* both small and large, and jokes about *ability or talent*. Many were similes, easily recognized, such as "Justin, you're like our Beatles. Not the band, but the bugs that live in shit." A few highly multivalent jokes were difficult to classify, such as the following *has been* joke: "Snoop was like a cool ass salamander, (and now he is like) a rejected mortal combat boss: 'now you have to fight fake crip'." This joke got laughs even though it was unusual for the roast and although its humor seems to go beyond the *has been* category. With a small number of the jokes (8 out of 292 jokes) we nonetheless had difficulty labeling their valencies or levels of multiple meaning. For example, Hannibal Buress got laughs for this line, "Justin, I don't like your music. I hate your music, man. I hate your music," and the reasons the audience laughed were probably multifarious – their discomfort at a forthright expression of dislike; their ironic appreciation of an insult that is a non-joke in a format where all insults are supposed to be jokes, etc. We also categorized jokes by the relative amount of audible laughter they received, although the majority of the time, each joke was received with at least a range of 2-3 out of a scale of 0-5, zero indicating no audience reaction and five extended laughter and standing ovation. In our analysis below, if laughter or lack of laughter impacted our interpretation of anything, we make a note of it. Appendix item one provides the categories of jokes created for our analysis, the number of jokes for this type of topic and an explanatory example, when necessary.

THE POST-RACE PREOCCUPATION WITH RACE: MOST COMMON JOKE TYPES AND TOPICS

Ultimately, the vast majority of the jokes were centered on race. Of these, there were jokes overtly about race (47), race stereotypes (7), the N-word (6), King-Kong/Donkey Kong (2), and black wannabes (11); they were also targeted at all present except for comedian Chris D'Elia and Roastmaster Jeffrey Ross, both of whom are phenotypically white in body, build, skin tone and speech. In an American roast program cast with five black celebrities, four white celebrities, one white guest celebrity, and featuring a target who is known for branding himself as a black wannabe, unsurprisingly, these race-based jokes constituted 24% of the total jokes. The next most frequently utilized category of jokes was about talent/skill/ability, which were 14% of the total jokes. There was a very large number of these jokes but nearly all had the same basic structures of either comparing the target of the joke (both Bieber and the other participants) to someone purportedly better or more famous, or highlighting the lack of talent or ability that impedes the addressee's achieving the pinnacle of success. Third, jokes about sexuality and gender were also quite common (slut/whore, 9; sodomy, 5; lesbian, 3; hermaphrodite, 3; gay, 10), totaling 10% of the jokes. For the purposes of this article we present details on the qualities of the race jokes below.

JOKES ABOUT RACE ON THE COMEDY CENTRAL ROAST

The 73 jokes or 24% of jokes about race on the roast were nearly always based on racial stereotypes and to be absorbed without conceiving as hateful, one had to be of the mindset, 'it's just a joke, don't be so sensitive.' An example would be "Like Superman, Shaq never met his real father" or "Look at Shaq, he has on a tie with… glitter? That's not diamonds, that graffiti" or "Shaq's dick is so big he has to use drop box to send a dick pic," or "(On Shaq's career) shattering 8 backboard and 79 cervixes," or "Shaq has a doctorate of education, but you wouldn't know it by how he pronounces doctorate of education." All of these jokes were what led the authors into discussing how a roast with such crafted black representation could be so full of profoundly simple racist jokes. All of these jokes and the two dozen others like them require the audience to know common racial stereotypes (black paternity is always in question; black people like tacky flashy clothing and create graffiti; black men have large penises and like to show off their sexuality; black men are hypersexual), and to mentally enact that stereotype in order to imagine the meaning of the joke. Likewise, to laugh at the joke is to recognize the inversion of the stereotype. In a very real sense, the inverted meanings of the jokes are the opposites of the stereotypes and a deliverer or an interpreter of such jokes can legitimately say that they are creating humor through inversion and do not intend the racist or the other bias-inducing meanings that coincidentally happen to appear on the surface level of the joke. And yet, these jokes do not acknowledge the structures or contexts out of which the stereotypes have emerged, and in toto they erase the signification of the historical nature of bias-inducing stereotypes and the harm they cause (Barthes 2013). Their effect therefore relies entirely on visualizing or otherwise reinforcing ugly stereotypes without critique or context. Moreover, they are perceived as defensible as harmless by the neoliberal interpreter who says, 'lighten up, it's just a joke.'

Several but by no means the majority of the jokes take account of wider structural issues or sometimes history and do indeed provide embedded critiques of the representational politics of race. In particular, they tend to satirize race-pandering in the media and in Justin Bieber's own persona. Here are a few examples. "All these rappers on stage and Martha Stewart has done the most jail time," is a complex joke with many interpretations, but these media jokes tend to hinge on the idea that the stereotype of rappers (as the media exemplary of black men) is indeed a media-generated stereotype, inviting the hearer to question what he or she sees in a deeper way. Another joke, "Kevin, I loved you as Black Annie," interestingly reinforces biases against short men and in that sense is a noncritical neoliberal joke with ugly implications for those who are not average in height or taller. And yet, the media critique is a deep and disturbing one of a media that panders to audience segmentation through segregated media, perhaps segregation within media, or even separate-but-equal media. Another similar critical joke that still perpetuates size-ism is "Is this a roast, or is it *Tyler Perry's Of Mice or Men*" lampooning the African-American filmmaker whose portrayals of black life try to work through cultural stereotype in a way similar to how mainstream television comedies that portray all white families. Another media critique joke seems to be interpretable from multiple political perspectives, in which Hannibal Buress remarks "(It's) good to see Comedy Central diversifying with whatever race Pete Davison is." To understand the joke, one has to generate a certain level of cynicism about controversies of equal opportunity and marketing diversity, and in that sense, this joke might require an anti-stereotyping, critical eye to be interpreted in the first place. However, such jokes also have a neoliberal interpretation which says that the media unnecessarily panders to diversity or secondarily that segregated media are about giving the people what they want (Pozner, 2010).

RACE JOKES AND JUSTIN BIEBER: WANNABES AND THE N-WORD

Highly salient to our discussion below is the phenomenon that Justin Bieber is frequently criticized for race-crossing in multiple jokes. He is likened to Michael Jackson with jokes like "(As) Michael Jackson got older, he acted whiter," which implies that Justin Bieber's career is aging him into acting blacker. Moreover, this joke heavily invokes stereotypes and the pick-and-choose quality of the blacker side of Justin's persona, when Snoop Dogg points out that, "most niggas like myself, we go crazy when we get famous. Buy some dope cars, date crazy women, but Justin, you bought a monkey." Additionally, Kevin Hart shows up contrasts when he tells Justin that "gangstas don't through eggs," a joke which got uproarious laughter. Overall, the black wanna be and N-word jokes were the most critical of both race stereotypes, and of media pandering to race and structural difference. This criticality is well summed up in this joke about the black experience delivered by Snoop Dogg, the comedian most often presented as being the most authentic of the black personas on stage: "Black people, we normally hate when white people steal our culture, be like us, minus the discrimination, police brutality and marching and shit… long list. Welcome to the family, my nigger." In those joke, race crossing and cultural appropriation without paying the price is directly attended to although this joke also harkens to authenticity, a critique that again, Snoop Dogg as the blackest of the black men, with a long career of black artistry in multiple black music genres and acting in critical race movies is entitled to say. By way of concluding this section, Kevin Hart's joke about the right to be black came early in the show, and was used to frame Justin Bieber's crafting of his persona through borrowing of black cultural forms, especially Bieber's repeated use of the N-word. Kevin says "(Justin), you said the N word on a video; that was gangster (although) a billion other black people say that every day." Other N-word jokes go along these lines, throwing into doubt Justin Bieber's authenticity as a representative of the black experience.

DISCUSSION

Outside of the comedy world and most specifically in the political arena, issues around colorblindness and neoliberal notions of post-race and gender identity are in a space of uncertainty. For those who choose to accept the neoliberalist narrative, the social milieu we live in provides much seemingly indisputable evidence that we have moved toward a more egalitarian and pluralistic world. African Americans, women, the sexually ostracized, those living with disabilities and other historically marginalized groups are more visible than ever before, with president Barack Obama symbolically leading a change of demographic perception of inequality and opportunity, and Hillary Clinton seeming to continue the walk toward diversity in power.

The format of comedy in the Justin Bieber Roast speaks specifically to the national imaginary of a world wherein the denial of social inconsistencies that come with the 'post' era are fully formed (Squires et al, 2010). The assumed new balance of power that arises from ignoring structural inequalities that come with identity difference has not been realized in the way that participants in the comedic discussion of race and gender assume. Hegemonic institutions, structures, and social positions remain in place so that forces of power and inequality go unchallenged. Such hegemony is perpetuated even as the millennial generation's consciousness is penetrated with popular culture scripts that assume there has been a significant change and the bringing in of an epoch/era of equality that affords humorous discussions of chauvinistic, misogynistic, homophobic and racist stereotypes.

THE POST-RACE PREOCCUPATION WITH RACE

The most important aspect of the roast observed was indeed the preoccupation with discussions of race. We argue that, ideally, one could interpret such a discussion as progressive acknowledgment of racial difference with the use of comedic media as a platform for discussions that are otherwise uncomfortable (Rossing, 2012). However, this is indeed a façade. The specific treatment of race within the context of *Comedy Central's Roast of Justin Bieber* provided a basis for assuming that racial inequality is no longer significant. In other words, the nature of the jokes and the framing of race communicate the idea that to make fun of one's race (or to a lesser extent gender identity, gender expression and/or sexuality) becomes the equivalent of making fun of one's career setbacks, embarrassing run-ins with the law or even one's height. The use of race as the foundation for systemic, institutionalized inequality through policy and legislation was only in three or four jokes out of 292 given the acknowledgment it deserves. The exceptions were key counterhegemonic moments, such as the brief critiques of media diversity or Snoop Dogg's challenge to Bieber's appropriation of black cultural forms without delving into the problems of discrimination and systematic discrimination out of which those forms grew. It is instead equated with other individual problems that are fair game for humor and ridicule. Much like neoliberal rhetoric in other aspects of social life, such minimization of race[1] in the context of comedy, provides basis for assuming that policies designed to address persistent inequality are simply no longer necessary. To be black and male is to be short, or to be a media foil for criminal behavior, or to be tacky. The roast's ongoing use of black stereotypes in jokes that are to be laughed away is how difference that can be joked about rather than a fact of life shaped by inequalities often supported by structural, social, political and institutional agents.

Additionally, the preoccupation with race in the context of the roast ironically further demonstrates the importance of race in shaping public discourse, social interaction, and politics of difference. The preoccupation with race in a post-racial world seems to function as an indication that race does indeed continue to shape the lives of whites and people of color alike. In other words, while race continues to function as a social fact, neoliberalism ideas that we are over race, living in an equal playing field were black men, white men, and white women take a stage to joke at each others' expense establishes a public dialogue and consciousness that is both racist and post-race, especially among millennial generation.

CONCLUSION

Research shows that comedy routines tend to create a space for open and honest discussions on social inequality and injustices in the public sphere (Rossing, 2010). As a completely subjective and culturally contextualized genre, comedians are often given a pass for acknowledging and humoring us about what we already know. While the contradictions of acknowledging race and forgetting race are serious, and paradoxical, concerns of (in)equality in American cultural life of the post-race era remain significant. An indication of the continued paradoxical anxiety is the fact that the popularity of comedy that openly discusses race has remained high. In the instance of Justin Bieber's roast, the roasters engage a number of racial jokes about Justin and other members of the roasting team. However, we argue that what appears to be a pop culture indication of a beyond race is instead working against a true move toward post-race reality. By calling attention to the ways in which race and gender jokes in the *Comedy Central Roast of Justin Bieber* reinscribe inequalities around race and gender identity, our study provides a foundation for understanding the communication of neoliberalist ideals in media designed for consumption by the millennial generation.

REFERENCES

Bahm, G. (2005). *The Daily Show:* Discursive Integration and the Reinvention of Political Journalism. *Political Communication, 22*(3), 259–276. doi:10.1080/10584600591006492

Barthes, R. (2013). *Mythologies: the Complete Edition, in a New Translation* (2nd ed.). (R. Howard & A. Lavers, Trans.). New York, NY: Hill and Wang.

Bell-Jordan, K. (2008). Black, White and a Survivor of the Real World: Constructions of Race on Reality TV. *Critical Studies in Media Communication, 25*(4), 353–372. doi:10.1080/15295030802327725

Bonilla-Silva. (2009). *Racism without Racists: Colorblind Racism and the Persistence of Racial Inequality in America* (3rd ed.). Lanham, MA: Roman and Littlefield.

Bucholtz, M. (2001). *White Kids: Language, Race and Styles of Youth Identity*. Oxford University Press.

Gallagher, C. A. (2003). Color-Blind Privilege: The Social and Political Functions of Erasing the Color Line in Post-Race America. *Race, Gender, & Class, 10*(4), 22–37.

Gill, R. (2011). Supersexualize Me! In G. Dines & J. Humez (Eds.), *Gender, Race, and Class in Media: A Critical Reader* (pp. 278–284). Thousand Oaks, CA: Sage Publications.

Goldberg, D. (2008). *The Threat of Race: Reflections on Racial Neoliberalism*. Malden, MA: Wiley-Blackwell. doi:10.1002/9781444304695

Hardy, J. (2015). Mapping Commerical Intertextuality: HBO's True Blood. In Gender, Race, and Class in Media: A Critical Reader. Thousand Oaks, CA: Sage Publications.

Kendall, D. E. (2011). *Framing class: Media representations of wealth and poverty in America*. Lanham, MD: Rowman & Littlefield.

Marwick, A., & boyd, . (2014). Networked privacy: How teenagers negotiate context in social media. *New Media & Society, 16*(7), 1051–1067. doi:10.1177/1461444814543995

Marwick & boyd. (2011). To See and Be Seen: Celebrity Practice on Twitter. *Convergence, 17*(2), 139-158.

McDonald, I. R., & Lawrence, R. G. (2004). Filling the 24×7 News Hole Television News Coverage Following September 11. *The American Behavioral Scientist, 48*(3), 327–340. doi:10.1177/0002764204268989

Nakamura, L. (2002). *Cybertypes: Race, Ethnicity and Identity on the Internet*. New York, NY: Routledge.

Nakamura, L. (2008). *Digitizing Race: Visual Cultures of the Internet*. Minneapolis, MN: University of Minnesota Press.

Pozner, J. (2010). *Reality Bites Back: The Troubling Truth about Guilty Pleasure T.V.* New York, NY: Seal Press.

Rossing, J. (2012). Deconstructing Postracialism: Humor as a Critical Cultural Project. *The Journal of Communication Inquiry*, *30*(1), 44–61. doi:10.1177/0196859911430753

Schiappa, E., Gregg, P., & Hewes, D. (2006). Can One TV Show Make a Difference? Will & Grace and the Parasocial Contact Hypothesis. *Journal of Homosexuality*, *51*(4), 15–37. doi:10.1300/J082v51n04_02 PMID:17135126

The Comedy Central Roast of Justin Bieber . (2015). Comedy Central.

Winograd, M., & Hais, M. (2011). *Millenial Momentum: How a New Generation Is Remaking America*. Rutgers University Press.

ENDNOTE

[1]   See Bonilla-Silva, 2009, for a detailed discussion on the minimization of race as a key in shaping the daily experiences of people of color.

APPENDIX

Table 1.

Category	Total Number of Jokes	Example
Age: Old	8	"Martha is so old her first period was in the Renaissance."
Age: Young	8	"(I've) never roasted somebody with a bedtime before."
Authenticity	4	"(I've) done a whole bunch of roasts, right? But they never let a real player on stage with me, Ludacris."
Bulimia	1	"(Justin), you've fucked more models than bulimia."
Racial Stereotypes	7	"That's right. That's what you call a fishing joke. I fish mutherfuckers." (Said by Snoop Dogg, highlighting the idea that white people like to fish but ganstas are not known for their fishing prowess). "Most niggas like myself, we go crazy when we get famous. Buy some dope cars, date crazy women, but Justin, you bought a monkey."
Black wannabe	11	"You are being kicked when down; want to be black get used to it."
Child exploitation	3	"I only wish the kid was a 9 year old." (referring to Justin getting publicity by assaulting a young person)
Child molestation	3	"(Scooter Braun) found Justin on the internet in the middle of the night, this little white boy."
Criminal Justice (about incarceration or run-ins with the law)	13	"All these rappers on stage and Martha Stewart has done the most jail time." (also racialized). And "I'm here to give Justin tips for when he ends up in prison."
Criminal Behavior (about being engaged in illegal activity but not including references to run-ins with the law or incarceration)	8	"I know I've been driving recklessly, smoking pot, abandoning monkeys."
Cuckoldry	1	"(Justin), you are about to get fucked harder than Orlando Bloom fucked Selena Gomez."
Dead Dad	3	"The only person that's inhaled more smoke than Snoop? Pete's dad inside the world trade center."
Driving	1	"(Justin has the) voice of Stevie Wonder and the driving skills of Stevie Wonder"
Drugs	4	"I ate three brownies right before they called and asked me to do this roast."
Fame	9	"(Introduction to Pete Davidson) newest member of Saturday Night Live whose intro is longer than his Wikipedia page."
Fetishism	1	"Marta, I want to fuck you so bad. I bet your pubic hair is Fifty Shades of Grey."
Gay (specifically around homosexual desire as being unmasculine)	10	"When J-Bird got arrested, (he) had a big smile, because he knows what happens in jail."
Has been	18	"Ludacris and Snoop, if I were 38, I'd be freaking out right now"
Hermaphrodite	4	"(That was an) impressive impression of Justin right down to the clit."
Immigrant	1	"Selena wanted to bang this guy; proving Mexicans willing to do disgusting jobs that American's just won't do."

continued on following page

Table 1. Continued

Category	Total Number of Jokes	Example
Immorality (or exploitation?)	1	"Hannibal Burress, you're the only Bill Cosby accuser that's making money off of it."
Infamy (i.e. being hated or loathed by the public)	3	"Justin was ranked fifth most hated; Kim Dong Il was not even rated that low; he uses your music to torture people."
King Kong/Donkey Kong	2	"…when Shaq takes a break from throwing barrels at super Mario."
Lesbian	3	"Lots are pointing fingers at you lately. Those are just lesbians showing the barber how they want their hair cut."
Marketing	1	After joke about Martha Stewart, "I'm sorry, will I no longer be getting free sheets?"
Masculinity (as in the opposite of embodying a real man's strength and sexual attractiveness)	14	"(About Justin in a strip club) dropped 75 gees, but when the DJ played one of your songs, the dancers complained about their pussies drying up." Example two: "(Justin was) arrested for a collision with a minivan in hometown in Ontario. (Later, he) beat up the minivan owner. Nice work."
Maturity	16	"Justin and Snoop, same problem. Like a teenage boy, he grew up but he stayed in high school."
Media Satire	7	"Is this a roast or is it Tyler Perry's of mice and men?"
Meta Joke (as in jokes about jokes at roasts),	11	Example "Mine was better, Ludacris (reference to dirty joke just told)."
Mumbling, specific to Shaquille O'Neal, who mumbles	2	"(Shaq) has a doctorate of education, but you wouldn't know it by how he pronounces doctorate of education."
N-word	6	There are two types of this joke. One is about Justin Bieber saying the word in rap song, and another is about whether it can be said on the Comedy Central channel repeatedly. "Justin, you know the word." And Snoop Dogg to Kevin: "You had your shot, this is my nigger (at Justin). N, N, N, N, N." (word repeated multiple times: later Kevin Hart says Snoop has used up their allotment of saying the word on television).
Nazis	2	You said Anne Frank would have been a Belieber. If Anne Frank had heard your music, should have ubered to Auschwitz.
Paternity	8	"Ludacris and I had a lot of hours making the Baby Song together. It was the only baby he made on purpose."
Michael Jackson	2	To Justin, "As Michael Jackson got older, he acted whiter."
Primitiveness	2	"Grrr. Grrr. Shaq. Grrr. I like to talk to him in his native tongue."
Quality/Skill/Ability	42	Example one: "You'll never end up like Curt Cobain and Amy Winehouse… respected." Example two: "(When they were) looking for a roast master, let's call Kevin Hart and see if he has Dave Chappelle's number." Example three: "A lot of Beliebers are upset that you haven't won a grammy. There's Martha Stewart, she can be your grammy."
Race	47	"Justin, you dainty wigger. They say you roast the ones you love." Or "Like superman, Shaq never met his real father." Or "Let me take a second explain to the black guys what a father is." Or "Pete, is the same race as whatever the Rock is and any parking attendant ever."
Rape	2	"Please welcome future rapist…"
Size:big	12	"Shaq is so big his toes are in different area codes."

continued on following page

Table 1. Continued

Category	Total Number of Jokes	Example
Size: small	20	"Kevin is only comedian with a star on the yellow brick road."
Slut/Whore	9	"I do a lot of gardening; you are the dirtiest, used up ho, I have ever seen."
Sodomy	5	"Best part about taking Justin from behind, shave half his head and pretend it's Miley Cyrus."
Stupidity	8	"You all got to excuse my retarded cousin." Example two: "Chris is here (and he is) Justin's favorite comedian. That's like being Shaq's favorite poet."
Ugly	14	"Jeff, looks like someone put Seth Rogen in the microwave."
Wealth	5	"But my worst regret was crashing my Maserati into Jeff's Saturn in the parking lot."

Chapter 3

The Personalized and Personal "Mass" Media – From "We-Broadcast" to "We-Chat":
Reflection on the Case of Bi Fujian Incident

Yu Zhang
New York Institute of Technology, USA

ABSTRACT

China's two major social media, the microblog Weibo and the messaging service WeChat have played important roles in representing citizens' voices and bringing about social changes. They often grow an ordinary event into a national debate as in the case of the Bi Fujian incident. They have also turned ordinary Chinese citizens into amateur reporters, empowering them to influence on issues that matter to them. An equalizer of power and discourse opportunity, the personalized and personal social media "weapons" are delivering the much needed social justice and consolation to the Chinese citizens amid widespread injustice, inequality, hypocrisy, indifference and corruption in the Chinese society.

INTRODUCTION

In a widely circulated home video on WeChat, according to the *Guardian* (Guardian, 2015), Bi Fujian, the host of a talent show at China's flagship state television station, the CCTV (China Central Television), was entertaining his companions at a private dinner by mimicking an old Chinese revolutionary song about Communist Party-led soldiers fighting bandits in northeastern China in the 1940s. Based on media reports, to the laughter of those guests, Bi inserted improvised comments in a speaking voice between the lyrics. After the part that mentioned China's late paramount leader Mao Zedong, he used a vulgar Chinese insult, and said "he has ruined us all" (Guardian, 2015). He also mocked the soldiers' battles as meaningless and the song's claim of victory boastful. The WeChat video went instantly viral across China. The incident renewed debate both on free speech and about Mao, who many Chinese blame for the disastrous 1959-1961 famine and the decade-long (1966-1976) chaotic Cultural Revolution. However, Bi's remarks also drew sharp criticisms from the state media and Mao's many loyal and vocal followers (Guardian, 2015) despite the fact that his policies have been discontinued and critiqued. The

DOI: 10.4018/978-1-5225-0212-8.ch003

revolutionary leader, whose portrait still hangs on Tiananmen Rostrum, remains a source of legitimacy for the Chinese Communist Party (CCP). The identity of the person(s) who taped and released the video remain a mystery.

In recent years, the Chinese microblog (Weibo), the Chinese version of Twitter, and WeChat (Weixin 微信) play an increasingly important role in transforming a local or trivial event into a national issue. Chinese netizens' intensive and extensive discussion often add provoking meanings and value to that event and frequently turn a seemingly insignificant issue into major national event. With the help of WeChat and Weibo, citizen journalism and online public opinion increasingly influence the behaviors of traditional media and government. This paper investigates the Bi Fujian parody case with regard to WeChat and Weibo. It argues that this kind of "silent" or less vocal expression, which differs from Weibo's "broadcasting" style, has become an influential way for netizens to engage in civic discourse. It also makes the state censorship less effective by upsetting the media and public agenda.

Following a literature review on Chinese social media, my study will use the Bi Fujian case and the phenomena of WeChat and Weibo to examine the following areas: 1), the differences between Weibo and WeChat, and why more people began to favor WeChat as their choice of social media. 2), the paper argues that not all censorship is political in nature and some may be legitimate and beneficial to the society. 3), social media upset as well as reset public agenda and media agenda. 4), balance, responsibility and compromise between the netizens and the state are needed when it comes to information and speech liberalization and legitimate limitations. 5), WeChat and Weibo serve as an equalizer of social and political power and discourse opportunity. 6), these personalized social media deliver the much needed social justice to the Chinese citizens amid widespread injustice, inequality, indifference and corruption in the Chinese society.

LITERATURE REVIEW

In China's communication and political systems, the media are instruments through which the Party propagates its ideologies and government policies (Pan, 2000). However, with the rapid development of the social media, optimism and even excitement about its ability to derail state agenda-setting capacity and transfer some of that agenda setting power to the public has been high (Chiu, Ip, & Silverman, 2012). As the "singing" incident demonstrates, citizen-generated events on social media has become an important news source for professional media, such as the official *Xinhua News Agency, People's Daily* and *CCTV*, which all have covered this case. Some other sensitive issues, such as the sudden collapsing of residential buildings, have also attracted national media who join the social media to demand the government agencies and authorities to be more accountable and transparent.

Some studies disagree on how effective social media can be. For example, a study by Pew Research Center and Rutgers University (Center, 2014) finds that social media actually weakens instead of enhancing people's engagement in expressing their opinions especially when they differ from their friends due to a spiral of silence impact (Center, 2014). However, other scholars have argued that discourses are more than expressions of meaning or emotion, they construct or build the world, and as such can serve as a form of an empowerment or power brokering (Poster, 1995; Stockmann D., 2014). Chinese civic discourse, which has been transformed by the emergence of the social media, is citizens' collective voice on public affairs regardless of their socio-economic class (Chen, 2014; Sullivan, 2012; King, Pan, & Roberts, 2013). It is both countering and complementary to the authoritative discourse and elitist discourse (Pell, 1995). Besides censorship, commercialization of Chinese media also deprives Chinese citizens of the opportunity for open civic discourse. Pressure from advertisers and ratings render the media programs and their contents to become hegemonic and homogenized and restrictions on length and content render making real statements near impossible (Xu, 2012).. Besides, the contents can be edited by the gatekeepers, thus distorting and degrading civic discourses.

The Chinese government's strict censorship policies, and control over Internet appear to have paradoxically resulted in a vibrant proliferation of online creative public discourse and folk narratives (Esarey & Qiang, 2011). For example, to bypass the censorship, netizens often uncensored alternative but similarly sounding Chinese words, taking advantage of the features of the Chinese language. One explanation for the paradox is that after years of censorship and suppression, Chinese citizens have finally found a discursive outlet on social media (Economist, 2013; Leibold, 2011). Citizen online discourse has become so popular even the CCP often listens to the comments, suggestions, and complaints (Luo, 2014). Weibo and WeChat articulate an individual-to-public agenda, which competes with the state agenda and expands these alternative public platforms. They also promote expression of personal emotions, concerns, and opinions on public affairs, and pushes the government for transparency and accountability (Wang, 2013; Chen, 2014). The intensive discussions on various events and accidents often triggered broader national debates on issues such as celebrity behaviors, product safety, official corruption, and government transparency (Gu, 2014; Xu, 2012). Weibo discussion on villagers' protests of local corruption, land seizure, and police power abuse have upset the state agenda in portraying a harmonious society through the mainstream media. Weibo and WeChat enable a self-organized network of contentious politics, simply by aggregating and scaling up grievances from ordinary citizens without conventional organization or a coherent collective identity (Chen, 2014). If a case trigged by social media quickly gains national attention and thus becomes more sustainable, it eventually generates discussions on the political system and development policy (Esarey & Qiang, 2011). Agenda-setting theory (McCombs, 2005) emphasizes the media's role as a central gatekeeper to construct the social reality in the public's mind and that the media can transfer the salience of issues on media agenda to the public agenda. According to Cairns (Cairns, 2013), agenda setting is a powerful tool the CCP relies on to influence public opinion. By directing toward and concentrating on reporting a particular topic, the media "help" the public find which issues and topics are important by virtue of the mere fact that they are reported on or not. While reporters do have some discretion to cover these topics, they nevertheless follow the Party line to avoid censorship or professional consequences (Cairns, 2013). It is argued that agenda setting as a form of soft-power, is superior to censorship when it comes to thought control (Cairns, 2013), as the latter often encounters resistance whereas the former can seep through people's minds and hearts to influence. Besides, while human censors can sometimes remove an online critical post almost as soon as it is created, but damaging messages may spread when a censor hesitates or consulting with their supervisors (Stockmann D., 2014; Stockmann & Gallagher, 2011). Thus, the Chinese government has realized that a more sophisticated way to exert state influence over public discourse is by allowing selective dissent that acknowledges the issue. For example, Xi's anti-corruption campaign encourages media to report on previous taboos, such as high-level CCP corruption to convince the public that this CCP leadership is very serious in curbing corruption. This serves to both dampen online rumors about a specific case and to take a preemptive strike against any criticisms. In this capacity, despite its temporary reputational costs, this proactive approach enhances the Party's long-term reputation and thus is able to influence the public in a positive way.

A TALE OF TWO SOCIAL MEDIA

The spectacular development of the Chinese social media is epitomized by the growth of Weibo and WeChat. Their unique niche and role in Chinese society lie in their abilities to reach and influence the masses in a personal way. In a society where information and media are still tightly controlled, the public quickly embraced the two "personal" and "personalized" media. Within two months of the launch of Sina Weibo in August 2009, it amassed one million users, and by its eighth month, 10 million (Millward, 2012). Within less than two years of Weibo's inception, numbers increased to 249 million in 2011 (CNNIC, Statistics report of Chinese internet development, 2012). The Sina Weibo as China's most popular "Twitter" has richer multimedia functionalities than Twitter (Chiu, Ip, & Silverman, 2012). Besides, Weibo's 140-Chinese-character limit allows more information to be transmitted than Twitter due to the nature and feature of the Chinese characters, which contain more information than the English words especially in permutation (Li J., 2014). The Twitter-like Weibo allows for immediate distribution of information from grassroots sources including photos and videos as a platform for snippets of interesting news and conversation flows on socially popular topics.

WeChat, on the other hand, resembles Facebook, but offers heightened privacy in communicating among an exclusive friend circle. Launched in 2011, WeChat, known as Weixin (微信) in Chinese, attracted 50 million users in the first year and over 400 million users globally (Hong, 2013). WeChat's identity as a private communication platform, to some degree, insulates it from censorship. Besides, the volume of explicit political discourse on WeChat is very small (Sloan, 2014). WeChat's privacy barriers has created a social networking space that respects the Chinese psyche and society against sharing some information and opinions in unlimited public (Simcott, 2014). This mobile messaging app focuses on communication among close friends and provides more intimate and private social-networking experiences than many other social media including Facebook (Millward, 2012; Zoo, 2014). However, beyond its appearance as a tool of one-on-one interaction, it is also a personal mass media. WeChat's easy-to-use feature and private nature are an efficient way to stay in touch with a personal but potentially enormous circle.

FROM TOWN SQUARES TO TEAHOUSES

Weibo, once China's major online oasis for vibrant debate, saw a drop of fifty-six million users in 2014 alone from 331 to 275 million accounts (CNNIC, Statistics report of Chinese internet development, 2014). Acting to ban posts that threatened national security, reputation or interests, the Chinese authorities closed the Weibo accounts of several prominent critics of government known as the Big Vs. One of them, Charles Xue, was arrested for soliciting prostitutes, although his role as a government critic on Weibo was a key reason he was targeted (Hatton, 2015). Another reason for Weibo's decline is the rise of WeChat, a mobile messaging platform, whose growing popularity and unmatched convenience, has quickly attracted millions of users. Its invitation-only format was disarming to government censors but its seeping power increasingly worries the authorities. If Weibo is a town square or concert stadium, WeChat resembles a chain of private tea houses, where conversation flows like tap water from home to home quietly but quickly. It thrives by filling the opinion void the government neglects and the public wants. For example, stopping local authorities from trampling citizens' rights, such as demolishing their homes or exposing hypocrisy of public figures is powerfully contagious. While these exposures constitute no threat to the CCP, the state is concerned with the power of online discourses and has implemented a new rule: Individuals could face up to three years in prison if their "rumor" posts are viewed 5,000+ times or forwarded 500+ times (Zhao, 2013).

The popularity of WeChat signifies a shift of the trend and paradigm of social media towards a more personal and private mass media model. While both Weibo and WeChat put facts and objectivity to test in a new type of social environment, where diverse incipient masses of civic discourses interpret the discourses as they are constructed and transmitted, WeChat users align themselves with their more personalized audiences to create an alternative civic and news discourse that differs from that of the dominant media. The most significant difference between WeChat and Weibo is in the convergence of their discourse production and consumption processes, which is a new participatory civic engagement model. Weibo allows users to post, share or broadcast brief and personal messages in a virtual town square where people can discuss almost anything. However, its huge user base and town-square format attract growing government scrutiny, resulting in many uncomfortable users switching to rival WeChat, which only lets people see posts from accounts they subscribe to. Because information spreads more slowly on WeChat, the platform has been less of a censorship target. The state media, which are renowned for their turgidity, especially in their print edition, now use social media to publish or promote their news in a livelier and more casual fashion, trying to broaden the party's reach by using unconventional language and popular language to appeal to the masses.

The anonymity to share one's ideas, opinions or videos, as in the Bi Fujian case, in an uninhibited manner make the netizens feel socially connected in an increasingly indifferent Chinese society. WeChat allows people to feel personal although users know that sharing within a small group always means the possibility to share with the masses outside this group--the message may even reach national masses as in the case of Bi Fujian. In the past, the Chinese citizens have few ways to be part of the media's agenda-setting process or start any collective action through the state controlled media (Gu, 2014). Therefore, when social media became available, Chinese citizens quickly realized its agenda-setting and agenda-upsetting power. As in the above case of celebrity Bi Fujian, the person who released this video does not even have to say a word to make his/her point—exposing the hypocrisy of a Party-state media host and the CCTV that made him a national celebrity, and triggered a storm. In other cases, government officials were dismissed or otherwise punished because of the public outcry on Weibo and WeChat, which have become the most dynamic personal mass media for Chinese netizens due to their agenda-setting ability. The quick communication model of Weibo and WeChat, from individual to intertwined groups and to the masses, allow them to seep and expand their boundaries to engage in civic journalism. Its many functions, from text and voice messaging to photo sharing, allow, for example, WeChat users to form a closely knit group, who might want to organize around any given idea or cause. According to *NewZoo* (2014) a social media monitoring website, Tencent, the Chinese Internet company that owns WeChat, also has a PC-based messaging app QQ, whose group chats has about 800 million active monthly users. The growth and consolidation of WeChat and QQ make its potential even more powerful.

IS STATE CONTROL ALL BAD?

The remarks by Bi Fujian, who is a public figure of the state CCTV, embarrassed both the state and CCTV and enraged millions of Chinese citizens. This and other incidents are magnified by the social media and often catch authorities and the masses by surprise. For many years, the Chinese government's dual strategies of information control target both domestic and foreign information contents and sources

(Economist, 2013). Its Great Firewall blocks foreign websites such as YouTube, Facebook and Twitter, while its Golden Shield watch Internet activity within China. Government agencies have invested heavily in manpower and software to track and analyze online behavior, both to gauge public opinion and to contain threats before they spread (Economist, 2013). The Bi Fujian case reminds the government that its "great firewall" and the "golden shield" could do nothing to prevent the release of information or image that could trigger a national debate about Chinese politics. Almost all Chinese internet users have a social media account and spend more time than netizens in other nations (Chiu, Ip, & Silverman, 2012).

China's big four internet service providers, Sina, Tencent, Sohu, and Netease were informed in March 2012 to enforce the state policy of registering users with their real identities (all four companies provide microblog or Weibo services), but the enforcement is so ineffective that the government has to remind them every year (Li, 2015; Lynch, 2015). The government outlaws anonymity in blogs, social networks, online forums and IM services, saying that fake accounts impersonate celebrity, government departments or pretend to be media organizations and release fake news (Hatton, 2015; Li J., 2014; King, Pan, & Roberts, 2013). The media and Western critics usually characterize these restrictions under the umbrella of censorship without seeing any legitimacy in this. However, what are considered unacceptable screen names by the Chinese government might not be welcome in the Western society either. These include anything harmful to the nation, fans ethnic discrimination, spreading rumor or relate to violence, etc. (Lynch, 2015). The identity of the person (s) who taped and released the video about Bi Fujian remains a mystery although the content of the video is not related to any of the banned category. It can be argued that many would like to know the identity of the person, but it can also be argued that if the person knows that he/she can be identified, the person might never have released the video. His freedom or restriction to "speak" affects the public's right to know and ability to debate about the contentious issue surrounding a public figure.

The government insists on identifying users of social media, requiring authentic names registration, and banning misleading personal handles such as "Clinton" or "Xinhua News" in blogs, microblogs, IM services, online forums, news comment sections and related services, according to the Cyberspace Administration of China (Li, 2015; Lynch, 2015). Netizens can still select their own personal usernames that do not involve "illegal, unhealthy or fake" contents and accounts that had "polluted the cyber environment, harmed the interests of the public, and seriously violated socialist values" (Lynch, 2015). The new regulations specifically ban nine categories of usernames and contents, including anything that harms or compromises national security, national secrets, incites ethnic discrimination/hatred, or harms national unity. Names that promote pornography, swindling, gambling, violence, terror, superstition, religious cults, and rumors are also banned (Lynch, 2015). CCP views the Internet as an ideological battleground it cannot afford to lose. Chinese President Xi Jinping has created and personally chairs a new high-level committee on Internet security (Annonymous, 2014).

Western media, scholars and politicians almost always view the Chinese crackdown as bad censorship by an authoritarian regime. The Chinese government has argued that identifying users and verifying their information and tracking their activities can bring increased credibility and integrity to the media and the online environment in general. Also, the Chinese government's blocking of Western social media players such as Twitter and Facebook is usually perceived in the West and academic community from the perspective of censorship only. However, the encouragement and protection of homegrown competitors are part of the reason for such blocking. For example, without the competition from Western social media, Sina Weibo has grown to be popular social network in China, with about 300 million active users and 600 million registered users (Simcott, R., February 27, 2014).. Its multimedia functions, displaying video and photos in timelines, even predated Twitter's rollout of these services. Sina Weibo's competitor Tencent Weibo has more than 230 million active users or a base of 507 million users, thanks to Tencent's instant messaging service, QQ. WeChat has become even more popular and competitive than Weibo with over 300 million users who are attracted by its combining features of Twitter, Facebook, Skype, Instagram and geo-location apps. (Simcott, R. February 27, 2014).

In contrast to the polarizing national debate about the freedom of public and private speech as indicated in the case of the video clip about Bi Fujian, a rare consensus between the Chinese masses and the Chinese government on censorship is in the area of pornography, rumor, fraud and violence. Over the years, the Chinese public have been creating social and psychological cyberspace to explore traditional taboo areas such as pornography and sexual identities as well as facilitating and promoting a porn culture, with widespread and lucrative sex entertainment across the nation (Jacobs, 2012). Ironically, even websites of state media such as the *Xinhua News* agency, *People's Daily* and *CCTV* contain links to provoking pictures and content. On the other hand, as the Bi video incident has shown, the fragmented, decentralized and anonymous nature of the social media postings and their posters makes it difficult to trace and verify their identities. As a result, unidentified and unverified malicious messages, such as rumors or computer viruses can cause harm and sabotage social integrity.

AGENDA UPSETTING

There is no doubt that the Chinese government is mixing "hard" censorship with a "soft" persuasive approach when it comes to social media. By allowing and encouraging critical views and discussion in the case of the video clip of Bi Fujian, the state actually benefits from the explosive critical comments against those who are disrespectful of Mao Zedong and the Party. On the other hand, this video exposed the hypocrisy of the politically correct image of CCTV and its host. Such silent but smart protests on Weibo and WeChat can potentially snowball from issue-specific criticisms into a sweeping denouncement of the CCP and its leadership reminiscent of the weeks leading to the 1989 Tiananmen event. While a crisis can prompt an outburst of public opinion in social media, how government responds can either alleviate or worsen an incident like this. In the Bi Fujian incident, the government took a balanced response, which has served to pacify both the Left, who criticized the defamation of Mao by a public figure, and the Right who insisted on protecting the freedom to speak. The state CCTV fired Bi but did not arrest or charge him. He could have been imprisoned or executed during the era of the Cultural Revolution.

Zhan Zhang and Gianluigi Negro argued that Weibo's roles as alternative media and new journalism foster civic engagement to achieve justice (Zhang & Negro, 2013). They believe that Weibo, as a platform for opinion leaders, maximizes individual power for social impact, and as a public administration tool, keeps netizens informed. The Weibo platform synergistically combines personal, interpersonal and mass communication elements in an intertwined way in disseminating information and creating new ways of communicating. According to Pan (2010), authoritarian regimes can, through content aggregation, generate collective opinion, turning a "private" opinion suddenly into a "public" opinion. What individuals say on the social media can ultimately contributes to and often becomes the collective opinions. Thus a few online activists can often lead or grow an army of critics to speak out on issues that matter to the public, such as corruption or environmental disaster. What is empowering is that individual Chinese citizens, whom the government usually ignores, can trigger overwhelming opinions from other netizens to collectively criticize the status quo, as in the case of the Bi Fujian incident. The state fears this phenomenon of a firestorm of criticism and commentary, especially when it is hard to identify those behind it and that the potential for those views to snowball into massive protest, online or offline, is huge and real.

Cairns (2013) argues that even without any spin, the media's ability to bring certain thoughts to the public can influence their political stances. Since media only reports on topics of which the government approves or tolerates to support CCP's claims to legitimacy, the result is to shift citizens' prioritization of issues and positions closer to the government's position. For example, two Chinese navy warships rescued 571 Chinese nationals stranded in the Yemen crisis in early 2015 (BBC, 2015). The state media reported that Chinese soldiers only ate pickles - while the citizens they rescued ate like kings. This triggered a wave of scorn on Chinese social media. Rather than being impressed, many Chinese netizens seemed furious and sarcastic about the story, calling the scenes either a misjudged publicity stunt, or simply a reflection of incompetence of navy officers. "Where is military expenditure going?" read one comment on Sina Weibo. If an eight course meal was on offer, the passengers and soldiers could have had four courses each, many pointed out. The story attracted tens of thousands of comments on Sina Weibo.

Despite the challenge, supervision and competition from the social media, the resilience of the "authoritarian" Chinese government has puzzled and impressed the world. The CCP is successful in persuading the public of its legitimacy as well as capable of balancing between censorship and producing exciting media content to keep it in power. For example, its recent state-led project, the China Dream, not only enhances CCP's political legitimization but also fosters heightened national identity and pride and cultivates a nationalistic chorus against Western ideologies and influences. It is not surprising that Bi Fujian is harshly criticized for attacking Mao, who remains a fetish, a national hero and a symbol for many Chinese. President Xi Jinping has fostered greater eagerness to cherish China's inner strength and historic glory to push for the realization of the China dream and to uncover China's historical and cultural past in a quest for a new identity and rejuvenation in the new era.

Social media as a nexus of revealed and disguised identity, ideology and people's everyday lives reflect Chinese collective inspirations for political representations. The voluminous chats surrounding the video clip of Bi Fujian on social media articulate the collective Chinese identity based on the memories of the Mao era. According to Chen Wenhong, social media reflects many contradictions and complexities of Chinese society (Chen, 2014). To resolve these social problems, WeChat and Weibo can help by pushing transparency and enhancing the visibility of oppressed groups by putting the control button in the hands of average Chinese citizens as demonstrated in a growing number of online incidents in recent years. While some studies have celebrated and praised social media, other scholars doubt whether they alone can achieve any genuine political or social changes, arguing that China has been successful in harnessing the power of the Internet without significant political changes (Whyte, 2010; Zhang, 2015; Luo, 2014).

However, the rising tide of activism and discourses on social media, despite state surveillance and control, challenge the legitimacy of the CCP's political power especially on issues that matter to the public such as livelihood, environmental, and social justice. The Chinese government has not only invested enormous technological and human resources on censorship but also on influencing public opinion, for example, using Weibo and WeChat for surveillance as well as mobilization of its citizens. Digital activism and civic engagement are safety valve (Chen, 2014) that allow people to vent their frustration and thus reduce the dangerous pressures felt by Chinese society and force a dialogue and negotiation between the state and civil community through social media. In B's case, the social media stormy discussion not only magnifies and adds fuel to the debates between conservatives and reformers, but also forces into the open the reconsideration of what constitutes private speech and what is not. While China regularly criminalizes certain political speech, it is also a nation where most people still feel they can talk freely among friends or at a dinner table. However, this case reminds the public that the pervasiveness of technology such as smartphones and social media can threaten the cozy social oasis more than state censorship. The combination of smartphones and WeChat could be a killer as well as savior. The Bi Fujian case raises the issue of behavior and speech on and in front of the social media and the consequences. In this case, it ended Bi's career with the prestigious CCTV.

LIBERALIZATION WITH LEGITIMATE LIMITATION

Chinese leaders have long been skeptical and dismissive of the Western style media freedom as trouble-inducing and damaging to China, believing that it will cause China chaos and to dissolve like the former Soviet Union. Despite still believing that complete liberalization of media, information and speech is bad for China, the Chinese leaders now also believe that a certain degree of freedom is actually needed and good for China. For example, the power of amassing public opinions to supervise officials and public figures for their misconducts and reevaluating problematic policies and practices are especially attractive to the CCP leadership who now focus on fighting rampant corruption in the Chinese society. The public's hatred and disdain towards corrupt officials and their abuse of power is a driving force that contributed to the gradual dissolving and loosening of the state monopoly of information and speech. In China's conventional media, the Party-state can easily control the information flow, and information becomes a privilege for authorities but luxury for common citizens (Shao, Lu, & Wu, 2012). Traditional media, where content are subject to extensive editorial review and political monitoring, were unlikely to release the video clip regarding Bi, which embarrasses a state media and the CCP. Gu (2014) argued that due to the lack of alternative information channels, Chinese citizens could only passively succumb to the imposed messages from state media, which usually ignore citizens' concerns and complaints. Petitioning and appealing their cases or causes further are often cost prohibitive and emotionally difficult, and protesting on the street is often not allowed or ignored. Their basic rights of being heard are frequently trampled.

Cases like Bi's video indicate that Weibo and other social media are capable of breaking the power and information asymmetry and empower citizens to collect, report, analyze, disseminate and petition information via "citizen journalism" without having to seek approval from authority (Han, 2011). Social media and their threaded comments attract users to create, repost, and comment, and public discourse of all types, topics, styles, and persuasions have blossomed and flooded the cyber space (Leibold, 2011; Xu, 2012). Paradoxically, the Chinese government's censorship and control have resulted in a vibrant proliferation of online public discourse and folk narratives (Xu, 2012). Blocking the bursting information flood may not be as effective as diverting and guiding it. Some citizens' online opinions have become so helpful and popular that even the CCP has adopted these opinions (Sullivan, 2012) to help make policy changes.

Despite its role in censorship, the Chinese government undisputedly plays a central role in driving the exponential growth of the Chinese internet, helping break its own monopoly of information, and paving the way for the social media to flourish as an influential and democratic media for political and social discourses. According to the China Internet Network Information Center survey, China had 3.2 million websites by the end of December 2013, a growth rate of 19.4% from 2012. The overall Chinese instant messaging users grew to 532 million, up by 64.4 million over the end of 2012 and with a utilization ratio of up to 86.2% (CNNIC, 2014). The Chinese government has also invested heavily in the promotion of e-government and e-commerce projects. Nearly all national and local government agencies now have Weibo and/or WeChat public accounts (CNNIC, 2014).

AN EQUALIZER OF POWER AND DISCOURSE

WeChat and Weibo have replaced one-way communication, equalizing everyone with access to the Internet, from the powerful and elite to average citizens to the same status, netizens. Citizens are motivated to carrying out their discursive discourses in a virtual space, which are facilitated by the increasing technological ease and their desire to speak their minds. They transformed the once elite power communication and put ordinary citizens on an equal footing with the elite, who either control or are favored by state or traditional media. As the video clip incident has ironically and clearly shown, that Bi and the person who released the video are reversed in their roles overnight: from envious power figure to powerless ordinary citizen, and vice versa. As such, power discourse and communication are no longer a privilege reserved just for the elite. Weibo and WeChat have equalized everyone into a writer, editor, journalist, commentator, producer and director all in one. However, as mentioned earlier, the colorful and dynamic discourses are not always matched with quality and value in some contents.

Social media exposure often forces overturn of unjust decisions and promptly investigates corruption, bureaucracy, inefficiency and waste. The only caveat is that while the state allows and encourages the media to supervise local officials and public figures, it prohibits challenging the central government and top national leaders, projecting a "nice central but bad local" image to divert public resentment (Stockmann, 2014) toward corrupt officials rather than the CCP in general. The central government such as the State Council, the CCP Central Committee and the Politburo, and other politically significant institutions are usually shielded from negative coverage. The media still serve as a propaganda tool, portraying the top political institutions and leadership as righteous and benign (Yang & Tang, 2010).

The popularization of social media such as Weibo and WeChat has led to the liberalization of public discourse and provided the Chinese citizenry with new opportunities for political advocacy. These social media spaces empowered China's netizens and diminished the state's ability to set public agenda and shape political preferences with unprecedented power to counter the might of China's propaganda state (Esarey & Qiang, 2011). The power of Weibo and WeChat to liberalize civic discourse and facilitate public supervision of the state actors has radically transformed the relationship between state and societal actors.

The above mentioned cases of the Chinese navy and the Bi Fujian incident have shown that WeChat and Weibo have effectively broken the party-state's monopoly on discourses and mobilization. According to Esarey and Xiao (2011), various exposures of social media have contributed to the abolition of the custody and repatriation system for migrant workers, the halting of environmental problematic development projects, the overhaul of the criminal justice system, the reconsideration of wrongfully convicted murder cases, and the investigation and dismissal of Party officials. As mentioned above, the CCP encourages netizens to challenge immoral practices and corrupt officials but not the power of the Party. Anytime when an online rant against the official abuses of power is about to change direction or grow bigger, the nervous attention of the censors are attracted. Because Weibo and WeChat have become a battleground where the state does not necessarily win just because they have monopoly over most resources in shaping public opinion. Moreover, the CCP's strategy to harness and guide the social media and the power of public opinion does not always work: the masses do not always think what the state wants them to think, and unintended outcomes do develop.

SOCIAL JUSTICE ON SOCIAL MEDIA

For people who despise Bi Fujian and other hypocritical public figures who "eat (Chinese Communist) Party's meals but breaks Party's Wok," the inequality and injustice in today's Chinese society has betrayed Mao Zedong's vision. The WeChat incident and Bi's firing from CCTV can be seen as an indirect revenge–that justice is carried out by a social media weapon on behalf of the disadvantaged, the marginalized and the disenfranchised. The Party-state has built its legitimacy on economic growth and political stability, but China's rapid economic growth has both alleviated and caused glaring social inequalities. The distribution of prosperity gained through decades of economic reform has become increasingly uneven. While Bi is not necessarily that rich or that bad, the netizens are just happy that they have caught red-handed another representative of a privileged group, who is part of the Party propaganda machinery. While some online protest cases have been driven by narrowly defined socioeconomic or environmental injustice rather than specific political claims, and protesters seek for solutions within the current Chinese political system, some participants are not necessarily direct victims of injustice or deprivation.

The right to freedom of speech is voraciously pursued and exercised by a population that previously had no outlet for such a type of critical public discourse (Xu, 2012). Pan (2010) argued that the competition and fight for the articulation between the state media and social media is common. Articulation on social media allows citizens to sustain, repair, or fortify as well as amend, resist, or erode an agenda. Social media's democratizing potentials to advance an agenda or a point of view, or simply coordinate some oppositional discourse or collective actions, are irresistible. Within the state-society framework, a vitalized and unofficially organized netizens strongly and creatively resist the authoritarian state to articulate their agenda or interests. To netizens, the opportunities to express is also an opportunity to impress and to make that voice matter. Viewed in this light, the persistent inequality and injustice in political and civic participation are alleviated with the help of social media such as WeChat and Weibo.

CONCLUSION

WeChat and Weibo have provided the Chinese citizens with an unprecedented ability and opportunity to challenge the dominance of the state discourses, without the limitation of time and space. As in the cases of Bi Fujian incident and the navy rescue, not only are the freedom and decisions of posting information generally controlled by posters themselves, the convenient, accessible, autonomous and interactive platform keeps citizens current on what is going on, often in real time. As an equalizer and highly grass-root technology, Weibo and WeChat allow netizens equal rights to freely narrate his/her own story and contribute to the social and civic dynamics by synergizing and combining individual voices to exert powerful impact. As a public oasis for citizens to engage in social and public affairs and vent dissatisfactions without physically protesting in the streets, they empower citizens to collect and analyze current social issues.

As a game-changer, WeChat and Weibo have turned the conventional one-way surveillance censorship into an engaging mutual monitoring, and empower Chinese citizens to supervise and comment on the conduct of public figures and officials. Despite state efforts at various censorship, WeChat and Weibo have boosted and contributed to China's democratization by breaking down the state information monopoly and providing citizens with more opportunities to access, analyze, post and exchange information. However, they defied the imagination and prediction of the Western technological determinants, who believed that information technology would compel the state toward a Western-style democracy.

The gradual shift and preference by Chinese netizens from town square styled "we broadcast" Weibo to tea-house kind of "we chat" personal, personalized and mass "conversation" are even more effective to evade and meander through censorship as in the case of Bi Fujian incident. Both the participatory and interactive nature of WeChat and Weibo force authorities to relax information censorship. Even the state news organizations now routinely leverage, publicize and rely on public comments from these social media to attract the public, which creates a new information environment where the participation of amateur citizen "journalists" are forcing the state and professional journalists to become competitive sense-makers instead of the parrots of the Party lines.

REFERENCES

Anonymous. (2014, February 28). *Xi to lead CCP group on Internet safety and information.* Retrieved from Sina News: http://news.sina.com.cn/o/2014-02-28/042029584155.shtml

Cairns, C. (2013). Air pollution, social media, and responsive authoritarianism in China. *UCLA Compass Conference.* Los Angeles, CA: UCLA.

Center, P. R. (2014, August 27). *The 'Spiral of Silence' on Social Media.* Retrieved from http://www.pewinternet.org/2014/08/27/the-spiral-of-silence-on-social-media/

Chen, W. (2014). *Taking stock, moving forward: The Internet, social network and civic engagement in Chinese societies.* Academic Press.

Chiu, C., Ip, C., & Silverman, A. (2012, April). Understanding social media in China. *McKinsey Quarterly.* Retrieved from http://www.mckinsey.com/insights/marketing_sales/understanding_social_media_in_china

CNNIC. (2012). *Statistics report of Chinese internet development.* Retrieved from China Internet Network Research Center: http://www1.cnnic.cn/

CNNIC. (2014). *Statistics report of Chinese internet development.* Retrieved from China Internet Network Research Center: http://www1.cnnic.cn/

Economist. (2013, April 6). China's internet: A giant cage. *Economist.* Retrieved from economist.com

Esarey, A., & Qiang, X. (2011). Digital communication and political change in China. *International Journal of Communication, 5,* 298–319.

Gu, Q. (2014). Sina Weibo: A mutual communication apparatus between the Chinese government and Chinese citizens. *China Media Research, 10*(2).

Guardian. (2015, April 10). *Chinese broadcaster apologizes for Mao Zedong insults.* Retrieved from The Guardian: http://www.theguardian.com/world/2015/apr/10/chinese-broadcaster-apologises-mao-zedong-insults-bi-fujian

Hatton, C. (2015, February 24). *Is Weibo on the way out?* Retrieved from BBC News: http://www.bbc.com/news/blogs-china-blog-31598865

Hong, K. (2013, July 3). *Tencent's WeChat chalks up 70 million users outside of China thanks to aggressive global marketing.* Retrieved from http://thenextweb.com/asia/2013/07/03/tencents-wechat-chalks-up-70-million-users-outside-of-china-thanks-to-agg

King, G., Pan, J., & Roberts, M. (2013). How Censorship in China Allows Government Criticism but Silences collective expression. *The American Political Science Review, 107*(2), 326–343. doi:10.1017/S0003055413000014

Leibold, J. (2011, November). Blogging alone: China, the internet, and the democratic illusion? *The Journal of Asian Studies, 70*(4), 1023–1041. doi:10.1017/S0021911811001550

Li, J. (2014, April 14). *'Twitter' and 'Facebook' of China are best frenemies.* Retrieved from Market Watch: http://www.marketwatch.com/story/twitter-and-facebook-

Li. (2015, January 14). *China to force social media users to declare their real names.* Retrieved from South China Morning Post: http://www.scmp.com/news/china/article/1679072/china-beefs-social-media-rules-forcing-people-use-real-name-registration?page=all

Luo, Y. (2014). The Internet and agenda setting in China: The influence of online public opinion on media coverage and government policy. *International Journal of Communication, 8*, 1289–1312.

Lynch, A. (2015, February 4). *China demanding real names be used on social media.* Retrieved from Lighthouse News Daily: http://www.lighthousenewsdaily.com/china-

McCombs, M. (2005). A look at agenda-setting: Past, present and future. *Journalism Studies, 6*(4), 543–557. doi:10.1080/14616700500250438

Millward, S. (2012, May 30). *The rise of social media in China with all new user numbers.* Retrieved from Tech in Asia: http://www.techinasia.com/rise-of-china-socialmedia-infographic-2012/

Pan, Z. (2010). *Articulation and Re-articulation: Agenda for understanding media and communication in China.* Academic Press.

Pell, C. (1995). Civil Discourse is Crucial for Democracy to Work. *Insight (American Society of Ophthalmic Registered Nurses), 11*(37), 13.

Poster, M. (1995). *The second media age.* Cambridge, MA: Polity Press.

Simcott, R. (2014, February 27). *Social media fast facts: China. Social Media Today.* Retrieved from Social Media Today: http://www.socialmediatoday.com/content/social-media-fast-facts-china

Sloan, A. (2014, March 19). *China's suprise freedom of speech crackdown on WeChat.* Retrieved from https://www.indexoncensorship.org/2014/03/chinas-suprise-freedom-speech-crackdown-wechat/

Stockmann, D. (2014). *Media commercialization and authoritarian rule in China.* Cambridge University Press.

Stockmann, D., & Gallagher, M. (2011). Remote control: How the media sustains authoritarian rule in China. *Comparative Political Studies, 44*(4), 436–467. doi:10.1177/0010414010394773

Sullivan, J. (2012). A tale of two microblogs in China. *Media Culture & Society*, 774–783.

Wang, W. Y. (2013). Weibo, framing, and media practices in China. *Journal of Chinese Political Science, 18*(4), 375–388. doi:10.1007/s11366-013-9261-3

Xu, Y. (2012). Understanding netizen discourse in China: Formation, genres, and values. *China Media Research, 8*(1).

Zhao, Y. (2013, September 23). *Anti-graft watchdog told to convey results*. Retrieved from China Daily: http://www.chinadaily.com.cn/china/2013-

Zoo, N. (2014). *Introduction to the Chinese games markets*. Retrieved from New Zoo: http://www.pro-elios.com/wp-content/uploads/2014/03/China-Games-Market-Newzoo-Report-2014.pdf

Chapter 4

Nothing Random about Taste:
Toni Morrison and the Algorithmic Canon

Jacqueline Wigfall
Independent Researcher, USA

ABSTRACT

In our digital age, "Is there an app for that?" gets asked and answered for books, but not the canon, until the invention of an online, tessellating medium of personal choice expansion called TasteKid. Its voter-influenced algorithm continuously updates users' personalized canons seeded from whatever writer or title they choose. This atypical engendering of literacy challenges—perhaps inadvertently—what the canon is and how it can be experienced for readers new to critical or cultural literacy and Toni Morrison fans alike. In fact, her works get linked to other media by the thumbs up or down responses of site visitors. In this way, technology eclipses the canon's previous assumption of "the center" because only a reader's choice can occupy it. Likewise, with the distance between authors decreasing, (at the pace of the site visitors' unpredictable orders), the obsolescence of "margins" effects a power shift.

INTRODUCTION

Catch a "shock of recognition," to use a phrase of Toni Morrison's, while reviewing the eerily predictive notion of Michel Foucault from 1969:

The frontiers of a book are never clear-cut: beyond the title, the first lines, and the last full stop, beyond its internal configuration and its autonomous form, it is caught up in a system of references to other books, other texts, other sentences: it is a node within a network. (Archaeology)

Today's network (the canon) has been exponentially transformed by the Internet which means that its nodes (literature) have been too. "Science and technology have always influenced the practice and materiality of culture and our technological landscape is increasingly becoming multimodal and multifocal. This has important implications for exploring the concept of so-called digital humanities within the larger framework of (multi)literacies" (Rutten & Vandermeersche, 2014). Consequently, to understand

DOI: 10.4018/978-1-5225-0212-8.ch004

Toni Morrison's canonization, we should consider the digitization of knowledge—how its future archaeologies are being uniquely configured today in cyberspatial clouds. As contemporary readers have grabbed up "intermediality," the publishing industry has readapted at the galloping pace of IT. From the book club's poststructural canon with a twist, to the Kindle queue (choose your own canon), and online communities that keep you 'cover(ed),' readers' choice has crossed paths with "the construction of a personal space in a web-based social environment" (Dettori, 2011). The experimental mix and match permits them to work through the canon asynchronously. How do these options shift Morrison's locations within it? What new intertextualities emerge? And on the university front—where her work magnetizes the practice of theory—how do sequent syllabi hold up against the surfing and searching done online?

Among the various "technologies" which go to make up any society, one in particular seems to me to have been much ignored, and that is what might be called "moral technology." A moral technology consists of a particular set of techniques and practices for the instilling of specific kinds of value, discipline, behavior, and response in human subject: and one rather important type of moral technology in our own day goes under the name of Literature (Eagleton 97).

Once a critical motif, technology is now literature's collaborator, for as pages are turned, readers update their status. Through this pair of disciplined behaviors, literacy refracts into reading, composing, and "publishing," in the Composition and Rhetoric sense, online, one digital footstep at a time. And when readers' paths are cross-analyzed (as well as traced), we might find that modern accessibilities are cracking the canon from within. Rather than digress from the issue of canonization, social and digital media's effect on book selection illuminates its terms, satisfies questions raised by its previous debates, and refreshes its premises altogether.

BACKGROUND

Remember when book clubs were the new discourse communities? Discussion questions, typically published at the end of printed editions, ferried authors and readers to their "destination." But unlike the meaning Roland Barthes had in mind, the "text's unity" was also bookended by its origin, the author. No reader made that clearer than Oprah Winfrey, who would go on to spotlight four of Toni Morrison's novels: *Song of Solomon*, *Paradise*, *The Bluest Eye*, and *Sula*. ("List") Undoubtedly America's most star-studded discourse community, "Oprah's Book Club" dramatized how real and embodied an author could actually appear while casting readers in the role of audience (whether studio, at home, or fan club). With its social revision of poststructuralism, the book club's popular canon drew authorship back into the reading process and amplified writers' celebrity.

Next, came the postmodern canon. As publications emerged in digital and online versions for rent, purchase, and trial, readers' consumption patterns began to determine not simply what went unread, but what went out of print and/or circulation. As a compass or divining rod, the canon continually shape-shifted with readers' selections via multisensory platforms including Audible and Nook. Meanwhile, "master works" showed up in cyberspace for free, their survival having exceeded the bandwidth of their copyright. Ironically, accessibility seemed to reduce value in the free market, and this further reshaped common knowledge about which titles needed to be read, and by whom, to prove or indicate what values. An important exception, perhaps, was the increased popularity of several genres of early African

American writing that universities began scanning and publishing online for a general public eager to read free of charge. Chief among these, "slave narratives" made it possible for humanities scholars and their students to increase the reach of their literacies while eliminating the costs previously associated with archival research. In absence of travel, photocopying, and expensive book buying, anyone seeking firsthand knowledge of the nineteenth century black experience, would. See, for example, Documenting the American South which began in 1996 as a "pilot project to digitize a half dozen highly circulated slave narratives" (About, 2014). These days, site visitors can kick it Old School or New by following DocSouth on Facebook or purchasing "DocSouth Books" through UNC Press.

Smartphone apps restored semiotic paradigms and aesthetic status to the book cover. In order to communicate which texts one has or wants to read, these phone apps prompt the user to display the cover associated with his sources. Tiled linearly (Goodreads and Tumblr) or spatially (Pinterest), book covers 'showed off' intellect crossed with photo album: more than a book shelf or personal library, one's "page" became engaging in an infographic way. For the follower, curiosity about the books one shelved together (on Goodreads) and the shelf's title is a discursive exercise consistent with its theory.

New Literacy Studies focused on the politics of traditional--Western--notions of "literacy" and also criticized the idea that literacy often only refers to reading and writing. **The focus has shifted to different kinds of literacies related to different media and networks.** *This critical perspective problematizes traditional concepts such as the literary canon: one form of literacy related to one specific medium, the book, and literature as a major genre. (Rutten & Vandermeersche, emphasis added)*

Online, it's not enough to read, or even to finish the book; the book is not enough and reading it does not prove "literacy." Much like a musical selection (or mixtape "track" of old), a direct quote also performs a distinct representation, an emotive one, how one felt on the day it was posted to one's Tumblr: "The function, the very serious function of racism" or "Toni Morrison on Creating Herself" number among the highlights tagged with her name. When scanning the "board" of one's favorite books, one's Pinterest followers will want to see what new logic one has mapped, e.g. "hand-picked," "novels and home," or "brought healing and understanding to my life." Rather than texts themselves, the aftereffects of literacy invite exchange, scrutiny, and (re)interpretations, all of which make the canon public and user-generated.

It was not always this way that a student, lay reader, or even a scholar was free to pick and choose books for the canon of literature written in English. Generally recognized as *The Canon*, the "great" or "master works" of English literature have been institutionally established and maintained as a list of written publications by authors who produced their work in set ways (poetry and prose), locations (Europe or North America), and eras (four):

- The Theocratic Age (2000 BCE-1321 CE);
- The Aristocratic Age (1321-1832);
- The Democratic Age 1832-1900); and
- The Chaotic Age (20th Century) (Jones)

Authors included were typically white and male and their readers were also. Book owners were book readers who had attended school and could afford tuition, personal libraries, and the homes in which to install them. On these shelves were Homer and Aristotle, Virgil and Ovid, Dante, Chaucer, and Shakespeare. "Modern American" literature signified Emerson, Poe, and Thoreau; "Modern English" evoked

Yeats, Joyce, and Lawrence. With the rarest of exceptions, literature written before (or beyond the land of) the ancient Greeks, or after by their descendants, was not included in the canon. After students and scholars of color (and their advocates) intervened upon such exclusions as an extension of wider social movements from Abolition and Suffrage to Civil Rights and Black Power, the literary canon began to contract and expand in unprecedented ways. Women writers of color, male writers of color, and women writers generally found their work incrementally selected for academic representation and commercial attention. This social advancement continued through Multiculturalism and the "Canon Wars" of the 1980s and 1990s, giving the canon its more contemporary shape reflecting a fuller range of human diversity. By the twenty-first century, writers not only come through diversely—in every way including how they racially identify; the global points of origin they claim or leave behind; and their genders by birth, conditioning, or self-construction—they self-publish, circulate, and sell their work independently too. Thus, mixed with Wi-Fi, reading Toni Morrison has become a distinctly symbolic + shared experience when, two years prior to Instagram, came "TasteKid," flanked by Tumblr and Pinterest.

2004: Facebook
2006: Goodreads, Twitter
2007: Tumblr
2008: TasteKid
2010: Pinterest, Instagram

In particular, TasteKid readers have been actively rebuilding even the multicultural canon, breaking it down, and configuring its alignments anew from wherever they happened to be searching. Cocooned in private residency or randomly populating cafes, the user-generated, literary canon is being formulated almost anywhere but church and university.

MAIN FOCUS OF THE CHAPTER

Hailed alongside Soovle and FastEagle when it appeared in 2008 (McGee, 2008), TasteKid has exemplified proletariat power by destabilizing traditional literary canons from within by sanctioning and facilitating how readers associate books with songs or bands and motion media favorites.

Unlike other recommendation services like GetGlue or Last.fm, you can simply tell TasteKid that, say, 'The Social Network' is your favourite movie and it can recommend not only other movies, but also music, shows, books and authors that you might be interested in. You can even enter in a list of things you like for even better results. (Bryant, 2010)

TasteKid works like a (free) crowdsourcing of public opinion about popular culture, which reciprocates with suggestions that reinforce a user's desire to be opinionated. It has put into the hands of the public the work of *norming*, which previously belonged to an elite class of academics. "You can help train the service by marking the things it suggests to you as 'Like', 'Dislike', 'Save' (to come back to it later) or 'Meh' (if you're not bother [sic] either way about it)" (Bryant, 2010), with or without an account because registering a profile is optional, thus TasteKid has enabled anyone with Internet access to treat the literary canon like "art in the age of reproduction," i.e. "reproducible" (Benjamin), perhaps per the intention of its founder Andrei Oghina.

Oghina, who is from Romania, earned his MS in Computer Science from Politehnica University of Bucharest, according to CrunchBase, and would have been well under thirty at the founding of TasteKid. Self-described as "a discovery engine," and critically classified as a "recommendation engine" (McGee, 2008), tastekid.com was immediately noted by the CEO of The Next Web for its "understated design" and quiet influence: "therein lies it's [sic] beauty… It just does it's [sic] job and does it remarkably well for a (very) new product" (Zee, 2008). Its algorithm is presented as the avatar "Emmy." (Emmy of 2015 is bespectacled and top-knotted; in 2014, she brandished a tank top and signature pixie-bob that draped one eye with the other generously framed by mascara). Emmy continues to humanize the search experience which, according to its own site, makes TasteKid "also a community of people that enjoy and consider exploration to be an important aspect of their lives." It is a website (that can be added as a search engine) for getting recommendations based on one's preferences in one of six categories, which run across the screen's top margin as tabs:

EVERYTHING | MUSIC | MOVIES | SHOWS | BOOKS | AUTHORS | GAMES

The search tool is defaulted to EVERYTHING. Type in *Toni* and the algorithm's initial recognition is *Braxton*. ("Toni"'n.d.) But, after one inputs the writer's full name, EVERYTHING and AUTHORS deliver a mostly American selection of popular writers:

Alice Walker; Sandra Cisneros; Joyce Carol Oates; bell hooks; Junot Diaz; Maya Angelou; E. Lynn Harris; James Baldwin; Zora Neale Hurston; Amy Tan; Michael Cunningham; Jeanette Winterson; Rita Mae Brown; Louise Erdrich; Richard Ford; Christopher Isherwood; Steve Martin. ("Toni," n.d.)

Each suggestion is followed by an information icon, which selected opens a descriptive pop up and includes the favorability ratings as well as the invitation for your vote. Curiously, Jamaica Kincaid, Gayle Jones, Edwidge Danticat, Arundhati Roy, and Cherrie Moraga are not listed. Morrison's TasteKid peers were not race or gender specific in 2014, but neither were their works known for Morrison's stylistic trademarks. Why Junot Diaz but not Danticat? Or, Garbriel Garcia Marquez, Eduardo Galeano, or Jean Toomer? Why not any of the feminist writers (Irigaray! Beauvior!) whose theories of feminine subjects and maternal genealogy arguably shape-shift throughout *Sula* and *Beloved*? Because "transformation of the superstructure," Benjamin might say in millennial syntax: "At any moment the reader is ready to turn into a writer. As expert, which he had to become willy-nilly in an extremely specialized work process, even if only in some minor respect, the reader gains access to authorship" (Benjamin, 1936).

"Books" was far more telling about the canon as a context for work by Morrison; Emmy recommended:

A Room of One's Own; My Antonia; Leaves of Grass; The Color Purple; Roots; When You Are Engulfed in Flames; The Namesake; Paradise Lost; Mrs. Dalloway; The World Is Flat; Much Ado about Nothing; Matilda; Everything Is Illuminated; A Portrait of the Artist as a Young Man; The Coldest Winter Ever; The Crucible; A Midsummer Night's Dream. ("Toni," n.d.)

It makes for challenging optics at first glance; each title signifies not one reading list, but many, covering an impressive, categorical spread. YA, Masterworks, Realism, Feminist Classics is a mashup begging the channel of Foucault: "One is confronted with concepts that differ in structure and in the rules governing their use, which ignore or exclude one another, and which cannot enter the unity of a logical architecture." In what universe does a 1970s television epic like "Roots" belong aside *Leaves of Grass*? Maybe the results were analogies. *Sula* is to *Mrs. Dalloway* as *Song of Solomon* is to *Everything Is Illuminated*. Maybe it is *mise en abyme*: *Tar Baby* nested in *The Namesake* nested in *My Antonia* nested inside *The Color Purple*. Or, maybe those books captured the most votes. So, as seed-texts, where did these titles come from? Through what media and experience did they arrive to readers in the first place? These TasteKid results, for a Toni Morrison search, could be someone's first selection along an originary booklist: *If You like Morrison, try Shakespeare*. For TasteKid tweens of 2014, Shakespeare's teleology is Toni Morrison, begging the question: is the canon really as unified as we were told?

We must ask ourselves what purpose is ultimately served by this suspension of all the accepted unities, if, in the end, we return to the unities that we pretended to question at the outset. In fact, the systematic erasure of all given unities enables us first of all to restore to the statement the specificity of its occurrence, and to show that discontinuity is one of those great accidents that create cracks not only in the geology of history, but also in the simple fact of the statement; it emerges in its historical irruption; what we try to examine is the incision that it makes, that irreducible - and very often tiny - emergence. (Foucault, 1972)

The question is, will we continue along present course, accumulating more and more unlikely nodes within the network? Over two hundred authors are (hyper)linked to Morrison's Amazon page, for example. Click on "William Shakespeare (1)" to order a "38 Titles" box set that includes *Othello* and *The Bluest Eye* ("Classroom Library"). Is TasteKid like this, one "event" of many, "subject to repetition, transformation, and reactivation" (Foucault, 1972)? And, if it is, has it foreshadowed a restoration of deconstruction? Popular culture could be intellectually debated; race was perceived as performance; and all interlocutors with anything to say approached everything as a text. Or, since user-generated "irruption" remains networked to "the statements that precede," (Foucault, 1972) perhaps the canonical order can never be faded because unlike the new, it is always linear. Historicizing logic has its place; an archaeology of knowledge requires dates.

Reading Morrison's work cultivates an appreciation for history. She is a writer for whom history is important. Tessa Roynon (2007) outlines the historical chapters for Morrison's novels in her article explaining that Morrison's ambivalent, yet purposeful, use of the classics "effects a rewriting of American history and a challenge to conservative conceptions of Americanness": *Tar Baby* and "American discovery;" *Paradise*, Puritans and "the New Republic;" "Slavery, the Civil War, Black Migration and Urbanization" for *Beloved* and *Jazz*; and the Civil Rights Movement for *Song of Solomon*. The research, detail, and logic of her thesis press historical criticism back into Morrison Studies. Whether 'a TasteKid' finishes *A Midsummer Night's Dream* after *The Bluest Eye* or before, perhaps a measure of reconciliation between chronological and thematic (or other algorithmically determined) orders is warranted.

That Morrison's ubiquity superseded identity politics—according to her TasteKid page of November 2014—bode well for the canon debates. Her authorship is female of color, on the one hand and on the other, informed by literary studies and her "role as *Senior editor* of Random House" (Bourdieu, 1998). Her presence among other greats projects a precious representation from the canon as "mirror" satisfying "a politics *of the image*" (Guillory, 1993, 7) or the "the spatio-temporal coordinates of [her] discourse" (Foucault, "What," 1969). "Situating literacy in the context of the power structures" made "important questions" relevant: "Whose literacies are dominant? Why are some literacies marginalized? What should we teach our students? What exactly do we mean by 'we'?" (Rutten & Vandermeersche, 2013).

Like the colonial power, like, say, France, Germany, or England, the canonical work acts as a center -- the center of the perceptual field, the center of values, the center of interest, the center, in short, of a web of meaningful interrelations. The noncanonical works act as colonies or as countries that are unknown and out of sight and mind. That is why feminists [hypertext unlinked] object to the omission or excision of female works from the canon, for by not appearing within the canon works by women do not appear. (Landow, n.d., emphasis added)

The canon as a network, or in this case webbed interrelationships, maps nicely against its current formations online. Clearly, a format like TasteKid's capitalizes on the hypnotic concept of books emanating, Koch snowflake-like, from elementary steps (author, title, genre). But, there are deep implications for how it spins the canon unrecognizable. If a reader brings his core preference—i.e. Toni Morrison—to tastekid. com, her texts act as "the center of [his] perceptual field," and establishes his baseline "values" *as hers.* She dominates, but is it *colonially,* as attributed to the traditional canon, "like, say, France, Germany, or England"? (Landow, n.d.) If Reader must broach *Tar Baby* to reach *Paradise Lost,* in the social media world order, Milton takes a bow. Consequently, Morrison's title continues its reach as both process and technical reproduction when socially circulating online to consumers new to reading, her work, or both. "[A]spects of the original that are unattainable" (Benjamin), to the solitary reader readily emerge after the algorithmic processing of user-generated likeability data, making *Tar Baby* no longer "out of reach" since TasteKid decreases the distance between readers and great works, i.e. like Benjamin's photograph or phonograph record, via TasteKid, the Nobel Laureate's works "meet the beholder halfway." Let's not forget that Morrison's well-earned, traditional canonization puts her writing in good company (or should) without concern that TasteKid's "technique of reproduction detaches the reproduced object from the domain of tradition" (Benjamin, 1936). Therefore, she can and should be read alongside Emmy's recommendations that offer exciting and meaningful insights to the well-nuanced literacies she independently evokes like Shakespeare: "linguistic, dramatic, social, political" (Smith, 1997, 455). From there, ripples nudge along a new course for canon's elder mission of bearing authorization and acceptance ("Canon"). It is the kind of requalification that happened at Georgetown in the mid-1990s when the university was "allowing English majors to graduate without studying any Shakespeare" (Honan, 1997).

ISSUES, CONTROVERSIES, PROBLEMS

Detractors of multiculturalism "were not so much *for* Shakespeare as *against* women's studies…. 'Shakespeare' was being used as a convenient antidote to the pluralism of contemporary American culture" (Smith, 1997, 453). After the dust settled, nobler principles prevailed. "What has changed is the context in which Shakespeare is being taught. The new curriculum in effect substitutes critical orientation for chronology as an organizing principle." (Smith, 1997, 453). Theory made this happen, 'hands-free,' without apps, before texting, and in absence of what today is an inescapable crush of e-mail. And yet, academia was equipped to resolve what some found to be difficult truths about cultural hierarchy. The center keeps moving, or is differently occupied by different parties. And every "wisdom" is a perspective-- categorical, *subjective,* and relative until it bumps against the irrefutably true. "And if changes in the medium of contemporary perception can be comprehended as decay of the aura, it is possible to show its social causes" (Benjamin, 1936). "Was this the wisdom of the ages?" the Shakespeare professor reflected, about the training he received for his field, "No, it was the wisdom of Modernism, something quite specific to the 1930s, '40s, and '50s" (Smith, 1997, 454).

For the Shakespeare professor at Georgetown: "It is in the meeting of past and present that education happens. The paradigm we need is not a matter of *either/or* but a matter of *both/and*" (Smith, 1997, 454). The media and venues have changed, but timeless remains the unfolding potential of a literary canon to enkindle pluralism. And if enthusiasts of rich, effective, multi-discursive literature have anything to say about literary curricula and the canon, the works earning "a continuing place" will offer "complex reflective surfaces." Morrison, in doing so has, for many readers "established an endless possibility of discourse," a compliment Foucault extends to authors like Freud, Marx and Ann Radcliffe, whose "texts opened the way for a certain number of resemblances and analogies which have their model or principle in her work. The latter contains characteristic signs, figures, relationships, and structures that could be reused by others…. They have created a possibility for something other than their discourse, yet something belonging to what they founded." (Foucault, "What," 1936).

SOLUTIONS AND RECOMMENDATIONS

An inflexible canon may find itself "ideologically bankrupt—though institutionally still extremely powerful," to appropriate Terry Eagleton's (1985) read on liberal humanism (100). Encyclopedia Britannica, for example, faced this situation head on in 2009 by adopting "user-generated content" and "user edits" for its website with the goal of approving them "within twenty minutes" for upload and public consumption. (Anderson, 2009) But when his company was compared to Wikipedia, the president of Britannica questioned Google's algorithm for producing Wikipedia "as a first link" (Cauz quoted in Anderson, 2009). The tension involved in the synthesis of modern and outmoded interfaces matches the complexity of what has come to be known as "the wisdom of the crowd." In his book of that title of 2005, James Surowiecki notes "one requirement for a good crowd judgement is that people's decisions are independent of one another. If everyone let themselves be influenced by each other's guesses, there's more chance that the guesses will drift towards a misplaced bias" (Ball, 2014). Here, TasteKid delivers and fans appreciate the bands and want more books (Appcrawlr, n.d.), but for a literary canon unprovoked by the highs and lows of user-generation, a former (formal) power may echo, and its "cultural capital" glow, but without the narcissistic charm and immediacy of social media, it could go the way of the "book collectors contest" ("2015").

"In *The Economics of Attention*, Richard Lanham explores what the current 'information age' can learn from the humanities…. Thus, in the new economy of attention the manipulation of attention is a basic skill" (Rutten & Vandermeersche, 2013). Understandably, the point is that "multimodal and multifocal" media rise to consumer demand; however, an equally compelling, subtextual implication is that consumers learn to become media users able to draw and maintain the attention of their followers. There is much the humanities "can learn from" the "information age," starting perhaps with the millennial expectation of self-centrality. At elemental levels programming delivers this power of the vote: "Even when users don't provide ratings you can still apply collaborative filtering techniques. For instance, you can use a binary representation where 1 means a user liked an item and 0 when they don't like it (or unknown)" (MsLovelace, 2011). Furthermore, holding the attention of the culturally literate will necessitate fluency in many languages and ease with multiple discursive registers. 'Tastekids' don't demand 'global perspectives,' they presume international perceptivities. TasteKid corporate presents multiculturally, with members who have studied and/or worked on two continents. Perhaps the canon should also allow readers to get there too, beyond ideological circumscriptions, by whichever means. Some will follow the path of their cellphone app's fractal behavior, and others may track the "recursion[s]" rescued—and deftly explicated—by literary theory like *Moorings and Metaphors*. "It seems that whatever its delivery system of its profit margin the practice of literature has certain traditional impulses that address and ameliorate the qualms that arise when contemplating its future" (Morrison quoted in Guariguata, 2000).

When Pierre Bourdieu asked Morrison about an in progress project on "heroines," she responds, in part, about a work that probably became *Paradise*:

How to describe the soul of a character without any reference to racial codes, without using this language secret, explicit or implied, that everyone uses to mark the race? And, at the same time, it must give the reader what it is never right: an immediate look, which allows him to see as he never sees. All of this requires a new speech, a new language. It is difficult, but I believe that it is rewarding. I really think that this language can be as subtle, just as hard, and get just as much emotions, without any reference to the color.

Though rhetorical, (cf. "Recitatif"), her question is ironically addressed earlier during the interview, in a comment she herself makes about discourse and rhetoric. "I think that there are exciting [moments] in writing in English in the 20th century, it is precisely this possibility to evolve between various levels of language, the vernacular language of the street to the lyrical or biblical language, passing *through the current register*" (my italics). Although the translation is roughly (digitally) rendered, it relays language as transformative and instructional, as *the* medium for humanistic expression. It is languages that seem malleable and multiple enough to present versions *through* which a writer may lead a reader. The moment parallels her quest for "a new language" for communicating "the soul of a character," for what is the pedagogical work of (canonical) literature if not to impart the lesson of empathy? With EQ (rather than IQ) as the endgame elicited by canonical engagements, literary studies and cognitive science can coexist, to wit, on the pages of Toni Morrison authored work and its tessellations.

CONCLUSION

Is it, therefore, difficult to believe that in 2015, books by Toni Morrison are still breaking new ground for higher education, doing the work of fomenting cultural literacy? Not to hear Bianca Brooks tell it when reflecting on "Masterpieces of Western Literature and Philosophy" and other first year literary experiences at Columbia University. Brooks recounts her introduction to the traditional authors and canonical titles familiar to students of color who major in English and go on to interrogate "the preservation of old ideas," yet doubt their own "place in academia." Along the way she hallmarks that at her alma mater, "for the first time since the inception of the core curriculum in 1919, freshmen will be required to read a book by a black female author, Toni Morrison's *Song of Solomon*." Incidentally, "[a]lso added to the syllabus is Milton's 'Paradise Lost,' Sappho's 'Lyrics,' Euripides' 'The Bacchae,' and the return of Bocaccio's 'The Decameron'" (Josi, 2015). But Brooks champions Columbia's act of canonical renewal with caution, urging "every university to frequently examine the implications of the books they require students to read. What does it mean to discuss the necessity of the slave in Plato's 'Republic'? What does it mean to praise the glory of war in Homer's 'Iliad'?" As new generations of readers, scholars, journalists, and writers are voicing critical thoughts like Brooks' ("questions that require us to venture outside the comfort of academia and into a realm of intellectual honesty," questions that indicate the necessity of Humanities defined by diversity), we see how richly the canon is being challenged by an episteme of Tweets and Likes.

Our digital age of canonical reformation features socially diverse choosing. Beyond marketable optics and political correctness is the assumption garnering crowd wisdom's success: "the wisest crowds are the most diverse" (Ball, 2014). At tastekid.com, the wide net is the best net. Upgraded over the course of the year during which this article was written, the website now opens with the status of EVERYBODY which unfurls the updates of users in real time above a list of media titles that are TRENDING NOW. Additionally, the logo naming the site has evolved from tastekid to TASTEKiD—with the lowercase "i" underscoring individuality for a site and source of micro yet influential considerations yielding collective, public change.

These days, "IF YOU LIKE" Toni Morrison, Emmy recommends *Beloved*, *Song of Solomon*, and *Sula*. (The kitschy reference to comedian Steve Martin is gone). Though streamlined and mostly self-referential, current TasteKid results for the Nobel Laureate indicate that her fans are partial to James Baldwin and Chimamanda Adichie's *Half of a Yellow Sun*, shot as a movie in 2013. The search experience still exemplifies the democratizing of Literature into *recommendations* the authority of which could change as speedily as their mentions go live, but Morrison's intellectual association with legendary authors persists, suggesting that while her writing iterates in the shapeshifting context of "an interplay of signs arranged less according to its signified content than according to the very nature of the signifier" (Foucault, "What," 1969), deciding whether to learn of her books will not be left to "a question of creating a space into which the writing subject constantly disappears" (Foucault, "What," 1969).

REFERENCES

2015 Andrew T. Nadell Book Collectors Contest. (n.d.). Duke University Libraries. Accessed November 10, 2014. http://library.duke.edu/support/friends/book-collectors-contest

About. (n.d.). Documenting the American South. Accessed November 11, 2014. Available: http://docsouth.unc.edu/support/about/

Anderson, N. (2009, January 22). Britannica opens up, aims the "literary canon" at Wikipedia. *Ars Technica*. Retrieved from http://arstechnica.com/business/2009/01/britannica-to-grind-wikipedia-beneath-its-heel-woth-small-moves-toward-openness/

Andrei Oghina. (n.d.). CrunchBase. Retrieved from https://www.crunchbase.com/person/andrei-oghina

Appcrawlr. (n.d.). *TasteKid*. Retrieved from http://appcrawlr.com/ios/tastekid

Ball, P. (2014, July 8). 'Wisdom of the crowd': They myths and realities". *BBC Future*. Available: http://www.bbc.com/future/story/20140708-when-crowd-wisdom-goes-wrong

Benjamin, W. (2005). The Work of Art in the Age of Mechanical Reproduction. (H. Zohn, Trans.). Random House. Accessed September 15, 2015. https://www.marxists.org/reference/subject/philosophy/works/ge/benjamin.htm

Bourdieu, P. (1998, January 2). Dialogue entre Pierre Bourdieu et Toni Morrison. *Vacarme*. Retrieved from http://www.vacarme.org/article807.html

Brooks, B. (2015, August 31). It's Not Just the Books, It's the Discussion. *The New York Times*. Retrieved from http://www.nytimes.com/roomfordebate/2015/08/31/what should-college-freshmen-read/its-not-just-the-books-its-the-discussion

Bryant, M. (2010, December 16). TasteKid now recommending movies, music and books to over 15,000 users. *TNW*. Accessed September 15, 2015, from http://thenextweb.com/eu/2010/12/16/tastekid-now-recommending-movies-music-and-books-to-over-15000-users/

Canon. (n.d.). In *Glossary of Literary Theory*. Accessed November 10, 2014, from http://www.library.utoronto.ca/utel/glossary/Canon.html

Dettori, G. (2011). Adolescents' online literacies – Edited by Donna E Alvermann. British Journal of Educational Technology, 42(2). DOI: doi:10.1111/j.1467-8535.2011.01173_1.x

Eagleton, T. (1985). Subject of Literature. *Cultural Critique*, (2). Available: http://www.jstor.org/stable/1354202

Foucault, M. (1972). *The Archaeology of Knowledge*. Routledge. Retrieved from http://www.marxists.org/reference/subject/philosophy/works/fr/foucault.htm

Foucault, M. (1969). *What Is An Author?* Lecture to Societé Francais de philosophie. Available: https://wiki.brown.edu/confluence/download/attachments/74858352/FoucaultWhatIsAnAuthor.pdf

Guariguata, L. (2000, October 3). Morrison Lectures on Digitization of Literature. *The Cornell Daily Sun*. Accessed September 15, 2015, from http://cornellsun.com/blog/2000/10/03/morrison-lectures-on-digitization-of literature/

Guillory, J. (1993). *Cultural Capital: The Problem of Literary Canon Formation*. University of Chicago Press.

Holloway, K. F. C. (1992). *Mooring and Metaphors: Figures of Culture and Gender in Black Women's Literature*. New Brunswick, NJ: Rutgers University Press.

Honan, W. H. (1996, April 2). Georgetown University Fills Shakespeare Gap. *The New York Times: Campus Journal*. Accessed September 16, 2015, from http://www.nytimes.com/1997/04/02/us/georgetown-university-fills-shakespeare-gap.html

Jones, J. (2014, January 28). Harold Bloom Creates a Massive List of Works in The 'Western Canon': Read Many of the Books Free Online. *Open Culture*. Accessed September 15, 2015, from http://www.openculture.com/2014/01/harold-bloom-creates-a-massive-list-of-works-in-the-western-canon.html

Josi, H. (2015, June 6). Toni Morrison added to Literature Humanities. *Columbia Spectator*. Retrieved from http://columbiaspectator.com/spectrum/2015/06/06/toni-morrisonadded-lit-hum-becomes-first-black-author-syllabus

Landow, G. P. (n.d.). *The Literary Canon*. Available: http://www.victorianweb.org/gender/canon/litcan.html

McGee, M. (2008, October 21). 7 Search Tools You May Not Know… But Should. *Search Engine Land*. Accessed September 15, 2015, from http://searchengineland.com/7-search-tools-you-may-not-know-but-should-15198

MsLovelace. (2011, July 31). 1 Answer. "how to categorize "tastekid" and "clerkdogs" recommender system." *StackExchange*. Retrieved from http://stackoverflow.com/questions/5026269/how-to-categorize-tastekid-and-clerkdogs-recommender-system

Oprah's Book Club List. (n.d.). Retrieved from http://oprahbookclublist.com/tag/toni-morrison/

Recitatif. (2001, August 9). *Literature, Arts, and Medicine Database*. New York University. Retrieved from http://litmed.med.nyu.edu/Annotation?action=view&annid=11854

Roynon, T. (2007). Toni Morrison and Classical Tradition. *Literature Compass*, *4*(6), 1514–1537. DOI: 10.1111/j.1741-4113.2007.00496.x

Rutten, K., & Vandermeersche, G. (2013). Introduction to literacy and society, culture, media and education. *CLCWeb: Comparative Literature and Culture*.

Scholastic. (2009). *Classroom Library (Grade 7-12): Monster; Twilight Series; Chosen Series; the House On Mango Street; to Kill a Mockingbird; Their Eyes Were Watching God; My Brother Sister & I; Othello; the Bluest Eye" on Books*. Accessed November 23, 2014, from http://www.amazon.com/Classroom-Library-Grade-7-12-Mockingbird/dp/1500256935/ref=sr_1_1?s=books&ie=UTF8&qid=1416722871&sr=1-1&keywords=toni+morrison

Smith, B. R. (1997). Teaching the Resonances. *Shakespeare Quarterly, 48*(4). Available: http://www.jstor.org/stable/2871255

Takaki, R. (2008). *A Different Mirror: A History of Multicultural America*. Little, Brown, and Company.

Toni Morrison. (n.d.). In *TasteKid*. Available: http://www.tastekid.com/like/Toni+Morrison

Zee. (2008, October 28). TasteKid Lets You Find Stuff Similar to Stuff You Like. *TNW*. Retrieved from http://thenextweb.com/2008/10/28/tastekid-lets-you-find-stuff-similar-to-stuff-you-like/

KEY TERMS AND DEFINITIONS

Canon Formation: An intellectual, political, process by which academic scholars choose and discuss choices of which books to teach and research or write about as literary and cultural exemplars.

Cultural Literacy: An academic neologism referring to a person's awareness of and ability to recognize, comprehend, and communicate about the history and details of a culture or social group.

Discourse: Language and patterns of language use that can be analyzed according to rules of grammar and various social norms.

Globalism: "Narrowly defined, globalism is intended to be an instant movement of capital and a rapid distribution of data and products operation on a politically neutral plain, shaped by multinational corporate demands" (Morrison quoted in Guariguata, 2000).

Hyperlink: A colorful or specially formatted word or phrase on a webpage or online document that, when clicked, opens to a source on the Internet because it is linked to it.

Multiculturalism: A social, political, and academic paradigm of racial and ethnic inclusion from the 1980s developed alongside "pluralism" to ensure increased public knowledge of identities, histories, and experiences in America that are not centrally, ostensibly, primarily, or wholly defined as racially white or of European heritage. Prior to multicultural intervention, society assumed the "popular but inaccurate story, [of how] our country was settled by European immigrants, and Americans are white…in the creation of our national identity, 'American' has been defined as 'white'"" (Takaki, 2008).

Multimodality: Reading and other cognitive processes that involve more than one type of literacy or uses a combination of online, digital, technological, offline, hardcopy, and other vehicles of information.

Status Update: A social media practice of sharing progress in work or lived experience with the public generally or personally selected online users specifically.

TasteKid: A twenty-first century, Internet-based search engine used to locate popular culture recommendations based on a user's registered interests.

YA: Young Adult, a publishing industry category that refers to books for the youth demographic corresponding to tween and teens, young people age 12 – 18, the target market for a genre of literature.

Chapter 5
Public History and National Identity:
The 1821 Revolution as Metaphor for the "Greek Crisis"

Eleni Andriakaina
Panteion University of Social and Political Sciences, Greece

ABSTRACT

In 2011, while the causes of Greek "crisis" started becoming the subject of public controversy, a documentary series aired on Skai channel vowing to challenge nationalist and populist accounts of the 1821 Revolution. By popularizing the main arguments of modernization theory, the "1821" documentary approached the past through the lens of "Cultural dualism" – the clash between a 'reformist' and an 'underdog' culture – and operated as a metaphor for contemporary Greece. Via the study of the media spectacle and the ways the history of 1821 goes public, historical inquiry can reflect on the normative/descriptive complex of rival historical narratives, exercise itself in perspectival seeing and self-reflexivity and move towards a history of the present.

FROM ACADEMIA TO THE MEDIA: THE PROBLEM OF GREEK MODERNITY

Taking as its object *Skai* channel's historical documentary on the 1821 revolution, this paper attempts to reflect on the ways Greece's modernization and cultural identity are approached, interpreted and contested in the old media and the new extended public sphere during the era of the crisis.

The eight-hour TV series on the birth of Greek nation attempted to popularize and disseminate the dominant, in the academic field, perspective of modernization theory and make it available to a wider audience. The decision for broadcasting such an ambitious and challenging TV series brought complex historical questions into contemporary debate. "1821" not only made the modernization perspective of the 1821 revolution relevant to a broad public audience but it also stimulated discussion in academic post-graduate courses and seminars.

DOI: 10.4018/978-1-5225-0212-8.ch005

Notwithstanding the differences in form and content, *Skai*'s intervention in public history via the creation of its historical documentary on the 1821 revolution was congruent with intellectual and political anxieties. Mainly, the concern for history's present relevance - that during the last decade forged a strong relationship between historians and program-makers in many other countries of Europe; such is the case of collaboration between the English historian Simon Schama with the *BBC* channel. Unlike however Simon Schama's revisionist history of the French revolution, exemplified i.e. in *BBC*'s documentary on Jacques-Louis David (2011) which railed against the *philosophes'* abstract ideals and the modern utopian projects for social engineering following the revolution, "1821" provided a framework of interpretation grounded on the opposition between a malign tradition and a benign modernity. In "1821" the focus of attention was the so called Greek peculiarity, the traumatic encounter of tradition and modernity· or otherwise, a narrative about the never-ending and always postponed modernity due to the burden of the country's Oriental, Ottoman and Byzantine past that makes convergence with Europe an aspiration unfulfilled.

The documentary's message that Greek independence was not the achievement of a heroic democratic people or the accomplishment of a glorious ancient nation but chiefly the outcome of the European power's intervention, was met by strong reactions expressed mostly via the new media, blogs and websites. Using new media, critics of the documentary entered the discussion arguing against an elite-driven historical rupture and in favor of national continuity. They did so either by essentializing (and thus de-historicizing) the struggles of the people against the powerful, foreign or indigenous elites (a quasi Marxist perspective); or by nationalizing (and thus de-historicizing) the social history of the people who, from the classical period and onwards, had inhabited the geographic regions incorporated within the territorial boundaries of the Greek 'nation-state' – (a nationalist perspective). In both cases, history becomes national rather than social.

Although reactions to *Skai's* documentary are of great importance for the overall understanding of the long-lasting debate over Greece's cultural identity, the paper does not focus on a detailed survey of such reactions, but rather opts to lay more emphasis on the core arguments of modernization theory that have been disseminated to a wide audience. This shift of attention to the effects of the popularization of modernization theory is not only due to the limited space of the paper but also to a number of substantial reasons: a. since the 80's modernization theory has been the most influential paradigm in Greek scholarship and its main assumptions remain largely unchallenged· notwithstanding its contestation by previous, Marxist and nationalist, paradigms that had inspired and stirred the reactions to *Skai*'s documentary, modernization theory's heuristic, descriptive utility as well as its normative premises have not been virtually questioned or deconstructed; b. during the crisis era the popularization of modernization theory and its concomitant ideals gained extra momentum; with the onset of financial crisis, the references to Greek modernization's *Other* evoked and homogenized multiple and various attitudes "that have been resistant towards neoliberal and other planks of Western-inspired modernization projects" (Xenakis, 2013, p. 173); and c. during the last years there is a growing tendency within the field of modern Greek studies towards questioning the essentializing perceptions of tradition, modernity, Europe or the Balkans (Triandafyllidou, Gropas & Kouki, 2013; Bogiatzis, 2009; Miliori 2002; Liakos, 2000). The need to rethink the binary opposition between a benign, progressive modernity versus a backward, traditional, "underdog" mentality can also lead to contemplate on the Janus face of modernization in general, as well as the ambivalences of Greece's modernization project from the early 19th century till the present day, in particular.

From the perspective of a rather optimistic approach within the field of public history and new media studies, the controversy over Greece's history and cultural identity could be seen as a sign of the democratization of the public domain in the digital age. Instead of lamenting the absence of consensus, the cyber-optimists, who address the extended public field as the promise of a democratic utopia, would rather welcome the debates over Greece's modernity and cultural identity as a sign of increasing political participation, pluralism and active citizenship. On the other side of the fence, the cultural pessimists would question the belief in the democratic potentialities of the digital age (Papacharissi, 2002, p. 10; Rozenzweig, 2011, pp. xix, 178) by focusing on "flaming", that is, the fragmented, polemical and heated nature of public debate.

The stance adopted by this paper, limited within the contours of the debate which is the object of analysis, neither share the optimism of the first group of scholars, nor do it embrace the pessimism of the second group. The paper argues that the use of media for the dissemination of academic history in the public domain and for its contestation not only reactivates older ideological conflicts and fosters new strifes associated with identity politics, but also tends to undermine the quest for the validity of historical interpretations giving priority to their political effectiveness. Instead of a historiographical pluralism, which could secure the dialogue between multiple and various perspectives on the past, the debate over history is prone to fostering polarization, shaping conflictual identities and forging divisive collective memories. However, the controversy over 1821 generated by *Skai's* documentary could offer an occasion for self-reflection. Turning the debate into an object of study rather than taking sides in it creates the opportunity to reflect on the normative/descriptive complex of rival historical narratives -not only those of national and Marxist history but those of modernization theory as well. Due to the very modality of media, new and old alike, the normative foundations and backward assumptions (Gouldner, 1971, pp. 31, 32)[1] of competing narratives, that are nowadays called upon to explain Greece's past, the origins of the present crisis and the ways out of it, are made focal and explicit, and thus, come to the fore.

By extending the participation of a multiplicity of actors in the public debate, the media offer a panoramic view of contending claims to truth, an all-encompassing view of exchange of arguments and counter-arguments and, thus, make possible a wide-ranging outlook on the battles between various narratives which exhibit totalizing ambitions with regard to the meaning of history. Instead of adopting a positivist perspective that distinguishes the competing explanations of Greek modernity and identity in accordance with a true/false dichotomy, the paper suggests a critical approach linked with the commitment not only to "reveal the error in half truth, but also to discover the truth in half wrong" (Lekkas, 2012, p. 263). Studying the media spectacle and focusing on how academic controversies gain publicity while engaging a wider audience in the debate over historical truth, contemporary historical inquiry could exercise itself in perspectival seeing and self-reflexivity; that is, "in 'accumulating different eyes', i.e. of multiplying various knowledge interests and sentiments about a subject without the prospect of final totalization" (Pels, 2000, p. xix).

The focus of attention here is on the relationship between what is selected as usable in the controversy and what is silenced and marginalized by the participants in the conflict. In this regard, the scholar who takes as an object of study the conflict of historical interpretations in the media appears as a tramp -*a la Michael De Certeau* (Weymans, 2004). A tramp who looks for the remnants, for what is useless and ineffective for the war of positions; who wanders seeking for the leftovers of historical experience· who is interested in those aspects of the past and the present which remain untapped and lie in the margins of media discourses and academic culture wars because they cannot be accommodated in the rival storylines without disturbing their certainties, coherence and ordered plots.

From the perspective described above then, this paper attempts to reconsider the dualistic opposition between tradition and modernity. Unlike *Skai*'s documentary, the paper argues that in the early 19th century tradition was not an obstacle to Greece's entrance to modernity. On the contrary, tradition, as lived experience, functioned as a lever for modernization; it made possible for abstract democratic ideals to be put into practice, for political rights and civil liberties to be incorporated in the actual practices of the people who revolted against the Ottoman Empire. Thus, instead of adopting the key opposition between an indigenous, stagnant tradition and an imported from the West modernity, the paper addresses the autochthonous customs, the traditional values and the communal institutions of the Greeks under the Ottoman Empire as resources rather than impediments to the project of modernization.

This line of investigation equally challenges the counter-arguments of the opponents of *Skai*'s documentary who also propagated the same dualistic understanding of modernity and tradition. Embracing the other pole of dualism, the vehement critics of "1821" claimed that modernization intrinsically precludes tradition. From the perspective of Greek primordialists, tradition is also perceived as the modernization's *Other*; as an authentic national culture to be celebrated and opposed to an imported Western modernity. For primordialists, tradition, understood as a fixed, timeless, changeless set of ideas and values abstracted from common life and concrete social practices, is essentialized, idealized and nationalized (Lekkas, 1992, pp. 80-84); by doing so, they "substitute an ideology, an abridgement of tradition, for tradition itself" (McIntyre, 2004, p. 56).

Clinging to the two poles of the conceptual opposition between modernity and tradition, both primordialists and modernists alike seem to exclude a third position beyond the dualism: that perhaps the revolution of 1821 could only be realized and achieved by grounding itself in some kind of continuity with the past, and that the project of modernization could only be sustainable by including tradition in the first place.

This third space-position enables perhaps a move beyond the *either or* logic of cultural dualism. It enables an understanding of the 1821, a decisive moment for the Greek entrance to modernity, neither in terms of an imported from the West modernity [an elitist modernist narrative], nor in terms of a supposedly timeless Greek nation [the primordialist populist narrative]. The third space-position, which is the perspective through which the story of the Greek revolution is being addressed here, is the fruit of a dialogue between concrete empirical studies in the field of modern Greek studies, on the one hand, and contemporary literature on modernization, on the other hand. As such, this phenomenology-inspired perspective is an attempt to come to terms with history as *process*, with the open, not-predetermined, lived history of the 1821 revolution; with the poetics of historical experience rather than the totalizing schemes through which it has been neatly ordered by the grand narratives of national and Marxist history during the 20th century; with the "more practical first-order discursive practices" (Mouzelis, 2008, pp. 1, 29, 101) and the modes of reflexivity (Lekkas, 2012, pp. 5-9) through which it has been understood by its historical protagonists rather than the essentializing dualistic oppositions by which we try nowadays to understand our past, to take positions towards our present and to master the future that eludes us.

THE RULES OF THE GAME: INTERVENTION AND REACTIONS

In January 2011 the first episode of the much acclaimed documentary "1821" on the history of Greek Revolution was aired. Long ago the released trailer had been announcing its objective. [2] The audience had been invited to celebrate an innovative and avant-garde interpretation of the War of Independence that was in agreement with expert knowledge and in accordance with the latest authoritative studies in the field. For the first time in history, according to *Skai* channel's rationale, Greek citizens would have the opportunity to be objectively informed about their past and reflect on their present and future: "it's about time to tell the truth about history", this was the call (Skai). The contributors of "1821" elucidated that the novelty of the series did not lie in the discovery of new historical evidence. "1821" was advertised as a radical interpretation of the Greek Struggle for Independence that made a serious claim to objectivity on the grounds that it recovered from the silences of history what was suppressed or distorted.

Thanks to the close cooperation of Greek and foreign scholars, the *Skai*'s series promised to offer an approach to 1821 free from ethnocentric bias and populist, right or left wing, distortions.[3] The main target of criticism was nationalist history but many of the arguments of left historiography about revolution were also to be challenged. With a cosmopolitan flair, an iconoclastic disposition and a spirited temperament the televised 1821 sought to revise the history of Greek revolution and discard the old orthodoxies. *Skai* channel actively responded to the challenges of the era declaring that its aim was to put the medium of television in the service of academic history and enlighten public audience beyond academia. It certainly did so in a certain manner -dramatic, impressive, vivid, assertive and sensational. The history of 1821 was narrativized and turned into a grand spectacle. Using a third person narrative mode and being visible to the audience, the narrator of "1821" supported the whole project with rhetorical coherence and eloquence. The series was advertised and its artistic qualities were highly praised.

Apart from its unquestionable literary and artistic qualities, the narration was imbued with a "confident certainty", a term used by John Tosh (2008, p. 133) in reference to the blocked reflexivity that often marks TV history. The documentary did not enter into a discussion about the problems of historical representation, the boundaries between literary and historical truth, the relation between personal experience, ideology and interpretation, the multiple and various modes of approaching the past. The engagement with such self-reflexive concerns would not only try the audience's patience, but it could also curtail the symbolic efficacy of *Skai*'s authoritative interpretation. "1821" highlighted the conflicts among different factions of the Greeks during the War of Independence; it downplayed the agency of autochthonous Greeks and praised instead the role of the Westernized intellectuals in the national movement; it brought to the fore the atrocities and massacres perpetrated by the indigenous Greeks against the Ottomans and it promoted an approach of the Ottoman Empire as a plural society marked by religious diversity and tolerance.

From first episode to last, the documentary provoked intense reactions and strong denunciations from part of the press but mostly from bloggers and internet sites. For the opponents of "1821" the approach of the documentary was in alignment with the political bias and ideological commitments of *Skai* channel and its scientific committee. They challenged the scientific authority of *Skai*'s consultants and stressed the close relationship between professional historiography and politics throughout Greek history. They also rejected the cognitive validity of the documentary arguing that "1821" was false, full of mistakes, misinterpretations and distortions. In this enterprise, they had support from other historians, some of whom were academics too. Now it was their turn to declare that they would *tell the truth about 1821* and show *how things did really happened*. The critics of "1821" meticulously dug into the archives, shuttled between their familiar primary sources and secondary literature, picked up the proper (from their perspective) facts, turned them into evidential material and argued their own authoritative account of the Greek revolution. In order to set the record straight, many of them wrote impressively detailed essays with numerous footnotes, hundreds of citations and lengthy lists of primary and secondary literature. After tracking many of the vulnerabilities, inconsistencies, indefensible arguments and contradictions of

"1821", they offered an interpretation that confirmed the class struggle between landowners and peasants or the uninterrupted historical continuity of the Greek nation since antiquity. [4]

Although they reached different conclusions about the past and its importance for the present, both parties in the controversy were committed to the idea that a truthful account of the past would provide them with an Archimedean point, a secure, stable, firm ground for their practices in the present – that is, for their choices, decisions, plans and aspirations. History was thus represented as a mode capable of providing certainty, a source of positive information that could be used to justify agendas and dictate policy –on, for instance, the proper relation with Turkey and Europe or appropriate measures for institutional reform. Lurking in the background of the controversy was a reductive strategy to reconcile fact and value, to deduce a single normative judgment from history, to derive *ought* from *is*. In other words, there was a tendency towards blurring the distinction between theory and practice, "theorizing and doing" (Nardin, 2015). So, the controversy over "the truth about 1821" took existential dimensions and was carried out with polemical zeal. The ongoing debate was driving towards the politicization of history and the de-politicization of politics.[5]

The reactions to "1821" did not come as a bolt out of the blue. In the last two decades, attempts inspired by the same agenda, the anti-nationalist, progressive revision of history, encountered similar responses.[6] From the perspective of past experience regarding the fate of previous similar interventions to reform historical consciousness, the circularity of the conflict's dynamics seems evident: the more intense, ambitious and grandiose the intervention, the more intense, robust and dynamic the reactions; and vice versa.[7] This repetitive process, which seems to have acquired a ritualistic aspect, reaches its peak as the public polarization between the agents of reform and their opponents necessitates an *either-or* choice: *either* with the reformers *or* with their opponents. The bipolar organization of public debate worked successfully. However, the result of this polarity was a loss; that is, the degradation of some dissentient voices that did not conform to this *either-or* logic and did not respond to the hailing, the interpellation process (Panagiotopoulos, 2011; Stathis, 2011; Sariyannis, 2011; Asdrahas, 2011).

Notwithstanding the reactions, or more precisely, because of them, *Skai*'s intervention in public history was successful. Apart from the validity of its historical interpretation and its cognitive impact, it had an important symbolic function. This can be understood if we move beyond a stimulus-response (reform-reaction) approach and adopt instead a relational perspective. In doing so, the object under study is not *Skai*'s intervention: it is neither the reactions to it, nor the interaction between the two parts of the conflict. It is their mutual constitution and close relationship in an ongoing circle of rivalry. *Skai*'s documentary set the stage not only for the enactment of the drama of Greek revolution, but for the re-enactment of the televised 1821 in the present. The "1821" event became the stage for dramatization of a paradigmatic struggle between the agents of Greece's modernization and reactions against them; in more familiar terms, the struggle between the "reformist" and the "underdog" cultures. This conflict (imaginary but real as well) determined the criteria of selectivity that govern the historical representation of the Greek War of Independence.

In *Skai*'s documentary the 1821 revolution worked as a metaphor for contemporary Greece. While "1821" was screening the obstacles encountered by the Westernized state intellectuals and politicians of the 19th in their effort to modernize the Greeks who had been living for centuries under the Ottoman rule, off the screen a similar scene was taking place: the drama of contemporary reformers and the obstacles they encounter. Taken as a whole *Skai's* event – the intervention to revise historical consciousness, the reactions towards it along with the responses to the reactions – had a symbolic power since it purported to be a performative confirmation of the *Cultural dualism* thesis; in other words, the clash between "reformist" and "underdog" culture that supports arguments about Greece's failed modernization. This thesis finds its formal expression and theoretical articulation in historical studies written during the era of Metapolitefsi (post-1974, after the dictatorship's fall). However, the key arguments of *Cultural dualism*, recycled, reshaped, decontextualized and often simplified, are disseminated in the public sphere. So, they constitute what we might call, following Giddens (2001, pp. 29-34), "lay knowledge" or, paraphrasing Michael Billig we could speak about modernization theory's arguments in its most banal, popular forms, as everyday, commonplace ideas.[8] Thus, the findings of modernization theories not only provide an explanation of its object, namely Greek modernity, but they also enter constitutively in the object they describe, that is, Greek society. In doing so, they set up a system of beliefs, convictions and practices that constitute a "habitus" which, functioning as a "structuring structure" (Bourdieu, 1990, pp. 96-98), guide the social actors to occupy a position and acquire a sense of identity in a polarized political field ("reformers" vs. "underdogs").

Seen from this perspective, the opposition between the agents of historical revisionism and their adversaries appears as the modern sequel to an older and familiar story. "1821" operated as a simulation of a story that occupies a central place in the grand narrative of Greece from Antiquity to the present. The first episode of the story is the battle of Hellenism (ancient Greeks) against barbarians. The second is a double fight, a fight on two fronts, given by the modernizers of the early 19th century against the Ottomans and the oriental mentality of autochthonous Greeks (the "underdog" culture). The third includes the Herculean efforts, precarious victories, continual frustrations and lost opportunities of the modernizers in their attempts to curb the resistances to modernization.[9]

MODERNIST IMAGINARIES: FROM *METAKENOSIS* TO *CULTURAL DUALISM*

Metakenosis is a term coined by Adamadios Korais (1748-1833), a major figure in the pantheon of Greece's Neo-Enlightenment movement. *Metakenosis* was the project of repatriation, transfusion or decanting, of Hellenic heritage from civilized Europe to Greece not only as a requirement for national liberation but as necessary for providing standards of conduct appropriate to civil society. The ideal of *Metakenosis* was turned into a national pedagogy and a technology for social reform especially when it was associated with problems of governmentality within the new state.

Metakenosis turned out to be an ambitious social engineering project undertaken by the educated strata to 'teach virtue' and establish a particular form of freedom and moral conduct from above, a type of individualization linked to the state. The precondition of this "civilizing process", a control-obsessed "gardening culture" (Bauman, 1987, p. 52), was the urgent need of the newborn state to extirpate old customs and deep-rooted traditions as possible sites of reaction and opposition, to eradicate signs of the Medieval, Byzantine and Ottoman past as locales of backwardness.

Metakenosis came to be the worldview of Greek intelligentsia to whom it provided a privileged position, a high vision, a *Great Idea* and a sense of mission: the modernization *qua* civilization of Greece, and more broadly of the Orient. This was the foundational idea of the first University of Athens, named as the Othonian University after Greece's first king Othon (Otto). Irredentism and the "civilizing project" represent two versions of a common, unifying dream, a national utopia: what the educated elite aspired to achieve by education, the fighters of Independence could achieve through war. In the literature on the Greek revolution of the early 19th century, the national tropes of mind/head and body were overwhelming: the body symbolized the armed fighters of the revolution and the mind/head the intellectuals (Andriakaina, 2013, pp. 49-70).

If *Metakenosis* conjures up the national dream, *Cultural dualism* alludes to the modernizer's nightmare. The *Cultural dualism* thesis, the grand narrative that gives shape to the self-representations, aspirations and modernizing ideals of Greek intellectuals, brings to the fore what *Metakenosis* tends to obscure and repress. As far as the former is committed to the implementation of the modernization ideal, it shifts the conflict (and the "civilizing project") within Greek society. In this case, a certain paradox arises: the oriental *Other* to be disciplined and civilized is not "out there", but inside the *social body*.

Theoretically articulated in the eighties, the era of Metapolitefsi (many decades after the "realization" of the Great Idea, the Asian Minor Catastrophe in 1922, and with the 1967-1974 military Junta still fresh in the collective memory), the motivating vision of *Cultural dualism* is the completion of modernization. After 2009, when the origins of the present crisis had become a hot topic of debate in the media and the public sphere, the *Cultural dualism* thesis gained momentum and extra popularity (Xenakis, 2013, p. 173). The key political issue was about responsibility and the burning question was *what is to be done* but also *who is to blame* for Greece's predicament. *Cultural dualism* provided a clear-cut answer grounded on historical arguments: the blame was put on tradition, the burden of the Ottoman past and the resistances to modernization emanating from the "underdog culture".

Cultural dualism provided not only justification for the intervention but also the narrative plot and interpretive scheme for *Skai*'s documentary series. This narrative sheds light on certain aspects of Greek history: the trauma of Greek modernity, the ambivalence of Greek identity towards Europe, the Balkans and the Orient. It is also an important attempt to fill in the silences of Marxist and nationalist historiography regarding the role of intellectuals and their contribution to the revolution. But it also faces certain limits which increasingly attract the attention of scholars (Tziovas, 2001, p. 201; Bogiatzis 2009; 2012, pp. 17-38); Delalande, 2012; Liakos, 2013; Mitsi & Muse 2013). The *Cultural dualism* thesis is a paradigmatic example of the whole set of projections and displacements that interfere in the dialogue with the past (LaCapra, 1980), –especially with those parts of it that are crucial for the present and take existential dimensions for the definition of individual or collective identity.

Cultural dualism resonates with the ideals, visions, anxieties and sentiments of the modernizing intellectuals of late twentieth-century Greece, of the era of Metapolitesfi. It was at the eighties, after the fall of junta, when they returned from abroad, with the hope that they would respond to Korais's project and achieve the fulfillment of the modernization ideal. The scholarly pursuits of the post-80s intellectuals along with their active involvement and engagement with the politics of Europeanization could perhaps provide an explanation why even within the field of modern Greek studies attention is focused on "the reactions to modernization" rather than the ambivalences or the ambiguities of modernity (Wagner, 1994). Still prevalent within the field is a version of modernization theory which regards the resistances to modernization as emanating from a previous or/and lower stage of historical development and not as part and parcel of the detraditionalization process, as a product of modernity itself, as an intrinsic part of the very same process of modernization.

Cultural dualism is a story about the Greek intelligentsia as the primary agent of the 1821 revolution, an avant-garde, modernizing elite that appears to have been caught in a previous stage of development, trapped inside a backward society. If we use the figurative tropes of early 19th century literature, the story of Greece's modernization depicts the rational head of Greece dwelling in an undisciplined body-society which, it tries, in vain, to control. No wonder then that it puts heavy emphasis on the role of great statesmen who stood out in the effort to reform Greek society and to put an end to the mind-body split. This is the perspective from which the story of Ioannis Kapodistrias, the first governor of Greece, was told by the 1821 documentary.

Authoritarian Modernization and Resistances

"1821" highlighted the spirit of Adamadios Korais and gave emphasis to his speculations regarding the civic maturity of the nation, the proper time for revolution, the moral and educational reform of Greeks as the fundamental preconditions for liberation.

Although after the outbreak of the revolution Korais strongly support it, in his early writings he assumed that the proper time was about fifty years later (Mackridge, 2009, p.123). He also never stopped expressing his worries that Greece, once liberated from the Ottomans, might end up being enslaved to "Turkified Christians" (or "Christians Turks"). Whom did Korais had in mind when he was writing about "Christian Turks"?[10] Committed to the *Cultural dualism* thesis, "1821" answered that the "Christian Turks" were the carriers of the "underdog culture" that since 1821 lingers on and blocks modernization. By reading the past in the light of present socio-political stakes, "1821" downplayed and silenced Korais's oppositional stance towards centralization of powers by Governor Kapodistrias, a former Joint Minister for Foreign Affairs to the Czar of Russia.[11]

Drawing on Orientalist discourses on the cultural backwardness, civic immaturity and incapability of self-government of autochthonous Greeks, the documentary engaged in apologetics for the Governor's initiative to suspend the Constitution of 1827.[12] *Chaos or order*? In the seventh episode entitled "Towards Independence" the Governor had to provide some kind of answer to this dilemma. In previous episodes, a number of scenes were dedicated to exposing the tribal nature of autochthonous Greeks, the fierceness and brutishness of their character, their vindictive rage, the ferociousness of their onslaught against Muslims, their brutalities during the war, the disorderly character of the irregular armies of Greeks contrasted with the disciplined of regular armies of the European *Great Powers* – in short, all the traits that could testify to the Oriental savagery and primitiveness of autochthonous population. Given this context, the suspension of the Constitution seemed justified on the grounds that civilization matters. In the last scene of the seventh episode the first Governor of Greece lies on the ground after being shot and stabbed by his enemies: two members of the Mavromichalis family, Peloponnesian notables, who had participated in the War of Independence.[13]

The documentary did not pay any attention to the ambivalence of contemporary historiography about Kapodistrias's policy - was he a tyrant as some scholars have argued *or* an assiduous modernizer, the great architect of modern Greece, as "1821" and many intellectuals still assume. A way out of this dilemma would necessitate a shift from the assumption of modernization as a benign process to a reflection on the tensions between modernity and modernization, the examination of the multiple paths to modernity and the means through which the modernization ideal has been planned, implemented and executed.

Kapodistrias inaugurated an authoritarian modernization from above (a project systematically launched in 1833 by the Bavarian regency). He embark on an effort to bring about a radical rupture with the past and construct a state *ex-nihilo*.[14] Instead of being explained as a sheer necessity imposed on him by the untamed Greek character, Kapodistrias's strong centralized administration was in tune with his paternalistic ideology, the theory and practice of enlightened despotism. Also in tune with the historicist arguments of the era, Kapodistrias consigned Greeks to "an imaginary waiting-room of history" (Chakrabarti, 2000, p. 8) claiming that the time was not ripe for revolution since the autochthonous were morally, socially and politically immature. Later on, however, he envisaged his task in terms that resonate with both the messianic dream of the prophet Isaiah as the "Anointed One", the righteous messiah-king with an unmediated authority over His people on the one hand, and the metaphor in Plato's ideal Republic, the philosopher-king, a dream so dear among many Enlightenment philosophers on the other. Having studied medicine in Italy, Kapodistrias conceived his rule in terms of pastoral power and understood himself as one who cares for the social body as a physician does. His ideas about the constitution as a "razor dangerous in the hands of immature people" (Dragoumis (1879/1973, pp. 151-152) reverberate with similar metaphors in colonial contexts. Instead of entrenching the rule of law and the core of common social life, Kapodistrias's attempt ended up to a huge bureaucracy, a sheer volume of elaborated, complicated and involuted laws, rules and regulations. His policy determined state - society relations and unleashed bureaucratic chaos that no one could navigate it all.

Assuming that a benevolent authoritarianism was needed to bring Greece closer to modernity, the necessary cost for convergence with Europe, *Skai's* documentary made Kapodistrias a symbol of the rational modern state and converted him into an early martyr of modernization: "From that moment on (the Governor's assassination) vested interests will bully for decades the Greek State and for any modernization effort there will be a bullet available" (*Skai*, 2009).[15] "1821" disregarded the strong opposition to Kapodistrias's policy by many Westernized intellectuals.[16] It also did not take into account that today Kapodistrias is the shared symbol of intellectuals with diverse and disparate political and ideological orientations. Paradoxically, *Skai*'s modernization idol, Kapodistrias, is also the icon of many who belong to the populist, religious right. [17]

The criteria of selectivity shaping the narrative of "1821" and fabricating the relevance of history to the present were determined by the necessities of contemporary political struggle, by the effort to shape public opinion rather than to cultivate the faculty of judgment, which is the aim of public history as argued by John Tosh (2008).[18] In "1821" the past's present relevance was synecdochically fabricated by picking and matching those parts of history which seemed to give apposite answers to contemporary political stakes: on the screen, 19th century Greece asking for help 'from outside', pleading the intervention of Europe; off-screen, protests and strikes following the news for the renewal of the loan programme to contemporary Greece.

The particular manner in which "1821" staged Kapodistrias's policy, and the oppositions to it, functioned as a metaphor for contemporary reforms and the responses to them. *Skai* not only homogenized the oppositions to the reforms [then and now], but it also debased and degraded them. By converting the conceptual heuristic distinction *modern - traditional* into the moralizing dichotomy of *progressive-backward,* "1821" placed social discontent and dissent in an inferior stage of historical development and so, it negated and vitiated recent opposition to austerity measures. *Skai* not only obscured political conflict and wiped out the contents of social struggle and protest (then and now), but it also addressed them as a social-engineering problem best solved by "experts". The documentary interpellated the historian as a social engineer, the *mind of the state* authorized to manage and discipline the *social body*, and apply 'neutral', abstract knowledge to the task of governing (Rose, 1999; Burchell, 1991). Viewing the *social body* as a mechanical entity, an object to be moulded from the state and shaped from above, *Skai* rather substituted for politics the administration of things.

Anti-Nationalist Constructivism Reconsidered

The documentary defined 1821 as a predominantly "European" accomplishment. This perspective, exaggerating the role of Westernized intellectuals in the historical process, was in tune with the main argument of *Cultural dualism* about 1821 as the foundational moment of Greece's failed modernity – a moment in which modern institutions were imported from the West into an undeveloped society. This argument, grounded on the idea of the singularity of modernity (Bhambra, 2014), is the product of a comparative analysis that examines the Greek case in contrast to a European transition to modernity (in general), which is viewed as exemplary.[19] From the second episode, "An Idea is Born", the audience watched the endless peripeteia (peripety) of abstract ideas towards their frustrated self-actualization, the drama of pure concepts that fall from their platonic realms into mundane life, the tragedy of the Enlightenment theories after meeting the messy reality of this world. The group of Westernized intellectuals, despite internal differences or rather because of them, did play a considerable part in the making of the national movement. However, in "1821" this particular grouping was regarded as the sole agent of the revolution: "a determined, purposeful elite who dragged all others into the War of Independence".[20]

The first episode seemed to promise a comprehensive historical approach that could place the 1821 events into a broad supra-national context; that is, a context that could provide an understanding of the 1821 beyond its borderlines as defined by the *Treaty of London for Greek Independence*. However, this promise was not carried out. Paradoxically, despite promises to offer a critical approach to nationalism, "1821" looked at the revolution through the lens of the nation-state. *Skai*'s perspective squeezed the explanatory depth and breadth of 1821 within Greece's national borders modeled arbitrary under the auspices of the Great Powers. In line with a positivist critique of ideology, striving to rebuff nationalist and Marxist accounts of the revolution, the documentary did not attempt to reinterpret the particular sorts of evidence used by national and Marxist narratives, but instead it singled them out as insignificant or as falsities in contrast to the "truth". In doing so, "1821" rather "threw the baby out with the bathwater".

The documentary was theoretically inspired from the constructivist theories of ethnogenesis, from the modernization theories of nationalism, which were used for the debunking of national myths. In their polemical responses, *Skai*'s opponents drew their argumentative armoury from primordialist theories which were used to ground a narrative of 1821 in the perspective of national awakening. The modernists tend to define nation as a pure modern form of consciousness and regard the state apparatus as the key mechanism through which national ideas are produced, spread and disseminated. For the constructivist "inventionist" approach, the nation is "a product of social engineering on the part of elites, and more especially of the intelligentsia" (Smith, 2001, p. 243). On the other side, the ethno-symbolist approach attempts to overcome the difficulties inherent in the stagist model of development by shifting the focus of analysis from structure to human agency and social interaction, from objective reality to subjective experience, and from historical discontinuities to continuities.[21] So, whilst the state-centric modernist theories regard nation as developed *from above,* a modern creation *ex nihilo* enforced by state elites on a *tabula rasa*, the ethno-symbolist approaches tend to privilege the community based, the horizontal, the *from below-popular* constituents of modern nations.

Pantelis Lekkas, in a paper written in 2005, offers a holistic, non-essentialist and non-teleological interpretation of the 1821 from the perspective of historical sociology. In a section entitled "Ethnic Awakening and Ethnogenesis: Betwixt or Beyond" Lekkas develops certain arguments regarding the debate between the two above-mentioned theses on nationalism which might provide insight on how to address the issue at hand –the anti-nationalist, anti-populist revision of Greek history by *Skai*'s documentary.

I deem worthy to quote herein the relevant argument in length: "The debate between the supporters of ethnic awakening and the adherents of ethnogenesis does not of course pertain to the Greek case alone. But it has certainly preoccupied recent Greek scholarship quite a lot, and the controversy rages to this day. Still, this conflict between national awakening and ethnogenesis poses a dilemma, which, on some reflection, seems generally misplaced and false (…). Its irremediable defect (..) is that it focuses on the nation, on its professed antiquity or modernity, and not on nationalism per se, on the intellectual and political movement that springs up in modernity and brings forward the concept of the supposedly antique nation as the only proper unit of state organization. Hence, both theses succumb, each in its own way, to the dominance of the very ideology that makes such a big issue out of the purported antiquity of the nation (…) both attitudes adopt the same loaded logic: a question posed by nationalism and yet concealing that it is the nationalist discourse itself which cries out for understanding (Lekkas, 2005, p. 165).

The dilemma of taking sides *for* or *against* arises when the participants in public debate draw their arguments from one theoretical perspective on nationalism only, while laying claim to its absolute validity. When that happens, the contingent nature of historical knowledge and the limited scope of theoretical perspectives from which the respective conflicting theses draw their armory is not acknowledged or accepted. In this case however, theoretical pluralism runs the risk of turning to its opposite (Craib, 1992, p. 7). Conflict then arises when the available theoretical perspectives are not used according to the degree of their explanatory force, their applicability to specific historical contexts, their capacity to withstand the test of falsification, their potential to stimulate further research or their potential to be employed in complementary fashion in order to shed light to different phases of the national phenomenon - i.e., Miroslav Hroch's (1985) work on nationalism exemplifies this kind of approach. Shifting the focus from the origins of nations to the formation of national movements, Hroch's analysis of the different phases of the national movement provides a theory of nationalism without resorting to dualistic oppositions between historical continuity and discontinuity, between intellectuals and the masses, between the national liberation ideal and material interests, between a *from above* and a *from below* approach of social change.

Wars over the history of 1821 break up when the definition of Greek identity is the main stake. In this case, the normative foundations of the various theoretical paradigms that guide historical interpretations block the readiness of the self to be open to "hostile information" and sharpen the tension between a scholar and a person in the world. As Gouldner (1971, p. 494) puts it, "news about the stability of a government is hostile information to a revolutionary but friendly information to a conservative. An openness to and a capacity to use hostile information is (...) inevitably linked, at some vital point, with an ability to know and to control the self in the face of threat". This seems particularly true for public history that becomes the site where different versions of the Greek nation and its history contested and conflicting views of national identity compete against each other. Through the contending, polarized historical narratives about 1821 the social and cultural identities of their producers are sustained and maintained, while the lines of demarcation between them are clearly delineated.

Fighting against the essentialism of national history and the populism of its opponents, the 1821 documentary set forth an extreme constructivist approach of the revolution: "[Nationalism] invents nations where they do not exist" (Gellner, 1983, p. 48). Extracted from Gellner's writings, this catch phrase became the slogan of the anti-nationalist agenda which highlighted the role of Westernized intellectuals in the modernization process. On the other side, the opponents of "1821" draw paradoxically their armory of opposition from a newer approach, the ethnosymbolist theory of Anthony Smith who has pinpointed the limitations of constructivism and rationalist analyses of institutional design.[22]

What is absent in the debate over the Greek revolution is a long-term perspective on the social, economic and cultural history of the geographic regions that revolted against the Ottomans and which were later incorporated within the territorial boundaries of the Greek 'nation-state'. Although "1821" promoted an approach of the Ottoman Empire against long established stereotypical and national images of the Turks, it rather underestimated the specific, historical results that the Ottoman state's religious tolerance and administrative diversity had for its non-Muslim subjects (Sakellariou, 2012/1939, pp. 61, 127-135, 186-190; Finlay, 1861/2014, 306-307; Jelavich, 1983, p. 36). So neither for the agents of *Skai*'s historical revisionism, nor for their opponents was the prehistory of 1821, the social history of Greek populations living under the Ottomans, addressed in terms beyond the lens of the 'nation-state', that is, in terms different from the national myths of origin. For the perennialists, the pre-1821 history is glorified as it testifies the existence of an ever-present nation resistant to Western modes of thought and forms of life; for the modernists, it is denounced as the locus of oriental customs and traditional backward mentality than hinders Greece's modernization. Thus, the age-long dispute about dispute over the meaning of 1821 revolution and the demolition of the traditional "municipal institutions" by the centralizing policies of Bavarian regency (1833), is still largely conducted in polarized terms of anti-nationalism versus nationalism and vice versa.

BEYOND CULTURAL DUALISM: THE POETICS OF HISTORICAL EXPERIENCE

Is 1821 a national *or* a social revolution? Is it a modern revolution *or* a traditional rebellion? Is it a European event *or* an indigenous accomplishment that drew inspiration from Balkan and Eastern traditions? Such questions, whenever formed within the contours of Greek modernity's grand narratives – whether nationalist, Marxist or modernizing – dictate answers in terms of *either-or*.

Despite their differences, the answers given to this set of questions share a common reductive logic. They insert order and coherence in historical experience by seeking a single center, a universal subject (the nation, the people, the bourgeoisie, the intelligentsia, Europeanism or anti-Europeanism) as the author of history. By totalizing historical experience in terms of a master voice, the grand narratives of Greek modernity follow the narrative plot of an adventure story revolving around a unitary, homogenous agent which embodies a utopian vision - an ideal nation, an idealized people or an idealized modernity.

Instead of a holistic, non teleological approach (Mouzelis, 2008, pp. 223-224; Lekkas, 2012, pp. 148-153) that could shed light on the various socio-political stakes of the conflicts, "1821" opted for an approach in terms of a cultural struggle whose stake was the attitude towards Europe. Had a broader context been chosen, the modernization of the Ottoman empire would not have been sacrificed in favor of an Oriental, multicultural, exoticism.[23] The diversity and historical particularities of the regions that rebelled against the Ottomans would not yield to the pressure of broad generalizations; and the modern nature of the 1821 national revolution along its social and popular content (Lekkas, 2005, p 166) could not be easily liquidated. Convergence with Europe and the anxiety over Greek identity were indeed among the main concerns and worries of the 19th century Greek intelligentsia (and they still are). But the causes of the revolution should also be sought at the level of the everyday life of 'reayas' under Ottoman rule during the era of great transformations, when differences in social status began to be perceived in terms of social inequalities and injustice. The shift from 'reayas' to a new subjectivity should be traced not only on the level of discourse, that is, in discursively articulated definitions of identity, but also on the level of situated social practices and contextual specific performances. It is obvious that now we have to shift our interest from the Greek diaspora (the Westernized intellectuals) to *the rest*, from the few and the famous to the ordinary, the common people.[24]

The people who participated in the war certainly cannot be regarded as experts in abstract rationalism and identity thinking. However, they did possessed practical wisdom and a rich poetic imagination, virtues that we could acknowledge and comprehend.[25] The appropriation and transformation of traditional institutions, longue duree customs and folk traditions was the creative response of the '*reayas*' to the great social and economic transformations occurring during the first decades of the 19th century (Galani, 2010; Chatziioannou, 2013).

In religious pamphlets and folk songs, in oral tradition and oracular literature, in apocalyptic myths, legends and sagas, the memory of the fall of Constantinople (1453) was kept alive throughout the centuries. Along with the memory of the fall, the eschatological promise of liberation, justice and resurrection, the deliverance of the *Genos of the Romans*, the egalitarian messages of the Gospels were being maintained as elements of real or fancied stories of hardship, heroic resistance, suffering and injustice. If for a large part of the intellectual elite the traumatic event was the Fall of Rome and the beginning of the Middle Ages, for the folk the traumatic event was the fall of Constantinople. The 'reayas', by blending, combining and mixing varied, heterogeneous, scrappy, incongruous elements from collective memory and past traditions (oracular literature, messianic myths, fairytales, eschatological prophesies) with new secular ideals and demands, actively participated in the Age of revolutions and modern ideologies.

What else other than a miscellaneous collection of heterogeneous motifs picked up from different traditions, a combination of radical ideas, values and ideals from various origins, was the revolutionary message of Rigas Velenstinlis (1757-1798)? With his works Rigas stirred up the spirit of rebellion in the region of the Balkans and invited subjects of the Ottoman Empire (Christians and Muslims alike) to fight against despotism as he combined secular Enlightenment thought, Jacobin subversive ideals and republican demands with Eastern Orthodoxy (i.e. the oracular prophecies of Agathagelos), religious symbols of Christianity (i.e. the Christian cross), and Ancient Paganism (i.e. the legend of Alexander the Great). (Manesis, 2009, pp. 146-1477; Kitromilides, 1999, pp. 309-310).[26] The same miscellaneous collection of revolutionary motifs from various traditions (elite and popular, high and low, Western and Eastern) was used by Filiki Eteria which, organized by three ordinary small-scale traders, played a prominent role in the initiation of the 'reayas' into the movement against social and religious discriminations.

What we have here, as the necessary precondition of 1821, is a rebellious culture, carnivalesque, hybrid and polyphonic; a culture that lies beyond the dualisms of "reformist" versus "underdog" cultures or between Westernizers and anti-Westernizers. The study of popular culture allows us to glimpse the complex nature of historical experience instead of the abstract categories of the contending ideologies through which it is tamed and neatly ordered.

"1821" downplayed Rigas Velestinlis's enterprising spirit and his vision of a 'multicultural' republic as well as the role of Filiki Eteria, its audacious project, its contribution to rebellious fermentation and its mass appeal. Their agency and their message was rather too messy. Their liminal, uncanny nature could not fit into the refined, clean conceptual schemes of *Cultural dualism*. The same goes for Papaflessas, a member of the Filiki Eteria who hurtled to Pelloponesos, spread the liberation message and played an important role in the outburst of revolution. Being both a priest of higher rank and office and a revolutionary, Papaflessas blurs the clear contours of a dualism that emphasizes the reactionary and conservative role of religion. Reveler, brawler, and womanizer, the rebellious priest Papaflessas with his Rabelaisian temperament not only shocked his contemporaries but still unsettles our rigid classification attempts.

"1821" not only effaced the agency of peasants and their active participation in the revolt. Most importantly, it completely wrote off the role of the middle social strata that had risen within the Ottoman Empire as a consequence of its nascent modernization. The documentary disregarded the urban character of the revolution in the islands, the maritime cooperatives or the 'protoindustrial clusters' (Petmezas, 1990, p. 584; Olympitou, 2003) in Eastern Thessaly and the crucial role of artisans, small craftsmen, ship owners, labourers, seamen in the 1821 revolution. These were anonymous people from the middling strata who, thanks to their geographical and social mobility, had been initiated into the Filiki Eteria and contributed to the preparation and conduct of the revolt, and especially to the dissemination of democratic and radical ideas. "1821" had no room for persons such as Antonis Oikonomou, a shipmaster from Hydra, or Panagiotis Karatzas, a shoemaker from Patra, who, fighting against priviledges and demanding justice (Kordatos, 1976, pp.189-199), contributed into the transformation of the '*reayas*'s every-day life.

A holistic, non-essentialist and non-teleological, framework might allow us to address not only the national character of the 1821 revolution, [27] but also these parts of historical experience which some Marxist accounts single out and highlight –such as, the struggle over land or, even the fight against property rights (McGrew, 1976, p. 125), without however resorting to reified and essentialist patterns of interpretation. By understating the social demands of the revolution around which the clashes during the war and after the formation of the Greek state were articulated, "1821" reduced the major reforms that marked early Greek history - constitutional establishment of equality before the law, democracy, parliamentarism, universal suffrage for men- into a paradox, as privileges conceded by enlightened elites to the masses.[28]

The piece of historical experience regarding the creative use of tradition, the artistry and inventiveness of human interaction, the hybridity of popular culture and the active role of autochthonous Greeks in the modernization process was the repressed element in *Skai*'s documentary. It does not conform to the reified opposition of traditional, backward society versus rational, modern state. It challenges the *either-or* identity logic of *Cultural dualism*, namely, the clash between high and low culture through which contemporary reformers define their identity, and acquire a sense of distinction from their opponents, left or right populists. It questions the conceptual purism and the clear-cut schemes of *Cultural dualism*, namely, the rigid opposition between civic and ethnic nationalism and the conflict between Westernism and Anti-westernism, though which Greek intellectuals approach past history and define their identity. As the 1821 revolution was framed in terms of modernity versus tradition, as a struggle between enlightened heterochthonous intellectuals and autochthonous populations, the agents, occurrences and developments which could not easily be accommodated to any of these polar opposites were expunged from history.

By reading early modern Greek history through the lens of *Cultural dualism*, "1821" succeeded in disseminating the message: *either* for the neoliberal type of social planning and technocratic reform *or* against reason and modernity. Certainly, this dilemma is itself a historical creation, and the set of responses it prescribes are integral parts of the history of early and late modernity. However, such a dilemma is not dictated by the inexorable laws of history as suggested by "1821", nor its dualistic alternatives exhaust the variety of intellectual responses which have been given to the challenges of detraditionalization, modernization and rationalization.

REFERENCES

Andriakaina, E. (2013). The Promise of the 1821 Revolution and the Suffering Body. Some thoughts on Modernisation and Anti- intellectualism. *Synthesis, 5*, 49-70.

Arvanitakis, D. (2011). *Η Επανάσταση του 1821 και ο 'ΣΚΑΪ TV*. Retrieved April 6, 2013, from http://www.rizospastis.gr/story.do?id=6157921&publDate=20/3/2011

Asdrahas, S. (2003). Τουρκοκρατία – Λατινοκρατία. Οι γενικοί χαρακτήρες της ελληνικής ιστορίας, 1453-1770. In V. Panagiotopoulos (Ed.), Ιστορία του Νέου Ελληνισμού 1700-2000, (vol. 1, pp. 17-38). Athens: Ellinika Grammata.

Asdrahas, S. (2011, March 26). Προϋποθέσεις της Επανάστασης του 1821. *Enthemata-Avgi Newspaper*.

Bauman, Z. (1987). *Legislators and Interpreters. In On Modernity, post-modernity and Intellectuals*. Polity Press.

Beaton, R. (2009). Introduction. In R. Beaton & D. Ricks (Eds.), *The Making of Modern Greece* (pp. 1–18). Ashgate.

Bhambra, G. (2014). Postcolonial and decolonial dialogues. *Postcolonial Studies, 17*(2), 115–121.

Billig, M. (1995). *Banal Nationalism*. London: Sage.

Bogiatzis, V. (2009). Παναγιώτης Κονδύλης και ελληνική νεοτερικότητα. *Σημειώσεις, 69*, 7-55.

Bogiatzis, V. (2012). Μετέωρος Μοντερνισμός. Τεχνολογία, ιδεολογία της επιστήμης και πολιτική στην. *E (Norwalk, Conn.)*, 1922–1940.

Bourdieu, P. (1990). *The Logic of Practice*. Polity Press.

Burchell, G. (1991). Peculiar Interests: Civil Society and 'Governing the System of Natural Liberty. In G. Burchell, C. Gordon & P. Miller (Eds.), The Foucault Effect: Studies in Governmentality (pp. 119-150). Chicago: University of Chicago Press.

Chakrabarty, D. (2000). *Provincializing Europe. Postcolonial Thought and Historical Difference*. Princeton University Press.

Chatziioannou, M. C. (2010). Mediterranean pathways of Greek merchants to Victorian England. T*he Historical Revue. La Revue Historique, 7*, 213–237.

Clogg, R. (2002). *A Concise History of Greece*. Cambridge, UK: Cambridge University Press.

Craib, I. (1992). *Anthony Giddens*. Routledge.

Delalande, N. (2012). The Greek State: Its Past and Future. An interview with Anastassios Anastassiadis. *La Vie des idées*. Retrieved April 6, 2012, from http://www.booksandideas.net/The-Greek-State-Its-Past-and.html

Dertilis, B. G. (2010). *Ιστορία του Ελληνικού Κράτους 1830-1920, vol. Α´- B*. Athens: Estia.

Diamandouros, N. (1972). *Political Modernization, Social Conflict and Cultural Cleavage in the Formation of the Modern Greek State: 1821-1828*. (PhD dissertation). Columbia University, New York, NY.

Diamandouros, N. (2000). *Cultural Dualism and Political Change in Postauthoritarian Greece*. Madrid: CEACS. (Original work published 1994).

Diamandouros, N. (2012). Politics, culture, and the state: Background to the Greek crisis. In O. Anastasakis & D. Singh (Ed.), Reforming Greece: Sisyphean Task or Herculean Challenge? (pp. 9-18). Oxford, UK: SEESOX.

Dragoumis, M. (2003). Review of J. Koliopoulos & Th. Veremis. (2002) Greece. The Modern Sequel: From 1821 to the Present. In Ιστορικά Κριτικά. Βιβλιοκριτικές των έργων του Θάνου Βερέμη (pp. 113-118). Athens: Kastaniotis.

Dragoumis, M. (2009). *Μεταρρυθμιστές όλων των κομμάτων αλληλοϋποστηριχθείτε*. Retrieved November 2, 2011, from http://e-rooster.gr/10/2009/1681

Dragoumis, N. (1973). *Ιστορικαί Α*. Athens: Ermis. (Original work published 1879)

Efthymiou, M. (2007). Instead of Introduction: The Communities of the Greek Peninsula Under Ottoman Rule. An Attempt of Schematic Classification, According to their internal economic and political function. *Eoa and Esperia*, 7, 239–245.

Filias, V. (2012). *Ποιοί πλαστογραφούν την αληθινή Ιστορία του 1821*. Retrieved April 2, 2013, from http://www.antibaro.gr/article/4250

Finlay, G. (2014). *History of the Greek Revolution* (Vol. 2). Campridge University Press. (Original work published 1861)

Galani, K. (2010). The Napoleonic wars and the disruption of Mediterranean shipping and trade: British, Greek and American merchants in Livorno. *La Revue Historique*, 7, 179–198.

Gellner, E. (1983). *Nations and Nationalism*. Oxford, UK: Blackwell.

Giddens, A. (1984). *The Constitution of Society: Outline of the Theory of Structuration*. Cambridge, MA: Polity Press.

Giddens, A. (1997). Living in a Post-Traditional Society. In Reflexive Modernization. Politics, Tradition and Aesthetics in the Modern Social Order (pp. 56-109). Cambridge, MA: Polity Press.

Giddens, A. (2001). *Modernity and Self-identity: Self and Society in the Late Modern Age*. Polity Press.

Gouldner, A. (1971). *The Coming Crisis of Western Sociology*. London: Heinemann Educational Books Ltd.

Gourgouris, St. (1996). *Dream Nation. Enlightenment, Colonization, and the Istitution of Modern Greece*. Stanford University Press.

Hatzopoulos, M. (2009). From resurrection to insurrection: 'sacred' myths, motifs, and symbolsin the Greek War of Independence. In R. Beaton & D. Ricks (Eds.), *The Making of Modern Greece* (pp. 81–94). Ashgate.

Holevas, K. (2014). *Από την κότα του Καποδίστρια στις μίζες του σήμερα.* Retrieved April 20, 2012, from http://www.antibaro.gr/article/9890

Hroch, M. (1985). *Social Preconditions of National Revival in Europe: A Comparative Analysis of the Social Composition of Patriotic Groups among Smaller European Nations.* Cambridge, UK: Cambridge University Press.

Jelavich, B. (1983). *History of the Balkans* (Vol. 1). Cambridge University Press.

Kitromilides, P. (1999). *Νεοελληνικός Διαφωτισμός. Ο.* Athens: MIET.

Kitromilides, P. (2010). Adamantios Korais and the dilemmas of liberal nationalism. In P. Kitromilides (Ed.), *Adamantios Korais and the European Enlightenment* (pp. 213–223). Oxford UK: Voltaire Foundation.

Kokkinos, G., & Gatsotis, P. (2010). Το σχολείο απέναντι στο επίμαχο ιστορικό γεγονός και το τραύμα. In G. Kokkinos, D. K. Mavroskoufis, P. Gatsotis & E. Lemonidou (Eds.), Τα συγκρουσιακά θέματα στη διδασκαλία της Ιστορίας (pp. 13-120). Athens: noogramma.

Koliopoulos, J., & Veremis, T. (2010). *Modern Greece. A Historiy since 1821.* Wiley-Blackwell.

Kordatos, Y. (1976). *Η Κοινωνική σημασία της Ελληνικής Επαναστάσεως του 1821.* Αθήνα: Εκδόσεις Διεθνούς Επικαιρότητας.

Koulouri, C., & Loukos, C. (2012). *Τα πρόσωπα του Καποδίστρια. Ο πρώτος Κυβερνήτης της Ελλάδας και η νεοελληνική ιδεολογία (1831-1996).* Athens: Poreia.

LaCapra, D. (1980). Rethinking intellectual history and reading texts. *History and Theory, 19*(3), 245–276.

Lekkas, P. (1992). *Η εθνικιστική ιδεολογία. Πέντε υποθέσεις εργασίας στην Ιστορική Κ.* Athens: EMNE-Mninon.

Lekkas, P. (1997, July 6). Οι Αντιδράσεις του Ορθολογισμού. *To Vima Newspaper.*

Lekkas, P. (2005). The Greek War of Independence from the Perspective of Historical Sociology. *La Revue Historique, 2,* 161–183.

Lekkas, P. (2012). *Abstraction and Experience: Toward a Formalist Theory of Ideology.* Athens: Topos.

Liakos, A. (2000). Encounters with Modernity: Greek Historiography Since 1974. *Cercles: revista d'història cultural, 3,*108-118.

Liakos, A. (2008). Hellenism and the Making of Modern Greece: Time, Language, Space. In K. Zacharia (Ed.), *Hellenisms. Culture, Identity, and Ethnicity from Antiquity to Modernity* (pp. 201–236). Aldershot, UK: Ashgate.

Liata, E. (2004). Οι Ελληνικές Κοινότητες (17ος - 19ος Αι.). Από την ιστορία των θεσμών στην ιστορία των τοπικών κοινωνιών και οικονομιών. In P. Kitromilides & T. Sklavenitis (Eds.), Ιστοριογραφία της νεότερης και σύγχρονης Ελλάδας 1833-2002, (vol. B, pp. 533-549). Athens: Κέντρο Νεοελληνικών Ερευνών-ΕΙΕ.

Loukos, C. (2003). Ο Κυβερνήτης Καποδίστριας. Πολιτικό έργο, συναίνεση και αντιδράσεις. In V. Panagiotopoulos (Ed.), Ιστορία του Νέου Ελληνισμού 1700-2000, (vol. 3, pp. 185-216). Athens: Ellinika Grammata.

Macridge, P. (2012). The heritages of the modern Greeks. *British Academy Review, 19*, 33–41.

Manesis, A. (2009). Η πολιτική ιδεολογία του P. In P. Kitromilides (Ed.), *Ρήγας Βελεστινλής. Ιδρυτές της Νεότερης Ελλάδας* (pp. 144–150). Athens: TA NEA-Istoriki Vivliothiki.

McGrew, W. (1976). The land issue in the Greek War of Independence. In N. Diamandouros, J. P. Anton, & J. Petropoulos (Eds.), *Hellenism and the First Greek War of Liberation, 1821-1830* (pp. 111–130). Thessaloniki: Institute for Balkan Studies.

McIntyre, K. (2004). *The Limits of Political Theory. Oakeshott's Philosophy of Civil Association.* Imprint Academic.

Miliori, M. (2002). Ambiguous partisanships. Philhellenism, turkophilia and balkanology in 19th century Britain. *Balkanologie, 6*(1-2), 127–153.

Millios, Y. (1988). *Ο Ελληνικός Κ.* Athens: Exandas.

Mitsi, Ef, & Muse A. (2013). Some Thoughts on the Trails and Travails of Hellenism and Orientalism: An Interview with Gonda Van Steen. *Synthesis, 5*, 159–178.

Mouzelis, N. (1996). The Concept of Modernization: Its Relevance for Greece. *Journal of Modern Greek Studies, 14*(2), 215–227.

Mouzelis, N. (2008). *Modern and Postmodern Social Theorizing: Bridging the Divide.* Cambridge University Press.

Nardin, T. (2015). Oakeshott on theory and practice. *Global Discourse, 5*(2), 310–322.

Olympitou, E. (2003). Τεχνικές και Επαγγέλματα. Μια εθνολογική προσέγγιση. In V. Panagiotopoulos (Ed.), Ιστορία του Νέου Ελληνισμού 1700-2000, (vol. 1, pp. 305-316). Athens: Ellinika Grammata.

Panagiotopoulos, V. (2004). Η αριστερή ιστοριογραφία για την Ελληνική Επανάσταση. In P. Kitromilides & T. Sklavenitis (Eds.), Ιστοριογραφία της νεότερης και σύγχρονης Ελλάδας 1833-2002, (vol. Α, pp. 567-577). Athens: Κέντρο Νεοελληνικών Ερευνών-EIE.

Panagiotopoulos, V. (2007, June 17). Ποιός θα διορθώσει ποιόν. *To Vima Newspaper,* 17- 06-2007.

Panagiotopoulos, V. (2011). *Εθνική Ιστορία ή μήπως εθνική μυθολογία.* Retrieved April 17, 2012, from http://politicalreviewgr.blogspot.gr/2011/03/blog-post_25.html

Papacharissi, Z. (2002). The virtual sphere: The internet as a public sphere. *New Media & Society, 4*(9), 9–27.

Papaderos, A. (2010). *Μετακένωσις. Ελλάδα –Ορθοδοξία –Διαφωτισμός κατά τον Κοραή και τον Ο.* Athens: Akritas.

Pels, D. (2000). *The Intellectual as Stranger. Studies in spokespersonship.* London: Routledge.

Petmezas, S. (1990). Patterns of Protoidustrulization in the Ottoman Empire. The case of Eastern Thessaly, ca. 1750-1860. *The Journal of European Economic History*, *19*(3), 574–603.

Pissis, N. (2011). Αποκαλυπτικός λόγος και συλλογικές ταυτότητες (17ος-18ος αι.). In A. Dimadis (Ed.), *Ταυτότητες στον ελληνικό κόσμο (από το 1204 έως σήμερα)* (Vol. 5, pp. 687–696). Athens: European Society of Modern Greek Studies.

Pizanias, P. (1987). Η εφαρμογή της θεωρίας για τις σχέσεις του 'καπιταλιστικού κέντρου' και της 'υπανάπτυκτης περιφέρειας' στην Ελληνική ιστοριογραφία. Ν. Ψυρούκης-Κ. Τσουκαλάς. *Mnimon*, *11*, 255–286.

Politis, A. (2007). *Το μυθολογικό κενό. Δοκίμια και σχόλια για την ιστορία, τη φιλολογία, την ανθρωπολογία και άλλα*. Athens: Polis.

Rose, N. (1999). *Powers of Freedom. Reframing Political Thought*. Cambridge University Press.

Rozenzweig, R. (2011). *Clio Wired. The Future of the Past in the Digital Age*. New York: Columbia University Press.

Rustow, D. (1968). Modernization and Comparative Politics. *Comparative Politics*, *1*(1), 37–51.

Sakellariou, M. (2012). *Η Πελλοπόνησος κατά την Δευτέραν Τουρκοκρατίαν, 1715-1821*. Athens: Herodotus. (Original work published 1939)

Sariyannis, M. (2011). *Παίζοντας με την κονσόλα της Ιστορίας*. Retrieved April 20, 2012, from http://enthemata.wordpress.com/2011/03/26/marinos/

Skai. (2009). *Μεγάλοι Έλληνες-Kapodistrias*. Retrieved April 20, 2012, from https://www.youtube.com/watch?v=7M0QyS7_Ml4

Smith, A. D. (1995). *The 1995 Warwick Debates on Nationalism*. Retrieved from http://gellnerpage.tripod.com/Warwick.html

Smith, A. D. (2001). Perennialism and Modernism. In A. Leoussi (Ed.), *Encyclopedia of Nationalism* (pp. 242–244). London: Transaction Publishers.

Stathakopoulos, D. (2011). *Τα Ημαρτημένα*. Retrieved April 20, 2012, from http://www.antibaro.gr/article/4025

Stathis, P. (2011). *Στα όρια επιστήμης και πολιτικής: το 1821 στον Σκάι*. Retrieved April 18, 2012, from http://enthemata.wordpress.com/2011/03/13/stathis/

Szabla, C. (2007). *George Finlay's Greece: Between East and West*. (Senior Thesis). Department of History, Columbia University, New York, NY.

Tambaki, A. (2004). Η ιστοριογραφική οπτική του μεταφραστικού εγχειρήματος: από τη 'μετακένωση' στη διαπολιτισμικότητα; In Ιστοριογραφία της νεότερης και σύγχρονης Ελλάδας 1833-2002, (vol. Α, pp. 419-431). Athens: Κέντρο Νεοελληνικών Ερευνών-ΕΙΕ.

Theotokas, N., & Kotaridis, N. (2006). *Η Οικονομία της Βίας. Παραδοσιακές και Νεωτερικές Εξουσίες στην Ελλάδα του 19*. Athens: Vivliorama.

Tosh, J. (2008). *Why History Matters*. Palgrave-MacMillan.

Triandafyllidou, A., Gropas, R., & Kouki, H. (2013). *The Greek Crisis and European Modernity*. Palgrave-MacMillan.

Tziovas, D. (2001). Beyond the Acropolis: Rethinking Neohellenism. *Journal of Modern Greek Studies*, *19*(2), 189–220.

Veremis, Th. (1982). Κράτος και Έθνος στην Ελλάδα: 1821-1912. In D. Tsaousis (Ed.), *Ελληνισμός και Ελληνικότητα. Ιδεολογικοί και Βιωματικοί Άξονες της Νεοελληνικής Κοινωνίας* (pp. 59–67). Athens: Estia.

Veremis, T. (2011a, February 6). Περί Εθνικισμού. *I Kathimerini Newspaper*.

Veremis, T. (2011b, February 13). Τα μηνύματα που μας διαφεύγουν. *I Kathimerini Newspaper*.

Wagner, P. (1994). *A Sociology of Modernity. Liberty and Discipline*. London: Routledge.

Weymans, W. (2004). Michael de Certeau and the Limits of Historical Representation. *History and Theory*, *43*(2), 161–178.

Xenakis, S. (2013). Normative Hybridity in Contemporary Greece: Beyond "Modernizers" and "Underdogs" in Socio-Political Discourse and Practice. *Journal of Modern Greek Studies*, *31*(2), 171–192.

ENDNOTES

[1]   This is the element that, according to Gouldner, makes a theory as being 'intuitively convincing' for the expert researcher and for a wider audience.

[2]   Sponsored by the National Bank of Greece, "*1821*" was presented by Petros Tatsopoulos. The chief consultant Thanos Veremis, a history professor at National and Kapodistrian University of Athens, collaborated with a team of historians including Iakovos Michailidis, William St. Clair, Fikret Adanir, Roderick Beaton, David Brewer, Spyros Sofos, Paschalis Kitromilides, Hans Eideneier, John Bintliff.

[3]   The eight hourly episodes were followed by panel discussions in which participated professional historians and a number of intellectuals from across the political spectrum. However important the panel discussions might have been (Tosh, 2008, p.135), this paper leaves them outside the scope of analysis in order to focus on how the documentary addressed the present-day political relevance of 1821, "its importance for present times", a point especially highlighted by *Skai*.

[4]   See among other, Filias (2012) and Stathakopoulos (2011).

[5]   The adversaries of "*1821*" accused the documentary producers of undermining the historical and cultural differences between the Greek and the Turkish nation, and thus, of becoming supporters of Turkey's candidacy for membership in the European Union (Arvanitakis, 2011). In their rejoinders, the consultants of "*1821*" made use of a vast array of historical examples (Veremis, 2011b). They spoke of the close connection between nationalist history and the "Metaxas dictatorship". They also stigmatized the "idiosyncratic nationalism" of the communist left in 1949 and decried its "fatal error" regarding "the Macedonian issue". (Veremis, 2011a). During the dispute between

contending parties, what was initially launched in terms of the Enlightenment project, namely, the dissemination of historical knowledge and the elimination of ignorance, began to be acknowledged as a conflict between different positions within the political spectrum. In this vein, the historian Thanos Veremis castigated the reactions complaining that the target was the "homeless center of the political spectrum that is sandwiched between two denunciators, the left and the right" (Veremis, 2011a).

[6]   For the controversy erupted in 2006 about the history textbook for sixth graders, see Kokkinos-Gatsotis (2010, pp. 13-120); Panagiotopoulos (2007).

[7]   For the political ineffectiveness of virulent anti-nationalism, see Lekkas (1997): "That (…) which, in my opinion, would be the most appropriate and effective attitude is the practical vitiation of nationalist ideologies, their reversal, even their perversion. Only in this way could be achieved, certainly not the crash of nationalism, but (…) its emasculation, the devitalization of its reactionary reflexes."

[8]   For the relation between the every-day knowledge of lay actors and the findings of social sciences, the 'double hermeneutic' as "a mutual interpretative interplay between social science and those whose activities compose its subject matter", see Giddens (1984, pp. xxxii, 284-288).

[9]   In the struggle to modernize Greece and achieve convergence with Europe since 1821 exemplary figures of the "reformist culture" stand out: Adamadios Korais, Charilaos Trikoupis, Eleftherios Venizelos, Konstantinos Karamanlis, Kostas Simitis. For the inclusion of Kapodistrias in the pantheon of modernizers, see Koliopoulos & Veremis (2010, p. 21).

[10]   According to Mackridge (2009), Korais was rather implying to the Fanariots and the local Greek notables, while Kitromilides argues: "Korais disapproved of Kapodistrias' initiative to suspend representative government and to govern dictatorially for a period until public order could be established in the new state. This development turned Korais actively against Kapodistrias, whom he now denounced as a new tyrant". However, Kitromilides (2010) holds that Korais's reaction to Kapodistrias's despotism, the denouncement of the Governor as a new tyrant was "probably a failure of judgment on the part of Korais, due to misinformation by the many enemies gained by the Governor's effort to impose due processes of government in a totally chaotic situation". Kitromilides (2010, p. 222). For the ambivalence of historiography towards Kapodistrias's rule, see Koulouri & Loukos (2012).

[11]   This was Korais's characterization of Kapodistrias's character in the most acute phase of his conflict with him (Loukos, 2003, p. 208).

[12]   Despite the acknowledgment that "Kapodistrias's authoritarian style and his beliefs that the Greeks were not capable of self-government had provoked the opposition of influential sections of society", Clogg (2002, pp. 41-43) concludes: "Kapodistrias (…) had little time for liberal provisions of the Troizene constitution or the factionalism of the assembly (…). This last he replaced by a twenty-seven members Panhellenion, which was under his direct control. He had a two-fold mission: to create the foundations of a state structure in a country ravaged by years of savage fighting and to secure as favorable borders as possible for the new state". It is worth mentioning that Diamandouros pinpoints "the authoritarian, paternalistic and eventually oppressive Kapodistrian regime" (1972: 188/2002: 256), and does not include him in the pantheon of Greek modernizers (1972: 249/2002:182). However, following the work of Dankwart Rustow regarding the three stages of political modernity, "the growth of authority, the formation of national identity, and the quest for political equality and participation", he argues that constitutionalism in Greece became a source

of "chronic instability and weakness" and shares the same faith about the indigenous Greek's immaturity for self-government. Furthermore, commenting on the Third Constituent Convention at 1826 and the decision of the modernizers to "opt for equality (constitutional change), he notes: "the granting of equality and civil rights to an essentially immobilized, passive, and traditional people before either identity or authority had been established, served to create a serious gap between state and society".

13 For a valuable distinction between elites and notables, see Asdrahas (2011). According to Millios (1988, pp. 192-194) the local notables of Peloponnese sought a decentralized, federal system. Diamandouros also notes that "the islands had traditionally been self-governing and had experienced no direct Ottoman rule for a long time, a fact which contributed to their stability and had allowed them to pursue economic enrichment" (1972, p. 293/ 2002, p. 215). The author also mentions that the local notables strongly opposed to centralization "by appealing to ancient democratic rights, the annual popular elections for the legislative and the executive branches of government". However, he contends that the appeal to democratic rights was a mask under which the notables hide their 'true' narrow self-interests (1972, pp. 291-20/2002, pp. 162, 215-220).

14 That is, without taking into account the tradition of self-governance and the relative autonomy that some regions had secured during the Ottoman Empire (Liata, 2004; Asdrahas, 2003, 2011; Efthymiou, 2007; Szabla, 2007).

15 *Skai*'s documentary, Μεγάλοι Έλληνες-Kapodistrias, January – May 2009. Retrieved April 20, 2012, from https://www.youtube.com/watch?v=7M0QyS7_Ml4, 3.22'-3.28'.

16 Kapodistrias's efforts towards the centralization of power provoked discontent and met resistance from many places, especially from Hydra, where many intellectuals had resorted. There, in consultation with the notables, they turned the island into the center of opposition demanding constitution (Loukos, 2003, pp. 204-208).

17 Holevas (2014): "What Greece and Europe need today is a 'Kapodistrias'". See also: Dragoumis (2009): "The slogan is: 'Reformers of all political parties be united (..). Maybe Kapodistrias's vision for Greece may eventually become a reality. For the populism of Kapodistrias, as one among many traditions that inspired his policy, see Loukos (2003).

18 Questions of interpretative consistency and coherence are often not the most relevant ones to ask in TV history, especially when its primary goal is to mould public opinion through framing and agenda setting, and to reach out and mobilize a wide audience. For instance, whilst the first episode of "1821" attempted to revise much of the nationalist and orientalist cliches about the Ottoman character, the "bad Turk" (and resulted in portraying the Ottoman Empire as a multicultural paradise of tolerance), the fourth episode, "the tail coat and the fustanella", took pains to expose the primitive, Ottoman-Oriental mentality of the autochthonous Greeks.

19 Although the modernization paradigm rejected Marxist historiography that interpreted 1821 in terms of class struggle, it implicitly adopted one of its main arguments about the Ottoman empire as a variant of feudalism (Diamandouros, 1972, pp. 215, 219/2002, pp. 187, 257). This assumption however contrasts with available historical studies according to which the condition of the 'reayas' in Ottoman Empire cannot be analyzed in terms of the economic, social, and political dependencies that characterized Western feudalism (Pizanias, 1987). By replacing socio-economic conflict with a cultural-political struggle as the engine of history, the modernization paradigm substituted the intellectuals (and Europe) for the people (or the nation) as the agent of revolutionary change (Panagiotopoulos, 2004, pp. 575-576).

[20]   Iakovos Michailidis, "1821", 4th episode: The tail coat and the fustanella:19.19-19.34 min. For the "unequivocal top-down view of social, cultural, and political formation, often articulated in terms of the will of an intellectual elite", see Gourgouris (1996, pp. 85-86).

[21]   It is no wonder then that Anthony Smith's perspective rather than Ernest Gellner's theory of nationalism is preferred by historians due their tendency to eschew generalizations and evolutionary historicist explanatory schemes. For the relation between the abstract theorizing of social sciences and the empirically oriented historical inquiries, see Bhambra (2011, p. 656); Mouzelis, (1996, pp. 223-225).

[22]   Roderick Beaton in his introduction to *The Making of Modern Greece* (2009, p. 9), albeit in favor of the modernist's claims, observes that from their perspective, "almost everything written by Greeks and their supporters can be dismissed as either 'perennialism' (…) or 'primordialist". The author also points out that since the 1980s, the modernist theories of nationalism "have undergone significant changes" that went rather unnoticed within the camp of Greek modernists; that is, Smith's ethnosymbolism that "emerged within the dominant 'modernist' paradigm, is now challenging "some of its cherished premises".

[23]   Even counter-modernizing tendencies, such as, the defense of religion, customs and traditional ways of life, are in need of justification and thus, are amenable to rationalization (Giddens, 1997). In this way, a new, reflexive, non-traditional relation to tradition was being formulated, a process which was further developed after the formation of the Greek state. Regarding the question whether the War of Independence can be subsumed under the classification of modern revolution, see among others, McGrew (1976: 111); Diamandouros (1972: 16 /2002: 272).

[24]   Historical scholarship in the field of social history has shed some light to folk culture and the worldview of the 'reayas' under the Ottoman rule offering an invaluable glimpse into their lives and mentalities: Theotokas-Kotaridis (2006); Pissis (2011: 687-696); Politis (2007); Hatzopoulos (2009, pp. 81-94). -

[25]   In a review of recent trends in Greek historiography Antonis Liakos (2000, p. 117) writes: "Neither popular culture nor the everyday life of the popular classes attracted the interest of Greek historians, as it did in Western Europe (…). In Greece the popular masses were considered anti-modern (…) and in juxtaposition to modernity".

[26]   For an important distinction between "two quite distinct legacies from Byzantium that are often conflated" that is, "Byzantium as the nurturer of the Christian Orthodox tradition, and Byzantium as empire", see Macridge (2012).

[27]   As Sakellariou notes (2012, p. 190), the 1821 revolution had both a national and a social character. The class of landowners became a revolutionary agent because opposition between Greek and Ottoman landowners was both a national and a social opposition.

[28]   "If one chose to study Greek institutional history, s/he would be tempted to consider Greece as the most advanced country in the world. However, what (…) is not visible and yet we must recognize, is the prevailing mentality of a society which is very far from all this (...)". Thanos Veremis in "1821", 4th episode: The tail coat and the fustanella: 18.42-17.48 min.

Section 2
Gender

Chapter 6
We All Scream for Ice Cream:
Positive Identity Negotiation in the Face of Cancer

Bryan McLaughlin
Texas Tech University, USA

Kang Namkoong
University of Kentucky – Lexington, USA

Shawnika Hull
George Washington University, USA

Dhavan Shah
University of Wisconsin – Madison, USA

David H. Gustafson
University of Wisconsin - Madison, USA

ABSTRACT

In the United States, women with breast cancer often find their identity confined by a sociocultural context that encourages them to adopt an overly optimistic outlook while hiding signs of their physical illness. Online social support groups offer a promising venue for breast cancer patients to take control of their self-definition and connect with individuals going through similar experiences. During the analysis of discussion board posts for an online breast cancer support group, ice cream unexpectedly emerged as a central component of group discussions. This included frequent sexual jokes about the deliverymen that brought the women ice cream. A grounded theory analysis revealed that ice cream symbolized the pursuit of everyday, physical desires, which allowed group members to construct a joyful, but forthright, shared identity. This paper demonstrates how online support groups can enable individuals facing a health crisis to use seemingly trivial symbols to take control over their self-definition.

INTRODUCTION

For many women, a breast cancer diagnosis changes everything. Breast cancer and the side effects of treatment create daunting physical and emotional challenges (National Cancer Institute, 2012) and pose unique threats to body image and femininity (Ehlers & Krupar, 2012; Oster, Astrom, Linda & Magnusson, 2009). Loss of hair, changes in body shape and functioning, and acute awareness of illness-related stigma might dramatically alter how a breast cancer patient perceives and feels about her body (Mathieson & Stam, 1995; Pelusi, 2006). Perhaps most jarring, women with breast cancer often have to deal with

DOI: 10.4018/978-1-5225-0212-8.ch006

existential concerns about their mortality (Kenne Sarenmalm, Toren-Jonsson, Gaston-Johnsson, & Ohlen, 2009). Because a cancer diagnosis can profoundly alter the way women view themselves and the world around them, patients often have little choice but to renegotiate their identity in relation to their cancer (Carpenter et al., 1999; Henriksen & Hansen, 2009). For many women in the United States, this identity negotiation is confined by a sociocultural context that encourages them to adopt an overly optimistic outlook while hiding signs of their physical illness (e.g., through the use of wigs and prosthetic breasts) (Broom, 2001; Wilkinson, 2001). This context can have a profound impact on how breast cancer patients view their illness, their relationships to it, and their identities as women with breast cancer.

Online support groups have received much attention for their potential to help cancer patients achieve positive health outcomes (e.g. Gufstason et al., 2005, 2008; Hawkins et al., 2010; Sandaunet, 2008). In particular, they offer women with breast cancer a promising venue wherein they can confront their negative emotions and take control of their self-definition. By connecting women who share similar experiences, online support groups have the capacity to build social networks outside of a particular sociocultural context (Pitts, 2004; Sandaunet, 2008; Van Uden-Kraan et al., 2008).

This study initially began with the intention of examining the degree to which members of an online breast cancer support group, enabled by the Center for Health Enhancement Systems Studies (CHESS), exchanged informational and emotional support messages and the effects these messages had on psychosocial outcomes. During the analysis of discussion board posts, *ice cream* unexpectedly emerged as a significant and central component of group discussions. This included frequent sexual jokes about the deliverymen that brought ice cream to the women. In the context of breast cancer, the topic of ice cream appeared rather trivial, yet group members appeared to be coalescing around this seemingly lighthearted topic in a meaningful way.

Due to a lack of a theoretical basis from which to speculate about this phenomenon, a grounded theory approach was employed. Grounded theory is appropriate when there is limited theoretical knowledge on a subject, as it outlines a systematic methodological process through which new theoretical accounts can arise inductively from the data (Glaser & Strauss, 1967). Grounded theory's origins lie in the interpretive tradition of symbolic interactionism (Benoliel, 1996; Jeon, 2004). Using this framework, *ice cream* was interpreted a symbol with a constructed meaning that may have important implications for the negotiation of identity. In doing so, this study address two important communication problems, (1) the potential for online support groups to allow individuals to construct an identity outside of the shared context of having a serious illness, and (2) how seemingly trivial symbols, such as ice cream, can have important implications for individuals facing a health crisis.

BACKGROUND

The Pervasive Culture of Optimism

At first glance, the joyful discussions about ice cream appeared to be at odds with the more dire experience of having breast cancer. At the same time, breast cancer has largely been ascribed a positive outlook in American culture, perhaps best exemplified by the symbolic pink ribbon (Ehlers & Krupar, 2012; Ehrenreich, 2009). In this regard, ice cream seemed to fit the optimistic and even cheerful portrait of breast cancer in the United States. This discourse of optimism has become so pervasive that negative accounts about the breast cancer experience are mostly disregarded by mainstream culture (Broom, 2001).

This context is important because the meaning a culture assigns to an illness can largely construct the parameters through which individuals can think about and react to their illness (Klehinman, 1988). The identity transformation that typically accompanies a breast cancer diagnosis occurs, and therefore should be understood, within the social context surrounding a breast cancer survivor (Mathieson & Stam, 1995). Contextual factors can include sociocultural, situational, interpersonal, and/or temporal contexts (Revenson & Pranikoff, 2005). The sociocultural context in which an individual with cancer is embedded can play a particularly important role because sociocultural forces shape an individual's interpretation of their health, and, consequently, their behavior in relation to their disease – ranging from their daily routines, to how they interact with others, to the type of treatments they seek out (Burke et al., 2009). The larger context in which breast cancer patients find themselves can have a profound impact on how they view their illness, their relationship to it, and their identities as women with breast cancer.

In the United States, the hopeful and positive culture surrounding breast cancer can therefore influence how women with breast cancer interpret their illness. Breast cancer patients in America often find that although they are initially allowed to "express initial distress, shock or horror," they are soon expected to project an idealistic aura of optimism (Wilkinson, 2001, p. 270). Although American culture actively trumpets the need to fight breast cancer, the commodification of breast cancer largely serves to marginalize and hide the realities of the disease from mainstream society (Ehlers & Krupar, 2012). American society encourages women to hide physical signs of their illness, as women with breast cancer are often encouraged to wear wigs and prosthetic breasts. As a result, "concealment of distress, anxiety and fear from others becomes part of the breast cancer experience" (Wilkinson, 2001, p. 271).

This context can make it difficult for women with breast cancer to construct an identity that allows for anger, disappointment, or fear. Many medical providers even discourage patients from participating in support groups because they allow for too much expression of negativity (Coreil, Wilke, & Pintado, 2004). Some scholars have called into question the conventional wisdom that women with breast cancer stand to benefit from thinking positively (Broom, 2001; Wilkinson, 2001). The upbeat image of breast cancer in America fails to account for the women who face grim long-term prospects (Ehlers & Krupar, 2012; Gray et al., 2001). For many, treatment is emotionally as well as physically trying, and for some women it is to no avail (Broom, 2001). Furthermore, the assumption that positive thinking can help beat cancer ultimately places the blame on victims who succumb to the disease (Ehrenreich, 2009).

This is not to say that thinking positively is necessarily a bad thing. Many American breast cancer patients do have much to gain from taking a more optimistic outlook (Coreil et al., 2004). At the same time, many women also stand to benefit from allowing themselves to struggle and admit negative emotions (Ehrenreich, 2009). A promising approach might be to come to terms with the health realities of breast cancer while still holding optimism for everyday life (Kenne Sarenmalm et al., 2009). Unfortunately, it can be difficult for women in America to find a space in which they can discuss the challenges and fears that accompany breast cancer.

Online Support Groups and the Renegotiation of Identity

Online support groups have received much attention for their potential to help cancer patients achieve positive health outcomes (Gufstason et al., 2005, 2008; Hawkins et al., 2010; Sandaunet, 2008), such as increased emotional well-being (Namkong et al., 2010), improved health self-efficacy (Shaw et al., 2006), reductions in cancer-related concerns (Han et al., 2008, 2011), and decreases in negative emotion (Shaw et al., 2007).

In particular, online social support groups offer women with breast cancer a venue in which they can confront their negative emotions and take control of their self-definition (Pitts, 2004; Sandaunet, 2008; Van Uden-Kraan et al., 2008). In these spaces, women often have supportive communications that include the act of acknowledging others' feelings and exchanging reassurance and encouragement (Kim et al., 2011). This understanding environment allows them a chance to speak, sometimes obliquely, about their changing identities. Online support groups therefore provide an opportunity for women with breast cancer to negotiate their identity on their own terms (Coreil et al., 2004; Pitts, 2004; Sandaunet, 2008). Online support groups can transcend geographic boundaries (Shaw, McTavish, Hawkins, Gustafson, & Pingree, 2000) and potentially allow a space where women with breast cancer have agency to construct their identity outside of a particular sociocultural context. By connecting women with similar experiences, online support groups have the capacity to build social networks with other individuals who can relate to the cancer experience (Rains & Young, 2009).

In this way, such groups can facilitate greater agency with respect to management of the disease and its side effects and social consequences. This might be particularly important in a context in which individuals with a serious illness, such as cancer, experience identity transformation vis-à-vis the illness imposed upon them or are viewed as stigmatized. That is not to say that individuals can ever fully transcend the context of their immediate social life but simply that imagined communities offer a chance to reconstruct the parameters within which individuals can understand their identity. In these online spaces, women with breast cancer can be afforded greater opportunity to carve out their own spaces and have more say in constructing the narrative that better fits their own experience rather than that which society assigns to them.

Ice Cream and Symbolic Interactionism

Given this context, it was clear that there was something significant about the way CHESS group members appeared to be coalescing around ice cream and the deliverymen who brought it, but there was a lack of previous work on this phenomenon. A grounded theory approach, which is appropriate when there is limited theoretical knowledge on a subject (Glaser & Strauss, 1967), was therefore employed. Grounded theory outlines a systematic methodological process through which new theoretical accounts can arise inductively from the data (Charmaz, 2006).

The origins of grounded theory are in the interpretive tradition of symbolic interactionism (Benoliel, 1996; Jeon, 2004), which is based on the view that all human action is mediated through symbol systems (Blumer, 1969). Symbols, such as language and signs, take on meaning through interaction, and people come to have shared interpretations of what message a symbol implies. The focus is therefore on interpreting the processes by which meaning is constructed and the consequences of that meaning on an individual's or group's actions (Joas & Knobl, 2004). Using the framework of symbolic interactionism entails placing an individual's perspectives at the center of the interpretive analysis, understanding each person as a socially situated, thinking being (Crooks, 2001).

Using this approach, ice cream was interpreted a symbol with a constructed meaning that may have important implications for the negotiation of identity. Symbolic interactionism is an appropriate theoretical framework from which to examine how individuals make sense of their experiences and the process through which they construct their identity (Aberg, Sidenvall, Hepworth, O'Reily, & Lithell, 2004). The meaning and implications of ice cream in this group might shed important insights into the processes of identity renegotiation and the healthy promotion of positive thinking.

METHOD

Participants

The data analyzed in this study were collected as part of the Center for Excellence in Cancer Communication Research's Mentor-Component study. Individuals who participated in this study were women diagnosed with breast cancer within the past two months who were given access to a private system of online resources, referred to as CHESS (Hawkins et al., 2010). Between April 2004 and April 2006, patients were recruited from three cancer institutions in different parts of the country. Participants were provided a laptop to use and compensation for Internet access fees for six months. Participants could access the online social support group service, an asynchronous bulletin board where fellow breast cancer patients shared experiences and advice. Of the 325 participants, analysis was limited to the 237 women who either wrote or read messages in online social support groups.

Data Construction and Preliminary Analyses

Prior to analysis all identifying information was removed from the data. The computer-aided content analysis program *InfoTrend* (for detailed descriptions of InfoTrend, see Han et al., 2011; Namkoong et al., 2010) was used throughout the analysis. The analysis initially began with the intention of identifying informational and emotional support expressions within discussion board posts. To develop coding rules that could capture these concepts, the first author read through all 18,064 posts from the discussion board. InfoTrend's keyword search function was employed to produce a random set of 100 posts containing the provided term. This function helped construct effective rule sets, which were developed inductively by looking at language use in context. During this process the authors discussed the language that signified informational and emotional support concepts and formulated ideas about how to capture these concepts. This allowed us to become intimately familiar with the data, including what was being said, the context of the dialogue, what latent meanings were shared, and how these messages were constructed syntactically. During this coding process ice cream emerged as a significant concept that warranted further investigation.

Grounded Theory Method

The grounded theory approach advocated by Charmaz was followed (2006, p. 9), which views grounded theory as "a set of principles and practices, not as prescriptions or packages." That being said, the approach used more closely followed the methodological practices prescribed by Strauss's version of grounded theory rather than Glaser's (for elaboration on this debate, see Walker & Myrick, 2006).

A number of principles and practices were employed in this grounded approach:

1. The constant comparative method, which includes meticulously checking developing codes, categories, and theories against the data and against each other;
2. Theoretical memos, the process of documenting one's thoughts, insights, and speculations about the emerging codes and categories;
3. Open coding, wherein the researcher goes through the data line by line, providing labels that represent the phenomenon being observed;

4. Axial coding, the process of constructing more inclusive categories that serve as axes around which open codes are clustered;

5. Selective coding, where the researcher identifies a core category that provides a central narrative that explains how the other codes and categories relate to each other;

6. Theoretical sampling, the process of selecting additional data for analysis based on emerging core categories; and

7. Negative case analysis, which involves purposefully looking for instances in which working categories or theories do not hold up (for elaboration on these practices see Charmaz, 2006; Glaser & Strauss, 1967; Strauss & Corbin, 1990).

RESULTS

Open Coding

Open coding was performed on 200 random posts that contained the words "ice cream," which were obtained using InfoTrend's keyword search. Every meaning unit that related to the topic of ice cream was assigned a label. After coding 200 posts it became clear that no new codes were emerging (additional posts were analyzed in subsequent coding procedures). The open codes were then organized and compared against each other. The initial analysis identified 75 codes. Through axial coding, 19 categories were established.

The relationships between the 19 categories were examined, noting the connections and the underlying concepts involved. Through this process the categories were continuously checked against the data, which included additional theoretical sampling. Theoretical sampling was achieved using InfoTrend's keyword search function. For example, to learn more about the deliverymen and sexual humor, the authors searched for posts including words such as "Schwan's," "yellow truck," "attractive," "crave," "kidnap," and so forth. This process resulted in the development of four notional categories:

1. Physical comfort,
2. Emotional support,
3. Delivery men as a symbol of sexual identity, and
4. Symbol of group identity.

Axial Codes

- **Ice Cream as Physical Comfort:** One thing that was patently clear was that most of the women of CHESS loved the feeling they got from eating ice cream. Members frequently proclaimed that ice cream was "really good," shared their eating experiences, and provided recommendations for flavors to try. But ice cream was revered for much more than taste; it was one of the most frequent suggestions for dealing with cancer- or treatment-related pain. Ice cream was said to "soothe the stomach" and seen as "good medicine," "better than pain pills," and "the secret cure for all ailments." In sum, group members constructed a commonsense portrait of ice cream as a truly unique source of physical pleasure and provider of comfort.

Figure 1. Initial categories from Axial Coding (with clustering Open Codes)

I. Basic Eating of Ice Cream (IC)

(1) Plans to eat IC
(2) Description of eating IC
(3) Description of/ recommendation for IC shop
(4) Description/ recommendation of IC flavor or IC recipe
(5) Questions about whether other members have had memorable IC eating experiences recently

II. Pleasure/Enjoyment of Eating

(6) Expression of enjoyment/ joy of eating IC
(7) Excitement over others eating IC

III. Ice Cream Addiction

(8) Can't stop thinking about IC
(9) Claims that one could not live without IC
(10) Explicit claims of being addicted to IC

IV. Ice Cream is Truly Unique

(11) Suggesting IC is the ONLY way to pick yourself up
(12) Proclamations that eating IC is the best experience
(13) Describing ideal heaven with reference to IC

V. Encouragement to Eat Ice Cream

(14) Encouragement to use IC to celebrate
(15) Encouragement to pamper oneself by eating IC
(16) Encouragement to keep eating IC

VI. Ice Cream and Health Concerns

(17) Desire to lose weight/ concerns that IC doesn't help
(18) Claims that IC is OK in moderation
(19) Claims that although IC puts weight on, it's worth it

VII. Lack of Will Power Towards Ice Cream

(20) Description of overeating IC
(21) Discussion of will power to not eat IC (for health)
(22) Encouragement to not stop eating IC despite health issues
(23) Sharing of low fat IC recipe/ ways to cut calories for IC

VIII. Taste of Ice Cream Remained after Treatment

(24) Claim that pickles & IC are the only foods that taste normal after treatments

IX. Ice Cream as Physical Support

(25) IC is the secret cure for all ailments/ is good medicine
(26) IC helps deal with fatigue
(27) IC helps deal with confusion
(28) IC helps after treatment
(29) IC makes headaches go away
(30) IC soothes the stomach/ helps with nausea

X. Ice Cream as Emotional Support

(31) IC is good therapy
(32) IC makes you feel better all around
(33) IC helps with positive thinking
(34) IC takes mind of BC problems
(35) IC provides joy
(36) IC gives hope
(37) IC helps with feelings of isolation
(38) Find comfort in picturing other members eating IC

Figure 2. Initial categories from Axial Coding (with clustering Open Codes) continued

XI. Explicit Encouragement of Others to Use IC for Emotional Support

(39) Encouragement to use IC as comfort when in pain
(40) Encouragement to eat IC to deal with bad prognosis
(41) Suggestions that IC can provide comfort after losing a loved one

XII. Ice Cream and Humor

(42) Members get giggly talking about IC/ describing IC experiences
(43) Using the topic of IC to make fun of others or oneself
(44) shared laughter/jokes about IC experiences

XIII. Schwans Man (SM) and Sexual Humor

(45) Claims of shyness/ embarrassment around SM
(46) Noticeable embarrassment about SM teasing
(47) Encouragement for other members to have SM bring them IC
(48) Jokes about a member kidnapping and/or stalking the SM
(49) Teasing member for being obsessed/ in love with SM
(50) Admission of lust for/ attraction to SM
(51) Use of sexual innuendo
(52) Use of explicit sexual jokes
(53) Jokes about competition for SM
(54) Feeling the need to keep love of SM secret from husband

XIV. Importance of Schwans in the IC Experience

(55) Questions about whether it is the SM or IC they crave
(56) Proclamations that IC without SM is not the same
(57) Claims that SM makes IC taste better

XV. Socializing over Ice Cream

(58) Plans to meet at IC shop/ Plans to get together over IC
(59) Desire (imagination) to socialize with Chesslings over IC/ IC social fantasy
(60) Excitement over getting IC together
(61) Discussion of sharing IC at Pillowfest

XVI. Overt Reflection on Ice Cream Stories

(62) Comments on frequency of ice cream stories
(63) Claims that IC stories make them want IC
(64) New member wants to understand the in-group discussion of IC

XVII. New Members and Ice Cream

(65) Welcoming new members by telling them IC is essential to the group identity
(66) Suggestions that new members should be required to love IC

XVIII. In-group/Out-group

(67) Comments that "ice cream" and "Schwans" have taken on new meanings
(68) Just saying words IC and SM leads to smiles and laughter
(69) Claims that others outside the group can't understand
(70) Claims to see the world through IC
(71) Overt discussion of IC as shared group bond
(72) Don't want to share SM with outsiders

XIX. Ice Cream and Outside Relations

(73) Discussion of eating IC with family and friends
(74) Discussion of husband bringing IC
(75) Asking members if their BF/husband likes IC

Figure 3. Axial Codes with Examples (Subcategories Correspond with Initial Categories from Figure 1.)

1. Ice Cream and Physical Enjoyment and Comfort

    I. Basic eating of ice cream
        Example: "Hey all you ice cream lovers I was at the Ice cream shop twice over the weekend, I had a colossal sundae yesterday."

    II. Pleasure/enjoyment of eating
        Example: "I bought a box of Dove bars and ate 3 of them in one day, ooooooh they were so good!"

    III. Ice cream addiction
        Example: "I have to do a non-dairy diet for two weeks. Worse part of that is NO ice cream. How can a woman survive?"

    VII. Lack of will power towards ice cream
        Example: "I think you should have had some triple fudge ice cream, but you had great will power with the chocolate chip cookie ice cream, I'd never be able to do that, HUGS"

    VIII. Taste of ice cream remained after treatment
        Example: "everything tasted like pennies. Since chocolate ice cream and pickles were the only foods that tasted like they should, that's what I ate."

    IX. Ice cream as physical support
        Example: "many of us on here truly believe it is the secret cure for all ailments."

2. Ice Cream as Emotional Support & Positive Thinking

    X. Ice cream as emotional support
        Example: "We cry and morn for the lose of the person because we are going to miss them but we also rejoice in his new life with Jesus. Have some ice cream and remember him with all of the good memories you have of him."

    XI. Explicit encouragement of others to use IC for emotional support
        Example: "When you get home from the hospital enjoy a little dish of your favorite ice cream to celebrate this step in your life!"

3. Ice Cream and Relationship Building/Maintenance

    V. Encouragement to eat ice cream
        Example: "Keep eating that ice cream!"

    XV. Socializing over ice cream
        Example: "Okay- Lets see who is all going to the Ice Cream place on XX Avenue?? Great food! Fun! Ice Cream Galore!!"

    XVI. Overt reflection on ice cream stories
        Example: "I find it interesting that the ice cream stories seem to keep going. I think its very positive. I dont know who started it but its good therapy!!!"

4. Sexual Humor/Reaffirmation of Sexuality

    XII. Ice cream & humor
        Example: "We can't feel guilty for wanting to rest so enjoy your naps, and maybe a little more ice cream would help, ha ha ha!"

    XIII. Schwan's man and sexual humor
        Example: "Well next time we don't hear from you for a few days we will just wait cause we don't want to interrupt the pickle, oh I am sorry, I mean the ice cream delivery."

    XIV. Importance of Schwan's in the IC experience
        Example: "I am jealous of your trip to the XX area though. and your homemade ice cream and shortcake with blueberries. The only problem there is no Schwan's man involved."

Figure 4. Axial Codes with Examples (Subcategories Correspond with Initial Categories from Figure 1.) continued

5. Ice Cream and Social Identity

IV. Ice cream is truly unique
Example: "ice cream is the only way to pick yourself up"

XVII. New members & ice cream
Example: "Welcome! Keep your spirits up! Take care of yourself! Enjoy some ice cream - a favorite of many on this network!!!"

XVIII. In-group/out-group
Example: "While we were getting directions to find the fish fry place, XXXX spots the schwans guy. this time her sister is with her so she doesn't want to follow him. some things sisters just don't share."

XIX. Ice cream and outside relations
Example: "how are you! i hear a new man?? does he like ice cream??"

- **Ice Cream as Emotional Support:** Ice cream also provided emotional support and encouraged positive thinking. In times of emotional distress, "ice cream is the only way to pick yourself up" and can "help everything seem a little less awful." Members encouraged each other to turn to ice cream in times of need, even during tragic moments. In one instance, a member shared with the group that she might have only six months to live. One member quickly responded, "I hope you are eating ice cream, and of course do not give up hope." Another member chimed in, saying, "You will continue to march because we need you. When you are in pain, just think of ice cream." Even for women in the face of death, ice cream provided a symbol of hope.

- **Delivery Men as a Symbol of Sexual Identity:** Members also spent a lot of time talking and joking about their attraction to the Schwan's deliverymen. This included teasing each other about stalking and kidnapping these providers of ice cream, such as when one member somewhat crudely joked, "I think she really, really, really wants the Schwan's guy to come to her house only. Come here little boy, I have some candy." One member pondered, "The Schwan's guy that I have is right up there in looks … Is it the ice cream or the Schwan's guy that we crave? Hmm?:) Yummy yum either way." Explicit jokes such as these were quite common. Group members clearly felt safe engaging in a candid discussion about their sexuality and physical desires, topics that can often be uncomfortable and embarrassing for women who are facing threats to their body image.

- **Ice Cream as a Symbol of Group Identity:** Ice cream was not just a symbol of hope and optimism, but also a signifier of group identity. This was demonstrated clearly when new members were welcomed into the group and told "We just need to get you into the Schwan's ice cream stuff. That will make you feel better." This type of welcome was common. Similarly, one member joked, "OF COURSE IT IS AN ABSOLUTE MUST! That anyone who joins CHESS has to love ice cream!" These quotes reflect an understanding that group members shared a passion for ice cream and newcomers were encouraged to adopt the same excitement to truly become part of the group. Group membership was therefore in part established and reaffirmed through their shared understanding of ice cream and the deliverymen. The importance of ice cream to the group was perhaps summed up best by one member's paraphrasing of the well-known song lyric, "You scream, I scream, we all scream for ice cream!"

Negative Case Analysis

At this point, ice cream's symbolic significance was becoming clear. Specifically, discussion of ice cream provided a way for the women of CHESS to construct a shared identity around lighthearted topics, rather than the negative shared experience of having breast cancer. Before moving forward with selective coding, however, it was important to perform a negative case analysis to check the developing insights and deepen the analysis.

Ice cream and sexual lust are rooted in a physical presence, so discussion of the afterlife and spirituality seemed to provide an important counterexample, especially because previous research has shown that religion was a big part of CHESS discussion (Shaw et al., 2007). In addition, because ice cream appeared to be a symbol of optimism, it was important to look for examples of members who were consumed with doubt and fear. The authors therefore searched for posts using words such as "God," "faith," "control," "plan," "death," "alone," and "afraid." This analysis made one thing clear: although members did struggle at times, they felt comfortable expressing negative emotions without fear of judgment. Members constantly encouraged others to be honest about their struggles, to "go ahead and cry if you need to," because "it feels good to get it all out." This demonstrated that the discussion board did not create unrealistic pressure to suppress negative emotions but still fostered an overall positive outlook.

The analysis also revealed that many of the women still had a hard time accepting their mortality and frequently expressed fears and doubts. One member admitted, "It is hard facing death. I still think the doctors are wrong." It was not surprising that many members struggled to fully accept their mortality. Many members dealt with this fear by putting their fate into "God's hands" and encouraged others to "trust God's plans." For example, one member proclaimed, "I have had many experiences with being so close to death and I tell you I am so calm as I give myself over to the doctors care and God's will." The conception of the sacred was clearly central to many members' coping strategies.

There was a crucial distinction between the ways religion and ice cream provided support; religion represented a "sacred," or otherworldly, response, whereas ice cream represented a "corporeal," or earthly, response. This did not suggest that ice cream was less important; instead, it highlighted the significance of having other means of reassurance outside of trust in God. Members claimed that cancer taught them to "live for today" and frequently reminded each other "life is for living and having fun!" Discussing and obsessing about ice cream and the deliverymen who brought it helped those who were trying to live "one day at a time" find meaning in everyday life.

Selective Coding

Next, the axial codes were used to perform a targeted analysis of the message posts looking for the underlying theoretical categories that connected the main categories. The analysis revealed two related underlying categories that together constructed a central narrative. The two core categories are: (a) ice cream as a positive symbol of group identity, and (b) ice cream as a symbol of living one day at a time.

- **Ice Cream as a Positive Symbol of Group Identity:** As discussed above, the dominant social construction of breast cancer encourages women to hide their physical and emotional struggles from the public eye. In contrast, the CHESS discussion group afforded members the opportunity to manage and share the wide variety of challenges experienced during treatment rather than simply focusing on "beating" the disease. This was, in large part, made possible through the use of ice cream as a symbol. Ice cream symbolized group membership, served as a mechanism to cope with the physical and emotional hardships associated with breast cancer, and helped group members provide emotional support to others.

Ice cream was an important mechanism for facilitating group bonds and constructing a shared narrative about the experience of having breast cancer. Ice cream symbolized the need for group members to confront the realities of their situation, while providing a sense of control in their ability to deal with their illness and find comfort and joy in life. By connecting the significance of ice cream directly to the experience of having breast cancer, the women of CHESS were able to construct a positive shared identity that addressed the challenges and needs that result from a breast cancer diagnosis.

- **Ice Cream as a Symbol of Living One Day at a Time:** Ice cream provided a symbol that was well situated to address the challenges and needs that arise from having breast cancer. Not only does a diagnosis result in physical and emotional hardship, it also makes the reality of human mortality salient and results in a range of threats to women's body image, sexuality and sexual functioning (Pelusi, 2006). In the CHESS group, the discussion of ice cream and deliverymen provided a means to openly discuss everyday, sensual desires, while confronting the physical and emotional hardships associated with breast cancer. Members claimed that cancer taught them to "live for today." Conversing about ice cream and the deliverymen who brought it helped those who were trying to live "one day at a time" find pleasure in everyday life.

Consuming ice cream and interacting with deliverymen were daily activities, or goals that could be readily achieved while at the same time leaving a craving for the next encounter. In short, these symbols embodied the philosophy that "life is for living and having fun!" For example, the provision of emotional support in the form of a suggestion to eat ice cream served as a reminder to continue to find comfort in daily life, even if, or especially if, the future is in doubt. Thus, desiring ice cream and/or the deliverymen was not just about physical pleasure but also about continuing to view oneself as a person with short-term desires and pleasures. This stands in opposition to the socialcultural context that encourages women with breast cancer to downplay their sexuality.

In this manner, the women of CHESS were able to establish a degree of control of their emotional and physical aspects of their identity. Thus, ice cream provided a symbol that did not repress the emotional and physical challenges associated with breast cancer, but still provided a means of finding joy and comfort.

Grounded Theory

The symbolic construction of ice cream served as a way for women with breast cancer to positively redefine their situation and foster a joyful group identity. This was achieved by expressing physical desires that provided meaning in everyday life without denying health realities.

CONCLUSION

Whereas previous CHESS studies have demonstrated that engagement in an online social support discussion board can lead to positive psychosocial outcomes, few examples of such work have closely examined the symbolic interactions through which these outcomes are achieved. For women with breast cancer, having an idealistically positive outlook is not always the healthiest way to cope, because it leaves many women unprepared to deal with the realities of their disease. The emergence of ice cream in the CHESS discussion group for American women with breast cancer provided an ideal opportunity to assess how optimistic outlooks are achieved, how the negative emotions and experiences associated with cancer are nonetheless confronted, and what implications these dynamics have for the negotiation of self-identity. The symbolic use of ice cream suggests that online groups provide a space in which identity can be negotiated with less sociocultural constraints than women with breast cancer typically face.

The results of the grounded analysis show that, through the discussion of ice cream and the delivery-men who brought it, group members were able to confront their situation while retaining their identity as women with everyday physical desires and emotions. The CHESS discussion board allowed women with breast cancer to remember that "life is for living," rather than promoting the necessity to transcend their situation. Having an identity marker based on everyday desires helped these women negotiate identities that were positive, joyful, and hopeful and that reaffirmed their sexual identity rather than focus only on the negative implications of having breast cancer.

In the United States, breast cancer identity is typically presented in a cheerful and hopeful light. Ice cream fits nicely into that framing of the disease. Other cultures might construct breast cancer differently, placing different constraints around the ways in which women with a breast cancer diagnosis can interpret their illness and their identity. This positive reframing of one's identity around a seemingly trivial or lighthearted topic might or might not be feasible—or even desirable—outside of U.S. culture. This study highlights the importance of considering the ways in which individual agency interacts with the cultural context in which women experience and manage a breast cancer diagnosis.

Although the circumstances of this discussion board are unique, these insights provide important implications. First, this study provides evidence that online support groups can simultaneously provide a space in which women can experience typical human emotions while encouraging them to maintain a positive outlook. This might be important for any individual facing a life-threatening illness who suffers from a lack of understanding in his or her immediate social surroundings. This is not to say that all online support groups adopt a healthy approach, because some groups discourage expression of negative emotions. The analysis demonstrates that online support groups at least have the potential to foster healthy coping habits by coalescing around lighthearted topics without denying the severity of the situation.

Second, the analysis demonstrates the potential benefits of having an identity marker situated squarely in physical everyday life and the role online groups play in facilitating the development of those identity markers. Whereas religious beliefs and spirituality can help with concerns and fears about mortality, the women of CHESS showed how powerful it can be to have an identity marker that is not based on their shared illness. In many cases, individuals facing life-threatening diseases can do nothing to prevent the illness from progressing. Regardless of how they interpret their ultimate fate, it is still vitally important that they find meaning in everyday life while they can. Connecting the experience of having breast cancer to the consumption of something situated in the everyday, physical world provides cancer patients with a degree of control over the experience that they do not have over their disease per se. Thus, for at least some individuals, healthy coping might be best served by defining the situation through the symbolic construction of shared consumption interests.

Although several scholars and breast cancer victims have rightfully expressed concern about the pervasive discourse of optimism surrounding breast cancer, this study highlights the potential for online support groups to promote positivity in a healthy manner, because they exist within a larger set of interactions that address the concerns, fears, and anxieties associated with breast cancer. Indeed, the positivity constructed by this CHESS group was not a form of escapism; instead, discussion of ice cream and the deliverymen helped achieve meaning by allowing women to feel comfortable expressing and pursuing natural physical desires. In this way, this study illustrates the potential for online support groups to provide individuals facing a health crisis the opportunity to form bonds outside of the shared context of their illness. Specifically, seemingly trivial symbols can be used to construct a positive and hopeful identity outside of the sociocultural constraints that may exist offline.

REFERENCES

Aberg, A. C., Sidenvall, B., Hepworth, M., O'Reily, K., & Lithell, H. (2004). Continuity of the self in later life: Perceptions of informal caregivers. *Qualitative Health Research*, *14*(6), 792–815. doi:10.1177/1049732304265854 PMID:15200801

Barni, S., & Mondin, R. (1997). Sexual dysfunction in treated breast cancer patients. *Annals of Oncology*, *8*(2), 149–153. doi:10.1023/A:1008298615272 PMID:9093723

Benoliel, J. Q. (1996). Grounded theory and nursing knowledge. *Qualitative Health Research*, *6*(3), 406–428. doi:10.1177/104973239600600308

Blumer, H. (1969). *Symbolic Interactionism: Perspective and Method.* Englewood Cliffs, NJ: Prentice-Hall.

Broom, D. (2001). Reading breast cancer: Reflections on a dangerous intersection. *Health*, *5*(2), 249–268. doi:10.1177/136345930100500206

Burke, N., Joseph, G., Pasick, R., & Barker, J. (2009). Theorizing social context: Rethinking behavior theory. *Health Education & Behavior*, *36*(5 Suppl), 55S–70S. doi:10.1177/1090198109335338 PMID:19805791

Carpenter, J., Brockopp, D., & Andrykowski, M. (1999). Self-transformation as a factor in the self-esteem and well-being of breast cancer survivors. *Journal of Advanced Nursing*, *29*(6), 1402–1411. doi:10.1046/j.1365-2648.1999.01027.x PMID:10354235

Charmaz, K. (2006). *Constructing Grounded Theory: A Practical Guide Through Qualitative Analysis*. London: Sage.

Coreil, J., Wilke, J., & Pintado, I. (2004). Cultural models of illness and recovery in breast cancer support groups. *Qualitative Health Research*, *14*(7), 905–923. doi:10.1177/1049732304266656 PMID:15296663

Crooks, D. (2001a). The importance of symbolic interaction in grounded theory research on women's health. *Health Care for Women International*, *22*(1-2), 11–27. doi:10.1080/073993301300003054 PMID:11813790

Crooks, D. (2001b). Older women with breast cancer: New understandings through grounded theory research. *Health Care for Women International, 22*(1-2), 99–114. doi:10.1080/073993301300003108 PMID:11813800

Donath, J. (1999). Identity and deception in the virtual community. In M. A. Smith & P. Kollock (Eds.), Communities in Cyberspace (pp. 29–59). New York: Routledge.

Ehlers, N., & Krupar, S. (2012). Introduction: The body in breast cancer. *Social Semiotics, 22*(1), 1–11. doi:10.1080/10350330.2012.640060

Ehrenreich, B. (2009). *Bright-Sided: How Positive Thinking is Undermining America.* New York: Picador.

Gall, T. L., Charbonneau, C., & Florack, P. (2011). The relationship between religious/spiritual factors and perceived growth following diagnosis of breast cancer. *Psychology & Health, 26*(3), 287–305. doi:10.1080/08870440903411013 PMID:20309779

Glaser, B., & Strauss, A. (1967). *The Discovery of Grounded Theory: Strategies for Qualitative Research.* New Brunswick, NJ: Transaction.

Gray, R., Sinding, C., & Fitch, M. (2001). Navigating the social context of metastatic breast cancer: Reflections on a project linking research to drama. *Health, 5*(2), 233–248. doi:10.1177/136345930100500205

Gustafson, D., Hawkins, R., McTavish, F., Pingree, S., Chen, W. C., Volrathongchai, K., & Serlin, R. et al. (2008). Internet based interactive support for cancer patients: Are integrated systems better? *Journal of Communication, 58*(2), 238–257. doi:10.1111/j.1460-2466.2008.00383.x PMID:21804645

Gustafson, D. H., McTavish, F. M., Stengle, W., Ballard, D., Hawkins, R., Shaw, B. R., & Landucci, G. et al. (2005). Use and impact of eHealth system by low-income women with breast cancer. *Journal of Health Communication, 10*(sup1), 195–218. doi:10.1080/10810730500263257 PMID:16377608

Han, J., Shah, D., Kim, E., Namkoong, K., Lee, S.-Y., Moon, T. J., & Gustafson, D. et al. (2011). Empathic exchanges in online cancer support groups: Distinguishing message expression and reception effects. *Health Communication, 26*(2), 185–197. doi:10.1080/10410236.2010.544283 PMID:21318917

Han, J., Shaw, B., Hawkins, R., Pingree, S., Mctavish, F., & Gustafson, D. (2008). Expressing positive emotions within online support groups by women with breast cancer. *Journal of Health Psychology, 13*(8), 1002–1007. doi:10.1177/1359105308097963 PMID:18987072

Hawkins, R., Han, J., Pingree, S., Shaw, B., Baker, T., & Roberts, L. (2010). Interactivity and presence of three eHealth interventions. *Computers in Human Behavior, 26*(5), 1081–1088. doi:10.1016/j.chb.2010.03.011 PMID:20617154

Henriksen, N., & Hansen, H. P. (2009). Marked bodies and selves: A literary-semiotic perspective on breast cancer and identity. *Communication & Medicine, 6*, 143–152. doi:10.1558/cam.v6i2.143 PMID:20635551

Hill, P., & Butter, E. (1995). The role of religion in promoting physical health. *Journal of Psychology and Christianity, 14*, 141–155.

Jenkins, R., & Pargament, K. (1995). Religion and spirituality as resources for coping with cancer. *Journal of Psychosocial Oncology, 13*(1-2), 51–74. doi:10.1300/J077V13N01_04

Jeon, Y.-H. (2004). The application of grounded theory and symbolic interactionism. *Scandinavian Journal of Caring Sciences*, *18*(3), 249–256. doi:10.1111/j.1471-6712.2004.00287.x PMID:15355518

Joas, H., & Knobl, W. (2004). *Social Theory*. Cambridge, UK: Cambridge University Press.

Kenne Sarenmalm, E. K., Thoren-Jonsson, A.-L., Gaston-Johnsson, F., & Ohlen, K. (2009). Making sense of living under the shadow of death: Adjusting to a recurrent breast cancer illness. *Qualitative Health Research*, *19*(8), 1116–1130. doi:10.1177/1049732309341728 PMID:19638604

Kim, E., Han, J. Y., Shah, D., Shaw, B., McTavish, F., Gustafson, D. H., & Fan, D. (2011). Predictors of supportive message expression and reception in an interactive cancer communication system. *Journal of Health Communication*, *16*(10), 1106–1121. doi:10.1080/10810730.2011.571337 PMID:22070449

Kleinmann, A. (1988). *The Illness Narrative. Suffering, Healing and the Human Condition*. New York: Basic Books.

Mathieson, C., & Stam, H. (1995). Renegotiating identity: Cancer narratives. *Sociology of Health & Illness*, *17*(3), 283–306. doi:10.1111/1467-9566.ep10933316

Namkoong, K., DuBenske, L., Shaw, B., Gustafson, D., Hawkins, R., Shah, D., & Cleary, J. et al. (2012). Creating a bond between caregivers online: Impact on caregivers' coping strategies. *Journal of Health Communication*, *17*(2), 125–140. doi:10.1080/10810730.2011.585687 PMID:22004055

Namkoong, K., Shah, D., Han, J., Kim, S. J., Yoo, W., Fan, D., & Gustafson, D. et al. (2010). Expression and reception of treatment information in breast cancer support groups: How health self-efficacy moderates effects on emotional well-being. *Patient Education and Counseling*, *81*, S41–S47. doi:10.1016/j.pec.2010.09.009 PMID:21044825

National Cancer Institute. (2012). *Coping with cancer: Managing physical effects*. Retrieved from http://www.cancer.gov/cancertopics/coping/physicaleffects/

Oster, I., Astrom, S., Linda, J., & Magnusson, E. (2009). Women with breast cancer and gendered limits and boundaries: Art therapy as a 'safe place' for enacting alternative subject positions. *The Arts in Psychotherapy*, *36*(1), 29–38. doi:10.1016/j.aip.2008.10.001

Pelusi, J. (2006). Sexuality and body image. *American Journal of Nursing*, *106*, 32–38. doi:00002820-200603002-00013

Pitts, V. (2004). Illness and Internet empowerment: Writing and reading breast cancer in cyberspace. *Health*, *8*(1), 33–59. doi:10.1177/1363459304038794 PMID:15018717

Rains, S. A., & Young, V. (2009). A meta analysis of research on formal computer mediated support groups: Examining group characteristics and health outcomes. *Human Communication Research*, *35*(3), 309–336. doi:10.1111/j.1468-2958.2009.01353.x

Revenson, T., & Pranikoff, J. (2005). A contextual approach to treatment decision making among breast cancer survivors. *Health Psychology*, *24*(4, Suppl), S93–S98. doi:10.1037/0278-6133.24.4.S93 PMID:16045426

Sandaunet, A.-G. (2008). A space for suffering? Communicating breast cancer in an online self-help context. *Qualitative Health Research, 18*(12), 1631–1641. doi:10.1177/1049732308327076 PMID:18955462

Shaw, B., Han, J., Kim, E., Gustafson, D., Hawkins, R., Cleary, J., & Lumpkins, C. et al. (2007). Effects of prayer and religious expression within computer support groups on women with breast cancer. *Psycho-Oncology, 16*(7), 676–687. doi:10.1002/pon.1129 PMID:17131348

Shaw, B., Hawkins, R., McTavish, F., Pingree, S., & Gustafson, D. (2006). Effects of insightful disclosure within computer mediated support groups on women with breast cancer. *Health Communication, 19*(2), 133–142. doi:10.1207/s15327027hc1902_5 PMID:16548704

Shaw, B. R., McTavish, F. M., Hawkins, R. P., Gustafson, D. H., & Pingree, S. (2000). Experiences of women with breast cancer: Exchanging social support over the CHESS computer network. *Journal of Health Communication, 5*(2), 135–159. doi:10.1080/108107300406866 PMID:11010346

Strauss, A., & Corbin, J. (1990). *Basics of Qualitative Research: Grounded Theory Procedures and Techniques*. Newbury Park, CA: Sage.

Van Uden-Kraan, C., Drossaert, C., Taal, E., Shaw, B., Seydel, E., & van de Laar, M. (2008). Empowering processes and outcomes of participation in online support groups for patients with breast cancer, arthritis, or fibromyalgia. *Qualitative Health Research, 18*(3), 405–417. doi:10.1177/1049732307313429 PMID:18235163

Walker, D., & Myrick, F. (2006). Grounded theory: An exploration of process and procedure. *Qualitative Health Research, 16*(4), 547–559. doi:10.1177/1049732305285972 PMID:16513996

Wellman, B. (1997). An electronic group is virtually a social network. In S. Kiesler (Ed.), Culture of the Internet (pp. 179–205). Mahwah, NJ: Erlbaum.

Wilkinson, S. (2001). Breast cancer: Feminism, representations and resistance—a commentary on Dorthy Broom's 'Reading breast cancer.'. *Health, 5*(2), 269–277. doi:10.1177/136345930100500207

Wright, K. B. (1997). Shared ideology in Alcoholics Anonymous: A grounded theory approach. *Journal of Health Communication, 2*(2), 83–99. doi:10.1080/108107397127806 PMID:10977242

Yoo, W., Chih, M.-Y., Kown, M.-W., Yang, J., Cho, E., McLaughlin, B., & Gustafson, D. et al. (2012). Predictors of the change in the expression of emotional support within an online breast cancer support group: A longitudinal study. *Patient Education and Counseling, 90*(1), 88–95. doi:10.1016/j.pec.2012.10.001 PMID:23122429

KEY TERMS AND DEFINITIONS

Grounded Theory: Grounded theory, developed by Glaser and Strauss (1967), is a systematic, methodological approach through which new theoretical accounts are derived inductively from data.

Identity Negotiation: Identity negotiation, which originates from the work of Erving Goffman, refers to the process through which an individual's role in society is established through an interaction between an individual's self-definition and the role and definition other social actors writ large wish to assign to that individual.

Online Support Groups: Online support groups are nonprofessional groups hosted on the Internet where members are united by a shared experience, illness, or identity without the constraints of space (the need to meet face-to-face) or time (the need to exchange messages in real time). Support may range from purely instrumental (sharing of pertinent information) to emotional.

Self-Definition: How an individual defines his or her own identity, personality, ability, and social standing.

Social Identity: Social identity is when two or more individuals are perceived to be members of a group based on a shared characteristic, attribute, or trait.

Sociolcultural Context: Socialcultural context refers to the social and cultural factors in which a social actor is situated. How an individual interprets their own actions, and how these actions are interpreted by others, depends upon the embedded meanings constructed by the societal and cultural context in which an individual finds themself.

Symbolic Interactionism: Symbolic interactionism, which originates from the work of George Herbet Mead, views all human action as mediated through symbol systems, such as language and signs. The meaning of these symbols derive are constructed collaboratively through human interaction, but each individual may interpret a symbol slightly differently depending upon their background and personal experiences.

Chapter 7
Social Media Affordances and the Capital of Queer Self-Expression:
Facebook, Ello, and the Nymwars

Greg Niedt
Drexel University, USA

ABSTRACT

This chapter presents an overview of the September 2014 controversy surrounding Facebook's enforcement of their "real name policy," the disproportionate targeting of drag performers for profile suspension, and the queer community's brief exodus to the network Ello. By drawing on research about identity in the online age, queer and subcultural theory, and the concept of affordances in social media, the author seeks to illuminate some of the causes of this incident, and the motivations of the actors involved. The online profile is framed as a locus for the construction of alternative identities—particularly those which challenge gender norms—as well as tension when that process is restricted. The author attempts to locate this concept of profiles, and the networked communities built from them, within a larger web of capital relations, exploring how the online and offline intersect therein.

INTRODUCTION

In September 2014, social media giant Facebook began enforcing the latest version of their profile name policy, which dictated that users use their legal name or some closely-related variant of it for their profiles. While the company's help center states that the purpose of the policy is to weed out "fake or malicious accounts," this wave of profile suspensions affected a disproportionate number of drag queens, queer performers, and other members of the queer community, particularly members of the Radical Faerie and Sisters of Perpetual Indulgence[1] groups in the San Francisco area. Word spread chiefly through the plight of well-known performer Sister Roma, who was forced to change her profile to her birth name, Michael Williams; she characterized the policy as "unfair, hurtful, discriminatory, and an invasion of privacy" (Holpuch 2014). A petition against the policy started by fellow performer Olivia LaGarce garnered over 40,000 signatures in support of the hundreds of users caught in the controversy. As long-term frustra-

DOI: 10.4018/978-1-5225-0212-8.ch007

tion with Facebook's privacy and account policies came to the foreground, and the company botched face-to-face meetings with Roma and other performers (offending many by suggesting that they simply subscribe to the pay-for-visibility "Fan Page" model), many sought a network that would be more accommodating of a self-defined online identity.

Into this vacuum stepped Ello, a no-frills social network that had entered beta testing some months before. With their small population, lax policies towards profile content, and insistence to not marketing user data, the site briefly became the darling of Facebook's discontents. At the height of the furor, thousands of users were leaving Facebook every hour for the junior network, partially due to tweets from queer celebrities such as RuPaul; founder Paul Budnitz expressed his support for the population boom, despite some concerns from new users that the site was technically inferior to Facebook in several ways (Sullivan 2014). Meanwhile, after refusing to alter their position for weeks, Facebook walked back several of their comments as a lead-up to a full apology by CPO Chris Cox on October 1. The company maintained their innocence against accusations of homophobia, and instead pointed to how their system for reporting fake profiles was exploited by one anonymous Internet user (@RealNamePolice), who boasted about their attacks against "secular sodomites" of all sorts (Hatmaker 2014). In light of their apology and re-instatement of suspended profiles, the animosity towards Facebook softened, and interest in Ello faded quickly in mid-October (Arthur 2014).

The entire situation may seem to be a simple skirmish in the "#nymwars"[2] or a community reacting to an isolated incident of prejudice from one homophobic user, but there are several aspects of how the situation developed worthy of examination. This chapter will explore why the name, as a symbol of gender subversion, became such a sticking point for these users. The different *affordances*[3] of Facebook and Ello will be considered through the lens of *capital*, following Bourdieu: "the set of actually usable resources and powers" (1984: 114), in a social or cultural context. The ways in which a presence on one site or the other was evaluated by members of the community furthermore demands a deeper understanding of the users in question: as online consumers (and producers) of social media data, as members of the queer community, and as a subset of drag performers. These users were coming from a shared history of challenging traditional conceptions of gender and sexuality, building new, alternative identities and social groups; Facebook's easy dismissal of all profiles not pegged to legal names as fake failed to account for the willingness to continue and defend that historical tradition.

While the focus of this chapter is gender identity, the analysis of how online affordances interact with capital in different contexts is one that can be extended to other aspects of the self as well. How do social networks enable control over the presentation of race, age, or class? What purpose do the choices users make in this regard serve? This chapter is also too brief to fully treat the underlying factors for why users might hold one ideology or another that influences the self-presentation choices they make; are there correlations between a user's personal politics and what they do with their profiles online? Certainly there is room to explore these topics, and as the saturation of new media increases, the urgency of that exploration will only continue to grow.

BACKGROUND: THE ONLINE SELF

Copious research has been dedicated to how the evolving Web has repeatedly disrupted notions of what it means to construct and enact an identity in different spaces. Early theoretical work on the Web by Sherry Turkle (1995) attempted to get at the deeper motivations of users in their construction of alternate selves online, by presenting interviews with users of several online *multi-user domains* (MUDs). These (mostly) text-based environments allow a user to separate to some degree from the "actual" world, manifesting instead as an *avatar* (with a *handle* rather than a name) which is not necessarily identical to the offline self. Within that slight distance, however, lies a high degree of emotional investment from the user. Turkle's assessment of one user, Stewart, and his character Achilles, sums up the simultaneous freedom and frustration of the avatar era: "He wants to feel that his real self lies somewhere between Stewart and Achilles. He wants to feel that his MUD life is part of his real life...MUDs simply allow him to be a better version of himself." (1995: 193) While this angle is rather psychoanalytic, the key notion is still helpful: there can be a highly affective dimension to the construction of the online self.

Beyond simply incorporating some of the same strategies used offline for self-presentation, online spaces allow for expressions of identity which might not otherwise be possible for the user. Following Turkle's line of inquiry, Boellstorff (2010) interviewed participants from the community Second Life to demonstrate more recent examples of such self-fashioning. He points out that the concept of *role* is an important one when considering identity, considering the self as multiple, subsumed into different roles from context to context. Second Life's combination of chatroom-style live communication with a graphical interface, wherein one has free rein to construct a new appearance, allows a user to become even further invested into the online identity. Moreover, the roles one is assigned in the "real world" can be suspended or altered online; the "gap between the virtual and the actual" leaves room for liberation (2010: 148-149). Members of these handle- and avatar-based communities have taken full advantage of that potential, especially in terms of gender; the user's "authentic" self is a matter of choice rather than an external imposition. (Rodino 1997, Danet 1998, Nip 2004, del-Toso-Craviotto 2008)

However, social media have come to occupy a peculiar moment in the history of online identity work, wherein the Web 2.0 mentality of user-as-producer necessitates what Marwick and boyd (2010) call the online "requirement to present a verifiable, singular identity." They point out that despite the theoretically boundless number of people who could view a page or read a post, users often present themselves or behave with a particular group of readers (what they call the *imagined audience*) in mind. On sites like Facebook, whose basic unit is the constantly visible profile featuring the user's offline appearance, the user cannot mediate their presentation from one audience member to another: all of them are always potentially present, in any given context. This results in a "lowest-common denominator effect" (2010: 122), where users will display only what appeals to the broadest swath of their viewership. As the audience widens, the polyvalent self that is tailored to each interaction becomes more and more flattened, a phenomenon Marwick and boyd call *context collapse*. Rather than fully develop each facet of their identities depending on the frames they're navigating, users are obligated to develop only those (very few) parts of themselves acceptable to everyone in every possible frame at once.

The knowledge that social media straddle this divide between online and offline life exerts a powerful undertow upon users. On the one hand, like countless network interfaces through the history of the Internet they have been geared primarily towards interaction *in absentia*, first asynchronously and more recently (with tools such as Chat, in Facebook's case) in real-time. Like other sites, there is a lingo and aesthetic that defines each brand; thanks to Facebook, specific denotations of "Like" and "unfriend" have become enfolded into common language. On the other hand, one's "actual" face *is* the avatar picture on profile-driven sites like Facebook, the content is primarily biographical rather than creative, and the structure resembles a searchable archive more than a "world." José van Dijck (2013) explains how this networked environment combines with the personal database feel to support Facebook's self-stated ideology of *sharing*. She further states that in the social media context, sharing is positioned as a value in opposition to *privacy*, and mentions Facebook CEO Mark Zuckerberg's "peculiar" reference to privacy as, legally, an "evolving norm." (45-46) The discourse surrounding these two terminologies speaks volumes about the company's attitude towards what should be on their site, and how people should interact with it: Zuckerberg has made no secret of his distaste for online users who attempt to deploy multiple named identities (Barmann, 2014).

Given this media landscape, this chapter attempts to shed some light on answers to the following research questions:

Q1: What qualities does an online self have for queer performers that may differ from their offline experience, or from the online experiences of others?

Q2: Why was the name such a sticking point for the performers embroiled in the controversy?

Q3: How does the frame of social media allow and/or disallow the aspects of identity which are essential to construct a queer identity?

Q4: What caused Ello to be adopted, and then cast off, with such speed? How was involvement with Ello as a form of protest against Facebook interpreted within/without the queer community?

Naturally, the community is not a monolith, and one person's reasons for joining Ello may be entirely different from the others. However, there are certain recurrent themes in the discourse that took place on and surrounding Ello, and aspects of the communities in question which provide some possible reasons for why the Facebook exiles proceeded the way they did.

QUEER CULTURE ONLINE

Out of the Closet, onto the Web

Implicit in the idea of context collapse is the notion that subcultures are more difficult to sustain, unless one operates one's entire life within a subculture. If the self that is presented online must be palatable to all possible audiences, then the user must account for the fact that some audience members—family, friends, coworkers—will discover some proclivity of the user's that causes them to re-evaluate the user they thought they knew more negatively. Hebdige (1979) talks about "resistance through style", and the way in which subcultures create new significations for objects to create such styles; resistance to the norms of society is constructed from the tools of society itself. Queer culture finds itself at a bewildering crossroads: even as great strides are made towards equality, the spectre of homophobia is constant. And even those strides tend to best serve the small sector of the population who generally conform to gender norms, at least outwardly, rather than the more radical sectors who seek to overcome gender norms entirely. At the same time, social media are becoming ever more pervasive and total; how should users "out" themselves online in a way that is true to themselves, but acceptable to all?

"Acceptable to all," it must be said, is an impossibly tall order. The indiscriminate profile-flagging by @RealNamePolice serves as an object lesson in how context collapse works the other way, too: the owner of the account saw no difference between users (Faerie, Sister, or neither) he or she interpreted as being untruthful about gender. Facebook's system for flagging objectionable profiles lent itself to abuse via the same homogenizing tendency; theoretically, all users are equal before the Report button. For the sake of Big Data[4], they must be—but this necessitates a lukewarm attitude towards individuality and distinctiveness. Users are reduced to aggregated bits of information; "social media tools [like Twitter] may be adept at mapping networks of people... [however,] they may not be as adept at identifying or forging the publics that emerge from those networks." (Gillespie 2012) The network does not equal a public, nor does it equal a community, save for the users' shared quality of being members. While some features such as size of the site's population work fine with that outlook, those that fall at least partially into the hands of users themselves have the potential to be used towards the same discriminatory ends as offline.

The fact that one bigoted user could flag hundreds of profiles and exercise so much power over a disenfranchised group exposes serious flaws in the way Big Data networks privilege policy over the experiences of users. This chapter focuses on the case of drag performers, but it's easy to see how Facebook's algorithms could facilitate prejudice against other groups. Legal considerations aside, the disruptive effects on users' sense of identity and participation online foment what Hebdige calls the "struggle for signification": a battle over the right to decide which signs (e.g., name) will refer to what (e.g., a stance on gender and sexuality) within the "lived ideology" of heteronormative discourse online (1979: 14, 17). Max H. Kirsch (2000) further points out the futility of attempting to completely banish queer community modes of thought from that heteronormative frame, given that queer individuals must daily navigate spaces where that frame is dominant, online and off, even by default in spaces that are unmarked (116-117).

Christopher Pullen (2009) complicates Kirsch's argument by stating, "concepts of gay citizenship and community are various...those representing the community do not necessarily reflect the same ideas or mobilise (sic) similar strategies." (78) He further examines the *assimilationist* and *pluralist* camps, where the former strives for equality and uniformity with the majority's norms, and the latter seeks to liquefy and distribute power evenly among groups with competing norms. The focus will remain on the latter here, the pluralists in this case being much more vocal and raising moral questions that apply beyond just the queer community. If there are those in and of the dominant frame who are actively seeking to further disenfranchise a community, then such discrimination must be addressed and resolved from every angle.

Gender Performance and Drag

The data-driven nature of social network sites encourages categorization: people are easier to cater to if they have discrete labels applied to their identity. Yet since Judith Butler's (1990) book *Gender Trouble*, queer theory has generally built on her initial view of gender as a *performance* which "[constitutes] the identity it is purported to be. In this sense, gender is always a doing, though not a doing by a subject who might be said to preexist the deed." (1990: 25) A static "Male/Female" label attached to a profile suggests an unchanging binary quality, which neither reflects gender performances that do not wholly correspond to either, nor the dynamic nature of a process that can change from context to context. (To the credit of some sites, the list of gender options has evolved over time, reflecting a greater diversity of non-heteronormative genders: Facebook's gender menu surpassed fifty items by February 2015, when they finally elected to simply add a freeform "Custom" option.) Butler is also clear to separate performative gender from biological sex—categories often conflated or combined by profile-building interfaces—which further suggests that an "authentic" gender presentation is a fallacy, online or off. She discusses the various strategies which are deployed in taking on one gender identity and/or another, and how the subject's agency comes to the forefront when taking conscious action that is socially interpreted as "gendered," in a Western normative frame, as male or female. "Such acts, gestures, enactments, generally construed, are *performative* in the sense that the essence or identity that they otherwise purport to express are *fabrications* manufactured and sustained through corporeal signs and other discursive means." (136)

Drag is merely one approach to that performance, but a notable one, both for its complicated history at the nexus of class, race, and gender (Drushel 2013), and for the way it simultaneously seems to be subversive of the whole notion of gender as an essential quality, yet draws on highly familiar ideas of gendered action to be effective. Butler sums this up by saying, "In imitating gender, drag implicitly reveals the imitative structure of gender itself," an imitation which, in the context of a live drag performance, or simply "wearing the face", is accomplished by the repetition of acts. (1990: 137-141) The success of a drag (queen) performance does not necessarily rely on how well the trappings of femininity obscure the biologically masculine reality of the performer; in many contexts, "passing" is not the goal, and the audience is under no illusion about the queen's underlying sex. Instead, success is measured by how precisely and hyper-emphatically the feminine actions are performed. Beyond the performance itself, Bill Rodgers (2006) also describes the "sacred" status of the drag queen as an icon in gay culture, being a catalyst of the Stonewall Riots and gay liberation, signifying political action in addition to simply challenging gender norms. The latter he further associates with shamanic tradition, to illustrate the Radical Faerie community's embrace of drag as religious, political, and social commentary, all at once. Although drag is perhaps the most visible genre of gender-bending, professional performers by no means have a monopoly on practices considered subversive by heteronormative standards.

In an online context, the bodily presence of the performer (the best option for demonstrating the accuracy of her performance) is flattened in two-dimensional photos and videos, whether from a show or not. The spatial effects of gesture and movement in which Butler promotes are mostly lost, leaving those verbal elements that constitute drag identity to bear the weight of the transition to online space. For example, Rusty Barrett (1999) describes how drag queens will use language marked as "white woman speech," both phonetically and discursively, to incorporate this element into their identity display, in some cases embellishing it into an even more precise persona, such as the use of religious lexicon to signify a churchgoing woman. The subversive aspect of the performance is emphasized in terms of setting, with the obvious displacement of a "ladylike" Christian woman into a gay bar; in the discourse itself, it is further emphasized by mixing a polished feminine register with outright vulgarity. Online, the sonic features (extreme changes of pitch, hypercorrect enunciation, etc.) are lost, but textual strategies may still be deployed to attempt to replicate them with the same content, and this constitutive text loses very little. Within the drag performance *field* (in Bourdieu's sense: "a certain distribution structure of some kind of capital" (1984: 138)), using all of these features shores up the performer's symbolic capital, as they indicate a level of authenticity and facility with the processes recognized as drag.

Such forms of capital, following Bourdieu's formulation, can usually be converted from one to another, for they all ultimately derive from *economic capital*, with some measure of effort required to effect a transformation. It is important to remember that capital is a transmutable resource in this way, but equally important to realize that the amount and form of effort required to shape it varies, depending on what particular expressions of capital are at play, who is manipulating it, and in what context/setting they are doing so. Power dynamics inform the distribution of these social resources, and unfortunately, a high level of resources within the queer community often corresponds to an inverse proportion in the mainstream community. Yet the capital of drag itself springs from specific resources, too, ranging from the physical (outfits, makeup) to the performative (a well-constructed persona, a successful act), to the abstract, when one considers the *drag name*.

The Drag Name

Anthony Giddens' (1991) comment that names lie at "the core of self-identity," reflecting what numerous researchers (e.g. Finch 2008, Pina-Cabral 2010, Palsson 2014) see as their positioning at the boundary between distinction from and connection with others, may seem like an obvious precept. As a result, names have not been given as much theoretical and analytical attention as some other socially-assigned aspects of identity; Palsson argues that they are as essential a "technology of the self" in Foucault's sense as any other, and calls for a more thorough answer to the question of why we bother to adopt names (2014: 619). Moreover, when we assign names to each other, and assign new names to ourselves, there are social moves being made which must be understood in context: the choice to adopt a spouse's name in marriage, for example, versus taking on a name with the intention of subverting traditional naming norms. Beyond this contextual level, an act of renaming also functions generally as an assertion of the right to anonymity and re-invention, a method of control over which aspects of identity will define the individual. As noted above with Mark Zuckerberg, presuming that right is often viewed with suspicion: why would anyone *want* to assume a new identity? However, this attitude does not account for the fact that just as birth names can encode gendered—as well as ethnic, (sub)cultural, or other demographic— information, so too can self-assigned names when their bearer feels a need to realign those backgrounds. The choice to rename is not necessarily borne out of a desire to be anonymous, nor do people become nameless; rather, they seek to have a name which more accurately reflects who they are or have become.

Constructing a drag name often requires the careful fusion of several elements: linguistic puns, references to well-known chanteuses, and vulgarity are all common. For those who are part of a "drag house", the last name can take on an adoptive connotation, with "mothers" and "children" going by and/ or performing under the surname of the house (Livingston 1990). Eden Sarid (2014) treats drag personas as separate individuals which are the intellectual property of the offstage male-presenting self, with the name functioning as a shorthand—a piece of symbolic *drag capital*—for that persona within the community, offline and online. Particularly clever names can showcase the performer's wit and creativity. Similarly, Peter Hennen describes the process by which Radical Faeries "discover" their names, albeit with more pagan overtones than the queens, and how they "[abandon] each when the feeling [is] right, in favor of one that more clearly [expresses] an emerging identity." (2004: 510) Both communities treat these names as wholly legitimate, as an element in a process of taking on and discarding identities or personas at will, names which are underpinned by and understood in relation to gendered practice, thereby signifying an attitude about gender in general.

The name thus resembles a bodily act of drag performance more than a static object, a performed piece of symbolic capital that can be judged as successful or not based on the criteria above. It becomes the "purest" expression of the drag persona, by which she can constitute herself via the name without relying on other bodily acts, signifying gender subversion in and of itself. It functions as a signifier for all the associated bodily acts. It is not the *only* element by which a performance or persona may be judged—one can't simply walk onstage with a drag name and expect applause—but it is necessary in order to coalesce all the other elements into a coherent *identity*. The name further reflects (and to some degree creates) the social capital one gains within the queer community, which recognizes and respects its inherent power of upward mobility; when the name itself is also recognized and respected (e.g. RuPaul), that entails high social capital. At the same time, there is also subcultural capital in creating and using a drag name, since it indicates a familiarity with the practices of the community, and an authenticity gained by understanding the "rules" in the field of queer production.

BUILDING THE ONLINE PERSONA

Names, being discrete bits of language, can easily be transferred from one context to another, i.e. from the stage of a West Village gay bar to a social media profile. Those stages, however, are containers which drag capital grew to fill; social media cannot accommodate the same panoply of resources a performer has at her disposal. Unlike the sensory stimuli of a live performance, names serve their purpose equally well onstage or off, or in any verbal/textual frame. This versatility, combined with the centrality of the name to a persona, makes it perhaps the key transferrable element for constructing an online self; consequently, to forbid or restrict it becomes a serious challenge to the rights of performers to build that self. Here, the idea of *affordances*, in a computer-mediated communication sense, comes into play: social networks can be evaluated based on the number of potential identity-building elements users have access to/are able to carry over into the online realm. The failure of Facebook to understand the value of chosen names and their significance to the queer culture lay at the root of the exodus from their site; the choice of Ello lay in what affordances it offered in Facebook's place.

Affordances

Boyd (2010) describes online communities as "networked publics", which are "simultaneously (1) the space constructed through networked technologies and (2) the imagined collective that emerges as a result of the intersection of people, technology, and practice." (2010: 39) She points out the importance of discourse and involvement from users as a kind of civic engagement in the social and cultural (but not necessarily political, going against the traditional definition of "public" set forth by Habermas) development of the online space, and argues that such participation in the space can be a way to develop an online identity. These "self-expressions and interactions" are bounded by four affordances regarding the management of content: *persistence*, *replicability*, *scalability*, and *searchability* (2010: 46). If digital content lasts for an indefinite amount of time, if it can be searched, copied, and replicated to increase visibility, users' participation in the network will account for those affordances when they, as all users do, create the content that keeps the network afloat.

Similarly, given that the ostensible purpose of a social network site is to join profiles together into a community, Parks (2010) outlines five themes in community-building that are applicable to social networks. These include: the ability to engage in collective action, rituals of sharing information, socially patterned interaction within the space, the awareness of being part of a community, and identification with that community. The community does not arise spontaneously, however; users must undertake particular actions (creating profiles as a ritualized sharing of information; messaging/posting as a socially patterned interaction) to develop and maintain that community. Parks suggests that the shared rituals and patterned interactions are more important than the other community-building elements in an online context, and further posits three kinds of "social affordances" that networks offer users: affordances of *membership* (how easy is it to join/maintain a profile on a network?), *personal expression* (how deeply can the profile be customized?), and *connection* (how many tools are there for interacting with other users?) (2010: 110). Therefore, a social network's success is determined by how well the affordances they offer facilitate community-building acts users may seek to undertake.

The tools a network provides for managing content have a direct bearing on how well the tools for creating community do their job. If the capacity to add certain content to a profile is stymied by confusing policies or lack of functionality, then how can communities centered on that content coalesce?

Additionally, the phenomenon of context collapse presents an even greater difficulty for the online formation of communities, such as the Radical Faeries, whose defining characteristics are outside the lowest-common-denominator social norms that one meets when facing an imagined audience of everyone. This was part of the attraction of Ello: compared with Facebook, its uninhabited space meant that queer users could present themselves for an imagined audience of their peers. Where there's a will, there's a way, and alternative communities have nevertheless flourished on Facebook, but how content and connection interact must be duly considered when assessing the choices networked users make. How then does this constitution of self and community translate into the affordances, in boyd and Parks' schemata, and compare what has been provided by Facebook and Ello, respectively?

Facebook

As the benchmark networked public, the unmarked case against which all other networks are judged, it can be difficult to assess the adequacy of Facebook's affordances, save for instances such as with the names controversy, when a feature previously offered is taken away. At the level of the profile, Facebook has a sizeable constellation of options that fall under Parks' header of *personal expression*: a user can list favorite movies and books, religious and political views, gender identity (for a time with an overwhelming menu of choices, as mentioned above), work history, and so on. Moreover, the "Wall" of user posts is essentially nothing but personal expression. There are two further distinctions to personal expression that are reflected in the structure of the Facebook profile: the *openness* of a particular feature (for example, free-response fields for gender and "About You" are more open than the "Interested in" section with its Women and Men checkboxes), and the *modularity* of features overall (the user can move, hide or show some of this information, but not all). A full exploration of each of these features' development over Facebook's history, in comparison with other networks, is beyond the scope of this chapter, but it is worth acknowledging that the presence or absence of a feature alone is too broad a distinction for how well that feature provides a community-building affordance.

For the affordances of *connection*, users on Facebook "friend" each other, create events with invitations, "Like"/comment on content around the network, post on each other's Walls, and have a scrolling feed that displays their friends' posts. There is a message app for cellular phones and Facebook email as well. For *membership*, a distinction should be made between the sign-up process (free, and touted as easy) and maintaining an active awareness of the frequently-changing terms of use (such as the privacy policy). The site has an extensive Help Center section dedicated to addressing user questions and problems, as well as providing walkthroughs to understand all the policies and processes on the site. (This also raises the question of *simplicity* as a dimension of affordances: if a feature for the user is obscured or difficult to understand, how useful is it?) There are other functionalities built into the site which lend themselves to developing a networked public in boyd's sense; the ability to share posts with other users demonstrates the *persistence* and *replicability* of content, while the use of hashtags and showing "trending" stories falls under *scalability*.

However, as boyd and Crawford (2012) point out, what the owners of the system afford its users and what they afford themselves are different things. The *searchability* of Facebook is a one-sided proposition, in that they offer "very poor archiving and search functions" to users, yet the company itself has complete access to all content (2012:666). The fact that these data are then leveraged for the purposes of ads and marketing, or manipulated for research purposes (Meyer 2014), not to mention that the *persistence* of content is ultimately out of the user's control, causes the affordances of the network to seem less and less advantageous. All of these features can also change, as the names policy and its enforcement has; the *stability* (how often does a feature mutate through different forms? to what end?) and *clarity* (is the user adequately notified of any change in how the feature works?) of each feature must also be considered. Legally, Facebook's defense lies in the terms of service agreement, and the fact that signing up (*membership*) subjects the user to all of these conditions, but as boyd and Crawford allude to in their piece, how Big Data networks handle the content and information of their users is mostly an ethical *terra incognita* that lies quite beyond a simple assessment of what a site can or can't do.

Ello

Ello began as a closed system, available only to the creators and their immediate circle of friends, with its public release in March 2014 accompanied by a contrarian manifesto stating "You are not a product." Their no-frills aesthetic and declaration to remain ad-free was openly opposed to other Big Data-driven networks; theoretically, their manifesto challenged the asymmetric distribution of affordances that marks Facebook. Initially, only tech commentators and bloggers seemed to be interested, though this interest was tempered with skepticism of yet another alternative entering the ring (Benson 2014). From an affordances perspective, this hesitation bore out: once the exodus surrounding the names controversy began, many users began reporting bugs, confusion about how to use the site, and frustration at the lack of features that they had become accustomed to from Facebook.

A key example is the ability to block other users, a functionality which the fledgling Ello lacked; Ello converts were skeptical of whether one group of third parties being unable to view their information was an adequate trade for the inability to manage the access of a different group, particularly since the catalyzing incident was an instance of cyber-discrimination (Sullivan 2014). From an affordances perspective, users wanted the ability to *not* engage in this variety of *connection*, à la Parks. The freedom to choose whether to use an affordance or not must also be considered while examining what a network offers. Jeffry van der Goot (2014) points out that the minimalist, black and white aesthetic of the site does indeed stand in stark contrast to Facebook—especially with the dearth of ads—but suggests that the designers were more interested in making the site look slick than adding some basic social network functionalities. Even that slickness occasionally fell short: because the site was still in beta testing at the time of its explosion, its animations and pages did not always load properly.

However, while Ello initially struggled to keep up with the influx of new users and their need for new features, developing them as fast as possible (Smith 2014), their laidback attitude concerning *personal expression* was an asset. The flexibility in terms of naming convention and what was shown to browsing users represented a departure from Facebook's insistence on legal name as display name. Ello's profile format also features a free-form text box where the user can optionally include any desired personal information, in any arrangement; on Facebook, this is broken into the discrete fields mentioned above and distributed around the modular page. (Several members of communities suspended from Facebook proclaimed their queer, drag, or faerie identities in this section.) Another celebrated element was the permission to post pornographic images (later hidden behind NSFW—"not safe for work"—filters) in header photos on the page, or within the content section. For communities rooted in queer subculture, that openness about alternative sexual norms fosters its own kind of connection; perhaps this is the sort of ritualized, patterned sharing of information that Parks says is essential to building community.

A cursory examination of profiles created in response to the Facebook suspensions reveals the use of Ello as a space to celebrate marginalized identities, with every tool the users have at their disposal.

Profile photos featuring drag and full beards, the open sharing of pornography, and commentary that made use of "dragspeak" in Barrett's sense are all common features of posts during that brief period from the leaders of the exodus to Ello. (Equally common are posts directed towards Ello's help page, to ask for assistance in navigating the unfamiliar interface.) The community created their own sense of ownership over the site, occasionally calling overt attention to their sudden hegemony; the giddiness that characterized Ello's adoption makes its wholesale abandonment of it all the more surprising.

DISCUSSION

In the profile era, the online self often becomes a reflection of the offline self. For some users, this unity is beneficial; for others, detrimental, if there is no space to explore the selves one cannot express offline, no alternative avatar to grow into. The drag community's use of their stage names for online profiles functions, in a way, as a successor to avatar handles. A well-inhabited drag persona online presents the same potential for growth and space to fill that the MUD identity does; "Gaysha Starr"[5] is just as rich with signification as "Achilles" from the Turkle study. Such profiles further point out two curious features of social media: the name is often the most inalterable piece (if the user wants to be consistently recognized, at least) and yet often, changing gender—or potentially race, or age, or another feature of identity—online is as easy as the click of a button. Beyond the level of personal preference, the choice to present one's drag self online becomes an implicit critique of the system itself, with its insistence on alignment between online and offline selves, enforced by (in Facebook's case) the real-name policy. Submission to such a policy represents the death knell of that avatar era dialectic between selves; to those for whom the legal name is repressive, shaming, or simply inaccurate (see for example Lloyd 2005, Mackenzie and Marcel 2009), resistance becomes an imperative. Hebdige sheds some light on the subtlety of this resistance: "The challenge to hegemony which subcultures represent is not issued directly by them... The objections are lodged, the contradictions displayed...at the profoundly superficial level of appearances: that is, at the level of signs." (1979: 17) One can read "signs" here as "names" with little difficulty.

Whether a given user struggling to maintain their name in the face of suspension was actively trying to break the top-down model of identity control depended on the user. If queer performers are a subculture, certainly there can be sub-subcultures of performers who are more open or less open about their motivations. In this specific instance, those targeted on Facebook tended to be very vocal about their dissatisfaction with the company's actions, expressing their opinions through any and all media outlets at their disposal. However, the performers' objection was not merely personal, but placed within the context of drag's larger point about the fluidity of identity. Facebook's intransigence became so frustrating because of the deep significance of this attitude and critique that drag embodies, and how the expressions of that critique, the symbolic capital that issues from its surface, fit into a user's conception of what her social media identity ought to be.

Drag capital becomes all the more precious within the community when considering that professional performers are, for the most part, disenfranchised in most other varieties of capital. RuPaul and the winners of her show Drag Race notwithstanding, rare is the wealthy drag queen (*economic capital*), and as part of the marginalized queer community, social capital outside the community is low as well. The offense at Facebook's suggestion that performers simply buy Fan pages for their alter egos stemmed not only from the company's assumption that the drag persona was an alter ego at all, but also that the persona is merely a commodity, and therefore the performers would want/could afford to promote it. Given that the name represents so much, both for its bearer and the community in which she uses it, yet costs so little to wear, it becomes easier to see why a performer would defend her right to use it. Especially since the drag persona quickly exhausts the other forms of capital which a performer often has so little of—wardrobes and makeup are expensive!—erasing the name does more damage than simply dismissing its symbolism. Because the symbolized acts are already nearly erased online, or at least missing much of the presence they have offline, the extra weight carried by the name as a result means that an attack on it places the whole persona's ability to exist online in jeopardy.

This kind of act is characteristic of subculture, with its ability to create new significations for items—or speech styles—beyond, and perhaps even to some degree supplanting, the mainstream ones. Hebdige's conception of subculture's remixing tendency puts this in more plainly subversive terms: "These 'humble objects'...[are] made to carry 'secret' meanings: meanings which express, in code, a form of resistance to the order which guarantees their continued subordination." (1979: 18) In this case, the humble gendered *practice* is what is given new, if rarely secret, meaning, which expresses resistance to the hegemony of heteronormativity. Unlike the punk culture Hebdige was analyzing, it is not enough to simply possess and display the objects in question; as performative acts, they must be enacted. Furthermore, skill in that enactment can be more valuable to the performer than actual sex/gender transformation, as leaving the stage, she has the option to divest herself of femininity and re-claim masculinity for what social capital is based on gender, all other things being equal.

Still, it would be too simplistic to say that Ello won its new user base solely because it set itself up as an anti-Facebook with total freedom of name and gender, and equally so to assume that it was abandoned by users just because Facebook finally made an apology. Certainly affordances played a role in how the new queer users made use of the site to construct identity once they got to Ello, but arguably, the undertow of social capital determined the overall pattern of comings and goings that characterized the site's rapid rise and fall. Previous research (i.e. Ellison, Steinfield, and Lampe 2007, 2011) has dealt extensively with the complex interactions of social capital and social networks; the key takeaway is perhaps that capital in a network does not exist in a vacuum. Ello became a space where the drag performers' symbolic capital was allowed, but to join the site in solidarity with the community even without a suspended Facebook profile served as a way to build in-group *social* capital.

Beyond the fact that social networks shape the form and processes of capital, at a more abstract level, they are themselves objects of those same processes. "Joining Ello" signified one's alignment with the drag queens, and carried status within that community, while "staying on Facebook" became devalued. Vivienne and Burgess (2012), in their study of queer digital storytelling, discuss Habermas' conception of the *public sphere* and recent theoretical objections to its exclusion of "minority groups who lack the cultural capital to participate." (2012: 366) The need to speak and display a chosen identity publicly does not vanish; instead, queer users are led to create (Vivienne and Burgess borrow Michael Warner's terminology here) a *counterpublic*, where the tools of social networks are used to foreground a specifically queer schema of capital. Affordances in the counterpublic are measured by different needs than those dictated by the public; control over the presentation of the self, à la Goffman, becomes the most valuable affordance of all.

Once it became clear, though, that Ello couldn't accommodate the full range of resources required to successfully compose the same identity online as off, Facebook had only to restore their capability to accommodate the name's centrality as an expression of capital. Again, the narrative changed: "joining Ello" became a relic of that particular historical moment, albeit one that did not entirely lose its significance. To remain on it, especially at the expense of Facebook, conveys no more status that having once been on it; yet it can continue to function as another expression of symbolic capital which signifies support of the community, for members and allies alike. It illustrated—and perhaps continues to illustrate—a stance in relation to queer identity politics that was, for its cultural moment, just as rich with meaning as using a drag name in the first place.

LIMITATIONS AND FURTHER RESEARCH

Any single paper can only be a brief overview of the issues of gender identity, the politics surrounding it, and how those politics translate into what individuals must navigate online; the subject is too enormous and complicated for any one researcher to circumscribe. Beyond that, there are several limitations to this study, to be addressed in the future. First, the study would have benefitted by presenting samples from profiles to delve further into the discourse used by members of the communities who decamped for Ello; understandably, many individuals approached by the author were reluctant to be part of any study about the topic. Following that, interviews with those users would go a long way to further elucidating the processes by which they decided to join—or not join, or abandon—Ello, as well as give a better sense of how they seek to construct an online self overall. Third, *capital* itself is another endless concept, but it's reasonable to say that these social choices—to join or not to join, to construct this or that kind of identity—are rooted not only in the forms of capital, but how it is transformed between contexts, and the equations by which individuals balance what choices they make in those contexts. (The question of what constitutes *drag capital* and how it influences a performer on- and off-stage is one that the author will have to address in a later paper.) Fourth, Facebook may still be the supreme social network, but there are myriad other sites of identity-building online. The more sites, active or defunct, are examined for the totality of their affordances, culture, and impact on what we understand as the virtual landscape, the more we can determine how and why we interact the way we do within it.

And of course, the experience of queer users discussed in this chapter is by no means unique. For example: not long after the drag queen controversy's quasi-resolution, Native American users such as Dana Lone Hill and Shane Creepingbear outlined their own frustrating experiences with Facebook name suspensions. It's unclear whether these were the result of racist discrimination-notably, Creepingbear's profile was suspended on Columbus Day-or poor algorithm control, but it took extraordinary measures, including the threat of a class-action lawsuit from one of Lone Hill's contacts, to address the problem (Bogado 2015). Although the Facebook policy has existed in some form since the site's inception, its efficacy is called into question whenever such incidents come to light. As of this writing, the policy is back in the news again, after Facebook's participation in the 2015 Gay Pride Parade in San Francisco. Critics of the network's ongoing insistence on "real names" included trans former employee Zoë Cat, who had worked to implement so many of the new gender-inclusion features on the network (Brogan 2015). Others have sought out new social networks (and Ello yet abides, with a minimal pool of active users), or undertaken other forms of protest, such as popularizing the "#MyNameIs" hashtag. Writing for The Guardian, Jillian York (2015) succinctly states: "As a society, we've arrived at a crossroads: identity is increasingly a part of our consciousness, while surveillance of our communications more invasive than ever. This presents a challenge for online service providers looking to create spaces that are free from harassment and other ills."

Furthermore, as several commentators pointed out, there are numerous populations besides those challenging traditional gender identity norms, who benefit from the security of a protean name on social media for a variety of reasons: abuse survivors, sex workers, public community figures, and so on. The real-name policy makes it easier for such populations to be targeted by stalkers, estranged family or spouses, and even, as seen here, anonymous bigots with no personal connection to the victims. If social media's purpose as a project is to make the world a more interlinked, intimate place—Zuckerberg's comments seem to indicate that Facebook's purpose instead is accuracy of data—then as a project it fails along these lines. Conflating the private and personal for the sake of accuracy is an example of what Daniel Bell (1976) defines as the *eclipse of distance* in the age of capitalism: "as an aesthetic, sociological, and psychic fact...there are no boundaries, no ordering principles of experience and judgment." (106) Not only is distance eclipsed technologically by social networks, but in terms of control over identity as well; when that control is distributed to the actor with the most capital (i.e., Facebook), the erasure of boundaries around the most individual of social processes, self-presentation, is complete.

Why is it important to examine such situations, and take them as warnings? From an impartial point of view, they provide an endlessly fascinating exercise in how capital is transformed, bought, and sold, moving through time across contexts, minuscule and grand alike. But from a moral point of view, the impartiality of capital(ism) coupled with the impartiality of data can clearly be used by the highly partial to cause trauma to others, from any community to any other. Kirsch, while musing whether Butler celebrates "the same ideal of the individual as self that capitalism has created", goes on to say: "a perception that we can reject binary systems of gender without rejecting all bases for identity, however temporary they may be, is necessary for true resistance and social change." (2000: 43) In this instance, that conception of gender in relation to identity holds true; but the quality "gender" could be replaced by race, age, religion, language, or any other categorization of what makes us who we are.

Finally, moving beyond the case discussed in this chapter, the social network affordances may be weighted differently for other groups with concerns about their online self-presentation. Consider the selfie: what opportunities do they offer users to construct an alternate self online? How have the aesthetics of self-portraiture changed, and how do they perpetuate ideologies that users see in the media, such as the sexualization of women? Or the profile options to choose a race, or list a birthday: why is it necessary for others to know a person's age or ethnic background (if the latter is even accurately categorized on a site)? Alternative social networks may insist that they are catering to one group or another by asking for this information—dating services, for example, may claim they need to accommodate the fetishes of users—but ultimately, this calls further attention to the structure of capital which permeates these sites. The online subject has been left with just as little power to dictate what a given aspect of their identity signifies as they do offline; all they can do is push against the evaluation of their self by manipulating whatever features a site offers to the best of their ability.

CONCLUSION

This chapter has presented a brief overview of the name-policy controversy which notably affected drag performers in 2014. Their objection grew from a legacy of queer subculture and a desire for self-expression given a particular shape from the history of the Web, but the move to Ello erupted instead from patterns of social capital, and how the affordances of networks reflect the capital of identity. The researcher has attempted to unpack the motivations for why they reacted the way they did, but also acknowledges that there are as many reasons as users, and this line of investigation might proceed to infinity. What remains is to take this moment as indicative of larger trends in where social media is going and what it means to have an online self. As long as we distinguish ourselves on the basis of personal characteristics and transmute them into data, allowing the system to reach total impartiality will eclipse the distance between private and personal to the point that we blind ourselves to the fact that there are real people at stake. We keep that future at arm's length by holding onto of our own power of self-determination; and our moral imperative, drag queen or not, is to stand our ground for the sake of our own identities.

REFERENCES

Arthur, C. (2014, October 14). Goodbye, Ello? Searches for new social network collapse. *The Guardian*. Retrieved from http://www.theguardian.com/technology/2014/oct/14/goodbye-ello-google-seacrhes-social-network

Barmann, J. (2014, September 19). Zuckerberg has always believed that we're only entitled to one identity. *SFist*. Retrieved from http://sfist.com/2014/09/19/zuckerberg_has_always_believed_that.php

Barrett, R. (1999). Indexing Polyphonous Identity in the Speech of African-American Drag Queens. In M. Bucholtz, A. C. Liang, & A. Sutton (Eds.), *Reinventing Identities: The Gendered Self in Discourse*. New York: Oxford University Press.

Bell, D. (1976). *The Cultural Contradictions of Capitalism*. New York: Perseus Books.

Benson, T. (2014, March 24). You are not a product: Ello wants to be the Anti-Facebook Social Network. *Motherboard*. Retrieved from http://motherboard.vice.com/read/you-are-not-a-product-ello-wants-to-be-the-anti-facebook-social-network

Boellstorff, T. (2010). *Coming of Age in Second Life*. Princeton, NJ: Princeton University Press.

Bogado, A. (2015, February 9). *Native Americans say Facebook is accusing them of having fake names*. Retrieved from http://colorlines.com/archives/2015/02/native_americans_say_facebook_is_accusing_them_of_using_fake_names.html

Bourdieu, P. (1984). *Distinction: A Social Critique of the Judgment of Taste* (R. Nice, Trans.). Cambridge, MA: Harvard University Press.

Bourdieu, P. (1986). The Forms of Capital. In *Handbook of Theory and Research for the Sociology of Education*. New York: Greenwood.

boyd, d. & Crawford, K. (2012). Critical questions for big data: Provocations for a cultural, technological, and scholarly phenomenon. *Information, Communication & Society*, *15*(5), 662–679.

boyd, d. (2010). Social Network Sites as Networked Publics: Affordances, Dynamics, and Implications. In *A networked self: Identity, community, and culture on social network sites*. New York: Routledge.

Brogan, J. (2015, July 6). *What's In a Real Name?* Retrieved from http://www.slate.com/articles/technology/future_tense/2015/07/facebook_s_authentic_name_policy_ensnares_zo_cat_a_trans_woman_who_tried.html

Butler, J. (1990). *Gender Trouble*. London, UK: Routledge.

Danet, B. (1998).Text as Mask: Gender, Play, and Performance on the Internet. In *Cybersociety 2.0: Revisiting Computer-Mediated Communication and Community*. Los Angeles, CA: Sage.

del-Toso-Craviotto, M. (2008). Gender and sexual identity authentication in language use: The case of chat rooms. *Discourse Studies*, *10*(1), 251–270. doi:10.1177/1461445607087011

Drushel, B. (2013) Performing Race, Class, and Gender: The Tangled History of Drag. *Reconstruction: Studies in Contemporary Culture*, *13*(2).

Ellison, N., Steinfield, C., & Lampe, C. (2007). The Benefits of Facebook "Friends": Social Capital and College Students' Use of Online Social Network Sites. *Journal of Computer-Mediated Communication*, *12*(4), 1143–1168. doi:10.1111/j.1083-6101.2007.00367.x

Ellison, N., Steinfield, C., & Lampe, C. (2011). Connection Strategies: Social Capital Implications of Facebook-enabled Communication Practices. *New Media & Society*, *13*(6), 873–892. doi:10.1177/1461444810385389

Finch, J. (2008). Naming Names: Kinship, Individuality, and Personal Names. *Sociology*, *42*(4), 709–725. doi:10.1177/0038038508091624

Gibson, J. (1979). *The Ecological Approach to Visual Perception*. New York: Psychology Press.

Giddens, A. (1991). *Modernity and Self-Identity*. Stanford, CA: Stanford University Press.

Gillespie, T. (2012). Can an algorithm be wrong? *Limn*, *1*(2).

Hatmaker, T. (2014, October 3). The single vigilante behind Facebook's 'real name' crackdown. *The Daily Dot*. Retrieved from http://www.dailydot.com/technology/realnamepolice-facebook-real-names-policy/

Hebdige, D. (1979). *Subculture: The Meaning of Style*. London, UK: Routledge.

Hennen, P. (2004). Fae Spirits and Gender Trouble: Resistance and Compliance among the Radical Faeries. *Journal of Contemporary Ethnography*, *33*(5), 499–533. doi:10.1177/0891241604266986

Holpuch, A. (2014, September 13). Facebook under fire from drag queens over 'real-name' rule. *The Guardian*. Retrieved from http://www.theguardian.com/technology/2014/sep/13/facebook-under-fire-drag-queens-real-name-rule

Kirsch, M. H. (2000). *Queer Theory and Social Change*. London, UK: Routledge.

Livingston, J. (1990). *Paris is Burning*. Miramax Films.

Lloyd, A. W. (2005). Defining the Human: Are Transgender People Strangers to the Law? *Berkeley Journal of Gender, Law & Justice*, 150.

MacKenzie, G., & Marcel, M. (2009). Media coverage of the murder of U.S. transwomen of color. In L. Cuklanz & S. Moorti (Eds.), *Local violence, global media: Feminist analyses of gendered representations*. New York: Peter Lang.

Marwick, A., & boyd, d. (2011). I tweet honestly, I tweet passionately: Twitter users, context collapse, and the imagined audience. *New Media & Society*, *13*(1), 114–133. doi:10.1177/1461444810365313

Meyer, R. (2014, June 28). *Everything We Know About Facebook's Secret Mood Manipulation Experiment*. Retrieved from http://www.theatlantic.com/technology/ archive/2014/06/everything-we-know-about-facebooks-secret-mood-manipulation-experiment/373648/

Nip, J. Y. M. (2004). The relationship between online and offline communities: The case of the Queer Sisters. *Media Culture & Society*, *26*(3), 409–428. doi:10.1177/0163443704042262

Palsson, G. (2014). Personal Names: Embodiment, Differentiation, Exclusion, and Belonging. *Science, Technology & Human Values*, *39*(4), 618–630. doi:10.1177/0162243913516808

Parks, M. (2010). Social Network Sites as Virtual Communities. In Z. Papacharissi (Ed.), *A networked self: Identity, community, and culture on social network sites*. New York: Routledge.

Pina-Cabral, J. (2010). The Truth about Personal Names. *Journal of the Royal Anthropological Institute*, *16*(2), 297–312. doi:10.1111/j.1467-9655.2010.01626.x

Pullen, C. (2009). *Gay Identity, New Storytelling and the Media*. Basingstoke, UK: Palgrave Macmillan. doi:10.1057/9780230236646

Rodgers, B. (2006). Becoming Radical Faerie: Queering the Spirit of the Circle. *Popular Spiritualities: The Politics of Contemporary Enchantment*, 117.

Rodino, M. (1997). Breaking out of Binaries: Reconceptualizing Gender and its Relationship to Language in Computer-Mediated Communication. *Journal of Computer-Mediated Communication*, 3.

Sarid, E. (2014). *Don't Be a Drag, Just Be a Queen – How Drag Queens Protect Their Intellectual Property Without Law*. Retrieved from http://ssrn.com/abstract=2511477

Smith, I. V. J. (2014, September 25). Ello's traffic deluge almost caused a total new user freeze-out, crisis averted. *The Observer*. Retrieved from http://observer.com/2014/09/ellos-traffic-deluge-almost-caused-a-total-new-user-freeze-out-crisis-averted/

Sullivan, G. (2014, September 25). *Social network Ello gets boost after Facebook boots drag queens*. Retrieved from http://www.washingtonpost.com/news/morning-mix/wp/2014/09/25/social-network-ello-gets-boost-after-facebook-boots-drag-queens/

Turkle, S. (1995). *Life on the Screen*. New York: Simon & Schuster.

van der Goot, J. (2014, September 24). *Ello: A Design Disaster*. Retrieved from https://medium.com/@jvdgoot/ello-a-design-disaster-d53022ab3a62

van Dijck, J. (2013). *The Culture of Connectivity*. New York: Oxford University Press. doi:10.1093/acprof:oso/9780199970773.001.0001

Vivienne, S., & Burgess, J. (2012). The Digital Storyteller's Stage: Queer Everyday Activists Negotiating Privacy and Publicness. *Journal of Broadcasting & Electronic Media*, *56*(3), 362–377. doi:10.1080/08838151.2012.705194

York, J. C. (2015, March 6). What to Facebook may be a 'fake name' may be the expression of your authentic self. *The Guardian*. Retrieved from http://www.theguardian.com/technology/2015/mar/06/facebook-internet-fake-name-authentic-self

ENDNOTES

[1] The Radical Faeries are a queer men's group with pagan overtones founded in the 1970s; the Sisters of Perpetual Indulgence, founded in 1979, are well-known for their "nun" drag and AIDS education programs.

[2] Refers to the debate over the right to pseudonymity online. The term gained popularity as a hashtag (#nymwars) on Twitter and elsewhere in response to Google+ introducing a similar name policy in 2011.

[3] James Gibson (1979) distinguished affordances as the various *potential* uses of an object (or system, in this case) which different users might perceive, as opposed to the actual qualities of the object.

[4] Refers to enormous data sets or, by metonymy, the industry of media companies who gather and use such sets for various purposes (such as selling it to third-party advertisers, or creating exhaustive user databases).

[5] aka Robert Matencio, a well-known Seattle-area performer and advocate for Asian-American representation in the queer community (hence the pun on "geisha")

Chapter 8
The #GamerGate Files:
Misogyny in the Media

Dustin Kidd
Temple University, USA

Amanda J. Turner
Temple University, USA

ABSTRACT

The GamerGate controversy exploded in late 2014 and seemed to pit feminist game critics against misogynistic male gamers who were defending their territory. GamerGate has been filled with intense anger on all sides, and has even resulted in threats of murder and rape. This chapter attempts to explain why so much hostility erupted over what appears to some to be a feminist critique of gaming and to others to be a misogynist-gamer critique of feminism. At heart is a surprising debate about mainstream gaming vs. indie gaming, and discomfort over changes to the notion of what counts as gaming and who counts as a gamer. The authors use online ethnographic methods to piece together the various elements of this cultural narrative from the online and social media contexts where it unfolded.

INTRODUCTION

On August 27, 2014, a Twitter user by the name of Adam Baldwin sends a short cryptic message composed almost entirely of a hashtag: #GamerGate. Below the tag are links to two YouTube videos posted on the account of someone named Internet Aristocrat. The videos are titled "Quinnspiracy Theory: In-N-Out Edition," parts 1 and 2. When viewed on a desktop computer, Twitter adds a preview of the video player with an image of an In-N-Out Burger franchise. The caption beneath the video reads "Whose [sic] a guy gotta fuck around here to get some fries with this?"

What is GamerGate? GamerGate is a culture war for the soul of the gaming industry. On the one hand, we have a nerd-centric gaming culture that is historically male dominated, whose members have been watching gaming transform as it goes mainstream and as women begin to join the ranks. On the other hand, we have a critique of gaming driven by feminist cultural critics who are increasingly gamers themselves, as players, designers, and game journalists (Hathaway, 2014). As the GamerGate Wiki site states: "Gamergate is a worldwide scandal" (GamerGate Wiki, 2015). Below, we provide on overview

DOI: 10.4018/978-1-5225-0212-8.ch008

of the history of video games, presented through the lens of the sociology of gender, before turning to the origin story of GamerGate itself. The GamerGate story is hard to reduce to text. As a supplement to this chapter, we have produced a collection of images, videos, and links related to GamerGate that can be found at https://www.pinterest.com/popculturefreak/gamergate/.

VIDEO GAME CULTURES AND MASCULINITIES

The computer games industry largely began with individual programmers or researchers tinkering with computer equipment as early as the late 1940s.[1] Primitive games developed along with burgeoning computer technology, largely as a hobby for technologically savvy students and workers. One major consequence of the historical development of video games as a field is its highly gendered, raced and classed nature. Because video game development, particularly multiplayer computer game development, stemmed from computer researchers in university settings (mostly in England), this industry bears the legacy of that origin. Those involved in computer research at universities would have been largely white, male, and upper-class. Those who created these games for fun were the ones who played them, and so this group was the original audience for video games.

After this first era of video game programming and play, commercial video games first became available in the early 1970's at home, before transitioning into public spaces such as bars, nightclubs, and arcades (Williams, 2006). After this initial success, and a spectacular crash in the late 1970s and early 1980s, video games experienced a final (and lasting) resurgence in the late 1980s. Throughout this time, discourses around video gaming have helped shape our cultural stereotype of who a gamer is. In an analysis of news media coverage of video games, Williams (2003) found that from the 1980s through the mid-1990s media fairly consistently referred to video games as both masculine and for the young, with strongly biologically deterministic language in reference to gender difference and language which positioned video game play as something adults should be ashamed to engage in. In each case, the message changes around 1995, with coverage after this point emphasizing both female and adult play (Williams, 2003). This stereotype this earlier coverage created seems to largely persist today, despite a wealth of industry and academic research to the contrary (Shaw, 2011), and it is only in the last few years that media has reported women achieving parity in numbers among game players (e.g., Entertainment Software Association 2014).

Video game and computer cultures have formed around the once reviled masculinity of the nerd. As larger changes in labor patterns have shifted middle class men from physical labor to mental, sedentary work in information technology (Connell, 1995:55), terms like nerd and geek are redefined in terms of hegemonic masculinity. Connell (1995) argues this is evidenced by discourse that positions technology as "powerful," and by the popularity of violent video games. In reframing "geeks" or "nerds" as part of a masculinity that enacts hegemonic values through virtual strength, skill, violence, and the domination of women, video game cultures embody a form of resistant masculinity that simultaneously rejects the dominant "real-world" hegemonic masculinity, while simply recreating it in a new environment. Kendall (2000:262) argues, "as an in-group term, it [nerd] can convey affection or acceptance. Even when used pejoratively to support structures of hegemonic masculinity, it can confer grudging respect for technical expertise." Video game cultures reframe their qualities as positive (in control of powerful technology) while enacting fantasies of, and remaining complicit in, a (virtually) violent hegemonic masculinity that subordinates women.

The concept of intersectionality provides a useful lens for thinking about the particular masculinity of gamer culture, including the men involved in GamerGate. Intersectionality was introduced by the legal scholar Kimberle Crenshaw as a way of explaining both the ways that forms of oppression like sexism and racism can work in concert, and the ways that these interlocking systems create unique relationships to the larger social world. Crenshaw argued that women's relationship to issues of discrimination (Crenshaw 1989) and violence (Crenshaw 1991) depend upon not only their gender but also their position in systems of race and class. Turning an intersectional lens to the men of video game culture allows us to recognize that these men are privileged by their gender, race, and sexuality, and they likely come from middle class backgrounds. Yet they do not feel privileged by their relationship to the economic and occupational system, and they may feel threatened precisely because of their gender and sexuality. One group of men involved in GamerGate, described below in the section on Wizardchan, identifies as a culture of male virgins over 30 who are not employed or in school. Gaming may be an outlet for escaping the realities of their economic position, but as an outlet it also creates a space of power where they exert control over the environment of the game. To that end, the gaming space may also be a space where they explore the possibility of exerting power over systems of gender, race, and sexuality that they feel are threatening not only their relationship to society but also their relationship to a leisure activity they love.

WOMEN IN TECHNOLOGY AND VIDEO GAMES

The hegemonic masculinity of virtual and technological worlds leaves little place for women in video game cultures. As fears about the impact of video games as a new form of media have abated, women's lack of participation in these areas and various explanations for the disparity between men and women have become a major source of concern to researchers. The increase in media attention to girls in the mid-1990s (Williams, 2003) is roughly timed with the emergence of "pink games" marketed to girls (Cassell & Jenkins, 1998, and the beginning of research focusing on the sexualization of women and hypermasculine violence in video game content (e.g., Dietz, 1998).

Game research over the past 20 years has established that women are both underrepresented and stereotyped within game content. In one of the earliest of these studies, sociologist Tracy Dietz finds that 30 percent of games had no female characters at all, and when women were present, they were most often portrayed as sex symbols (33.33%), or victims (21%) (Dietz, 1998). Data that is more recent uses game *characters* as the unit of analysis, rather than video games, but similarly finds that women are approximately 14% of characters across the games studied, and when women are present in games, about 12% were primary characters (Downs & Smith, 2010). Additionally, Downs and Smith (2010) find that female characters were much more likely to display hypersexualized traits such as revealing clothing, nudity, unrealistic body proportions, and inappropriate clothing.

Despite this, the share of women has been increasing; the latest Entertainment Software Association (2014) player data finds that women are nearly half of video game players (48 percent), and media outlets boasted headlines such as, "Study: More women than teenage boys are gamers" (Sullivan, 2014). Yet this demographic equality belies a more complicated relationship between gender, video games, and video game cultures. Shaw (2013) looks at how sexual, gender, and racial minority groups relate to the identity of "gamer" (and therefore gamer cultures). She identifies the importance of appropriate consumption of video games, as well as the social and cultural "video game" capital that players possess in order to identify as a member of video game culture, but argues that female players are less likely to achieve these hallmarks of the gamer identity. Female players' identification with video gaming (and therefore gamer cultures) was shaped by the stigma of games as a (juvenile) masculine practice, as well as women's exclusion from the imagined "audience" for video games (at the level of game production). Games, her subjects argued, are created for and marketed to groups who are expected to buy them, and women existed largely outside of these market logics. These factors then discourage women (and other minority groups) from identifying as video gamers, and accepting that the constructed nature of the video game audience as "adolescent, white, heterosexual, cisgendered [and] male" (Shaw, 2013: para. 30) is the logical outcome of rational market logic keeps these groups in a marginalized position within gaming communities.

Partially due to these cultural associations and market logics, women's relationships to gaming are formed based on a binary formation of gaming that is both constructed and shifting. Kubik (2012) argues that video game cultures and industry leaders imagine a hardcore center to video gaming, which is masculine in nature. These ideologies tie to larger social patterns and conceptions of who is (and is not) considered technologically competent, presented as a legitimate, competent (masculine) hardcore gamer in contrast to an illegitimate, unskilled (feminine) casual gamer. As a result, female video game players and experts constantly have to assert their legitimacy in these arenas. However, Kubik (2012) does emphasize that the dichotomy of casual/hardcore has little to do with the actual skills involved in playing the games. She notes that often games with similar gameplay will be placed in one category or the other based on factors that signal a masculine audience (such as style, or adult content) rather than the skills needed to play them.

The dichotomization of "men's" and "women's" play into hardcore/casual is echoed in a piece by Vanderhoef (2013), who argues that causal gaming is deeply associated with the feminine. Through this feminization, casual games are positioned as inconsequential and "less than" hardcore (masculine) games, which Vanderhoef ties to larger cultural patterns of the way that the feminine is devalued in larger cultural discourse. This larger cultural discourse asserts that "technologies are *gendered*" (Jenson and de Castell, 2010, emphasis in original). So, as video games are artificially segmented into hardcore and casual, Jenson and de Castell (2010) claim that women have not been as alienated from technology as some argue, and that women's use of technologies and contributions to technological advancements have been actively ignored. Furthermore:

Masculinity can be seen, on this view, to be constructed, at least partially, through assumptions related to technological skills and competence. Technological competence, so seen, has less to do with actual skills and more to do with construction of a gendered identity—that is, women lack technological competence to the extent that they seek to appropriately perform femininity; correlatively, men are technologically competent by virtue of their performance of masculinity. (Jenson & de Castell, 2010:54)

It follows then that participating in video gaming is a performance of masculinity, whether undertaken by men or women, and this conclusion is supported by games research (Kendall, 2000; Cote, 2015).

GENDER-BASED CONFLICT IN VIDEO GAMES

Video gaming, as an extension of the broader category of "technology," is culturally associated with the masculine. As Jenson and de Castell (2010) argue, engaging with this technology can be framed as a performance of masculinity, so the fact of women's gaming has to be rationalized. Women's presence in video game cultures is framed as "not gaming" through the creation of the hardcore/casual dichotomy, and women's presence in gaming is "forgotten."

Originally intended to reframe women's gaming as "not gaming" and therefore positioning women outside of gaming culture, the social construction of the broad category of "casual" gaming has had a major unintended consequence for the "hardcore" center of gaming. While hardcore video gamers themselves seem to view casual games as outside of gaming and of little consequence, the creation of casual genres and machines (such as the Nintendo Wii) which cater to casual players has been profitable, making "casual" gaming a valid segment of the video game market (Entertainment Software Association, 2014). Through trying to exclude "feminine" gaming by marking it as different, and less important, than the hardcore masculine gaming center, casual gaming and gameplay which does not fit the hegemonic masculine ideal has been legitimized through profitability. Somewhat ironically, this disrupts the stereotype of the young, straight, white male gamer in a very visible way and, according to Vanderhoef (2013), this "feminine" casual play is then is seen as a threat to hardcore gaming. The validity of casual gaming as a market segment detracts from the power and privilege previously monopolized by masculine hardcore gamers, as game companies can develop these casual games much more quickly and cheaply than a more traditional title.

In addition to the splintering of video gaming and game cultures into "hardcore" and "casual," women are moving into traditionally male "hardcore" gaming spaces. Visible groups of female gamers such as PMS (Pandora's Mighty Soldiers) clan who aim "to provide a fun, competitive, and positive environment to female gamers while promoting respect for women in matches and tournaments" (PMS Clan, 2011) or simply all-women guilds such as "Puerto Reekan Killaz" or "Conscious Daughters," (from Gray's 2013 ethnographic study of Xbox Live gamers) actively challenge the notion that gaming spaces are inhabited solely by men. As women move into these spaces, they challenge existing "beliefs about the abilities and proper place of female players, and [lead to] fears about the changing nature of the game industry" (Consalvo, 2012: para 8) which Mia Consalvo argues are central factors shaping the aggression towards them. Changes in the organization of video game communities, and moves away from pleasing only the "hardcore" audience, are laid at women's feet, garnering ire from some masculine gaming communities.

Perhaps due to the challenge they present to the norms of hegemonic masculinity in video game cultures, various women in gaming have spoken out about being marginalized and mistreated, particularly while gaming online. For example, blogs like "Not in the Kitchen Anymore," and "Fat, Ugly or Slutty," began (in 2010 and 2011, respectively) to post pictures of harassing electronic messages, or post audio from abusive chat within games (Haniver, 2014; Fat, Ugly or Slutty, 2014). Feminist news sites such as Jezebel have repeatedly reported on women who are demeaned or marginalized within gaming cultures (Baker, 2012), and even traditional news sites such as the BBC have reported on sexual harassment in gaming (Fletcher, 2012). One recent study suggests that women face a greater amount of hostility gaming online than do men (Kuznekoff & Rose, 2013).

These various sites of gender conflict online and in video game cultures contribute to what Consalvo (2012) terms a "toxic gamer culture," where the meanings of what a video game is and who counts in gaming cultures is contested, and the future of video gaming is up for debate. It was in the midst of this toxic gamer culture that game developer Zoe Quinn found herself at the origins of the culture war that has become GamerGate.

DEPRESSION QUEST

Zoe Quinn released the game *Depression Quest* in 2013. It is a text-based game that is designed to demonstrate the experiences of depression, while also designed with the intent of helping people fight the effects of depression. Its style is reminiscent of the *Choose Your Own Adventure* novels, but the most important choices are the ones that the designer has stricken through. Those options cannot be selected by the player, and they highlight the fact that good options often feel unavailable to people who suffer from depression.

Depression Quest is found online at www.depressionquest.com, but it has also been released through Greenlight, a component of the online gaming platform Steam. Greenlight is a tool by which the Steam community can review new games and help good games find a wider audience. In an interview for *Vice* magazine, Quinn described what happened when she first released *Depression Quest* on Greenlight:

When it hit Greenlight, people were leaving foul comments there, and suddenly I started getting stuff sent to my email. "Oh I saw your game on Greenlight and I hope you kill yourself." I guess somebody who thought they were really clever figured out my address and sent a very detailed rape threat to my house. That was when I decided to pull it off [Greenlight]. I just didn't have the emotional time and effort to spend on it. Putting something on Greenlight, you have to manage this whole campaign, promotion. It's exhausting when you also have people telling you that they want you to die. (Kotzer, 2014)

The article, entitled "Female Game Designers are Being Threatened with Rape," was published on January 23, 2014, and was written by gaming journalist Zack Kotzer. As GamerGate eventually unfolded, later in 2014, the field of gaming journalism would turn out to be a central issue. While many would respond to this by scoffing at the very concept of gaming journalism, others would argue that if there is no integrity in gaming journalism then there is no integrity in journalism at large and no integrity in gaming. A few weeks before Kotzer's article appeared in *Vice*, another gaming journalist included *Depression Quest* in a piece he published online at the site Rock, Paper, Shotgun. That piece, written by Nathan Grayson and published on January 8, 2014, consisted of little more than a list 50 new games released on Greenlight. The games were not reviewed or rank ordered. However, the list was illustrated with a screen capture from *Depression Quest*. At the end of the opening paragraph, the last line before the list reads: "Anyway, standouts: powerful Twine darling *Depression Quest*, surrealist Thief usurper Tangiers, and sidescrolling epic Treasure Adventure World" (Grayson, 2014a). Twine is an open source platform used in game development, including Depression Quest.

On social media, Quinn alleged that Depression Quest was particularly attacked by members of Wizardchan. Wizardchan is an online discussion board, found at wizchan.org, that describes itself as follows:

Wizardchan is a Japanese-inspired image-based forum (imageboard) for male virgins to share their thoughts and discuss their interests and lifestyle as a virgin. The name of our website is inspired by the wizard meme, which refers to someone who has maintained his virginity past the age of 30. In contrast to other imageboards, Wizardchan is dedicated exclusively to people who have no sexual experience and may be NEET or hikkikomori.[2]

NEET stands for Not in Education, Employment, or Training. Hikikomori is a Japanese term for socially withdrawn. Wizardchan users have denied the claims that they attacked Depression Quest and allege that Quinn invented the attack to garner more press for her game.

The trail to GamerGate goes quiet for a couple of months, until Rock, Paper, Shotgun posts a video on its YouTube account at the end of the Game Developers Conference (GDC) in San Francisco.[3] The video appeared on March 22, 2014, and featured Nathan Grayson sitting on a bed interviewing Hayden Dingman from *PC World*; Lucas Pope, the developer of the game *Papers, Please*; Zoe Quinn, developer of *Depression Quest*; and Matthew Ritter, developer of the game *Boon Hill*. They seem to be sitting around someone's bedroom, having a casual conversation about their current game interests. Each person is featured for a few minutes. Quinn talks for about three minutes (in a 30 minute video) about sharing her game at the GDC. She discusses a talk she gave about what it is like to release a game that is so personal. The discussion of *Depression Quest* is pretty limited. At one point, the other interview participants congratulate Quinn on her success. When she expresses discomfort with the positive comments, Ritter says "We take it back. Your game sucks." But when you watch the interview, it's clear that he is joking and the general spirit is one of support for Quinn. But there is no indication that the other participants have even played the game.

GAME_JAM

The next major event in the path to GamerGate happened in the week that followed the Rock, Paper, Shotgun video. Quinn was recruited to participate in a reality television show called *GAME_JAM* that would pit teams of game developers against each other as they raced to create new games. The premise of the show is a core element in indie game culture: the game jam. The show was being sponsored by Mountain Dew and produced by a production company called Polaris (owned by Maker, which is owned in turn by Disney) (Campbell, 2014). The host for the show was Matti Lesham, whose previous credits include, according to the Internet Movie Database (IMDB), *Dewmocracy* (2008), "A web-based fantasy game that allows gamers to create a Mountain Dew soft drink, including its flavor, color and label."[4] Each team of developers also included a YouTube star, such as the video blogger (or vlogger) JonTron, of the JonTronShow.[5]

Production of *GAME_JAM* did not go well, according to pretty much everyone involved. Not surprisingly, the reality television style of the show resulted in pressures to create conflict between gamers. When these conflicts failed to materialize, Lesham began asking competitors questions about whether women could succeed in gaming. He is quoted in one article about the production as follows:

Two of the other teams have women on them. Do you think they're at a disadvantage?

And then:

Do you think you're at an advantage because you have a pretty lady on your team? (Grayson, 2014b)

Participants left the set soon after this incident, and refused to participate in the production any further. The production was derailed and the show never happened.

The article that I use above to quote Lesham was written by Nathan Grayson, so it provides the next key point in a series of connections between Grayson and Quinn that would later become the linchpin for GamerGate. By this time, Grayson has started writing for Kotaku, a gaming blog owned by Gawker.

After *GAME_JAM* fell apart, Quinn took to her blog, Dispatches from the Quinnspiracy, to reflect on the experience:

It's a weird time for games, and it can be easy to lose sight of that when you're working in the industry.... I've taken every speaking gig offered to me because I've read so much on how having someone who looks like you being visible in places you'd like to be in someday can do really powerful stuff for traditionally marginalized groups. A lot of these panels and places I've been going, if I had said no there wouldn't be any women present at all, much less an openly queer one. I'm tired and sick and stressed but really happy that I can do this thing that I care about and maybe, hopefully, help someone else feel more welcome or able to do this thing that I care about so much. (Quinn, 2014)

She does not directly speak about the show, which she explains is a result of a contractual obligation. But clearly the show's failure led her to examine the culture of gaming, including indie gaming, and the intersecting issues of gender.

Quinn noted in Grayson's article that the experience made her want to start her own game jam, and she began using the name Rebel Jam to refer to that goal. She was accused of derailing *GAME_JAM* as a way of promoting Rebel Jam.

A note on the use of quotes from social media and online sources: such quotes are used throughout this essay. From an ethical standpoint, these are publicly available sources so they are fair game for quoting. A pattern emerges when we look across these sources. Targets of GamerGate, primarily women, who post online about their experiences choose to forego the anonymity that the internet and social media allow, making them even more vulnerable to online harassment. By contrast, participants in GamerGate, primarily men, frequently use profiles that do not include real names or photographs, making it easier to engage in harassing behavior without being held accountable for their actions.

THE FINE YOUNG CAPITALISTS

Across 2014, Zoe Quinn was also engaged in a somewhat public battle with a group that identifies as The Fine Young Capitalists. On Wikipedia, the Fine Young Capitalists are described as radical feminists (Wikipedia, 2015b). But an article on CinemaBlend describes them simply as pro-feminist (Usher, 2014). The group operates as an anonymous collective whose goal is to help women and minorities become more involved in gaming. The origins of the group are described in a YouTube video that features the group's founder Matthew Rappard. He is the only publicly identified member of the group and he claims that he has only gone public as a result of Zoe Quinn and others sharing his personal information online—a practice referred to in the Reddit and 4chan communities as 'doxxing'.

So an anonymous pro-feminist organization, founded by a male, and possibly consisting of mostly men, set out to reward female game designers.[6] They recruited the help of a Colombian "transmedia production company" called Autobótika to help them launch a campaign. A video on The Fine Young Capitalists' YouTube page features Autobótika's Lola Barreto, which gives the impression that women are actively involved in the campaign. Perhaps they were; it is difficult to ascertain the group's demographics. But there is no clear indication that women were active with the group from the start. In a defense of The Fine Young Capitalists on their Tumblr account, Barreto is one of several women listed, even though she is part of Autobótika (The Fine Young Capitalists, 2014). In one interview, Barreto clearly says that she is not part of The Fine Young Capitalists and that her company was contracted for its services (Morley, 2014). The central premise of the group is that men, a group that is privileged in gaming, can reach out and lend a hand of support to help more women and other "under represented labor"[7] become game developers. Rappard does say in an online video that there were women involved as well, but those women are not named. The campaign that they launched with Autobótika solicited ideas for games from women. The women whose ideas were considered the best were then matched with concept artists to storyboard the game (Morley, 2014). These storyboards were then made available online so that a broad audience could vote on which of the games should actually get made, with the plan to make the games and sell them, giving 8% of the proceeds to the women who created the games and the rest of the money to charity.

Quinn became aware of The Fine Young Capitalists project in February 2014 and contacted them with concerns. First, she was bothered that they were basically asking women to work for free as they volunteered their creative gaming ideas (Seraphita, 2014). Rappard says in his YouTube video that he does not understand why this is a problem, because the group is essentially trying to help women and the winner would be offered 8% of the proceeds. Quinn's critique does seem legitimate though, as it is basically using a contest to generate free research & development ideas. Later in the year, Stephen Daly at Gameranx would publish an op-ed that shared Quinn's concerns (Daly, 2014).

Second, Quinn asked questions about The Fine Young Capitalists' policy regarding trans people. The question wasn't random. They had a stated policy on their website. The name of the HTML document bearing the website is "TransgenderPolicy" and the headline at the top of the policy reads "Are you a boy or a girl?" The policy is as follows:

Although it has become an Internet meme, the question "Are you a boy or a girl?" is actually quite a complicated question. As TFYC is based in Canada we use the theory of self identification, where a person will be considered a man or a woman based upon on their own view of how they should be perceived in society. This can bother some people for some reason, so to put the record straight let's lay out what exactly that means. The only question regarding gender we ask is.

Participant has self identified as Woman before the date of March 11, 2014.[8]

Quinn claimed that the policy was transphobic. Rappard defended the policy saying it was a necessary way to prevent men from gaining access to the award by suddenly claiming they identify as women. In an email to a journalist, Rappard said "the text was approved by a lawyer and signed by a sociology student."[9]

The theory of self-identification seems to be a fairly progressive approach. However, the fear that men would embrace a trans identity and declare themselves women simply to gain access to this award is unfounded, and does hint at a fear that trans identities could destabilize social action.

Zoe Quinn took her concerns to Twitter. It is at this point that Rappard says he was doxxed, when Quinn's friend and associate Maya Felix Kramer released his name and Facebook account on Twitter. He says that Quinn's reply to that tweet effectively alerted her followers as well, making her complicit with the doxxing. The launch of the fundraising campaign for The Fine Young Capitalists was delayed as a result. Quinn tweeted: "I love how a conversation between me and @legobutts resulted in accidentally killing an exploitative startup's website."[10] @legobutts is the Twitter handle for Maya Felix Kramer.

The launch was delayed into the summer. During this time, Rappard says that Quinn was contacted and even offered a chance to work with The Fine Young Capitalists as a consultant, but she rebuffed their offers.

By the time the fundraising campaign launched, the battle between Zoe Quinn and The Fine Young Capitalists had been waged fairly publicly, especially on Twitter and 4chan. Two of the boards on 4chan, /pol/ or Politically Incorrect and /v/ or Video Games began organizing donations to The Fine Young Capitalists, explicitly to spite Zoe Quinn. According to Rappard, the 4chan portal on the giving site IndieGoGo was the strongest source of donations for their program. The Fine Young Capitalists and the 4chan users worked out a deal whereby the 4chan /v/ board could place its logo on the resulting game *and* choose the charity that would receive the donated proceeds from the game.[11] They were even allowed to create a character that would be inserted into the winning game. 4chan users selected the Colon Cancer Alliance as the charity recipient. CCA was one of six choices presented in a 4chan poll, the others being the Prostate Cancer Foundation, the Mankind Initiative (described as a "charity for abused men"[12]), Survivors UK ("male rape and sexual abuse support"), the Jewish Internet Defense Force (a group described on Wikipedia as "an organization that uses social media to mobilize support for campaigns against websites and Facebook groups that promote or praise what it regards as Islamic terrorism or anti-Semitism" [Wikipedia, 2015a]), and the Friends of the Israel Defense Forces (a New York City based organization that provides support for veterans of the Israel Defense Forces). The selection of possible charities is telling. If Zoe Quinn is seen as a social justice warrior—a hot button term in this debate—then these charities are meant to present an alternative vision of social justice that emphasizes the victimization of men.

4chan is an online image and message board that was started in 2003 by a 15 year-old named Christopher Poole. The primary purpose of 4chan is to share images and to create dialog about those images. It was modeled on Japanese websites, particularly 2chan, and originally focused on Japanese popular culture. Its original catchphrase according to an August 18, 2005, screen capture was: "What you need, when you need it."[13]

4chan allows users to post images without registering. They can use any identity they choose, or they can post entirely anonymously. 4chan has been linked to the worldwide anonymous collective of hacktivists (hacker activists) known as Anonymous, and it is widely described as their original creation point. Anonymous has been linked to campaigns against Scientology and the Westboro Baptist Church, as well as attempts to garner greater media attention to a number of crimes (Gilbert, 2014). 4chan explains its concept of anonymous on an FAQ board:

"Anonymous" is the name assigned to a poster who does not enter text in to the [Name] field. Anonymous is not a single person, but rather, represents the collective whole of 4chan. He is a god amongst men. Anonymous invented the moon, assassinated former President David Palmer, and is also harder than the hardest metal known the (sic) man: diamond. His power level is rumored to be over nine thousand. He currently resides with his auntie and uncle in a town called Bel-Air (however, he is West Philadelphia born and raised). He does not forgive.[14]

A stroll through 4chan's boards reveals a sustained interest in Japanese anime and manga, as well as a variety of adult boards. Its most popular board is the random board, known popularly as /b/ (because that is the URL extension where it is found, i.e., http://boards.4chan.org/b/). Frequent users of /b/ call themselves /b/tards, a play on the slur retards, and they are known for making heavy use of the word fag.

The character created by the 4chan users for the game selected by The Fine Young Capitalists is named Vivian James. She will appear in the game After Life Empire, which is being developed by Autobótika. The Fine Young Capitalists have a video about the game development on their YouTube account. In the video, 5 game designers and technicians—4 male and 1 female—discuss the process of developing the game. The women who created the game are not named, but one of the men in the video comments on them. The comment is in Spanish but translated in the subtitles as "What I like about this project that the ideas come from women."[15]

TFYC have come under fire for taking money from 4chan (Daly, 2014), but at the request of 4chan users, TFYC are now making videos about female game designers and have already released videos about Anna Kipnis[16] and Corrinne Yu.[17] More recent projects by TFYC are being funded by an online porn stream, in partnership with the porn start Mercedes Carrera.

TL;DR

As the controversy over The Fine Young Capitalists is reaching its zenith in August 2014, Zoe Quinn faces a new battlefront, this one much more personal than the others. This is the same month that Quinn is also re-releasing Depression Quest on Steam's Greenlight service, after pulling it a year earlier due to harassing comments. As all of this is happening, her romantic relationship with boyfriend Eron Gjoni is ending. They had taken a break, gotten back together, and then called it quits again. Gjoni is also a game developer and was very aware of Quinn's struggles with Depression Quest, *GAME_JAM*, and The Fine Young Capitalists.

He started a blog to publicly express his anger towards his ex-girlfriend, naming the blog The Zoe Post. The first post on the blog, dated August 16, 2014, was titled "TL;DR." This is a shorthand term used on Reddit and other sites (Sheets, 2012). It stands for "Too Long; Didn't Read." If you jump in mid-stream to a lengthy thread, you need a summary to catch you up and save you from reading the full thread. Look for a post labeled "TL;DR" and you should find a summary of the thread up to that point. Gjoni's post about his relationship was meant to provide a summary of their break up. He opens with a concise statement of his feelings towards Quinn:

I dated Zoe Quinn. I thought she was the most amazing, kind hearted person in the world.

Turns out she was bullshitting pretty much everything I fell in love with her for, and is actually an unbelievable jerk. (Gjoni, 2014)

Gjoni makes a list of 24 things he is holding against Quinn, including an accusation that she had a sexual affair with games journalist Nathan Grayson. In fact, he identifies five men (some named, some left anonymous) who he believes Quinn slept with during their relationship, or during a period when they were on a break but had a supposed commitment not to sleep with others. "TL;DR" was one of 9 posts that Gjoni published on August 16 on The Zoe Post. The others are the "too long" versions that elaborate on the breakdown of the relationship in great detail.

Within days, the blog made national headlines. *Daily Dot* broke the story on August 20. Their coverage of the story highlighted the ways that an online gaming community had used Gjoni's blog to construe a claim that Quinn had traded sex for professional success.

All week, gamers have accused Quinn of trading sexual favors for career advancement from industry professionals and positive reviews from gaming journalists. Despite the lack of evidence for either of these claims—again, Gjoni's post never makes either allegation, and the gaming journalist he names never reviewed Quinn's game, Depression Quest—the idea has taken firm hold within the gaming community. (Romano, 2014)

Vice would publish an article less than two weeks later that featured an interview with Gjoni, calling him "the guy whose tell-all blog entry about his ex-girlfriend sparked the recent flare-up of the notorious Quinnspiracy debacle" (Pearl, 2014). The *Vice* article does note that Gjoni allies himself with the social justice side of the controversies, but separates that issue from his personal romantic problems with Quinn.

MUNDANE MATT AND THE INTERNET ARISTOCRAT

After the launch of The Zoe Post, gamers began using the details offered by Gjoni to piece together a case against Zoe Quinn. YouTuber MundaneMatt posted a nearly 16 minute video later the same day, August 16. He opens with a lament about the accusations of sexism that have been leveled against the gaming industry. Then he turns to The Zoe Post as evidence, he believes, that the accusations of sexism are coming from a corrupt relationship between gaming journalism and "SJW" gamers. SJW stands for Social Justice Warriors, a term that is often used with contempt in a community that is now known as the GamerGate community, a group of gamers who want to rid the gaming industry of questions related to gender, race, and inequality.

MundaneMatt's video was titled "Hell hath no fury like a lover's scorn (Zoe Quinn and Eron Gjoni)." He reads the "TL;DR" from The Zoe Post and then begins his case against Zoe Quinn, asking: "How much of Zoe's coverage for Depression Quest lately has been from actual merits—you know, 'she earned it'—or people she was fucking to get it?"[18] He argues that Quinn is

1. Sleeping with reporters to generate positive coverage of her work, and
2. Sleeping with reporters to protect herself from negative coverage.

He cites Grayson's pieces on Quinn from Rock Paper Shotgun and Kotaku as proof that the sexual relationship was generating coverage for Quinn. However, he never reads from those sources. The RPS piece, as mentioned above, is just a list of 50 new games released through Greenlight. The Kotaku piece was about *GAME_JAM*. But it seems to be the existence of these pieces, and not their tone, that infuriates MundaneMatt.

In MundaneMatt's YouTube video, we hear his voice but we don't see his face. The visual part of the video is a screen capture from Depression Quest. Quinn used that screen capture to claim to YouTube that the video violated her rights, according to the Digital Millennium Copyright Act (DMCA). The video is removed a day after it is posted, but then restored a week later when YouTube determines that DMCA claim is invalid.

While the video was down, and partly in response to the video's removal, another YouTuber posted his case against Zoe Quinn in a pair of videos. Internet Aristocrat posted "Quinnspiracy Theory: The Five Guys Saga" and "Quinnspiracy Theory: The In-N-Out Burger Edition"[19] on August 19 and August 22, respectively. The name of the videos is based on an element from The Zoe Post. Reflecting on the fact that he had a list of five guys with whom Quinn had allegedly cheated, Eron Gjoni joked that he couldn't stop thinking of her as "burgers and fries." Thus, Internet Aristocrat names his first video after the Five Guys burger chain and chooses a second hamburger restaurant, In-N-Out Burger, for the second video. At one point in the first video, he even posts pictures of the five men in question and steps through their links to Zoe and how those links suggest problems in the worlds of gaming and journalism.

Internet Aristocrat largely repeated the arguments put forward by MundaneMatt. He says: "Gaming journalism has reached a low point…. It started to travel off into the areas of social justice and feminism and opinion pieces, and op-eds that had nothing to do with gaming."[20] In comparison to MundaneMatt, Internet Aristocrat is even more focused on using the controversy to expose problems in journalism. He uses apocalyptic language, comparing problems in gaming journalism to Watergate, and saying "We watch as the fifth estate burns in front of our eyes." He suggests that if Quinn and Grayson had a sexual relationship, perhaps another Kotaku editor Stephen Totilo was sleeping with cultural critic Anita Sarkeesian.

In keeping with his focus on journalism, Internet Aristocrat gives more attention to Grayson than did MundaneMatt, calling Grayson "the biggest fucking issue that we're looking at…." He discusses the same RPS and Kotaku articles that were mentioned by MundaneMatt, also failing to actually read from them to indicate how the articles present Quinn's game favorably. He adds a discussion of an item he found posted on Reddit by a user named SillySlader, who was later revealed to be Matthew Rappard,[21] describing Quinn's takedown of TFYC. The video is a case not only against Quinn, but also against those he considers SJWs. Perhaps his frustration is best summed up with the line "They have ruined our hobby." It should be noted that Internet Aristocrat has since removed his YouTube and Twitter accounts, although the videos are reproduced elsewhere, and he has functionally left GamerGate saying that he is uncomfortable with the notoriety and with the viciousness that occurs online (The Ralph Retort, 2014).

Another video released on August 19 was called "Lies, Damned Lies and the Video Game Press" by Sargon of Akkad. Sargon is also angry about both Zoe Quinn and gaming journalism, but he targets his attacks towards SJWs.

The fundamental problem with social justice in video games is that social justice revolves around the concept of demonizing straight white men. As you can imagine, since the video games industry was created by straight white men, this leaves social justice warriors on the outside. Or at least, it should do if blatant lying, nepotism, bigotry, and corruption hadn't overrun the video game press.[22]

Sargon expresses grave concerns about how SJW journalism has misconstrued the very concept of gaming. He picks apart published data that indicates women are half of all gamers by pointing to other reports that indicate women play very different games from men. High numbers of women, for instance, play Candy Crush and Farmville. "No one who calls themselves a gamer plays Farmville of Candy Crush." He insists that gaming only truly refers to competitive games and that women are averse to such games because of "inherent biological differences." What does he think true gamers want? "They want to be left alone to enjoy their games and they want objective video game reviews."

On August 20, Kotaku spoke up about the controversy and the implied role of their employee Nathan Grayson. They conclude that he never reviewed Depression Quest and that he had only written about Quinn in the article about *GAME_JAM*, in March, prior to the beginning of Grayson's romantic relationship with Quinn in April 2014 (Totilo, 2014). The post on Kotaku was by editor Stephen Totilo.

ME JAYNE

We finally get to the hashtag that launched a thousand tweets: #GamerGate. That hashtag was sent in a tweet by the actor Adam Baldwin. Baldwin has 114 film, television, and video game credits to his name, according to IMDB,[23] but in nerd culture he is best known for playing Jayne Cobb on the science fiction show *Firefly*. *Firefly* had just 14 episodes in 2002-2003, but it acquired a huge cult following that led to a film in 2005 called *Serenity*. Baldwin's character offered a particular archetype of masculinity, despite the name Jayne, that was gruff, quiet, and resistant to change. It was a personality that suited Baldwin as well. He opposes gay marriage, is skeptical about climate change, and he's a gun enthusiast who is an occasional contributor to Breitbart. (Breitbart posted an article about GamerGate on September 1, 2014, with the headline "Feminist Bullies Tearing the Video Game Industry Apart" [Yiannopoulos, 2014]) Baldwin is active on Twitter with over 209,000 followers. That's an increase from the 186,000 followers reported on August 28, 2014 (McNally, 2014). His Twitter feed is filled with political observations and stances against gay rights and feminism.

On August 27, 2014, Baldwin tweeted links to both of Internet Aristocrat's videos, along with the hashtag (#) GamerGate. The size of Baldwin's Twitter audience allowed this issue to reach a much wider audience, well beyond the limits of gaming culture. Baldwin is credited with essentially breaking the story with his simple tweet.

That same day, Anita Sarkeesian received a series of violent threats on Twitter. Anita Sarkeesian is a feminist media critic who operates as a public intellectual using social media spaces like YouTube, Tumblr, and Twitter. She holds a Master's degree in social and political thought from York University in Toronto, where she graduated in 2010. In 2009, while still a student, she launched the Feminist Frequency project, which began as a website that offered feminist media and media criticism. Her videos have covered a range of topics in commercial popular culture, including applications of the Bechdel Test to the Academy Award Nominees, and feminist critiques of children's toys. She gained significant public attention in 2012 when she began a Kickstarter campaign to pay for a series of videos called "Tropes vs. Women in Video Games." Her goal was to raise $6,000. She raised over $150,000. The video series, and other similar series that she has released since, have been very popular and they are often used in college classrooms. Sarkeesian has appeared on numerous media outlets, including a widely seen interview with Stephen Colbert on the Colbert Report. Sarkeesian had just released a new video on August 25, two days before the threats happened.

The threats that Sarkeesian received allude to rape and murder, and they reference her home address and the address of her parents. The account was listed as Kevin Dobson (@kdobbsz), and it was a newly created account. Sarkeesian tweeted a pic of the tweets, called authorities, and fled her home. Initially, the group that came to be known as GamerGate insisted that she had posted the offending tweets herself. Two months later, GamerGaters claimed to have tracked down the harasser and discovered that he was a games journalist in Brazil (Schreier, 2014). The timing of the incident in conjunction with Baldwin's tweet made GamerGate a story that supersedes the series of events surrounding Zoe Quinn. Quinn also fled her home around this same time, after receiving multiple threats of rape, violence, and murder, and she stayed away from her home for several months (Lee, 2014). She spoke from England with the Guardian in December: "What am I going to do – go home and just wait until someone makes good on their threats? I'm scared that what it's going to take to stop this is the death of one of the women who's been targeted" (Stuart, 2014).

In September, 2014, Quinn along with several journalists and a few Internet detectives, scoured the boards of 4chan to trace back the origins of GamerGate. The findings are summarized in an article on Ars Technica (Johnston, 2014). The boards indicate that a few posters coordinated the controversy on 4chan and used fake Twitter accounts—known as sock puppets—to generate online attention. One 4chan user, OperationDunk, congratulates the group on their success in generating media attention saying "It took a few days of 4-5 of us doing it but it's taking off." According to the discussion boards, the group planned out a new hashtag to add to the conversation: #NotYourShield. The implication was that the women they called Social Justice Warriors were using male gamers as a shield against attacks on their own integrity. 4chan responded by producing logs of its boards, claiming that the full logs would exonerate 4chan. Blogger David Futrelle examined the logs and came to the following conclusion:

The 4channers express their hatred and disgust towards her; they express their glee at the thought of ruining her career; they fantasize about her being raped and killed. They wonder if all the harassment will drive her to suicide, and only the thought of 4chan getting bad publicity convinces some of them that this isn't something they should hope for. (Futrelle, 2014)

One week later, on September 17, 4chan began shutting down all discussion of GamerGate. Threads where the term was mentioned were deleted and users who posted about it were reportedly banned from the site (Gaming Admiral, 2014).

8CHAN

The next major event in the GamerGate saga occurred in October when indie game developer Brianna Wu tweeted pics of a meme that someone had sent her. The meme—of the sort often found at meme-generator.com—pictures a little boy who seems angry and close to tearing his hair out. Text appearing above and below his head uses tweets from Wu to present a series of jokes about Gamergaters:

- *GamerGate is not*
  - *About oppressing women.*
- *This is about corruption*
  - *Tweets 500 things attacking women.*
- *Says "go start your own game studio"*
  - *To a woman who owns a game studio.*
- *Lectures women on how to respond*
  - *To the problems he causes.*
- *Fighting an apocalyptic future*

○   *Where women are 8% of programmers, and not 3%.*
- *Bases entire identity in video games*
  ○   *Feels like a badass (Scimeca, 2014).*

Wu tweeted out the meme on October 9th, 2014, at 2:39PM. Immediately, GamerGaters took the meme and flipped the script, prompting Wu to send a new tweet at 6:44 meme that read: "A fan made a meme of 6 of my Tweets. #Gamergate spent day filling it with 36 pages of garbage."[24] The new variants of the meme were created by users of 8chan, an offshoot and competitor to 4chan. When 4chan had banned conversations about GamerGate in September, many users simply migrated to 8chan because 8chan promises to not to impose any rules other than the law. Child pornography is banned on 8chan, but not much else. The quick response to from GamerGate to Wu's tweeted meme was, at this point, all fun and games.

By the next evening, it was a different story. A newly created Twitter account called Death to Brianna (@chatterwhiteman) sent a series of threatening messages directed to Wu's Twitter account @ spacekatgal. Some highlights:

- *@spacekatgal Guess what bitch? I know where you live. You and Frank live at {REMOVED}.*
- *@spacekatgal I'm going to rape your filthy ass until you bleed, then choke you to death with your husband's tiny Asian penis.*
- *@spacekatgal If you have any kids, they're going to die too. I don't give a fuck. They'll grow up to be feminists anyway.*

At 8:57PM on the night of October 10 Brianna Wu tweeted an image of the tweets from Death to Brianna, with the message: "The police just came by. Husband and I are going somewhere safe. Remember, #gamergate isn't about attacking women" (Scimeca, 2014). Death to Brianna was shut down by Twitter.

Wu's story was the basis of an episode of *Law & Order: Special Victims Unit* that aired on February 11, 2015. The episode was called "Intimidation Game." In an essay on Bustle just before the episode premiered, Wu described how the intimidation she felt from a long series of threats had impacted her career. "The reality is, this circus has sucked every bit of joy from a career I once felt destined for…. There's not a single day I don't ask myself why I'm here" (Wu, 2015). Since the initial threats came in October, 2014, Wu has received over 40 more threats and has reported all of them to the police.

OPEN CARRY

Just days after the threats against Brianna Wu, a new threat was lodged against Anita Sarkeesian. Sarkeesian was scheduled to speak about women in video games at Utah State University on October 15, 2014. The school received three different threats in the days leading up to the event. One threat, received on October 13, promised that unless the talk was canceled there would be a "Montreal Massacre-style attack," referencing the 1989 tragedy when Marc Lepine killed 14 women under the banner of 'fighting feminism' (Hern, 2014). A second threat, received on October 14, claimed affiliation with GamerGate. Then a third threat came in that claimed to be from a USU student, saying:

Anita Sarkeesian is everything wrong with the feminist woman, and she is going to die screaming like the craven little whore that she is if you let her come to USU. I will write my manifesto in her spilled blood, and you will all bear witness to what feminist lies and poison have done to the men of America. (Alberty, 2014)

Since the threats promised violence, and one of them mentioned guns and pipe bombs, Sarkeesian asked for metal detectors at the talk. The school refused, saying that Utah's open carry laws prohibited them from removing any weapons they might find. An additional Utah law restricts schools from banning weapons. Sarkeesian says that she could not guarantee the safety of her audience, so she canceled the talk.

CONCLUSION

The FBI confirmed in December that is investigating GamerGate and the threats that have been associated with it (Rogers, 2014). So far, there have been no arrests related to the threats against Quinn, Wu, or Sarkeesian.

According to some, the beginning of GamerGate was the end of gaming as we know it. The Gamer-Gate wiki page, which is clearly maintained by Gamergaters, provides a list of 10 articles and blog posts that declare the death of gaming (GamerGate Wiki, 2015). On Gamasutra, Leigh Alexander says: "'Gamer' isn't just a dated demographic label that most people increasingly prefer not to use. Gamers are over. That's why they're so mad" (Alexander, 2014). Also on Gamasutra, Devin Wilson offered what he called a "Guide to ending gamers" (Wilson, 2014). He presents a series of 18 steps that gamers can take to transform the gaming culture, including more self-reflection about the games they play and ending with "we all grow up." Kotaku predicted that GamerGate would be the end of the gamer identity (Plunkett, 2014). Other articles raised grave concerns about the subculture of male gamers (Chu, 2014).

Of course, gaming has not ended. Mainstream commercial games are just as successful as ever. Indie gaming persists as well. GamerGate may not have transformed the gaming journalism culture as GamerGaters has hoped, and it may not have eradicated misogyny from gaming culture the way that feminist critiques may have wished. But it has brought mainstream media attention to gaming culture and it has helped to renew attention to gender disparities across cultural genres. The world of gaming is now heavily intertwined with the anonymous world of social media and the Internet. That has created a culture in both places that is rampant with bullying and threats—an upsetting but logical result of the culture of anonymity. Anonymity, like the hacktivist group Anonymous, can be powerful and can effect change that might not otherwise happen. But it is difficult to hold accountable.

Jennifer Allaway, now a recent graduate Willamette University, conducted a study of gender issues in gaming as part of a funded undergraduate research project. She interviewed 34 games professionals and conducted a survey of 344 respondents. She then began a new project, using an online survey method, studying the role of diversity in game development. In a post on Jezebel from October 13, 2014, she says she was close to completing her data collection when GamerGate caught wind of it (Allaway, 2014). She received an email on September 25 warning her that she had been targeted for "vote-brigading," which is a coordinated attack of something posted on social media to get it voted down or taken down. One discussion I found of the practice described it as "the Reddit form of a lynch mob."[25] In Allaway's case, vote brigading resulted in a lot of fake survey responses. She explains: "In under four hours, the developer survey jumped from around 700 responses, which had been collected over the course of a month, to over 1100 responses. The responses… ranged in their degree of racism and misogyny, but they all ridiculed the project with dishonest mockery." The new surveys that she collected were filled with phrases like "suck my dick" and "kill yourself." Allaway concludes that GamerGate is a hate group, with Eron Gjoni as its initial leader, a series of recruitment practices online, propaganda tools that include YouTube videos and memes, and a practice of dehumanizing its victims.

Erik Kain, a gaming blogger for *Forbes*, has argued that GamerGate is not a hate group, but rather a consumer movement. He credits GamerGaters with organizing a revolt against a deeply unsatisfying marketplace by loyal consumers who deserve better. GamerGate, he argues, is "the natural outcropping of upset consumers who have long been at odds with the video game media" (Kain 2014). Is GamerGate a hate group, or a consumer movement? Can it be both?

Turning the lens from GamerGaters to feminist critics of the gaming industry, how do we make sense of the women who embrace a gamer identity while also challenging what that identity means? Do the women who make and play indie games like Depression Quest also participate in what GamerGaters call hardcore point and shoot games? If these women are part of gamer culture, what are the common threads across that culture? How does a feminist participation in the gaming industry transform the practice of feminism? Can games be a useful tool for addressing questions of inequality?

REFERENCES

Admiral, G. (2014, September 17). 4Chan mods shutting down #GamerGate discussions. *Attack on Gaming*. Retrieved June 28, 2015, from http://attackongaming.com/gaming-talk/4chan-mods-shutting-down-gamergate-discussions/

Alberty, E. (2014, October 16). Anita Sarkeesian explains why she canceled USU lecture. *The Salt Lake Tribune*. Retrieved June 28, 2015, from http://www.sltrib.com/sltrib/news/58528113-78/sarkeesian-threats-threat-usu.html.csp

Alexander, L. (2014, August 28). *'Gamers' don't have to be your audience. 'Gamers' are over.* Retrieved June 28, 2015, from http://gamasutra.com/view/news/224400/Gamers_dont_have_to_be_your_audience_Gamers_are_over.php

Allaway, J. (2014, October 13). #Gamergate trolls aren't ethics crusaders; they're a hate group. *Jezebel*. Retrieved June 28, 2015, from http://jezebel.com/gamergate-trolls-arent-ethics-crusaders-theyre-a-hate-1644984010

Baker, K. J. M. (2012). The Fight Against Misogyny in Gaming Enlists Some Big Names. *Jezebel*. Retrieved April 9, 2014, from http://jezebel.com/5922961/the-fight-against-misogynism-in-gaming-enlists-some-big-names

Campbell, C. (2014, March 31). How 'Game Jam,' an indie game dev reality show, collapsed on its first day of filming. *Polygon*. Retrieved June 28, 2015, from http://www.polygon.com/2014/3/31/5568362/game-jam-reality-show-maker-studios

Cassell, J., & Jenkins, H. (Eds.). (2000). *From Barbie to Mortal Kombat: Gender and Computer Games (Reprint edition)*. Cambridge, MA: The MIT Press.

Chu, A. (2014, August 28). It's dangerous to go alone: why are gamers so angry? *The Daily Beast*. Retrieved June 28, 2015, from http://www.thedailybeast.com/articles/2014/08/28/it-s-dangerous-to-go-alone-why-are-gamers-so-angry.html

Connell, R. W. (2005). Masculinities (2nd ed.). Berkeley, CA: University of California Press.

Consalvo, M. (2012). Confronting toxic gamer culture: A challenge for feminist game studies scholars. *Ada: A Journal of Gender, New Media, and Technology*, (1). Retrieved June 28, 2015 from http://adanewmedia.org/2012/11/issue1-consalvo/

Cote, A. C. (2015). 'I Can Defend Myself' Women's Strategies for Coping With Harassment While Gaming Online. *Games and Culture*, *1555412015587603*. doi:10.1177/1555412015587603

Crenshaw, K. (1989). Demarginalizing the Intersection of Race and Sex: A Black Feminist Critique of Antidiscrimination Doctrine. *University of Chicago Legal Forum*, *1989*, 139–168.

Crenshaw, K. (1991). Mapping the Margins: Intersectionality, Identity, and Violence Against Women of Color. *Stanford Law Review*, *43*(6), 1241–1300. doi:10.2307/1229039

Daly, S. (2014, September 3). The Fine Young Capitalists' noble goals don't excuse them from scrutiny. *Gameranx*. Retrieved June 28, 2015, from http://www.gameranx.com/features/id/23968/article/the-fine-young-capitalists-seemingly-noble-goals-don-t-excuse-them-from-scrutiny

Dietz, T. L. (1998). An Examination of Violence and Gender Role Portrayals in Video Games: Implications for Gender Socialization and Aggressive Behavior. *Sex Roles*, *38*(5-6), 425–442. doi:10.1023/A:1018709905920

Downs, E., & Smith, S. (2010). Keeping Abreast of Hypersexuality: A Video Game Character Content Analysis. *Sex Roles*, *62*(11), 721–733. doi:10.1007/s11199-009-9637-1

Entertainment Software Association. (2014). *Essential Facts about the Computer and Video Game Industry: 2014 Sales, Demographic and Usage Data*. Retrieved June 28, 2015, from http://www.theesa.com/wp-content/uploads/2014/10/ESA_EF_2014.pdf

Fat, Ugly or Slutty. (2014). *Fat, Ugly or Slutty*. Retrieved April 9, 2014, from http://fatuglyorslutty.com/

Fine Young Capitalists. (2014, September 3). *On apologizing for getting punched in the face*. Retrieved June 28, 2014, from http://thefineyoungcapitalists.tumblr.com/post/96578864050/on-apologizing-for-getting-punched-in-the-face

Fletcher, J. (2012). *Sexual harassment in the world of video gaming*. Retrieved April 9, 2014, from http://www.bbc.co.uk/news/magazine-18280000

Futrelle, D. (2014, September 8). Zoe Quinn's screenshots of 4chan's dirty tricks were just the appetizer. Here's the first course of the dinner, directly from the IRC log. *We Hunted the Mammoth*. Retrieved June 28, 2015, from http://wehuntedthemammoth.com/2014/09/08/zoe-quinns-screenshots-of-4chans-dirty-tricks-were-just-the-appetizer-heres-the-first-course-of-the-dinner-directly-from-the-irc-log/

GamerGate Wiki. (2015). *Timeline*. Retrieved June 28, 2015, from http://wiki.gamergate.me/index.php?title=Timeline

Gilbert, D. (2014, October 31). Hacker, hoaxer, whistleblower, spy: the many faces of Anonymous – review. *The International Business Times*. Retrieved June 28, 2015, from http://www.ibtimes.co.uk/hacker-hoaxer-whistleblower-spy-many-faces-anonymous-review-1472581

Gjoni, E. (2014, August 16). TL;DR. *The Zoe Post*. Retrieved June 28, 2015, from https://thezoepost.wordpress.com/2014/08/16/tldr/

Gray, K. (2013). Collective Organizing, Individual Resistance, or Asshole Griefers? An Ethnographic Analysis of Women of Color in Xbox Live. *Ada: A Journal of Gender, New Media, and Technology*. Retrieved June 28, 2015, from http://adanewmedia.org/2013/06/issue2-gray/

Grayson, N. (2014a, January 8). Admission quest: Valve Greenlights 50 more games. *Rock, Paper, Shotgun*. Retrieved June 28, 2015, from http://www.rockpapershotgun.com/2014/01/08/admission-quest-valve-greenlights-50-more-games

Grayson, N. (2014b, March 31). The indie game reality TV show that went to hell. *Kotaku*. Retrieved June 28, 2015, from http://tmi.kotaku.com/the-indie-game-reality-tv-show-that-went-to-hell-1555599284

Haniver, J. (2014). *Not in the Kitchen Anymore*. Retrieved April 9, 2014, from http://www.notinthekitchenanymore.com/about/

Hathaway, J. (2014, October 10). What is Gamergate and why? An explainer for non-Geeks. *Gawker*. Retrieved June 28, 2015, from http://gawker.com/what-is-gamergate-and-why-an-explainer-for-non-geeks-1642909080

Hern, A. (2014, October 15). Feminist games critic cancels talk after terror threat. *The Guardian*. Retrieved June 28, 2015, from http://www.theguardian.com/technology/2014/oct/15/anita-sarkeesian-feminist-games-critic-cancels-talk

Jenson, J., & de Castell, S. (2010). Gender, Simulation, and Gaming: Research Review and Redirections. *Simulation & Gaming*, *41*(1), 51–71. doi:10.1177/1046878109353473

Johnston, C. (2014, September 9). Chat logs show how 4Chan users created #GamerGate controversy. *Ars Technica*. Retrieved June 28, 2015, from http://arstechnica.com/gaming/2014/09/new-chat-logs-show-how-4chan-users-pushed-gamergate-into-the-national-spotlight/

Kain, E. (2014, October 9). #GamerGate Is Not A Hate Group, It's A Consumer Movement. *Forbes*. Retrieved June 28, 2015, from http://www.forbes.com/sites/erikkain/2014/10/09/gamergate-is-not-a-hate-group-its-a-consumer-movement/

Kendall, L. (2000). 'OH NO! I'M A NERD!' Hegemonic Masculinity on an Online Forum. *Gender & Society*, *14*(2), 256–274. doi:10.1177/089124300014002003

Kotzer, Z. (2014, January 23). Female game designers are being threatened with rape. *Vice*. Retrieved June 28, 2015, from http://www.vice.com/en_ca/read/female-game-designers-are-being-threatened-with-rape

Kubik, E. (2012). Masters of Technology: Defining and Theorizing the Hardcore/Casual Dichotomy in Video Game Culture. In *Cyberfeminism 2.0* (pp. 135–152). New York, NY: Peter Lang Pub.

Kuznekoff, J. H., & Rose, L. M. (2013). Communication in multiplayer gaming: Examining player responses to gender cues. *New Media & Society*, *15*(4), 541–556. doi:10.1177/1461444812458271

Lee, D. (2014, October 29). Zoe Quinn: GamerGate must be condemned. *BBC*. Retrieved June 28, 2015, from http://www.bbc.com/news/technology-29821050

McNally, V. (2014, August 28). A disheartening account of the harassment going on in gaming right now (and how Adam Baldwin is involved). *The Mary Sue*. Retrieved June 28, 2015, from http://www.themarysue.com/video-game-harassment-zoe-quinn-anita-sarkeesian/

Morley, J. (2014, August 26). Autobótika's Lola Barreto Discusses The Fine Young Capitalists. *Cliqist*. Retrieved June 28, 2015, from http://cliqist.com/2014/08/26/autobotikas-lola-barreto-discusses-the-fine-young-capitalists/

Pearl, M. (2014, August 29). This guy's embarrassing relationship drama is killing the 'gamer' identity. *Vice*. Retrieved June 28, 2015, from http://www.vice.com/read/this-guys-embarrassing-relationship-drama-is-killing-the-gamer-identity-828

Plunkett, L. (2014, August 28). We might be witnessing the 'death of an identity'. *Kotaku*. Retrieved June 28, 2015, from http://kotaku.com/we-might-be-witnessing-the-death-of-an-identity-1628203079?utm_

PMS Clan. (2011). *Our Mission*. Retrieved June 28, 2015, from http://www.pmsclan.com/

Quinn, Z. (2014, March 31). Unreality: my takeaways after being on and subsequently walking off a reality show about game jams. *Dispatches from the Quinnspiracy*. Retrieved June 28, 2015, from http://ohdeargodbees.tumblr.com/post/81317416962/unreality-my-takeaways-after-being-on-and

Ralph Retort. (2014, November 29). *The Ralph's exit interview with Internet Aristocrat*. Retrieved June 28, 2015, from http://theralphretort.com/theralph-s-interview-with-internet-aristocrat/

Rogers, K. (2014, December 18). The FBI is investigating #GamerGate. *Motherboard*. Retrieved June 28, 2015, from http://motherboard.vice.com/read/the-fbi-is-investigating-gamergate

Romano, A. (2014, August 20). The sexist crusade to destroy game developer Zoe Quinn. *The Daily Dot*. Retrieved June 28, 2015, from http://www.dailydot.com/geek/zoe-quinn-depression-quest-gaming-sex-scandal/

Schreier, J. (2014, November 13). The Anita Sarkeesian hater that everyone hates. *Kotaku*. Retrieved June 28, 2015, from http://kotaku.com/the-anita-sarkeesian-hater-that-everyone-hates-1658494441

Scimeca, D. (2014, October 13). *Indie developer mocks GamerGate, chased from home with rape and death threats*. Retrieved June 28, 2015, from http://www.dailydot.com/geek/brianna-we-gamergate-threats/

Seraphita, N. (2014, September 9). Truth in gaming: an interview with The Fine Young Capitalists. *APG Nation*. Retrieved June 28, 2015, from http://apgnation.com/articles/2014/09/09/6977/truth-gaming-interview-fine-young-capitalists

Shaw, A. (2011). Do you identify as a gamer? Gender, race, sexuality, and gamer identity. *New Media & Society*, *14*(1), 28–44. doi:10.1177/1461444811410394

Shaw, A. (2013). On Not Becoming Gamers: Moving Beyond the Constructed Audience. *Ada: A Journal of Gender, New Media, and Technology*, (2). Retrieved June 28, 2015, from http://adanewmedia.org/2013/06/issue2-shaw/

Sheets, C. A. (2012, March 29). What does TLDR mean? AMA? TIL? Glossary of Reddit terms and abbreviations. *The International Business Times*. Retrieved June 28, 2015, from http://www.ibtimes.com/what-does-tldr-mean-ama-til-glossary-reddit-terms-abbreviations-431704

Stuart, K. (2014, December 3). Zoe Quinn: All gamergate has done is ruin people's lives. *The Guardian*. Retrieved June 28, 2015, from http://www.theguardian.com/technology/2014/dec/03/zoe-quinn-gamergate-interview

Sullivan, G. (2014, August 22). Study: More women than teenage boys are gamers. *The Washington Post*. Retrieved June 28, 2015, from http://www.washingtonpost.com/news/morning-mix/wp/2014/08/22/adult-women-gamers-outnumber-teenage-boys/

Totilo, S. (2014, August 20). From the EIC. *Kotaku*. Retrieved June 28, 2015, from http://kotaku.com/in-recent-days-ive-been-asked-several-times-about-a-pos-1624707346

Usher, W. (2014, September 10). TFYC discuss #GamerGate, recovering from hacks, 4chan support. *Cinema Blend*. Retrieved June 28, 2015, from http://www.cinemablend.com/games/TFYC-Discuss-GamerGate-Recovering-From-Hacks-4chan-Support-67239.html

Vanderhoef, J. (2013). Casual Threats: The Feminization of Casual Video Games. *Ada: A Journal of Gender, New Media, and Technology*. Retrieved June 28, 2015, from http://adanewmedia.org/2013/06/issue2-vanderhoef/

Wikipedia. (2015a). *Jewish Internet Defense Force*. Retrieved June 28, 2015, from http://en.wikipedia.org/wiki/Jewish_Internet_Defense_Force

Wikipedia. (2015b). *The Fine Young Capitalists*. Retrieved June 28, 2015, from http://en.wikipedia.org/wiki/The_Fine_Young_Capitalists

Williams, D. (2003). The Video Game Lightning Rod. *Information Communication and Society*, 6(4), 523–550. doi:10.1080/1369118032000163240

Williams, D. (2006). A brief social history of game play. In P. Vorderer & J. Bryant (Eds.), *Playing video games* (pp. 197–212). Mahwah, NJ: Erlbaum. Retrieved June 28, 2015, from http://is.muni.cz/el/1421/podzim2013/IM082/um/WilliamsSocHist.pdf

Wilson, D. (2014, August 28). A guide to ending 'gamers'. *Gamasutra*. Retrieved June 28, 2015, from http://gamasutra.com/blogs/DevinWilson/20140828/224450/A_Guide_to_Ending_quotGamersquot.php

Wu, B. (2015, February 11). I'm Brianna Wu, And I'm Risking My Life Standing Up To Gamergate. *Bustle*. Retrieved June 28, 2015, from http://www.bustle.com/articles/63466-im-brianna-wu-and-im-risking-my-life-standing-up-to-gamergate

Yiannopoulos, M. (2014, September 1). Feminist bullies tearing the video game industry apart. *Breitbart*. Retrieved June 28, 2015, from http://www.breitbart.com/london/2014/09/01/lying-greedy-promiscuous-feminist-bullies-are-tearing-the-video-game-industry-apart/

ENDNOTES

1   The history in this paragraph is summarized from: http://en.wikipedia.org/wiki/History_of_video_games.

2   As quoted on the opening page of Wizardchan: https://wizchan.org/.

3   The video is available on YouTube at: https://www.youtube.com/watch?v=xIKEJBHbLgg.

4   His filmography can be found on IMDB at: http://www.imdb.com/title/tt1139308/?ref_=nm_flmg_prd_3.

5   His YouTube channel is found at: https://www.youtube.com/user/JonTronShow/.

6   The video is available on YouTube at: https://www.youtube.com/watch?v=1d6Q3VpqXyk.

7   The video and online campaign can be found on Indigogo at: https://www.indiegogo.com/projects/the-fine-young-capitalists--2.

8   The policy is described on their website at: http://www.thefineyoungcapitalists.com/Transgender-Policy.

9   A screen capture of an email explaining this is found at: http://knowyourmeme.com/photos/816444-quinnspiracy.

10   A screen capture of the tweet is found at: http://imgur.com/PFO1zJB,CU55Sd5,OH8fIpw,Dwm6vvx#1.

11   An image and overview of Vivian James is found at: http://knowyourmeme.com/memes/vivian-james.

12   An image capture of the straw poll can be found online at: http://knowyourmeme.com/photos/816470-vivian-james.

13   The page can be viewed through the Web Archives at: https://web.archive.org/web/20050818191647/http://dp.information.com/?a_id=35&domainname=4chan.com.

14   The FAQ is found on the 4chan website at: http://www.4chan.org/faq.

15   The video is available on YouTube at: https://www.youtube.com/watch?v=FCRuu82DxcI

16   The video is available on YouTube at: https://www.youtube.com/watch?v=QAHdntHbPM8.

17   The video is available on YouTube at: https://www.youtube.com/watch?v=OQk_z_vnGGg.

18   The video is available on YouTube at: https://www.youtube.com/watch?v=O5CXOafuTXM.

19   The video is available on YouTube at: https://www.youtube.com/watch?v=TezNpsXvUoo.

20   The video is available on YouTube at: https://www.youtube.com/watch?v=dH1052F2ZaY.

21   The connection between Rappard and SillySlader is examined in the blog post "How not to run your games education programs." Retrieved June 28, 2015, from http://robowitchery.tumblr.com/post/104085628388/how-not-to-run-your-games-education-programs.

22   The video is available on YouTube at: https://www.youtube.com/watch?v=bAJYmrKR8WE.

23   Baldwin's filmography can be found on IMDB at: http://www.imdb.com/name/nm0000284/?ref_=tt_cl_t5.

24   The tweet can be seen at https://twitter.com/Spacekatgal/status/520344200249090048.

25   This comment was found in a Reddit discussion board retrieved June 28, 2015, from http://www.reddit.com/r/OutOfTheLoop/comments/24d8cj/whats_vote_brigading_and_why_is_it_illegal/.

Chapter 9
Digitizing Consumer Activism:
A Thematic Analysis of Jezebel.com

Veronika Novoselova
York University, Canada

ABSTRACT

Charting connections between consumer protest, feminist activism and affordances of digital media, this chapter argues that social media and blogging platforms are becoming instrumental in creating new spaces for feminist action. Women's blog Jezebel (www.jezebel.com) has been chosen as a case study to examine how feminist bloggers use the dialogical environments of digital media to construct narratives of involvement in consumer culture. The chapter provides a critical overview of the major thematic categories identified on Jezebel. Such an analysis is particularly important for situating the blogosphere as a site of ongoing cultural negotiations while marking the limits of feminist consumer mobilization under the conditions of neoliberalism. The chapter concludes with the discussion of how Jezebel.com establishes a feminist networked space where bloggers construct diverse narratives of consumer activism.

INTRODUCTION

Feminism's relation to commercial culture and consumer activism has always been conflicted. The 1970s were marked by anti-consumerist and anti-marketing tendencies in the women's movement; feminist thought of the 1980s and the 1990s brought to the fore the complex meanings that consumers attach to commercial products and consumer practices (Catterall, Maclaran, & Stevens, 2005). Although contemporary feminist scholarship exhibits a continuous interest in the intersections of gendered, sexual and consumer citizenship (Cronin, 2000; McRobbie, 2009), there has been little discussion of how feminism reshapes the contours of consumer activism and develops new modes of citizen-consumer agency in the context of digital cultures.

Scholars of feminism and consumer culture have been largely skeptical of politics aligned with consumerist logics of the neoliberal marketplace. Angela McRobbie (2009), for example, tackles the impact of neoliberal demands on young womanhood in her book *The Aftermath of Feminism: Gender, Culture and Social Change*. In particular, McRobbie contends that feminist concerns with sexual politics are

DOI: 10.4018/978-1-5225-0212-8.ch009

rendered irrelevant in the terrains of capitalist economy, mainstream media and popular culture. According to McRobbie, the prevailing paradigms of individual empowerment create modes of sexual and economic regulation that curtail possibilities of collective feminist actions. Informed by these critiques, this chapter offers a different perspective on the possibilities of feminist collective mobilizing from within consumer culture. After providing a brief overview of the literature on consumer activism, the chapter offers a thematic analysis of Jezebel blog (www.jezebel.com) to examine the roles of feminist networked publics in advancing and reshaping the existing modes of consumer protest.

As a number of academics have pointed out, consumption has become a legitimate, although not unproblematic, form of political action (Kang, 2012; Lekakis, 2012). Consumption-based or consumer activism is an umbrella term for various ways in which consumers attempt to challenge and sway producers through displays of discontent: letters, street demonstrations, petitioning, lobbying, boycotting and the practice of ethical consumption, or "buycotting", involving purchases based on ethical concerns around trade, environmental sustainability and the political meanings of products (Hawkins, 2010). As Richard A. Hawkins (2010) points out in his overview of historical and global dimensions of consumer activism, "boycotts, buycotts and other forms of consumer activism provide an opportunity for the relatively powerless individual consumers and workers to redress the imbalance in the marketplace" (p.123).

Given an increasing consumer awareness of the intersections in purchasing and political power, it is counterproductive to dichotomize between active civil duty and self-interested, individualistic consumerism (Banet-Weiser & Mukherjee, 2012; Scammel, 2000). Instead, a more fruitful approach is to frame consumer citizenship as a form of political involvement based on consumption and implicated in consumer culture. Such framing of consumer practices implies that neoliberal consumer-citizens realize their political subjectivities from within rather than from outside of consumer culture (Mukherjee, 2012). Rejecting the notion that all forms of consumer activism are inherently futile or hypocritical, Sarah Banet-Weiser and Roopali Mukherjee (2012) reconsider the productive potential of consumer mobilization in their introduction to *Commodity Activism: Cultural Resistance in Neoliberal Times*:

… commodity activism may illuminate the nettled promise of innovative creative forms, cultural interventions that bear critically, if in surprising ways, on modes of dominance and resistance within changing social and political landscapes (p.3).

Social media and the blogosphere are becoming *the* key spaces where voices of feminist resistance come into being. While consumer activists use a variety of digital media to reach their aims, the focus on the role of bloggers in consumer movements is particularly significant because blogs have become a major form of online communication and a default format of Web publishing (Rosenberg, 2010). Current blog studies, coupled with popularity logic of search indexing, tend to devote more attention to "serious" political blogs, tacitly reinforcing the notion that the political sphere is a domain of white masculinity where women and minorities cease to be political subjects (Pham, 2011). Given the limited visibility of women in mainstream blog studies, it is important to recognize political agendas and activist impulses behind women-authored content that covers not only governance and formal political institutions, but also a range of topics that pertain to popular commercial culture. Techno-cultural studies scholar Minh-Ha T. Pham (2011), who has written extensively on the economy of social media, argues that the high compatibility of fashion blogs with the neoliberal values does not preclude them from being politically significant, but creates political subjectivity as performed in and through consumption. Drawing on these insights, the chapter claims that Jezebel, a popular women's blog, is involved in a constant negotiation with consumer culture; this negotiation has the capacity to channel dissatisfaction into practices of consumer activism.

At this point, the question emerges as to what it means to engage in Internet-based, feminist consumer activism. Jessalynn Marie Keller's (2012) conceptualization of online feminist activism helps to understand the new articulations of feminist activism on social networks. In her work on virtual feminisms, Keller argues that young women and girls engage in the new type of Internet-based activism by creating online communities and social networks, producing media criticism, sharing personal lived experiences, and taking part in critical dialogues with fellow bloggers and commentators. As Keller puts it, rethinking the Internet as a space for public engagements allows one to see teenage feminist bloggers "as active agents, cultural producers, and citizens rather than passive victims and cultural dupes in the online world" (p.440). Building upon Anita Harris's (2004) work on young women's consumer-citizen identities, Keller argues that Internet allows for new understandings of both feminism and activism as centered on the establishment of public selves that destabilize gender dynamics. Within this paradigm, feminist consumer activism can be understood to encompass a variety of networked engagements with consumer culture including media criticism, public discussions and awareness raising campaigns.

BACKGROUND

The role of digital media in citizens' public protest is a matter of contestation within academic and activist terrains. It has been observed that blogs, mass emails, listserves, online petitions and video-sharing websites have made consumer activism less labour-intensive and less time-consuming than it used to be (Albinsson & Perera, 2012). Some critics, however, have charged that efforts to enact change through social media are best summed up as "slacktivism" or "clicktivism": a laid-back campaigning that requires little commitment to "real life" action and has a limited sociopolitical impact (Morozov, 2009). What is problematic about such critiques is that they implicitly operate within the framework of digital dualism. This framework, rooted in the cyberculture discourses of the 1990s and the 1980s, dichotomizes between the actual and the virtual instead of recognizing them as interwoven and co-constitutive elements of one reality (Jurgenson, 2012). The workings of digital dualism have been largely rejected by scholars who analyze online media as extensions of prevailing discourses and systems of knowledge (Daniels, 2009; Passonen, 2011). In other words, it is productive to examine the digital and the physical as integral parts of contemporary life where "offline contexts always permeate and influence online situations, and online situations and experiences always feed back into offline experiences" (Baym, 2006, p.86).

Unlike the offline/online dichotomy, a more nuanced approach to digital communication emphasizes a continuity between online activism and traditional campaigning. Mass emails, for instance, are a contemporary modification of conventional tactics of political protest such as postcards and petitions (Karpf, 2010). The problem with a dismissal of Internet-based organizing as "clicktivism" is twofold: first, it obscures connections between the existing activist practices and new technologies that transform or enhance these practices, and second, it downplays the significance of Internet-based consumer campaigns for eliciting concrete responses from commercial institutions and other market actors.

The term *convenience activist*, suggested by Pia A. Albinsson and B. Yasanthi Perera (2012) in their work on social media and consumer movements, designates a particular type of Internet-based protest within online cultures. In contrast to "clicktivism", "slacktivism" and other dismissive labels, the framework of convenience activism highlights a low cost but active commitment of social media users to promote a cause of their choice. The framework of convenience activism proves useful for analyzing feminist consumer protest on Jezebel.com where contributors do not initiate coordinated consumer campaigns, but channel and legitimize attempts of other activists to influence the commercial sphere (this is not to say that *all* feminist bloggers are convenience activists or that convenience activism is the dominant mode of civic engagement among feminists in the North America). Ultimately, convenience activism might not be profound in terms of impact, but it defines the contours of contemporary consumer protest and belongs to a spectrum of civic engagement alongside fund raising, crowd-sourcing, advocacy and other forms of Internet-based political participation.

METHODS

Jezebel is a women's blog launched in 2007 as a part of Gawker Media blog network. According to the Internet traffic estimates made by Google Ad Planner (2012), Jezebel receives 230,000 unique daily visitors mostly from the United States, Canada, and the United Kingdom. Technically, Jezebel's format aligns with the conventional definition of a blog as a website with dated entries arranged and archived in a reverse chronological order (Rosenberg, 2010). However, as a part of the larger Gawker Media network, Jezebel has an extended editorial team, including staff writers and reporters. Since the high level of institutionalization and frequent daily of updates allow Jezebel to compete for online traffic with more established media, Jezebel can be considered a professional multi-author blog. While Jezebel's mode of operation vastly differs from that of personal blogs, it still falls under the blogging format. With regard to what counts as a blog, it is important to remember that blogging was not invented at a particular moment, but evolved overtime, encompassing a multitude of technological formats and creative approaches (Rosenberg, 2010) and that bloggers tend to conceptualize blogging as an act of writing on the Internet, rather than a commitment to a particular type of web page (Baumer, Sueyoshi & Tomlinson, 2008).

With the tag line "Celebrity, Sex, Fashion for women. Without Airbrashing", Jezebel covers celebrity gossip, shopping tips, fashion advice and relationships issues; the question of whether Jezebel is a feminist website is open for a debate. In particular, there is a certain level of suspicion among some feminists around the transformative potential of engaging with consumer culture. To broaden the definition of what it means to be a feminist in contemporary Western society, Katelyn M. Wazny (2010) analyzes the content and interactions on Jezebel, concluding that it is, indeed, a feminist website:

> ... *the user community that had grown up around the website had implicitly become a feminist website due to the commenters understanding of feminism and how that applied to the content and conversations taking place on the website (p.15)*

While its coverage of popular culture is not unproblematic, Jezebel differs from mainstream women's magazines in its explicit stance against sexism, racism, homophobia, sexual double standards, and sexual objectification. Although Jezebel is not explicitly marketed as a feminist resource, it is safe to assume that the overreaching political stance of Jezebel's contributors and commentators makes it a feminist blog that critiques, among other issues, the habitual representations gender and workings of power.

To find out how Jezebel bloggers draw on and rework strategies of consumer activism, a thematic analysis of 120 blog posts was conducted. Overall, 120 posts published over the period of November and December of 2012 were sampled by keywords and analyzed for repeated patterns and themes pertaining to consumer activism, consumerism and consumer culture. Out of 120 sampled blog posts, 85 posts offered little critical commentary on consumer culture while 35 posts were classified as fitting in a broad category of consumer activism. The discussion below provides an overview of the major thematic categories identified in these 35 posts. The data suggests that Jezebel writers utilize four broadly-defined strategies of consumer activism:

1. Direct expressions of consumer dissatisfaction with a particular product or service (10 posts);
2. Criticisms of unfair practices in the retail and apparel industries (9 posts);
3. Criticisms of consumerism and consumer culture (10 posts);
4. Assignment of subversive meanings to commercial products and wider consumption practices (6 posts).

The following sections provide several examples from each category and discuss their significance for making consumer politics a part of the larger landscape of feminist mobilizing and social change.

"AS A CUSTOMER, I AM LIVID": CHALLENGING CORPORATIONS THROUGH COLLECTIVE ACTION

The first strategy of consumer activism identified on Jezebel includes blog posts in which bloggers publicly express their dissatisfaction with a particular brand, a product, a service, an advertisement and a marketing strategy; some of these expressions also call for collective actions targeting specific actors in the commercial scene. In particular, one way for Jezebel bloggers to critically engage with consumer culture is to pinpoint gendered, racialized and otherwise problematic underpinnings of commercial products and consumer practices. Through strategic information sharing and calls for collective actions, bloggers attempt to hold corporations accountable for their role in sustaining and profiting from the existing categories of inequality.

A number of Jezebel bloggers call for petitioning and boycotting major corporations as a way to intervene in the patterns of racial othering, cultural appropriation and sexist stereotyping. Below are several examples of such initiatives that confront the troubling dimensions of dominant discourses around race and gender. The first example is the blog post by Laura Beck (2012b) who draws attention to racial meanings encoded in "Make Me Asian" and "Make Me Indian" applications for Google smartphone. Reminiscent of "blackface" - a notorious practice of racial signification - these applications are designed to "racialize" users' photos by coloring their skin and applying stereotypical imagery such as slanted eyes, a rice paddy hat or war paint. Calling the applications "incredibly racist" and "egregious", Beck provides a link to an online petition asking Google to remove them from its Play store. This petition, started by Peter Chin, was a confirmed victory with 8450 people digitally asking Google to take down the application (Chin, 2012).

Petition websites work by automatically sending an email to a decision-maker every time a supporter leaves his or her signature under a petition. More than 100 million people from 196 countries have used Change.org (https://www.change.org/about), one of the most popular petition platforms. The popularity of online petitions emerges from their user-friendly interfaces, the ease of access and an opportunity to insert one's voice into the activist discourse without significant time or monetary commitments. Similar to their paper predecessors, online petitions pressure decision makers, whether in business or government, to facilitate social change. Besides fulfilling an important function of citizen mobilization, online petitions bring feminist causes into public consciousness through enabling their circulation on social media and in the blogosphere. This point about networked circulation is particularly important for the analysis of Jezebel's role in consumer activism. Since online environments thrive on mutual linking, endorsing petitions becomes an important and convenient way to participate in the networked activism. When Jezebel bloggers link to online petitions, they use their authority as opinion leaders and highly-visible networked subjects to signal what issues matter and how these issues ought to be addressed. Thus, the dialogical environment of the blogosphere becomes a new terrain where the reshaping and refiguring of feminist actions take place.

Along with petitioning, boycotting is a common form of feminist consumer protest that can be facilitated through online networks. As a form of consumer resistance, boycotting has a long history in feminist movements. During the 18th and 19th centuries, when British women were largely disenfranchised from mainstream political processes, they made their voices heard through consumer-based activism such as organized boycotts of slave-produced cotton and sugar (Jubas, 2008). As a feminist practice, boycotting reached its heyday during the women's liberation movement of 1970s when women's groups called for boycotts of products whose advertisements appeared to be offensive or demeaning to women. In the United States, boycotted brands included Cosmopolitan magazine, Silva Thins cigarettes, and Ivory Liquid detergent, just to name a few (Craig, 1997).

Currently, boycotts continue to be a vehicle for criticisms of market actors (Lekakis, 2012). Jezebel, as a media centered on the themes of fashion, relationships and celebrity gossip, becomes a space conducive to articulating and exploring the politics behind the boycotting of consumer products. The following excerpts serve as good examples of how feminist bloggers articulate consumer dissatisfaction and, through these articulations, establish discursive ties to earlier forms of feminist praxis.

Jezebel's blogger Ruth Hopkins (2012) puts forward a call for boycotting the lingerie retailer Victoria's Secret for its appropriation of a Native American symbol at a fashion show in New York. During the show, a white model wore a replica of a Native American head-piece, igniting criticisms of Victoria's Secret brand on social media. Hopkins writes the following in response to the fashion show:

As a Victoria's Secret customer, I am livid. After years of patronage and loyalty to the Victoria's Secret brand, I am repaid with the mean-spirited, disrespectful trivialization of my blood ancestry and the proud Native identity I work hard to instil in my children. Well, I've got news for you, Victoria's Secret. Consider yourself boycotted. Perhaps it's time for us to resume the feminist practice of bra-burning. Regardless, this Native girl is ready to go commando (para.7)

By "talking back" to Victoria's Secret, Hopkins articulates a consumer-citizen subject position, "through which the mix of lifestyle, identity, belief and practice is brought to bear through market mechanisms" (Parker, 1999, p. 69). This position embodies a clash between the blogger's identity as a Native American woman and an identity as a loyal Victoria's Secret customer. Articulating political reasons behind her rejection of the brand, Hopkins attempts to stir collective action through the call for boycotting. Hopkins' reference to "the feminist practice of bra-burning" serves a dual conceptual purpose: it is a humorous pun in her critique of the lingerie retailer as well as a metaphor for feminist resistance and the discursive bridge between past and present feminist movements. While it has been claimed that young women tend to reject the collective politics of the earlier feminist movement (McRobbie, 2009), this blog post exemplifies the ways in which consumer decisions become entangled with feminist politics and presented to the networked audience for comment and debate.

Admittedly, Hopkins' short piece did not translate into a wider consumer mobilization; it did, however, initiate a critical discussion among Jezebel's networked public. Her post received more than 600 comments in which some readers enthusiastically supported the idea of boycotting, some rejected it, and others started debating the conceptual complexity of cultural appropriation. Overall, the networked space of Jezebel showcased the diversity of feminist understandings of consumer culture and provided a productive ground where these understandings can be contested.

Another example of a networked participation in consumer politics is a blog post by Laura Beck (2012a) who informs Jezebel's audience about a petition urging Hasbro, the toy and board game company, to manufacture a toy oven in a "gender neutral" color, that is, a color not traditionally associated with femininity. This initiative was started by a 13-year old New-Jersey girl McKenna Pope after she realized that her 4-year-old brother would love to play with a toy oven if it was not pink. Endorsing the initiative to expand the marketing reach to include boys and girls, Beck links to change.org petition that gathered 45,502 supporters (Pope, 2012).

Beck's blog post invites a heterogeneity of feminist voices and showcases the robustness of disagreements in the comment section. Although Beck endorses the petition, some Jezebel commentators doubt whether re-defining cooking as a less female-centric activity is indeed a laudable feminist goal. For example, commentator CinnamonSpice (2012) writes that it is "definitely not on any kind of revolutionary gender frontier by encouraging boys to partake in an activity which they currently dominate professionally" (n.p). To this, user JustTheTippiHedren (2012) replies that this initiative troubles the divisions of domestic labor and "is immediately relevant to the lives of hundreds of millions of people in ways that the gender divide in professional cooking is not" (n.p.). These and similar comments indicate that Jezebel readers actively take up the digital space to contest the meanings, goals and directions of feminist consumer activism. Although comments on popular websites are commonly critiqued for their low level of critical engagement and the lack of civility, the case study of Jezebel points out potentialities of comments cultures for expanding and troubling the dimensions of feminist consumer politics.

Direct calls to consumer action can produce tangible results: Google pulled the "Make Me Asian" and "Make me Indian" applications from its Play store, Victoria's Secret apologized for including a Native American head piece in its show, and Hasbro promised to produce blue and silver Easy Bake Ovens which would be marketed to boys and girls alike. However, there are two important reservations regarding the apparent success of Internet-based consumer campaigns. First, it is important not to overestimate the transformative extent of these changes; neither of the companies made a serious commitment to addressing the structural issues around race and gender. Second, it is difficult to assess the role of the blogosphere in these campaigns. Although it has been argued that the role of social media in accelerating a two-way communication between consumers and producers is growing (Albinsson & Perera, 2012), it is not entirely clear how the influences of the feminist blogosphere compare to the publicity generated by mainstream media outlets.

CRITICISMS OF RETAIL AND APPAREL INDUSTRIES

The second category of consumer activism includes critical commentaries aimed at raising awareness around hiring bias, harassment, and occupational occupational safety in retail and manufacturing industries, primarily the fashion sector. Blog posts in this section do not outline strategies for collective resistance and direct protest, but rather inform readers about problematic issues concerning women and work.

Jezebel bloggers repeatedly voiced their concerns around working conditions in Zara, a clothing chain store. Calling conditions in Zara factories "slave-like", Anna Breslaw (2012, para.1) links to Jenna Sauers's (2011) short piece on precarious working conditions of undocumented immigrants from Peru and Bolivia who were forced to work long shifts in Zara factory in Brazil. These kinds of social commentaries differentiate Jezebel from the majority of mainstream women's magazines that rarely discuss the issues of worker exploitation; when mainstream women's magazines do take up such topics, it is largely to assuage consumer anxiety rather than to provide a substantial critique of the retail industry under conditions of neoliberalism. It is important, however, to note that Jezebel bloggers neither offer in-depth critical analysis of the retail industries nor do they provide any original investigative journalism on this topic, basing their brief commentaries on articles published in mainstream newspapers such as *The New York Times*.

It is important to recognize the limitations of criticisms published by Jezebel bloggers. While drawing attention to the problems in these sectors, bloggers rarely go so far as to discuss how neoliberal politics and consumerist ideologies are implicated into the systematic marginalization of precarious workers. In fact, just like the content in mainstream women's magazines, Sauers' piece on the working conditions in Zara is immediately followed by stories about latest makeup trends and gossip from the fashion industry. Thus, despite its attempt to draw the audience's attention to a current social problem, Jezebel creates a discursive space that does not emphasize the importance of such critiques compared to more trivial content. In addition, the blog post gathered only 15 comments, indicating that the majority of the Jezebel commentators have a weak interest in discussing the issue.

CONDEMNING AND CONDONING: CRITICISMS OF CONSUMERE CULTURE

Blog posts under the third thematic category are focused on the criticisms of consumer culture and consumerism as a predominant mode of self-making. Here, the term *consumer culture* refers to culture where consumption becomes as a signifier of personal worth; *consumerism* refers to a set of values that promotes an excessive accumulation of commercial products. Posts that fall under this category seek to explain negative impact of consumerist ideologies on self-making, body image, sustainability, gender relations and community development.

In a piece titled "What the Hell is Black Friday for?", Lindy West (2012) problematizes Black Friday as a ritualized consumption practice. She asks:

So is Black Friday purely a money thing? Are the throngs outside of Wal Mart really drawn there by the promise of indispensable savings in lean economic times? If so, there's something incredibly dehumanizing and degrading about luring people in with irresistible savings and making it worth it to them to prostrate themselves before the doors of K-Mart and literally stampede in herd-form to acquire pieces of plastic garbage that will be forgotten by the following Christmas. REALLY. UPSETTING (para. 10).

Acknowledging her own momentary pleasures of experiencing consumer culture through fashion and technology, West questions her own authority to critique the materialistic pursuits of others.

I don't get to complain about other people's personal brands of materialism until I stop buying polka-dotted iPhone cases and high heels I wear one time and then give away because they make my feet look "loaflike" (para.12)

Here, West's consumer subject position is contradictory: it underscores the opposition towards unbridled consumerism, yet verbalizes failures to resist the seductive allure of consumer culture.

Another example of a blog post is this category is Erin Gloria Ryan's critique of the culture of conspicuous consumption contrasted with the post-hurricane Sandy devastation:

Even in the face of tragedy, the buying of expensive crap must go on. At least, if you're Oprah. And so, while entire towns are still closed off in New Jersey and children in Staten Island don't have shoes, Oprah released a resurrected version of her famed Favorite Things list filled with even higher frivolity-level tchotchkes than usual. WORST TIMING EVER, OPRAH. Couldn't you at least wait for the smoke over Breezy Point to clear? (Ryan, 2012, para 1)

Ironically, Ryan proceeds to list Oprah Winfrey's favorite items such as $250 set of skincare products. The critical opening and a sarcastic tone of this blog post grant readers a "guilt-free" experience of consuming celebrity gossip that to the large extent attracts Jezebel's readership. What is significant here is that Ryan's post exemplifies an ambiguous position occupied by Jezebel bloggers: they are resisting certain aspects of consumerism while at the same time legitimizing consumerist logics through contributing to the hyper-visible mode of commodified celebrity. These engagements, however, open a new angle of inquiry for research on feminist self-making and community building in the age of social networks. As production and consumption of commodified celebrity become structurally important for the media industry (Turner, 2010), questions for future research include what discursive effects does celebrity have on feminist publics and how does feminist media take up, rework and appropriate the celebrity discourse.

FEMINIST BARBIES AND SUBVERSIVE CONSUMPTION

The final and the most creative category of feminist consumer activism includes blog posts which assign alternative meanings to commercial products and attribute a subversive potential to certain consumption practices. Playful and insurgent, an appropriation of brand culture by feminist activists can be thought of as a strategy of defiance in the media-saturated environment. As Stuart Ewen and Elizabeth Ewen put it, "in the society predicated upon the marketing of images, images become a weapon of resistance" (as cited in Nava, 1992, p.163).

For example, the Barbie doll has long been critiqued by feminist academics for promoting unrealistic and sexualized bodily proportions, heterosexism and hegemonic whiteness (Hegde, 2001; Rogers, 1999). In a Jezebel blog post titled "The Gender Politics of the Dollhouse" Lisa Wade (2012) rethinks the terms in which the Barbie doll has been conceptualized, arguing that a new Barbie house represents female-independence by underscoring themes of "female home-ownership and female-dominated social interaction" (Wade, 2012, para. 4). Wade's statement stresses interpretative flexibility of consumer products that can be re-positioned to challenge traditional gender hierarchies.

The dominant meanings encoded in advertizing and marketing can be further subverted by the practice of culture jamming. Christine Harold (2004) defines culture jamming as a movement that "seeks to undermine the marketing rhetoric of multinational corporations, specifically through such practices as media hoaxing, corporate sabotage, billboard "liberation," and trademark infringement" (p.190). Digital media cultures become a fertile ground for the development of culture-jamming practices. Naomi Klein (2002) suggests that digital technologies create "a culture of constant, loosely structured, and sometimes compulsive information-swapping" (p.4) where people establish social networks in order to engage in anti-corporate activism through culture jamming, ad parodies and "hacktivism".

The intersections of the culture jamming ethos and feminist politics are exemplified by Jezebel's positive coverage of the "PINK loves consent" campaign organized by FORCE: Upsetting a Rape Culture (http://upsettingrapeculture.com). FORCE is a feminist collective based in Baltimore, Maryland that promotes consent through art, workshops and public talks. One of their tactics was to direct public attention to the issues of sexual violence by secretly putting consent-themed underwear, such as thongs that say "Ask First", in Victoria's Secret stores. FORCE members also created a mock website where they attributed a line of consent-themed underwear to Victoria's Secret. Through this campaign, FORCE troubled mainstream narratives around women's sexuality and disturbed the commercial space that maintained these narratives. Their campaign was a "rhetorical sabotage" (Harold, 2004, p.190) used to draw attention to and subvert the dominant rhetoric around women's bodies as a site of pleasure for others.

Here one can see the difference in how mainstream media takes up nonthreatening feminist discourses while ignoring more radical calls for social change. ABC News, USA Today and other news media outlets covered the feel-good, "boy-friendly" consumer campaign around Hasbro's toy oven, yet the FORCE initiative, targeting a commercial establishment that has long been criticized for its problematic depictions of women, was largely overlooked by mainstream media. In contrast, this initiative made headlines in the blogosphere. By encouraging readers to make their own "consent panties" and providing a link to the FORCE website, Jezebel blogger Katie J.M. Baker (2012) signaled her support of the group. In this context, Jezebel, along with Feministing (www.feministing.com) and other feminist blogs that linked to the FORCE website, became — at least temporarily — allies and participants in feminist consumer activism.

CONCLUSION

The use of social media and blogging platforms in collective mobilizing is being increasingly taken up as a subject of inquiry, but the role of feminist bloggers in consumer activism and the scope of their influence on political discourse has yet to be fully assessed. This thematic analysis of Jezebel has been chosen as an entry point to approach this gap. The analysis reveals that Jezebel is a heterogeneous space where bloggers reflexively position themselves in relation to certain brands and consumption practices; this space provides a discursive platform for individual and collective voices of consumer resistance.

As a type of public writing, blogging contributes to feelings of individual empowerment through an external validation of a blogger's voice by communicative agents (Stavrositu & Sundar, 2012) and through shared negotiations of and reflections on competing gender discourses (Lovheim, 2011). Still, it has been argued that bloggers have little collective power compared to such public figures as politicians, bureaucrats and special interest groups, and thereby they exert a limited influence on the political landscape and decision-making (Mowles, 2009). In her analysis of Feministing, Jessica M. Mowles (2009) acknowledges the potential of digital media to change the prevailing political discourses, yet maintains that bloggers are yet to establish solid ties to direct forms of activism. As this analysis makes evident, the use of digital tools for a consumer mobilization makes corporations respond to collective protests realized through feminist social media networks.

Besides drawing the audience's attention to the gendered meanings attached to consumer products and practices, Jezebel brings to the fore the intersectional concerns of young feminists. As an analytical category, intersectionality aims at analyzing multiple dimensions of identities and social locations (Crenshaw, 1989). An example of an intersectional approach to feminist consumer activism is Ruth Hopkins' (2012) self-identification as a Native American at the centre of her critique of the Victoria's Secret fashion show; Lindy West's (2012) piece, while not explicitly intersectional, maintains that her critique of Black Friday is complicated by the privilege of being in a position to enjoy consumer products. As these examples demonstrate, given the multiplicities of one's social positionings, feminist consumer efforts require an intersectional awareness.

Consumer activism is played out within the field of feminist blogging in a multitude of ways: some bloggers invoke the discourses of individual empowerment in the attempt to stop buying a particular brand, others rely on collective actions such as petitions and boycotts, and many of them start critical conversations on gendered aspects of consumer culture. However, the radical potential of such efforts is limited in so far as Jezebel thrives upon recycled celebrity narratives and offers only a surface critique of capitalist production and conspicuous consumption.

One of the defining characteristics of blogging as a social practice is a significance of mutual linking that allows multiple interconnected publics to take up, share and debate consumer activist initiatives in overlapping participatory platforms. When it comes to Internet-based publicity, peer support through linking – or "link love" (Rosenberg, 2010, p.320) – is a crucial way for feminist activists to influence public opinion. Jezebel, along with other social media, serves as a digital tool for publicizing feminist campaigns and generating debates around their effectiveness, messages, and directions. Jezebel's engagements with grassroots activists affirm the idea that the digital and the physical are interwoven elements in manifold strategies of consumer activism.

Three limitations of this study should be considered. First, Jezebel is not representative of the feminist blogosphere's diversity. Feminist blogs are built around various shared activities, intersections of identities, geographical locations, and theoretical stances. They differ not only in content, but also in the kinds of reading practices they allow and what network building tools available to users. Therefore, a larger sample of blogs is needed to generalize the patterns of Internet-based consumer activism among feminist publics. Second, privileging high-traffic blogs such as Jezebel constructs a consumer-driven notion of success as measured by the number of links and visitors. This definition of success is potently restrictive if one takes into account blogs that have minimal traffic yet offer important insights. Low-profile, diary-style blogs that aim at creating intimate communities deserve their share of scholarly attention. Documenting the mundane and the transient - "the prosthetic memories" that would otherwise remain unpublished (Rosenberg, 2010, p.348), personal blogs can illuminate how feminist consumer-citizen identities are constructed and negotiated in everyday life. Finally, this chapter has only tangentially touched upon the interactions that happen in the comment sections. A digital text is physically co-created by audiences (Kirby, 2009), and the meanings of a blog exist "neither solely in the blog itself nor solely in the reader, but rather in the reader's active interpretation of, and interaction with, the blog" (Baumer et al., 2008, p. 5). Commentators play a crucial part in the blogosphere, and future research should explore how feminist publics use the dialogical environments of digital media to actively construct narratives of critical involvement in consumer culture.

REFERENCES

Albinsson, P. A., & Perera, B. Y. (2012). Consumer activism through social media: carrots versus sticks. In A. Close (Ed.), *Online consumer behavior: Theory and research in social media, advertising, and e-tail* (pp. 101–132). New York: Routledge.

Baker, K. J. M. (2012, December 13). *Feminist Group Continues to Fuck With Victoria's Secret By Sneaking 'Consent Panties' Into Stores.* [Web log post]. Retrieved April 1, 2013 from http://jezebel.com/5968192/feminist-group-continues-to-fuck-with-victorias-secret-by-sneaking-consent-panties-into-stores

Banet-Weiser, S., & Mukherjee, R. (2012). Introduction. In R. Mukherjee & S. Banet-Weiser (Eds.), *Commodity activism: Cultural resistance in neoliberal times* (pp. 1–17). New York: New York University Press.

Baumer, E., Sueyoshi, M., & Tomlinson, B. (2008). Exploring the role of the reader in the activity of blogging. In *Proceedings of the SIGCHI Conference on Human Factors in Computing Systems* (pp. 1111-1120). ACM. doi:10.1145/1357054.1357228

Baym, N. K. (2006). Finding the Quality in Qualitative Research. In D. Silver & A. Massanari (Eds.), *Critical Cyberculture Studies* (pp. 79–87). New York: New York University Press.

Beck, L. (2012a, December 17). *Awesome Teenager Successfully Petitions Hasbro For Gender Neutral Easy-Bake Oven.* [Web log post]. Retrieved April 1, 2013, from http://jezebel.com/5969299/awesome-teenager-successfully-petitions-hasbro-for-gender-neutral-easy+bake-oven

Beck, L. (2012b, December 27). *Google Selling Ridiculous "Make Me Asian" and "Make Me Indian" Apps in Their Store* [Web log post]. Retrieved April 1, 2013 from http://jezebel.com/5971663/google-selling-ridiculous-make-me-asian-and-make-me-indian-apps-in-their-store

Breslaw, A. (2012, November 10). *Factory Conditions at Zara Look To Have Improved Since Last Year (Kinda).* [Web log comment]. Retrieved April 1, 2013, from http://jezebel.com/5959456/factory-conditions-at-zara-look-to-have-improved-since-last-year-hopefully

Catterall, M., Maclaran, P., & Stevens, L. (2005). Postmodern paralysis: The critical impasse in feminist perspectives on consumers. *Journal of Marketing Management*, *21*(5-6), 489–504. doi:10.1362/0267257054307444

Chin, P. (2012, January 17*). Google: Remove the racist "Make Me Asian" & "Make Me Indian" apps from @GooglePlay.* Retrieved January 17, 2012, from https://www.change.org/p/google-remove-the-racist-make-me-asian-make-me-indian-apps-from-googleplay

CinnamonSpice. (2012, December 18). *Please someone enlighten me.* [Web log comment]. Retrieved December 18, 2012, from http://jezebel.com/5969299/awesome-teenager-successfully-petitions-hasbro-for-gender-neutral-easy+bake-oven

Craig, S. (1997). *Madison Avenue versus The Feminine Mystique: How the Advertising Industry Responded to the Onset of the Modern Women's Movement*. Paper presented at the Popular Culture Association conference, San Antonio, TX. Retrieved April 13, 2013 from http://www.rtvf.unt.edu/people/craig/madave.htm

Crenshaw, K. (1989). Demarginalizing the intersection of race and sex: A black feminist critique of antidiscrimination doctrine, feminist theory, and antiracist politics. *University of Chicago Legal Forum, 1989*, 139–167.

Cronin, A. M. (2000). *Advertising and consumer citizenship: Gender, images, and rights*. London: Routledge.

Daniels, J. (2009). Rethinking Cyberfeminism(s): Race, Gender, and Embodiment. *Women's Studies Quarterly, 37*(1/2), 101-124.

Google Ad Planner. (2012). *Google Display Network*. Retrieved from https://www.google.com/adplanner/#siteSearch?uid=Jezebel.com&geo=US&lp=false

Harold, C. (2004). Pranking rhetoric: "Culture jamming" as media activism. *Critical Studies in Media Communication, 21*(3), 189–211. doi:10.1080/0739318042000212693

Harris, A. (2004). *Future Girl: Young Women in the Twenty-first Century*. New York: Routledge.

Hawkins, R. A. (2010). Boycotts, buycotts and consumer activism in a global context: An overview. *Management & Organizational History, 5*(2), 123–143. doi:10.1177/1744935910361644

Hegde, R. S. (2001). Global makeovers and maneuvers: Barbie's presence in India. *Feminist Media Studies, 1*(1), 129–133. doi:10.1080/14680770120042918

Hopkins, R. (2012, November 12). *Victoria's Secret's Racist Garbage Is Just Asking for a Boycott*. [Web log post]. Retrieved April 1, 2013, from http://jezebel.com/victoria.s-secret-fashion-show/

Jubas, K. (2008). Adding Human Rights to the Shopping List: British Women's Abolitionist Boycotts as Radical Learning and Practice. *Convergence, 41*(1), 77.

Jurgenson, N. (2012). When atoms meet bits: Social media, the mobile web and augmented revolution. *Future Internet, 4*(1), 83–91. doi:10.3390/fi4010083

JustTheTippiHedren. (2012, December 18). *The vast majority of folks will never pursue a career as a chef*. [Web log comment]. Retrieved April 1, 2013, from http://jezebel.com/5969299/awesome-teenager-successfully-petitions-hasbro-for-gender-neutral-easy+bake-oven

Kang, J. (2012). A Volatile Public: The 2009 Whole Foods Boycott on Facebook. *Journal of Broadcasting & Electronic Media, 56*(4), 562–577. doi:10.1080/08838151.2012.732142

Karpf, D. (2010). Online Political Mobilization from the Advocacy Group's Perspective: Looking Beyond Clicktivism. *Policy & Internet, 2*(4), 7–41. doi:10.2202/1944-2866.1098

Keller, J. M. (2012). Virtual feminisms: Girls' blogging communities, feminist activism, and participatory politics. *Information Communication and Society, 15*(3), 429–447. doi:10.1080/1369118X.2011.642890

Kirby, A. (2009). *Digimodernism: How new technologies dismantle the postmodern and reconfigure our culture*. New York: Continuum.

Klein, N. (2002). Farewell to the 'End of History': Organisation and Vision in Anti-Corporate Movements. *Socialist Register, 38*(38).

Lekakis, E. J. (2012). Will the fair trade revolution be marketised? Commodification, decommodification and the political intensity of consumer politics. *Culture and Organization, 18*(5), 345–358. doi:10.1080/14759551.2012.728392

Lövheim, M. (2011). Young women's blogs as ethical spaces. *Information Communication and Society, 14*(3), 338–354. doi:10.1080/1369118X.2010.542822

McRobbie, A. (2009). *The aftermath of feminism: gender, culture and social change*. Los Angeles, CA: SAGE.

Morozov, E. (2009, May 19). The brave new world of slacktivism. *Foreign Policy*. Retrieved July 10, 2015, from http://www.foreignpolicy.com

Mowles, J. M. (2008). Framing Issues, Fomenting Change, 'Feministing': A Contemporary Feminist Blog in the Landscape of Online Political Activism. *International Reports on Socio-Informatics, 29*.

Mukherjee, R. (2012). Diamonds (are from Sierra Leone): Bling and the promise of consumer citizenship. In R. Mukherjee & S. Banet-Weiser (Eds.), *Commodity Activism: Cultural Resistance in Neoliberal Times* (pp. 114–133). New York: New York University Press.

Nava, M. (1992). *Changing cultures: Feminism, youth and consumerism*. London: Sage Publications.

Parker, G. (1999). The role of the consumer-citizen in environmental protest in the 1990s. *Space and Polity, 3*(1), 67–83. doi:10.1080/13562579908721785

Passonen, S. (2011). Revisiting Cyberfeminism. *Communications, 36*, 335–352.

Pham, M. H. T. (2011). Blog ambition: Fashion, feelings, and the political economy of the digital raced body. *Camera Obscura, 26*(76), 1-37.

Pope, M. (2012, December 19). *Hasbro: Feature boys in the packaging of the Easy-Bake Oven*. Retrieved December 19, 2012 from https://www.change.org/p/hasbro-feature-boys-in-the-packaging-of-the-easy-bake-oven

Rogers, M. F. (1999). *Barbie culture*. London: SAGE Publications.

Rosenberg, S. (2010). *Say everything: How blogging began, what it's becoming, and why it matters*. New York: Crown.

Ryan, E. G. (2012, November 2). *The Least Practical Items From Oprah's $18,000 Favorite Things List, Measured in Gwyneth Paltrows*. [Web log post]. Retrieved April 1, 2013, from http://updates.jezebel.com/post/34842276933/the-least-practical-items-from-oprahs-18-000-favorite

Sauers, G. (2011, August 19). *Zara Says It Really Had No Idea Its Clothes Were Being Manufactured In "Slave-Like Conditions"*. [Web log post]. Retrieved April 1, 2013, from http://jezebel.com/5832541/zara-says-it-really-had-no-idea-its-clothes-were-being-manufactured-in-slave+like-conditions

Scammell, M. (2000). The internet and civic engagement: The age of the citizen-consumer. *Political Communication, 17*(4), 351–355. doi:10.1080/10584600050178951

Stavrositu, C., & Sundar, S. S. (2012). Does Blogging Empower Women? Exploring the Role of Agency and Community. *Journal of Computer-Mediated Communication, 17*(4), 369–386. doi:10.1111/j.1083-6101.2012.01587.x

Turner, G. (2010). Approaching celebrity studies. *Celebrity Studies, 1*(1), 11-20.

Wade, L. (2012, November 20). *The Gender Politics of Doll House*. [Web log post]. Retrieved April 1, 2013, from http://jezebel.com/5962277/the-gender-politics-of-the-dollhouse

Wazny, K. M. (2010). Feminist Communities Online: What it means to be a Jezebel. *B Sides, 8*. Retrieved from http://ir.uiowa.edu/cgi/viewcontent.cgi?article=1012&context=bsides

West, L. (2012). *What the Hell is Black Friday for?"* [Web log post]. Retrieved April 1, 2013, from http://jezebel.com/5961936/in-which-i-try-to-figure-out-what-the-fuck-black-friday-is-for

KEY TERMS AND DEFINITIONS

Consumer Activism: Campaigns aimed at challenging commercial institutions through displays of consumer discontent. Consumer activism may involve letters, rallies, petitions, lobbying, boycotts and ethical consumption practices.

Consumer Culture: A culture where consumption is a central feature of social life and a signifier of personal worth.

Consumerism: A set of values promoting an excessive accumulation of commercial products.

Digital Dualism: A notion that "the offline" and "the online" are two separate spheres.

Section 3

Age

Chapter 10

The Phrase Has Been Hijacked:
Studying Generational Communication on Feminism through Social Media

Alison N. Novak
Rowan University, USA

Julia C. Richmond
Drexel University, USA

ABSTRACT

Previous scholarship has identified that as digital media platforms evolve, the potential of intercultural and cross generational communication continues to grow. Digital social media, in particular, has proven to be a valuable channel for users of different backgrounds (and ages) to communicate and speak with each other, often articulating and discussing cultural tensions. Previous research has identified the ubiquitous nature of digital social media as benefiting cross generational communication, as generational groups are often isolated from each other in the physical world, but connected in the digital field. This connection, therefore, provides an opportunity for intergenerational communication to take place, giving a platform for users of different age backgrounds to discuss topics previously quiet in the limited physical interactions.

INTRODUCTION

The popularity and growth of digital media and social networks provides scholars a unique insight into intergenerational communication and feminist identity formation. The Tumblr page, "Women Against Feminism" was one such instance of Millennial users sharing their views on historical and current waves of Feminism. Through a frame analysis, this study explores how young users articulate and describe their views on Feminism. This study finds a set of six frames used by users to describe feminism: representation, I don't hate men, Feminism failed(s), Feminism succeeded(s), no reason, and countenance. The analysis concludes that although many Millennials reject the label of Feminist, they enact the practices of the group.

DOI: 10.4018/978-1-5225-0212-8.ch010

Previous scholarship has identified that as digital media platforms evolve, the potential of intercultural and cross-generational communication continues to grow (DeRidder, 2015). Digital social media, in particular, has proven to be a valuable channel for users of different backgrounds (and ages) to communicate and speak with each other, often articulating and discussing cultural tensions (Aarsand, 2007). Previous research has identified the ubiquitous nature of digital social media as benefiting cross-generational communication, as generational groups are often isolated from each other in the physical world, but connected in the digital field (Correa, 2014). This connection, therefore, provides an opportunity for intergenerational communication to take place, giving a platform for users of different age backgrounds to discuss topics previously quiet in the limited physical interactions.

In summer 2014, one such iteration of intergenerational communication occurred facilitated through the social media platform Tumblr. The Tumblr page "Women Against Feminism" asked users to submit images of themselves holding up signs that explained why they felt they "no longer needed Feminism." Since this initial request, the page received approximately 5,000 posted images submitted from women around the world. Further, the page was shared over 1.5 million times (as of October 2015). These primarily young women were not just sharing messages for the good of other submitters, they were writing as if in a conversation with another generational group: Feminists from the second wave.

This study uses the Tumblr page "Women Against Feminism" as a case study to look at the perception of Feminism by the Millennial generation. Particularly, it uses the archived images to interpret how young women perceive previous Feminist movements (and leaders) and their role in contemporary society. Further, it gives insight into how Millennial women choose to represent themselves in relationship to contemporary issues facing women which are traditionally addressed through Feminism. These include inequality in pay, traditional gender roles in romantic relationships, and family planning. Important questions addressed in this study include: Who is the intended audience of these messages? How do these messages incorporate and discursively construct age in Feminist movements? How does the social media platform facilitate these messages and provide a space for potential collective reflection on Feminism?

Through a frame analysis of the complete corpus of images and messages shared on the "Women Against Feminism" page, this study seeks to build deeper understanding of how Millennial women view the role of Feminism in contemporary society. Further, by researching the messages shared on the social media platform, the study also contributes to the understanding of how social media facilitates intergenerational communication. Importantly, this study challenges previous theoretical work that concludes the internet is a place of intergenerational conversation, equality, and understanding (Correa, 2014; Cullen & Fischer, 2014). This research holds findings relevant to scholars in Feminist and Media Studies, generational and age communication, and computer mediated communication.

REVIEW OF THE LITERATURE

Tensions between Feminist Movements

Feminist movements closely delineate social norms, intentions, and aims of Feminists at different periods of time (Byers & Crocker, 2012). While there has been much scholarly debate over the names, dates, and points of transition are for historical "waves" of Feminism, there is agreement that each wave is associated with a different generation of Feminists (Cullen & Fischer, 2014). Each wave represents the energy, intentions, and political nature of a generation of Feminists. In America, most scholars agree that there have been three historical waves of Feminism, beginning with the Suffragettes in the late 1800s and early 1900s (Evans, 2011). This group of (primarily) women, fought for women's suffrage through protest and legal challenges to the current set of laws. Decades later, the second wave, associated with a more social agenda, such as getting women's athletics recognized by Universities and eliminating unfair hiring practices, was known for their social protests and aggressive and outspoken messages (Maeckelberghe, 2000). Today, a third wave of digitally-savvy Feminists seeks to continue the work of the second wave Feminists, but instead protest through social organizations, digital spaces, and social media (Fotopoulou, 2014). This paper uses this somewhat controversial framework of waves to look at how women from the third wave perceive earlier movements and their supporters.

Noted in these transitions of Feminist waves, there are also generational transitions. Throughout Feminist history, there are different generations of women (and men) responsible for shaping the contemporary efforts and approaches of the movement. Van der Tuin (2009) notes that each generation shapes Feminism in accordance with the norms, practices, and needs of the current time period they operate within. Pinto (2009) adds that the waves are shaped and constructed by the individuals supporting, engaging, and identifying with them. Thus the practices of a Feminist movement are shaped by the inclusion of new (younger) generations and loss of older ones.

Evans (2011) adds that this generational identification within Feminist wave contributes to tensions within the larger Feminist movement and identity. Because each generation brings their own perception and goals for Feminism, differences across generations contribute to tensions within the Feminist identity. Maeckelberghe (2000) identifies that in a digital era, challenges and tensions exist between the members of the second and third wave of Feminism because the two movements reflect somewhat contradictory goals and methods. For example, second wave Feminism was founded on "shock-politics," with a goal of creating noise in the political machinery to direct attention and enact policy changes for the needs of women (Evans, 2011). Alternatively, third wave Feminists tend utilize more inclusionary practices to work within a system to create positive social changes for women (McNeil, 2010). Janus (2012) notes that third wave Feminists often critique the outspoken, revolutionary nature of second wave Feminists. Third wavers reflect that the methods of second wavers may have had negative effects on the overall position of women in American society (Janus, 2012). Often cited, are the "bra-burning" reputation of second wavers, as well as the exclusionary practices of men in the second wave (something that is largely contested academically) as being counter-productive and problematic in the eyes of third wave Feminists (Janus, 2012). Palmer (2013) adds that many third wave Feminists believe they have to "clean up the reputation of Feminism" as it was tarnished during the 1960s and 1970s (p. 140). Today's third wave Feminists identify themselves based on disassociation with second-wave Feminists (Palmer, 2013). Byers and Crocker (2012) note that this has produced resentment between Feminist generations, but one that rarely is communicated explicitly. When looking at conversations between members of different Feminist generations, rarely was this tension or resentment discussed directly. Instead, it could be found in short, off-the cuff remarks about the other group, or implied in the discussions of how to fix Feminism's reputation (Byers & Crocker, 2012).

While the movements of American Feminism are largely separated by differences in membership and practice, there are similarities that unite the three waves. Janus (2013) notes that Feminism across the waves is defined by its attempt to define, assist, and promote the position of women. How each wave recognizes what that contemporary position should be, is what changes. How Feminism defines women is negotiated by membership through actions and texts. While not a consensus among all members, there is some unity in this goal (Palmer, 2003). In the past, this act of negotiation has been studied by anthropologists who research Feminist organizations and social groups (Van der Tuin, 2009). It is suggested today, that this negotiation process may take place in digital spaces, but much more research is necessary to study this possibility.

This tension is also exhibited by older Feminists towards younger ones. It is common for generational groups (particularly older ones) to have some resentment towards younger groups (Pinto, 2009). This is implied in Stuart Hall's (1997) classical cycle of representation, where newer generations are almost always represented negatively in the media as a way to express this tension and resentment. Within Feminism, older generations often find resentment with what they perceive to be a "slacktivist" approach to fighting for women's' needs (Peltoa et al., 2004). The focus on digital activism, such as creating Facebook campaigns to protest a company with unfair labor practices towards women, is often termed "lazy" or "probably unsuccessful" by older Feminists who disapprove of the tactics of third wave Feminists (Yang, 2014).

Scholars note that technology is often a frequent source of tension between generations (Yang, 2014; Tiidenberg, 2015). New generations are often framed as being too dependent on technology for practices that were previously carried out in physical spaces (Passey, 2014). For example, Millennials are often criticized for their use of social media to interact with friends, organize, or do work. This tension surrounding technology is echoed in the discourses of older Feminists as they reflect on the third wave. However, few studies have looked at how technology may serve a platform for conversations on the tensions between Feminist movements. Or, specifically, how technology may allow newer generations of women to voice tension and frustration with the efforts of previous waves? Through the Tumblr page, this study seeks to fill this void.

Feminism in Digital Spaces

As digital technology evolved throughout the late 1990s and early 21st century, the nature and use of Feminism has similarly changed. Benn (2013) argues that Feminism has a symbiotic relationship to contemporary digital media, suggesting that Feminism is shapes and is shaped by these new technologies. For example, since the chat rooms of the 1980s, digital media that facilitates discussion and interaction between users has documented postings and conversations regarding Feminism (Flottemesch, 2013). These online spaces, which have evolved dramatically over the past 35 years, have hosted debates over the use and value of Feminism, the transition between the second and third wave, and even the possibility of the extinction of Feminism. Luckman (1999) argues that these digital spaces both bear witness to discussions regarding Feminism, but also host debates and conversations that set boundaries for the physical parameters and expression of Feminist values, identity, and culture. The digital space allows Feminists to construct the modern identity of their shared culture, which is then demonstrated in physical interactions, expressions, and roles (Davis, 2011). In short, the digital space helps facilitate Feminist conversations that then shape the way Feminism is carried out in a physical space.

As scholars have noted, the digital space, while providing a medium for these conversations, also influences the very nature of Feminism. Fotopoulou (2014) argues that through affordances within digital media (i.e. liking on Facebook, or retweeting on Twitter), these interactions and conversations are shaped. For example, most social media require a network connection, such as a "friend" on Facebook, in-order for users to see each other's posts and communicate. In this sense, the Feminist network, which has previously benefited from both formal and informal connections, is strictly formalized in digital spaces that require a mutual connection in order to communicate (Fotopoulou, 2014). This structures the conversations about Feminism and limits them to individuals who share a friendship. Fotopoulou (2014) argues this may limit Feminist conversations between insular communities, and limit their ability to expand the Feminist network to include intercultural communication. Fotopoulou (2014) calls for more research that looks for the possibility of intercultural Feminist communication on social media specifically focused on cross-racial, age, or gender identities.

Feminism is also identified as a cultural force that shapes digital media technologies. Prieto (2015) argues that Feminism and Feminist groups have influenced the development of specific sites and content, such as using Internet meme's to critique Presidential nominee Mitt Romney's "Women-First" campaign platform. By developing and promoting memes of "Binders full of Women" created and shared by other Feminists, digital media was used to oppose potential policies that did not align with the aims of Feminism in 2012. Again, these studies call for more research looking at how other cultural groups, such as generational groups may influence this practice and similarly shape the developing of digital media (De Ridder, 2015).

Intersections of Age and Feminism

Digital media also provides a space to explore the intersections of age and gender, through the lens of Feminism. Especially within the context of third wave Feminism, intersectionality has developed into a framework for understanding the multiple identities operating within a single individual (Davis, 2008). While this framework is frequently applied to sociological considerations of race, gender, and class it has also been extended to all social divisions such as age (Crenshaw, 1991;Yuval-Davis, 2006). The politicization of Feminism in digital media is informed by the intersectionality of identity categories.

While age is a political identity within the Feminist intersectionality framework, it is also a crucial consideration within the overarching Feminist dialogue. Due to the fluidity of the Feminism, there have been considerable changes in terminology within the movement. Changes in language have been a key factor in creating differences in situated knowledge among Feminists (Haraway, 1988). As Haraway (1988) argues, Feminism is affected by issues of translation which she argues are always interpretive, critical, and partial. She offers Feminism is not a single standpoint due to the multiplicities within the interpretation (Haraway, 1988). Even the word "Feminism" needs to be broken into different "waves" due to the evolution of the movement depending on situated knowledge with regard to historical context (Byers & Crocker, 2012). As a result, Feminism is fractured along generational lines which can cause noise within intergenerational dialogue.

Intergenerational Communication in Digital Spaces

Digital spaces also provide a facilitator for intergenerational communication (Flottemesch, 2013). Because generations are often isolated and insular in physical settings (such as in schools or nursing-homes), digital spaces allow for connection and communication across age groups (Passey, 2014). Further, cultural norms and values, such as not challenging elders, often prohibits younger groups from challenging or questioning older generations, thus limiting conversations (Davis, 2011). While physical interactions often limit the honesty, transparency, or scope of inter-generational communication, digital media provides a platform for more open discourse, as well as a space for younger groups to vent frustrations they have with older groups (Davis, 2011). Often, this form of inter-generational communication develops in one-way channels, where individuals post messages that are directed to other age groups, despite their limited (or non-existent) presence on a site. The Tumblr page, "Women Against Feminism" fits this description, as the majority of users on the page and larger site are under the age of 30, and Tumblr reports that only 5% of its users are over the age of 50 (Tumblr.com). Further, the intention of these types of inter-generational communication is not to stimulate or create a conversation, but rather vent and post one-way messages that will hopefully be shared among other users. While previous studies have identified this phenomenon, none have explored how these one-way messages, intended for an inter-generational audience, materialize and are framed by users. This study aims to begin the exploration of how these messages are framed and shared across social media.

Most research on intergenerational communication in digital spaces focuses on interactions that build understanding over difficult topics, debates, and controversies. Aarsand (2007) notes, that in particular, youth use online spaces to voice concerns over salient topics such as violent video game policies or student loan reform. While they share the messages directly for their fellow users, the hope is that by building an online community of other youth, their messages may eventually penetrate older groups who have the power to influence these issues formally (Aarsand, 2007).

Tumblr

Hart (2015) documented the popularity of Tumblr and explored how these youth-generated messages appear on Tumblr. The social network was created in 2007 as a microblogging site where users could add text or visuals (called notes) to pages dedicated to specific topics (called blogs). In August 2015, the site hosted over 248 million blogs and was named one of the five most popular and accessed social media platforms in the world (Tiidenberg, 2015). Tumblr's affordances allow users to vote for popular blogs that are then categorized as "trending" and then appear on the sites homepage and be instantly viewed by anyone who logs-in, thus reifying the blogs popularity and access. The Tumblr page "Women Against Feminism" appeared on Tumblr's trending pages for 14 days in 2014, thus captivating the attention of other media such as the *Today Show*. Hart's (2015) work described users that added notes to popular blogs as a type of community, thus forming intimacy over shared views or interest in a topic. These communities build trust and shared values over their one-way messages, which although not directed to any specific user, help the group construct an identity and set of practices. Fink and Miller (2014) argue that Tumblr, like Facebook and Twitter, facilitates the emergence of salient and popular topics by their users. As a blog is voted for and becomes features as "Trending," the topic is often shared beyond the youth-centered limits of Tumblr, thus becoming accessible to an audience beyond the initial group. "Women Against Feminism" similarly reached outside audiences and older populations when it was picked up as a news story. The possibility of the site being seen by older audiences, or older Feminists is precisely why the topic requires scholarly insight.

METHOD

In an effort to study how the young Tumblr users described and discussed Feminism across the "Women Against Feminism" blog, a frame analysis was conducted. Framing, while traditionally a technique applied to journalism, is a helpful lens for studying how the users articulated their personal reactions and feelings on the topic. Wayne, Atkin, and Lau (2014) identify individual frames as a type of personal framing system that users invoke to shape their comments, responses, and social media content.

Similar to media frames, individual frames allow a user to select and create a message that invokes a theme, position, or underlying meaning for the audience (Wayne, Atkin, & Lau, 2014). Young (2010) adds that analyzing individual frames also allows researchers to see larger trends among many users regarding the public opinion on a subject or issue. Further, by exploring how many users individually frame a topic, such as Feminism, it is possible to understand the intrapersonal relationships that exist between users and the subject (Aroopala, 2011). In a study of building identity of collective movements in social media, Aroopala (2011) used individual frames to look at how members related to each other, in addition to the social causes they supported. Similarly, this study seeks to identify and analyze the presence of individual frames on Tumblr' page "Women Against Feminism" to study both how users frame Feminism, as well as Feminists.

No previous studies have looked at how online users frame Feminism, particularly through an intergenerational context. As a result, the researchers developed a priori frames based upon the 5,434 current posts on "Women Against Feminism." To do this, the researchers individually randomly sampled and read 100 posts, then developed their own exhaustive list of frames that fit their sample. The authors met and negotiated a final set of six frames: representation, I don't hate men, Feminism failed(s), Feminism succeeded(s), no reason, and countenance. After identifying the six frames, the researchers then read the 5,334 remaining posts to ensure that all posts fit thoroughly and exhaustively within the frames.

Despite the presence of initial sampling to identify the sets of frames, this analysis remains primarily qualitative. Rather than reporting on the statistical frequency of each frame, this study's findings introduce the nuances of how each frame is used, and how this lends insight into the intergenerational relations exhibited within. For reliability purposes, each frame described in detail below includes several examples of posts.

FINDINGS

Representation

Easily the most common way women framed Feminism and why they felt it was no longer necessary was because of the inappropriateness of the term "Feminist." Often users described the Feminist terminology as ill-fitting their views of society and relationship to others. For example, one user posted, "I don't need Feminism because I don't think being a woman is a disadvantage." Here, it is the perception of the ideology of Feminism that users oppose, particularly invoking earlier Feminist movements that argued society's positioning of women as inferior to men. Users invoking an individual frame of representation argued that the term Feminism failed to represent the current status of women or their views of women's equality. Immediately, it is clear that this is not just a criticism of Feminism, but also those who historically supported earlier waves that centered on inequality and status issues.

Similarly, the terms Feminism and Feminist were problematic for the users who felt that they did not want to be identified as a Feminist. They saw this label not just as poorly representing their own views, but also one that would hold them back or carry a stigma. For example, "I do not need Feminism because I am a strong, young girl who does NOT need special treatment." Again, this amplifies the argument that "Feminist" not only misrepresents the users, but also would actually hurt their overall acceptance in society. The representation frame suggests that the users do not feel that Feminism is a term or ideology that is of positive value in their daily lives.

There is also evidence of the representation label used to examine the changing notions of Feminism across the decades. Although most users are young women (denoted by their shared photos and profiles), women who identified as former Feminists now reflected that the current ideologies no longer represented their interests or needs. One user posted, "I was an active Feminist in the 70s. I am no longer a Feminist because I do not embrace political ideologies." Like similar users, this post suggests that the term Feminist has held different meanings over time, and today's definition did not accurately or adequately fit older values. This was often paired with specific reflections on the ideologies that the users opposed, such as the view of men as socially superior to women. One user reflected on the deeper ideologies that underscored these new changes, "Because, while I believe that Feminists mean well, Feminist ideologies create division, fear and anger between men and women and prevent us from seeing one another clearly." The specific identification of Feminists relationship with men is also its own frame independent of representation.

I Don't Hate Men

Outside of representation of females there were also posts that questioned Feminism in its approach to masculinity. Users challenged Feminist categorization of men as oppressive agents in the marginalization of women. Many posts asserted that Feminism unfairly demonizes men in pursuit of gender equality and further questioned how ostracizing men could contribute to a more egalitarian situation. Frequently, users celebrated the role of men in their development as critical social thinkers.

Posts such as "I don't need Feminism because my masculine old-fashioned father is my favorite person in the world" include personal connections with men such as fathers, brothers, boyfriends or husbands. By citing examples from the nuclear family, the users are confronting Feminism from a personal stance rather than on a structural or social level. This distinction is important because personal interactions do not account for social problems.

While many of the post did reference specific male family members, other users criticized Feminism in its treatment of all men. Posts such as "I don't need Feminism b/c men are not our enemy, they are our fathers, sons and brothers, belittling them helps no one" challenged perceived Feminist anti-male stance. Users rejected depictions of men as adversaries to the Feminist movement and deemed such depictions as counterproductive to a meaningful gender dialogue.

Some posts extended the male-positive vein by considering the challenges met by men as a result of gender inequality. One user claimed, "I don't need Feminism because men's problems matter as much as mine, and playing victim is not empowering." Here the user maintained that men and women both face obstacles relative to their gender identity. Further, the post identifies the victimization of women by Feminist as a major weakness to the movement. Such posts acknowledge the problems and needs of men as equal to those faced by women. Users warn Feminists against persecuting men in the name of empowerment. Many cite egalitarianism as an alternative to Feminism, which in their view would level the playing field for men, women and trans-individuals.

Feminism Failed(s)

It is not just that users frame the term Feminist and its ideologies as ill-fitting; there is also an individual frame that suggests that Feminism itself has failed and will continue to fail to accomplish its goals. Largely, these posts generally framed Feminism's aim to help women as a failure, without citing specific reasons. For example, "I no longer need Feminism because it is hurting men and is not helping women." Again, this generally refers to Feminism as a failure by invoking its overall mission of helping women, but not addressing specific aims (such as reducing wage discrepancies).

There is also an effort to distinguish modern Feminism's failures and those of Feminism's past. For example, "Modern Feminism cannot stand behind its own record of action. That's why Feminists hide behind definitions so much." In posts like this one, it is modern Feminism and the frustration of the perception of inaction that causes it to be labeled as a failure. Similar posts criticized that modern Feminists did not host physical events, and instead were too caught up around the Feminist ideology, terminology, and definition.

This is not to say that past Feminism was viewed inherently as a success. In an effort to summarize frustrations and declare Feminism as a failure, several posts cited scholars, social critics, and even actors and actresses to summarize their own feelings. In one quote from scholar Camille Paglia, "Feminism is dead. The movement is absolutely dead. The women's movement tried to suppress dissident voices for way too long. There is no room for dissent."

Feminism Succeeded(s)

While some users believed that Feminism was unnecessary in modernity, others thought the movement was completed by past efforts. To these users, Feminism was no longer relevant because past movements had successfully gained equality to men. Individuals did not identify themselves as members of a marginalized group and questioned the arguments of current Feminist scholarship. The posts within this frame argued that women were not oppressed and enjoyed equal privileges to men. Some posts acknowledged the need for Feminism historically but claimed the current social movement was inappropriate.

One user posted "I don't need Feminism because I don't think being a woman is still a disadvantage." Here the user is claiming that Feminist critique is no longer suitable because women are not in a marginalized position. These posts focused on the success that second-wave Feminism had in equalizing the role of women in society. Here, they challenged that the Feminist label was problematic because it reinforced earlier notions of inequality. Users argued, that by calling themselves Feminists, they may invoke a time-period where women were unequal to men, thus accidentally disadvantaging themselves.

Again, particularly notable in this frame is the current treatment of women compared to their historical position. Several users asked viewers "Do I look oppressed to you?" and contextualized it by saying that today's women were not oppressed like they were in the past. This also placed the focus on the visual nature of Tumblr, as many of the women shared images of them looking strong or carrying out physical tasks. For example, several women mimicked the classic wartime poster of Rosie the Riveter, by standing with their arm raised showing an arm muscle. These posts reinforced the past success of Feminist icons (like Rosie) or movements (like the second wave) by saying that Feminism was so successful, today's society no longer has the needs it once addressed.

No Reason

Most posts included reasons for rejecting Feminism as a political or social movement of the past. However, there were a notable amount of posts that either claimed to have no reason to reject it or stated a desire to keep their reasons secret. Many of these posts simply read, "I don't need Feminism" or "I don't need Feminism. period." From these posts, it seems like the users imply that they either agree with the other users in their reasoning, or that the reasons for rejecting Feminism should be obvious enough and no words are necessary.

This was also one of the frames that reflected hostility towards other users or readers. For example, many users used swear words when invoking this frame: "I don't need Feminism so fuck off." Or "This is what anti-Feminist looks like" (the accompanying image was a woman giving the camera the middle finger). These acts of hostility reinforce the passion that many users felt as they posted their explanations online. It perhaps also represented frustrations with the definitions of Feminism that they felt did not apply or fit their perception of women. Without talking directly to these users, or looking at their posts on other pages, it is difficult to understand their exact motivation for this hostility.

Other users simply stated that the reasons they didn't need Feminism were personal and secret, not meant to be shared in a public online space. It is interesting that these users often accompanied their posts with pictures of themselves, and they made no effort to hide or anonymize their posts. It is interesting that these users would devote the time and energy into creating a post, just to say that they won't share their own perspectives. Again, without directly talking to these women, it is difficult to surmise why they engaged in this behavior, but the presence and frequency of the frame makes it worth identifying.

Counterance

Although the posts were primarily supportive of the criticism of Feminism, there were also a small subset of posts that were intended as sarcasm or even critique of the page. In these cases, users appropriated the "I no longer need Feminism…" portion of the post, but instead filled in the remainder with content that justified the continual presence and ongoing need of Feminism in their lives. For example, "I don't need Feminism because commenting on a man's looks is sexualization but doing the same to woman is a-okay in their books." Here, the user sarcastically points out that inequality still exists, particularly when considering the female versus male body and mindset. Importantly, by using sarcasm, these posts still operated within the norms of the page, but were able to co-opt it to provide their own definitions and perspectives.

The co-opting of the page became a type of internal negotiation with the other users over the definition of Feminism. Posts framed through countenance, provided challenges to other users who framed Feminism as being anti-male or unnecessary because it had already accomplished everything it needed to do. Importantly, these posts were also some of the only ones that cited evidence or personal stories to bolster arguments. For example, several women shared stories of their own sexual abuse, arguing that it was the successes of Feminism that helped them gain vindication against their abusers. By sharing personal stories, these women provided evidence for the continued use of the "Feminist" label, especially trying to dispel arguments that it was harmful to women's needs.

Countering was also primarily a frame that was used by women who identified as "young." Rather than having representatives of the second-wave counter these claims, these frames of counteract were used by the same demographic of users who were fighting the Feminist label and movement. Although it is likely that other (older) readers would have countered the messages shared on the page, the actual users invoking the frame were young.

REFLECTION

Tumblr served as a platform for young women to address their frustrations and anger towards previous Feminist movements and the traditional definition of Feminism. Within the 5,434 posts, women framed their reactions to women and Feminism by providing images and posters with contemporary criticism. Working together, these frames provide vital information about how users react to the historical definition of Feminism.

First, it is clear that this is a generationally defined page. Many of users identified themselves as "young," "Millennial," or "YA's" (young adults). Importantly, it was also clear that these users were not addressing other youth, but instead voicing frustrations over the historical definition and practices of Feminism. By referring to Feminism in the past tense, or referencing actions of the second wave Feminists, this Tumblr page became a sounding-board for intergenerational tension. Some posts even addressed famous second-wave Feminists by name or by specific protest/act. The frustrations over Feminism were not regarding recent issues, but instead historical ones. Importantly, Tumblr markets itself as a "Millennial" platform, intended for users between the ages of 13 and 33. According to Tumblr, it is likely that most second-wave Feminists do not use the site. Therefore, the posts criticizing the actions of past Feminists were not intended for replies or to inspire a type of intergenerational conversation. Instead, they were meant as a release-valve for the frustrations that young women felt towards the historical movements.

Although there were clear patterns of framing within the posts, there was relatively little evidence cited to support each author's arguments. For example, there were almost no statistics referenced when discussing "women centered issues" such as sexual abuse, equal pay, or the role of women in marriage. Beyond statistics, there were also few personal stories shared to support their arguments, despite many women using qualifiers that demonstrate they were voicing their own opinions. The lack of evidence may be a product of the Tumblr platform itself. While the platform does not have a size limit to the number of words or characters a user can include in a post, the social norms of the site dictate that posts need to be short enough for a reader to skim. Further, because this page asked women to post pictures of themselves, the amount of words included in a post was limited to what they could physically list on a piece of paper.

The lack of evidence within the page may also be emblematic of generational changes in argumentation as well. Palmer (2003) notes that Millennial Feminists of the third wave are less likely to provide research-based information for the changing role of women, and instead focus on advocacy through sheer size (the larger the group, the more powerful the movement). What is complicated in this Tumblr page, is the fact that these women were not identifying as Feminists, and, in fact, were actually identifying as non-Feminists, or anti-Feminists. This label, too, may be explained by generational identity literature and research. Millennials often reject historically-based labels for themselves in an effort to prove independence, uniqueness, and individuality, despite often advocating and positioning themselves similarly to historical groups (McNeil, 2010). Millennials may actively protest a label, like Feminist, in an effort to distance themselves from what they perceive as historical problems (Van der Tuin, 2009). McNeil (2010) adds that although they may not like the label, their rejection of it perhaps is an indicator of that very identity. Despite their criticisms, these women may actually be fulfilling the role of contemporary Feminists, by advocating for their own definition of the movement.

The struggle to define Feminism as a term of reference for Millennials is precisely what is problematized and brought to life through this Tumblr page. Here, the Millennials, while protesting Feminism, are actually just advocating for a different definition than the one used during the second wave. Through their vocal rejection of Feminism, they are using the digital space to redefine the term and redefine what the movement should focus upon. While not explicitly negotiating a set of actions or practices, their criticism of the historical reputation of second wave Feminism simultaneously allows users to identify what they believe appropriate and current needs of women are. This is communicated in three ways. First, they address the need to revamp and fix the current perception of Feminists as anti-male. A majority of the posts challenged the need to be divisive in the consideration of women and male needs. The user's promoted the idea that in order to help or be fair to women, did not mean that women had to work against men. Instead, they encouraged the fair treatment of men, while simultaneously identifying, respecting, and helping women. Second, these users took on the classic concern of Feminism by examining the representation of women in media, the workplace, and larger social situations. Here, they rejected the way the second wave positioned the representation of women as negative, and instead challenged the reader to seek out and support positive representations of women in society. Finally, a subset of users co-opted the Tumblr page to advocate for other personal issues or fight the outspoken majority who criticized the role of Feminism.

At the heart of the definition of Feminism is the goal of defining and promoting the place of women in society. While this Tumblr page is full of reasons to not be a Feminist, by describing and attempting to promote the contemporary position of women, they are enacting Feminist practices. Even as a small subset co-opted the digital platform for their own use, they again reinforced a traditional practice of Feminism- by working inside the space to enact change.

A terse reading of the Tumblr page suggests that the young, female users rejected the aims of Feminism, especially its second wave. However, when looking at the practices, goals, and frames of the users as they attempted to define the contemporary position of women, it is clear they were actually enacting some of the historical definition of Feminism. In fact, this digital space seems to fit Janus (2013) call for exploration of how the current position is negotiated by third-wave Feminists. Similar to anthropological studies looking at Feminist groups and organizations of the second wave, these users struggle to provide a consistent definition of the current position of women, despite there being an overwhelming consensus that all users are concerned.

If this Tumblr page is one of the current spaces where the definition and place of women and Feminists is being explored, challenged, and negotiated, the space itself must be studied for issues of access and literacy. Tumblr, while an established social network by the time of this page's creation, still requires the user to have an intricate knowledge of its normative practices, such as uploading images, commenting on other posts, and even the normal length of posts. The affordances of the site suggest that someone with a more intricate knowledge of Tumblr may be able to get more followers, generate more shares, and push their post to the top of the page (thus more likely to be read). Further, the digital space has access issues that stem from the ability to contribute to the medium. For this page alone, users needed access to a computer, a digital camera, and materials for making the physical sign. Furthermore, in order to participate, users needed to have a Tumblr account. While most posts were from the United States on this page, Tumblr is not accessible everywhere around the world, thus eliminating some regions from the conversation. Finally, although often derogatorily termed "slacktivism," users had to feel comfortable and brave enough to post an image of themselves with their reasons for not wanting Feminism. It is likely that some individuals who would want to contribute to the conversation either did not have the digital resources or the courage to contribute to the space, despite having an opinion on the subject. These types of issues stemming from access and affordances are a necessary focus of future research, particularly if the modern definitions of women and Feminism are routinely negotiated here.

"Women Against Feminism" is an ongoing Tumblr page, that even as of October 2015, was generating posts. It is possible that the page will continue to serve as a digital space of negotiating the contemporary definition of women and the practices of Feminism. As this negotiation continues, it will be important to look at how it may influence intergenerational relationships, communication, or perceptions as they relate to the newest actions and perspectives of third wave Feminism.

REFERENCES

Aarsand, P. A. (2007). Computer and video games in family life: The digital divide as a resource in intergenerational interactions. *Childhood*, *14*(2), 235–256. doi:10.1177/0907568207078330

Aroopala, C. (2012). 2011). Mobilizing collective identity: Frames & rational individuals. *Political Behavior*, *34*(2), 193–224. doi:10.1007/s11109-010-9155-4

Benn, M. (2013). After post-Feminism: Pursuing material equality in a digital age. *Juncture*, *20*(3), 223–227. doi:10.1111/j.2050-5876.2013.00757.x

Byers, M., & Crocker, D. (2012). Feminist cohorts and waves: Attitudes of junior female academics. *Women's Studies International Forum*, *35*(1), 1–11. doi:10.1016/j.wsif.2011.09.003

Correa, T. (2014). Bottom-up technology transmission within families: Exploring how youths influence their parents' digital media use with dyadic data. *Journal of Communication*, *64*(1), 103–124. doi:10.1111/jcom.12067

Crenshaw, K. (1991). Mapping the margins: Intersectionality, identity politics, and violence against women of color. *Stanford Law Review*, *43*(6), 1241–1299. doi:10.2307/1229039

Cullen, P., & Fischer, C. (2014). Conceptualising generational dynamics in Feminist movements: Political generations, waves and affective economies. *Social Compass*, *8*(3), 282–293. doi:10.1111/soc4.12131

Davis, D. (2011). Intergenerational digital storytelling: A sustainable community initiative with inner-city residents. *Visual Communication*, *10*(4), 527–540. doi:10.1177/1470357211415781

Davis, K. (2008). Intersectionality as buzzword: A sociology of science perspective on what makes a Feminist theory successful. *Feminist Theory*, *9*(1), 67–85. doi:10.1177/1464700108086364

De Ridder, S. (2015). Are digital media institutions shaping youth's intimate stories? Strategies and tactics in the social networking site netlog. *New Media & Society*, *17*(3), 356–374. doi:10.1177/1461444813504273

Evans, M. (2011). *Feminist waves, Feminist generations*. Basingstoke, UK: Palgrave MacMillan LTD; doi:10.1057/fr.2010.41

Fink, M., & Miller, Q. (2014). 2013). Trans-media moments: Tumblr, 2011–2013. *Television & New Media*, *15*(7), 611–626. doi:10.1177/1527476413505002

Flottemesch, K. (2013). Learning through narratives: The impact of digital storytelling on intergenerational relationships. *Academy of Educational Leadership Journal*, *17*(2), 53.

Fotopoulou, A. (2014). Digital and networked by default? Women's organisations and the social imaginary of networked Feminism. *New Media & Society*. doi:10.1177/1461444814552264

Hall, S. (1997). *Representation: Cultural representations and signifying practices*. London: Sage Publications Ltd.

Janus, K. K. (2013). Finding common Feminist ground: The role of the next generation in shaping Feminist legal theory. *Duke Journal of Gender Law & Policy*, *20*(2), 255.

Luckman, S. (1999). (En)Gendering the digital body: Feminism and the internet. *Hecate*, *25*(2), 36–47.

Maeckelberghe, E. (2000). Across the generations in Feminist theology: From second to third wave Feminisms. *Feminist Theology*, *8*(23), 63–69. doi:10.1177/096673500000002312

McNeil, M. (2010). Post-Millennial Feminist theory: Encounters with humanism, materialism, critique, nature, biology and darwin. *Journal for Cultural Research*, *14*(4), 427–437. doi:10.1080/14797581003765382

Palmer, L. (2003). *The next generation: Third wave Feminist psychotherapy*. Malden, MA: Blackwell Publishers.

Passey, D. (2014). Editorial on intergenerational learning and digital technologies: New perspectives from research. *Education and Information Technologies*, *19*(3), 469–471. doi:10.1007/s10639-014-9339-3

Peltola, P., Milkie, M. A., & Presser, S. (2004). The "Feminist" mystique: Feminist identity in three generations of women. *Gender & Society*, *18*(1), 122–144. doi:10.1177/0891243203259921

Pinto, J. (2009). *Feminist waves, Feminist generations: Life stories from the academy*. Thousand Oaks, CA: Sage Publications INC.

Prieto, R. R. (2015). From margin to center: Applying the theoretical framework of postcolonial Feminism to human rights. *Athenea Digital (Ed. Impresa)*, *15*(2), 81–110. doi:10.5565/rev/athenea.1363

Tiidenberg, K. (2015). Boundaries and conflict in a NSFW community on Tumblr: The meanings and uses of selfies. *New Media & Society*. doi:10.1177/1461444814567984

Van der Tuin, I. (2009). Jumping generations: On second- and third-wave Feminist epistemology. *Australian Feminist Studies*, *24*(59), 17–31. doi:10.1080/08164640802645166

Wang, K. Y., Atkin, D. J., & Lau, T. (2014). Media versus individual frames and horizontal knowledge gaps: A study of the 2010 healthcare reform debate online. *Electronic News*, *8*(1), 30–48.

Yang, H. (2014). Young people's friendship and love relationships and technology: New practices of intimacy and rethinking Feminism. *Asian Journal of Women's Studies*, *20*(1), 93–124. doi:10.1080/12259276.2014.11666174

Young, A. A. (2010). New life for an old concept: Frame analysis and the reinvigoration of studies in culture and poverty. *The Annals of the American Academy of Political and Social Science*, *629*(1), 53–74. doi:10.1177/0002716209357145 PMID:24489382

Yuval-Davis, N. (2006). Intersectionality and Feminist politics. *European Journal of Women's Studies*, *13*(3), 193–209. doi:10.1177/1350506806065752

Chapter 11
Re-Routing the Masculinity Myths in Bangladeshi Fashion Adverts:
Identifying a New Wave among the Youths

Nusrat Zahan Mou
International University of Business, Agriculture, and Technology (IUBAT), Bangladesh

Md. Shafiqul Islam
United International University, Bangladesh

ABSTRACT

This chapter aims to focus on the impacts of some particular fashion adverts which are breaking the prevalent ideas regarding 'the representation of men' on Bangladeshi youths of different ages and areas by making a survey on the youths studying at different Bangladeshi universities. The media of the western countries are acquainted with these types of representation of men while the Bangladeshi media has let its viewers know about this lately through different advertisements specially fashion adverts. This new type of representation of men and "masculinity" or the emergence of "Metrosexual men" in the Bangladeshi media has its own impacts on the youths of Bangladesh whether it is about creating a new concept or it is only about dealing with the consumer culture. However, this chapter points to highlight on the fact that to what extent the concepts of the urban Bangladeshi youths (both male and female of different ages and areas) are molded by the emergence of this type of adverts in Bangladeshi media.

INTRODUCTION

Culture is dynamic that evolves with the passage of time. Thus, the definitions, concepts, psychology and the ability of acceptance change too. These days, culture is gradually getting involved with the social media platforms, and newer concepts of networking are coming into being every day. The viral ads have become one of the mediums of publicizing the products. By spreading the advertisements not only the brand names, information and the products are getting the publicity but also the concepts regarding various stuffs are getting different dimensions gradually (Huang et al, 2012). Through the viral ads spread in the social media networks, the ideas regarding fashion, the boundaries regarding gender are changing lately.

DOI: 10.4018/978-1-5225-0212-8.ch011

Likewise, the ideas of the representations of 'men' in the viral ads are re-forming with the identity of stereotyped idea of 'men'. The definitions, myths and concepts regarding 'men' are gradually altering with the ideas regarding 'fashion' through the viral ads of different consumer products like clothes and accessories and other commodities (Nixon, S, 1997). However, this paper focuses on the ideas regarding masculinity which is changing these days through the viral ads which are circulated in the social media networks in Bangladesh.

This chapter aims to focus on the impact of some particular fashion adverts on Bangladeshi youths of different ages and areas. It also focuses on the aspect that whether there are new ideas or concepts regarding "masculinity" is creating through the adverts and what the impacts of these adverts are on to-day's youths by making a survey on the youths studying at different universities of Bangladesh. It seems that these adverts are breaking the prevalent concepts regarding the representation of men in media. The media of the western countries are acquainted with these types of representation of men while the Bangladeshi media has let its viewers know about this lately. This new type of representation of men and "masculinity" in the Bangladeshi media has its own impact on the youths of Bangladesh whether it is about creating a new concept or it is only about dealing with the consumer culture. However, this chapter points to highlight on the fact that to what extent the concepts of the urban Bangladeshi youths (both male and female of different ages and areas) are molded by the emergence of this type of adverts in Bangladeshi media.

It is an analytical, qualitative field research in the field of Cultural Studies. Therefore, it requires both empirical study and library research. This chapter takes the help of some specific adverts shown in the Bangladeshi media which can create some scopes to re-channel the common notions regarding masculinity in terms of tradition, trends, professional jobs, domestic chores and language. To accomplish the research, a survey is conducted among the Dhaka living youths of different ages and areas of Bangladesh who are studying at different Universities and affluent. This chapter also studies different feminist, Psychoanalytic and other theories apart from the term and use of the concept of the "distinctive new version of men" presented by Sean Nixon (1997) and "the re-gazing of masculinity" (in terms of Bangladesh) presented by Hossain and Hossain (2011).

The aim of the chapter is fourfold. The first section deals with the "Operational Definition and Theoretical Frameworks" which discusses about the different definitions regarding "masculinity" and shows the different faces of masculinity. It also investigates the background and the scenario of Bangladesh. The second section investigates the scenario of Bangladesh regarding the title of the chapter through a survey. The third section analyses the survey and confers about the impacts on both male and female youths of Bangladesh. Finally, it discusses about the scope for further research in the related areas and in conclusion it summarizes the major discussion.

BACKGROUND: "MYTHS OF MASCULINITY" AND THEIR REPRESENTATION IN MEDIA

"The Myths of Masculinity"

According to Norman Mailer (1966), "Masculinity is not something given to you, but something you gain. And you gain it by winning small battles with honor." This single sentence is not enough to define masculinity; but it simply represents the main idea that "masculinity" is not the "natural behavior of a man" rather it is the set of attitudes and behaviors that is expected to be performed by a male person in a particular social setting. Therefore masculinity does not have a universal definition rather the definition of masculinity varies from society to society.

Masculinity is not a biblical term. The ideas and notions which were pre-dominant over the years regarding masculinity are that they are a fixed set of ideas which is related to some particular aspects. The definition of masculinity is not something static. However, the noticeable aspect is that, the features of masculinity always deal with some common objects like "aggression, competitiveness, emotional ineptitude and coldness, and coldness dependent upon an overriding and exclusive emphasis on penetrative sex". Nixon (1997)

The ubiquitous myths of masculinity also focus on these points. Gary Oliver and Jim Burns (2012) presented five fundamental myths of masculinity which have been further discussed by Gary and Carrie Oliver (2012) in the book *Raising Sons and Loving It!* The myths of masculinity presented by them are:

Myth 1: *A Man's Man is Big, Brave and Strong.*
Myth 2: *A Man's Man Isn't Emotional and Doesn't Express Affection.*
Myth 3: *A Man's Man Isn't Weak and Shouldn't Cry.*
Myth 4: *A Man's Man is an Expert on Sex.*
Myth 5: *A Man's Value is Determined by What He Does and How Does and How Much He Earns.*

"Be a Man"

It has always been thought as natural that 'sex' is biologically fixed where 'gender' is culturally constructed. However, Judith Butler (2000), in her book *Gender Trouble: Feminism and the Subversive of Identity*, focuses on the point that the total process is 'culturally constructed' as the society and culture decide what the folks who hold a particular gender identity should do. Butler's argument is that whether a person is male or female that depends on her/his performance and the tasks s/he does.

When "sex" is not "biologically fixed" then a boy's/girl's features depend on the way they are being raised up. Boys are always raised up in a way where he is taught to 'be a man'. His parents teach him the ways of being a man so that he can fit in the patriarchal society. Boys are strictly taught to avoid or suppress the aspects which are thought as 'girly' by the society. Gary Oliver points out some of the advices that a boy often has to listen from his father a that girl never has to hear or learn which includes:

- "Suck it up."
- "No pain, no gain."
- "Are you a man or a mouse?"
- "Act like a man."

Another point that is presented by Judith Butler (2000) is "performativity". Butler contends that sex and gender depend on the holder's "performativity"; she adds that a baby is taught from her/his very childhood that what s/he should do. S/he follows the ways the folks of her/his gender follow and maintain. What Butler wants to convey is – sex or gender is not created by the God rather both of those are constructed by the society.

However, since the definition or characteristics of masculinity are not fixed and unitary, it has changed and re-shaped in different centuries in different ways.

Plural Masculinities

Different versions and definition of masculinities are found in different ages which have changed and re-shaped in another century consistent with that century's variables. Hossain and Hossain (2011) in their essay "From 'Nabab' to *kebab*: the re-gazing of masculinity in Bangladeshi fashion photo-discourse" point out the two major reasons behind the problematization of conceptualizing masculinity. They describe, "One, the model of patriarchy proves to be insufficient to explain masculinity and the power operation involved in it. Different socio-political variables – history, class, ethnicity, age – have had much to do with the process of conceptualizing masculinity" (p. 164)

The term "Plural Masculinities" is found in Sean Nixon's (1997, p. 297) essay "Exhibiting Masculinity". He presents the term asserting that "… masculinity is not a fixed and unitary idea". (p 301) He again borrows Jeffery Week's phrase "invented categories" (Weeks, 1991, cited by Nixon (1997), p. 301) to describe masculinity. Nixon also gives examples of different variables on which the definition and characteristics of masculinity depends in his essay "Exhibiting Masculinity". While presenting this issue Nixon introduced the readers with a term 'New Man' through his essay "Exhibiting Masculinity". Here, he explains the new representation of masculinity "as a distinctive new version of masculinity" (p. 295).

"Metrosexual Man"

The term "metrosexual man" indicates "an urban-living fashion-conscious man; a heterosexual with many attributes commonly attributed to gay men". This definition that is found in WordWeb, an online dictionary, gives an idea about "metrosexual men". Simpson (2003) used this term in his essay "Metrosexual? That rings a bell…" as "man with money and an interest in fashion and beauty who lives within easy reach of a city". Simpson (2003) says all he found about "metrosexual men" is "A dandyish narcissist in love with not only himself but also his urban lifestyle…. Mark Simpson invented this term in 1994 [in the *Independent*], but it has been picked up by numerous media outlets, including the *Observer*, the *Herald* and *Maclean's* magazine." The essay again says when Simpson continued his search, he found:

The typical metrosexual is a young man with money to spend, living in or within easy reach of a metropolis – because that's where all the best shops, clubs, gyms and hairdressers are. He might be officially gay, straight or bisexual, but this is utterly immaterial because he has clearly taken himself as his own love object and pleasure as his sexual preference. Particular professions, such as modelling, waiting tables, media, pop music and, nowadays, sport, seem to attract them but, truth be told, like male vanity products and herpes, they're pretty much everywhere (Salon.com July 22, 2002).

Simpson (2003) again discusses about the emergence of "metrosexual men":

Truth is, I was not being entirely serious when I first wrote about metrosexuality back in 1994, shortly after the publication of my book about contemporary masculine identity, 'Male Impersonators: Men Performing Masculinity'. That's to say, when I wrote about how male metrosexuality was coming out of the closet and taking over the world, I was being slightly satirical about the effect of consumerism and media proliferation, particularly glossy men's magazines, on traditional masculinity. But then, this wouldn't be the first time a satire on consumerism was appropriated by consumerism to hasten the process it sought to critique.

The Portrayal of Masculinities throughout Centuries

From the Greek mythologies to Michelangelo's paintings, the indication that masculinity can be identified with beauty has been found. While the Greeks' concept of masculinity was not very aloof from beauty, the Western concept of masculinity was also mingled with beauty as the portrayal of the knights were found "indicative of ability, nobility, and fashion as well" (Hossain and Hossain, 2011, p. 165) and the Eastern concept of masculinity was also more or less alike. As the authors say, "Even though characteristically different, a similar stylization of body was evident among the Samurais."(Hossain & Hossain, 2011, p. 165)

The first half of the twentieth century presented the "masculine and heteronormative" portrayal of men. The Hollywood films especially the western films portrayed the male prowess undercutting sexualization. The last half of the twentieth century presented men as "strong, muscled, and powerful." However, the concept of beauty associated with masculinity in later days which was around 1970 which emerged with the Calvin Klein adverts. From there, men were represented as the objects to be desired and eroticized in the mainstream culture and media. (Hossain and Hossain, 2011, p.165)

The Scenario in Bangladesh

Though Mr. Bangladesh competition began in 1973, the representations of men as eroticized or fetishized objects are not a very old idea. In Bangladeshi media, the stereotyped representation of men and masculinity was noticeable. In '60s and '70s, Hollywood and Bollywood experienced with the male bodies. Nevertheless, Bangladeshi media was not very experimental regarding the representation of men. Rather the Bangladeshi stars like Sohel Rana and Wasim presented the macho, aggressive, strong male characters while the then film icons Razzaq and Rehman presented the "good boy" image by representing the gentleness. The tv and the satellites were not very available then. Later on, another famous star Zafar Iqbal introduced a new trend where he represented the lover-boy image with a new look and style. One of the most popular stars of Bangladesh Salman Shah introduced a new style in the later days. However, actor Afzal Hossain popularized this lover-boy trend in TV media. (Hossain & Hossain, 2011, p. 166)

Nevertheless, the media always skipped the erotic representation of the male bodies unless a new trend in advertisement media emerged after the advent of the satellite channels. While the use of beauty products was only an aspect regarding women, after the advent of the satellite channels the awareness of health and beauty increased and even in Bangladesh, male audiences were the targets and the beauty products of men emerged. "Good looking" and "Well-built" Bangladeshi models like Nobel were presented in the Bangladeshi media who introduced a new trend.

These representations of men and masculinity do not necessarily contradict the conventional portrayal and representation of men and masculinity but obviously these brought a new style. Later on the fashion houses took this advent of satellite as a blessing and started 'mainstreamizing' a new trend as Hossain says – "The fashion and grooming industry took the lead and soon made it a phenomenon: self-aware metrosexual men craving for approving look." (Hossain & Hossain, 2011, p. 166)

While the Western media was letting its viewers be acquainted with the representation of the "distinctive new version of masculinity", the Bangladeshi media was not very progressive regarding this issue. However, Bangladeshi media has let its viewers know about this trend lately. Sean Nixon in his essay "Exhibiting Masculinity" presents three important looks which were produced across the "new man" images. Hossain and Hossain (2011) identified four 'new' visual codes of masculinity found in recent Bangladeshi fashion adverts in their essay "From 'Nabab' to *kebab*: the re-gazing of masculinity in Bangladeshi fashion photo-discourse", which are – "the Charming Lad Style, the Free-Spirit Youth Style, the Cool Dude Style, and the Hot Hunk Style."

According to the authors, 'the Charming Lad Style' is "a *deshi* and relatively less erotic form of visual code of masculinity." As the name suggests, a charming, gentle, good looking male model wearing semi-formal dresses; in most cases, traditional dresses like fotuas or Punjabis are being presented in the adverts in this code. The gesture and the posture of the model give the ideas of his mildness which is "playful, yet responsible" and goes with the 'feminine' characteristics.

The authors divide the second code "Free-Spirit Youth Style" into two types as the "Frolic" and the "Attitude". The 'Frolic' models are shown wearing colorful shirts and T-shirts which show their care-free attitude whereas the "Attitude" models are presented in dark shaded dresses and they are direct and somewhat aggressive. At the same time, using dark glasses adds a mysterious aspect while these models are presenting in between the play of black and white light and shadow.

The authors next present the "Cool Dude Style" while an "equally elegant and exciting, desirable and attainable" model is presented. His gesture and posture invoke eroticism and clearly depict his self-confidence. The attire of the "Cool Dude" are well organized which is shown somewhat unbuttoned and the well-shaped body of the model is presented thus.

The last code identified by the authors is "Hot Guy Style" which shows the totally different version of masculinity and the authors found "In this code of style, the concept of masculinity is problematized." The model is topless in most cases that shows his muscular, gym-shaped lean body and these aspects invoke the viewers. He is presented as the "'passive' object of desire" which role was used to be played by the female models in the early days.

In this light, this research aims to study and analysis the impact of these fashion adverts on the youths of different ages and areas of Bangladesh. A survey has been conducted based on these four codes of masculinity prevalent in Bangladeshi fashion adverts and their impact on the youths of Bangladesh to identify this aspect.

The Methodology of the Survey

The chapter adopts the process of field research. To execute the field research, the primary data has been collected through a survey on the basis of a structured questionnaire on some students of different Universities of Bangladesh. The questionnaire has been formulated consisting with the psychological rules and regulation. Structured questionnaire has been the way of conducting the survey as unstructured questionnaire cannot fulfill the purpose of exploring the fact that how and to what extent the perspective and gazes of urban Bangladeshi youths are being molded by these adverts. To analyze the questionnaire, MS Excel has been used.

DATA COLLECTION AND ANALYSIS

Data Collection Procedure

A survey has been conducted to find out the impacts of the fashion adverts on the youths. For conducting the survey a questionnaire has been sent with 15 questions. The questionnaire was sent at different universities of Bangladesh, mainly Jahangirnagar University, University of Dhaka, North South University, East West University and others Universities. The respondents are both male and female, students and are between 19 to 24 years. The respondents are also Dhaka living and enough well-off to have the ideas regarding global and Bangladeshi fashion and new trends.

Response Rate

320 questionnaires were sent at different universities of Bangladesh. 168 questionnaires were collected. Among 168, 12 questionnaires were unusable because of incomplete and improper information. Therefore, 156 responses have been used to analyze the data. So, the respondent rate is 49%. 78 respondents are male and 78 respondents are female.

Data Analysis

The questions are based not only on the television adverts which are shown on Bangladeshi television channels but also on the adverts or photos published on the internet, such as Facebook fashion fan pages in order promote the products. The questions focus on some particular adverts where the four codes of masculinity are dominant and these four codes are identified by Hossain and Hossain (2011) in their essay "From 'Nabab' to *kebab*: the re-gazing of masculinity in Bangladeshi fashion photo-discourse". The first photo was taken from Le Reve's Facebook fan page which portrays the "Charming Lad Style". The second photo was taken from Asif Azim's Facebook Fan Page which portray the "Free-spirit Youth Style". The forth and the last photos were taken from Artisti's Facebook fan page. The fourth and last photo was taken from Artisti's Facebook fan page which go with the "Cool Dude Style" and the "Hot Guy Style". The analysis of the collected data has been presented in Table 1.

FINDINGS AND DISCUSSION

Consumer Culture

The representations of beautiful female models were very common in the media of Bangladesh which was very similar to the global trends.

The aspect which sprinkles a new spice on this old issue is that while the viewers of the Bangladeshi media found some new sorts of adverts shown in the TV through the advent of the satellite. This was an advert of Lux, one of the leading soaps produced by one of the most famous companies throughout India, Bangladesh and other countries, Unilever Limited. After almost 50 female stars of India, Hindustan Unilever Ltd. Chooses a male star Shahrukh Khan as the model of their product Lux. This advert obviously presented a different sort of representation of men; and later Indian male film stars recurrently came in the media with different types of beauty products like Shahrukh Khan had demonstrated while advertising 'Imami Fair and Handsome', John Abraham in publicizing 'Garnier men face wash', Shahid Kapoor in the adverts of 'Vaseline men face-wash' and Virat Kohli in the adverts of 'Fair and Lovely Max Fairness cream'. With these representations of male stars as the models of beauty products the audiences gradually become acquainted with the new concept regarding masculinity. However, Bangladeshi media influenced by these satellite cultures came up with the adverts of beauty products done by

Table 1. The result of the survey

Questions		Yes		No		Sometimes		Never	
		M	F	M	F	M	F	M	F
Q1. Influence of stars to use the beauty products.		11%	23%	63%	23%	15%	54%	11%	0%
Q 2. Identification with the model (consumer's psychology)		11%	9%	26%	27%	56%	55%	7%	9%
Q 3. Finding out the model with whom the respondent can identify. (See the figure from appendix)	1.	17%	28%						
	2.	9%	0%						
	3.	17%	29%						
	4.	0%	14%						
	No one	57%	29%						
Q 6. Finding out the model attractive/ desirable.	1.	36%	24%						
	2.	4%	0%						
	3.	39%	47%						
	4.	7%	5%						
	No one	14%	24%						
Q 7. Keeping the adverts while shopping		7%	21%	31%	16%	58%	58%	4%	5%
Q 9. Respondent's opinion whether these adverts contradict the conventional portrayal.		27%	39%	42%	28%	31%	33%	0%	0%
Q 10. Finding out whether any of the model is 'odd'.		46%	45%	19%	14%	27%	41%	8%	0%
Q 13. Investigating of getting any hint of homosexuality through this adverts.		18%	14%	61%	59%	17%	23%	4%	4%
Q 14. Finding out the most 'proactive' model.	1.	0%	0%						
	2.	17%	0%						
	3.	8%	12%						
	4.	75%	88%						

*F = Female and M = Male.

the male models like Nobel, Moin. The satellite culture's effect is again found when the commercial of 'Fair and Lovely Menz Active' was shown in the different channels of Bangladesh where Tamim Iqbal, a famous Bangladeshi cricketer has been shown to use the beauty product.

From the analysis of the first question, an interesting fact has been found. Not a single girl says "never" to the first question and that indicates that, no one of the girls accept that they are never motivated to use the beauty products when they see any stars to use those while 11% of the boys say "never".

The majority of the respondents say "no" and among them, the number of the boys is greater than the number of the girl respondents. By analyzing the answers of this question, one fact becomes clear that, in countries like Bangladesh, the beauty products for male are yet to expand their market and customers while the market of the beauty products for female has already created its space.

The male beauty products present the 'importance' of using 'Emami Fair and Handsome' – a complexion enhancing beauty product through its commercials by identifying the technical aspects. Most of the commercials show or the products are launched with the dialogues that, men have to spend much more times in sun and as they have tougher skin than women they need something extra. These factors have been emphasized by showing the presence of the experts, scientists or doctors and pointing to the UV rays and other issues like tension, stress etc. (This advertisement technique is called "testimonial". According to 'Advertisement Techniques', when "a famous personality is used to endorse the product – *e.g. a famous basketball player (Michael Jordan) recommends a particular brand of skates*" then it is called testimonial). In this continuation, when 'Fair and Lovely Menz Active' was launched in Bangladesh, the need of using the beauty products among the males has been come to the limelight. Therefore, 11% of the boys are found to say "yes" and that was not a very common scenario even before a decade. Girls were very used to know about the beauty products and if 23% of the girl respondents say that they are motivated to use the products when they see any stars using those, it is not something very shocking rather seems quite natural. Like this issue, boys would say "no" to this answer or frown reading this question seemed quite ok before some years or like a decade. Nevertheless, 11% of the boys' acceptance show that the scenario is changing these days.

36% of the total respondents say "sometimes" where 15% of the boys say "sometimes" and 54% of the girls say "sometimes". This data can be given an interesting reading. Some of the boy respondents were not very willing to mark the "yes" option. There was a denial to the fact that, "yes, I am a boy and I use beauty products." So, those who are thinking that most of the boys say "no" and that means there is no presence of "metrosexual men" in Bangladesh, are wrong. The number of the beauty salons, spa salons and beauty products for men are the evidence of the emergence of "metrosexual men" in Bangladesh even some other important aspects are kept away from counting. It is quite unquestionable that, the commercials of the products are successful in making their market accepting the strategy of showing some stars or reliable sources to create the 'need' among the male consumers.

Consumers' Psychology

Sean Nixon in his essay "Exhibiting Masculinity" focuses on three concepts of psychoanalysis which help to conceptualize the relationship between the "new man" images and the consumers of these images. The three concepts identified by Nixon are identification, scopophilia and narcissism. To explore and understand the relation between the fashion adverts of Bangladesh and its consumers, this chapter tries to focus on the concepts presented by Nixon. In Nixon's language

Identification is the central of the three concepts and carries precise meanings in Freud's writing. In his essay 'Group Psychology and the analysis of the ego' (Freud, 1977/1921), for example, he explicitly distinguishes between two kinds of relationship which individuals enter into with the external world of objects around them. On the one hand, he says, there is a relationship with the object which involves the focusing of libidinal investments (the sexual drives) upon, usually, another person. On the other hand, there is identification which involves some projection based on a similarity between the individual and an external person and, from that, the moulding of the ego after that person. Freud summarizes this distinction between two kinds of desire: a desire to have the other person (which he calls object cathexis) and a desire to be the other person (identification) (p.135) (Nixon, 316, 317).

The second question of the survey is based on one of these two terms that is "identification" identified by Freud. This question tries to find out how these fashion adverts work on the psychology of the consumers or the youths of Bangladesh.

The interesting fact which has been found from this survey is that the percentage of the boys who say "never" is comparatively low than those who say "no". When this aspect was almost thought as ridiculous that guys would go for shopping, let alone for themselves; it has been quite acceptable these days that, guys will go for shopping. Hossain (2011) discusses about this issue in the chapter "Guys Going Shopping" in his essay "*Ecstasic Dance! Artistic Bang!!*: Economics of Metrosexual Masculinity in Bangladeshi haute couter Visual Discourse". Here he shows that guys go for shopping has become a very common phenomenon in Bangladesh in recent days. Hossain here discusses about "metrosexual men" and this survey also presents a clear evidence that in Bangladesh "metrosexual men" have emerged and that is why most of the boy respondents say that "sometimes" they can identify themselves with the models of these fashion adverts and that provoke them to buy such clothes which are presented in these adverts.

From the analysis of the answers of the respondents, one thing is clear that, most of the boy respondents are influenced by these fashion adverts. Consciously or subconsciously these images affect them. This can be also read as the strategy of the advertisement that, advertisements create "needs" and then consumers feel that they have to fulfill them.

Now, if the answers of the girl respondents are analyzed then another interesting aspect can be found and that is almost all the girls think alike the boys. However, 27% of the girls say that they cannot relate these images of the models with the persons they are shopping for while 55% of them say "sometimes" and 9% of them say "yes".

This is an important aspect in the context of Bangladesh as girls go for shopping for the male members of the family or their counterparts are quite natural in Bangladesh. These adverts attracts "female gaze" where guys are the objects to be looked at and girls are the subjects which counters Laura Mulvey's discussion regarding "male gaze". Hossain discusses in detail regarding this issue in the above mentioned essay in the part called "female gaze".

The important aspect is that when the respondents are given four images of the models where "new visual codes of masculinity" are represented, 57% of the boys say they find none of the models with whom they can identify themselves where almost half of this number that is 29% of the girls say "no one". In this case of boys, they are giving contradictory answers. While answering the second question, they say "sometimes", they are highlighting "no one" among the five options. Another aspect is that, there is a sheer denial of the fact that they are influenced by these adverts. There is a sort of dilemma working in their minds which keep aloof them highlighting the answer they want. Some kinds of fear is working in their thoughts which can be something like that – if he says that he is influenced by these adverts that can put his 'manliness' in danger.

Another evidence of this aspect is that, none of the boys go for the fourth image where the model is topless, though 14% of the girls say they can identify with the person they are shopping for with this model. This can be explained in the light of the explanation given by Hossain (2011). The model is showing his beefcake, but his topless body reminds the girls that showing/ presenting body is not a very 'masculine' job.

Metrosexual masculinity negotiates between the masculine – just being a man – and feminine – 'feminized' because subject to the gaze – aspects of masculinity. Thus, the eroticism of men displayed triggers female voyeurism pleasure while the guy's so-called feminization helps women disavow the pleasure.

This simultaneous operation of contradictory but complementary impulses renders these men attractive and acceptable, leaving women buyers evoked and convinced at once (p. 46).

Again, none of the girls goes for the second image of the model that represents the "Free-spirit Youth Style" where 9% of the boys go with this 'macho'/ 'yo' types of look. Girls are yet to be ready to find these kinds of looks in their male counterparts where somehow boys think that they go with this 'yo' type of look and these types of looks makes them more macho by removing the boyish looks which undercuts the charming/ feminine aspects.

The fourth question of the survey needs explanation from the respondents. Some very interesting answers have come from the respondents. Most of the boys' say that the fashion houses often fail to produce clothes they want to buy/ wear. Thus, the adverts cannot fulfill their 'needs'. They want something different. Many of the boy respondents think that, if they follow the trends then they cannot show their uniqueness and following the trends started by the fashion houses make them look like a bunch of school-boys wearing uniforms.

Many of the boys say that, they buy products if the quality is good. They do not even notice the models of the adverts rather than go for the quality. To them, models of the fashion adverts are merely the "productions of the consumer media" to sell their products.

Following the trends is not always very welcome to many of the boys of today. Some think that, they do not look alike the models and therefore there is no need to buy/ wear the clothes they wear to promote the fashion houses.

The girl respondents' ideas are not very different from the boys in this manner. The noticeable aspect is that, most of the girls who said "no" to the second question say that they do not go shopping for boys. So, they really do not need to watch these adverts or know which trends among the boys are going on these days.

Some of the girls say that they do not want their counterparts to look like these models. So, they do not want to go for any of the models. Accept these answers; all the answers of them are very much alike with the answers of the boys. Most of them think that, these models and even the trends are created by the consumer media or the fashion houses, to create the 'needs' just to sell their products.

The next question they have been asked is if they do not watch the fashion adverts then whom do they think are the target audiences of these adverts. Most of the respondents say that, those who are very trendy or like to follow the fashion watch and follow the fashion adverts. Some of them say that, the people who want themselves or their counterparts or family members to look like the models watch these adverts and are the main consumers of these fashion houses.

Though the survey is conducted among some people of a very specific class who can afford these clothes and seem to have knowledge regarding fashion and trends; many of the respondents say that, they are not the target audiences of these adverts. Rather, they think that, "rich", and "fashionable" people are the target customers of these fashion houses and these adverts of the models.

An interesting fact which is found from the survey is that, many of the respondents say that, teenagers or young people are the target audiences of the fashion industry as they can easily be motivated by the adverts. Another thing the respondents say that, teen people usually have a common issue that is keeping pace with the recent trends. Although, the respondents of this survey are among 19 to 24, they think themselves someone not shallow and thus they do not just want to go with the trend. They think themselves "unique" and thus follow their own "style".

Some of the respondents say that the target audiences of these fashion adverts are the "superficial" people. In this case, the previous discussion is also applicable. Another group of respondents answers that, people who seek external beauty or try to enhance their beauty all the time are the target of these adverts. These groups of youths think they do not "seek for external beauty" and thus these adverts are not for them and they do not pay attention to these fashion adverts. They also think that, "seeking for beauty" or paying attention to these beauty enhancing products are so "un-masculine" or "feminine" that it can hamper their "masculine" identity if they go for these issues.

Few of the respondents think that, these adverts are targeted to the "gays" as only the "girly, effeminate "homos' want to take care about their skins and think again and again before buying clothes. Straight guys don't have that much time to watch the adverts, think and then go shopping clothes." This group of youths thinks that, in Bangladesh queer or homosexuality is being mainstreamed through these adverts and they are the intended audiences. The fashion industry creates the 'needs' for the products by making the audiences realize that the products are useful in order to make them beautiful and the adverts play the most important role in this regard. This aspect can be explained in the light of Hossain's (2011) discussion. In his essay, "Ecstatic Dance! Artistic Bang!!: economics of metrosexual masculinity in Bangladeshi haute coutre visual discourse" (2011) he discusses how the consumerist culture is mainstreaming the "queer consumption" to fulfill their purpose of expanding market and making business –

Who is the intended audience of this images? – straight men? gay men? women? for Straight guys, these metrosexuals provide techniques of self through which to inhabit masculine subject-positions. For gay guys, it is more: these images offer scopophilic pleasure and corresponding subjectivization. Businesses are alert in identifying the consumer behavior of gay men. Traditionally, gay guys are (thought to be) devoted to grooming, to look good and feel confident, which do bring about change in their life-styles. Many of them frequent gyms to gain chiseled biceps, triceps, chests, abs, and asses. And they spend a lot in this kind of grooming. ... This buying power of gay men must have impacted upon the nature of adverts for male beauty products (p. 45).

The sixth question is a very technical question which has the purpose to find out if the boy respondents get the point that they are asked to answer if any of the/ some of the/ all of the models seem attractive/ desirable to them. The question of the survey just wants to explore how the adverts affect the consumers (youths) of Bangladesh and how the psychoanalysis of "object cathexis" (Nixon, 1997, p. 317) helps to "conceptualize" the relationship between the models of these fashion adverts and the consumers.

Freud's idea regarding this psychoanalysis is found in Nixon's essay where he discusses that Freud says "there is a relationship with the object which involves the focusing of libidinal investments (the sexual drives) upon, usually, another person". Freud also identifies a desire other than "identification" which is "object cathexis" to understand the relationship between these images of the adverts and the spectators. By "object cathexis", Freud indicates "a desire to *have* the other person."

However, very few of the respondents say that 'no one' of the models is attractive/ desirable. The total number of the respondents who goes for "no one" option is 21%. The striking matter is that 24% of the girls find "no one" of the models is attractive/ desirable whereas 14% of the boy respondents find "no one" of the models attractive/ desirable. This analysis indicates that only 14% of the boys do not find any of the models either attractive or desire and the rest of the boys find any of the / some of the models attractive/ desirable.

Well, the boys of Bangladesh have started finding male models attractive/ desirable. That is certainly a remarkable aspect. This analysis indicates that, with the emergence of "metrosexual men", in Bangladesh, the mainstreamization of homosexuality and queer is also in the process.

The seventh question of the survey is intended to find out if the youths of Bangladesh keep these adverts in their minds. Most of the respondents say they "sometimes" keep these adverts in their minds while shopping. This again indicates the effect of "metrosexual men" when the majority of them that is 58% say "sometimes" and 7% of them say "yes". These adverts affect girls when they go shopping for the boys. The rest of the respondents' answers can be analyzed in the light of the analysis of the fifth question.

In answering the eighth question, most of the respondents answer that, these fashion adverts are the "traps" for the consumers and the motives of the adverts are to trap them in their strategies. These adverts are to attract those who are very beauty conscious. Those who think they are the "real man", do not go for these adverts or trends. Thus they think these adverts as only the tactic of selling their products by creating 'needs' among the consumers. While wearing attires are thought as totally 'girly', these days, guys are seen wearing those very often. Even, it is not like that they are thought as 'homos', rather buying and wearing accessories have become a very usual aspect. Hossain says about this issue in his essay, "*E*cstatic *D*ance! Artistic *B*ang!!: economics of metrosexual masculinity in Bangladeshi haute coutre visual discourse"(2011) – "Men these days are aware of and fussy about the clothes, the accessories, the hair style, the skin, and the body." (p. 44)

The ninth question of the survey tries to hear about from the respondents whether in any way these fashion adverts contradict the conventional portrayal of masculinity or their ideas regarding masculinity. The most interesting fact which has been found from the analysis of the answers of this question is, 0% that means none of the respondents says "never".

The majority of the respondents vote for "no" and "sometimes" among the four options. This is a clear indication that the ideas regarding masculinity have been changed even in countries like Bangladesh. People, especially the youths are very much acquainted with these representations of masculinity. They have started thinking that men can be beauty conscious and there is nothing very shocking in this aspect.

Again, in this respect, girls' ideas do not match with the answers of the boys'. 28% of the girls say that, these adverts do not contradict their ideas regarding masculinity which is lesser than the percentage of the boys. 33% of the girls say "sometimes".

However, 27% of the boys say that these adverts contradict their ideas their ideas regarding masculinity while 39% of the girls say "yes". This indicates that, girls are not yet very ready to take this representation of masculinity easily like the boys. 'Boys going parlor' is not a very welcomed scene to them yet.

The next question of the survey is asked to the respondents to find out if they find any of the models odd. Girls are a bit ahead in this manner from the boy respondents. None of the girls say "never" where 8% of the boys say "never". 27% of the boys say "somehow" where 41% of the girls say "somehow".

Again, 46% of the boys say "yes" and 45% of the girls say "yes". When, in the next question, they are asked why they are thinking so, some very interesting facts have come out.

Many of the respondents think that, these adverts are nothing to be bothered but these make themselves to think that why the fashion industry is showing their models like these adverts which in no way goes with the Bangladeshi tradition. They think that, these adverts and the products are only produced to keep pace with the foreign culture. This is just their strategy to advertise and sell their products. A respondent answered that, "I have never seen any normal regular guy wearing these accept the models".

Many of them say that the fourth model looks a bit odd because he is "half-naked". They say that, it is very unusual in countries like Bangladesh that, models would go so far like showing their bodies.

Someone find it "vulgar" and "meaningless". Some of them was very surprised and said, "if the guy would promote a shoe, then would he be totally undressed and wore only a pair of shoes?"

However, the respondents were also asked to explain if they find the models usual. Most of them say that, these representations are very usual to them. They are very used to watch these sorts of adverts and models. They also think the ideas of Bangladesh are changing and have already been changed a lot. People are ready to accept the changes.

Rest of the respondents says that, "the models are not real" which means the models are not representing the real picture of masculinity or even real portrayal of themselves. They are doing it because they are told to promote the products and it's just the strategy to expand the men's market.

The next question they are asked to answer if they think these adverts are showing any hint of homosexuality. Very few of them say "never" which indicates they are not very sure regarding this aspect.

Most of them say "no" and some say "sometimes" while a very few of them say "yes". An interesting fact is noticed while conducting the survey that is the respondents are not very ready to say "yes" even if they feel it. Some of them even said that, "why would I let everyone know that homosexuality is not something unknown to us anymore. This issue should not be exposed publicly." From this remark, one thing have become clear that, the people of Bangladesh are not taking this issue like some other frequent issues. However, there are also some, to whom this is a very usual aspect.

Almost all the respondents say that they find the fourth image of the model very provocative when they say "yes" to the question that these images provoke homosexuality. The "half-naked" model seems to be threatening to 75% of the boys and 88% of the girls also go for this image of the model. 8% of the boys and 12% of the girls think the third image of the model provoke homosexuality. His clean-shaved chest and the posture seem provocative to them. 17% of the boys think, "homos" have the characteristics like girls and like girls they will find the extreme-masculine "goon" looking model of the second image "seducing" while none of the girls think alike and 0% of them go for this image. No one of the respondents think the "Charming lad" of the first image can be a threat or provoke homosexuality. They think that this model of the image himself looks like a "sissy" and thus he cannot be a threat.

The respondents have given some very contradictory explanations. A respondent says that, "These commercials are intended to attract boys. The models are represented in a provocative way." Some other respondents think that, homosexuality is an internal psychological aspect. These adverts do not have any hint of homosexuality but if the watchers want to find out that, they can find it. Some think that, in countries like Bangladesh, provoking commercials cannot be shown in the media.

The aspects which have been found from the analysis of the answers found after conducting the survey among the youths can be explained in the way, the concepts and ideas of the youths of Bangladesh are changing. They are being globalized. They have the knowledge regarding today's world. But, the age old traditions and conventions of Bangladesh need time to be changed. Another point is that, whatever the fashion industry is doing, it is something more than changing the concepts. Even if they are trying to change the concepts of the people, it is one of their strategies to expand their market. Hossain says about this issue in the sub-chapter "Men Market" in his essay, *Ecstatic Dance! Artistic Bang!!: economics of metrosexual masculinity in Bangladeshi haute coutre visual discourse*" (2011) –

Four aspects that I identified as crucial to understand metrosexuality cater to consumerism. Thus, a man requires updating his wardrobe and follow fashion seasons (e.g. Pahela Baishakh or winter); he feels like piling accessories and jewelry to suit different events; he needs to try a range of skin and hair care products to leave his skin lively and get his shoulder dust-free; he has to visit gyms or practice yoga so that he looks fit. Further boosted by fashion magazines like Canvas and beauty contests like "YGTL", men's grooming now has a huge market: there are many men's salons like Persona Adams and Face-wash; the super-shops boast of special for men's body care products ranging from School foot-care to 'Max' fairness cream; there are numerous shops that sell only men's accessories; and there's gym in almost every para in Dhaka. The well-proportioned male bodies- attainable but tough to gain- have also encouraged the use of steroids and cosmetic surgery, thus ensuring quick success and approbation. So the re-fashioning of men that is often seen as a way of queering masculinity can, from another point of view, be seen as a postmodernist ploy for consumption. Adverts have a 'legitimate' goal, that is, to create desire for what you don't need or never thought of. The metrosexual men in the fashion ads boost the men market (p. 45).

However, provocation can be a good way of advertising a product. It can be a good strategy to sell the products and expanding market. Provocation can be embedded in the adverts when some important features can be embedded in adverts successfully. Richard Vezina and Olivia Paul (1997) mention that the good combination of distinctiveness, ambiguity and the transgression of norms and taboos can be used as a provocation for the consumers. They mentioned that a large number of the same types of advertisement bore the consumers and audiences. Therefore, distinctiveness is necessary. Very often a clear message of the ad represents the commercial purpose to the consumers as well as the audiences. And thus, ambiguity or a tiny and well indicating scope for thinking can enhance the appeal of the adverts. Though distinctiveness is required, transgression of norms and taboos should be considered carefully. Society as well as his members have not always stood alone ready to take the big change violating the social norms. A small level of change has been accepted by the society at the every time of the history of human civilization. And the role of advertising has been investigated in this case also. Pollay (1986) mentioned that Standards of public decency have changed much in the twentieth century, and adverting has been one of the elements contributing to changed norms (p. 28).

The use of sexual appeal in the advertising can be considered as an example of transgression of norms and taboos. Sexuality is considered as taboos at different degree throughout the world. But the fact is sexual content of advertisements increase the amount of attention and interest garnered by the ads (Bello et al., 1983). Severn et al (1990) mentioned that sexual content has an impact on the purchase intention despite the controversy surrounding these appeals. Although Richard Vezina and Olivia Paul (1997) suggests on the consistency of the adverts content and product, the fact is transgression of norms is taking place in society through advertising. Therefore the opinions of the respondents that have been explored by the survey to undertake this research are not negligible.

Another point is that, Trends of Viral adverts are increasing in Bangladesh. Viral adverts indicate the adverts those are shareable by the users of social networks like facebook, youtube, twitter, orkut and other. Researchers mention that (e.g., Jinsong, Huang, Song Su et al., (2013)) the contents of the viral adverts are working as a prime motivator to share with the user. Contents are attractive to the user when these comply with different components like ambiguity, distinctiveness, transgression of norms and taboos and others (Richard Vezina., Olivia Paul., 1997).

Therefore, the increasing amounts of viral adverts in Bangladeshi cyber space indicate the interests and willingness of the users to give the scope and accept the change of culture in this digital era.

SCOPE FOR FURTHER STUDIES

This chapter explores the area of future research related to the emergence of "metrosexual men" in Bangladesh, how "metrosexual Men" emerges in Bangladesh through the fashion adverts and the commercials of beauty products help them to emerge or the emergence of them gave birth to such adverts can be given a reading in future. The ramp fashion can also be given a reading under the light of cultural studies.

CONCLUSION

Bangladeshi fashion adverts have changed radically in the recent few years. The aim of the chapter was to highlight on the fact that to what extent the concepts of the urban Bangladeshi youths are molded by the emergence of the representation of "distinctive new type of men" in the adverts in Bangladeshi media. After conducting the survey, one thing has become clear that, the representation of masculinity has gone through a huge modification in these few years. Somehow, the ideas regarding the identity of 'being masculine' or 'masculinity' are getting re-shaped and people are making their minds to accept the changes of culture in this digital era.

REFERENCES

Advertising Techniques. (n.d.). Retrieved March 1, 2013, Retrieved April 8, 2013 from http://www.foothilltech.org/rgeib/english/media_literacy/advertising_techniques.htm

Artisti Collection's Photos. (2011). Retrieved March 14, 2013 from http://www.facebook.com/photo.php?fbid=10150121738826259$set=pu.45324601258$type=1&theater%3Eweb

Artisti Collection's Photos. (2012). Retrieved February 4, 2013, from http://www.facebook.com/photo.php?fbid=10151141313996259&set=pb.45324601258.-2207520000.1364583379&type=3&theater

Bangladesh, Tumbir. (2012a). Retrieved March 16, 2013, from http://fyeahbangladesh.tumblr.com/post/4620112214/asif-azim

Bangladesh, Tumbir. (2012b). Retrieved March 16, 2013, from http://fuckyeahethnicmen.tumblr.com/post/4283724312/asif-azim-is-a-top-ramp-model-of-bangladesh-and

Bello, D. C., Pitts, R. E., & Etze, M. J. (1983). The Communication Effects on Controversial Sexual Content in Television Programs and Commercials. *Journal of Advertising*, *12*(3), 32–42. doi:10.1080/00913367.1983.10672846

Bordo, S. (2006). Beauty (Re) Discovers the Male Body. In R. K. Miller (Ed.), *Motives for Writing*. New York: McGraw-Hill.

Brace, I. (2004). *Questionnaire Design: How to Plan, Structure and Write Survey Material for Effective Market Research*. London: Kogan Page Ltd.

Butler, J. (1990). *Gender Trouble: Feminism and the Subversion of Identity*. Taylor and Francis Group.

Butler, J. (2000). Subjects of Sex/Gender/Desire. In S. During (Ed.), *The Cultural Studies Reader* (2nd ed.; pp. 340–353). New York: Routledge.

Carlo, M. M. (2009). Advertising time expansion, compression, and cognitive processing influences on consumer acceptance of message and brand. *Journal of Business Research, 62*(4), 420–431. doi:10.1016/j.jbusres.2008.01.019

Clare, A. (1998). *A Semiotic Analysis of Magazine Ads for Men's Fragrances.* Prifysgol Aberystwyth University. Retrieved March 5 2013, from http://www.aber.ac.uk/media/Students/awc9401.html

Connell, R. W. (2006).Understanding Men: Gender Sociology and the New International Research on Masculinities. In *The Sage Handbook of Gender and Education*. London: Sage Publication.

During, S. (1999). *The Cultural Studies Reader* (2nd ed.). New York: Routledge.

Gill, R. (2009, Dec.). *Rethinking Masculinity: Men and Their Bodies.* Seminar, The London School of Economics and Political Science. Retrieved February 20, 2013 from, http://fathom.lse.ac.uk/Seminars/21701720/21701720_session2.html

Hickey, A. M. (2001). Understanding Men: Gender Sociology and the New International Research on Masculinities. *Social Thought & Research, 24*(12), 33–35.

Hooks, B. (2004, July). *Understanding Patriarchy.* Louisville Anarchist Federation.

Hossain, M. S. (2011). Ecstatic Dance! Artistic Bang!!: Economics of metrosexual masculinity in Bangladeshi haute coutre visual discourse. *Nrivijnana Patrika, 16,* 1–16.

Hossain, M. S. and Hossain, T.T. (2011). From Nabab to Kebab: the re-gazing of masculinity in Bangladeshi haute couture visual discourse. *Harvest, 26.*

Huang, J., Su, S., Zhou, L., & Liu, X. (2013). Attitude Toward the Viral Ad: Expanding Traditional Advertising Models to Interactive Advertising. *Journal of Interactive Marketing, 27*(1), 36–46. doi:10.1016/j.intmar.2012.06.001

Le Reve wear your dream's photos. (2012). Retrieved March 15, 2013 from http://www.facebook.com/photo.php?fbid=414238065301562&set=pb.134736613251710.-2207520000.1364582065&type=3&theater

Le Reve wear your dream's photos. (2013). Retrieved March 20 2013, from http://www.facebook.com/photo.php?fbid=513198755405492&set=pb.134736613251710.-2207520000.1364581878&type=3&src=http%3A%2F%2Fsphotos-c.ak.fbcdn.net%2Fhphotos-ak-prn1%2F28170_513198755405492_1277405004_n.jpg&size=533%2C800

Mailer, N. (1966). *Cannibals and Christians.* New York: Dial Press.

Metcalf, A., & Humphries, M. (1985). *Sexuality of Men.* London: Pluto Press.

Mulvey, L. (2004). Visual Pleasure and Narrative Cinema. In L. Braudy & M. Cohen (Eds.), *Film Theory and Criticism.* Oxford, UK: Oxford U P.

Nixon, S. (1997). *Exhibiting Masculinity. Cultural Representation and Signifying Practices. Stuart Hall* (pp. 291–336). London: Sage Publication.

Orth, U. R., & Denisa, H. (2004). Men's and women's responses to sex role portrayals in advertisements. *International Journal of Research in Marketing, 21*(1), 77–88. doi:10.1016/j.ijresmar.2003.05.003

Paul, O., & Vezina, R. (1997). Provocation in Advertising: A conceptualization and assessment. *International Journal of Research in Marketing, 14*(2), 177–192. doi:10.1016/S0167-8116(97)00002-5

Pollay, R. W. (1986). The Distorted Mirror: Reflections on the Unintended Consequences of Advertising. *Journal of Marketing, 50*(2), 18–36. doi:10.2307/1251597

Puranik, A. (2012). *Meaning, Definition, Objective and Functions of Advertising.* Retrieved March 8, 2013, from http://www.publishyourarticles.org/knowledge-hub/business-studies/advertising.html

Re-channeling the myth of masculinity: the emergence of androgyny in the Bangladesh media. (n.d.). Retrieved on 22 February, From http://www.lawyersnjurists.com/articles-reports-journals/others-articles-reports-journals/re-channeling-myth-masculinity-emergence-androgyny-bangladeshi-media/

Rose, G. (2001). *Visual Methodologies.* London: Sage Publication.

Severn, J., Belch, G. E., & Belch, M. A. (1990). The Effects of Sexual and Nonsexual Advertising Appeals and Information Level on Cognitive Processing and Communication Effectiveness. *Journal of Advertising, 19*(1), 14–22. doi:10.1080/00913367.1990.10673176

Simpson, M. (2003). *Metrosexual? That rings a bell...* Retrieved from http://www.marksimpson.com/pages/journalism/metrosexual_ios.html

Vezina, R., & Paul, O. (1997). Provocation in Advertising: A Conceptualization and an Empirical Assessment. *International Journal of Research in Marketing, 14*(2), 177–192. doi:10.1016/S0167-8116(97)00002-5

Woodruffe-Burton, H. (1998). Private desires, public display: Consumption, postmodernism and fashion's "new man". *International Journal of Retail & Distribution Management, 26*(8), 301–310. doi:10.1108/09590559810231760

Yin, R. K. (1984). *Case Study Research: Design and Methods.* Beverly Hill, CA: Sage Publication.

Your life your rules . (2011). Retrieved February 22, 2013, from http://www.youtube.com/watch?v=egseZdgVo0k

KEY TERMS AND DEFINITIONS

Consumer Culture: A cultural phenomenon where buyers of particular products focus more on the recent trends in purchasing products rather than focusing on the monetary or aesthetic values.

Cultural Impact: The impacts on the people of the adverts which represent the "new version of men".

Cultural Studies: A study of the culture to find out the variables and different aspects, changes, incidents etc.

Masculinity: Not a unitary or God created term, rather a term which depends on different variables (performance, age, society etc) and has different faces.

Metrosexuality: Typical males living in urban areas who spend significant amounts of time shopping and grooming themselves; often attributed with homosexual orientations.

Myths of Masculinity: The myths regarding masculinity which makes a person a "man".

Plural Masculinity: The idea of pluralizing male-selves depending on social and cultural roles.

Viral Ads: Advertisements which are spread through the internet or social networking sites like facebook, twitter etc.

APPENDIX: QUESTIONNAIRE

Your basic information:

Institution: Position: Student

Age: Gender:

Please "Mark" or "Highlight" the appropriate answer with "√". (You can choose multiple answer, but please avoid contradictory answers.)

1. Are you motivated to use the beauty products when you see any stars to use those?
   a. Yes
   b. No
   c. Sometimes
   d. Never
2. How do you feel when you see the adverts? Can you identify/relate yourself (for boys) / the person you are shopping for with any of the models of the photos (for girls) (See Box 1)?
   a. Yes
   b. No
   c. Sometimes
   d. Never
3. If the answer is "yes", then mention with which model you can identify yourself (for boys) / the person you are shopping for girls)?
   a. 1
   b. 2
   c. 3
   d. 4
   e. No one
4. If the answer is "no", then explain briefly?

   _____

5. If the answer is "no" then whom do you think are the target audiences of these adverts?

   _____

6. Which of the models is more attractive/ desirable?
   a. 1
   b. 2
   c. 3
   d. 4
   e. No one
7. Do you keep thes adverts on your mind when you go for shopping?
   a. Yes
   b. No
   c. Sometimes
   d. Never

Box 1.

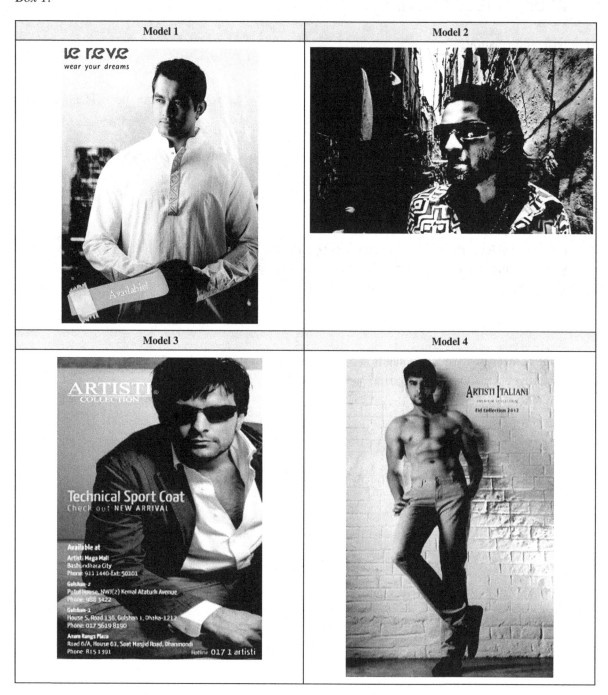

8. If the answer is "no" then what do you think about the motives of these adverts?

    _____

9. Do you think these adverts contradict the conventional portrayal of masculinity/ your ideas regarding masculinity?
    a. Yes
    b. No
    c. Somehow
    d. Never
10. Do you think any of the models 'odd'?
    a. Yes
    b. No
    c. Somehow
    d. Never
11. If the answer is "yes", explain briefly.

    _____

12. If the answer is "no" explain briefly.

    _____

13. Do you think these adverts show any hint of homosexuality?
    a. Yes
    b. No
    c. Somehow
    d. Never
14. If the answer is "yes" then which one(s) do you think is/are the most provocative? Explain briefly.
    a. 1
    b. 2
    c. 3
    d. 4

    _____

15. If the answer is "no", explain briefly.

    _____

The survey ends here! Thank you for your participation.

Chapter 12
The Roles of Age, Gender, and Ethnicity in Cyberbullying

Michelle F. Wright
Masaryk University, Czech Republic

ABSTRACT

Children and adolescents have become active users of electronic technologies, with many of them blogging, watching videos, and chatting via instant messenger and social networking sites. Many of these activities have become a typical part of their lives. Electronic technologies have brought many conveniences to the lives of children and adolescents. Along with the opportunities associated with these technologies, children and adolescents are also susceptible to risks, including cyberbullying. Therefore, many researchers have become concerned with identifying which factors might predict children's and adolescents' involvement in these behaviors. Some predictors that researchers have focused on include age, gender, and ethnicity, but the findings were mixed. This chapter draws on research to review studies on the relationship of age, gender, and ethnicity to children's and adolescents' cyberbullying involvement and concludes with solutions and recommendations as well as future directions for research focused on these predictors and cyberbullying.

INTRODUCTION

Millions of children and adolescents utilize electronic technologies everyday (e.g., cell phones, the internet) (Madden, Lenhart, Duggan, Cortesi, & Gasser, 2013). Such technologies offer many conveniences, including the opportunity to communicate with friends and family, the ability to research and access information for personal and educational use, watch videos, and play online games. Although electronic technology use offers children and adolescents many benefits, there are some notable risks, including exposure to unwanted electronic content through video, images, and text, identify theft, sexual predators, and internet addiction. Cyberbullying is another risk associated with children's and adolescents' electronic technology use.

Cyberbullying has gained increased attention among researchers, educators, parents, and the general public. Defined as an extension of traditional bullying, cyberbullying involves bullying behaviors

DOI: 10.4018/978-1-5225-0212-8.ch012

using electronic technologies, like instant messenger, social networking websites, email, and text messages (Grigg, 2010, 2012; Nocentini et al., 2010). Because cyberspace offers the opportunity to remain anonymous, those engaged in cyberbullying are able to harm their victims without experiencing the consequences associated with their actions (Wright, 2014b).

Researchers have proposed that the online disinhibition effect is also present in the cyber context (Moore, Nakano, Enomoto, & Suda, 2012; Suler, 2004; Wright, 2014a). This effect leads many children and adolescents to say and/or do things through electronic technologies that they would never do or say in the offline world. Cyberbullying can also involve more bystanders than traditional school bullying in the offline world. In particular, posting a video online can receive thousands of watches and be shared amongst other people over and over again. Researchers have recognized the importance of focusing their attention on cyberbullying, and many of them have investigated the predictors associated with children's and adolescents' involvement in these behaviors. Three predictors: age, gender, and ethnicity, have proven to be inconsistent predictors of cyberbullying involvement (Barlett & Coyne, 2014; Fredrick, 2010; O'Neil & Dinh, 2013; Pornari & Wood, 2010; Shapka & Law, 2013; Wright & Li, 2013b).

This chapter draws on research from a variety of disciplines, including psychology, education, sociology, communication, computer science, and media studies in order to describe the roles of age, gender, and ethnicity in cyberbullying among children and adolescents from elementary, middle, and high schools. This chapter is divided into seven sections:

1. Description of cyberbullying including the definitions, technologies used, the role of anonymity, and prevalence rates of cyberbullying,
2. Discussion of the role of age in children's and adolescents' cyberbullying involvement,
3. Explanation of the research related to the role of gender in children's and adolescents' cyberbullying involvement,
4. Summary of the studies examining cyberbullying among children and adolescents of different ethnicities,
5. **Solutions and Recommendations:** A discussion of the strategies that can be used to prevent cyberbullying among children and adolescents,
6. **Future Research Directions:** A description of various recommendations to further research on the role of age, gender, and ethnicity in children's and adolescents' cyberbullying involvement, and
7. Final remarks about the current state of cyberbullying literature and how age, gender, and ethnicity impact children's and adolescents' involvement in these behaviors.

The studies reviewed in this chapter utilize a variety of research designs, including cross-sectional, longitudinal, qualitative, and quantitative.

WHAT IS CYBERBULLYING?

In the literature, cyberbullying is defined as utilizing electronic technologies (e.g., email, text messages via mobile phones, social networking websites) to intentionally harass, embarrass, and intimidate others (Arslan, Savaser, Hallett, & Balci, 2012; Ferdon & Hertz, 2007; Joinson, 1998; Kowalski & Limber, 2007; Mouttapa, Valente, Gallagher, Rohrbach, & Unger, 2004; Slonje & Smith, 2008; Topcu, Erdur-Baker, & Aydin, 2008; Ybarra, West, & Leaf, 2007). Cyberbullying behaviors might include sending unkind, harassing, or humiliating text messages and emails, social exclusion, stealing someone's identity information, pretending to be someone else (e.g., impersonation), making anonymous, insulting, and harassing phone calls, sharing a victim's secret without permission by posting or sending it to someone else, spreading nasty and untrue rumors about someone using social networking websites or other sources, threatening to harm someone physically, and the creation of defamatory websites (Chisholm, 2006; Rideout, Roberts, & Foerhr, 2005; Wright & Li, 2012; Ybarra & Mitchell, 2004). Another form of cyberbullying is happy slapping (Gillepsi, 2006; Smith, Mahdavid, Carvalho, Fisher, Russell, & Tippett, 2008). Happy slapping involves filming a group of people who randomly insult another person and then post the images or videos online. Flaming is another type of cyberbullying behavior, and it involves posting provocative, offensive, or hostile messages in a public forum with the desire to trigger an angry response or an argument from members of the forum. Similar to the definitional components of traditional school bullying, cyberbullying behaviors are those that are repetitive in nature and include an imbalance of power between the bully and the victim. Repetition can include cyberbullying acts that involve harassing the victim multiple times on various platforms or sharing humiliating videos of the victim (Vandebosch & Van Cleemput, 2008). For example, a humiliating video of someone can be shared multiple times by different people in cyberspace, which perpetuates the cyber of victimization.

Many of the earlier investigations of cyberbullying focused on the frequency rates of children's and adolescents' involvement in these behaviors. A few studies have found high prevalence rates. For instance, Wolak and colleagues (2007) found that 50% of American children and adolescents in their sample reported to being victimized by cyberbullying. In another study, utilizing an older sample of Hawaiian adolescents (grades 9-12th), Goebert and colleagues (2011) found that 56.1% of these adolescents experienced cyber victimization. Some slightly lower rates of cyberbullying have been found as well. For instance, Patchin and Hinduja (2006) found that 29% of children and adolescents in their sample were victims of cyberbullying, with 47% in this sample reporting that they had witnessed these behaviors. Similarly, Kowalski and Limber (2007) found that 11% of adolescents in their sample had been cyberbullies, 4% had bullied other adolescents, and 7% were involved in cyberbullying as both the victim and the bully. In another study, Hinduja and Patchin (2012) also found lower levels of cyberbullying, similar to Kowalski and Limber. In their sample, 4.9% of children and adolescents perpetrated cyberbullying in the past 30 days. Differences in these prevalence rates reflect variations in sampling techniques, definitions of cyberbullying, and measurement techniques. Despite these differences, it is clear that cyberbullying occurs among children and adolescents, and that additional investigations should be conducted to better understand the predictors of their involvement in these behaviors.

One frequently examined predictor of cyberbullying involvement is children's and adolescents' involvement in traditional school bullying. Among these studies, researchers have consistently found associations between cyberbullying and traditional school bullying, cyber victimization and traditional school bullying victimization, and traditional school bullying victimization and cyberbullying (Barlett & Gentile, 2012; Cappadocia, Craig, & Pepler, 2013; Corcoran, Connolly, & O'Moore, 2012; Fanti, Demetriou, & Hawa, 2012; Heirman & Walrave, 2012; Mitchell, Ybarra, & Finkelhor, 2007; Steffgen, Konig, Pfetsch, & Melzer, 2011). Children's and adolescents' electronic technology usage is also another predictor of cyberbullying perpetration and victimization. In this literature, researchers have found that higher levels of internet usage were related to cyberbullying involvement among children and adolescents (Aricak, Siyahhan, Uzunhasanoglu, Saribeyoglu, Ciplak, Yilmaz, & Memmedov, 2008; Ybarra & Mitchell, 2004). Other research has focused on comparing the risk of cyberbullying victimization based on victimization status. Findings revealed that cybervictims reported higher levels of instant messaging, email, blogging sites, and online gaming usage when compared to non-victims (Smith et al., 2008; Ybarra & Mitchell, 2004). One explanation for the positive relationships between electronic technology usage and cyberbullying involvement is the disclosure of personal information. Children and adolescents who disclose more personal information online are at a greater risk for experiencing cyber victimization (Ybarra et al., 2007).

Other risk factors associated with children's and adolescents' involvement in cyberbullying are internalizing (e.g., depression, anxiety, loneliness) and externalizing (e.g., delinquency, alcohol use) difficulties. Researchers argued that internalizing difficulties inhibit children's and adolescents' ability to cope with negative experiences, making them more vulnerable to cyberbullying involvement (Cappadocia et al., 2013; Mitchell et al., 2007; Ybarra & Mitchell, 2004). Additional variables linked to children's and adolescents' cyberbullying perpetration and cyber victimization include higher normative beliefs regarding bullying (i.e., believing that bullying is acceptable), diminished pro-victim attitudes (i.e., believing that bullying is unacceptable and that one must defend victims), lower levels of peer attachment, less self-control, less empathy, and greater moral disengagement (Ang, Tan, & Manser, 2010; Burton, Florell, & Ygant, 2013; Elledge, Williford, Boulton, DePaolis, Little, & Salmivalli, 2013; Lazuras, Barkoukis, Ourda, & Tsorbatzoudis, 2013; Robson & Witenberg, 2013; Steffgen et al., 2011; Wright, Kamble, Lei, Li, Aoyama, & Shruti, 2015; Wright & Li, 2013a).

Parenting is another important predictor of cyberbullying involvement. Children and adolescents who report that their parents utilized indifferent-uninvolved parenting styles as well as inconsistent monitoring of their children's online activities had children with a greater risk of being involved in cyberbullying as either the bullies or victims (Aoyama, Utsumi, & Hasegawa, 2011; Duncan, 2004; Totura, MacKinnon-Lewis, Gesten, Gadd, Divine, Dunham, & Kamboukos, 2009). Neglectful parenting styles increase children's and adolescents' susceptibility to cyberbullying involvement when compared to those children and adolescents who report uninvolved parenting styles (Dehue, Bolman, Vollink, & Pouwelse, 2012). Another extreme form of parenting is linked to the involvement in cyberbullying among children and adolescents. In particular, children and adolescents who were from families who were overprotective or utilized authoritarian parenting styles had a greater likelihood of experiencing cyber victimization (Mesch, 2009; Navarro, Serna, Martinez, & Ruiz-Oliva, 2013). Such families do not allow their children to develop autonomy, become more assertive, or practice social skills which makes it likely that they have poor interactions with their peers, putting them at risk for victimization by cyberbullying. A lack of parental monitoring of online activities and lower emotional bonds with caregivers increases children's and adolescents' cyberbullying involvement. Parental mediation is also linked to these behaviors. In this literature, parents often overestimate the amount of monitoring they engaged in concerning their children's online activities (Mason, 2008). Wright (2015a) also found that cybervictims experienced more cyberbullying when their parents engaged in lower levels of parental monitoring and these adolescents also had greater levels of depression and anxiety. Thus, parental mediation might mitigate the psychosocial adjustment difficulties associated with children's and adolescents' involvement in cyberbullying. Children and adolescents who believe that their parents will punish them for negative online behaviors are less likely to engage in cyberbullying (Hinduja & Patchin, 2013). When parents are unconcerned with appropriate online behaviors and do not implement effective mediational practices for technology usage, they are likely to have children who engage in more negative behaviors in the cyber context, like cyberbullying. Parents must be willing to discuss appropriate technology practices, set rules for technology consumption, and to stay current on modern technological trends in order to reduce their children's exposure to cyberbullying.

Schools and peers also have a role in children's and adolescents' involvement in cyberbullying. The role of schools in cyberbullying has been hotly debated as many cases of cyberbullying occur off school property. Because of this, it is difficult for schools to become aware of these situations, particularly given victims' reluctance to report cyber victimization (Mason, 2008). The involvement of schools is further complicated because there is a lack of consensus concerning schools' implementation of consequences regarding cyberbullying, especially when the schools' code of conduct does not include specific language addressing these behaviors (deLara, 2012). Despite the complicated nature of the relationship between schools and cyberbullying, it is clear that incidences of these behaviors typically involve children and adolescents who attend the same school. Because the perpetrator and victim might attend the same school, the cyberbullying incidence could spread from the cyber context to the school environment, potentially leading to these two individuals and others engaging in negative interactions on school grounds. Such events have potential to disrupt the learning process. Despite the possible "spill over" effect onto school grounds, administrators' and teachers' perceptions and awareness of cyberbullying vary, with some not perceiving these behaviors as problematic or particularly serious when compare to physical forms of bullying (Kochenderfer-Ladd & Pelletier, 2008; Sahin, 2010). This is probably because cyberbullying is considered an indirect form of bullying, like relational bullying, and many educators do not understand the harmful consequences associated with these forms of bullying.

In order for schools to "tackle" cyberbullying, teachers must be current on new technologies. However, Cassidy and colleagues (2012a) found that many Canadian teachers were not familiar with newer forms of technologies, making it difficult for them recognize and deal effectively with cyberbullying. Because of their unfamiliarity with these technologies, they were unsure of how to respond to cyberbullying or what strategies to utilize in an effort to alleviate the incident. When teachers were concerned with their students' involvement in cyberbullying, many found it difficult to implement solutions and strategies to reduce these behaviors due to few policies and programs developed at the school level (Cassidy, Brown, & Jackson, 2012b). Tangen and Campbell (2010) found that teachers were more likely to encourage prevention programs designed to eliminate or reduce students' involvement in traditional school bullying rather than cyberbullying. Such a finding might suggest that cyberbullying is not a serious concern warranting their attention. However, it is extremely important for schools to understand the importance of implementing policies regarding cyberbullying as such behaviors have a profound impact on the learning environment (Shariff & Hoff, 2007). Furthermore, educators should also receive training on how to effectively deal with students' involvement in cyberbullying. A lack of policies might leave children and adolescents to be fearful of their classmates as they might be concerned about their peers acting as cyberbullies. This fearfulness can make it difficult for them to concentrate, impacting their ability to learn and reducing their academic attainment and school functioning (Eden, Heiman, & Olenik-Shemesh, 2013; Wright, in press). Negative school climate and lower school commitment make children and adolescents feel less connected to their school, increasing their perpetration of cyberbullying. Receiving additional training improves teachers' confidence in their teaching abilities and their commitment to their school (Eden et al., 2013). Such changes might increase the likelihood that teachers will learn about cyberbullying, which engenders a greater awareness of these behaviors and confidence when dealing with cyberbullying. This greater confidence relates to teachers being more likely to intervene in cyberbullying incidences, protecting children and adolescents from victimization by these behaviors (Elledge et al., 2013).

Another strategy helpful for reducing cyberbullying is when teachers are motivated to learn about these behaviors, either through self-study or professional development. In elementary school, teachers are motivated to learn about cyberbullying, but this motivation diminishes among teachers in middle school. This is especially problematic as cyberbullying involvement typically increases during these school years (Ybarra et al., 2007). More training should be offered for middle school teachers in order to increase their awareness of cyberbullying.

Providing socialization about acceptable and unacceptable behaviors, peers represent an important developmental context for children and adolescents. Consequently, these social norms dictate the type of behaviors that they engage in, even if the behaviors are considered negative. In one study, Festl and colleagues (2013) found that adolescents' risk of cyberbullying involvement increased when they were from classrooms with high rates of cyberbullying perpetration and victimization. They argued that the climate of the classrooms served to promote and encourage cyberbullying behaviors. Similarly, children and adolescents who believed that their friends perpetrated cyberbullying were more likely to also engage in these behaviors (Hinduja & Patchin, 2013). Peer attachment also relates to children's and adolescent's involvement in cyberbullying. Lower levels of peer attachment predicted both cyberbullying perpetration and cyber victimization (Burton et al., 2013). In addition, research by Sevcikova et al. (2015) and Wright and Li (2013b) suggests that peer rejection increases the relationship between adolescents' cyber victimization and cyberbullying perpetration. Wright and Li (2012) proposed that peer rejection is a negative experience, which triggers negative emotions and in order to alleviate such emotions adolescents engage in cyberbullying. Other research has also focused on cyberbullying as a behavior which can promote or boost children's and adolescents' social status among their peers. In this research, Wright (2014c) found that higher levels of perceived popularity, a reputational form of popularity in the peer group, which is typically associated with school bullying perpetration, was related to adolescents' engagement in cyberbullying. Wright (2015b) proposed that electronic technologies might be used as tools to promote and maintain adolescents' social standing.

Most of the previously reviewed studies utilized concurrent research designs, making it difficult to understand the longitudinal associations of various risk factors to cyberbullying involvement. In one of the few studies to investigate these behaviors utilizing a longitudinal design, Fanti and colleagues (2012) examined children's and adolescents' exposure to violent media, their callous and unemotional traits, and their cyberbullying involvement one year later. Their findings revealed that media violence exposure was linked to subsequent cyber victimization. In addition, perceived stress from parents, peers, and academics increased adolescents' cyberbullying perpetration one year later (Wright, 2014a).

As described in this section, there are a variety of risk factors which make children and adolescents vulnerable to cyberbullying involvement. Researchers are beginning to move beyond individual predictors of cyberbullying involvement to the role of parents in children's and adolescents' perpetration and victimization by these behaviors. The previously reviewed literature suggests that there are a variety of consistent predictors of cyberbullying perpetration and cyber victimization. Research has also focused on variables (i.e., age, gender, ethnicity) which are not consistent predictors of children's and adolescents' involvement in these behaviors. Therefore, the next sections of the chapter will review studies on age, gender, and ethnicity as they relate to cyberbullying involvement in an order to highlight the inconsistent findings regarding these variables.

AGE AND CYBERBULLYING

Age was proposed as a potential predictor of cyberbullying due to differences in children's and adolescents' involvement in traditional forms of bullying. In this literature, younger children, particularly those in elementary school, are more likely to engage in greater levels of physical aggression when compared to adolescents (Coyne, Nelson, & Underwood, 2010). As children develop better verbal skills, they began to utilize more verbal forms of aggression. Furthermore, as children begin to interact with their peers more, they form more peer relationships, leading to increases in relational aggression and indirect aggression. These forms of aggression increase more from childhood to adolescence as peer relationship become a major focus among adolescents and they develop better abilities to understand social situations. Sometimes cyberbullying is conceptualized as an indirect form of bullying (Barlett & Coyne, 2014). Therefore, researchers suggest that cyberbullying involvement might increase in adolescence, similar to the increases in relational and indirect forms of aggression from childhood into adolescence. This proposal is even more complicated as electronic technology usage relates to cyberbullying involvement, and therefore children are susceptible to perpetrating and/or being victimized by these behaviors as soon as they begin to utilize these technologies (Arslan et al., 2012; Mouttapa et al., 2004; Olweus, 1999). Children are beginning to use technologies at an earlier age, with some researchers identifying cyberbullying among children as young as nine years old (O'Neill & Dinh, 2013).

Although research on the longitudinal examinations of cyberbullying involvement are increasing, there are few studies which examine age-related differences to determine the risk associated with perpetrating and/or experiencing these behaviors. In this literature, early adolescence engage in and are victimized by higher levels of cyberbullying when compared to younger children and late adolescence (Sevcikova & Smahel, 2009). Another study focused on hacking, with findings revealing that this behavior increased during middle school (grades 6th through 8th) but later declined in high school (Williams & Guerra, 2007). On the other hand, age is not always a consistent predictor of cyberbullying involvement. In one study, Wade and Beran (2011) found the highest levels of cyberbullying perpetration and cyber victimization among 9th graders in high school in comparison to adolescents in middle school.

There are some possible explanations as to why there might be conflicting findings regarding age differences in children's and adolescents' cyberbullying perpetration and cyber victimization. One possibility might be that many of the previous studies do not take into account electronic technology saturation or the amount of time and number of technologies utilized by their participants. Consequently, this research might reflect electronic technology increases among an age group instead. Another possibility is that many of these studies do not consider potential gender and age interactions, which could also clarify inconsistent findings. The next section reviews the literature on gender as a factor, which impacts cyberbullying involvement.

GENDER AS A PREDICTOR OF CYBERBULLYING INVOLVEMENT

Like the focus on age, gender has been examined as another factor which might predict cyberbullying involvement. However, studies focusing on gender have found more conflicting findings than those concerning age. Gender receives particular attention when it comes to cyberbullying because the literature suggests that boys have more technological skills when compared to girls, and such skills are associated with the involvement in these behaviors. In the literature on gender differences in cyberbullying, some researchers (e.g., Boulton et al., 2012; Li, 2007; Ybarra et al., 2007) have found that boys were more often engaged in cyberbullying as the aggressor when compared to girls. On the other hand, other researchers (e.g., Adams, 2010; Hinduja & Patchin, 2007; Kowalski & Limber, 2007) have suggested that the perpetrators of cyberbullying were more often girls whereas boys were most likely to report cyber victimization (e.g., Akbulut, Sahih, & Eristi, 2010; Dehue, Bolman, & Vollink, 2008; Erdur-Baker, 2010; Huang & Chou, 2010; Pornari & Wood, 2010). Other research has found no gender differences in cyberbullying involvement (e.g., Beran & Li, 2005; Didden, Scholte, Korzilius, de Moore, Vermeulen, O'Reilly, Lang, & Lancioni, 2009; Fredrick, 2010; Marcum, Higgins, Freiburger, & Ricketts, 2012; Wright & Li, 2013b).

Some studies have focused on gender differences in cyberbullying involvement based on the types of electronic technologies. In particular, Dehue and colleagues (2008) found that boys were more likely to engage in cyberbullying through online games, while girls were most often cyberbullies through MSN messenger. Their findings also suggested that girls were also more often victimized through MSN messenger. Other research has revealed that girls were more likely to be victimized through mobile devices (Gorzing & Frumkin, 2013; Ortega et al., 2009). Contrary to these findings, Raskauskas (2010) found no gender differences in victimization via text messages.

Similar to the research on the electronic technologies used to harm others, some researchers have investigated gender differences in the type of behaviors involved in cyberbullying. Popovic-Citic and colleagues' (2011) findings suggested that boys were more likely to engage in and experience cyber harassment, denigration, and outing (i.e., the act of revealing something about another person without this person's permission). Furthermore, girls were more likely to engage in cyberbullying using gossiping and ignoring behaviors and they also experienced more victimization by these behaviors as well (Dehue et al., 2008). Less attention has been given to whether electronic technology and behavior might interact when considering gender differences in cyberbullying involvement. In one of the few studies to investigate this topic, Wright (in press) found that boys engaged in and were victimized more by verbal aggression via online games, while girls perpetrated and were victimized more by relational and verbal aggression through social networking sites. Therefore, research on gender differences in cyberbullying involvement should move beyond mean level comparisons and focus instead on how electronic technologies and behaviors interact to explain variations in rates of these behaviors.

ETHNICITY AS A PREDICTOR OF CYBERBULLYING INVOLVEMENT

Although some attention has been given to age and gender as predictors of cyberbullying, little attention has focused on ethnicity differences. Among this sparse literature, there are also conflicting findings, similar to the research on age and gender. Shapka and Law (2013) found that East Asian Canadian adolescents engaged in less cyberbullying when compared to Canadian adolescents of European decent. In addition, East Asian Canadian adolescents perpetrated greater levels of proactive cyberbullying (i.e., goal-directed behavior), while Canadian adolescents of European decent engaged in more reactive cyberbullying (i.e., response to provocation). To explain these findings, Shapka and Law proposed that adolescents from East Asia are socialized by their parents to have collectivistic values. Therefore, they value social harmony, making them less likely to engage in direct forms of bullying. However, their culture includes large power distances, which increase corruption and coercion, leading these adolescents to engage in more proactive forms of bullying. It is important to note that Shapka and Law did not assess adolescents' cultural values, and consequently they provided generalizations about the type of values they might endorse based on their country of origin.

In research conducted in the United States, Low and Espelage (2013) investigated differences in cyberbullying perpetration among African American and Caucasian European American adolescents over a six month period. Ethnic differences were found for cyberbullying perpetration at Wave 1, but not at Wave 2, with these results suggesting that African American adolescents engaged in more of these behaviors when compared to Caucasian adolescents. Other research in the United States has focused on Caucasian, Filipino, Samoan, and Native Hawaiian adolescents' differences in cyber victimization. These findings indicated that Native Hawaiians reported lower levels of cyber victimization when compared to the three other groups. Like studies on age and gender differences in cyberbullying involvement, Hinduja and Patchin (2008) did not find any ethnicity differences in their study conducted among adolescents in the United States. Heirman et al. (2015) also found no ethnicity differences among adolescents in their study conducted in the Netherlands. More attention needs to be given to understanding ethnicity differences related to cyberbullying. Some of the previously reviewed literature did not explain why differences were found. Like research on cross-cultural differences in cyberbullying, research on ethnicity differences should take into account cultural values as well as socioeconomic status in order to better understand the nature of the differences found in these behaviors.

SOLUTIONS AND RECOMMENDATIONS

Cyberbullying is a concern among all members of our community. Attention should be given to educational curriculum, particularly to designing this curriculum to focus on teaching children and adolescents about the positive uses of electronic technology, empathy, self-esteem, social skills, cyberbullying, digital literacy skills, and citizenship (Cassidy et al., 2012b). Schools should also focus on improving school climate (Hinduja & Patchin, 2012). They can do this by developing and adopting a code of conduct which addresses technology usage, learning students' names, recognizing and praising good behavior, and staying current on electronic technologies. When schools implement a code of conduct, it is important that administrators and teachers enforce these policies.

Parents also serve an important role in helping to reduce cyberbullying. For instance, parents need to join forces with their children's school and to increase their awareness and knowledge of electronic technologies and cyberbullying (Cassidy et al., 2012a; Diamanduros & Downs, 2011). Knowledge about electronic technologies will help them understand the range of their children's cyber behaviors as well as the potential risks and opportunities associated with their children's usage of these technologies. Having more knowledge of electronic technologies can make it easier for parents to develop and implement parental monitoring strategies, which reduces their children's risk of experiencing or perpetrating cyberbullying. Furthermore, this knowledge can also help parents to engage in open communication with their children about the risks and opportunities related to electronic technologies. Guidelines for children regarding the amount of time that they should spend online and how their children should behave online are also important techniques for reducing their children's risk of cyberbullying involvement. In addition, parents also need to be mindful of their electronic-related behaviors as well in order to serve as role models for their children.

Communities also have an impact on children's and adolescents' involvement in cyberbullying. In our communities, many of us take on the role of bystanders, not noticing someone in need and how to help this person. We might not do anything, leaving the intervening to someone else, who also do not end up helping. We should help others in order to serve as role models for appropriate behaviors. Children and adolescents can learn through our example. As a society, we need to recognize that cyberbullying undermines our values and as a result we need to understand that this behavior impacts everyone. Thus, we all must be united when it comes to tackling this threat.

FUTURE RESEARCH DIRECTIONS

After the review of the age-related differences in cyberbullying, it is clear that little attention has been given to the developmental trajectory of children's and adolescents' involvement in these behaviors. Therefore, studies should be conducted with longitudinal designs, especially accelerated longitudinal designs, to better understand age differences associated with cyberbullying. Because of the lack of research on younger age groups, specifically those in elementary school, and studies conducted across transitions from elementary to middle school and from middle school to high school, it is not clear whether certain variables are stronger predictors of these behaviors. In addition, longitudinal designs can also help to explain the developmental trajectory of traditional school bullying and cyberbullying. Additional research attention should be given to understanding gender differences in cyberbullying by taking into account different behaviors and technologies. The literature reviewed in the gender section revealed that some studies have found complex differences in regards to different cyberbullying behaviors as well as technologies. However, little attention has been given to the interactions among gender, behaviors, and technologies. Like research findings on gender and age, research exploring ethnicity differences in cyberbullying are also mixed. More attention should be given to exploring ethnicity-related differences and predictors of cyberbullying involvement as well as those designed to investigate cultural values and socioeconomic status as potential confounding variables.

CONCLUSION

Based on the review of the literature, it is clear that there are a variety of predictors of cyberbullying, with some predictors being more consistently related to children's and adolescent's involvement in these behaviors. Research on age, gender, and ethnicity has yielded incredibly mixed results, making it difficult to identify the meaningfulness of these particular predictors. It is imperative that additional research be conducted on these variables in an effort to fully understand the risks associated with children's and adolescents' involvement in cyberbullying.

REFERENCES

Adams, C. (2010). Cyberbullying: How to make it stop. *Instructor*, *120*(2), 44–49.

Akbulut, Y., Sahin, T. L., & Eristi, B. (2010). Cyberbullying victimization among Turkish online social utility members. *Journal of Educational Technology & Society*, *13*, 192–201.

Ang, R. P., Kit-Aun, T., & Mansor, A. T. (2010). Normative beliefs about aggression as a mediator of narcissistic exploitativeness and cyberbullying. *Journal of Interpersonal Violence*, *26*(13), 2619–2634. doi:10.1177/0886260510388286 PMID:21156699

Aoyama, I., Utsumi, S., & Hasegawa, M. (2011). Cyberbullying in Japan: Cases, government reports, adolescent relational aggression and parental monitoring roles. In Q. Li, D. Cross, & P. K. Smith (Eds.), *Bullying in the global playground: Research from an international perspective*. Oxford, UK: Wiley-Blackwell.

Aricak, T., Siyahhan, S., Uzunhasanoglu, A., Saribeyoglu, S., Ciplak, S., Yilmaz, N., & Memmedov, C. (2008). Cyberbullying among Turkish adolescents. *Cyberpsychology & Behavior*, *11*(3), 253–261. doi:10.1089/cpb.2007.0016 PMID:18537493

Arslan, S., Savaser, S., Hallett, V., & Balci, S. (2012). Cyberbullying among primary school students in Turkey: Self-reported prevalence and associations with home and school life. *Cyberpsychology, Behavior, and Social Networking*, *15*(10), 527–533. doi:10.1089/cyber.2012.0207 PMID:23002988

Barlett, C., & Coyne, S. M. (2014). A meta-analysis of sex differences in cyber-bullying behavior: The moderating role of age. *Aggressive Behavior*, *40*(5), 474–488. doi:10.1002/ab.21555 PMID:25098968

Barlett, C. P., & Gentile, D. A. (2012). Long-term psychological predictors of cyber-bullying in late adolescence. *Psychology of Popular Media Culture*, *2*, 123–135. doi:10.1037/a0028113

Beran, T., & Li, Q. (2005). Cyber-harassment: A new method for an old behavior. *Journal of Educational Computing Research*, *32*(3), 265–277. doi:10.2190/8YQM-B04H-PG4D-BLLH

Boulton, M., Lloyd, J., Down, J., & Marx, H. (2012). Predicting undergraduates' self-reported engagement in traditional and cyberbullying from attitudes. *Cyberpsychology, Behavior, and Social Networking*, *15*(3), 141–147. doi:10.1089/cyber.2011.0369 PMID:22304402

Burton, K. A., Florell, D., & Wygant, D. B. (2013). The role of peer attachment and normative beliefs about aggression on traditional bullying and cyberbullying. *Psychology in the Schools*, *50*(2), 103–114. doi:10.1002/pits.21663

Cappadocia, M. C., Craig, W. M., & Pepler, D. (2013). Cyberbullying: Prevalence, stability and risk factors during adolescence. *Canadian Journal of School Psychology*, *28*, 171–192.

Cassidy, W., Brown, K., & Jackson, M. (2012a). "Making kind cool": Parents' suggestions for preventing cyber bullying and fostering cyber kindness. *Journal of Educational Computing Research*, *46*(4), 415–436. doi:10.2190/EC.46.4.f

Cassidy, W., Brown, K., & Jackson, M. (2012b). "Under the radar": Educators and cyberbullying in schools. *School Psychology International*, *33*(5), 520–532. doi:10.1177/0143034312445245

Chisholm, J. F. (2006). Cyberspace violence against girls and adolescent females. *Annals of the New York Academy of Sciences*, *1087*(1), 74–89. doi:10.1196/annals.1385.022 PMID:17189499

Corcoran, L., Connolly, I., & O'Moore, M. (2012). Cyberbullying in Irish schools: An investigation of personality and self-concept. *The Irish Journal of Psychology*, *33*(4), 153–165. doi:10.1080/0303391 0.2012.677995

Coyne, S. M., Nelson, D., A., & Underwood, M. K. (2010). Aggression in childhood. In P. K. Smith & C. H. Hart (Eds.), *The Wiley-Blackwell handbook of childhood social development* (pp. 491-509). Chichester, UK: Wiley-Blackwell.

Dehue, F., Bolman, C., & Vollink, T. (2008). Cyberbullying: Youngsters' experiences and parental perception. *CyberPscyhology & Behavior*, *11*(2), 217–223. doi:10.1089/cpb.2007.0008 PMID:18422417

Dehue, F., Bolman, C., Vollink, T., & Pouwelse, M. (2012). Cyberbullying and traditional bullying in relation to adolescents' perceptions of parenting. *Journal of Cyber Therapy and Rehabilitation*, *5*, 25–34.

deLara, E. W. (2012). Why adolescents don't disclose incidents of bullying and harassment. *Journal of School Violence*, *11*(4), 288–305. doi:10.1080/15388220.2012.705931

Diamanduros, T., & Downs, E. (2011). Creating a safe school environment: How to prevent cyberbullying at your school. *Library Media Connection*, *30*(2), 36–38.

Didden, R., Scholte, R. H. J., Korzilius, H., de Moor, J. M. H., Vermeulen, A., & O'Reilly, M. et al. (2009). Cyberbullying among students with intellectual and developmental disability in special education settings. *Developmental Neurorehabilitation*, *12*(3), 146–151. doi:10.1080/17518420902971356 PMID:19466622

Duncan, D. R. (2004). The impact of family relationships on school bullies and victims. In D. L. Espelage & S. M. Swearer (Eds.), *Bullying in American schools* (pp. 277-244). London: Lawrence Erlbaum Associates.

Eden, S., Heiman, T., & Olenik-Shemesh, D. (2013). Teachers' perceptions, beliefs and concerns about cyberbullying. *British Journal of Educational Technology*, *44*(6), 1036–1052. doi:10.1111/j.1467-8535.2012.01363.x

Elledge, L. C., Williford, A., Boulton, A. J., DePaolis, K. J., Little, T. D., & Salmivalli, C. (2013). Individual and contextual predictors of cyberbullying: The influence of children's provictim attitudes and teachers' ability to intervene. *Journal of Youth and Adolescence*, *42*(5), 698–710. doi:10.1007/s10964-013-9920-x PMID:23371005

Erdur-Baker, O. (2010). Cyberbullying and its correlation to traditional bullying, gender and frequent and risky usage of internet-mediated communication tools. *New Media & Society*, *12*(1), 109–125. doi:10.1177/1461444809341260

Fanti, K. A., Demetriou, A. G., & Hawa, V. V. (2012). A longitudinal study of cyberbullying: Examining risk and protective factors. *European Journal of Developmental Psychology*, *8*(2), 168–181. doi:10.1080/17405629.2011.643169

Ferdon, C. D., & Hertz, M. F. (2007). Electronic media, violence, and adolescents. An emerging public health problem. *The Journal of Adolescent Health*, *41*(6), 1–5. doi:10.1016/j.jadohealth.2007.08.020 PMID:17577527

Festl, R., Schwarkow, M., & Quandt, T. (2013). Peer influence, internet use and cyberbullying: A comparison of different context effects among German adolescents. *Journal of Children and Media*, *7*(4), 446–462. doi:10.1080/17482798.2013.781514

Fredrick, K. (2010). Mean girls (and boys): Cyberbullying and what can be done about it. *School Library Media Activities Monthly*, *25*(8), 44–45.

Gillespie, A. A. (2006). Cyber-bullying and harassment of teenagers: The legal response. *Journal of Social Welfare and Family Law, 28*(2), 123–136. doi:10.1080/09649060600973772

Goebert, D., Else, I., Matsu, C., Chung-Do, J., & Chang, J. Y. (2011). The impact of cyberbullying on substance use and mental health in a multiethnic sample. *Maternal and Child Health Journal, 15*(8), 1282–1286. doi:10.1007/s10995-010-0672-x PMID:20824318

Gorzig, A., & Frumkin, L. A. (2013). Cyberbullying experiences on-the-go: When social media can become distressing. *Cyberpsychology: Journal of Psychosocial Research on Cyberspace, 7*(1), article 1. doi: 10.5817/CP2013-1-4

Grigg, D. W. (2010). Cyber-aggression: Definition and concept of cyberbullying. *Australian Journal of Guidance & Counselling, 20*(02), 143–156. doi:10.1375/ajgc.20.2.143

Grigg, D. W. (2012). Definitional constructs of cyberbullying and cyber aggression from a triangulatory overview: A preliminary study into elements. *Journal of Aggression, Conflict and Peace Research, 4*(4), 202–215. doi:10.1108/17596591211270699

Heirman, W., & Walrave, M. (2012). Predicting adolescent perpetration in cyberbullying: An application of the theory of planned behavior. *Psicothema, 24*, 614–620. PMID:23079360

Heirman, W., Angelopoulos, Weege, D., Vandebosch, H., Eggermont, S., & Walrave, M. (2015). Cyber-bullying-entrenched or cyberbully-free classrooms? A class network and class composition approach. *Journal of Computer-Mediated Communication, 20*, 260-277.

Hinduja, S., & Patchin, J. W. (2007). Offline consequences of online victimization. *Journal of School Violence, 6*(3), 89–112. doi:10.1300/J202v06n03_06

Hinduja, S., & Patchin, J. W. (2012). Cyberbullying: Neither and epidemic nor a rarity. *European Journal of Developmental Psychology, 9*(5), 539–543. doi:10.1080/17405629.2012.706448

Hinduja, S., & Patchin, J. W. (2013). Social influences on cyberbullying behaviors among middle and high school students. *Journal of Youth and Adolescence, 42*(5), 711–722. doi:10.1007/s10964-012-9902-4 PMID:23296318

Huang, Y., & Chou, C. (2010). An analysis of multiple factors of cyberbullying among junior high school students in Taiwan. *Computers in Human Behavior, 26*(6), 1581–1590. doi:10.1016/j.chb.2010.06.005

Joinson, A. (1998). Causes and implications of behavior on the Internet. In J. Gackenbach (Ed.), *Psychology and the Internet: Intrapersonal, interpersonal, and transpersonal implications* (pp. 43-60). San Diego, CA: Academic Press.

Kochenderfer-Ladd, B., & Pelletier, M. (2008). Teachers' views and beliefs about bullying: Influences on classroom management strategies and students' coping with peer victimization. *Journal of School Psychology, 46*(4), 431–453. doi:10.1016/j.jsp.2007.07.005 PMID:19083367

Kowalski, R. M., & Limber, S. P. (2007). Electronic bullying among middle school students. *The Journal of Adolescent Health, 41*(6), 22–30. doi:10.1016/j.jadohealth.2007.08.017 PMID:18047942

Lazuras, L., Barkoukis, V., Ourda, D., & Tsorbatzoudis, H. (2013). A process model of cyberbullying in adolescence. *Computers in Human Behavior*, *29*(3), 881–887. doi:10.1016/j.chb.2012.12.015

Li, Q. (2007). Bullying in the new playground: Research into cyberbullying and cybervictimization. *Australasian Journal of Educational Technology*, *23*, 435–454.

Low, S., & Espelage, D. (2013). Differentiating cyber bullying perpetration from non-physical bullying: Commonalities across race, individual, and family predictors. *Psychology of Violence*, *3*(1), 39–52. doi:10.1037/a0030308

Madden, M., Lenhart, A., Duggan, M., Cortesi, S., & Gasser, U. (2013). *Teens and technology 2013.* Retrieved from: http://www.pewinternet.org/2013/03/13/teens-and-technology-2013/

Marcum, C. D., Higgins, G. E., Freiburger, T. L., & Ricketts, M. L. (2012). Battle of the sexes: An examination of male and female cyber bullying. *International Journal of Cyber Criminology*, *6*(1), 904–911.

Mason, K. (2008). Cyberbullying: A preliminary assessment for school personnel. *Psychology in the Schools*, *45*(4), 323–348. doi:10.1002/pits.20301

Mesch, G. S. (2009). Parental mediation, online activities, and cyberbullying. *Cyberpsychology & Behavior*, *12*(4), 387–393. doi:10.1089/cpb.2009.0068 PMID:19630583

Mitchell, K. J., Ybarra, M., & Finkelhor, D. (2007). The relative importance of online victimization in understanding depression, delinquency, and substance use. *Child Maltreatment*, *12*(4), 314–324. doi:10.1177/1077559507305996 PMID:17954938

Moore, M. J., Nakano, T. N., Enomoto, A., & Suda, T. (2012). Anonymity and roles associated with aggressive posts in an online forum. *Computers in Human Behavior*, *28*(3), 861–867. doi:10.1016/j.chb.2011.12.005

Mouttapa, M., Valente, T., Gallagher, P., Rohrbach, L. A., & Unger, J. B. (2004). Social network predictor of bullying and victimization. *Adolescence*, *39*, 315–335. PMID:15563041

Navarro, R., Serna, C., Martinez, V., & Ruiz-Oliva, R. (2013). The role of Internet use and parental mediation on cyberbullying victimization among Spanish children from rural public schools. *European Journal of Psychology of Education*, *28*(3), 725–745. doi:10.1007/s10212-012-0137-2

Nocentini, A., Calmaestra, J., Schultze-Krumbholz, A., Scheithauer, H., Ortega, R., & Menesini, E. (2010). Cyberbullying: Labels, behaviours and definition in three European countries. *Australian Journal of Guidance & Counselling*, *20*(02), 129–142. doi:10.1375/ajgc.20.2.129

O'Neill, B., & Dinh, T. (2013). *Cyberbullying among 9-16 year olds in Ireland.* London, UK: EU Kids Online.

Olweus, D. (1999). Sweden. In P. K. Smith, Y. Morita, J. Junger-Tas, D. Olweus, R. Catalano, & P. Slee (Eds.), *The nature of school bullying: A cross-national perspective* (pp. 7-27). New York, NY: Routledge.

Ortega, R., Elipe, P., Mora-Merchán, J. A., Genta, M. L., Brighi, A., & Guarini, A. et al. (2012). The Emotional Impact of Bullying and Cyberbullying on Victims: A European Cross-National Study. *Aggressive Behavior*, *38*(5), 342–356. doi:10.1002/ab.21440 PMID:22782434

Patchin, J. W., & Hinduja, S. (2006). Bullies move beyond the schoolyard: A preliminary look at cyberbullying. *Youth Violence and Juvenile Justice, 4*(2), 148–169. doi:10.1177/1541204006286288

Pornari, C. D., & Wood, J. (2010). Peer and cyber aggression in secondary school students: The role of moral disengagement, hostile attribution bias, and outcome expectancies. *Aggressive Behavior, 36*(2), 81–94. doi:10.1002/ab.20336 PMID:20035548

Raskauskas, J. (2010). Text-bullying: Associations with traditional bullying and depression among New Zealand adolescents. *Journal of School Violence, 9*(1), 74–97. doi:10.1080/15388220903185605

Rideout, V. J., Roberts, D. F., & Foehr, U. G. (2005). *Generation M: Media in the lives of 8-18-year-olds: Executive summary.* Menlo Park, CA: Henry J. Kaiser Family Foundation.

Robson, C., & Witenberg, R. T. (2013). The influence of moral disengagement, morally based self-esteem, age, and gender on traditional bullying and cyberbullying. *Journal of School Violence, 12*(2), 211–231. doi:10.1080/15388220.2012.762921

Sahin, M. (2010). Teachers' perceptions of bullying in high schools: A Turkish study. *Social Behavior and Personality, 38*(1), 127–142. doi:10.2224/sbp.2010.38.1.127

Sevcikova, A., Machackova, H., Wright, M. F., Dedkova, L., & Cerna, A. (2015). Social support seeking in relation to parental attachment and peer relationships among victims of cyberbullying. *Australian Journal of Guidance & Counselling, 15*, 1–13. doi:10.1017/jgc.2015.1

Sevcikova, A., & Smahel, D. (2009). Online harassment and cyberbullying in the Czech Republic: Comparison across age groups. *The Journal of Psychology, 217*(4), 227–229.

Shapka, J. D., & Law, D. M. (2013). Does one size fit all? Ethnic differences in parenting behaviors and motivations for adolescent engagement in cyberbullying. *Journal of Youth and Adolescence, 42*(5), 723–738. doi:10.1007/s10964-013-9928-2 PMID:23479327

Shariff, S., & Hoff, D. L. (2007). Cyber bullying: Clarifying legal boundaries for school supervision in cyberspace. *International Journal of Cyber Criminology, 1*, 76–118.

Slonje, R., & Smith, P. K. (2008). Cyberbullying another main type of bullying? *Scandinavian Journal of Psychology, 49*(2), 147–154. doi:10.1111/j.1467-9450.2007.00611.x PMID:18352984

Smith, P. K., Mahdavi, J., Carvalho, M., Fisher, S., Russell, S., & Tippett, N. (2008). Cyberbullying: Its nature and impact in secondary school pupils. *Journal of Child Psychology and Psychiatry, and Allied Disciplines, 49*(4), 376–385. doi:10.1111/j.1469-7610.2007.01846.x PMID:18363945

Steffgen, G., Konig, A., Pfetsch, J., & Melzer, A. (2011). Are cyberbullies less empathic? Adolescents' cyberbullying behavior and empathic responsiveness. *Cyberpsychology, Behavior, and Social Networking, 14*(11), 643–648. doi:10.1089/cyber.2010.0445 PMID:21554126

Tangen, D., & Campbell, M. (2010). Cyberbullying prevention: One primary school's approach. *Australian Journal of Guidance & Counselling, 20*(02), 225–234. doi:10.1375/ajgc.20.2.225

Topcu, C., Erdur-Baker, O., & Capa, A. Y. (2008). Examination of cyber-bullying experiences among Turkish students from different school types. *Cyberpsychology & Behavior, 11*(6), 644–648. doi:10.1089/cpb.2007.0161 PMID:18783345

Totura, C. M. W., MacKinnon-Lewis, C., Gesten, E. L., Gadd, R., Divine, K. P., Dunham, S., & Kamboukos, D. (2009). Bullying and victimization among boys and girls in middle school: The influence of perceived family and school contexts. *The Journal of Early Adolescence, 29*(4), 571–609. doi:10.1177/0272431608324190

Vandebosch, H., & van Cleemput, K. (2008). Defining cyberbullying: A qualitative research into the perceptions of youngsters. *Cyberpsychology & Behavior, 11*(4), 499–503. doi:10.1089/cpb.2007.0042 PMID:18721100

Wade, A., & Beran, T. (2011). Cyberbullying: The new era of bullying. *Canadian Journal of School Psychology, 26*(1), 44–61. doi:10.1177/0829573510396318

Williams, K. R., & Guerra, N. G. (2007). Prevalence and predictors of Internet bullying. *The Journal of Adolescent Health, 41*(6), s14–s21. doi:10.1016/j.jadohealth.2007.08.018 PMID:18047941

Wright, M. F. (2014a). Cyber victimization and perceived stress: Linkages to late adolescents' cyber aggression and psychological functioning. *Youth & Society.*

Wright, M. F. (2014b). Predictors of anonymous cyber aggression: The role of adolescents' beliefs about anonymity, aggression, and the permanency of digital content. *Cyberpsychology, Behavior, and Social Networking, 17*(7), 431–438. doi:10.1089/cyber.2013.0457 PMID:24724731

Wright, M. F. (2014c). Longitudinal investigation of the associations between adolescents' popularity and cyber social behaviors. *Journal of School Violence, 13*(3), 291–314. doi:10.1080/15388220.2013.849201

Wright, M. F. (2015a). Cyber victimization and adjustment difficulties: The mediation of Chinese and American adolescents' digital technology usage. *CyberPsychology: Journal of Psychosocial Research in Cyberspace, 1*(1), article 1. Retrieved from: http://cyberpsychology.eu/view.php?cisloclanku=2015 051102&article=1

Wright, M. F. (2015b). The role of the media and the cyber context in adolescents' popularity. In P. Lorentz, D. Smahel, M. Metykova, & M. F. Wright (Eds.), *Living in the Digital Age: Self-Presentation, Networking, Playing, and Participation in Politics*. Brno: Muni Press.

Wright, M. F. (in press). Adolescents' cyber aggression perpetration and cyber victimization: The longitudinal associations with school functioning. *Social Psychology of Education.*

Wright, M. F. (in press). Understanding gender differences in cyber aggression: The role of technology, behaviors, masculinity, and femininity. *Sex Roles.*

Wright, M. F., Kamble, S., Lei, K., Li, Z., Aoyama, I., & Shruti, S. (2015). Peer attachment and cyberbullying involvement among Chinese, Indian, and Japanese adolescents. *Societies, 5*(2), 339–353. doi:10.3390/soc5020339

Wright, M. F., & Li, Y. (2012). Kicking the digital dog: A longitudinal investigation of young adults' victimization and cyber-displaced aggression. *Cyberpsychology, Behavior, and Social Networking, 15*(9), 448–454. doi:10.1089/cyber.2012.0061 PMID:22974350

Wright, M. F., & Li, Y. (2013a). Normative beliefs about aggression and cyber aggression among young adults: A longitudinal investigation. *Aggressive Behavior, 39*(3), 161–170. doi:10.1002/ab.21470 PMID:23440595

Wright, M. F., & Li, Y. (2013b). The association between cyber victimization and subsequent cyber aggression: The moderating effect of peer rejection. *Journal of Youth and Adolescence, 42*(5), 662–674. doi:10.1007/s10964-012-9903-3 PMID:23299177

Ybarra, M. L., Diener-West, M., & Leaf, P. (2007). Examining the overlap in internet harassment and school bullying: Implications for school intervention. *The Journal of Adolescent Health, 1*(6), 42–50. doi:10.1016/j.jadohealth.2007.09.004 PMID:18047944

Ybarra, M. L., & Mitchell, K. J. (2004). Online aggressor/targets, aggressors, and targets: A comparison of associated youth characteristics. *Journal of Child Psychology and Psychiatry, and Allied Disciplines, 45*(7), 1308–1316. doi:10.1111/j.1469-7610.2004.00328.x PMID:15335350

Section 4
Intersectionality

Chapter 13

Feminist Uses of Social Media:
Facebook, Twitter, Tumblr, Pinterest, and Instagram

Stine Eckert
Wayne State University, USA

Linda Steiner
University of Maryland, USA

ABSTRACT

The internet has clearly become crucial for feminist organizing, enabling feminist associations to undertake both campaigns and counter-campaigns. Feminist groups and individuals are using social media to advocate policy, fight policy, promote discussions of problems, and argue against anti-feminist, misogynist and anti-progressive ideologies. This textual analysis of feminist accounts on Facebook, Twitter, Instagram, Tumblr and Pinterest demonstrates that feminist individuals and groups used these platforms to discuss structural gender issues, aspects of identity, daily practices, provide motivational material, and both justify and defend intersectional feminisms. Few groups on and site were anti-feminist. Using the theory of fluid public clusters, this chapter argues that social media are especially significant for minority feminists and feminists of color; they enable White and majority feminists to go beyond rhetorical proclamations of intersectionality and to enact alliances.

INTRODUCTION

The internet has become crucial for feminist organizing, enabling feminist associations to undertake campaigns and counter-campaigns. Feminist groups are using social media (Facebook, Twitter, Tumblr, Pinterest, Instagram and others) to advocate and fight policies, promote discussions of problems, and argue against anti-feminist, misogynist and anti-progressive ideologies. Every major feminist organization is present online; many feminist groups organize their work entirely online. The Black Power movement slogan of the 1960s insisted "The revolution will not be televised." But, if social media-friendly activists have their way, "the feminist revolution will be tweeted, hashtagged, Vined and Instagrammed" (Irwin, 2013, para 1).

DOI: 10.4018/978-1-5225-0212-8.ch013

This chapter focuses on the extent to which Twitter, Facebook, Tumblr, Pinterest and Instagram enable feminists, especially collectives and organizations, to explain, critique, debate, question, challenge or push for feminist policies. Where, when, and how do social media operate for feminists? How well do social media serve digital feminists from various backgrounds, especially for advocating (whether individually or in organizations) on behalf of larger, collective goals? In recent years, the pendulum seemingly swung from huge optimism about social media's democratic potential for leveling informational playing fields to fears that the online environment was toxic for feminists and feminisms. Problems are sometimes attributed to sexist trolls or online abuse and open attacks on feminists, as seen in the #Gamergate controversy, when feminists who critiqued sexism in video games and advocated for more women in the gaming industry (Wingfield, 2014) drew highly sexist attacks – to which they responded. Internally, philosophical tensions and fights among feminists are often compounded by generational differences (in terms of age as well as in "waves" of feminisms) over the meaning, goals, and appropriate methods and strategies of feminisms.

Other explanations concern whether the design of social media itself reflects and serves men's and patriarchal interests. The fact that relatively few women work at Intel, Cisco, Google, Yahoo, LinkedIn, Twitter and Facebook, especially in high status executive and technology jobs, is also relevant (Khazan, 2015; Lien, 2015). Moreover, social media are not only increasingly consolidating under the umbrellas of a few corporations, but are becoming potentially colonized to suit commercial agendas. For example, in 2013 Yahoo! acquired Tumblr for $1.1 billion in cash. Unhappy Tumblr users collected nearly 170,000 signatures in protest, but the deal went through. Famously launched in 2004 by Harvard students, Facebook turned cash-flow positive five years later; when it went public in 2012 it reached a peak market capitalization of $104 billion, and more than doubled this by 2015. In 2012, Facebook bought Instagram for approximately $1 billion in cash and stock. Twitter has similarly purchased many other companies and applications, such as the video sharing service Vine. In 2013, when Twitter was first traded on the New York Stock Exchange, Twitter had a valuation of around $31 billion (BBC, 2013). Social media are becoming increasingly interlinked not only online via cross-posting settings but also in ownership structure. Not everyone will accept Fuchs's (2014) claim that participatory democracy requires ownership democracy, but ownership over-determines participation. Insisting that participation must be understood in terms of political economy, Fuchs argued that a participatory democratic public sphere requires that everyone has equal access to resources of cultural production, distribution, and visibility. Looking at Twitter in particular, he complained that social media favor corporations and powerful political figures.

Nonetheless, this does not rule out the possibility that feminists can use social media to debate feminisms, embody feminist values and engage with feminists, and, for that matter, anti-feminists. For instance, in 2014-2015, *Feminist Media Studies* (14:6, 15:1, and 15:2) carried 24 brief essays on feminist uses of Twitter. These demonstrated how feminists use hashtags to draw attention to (sexual) violence against women (especially rape and rape culture, particularly against women of color and trans women); harassment in public spaces; sexism; bias and misrepresentation of women, especially women of color in advertising, games, and news; men as feminists and allies; and victim blaming. The exploitation of people's unpaid labor and the persistence of "asymmetrical visibility," as Fuchs (2014) put it, have not dampened activists' enthusiasm to exploit social media. Feminists have always been eager to experiment with new media. Already in 1989 Felski posited that the distinct oppositional style of feminist counterpublics in the so-called third wave was to resist the homogenizing and universalizing logic of the global culture of mass media. Now the opportunities for working both, alone and collectively, synchronously and asynchronously, within geographic areas and outside, or across them all, suggest that social media could be more effective (which is <u>not</u> to say perfect) tools for feminists than print, broadcast, and cable. The point is that these evolve in response to historical context.

To gauge how much currency, use, and meaning the "label" of feminism carries in social media discourse, this analysis focused on the many English-language feminist online projects that self-identify as feminist, using the terms "feminist" or "feminism" (or parts and puns thereof) in blog/account/group names on Facebook, Twitter, Tumblr, Pinterest and Instagram. This does not mean that feminists are only active within these social media. Others may identify as feminist without using this label, perhaps out of concerns about stigmatization and a perception that the "f-label" narrows or limits their effectiveness in advocacy or in forming alliances (Walby, 2011).

Although social media, including in the very language of that term, seem oriented to self-expression and personal and public interaction, feminist projects can and should be understood and analyzed as political expressions for collective purposes. Since increasingly feminisms must be pluralized rather than treated as monolithic, this study examines which feminists are able to use social media more or less effectively for which purposes. How do race, ethnicity, sexuality and religion intersect with feminist identities in this context? This chapter highlights differential but intersectional uses by Black, Asian American, Native American and Latina as well as lesbian, gay, bi-sexual, transgender and queer feminists. Feminist social media use also implicates generation in terms of literal age and feminist movements affiliations. Building on work described below around feminists' use of (micro-)blogs for debates on feminisms in the United States, Europe, Asia and Africa, this chapter highlights lesser studied issues regarding race, ethnicity, sexuality, religion and generations on Facebook, Twitter, Tumblr, Pinterest and Instagram.

This chapter is not about how many women use social media. That said, to no one's surprise, Pew Research Center (2014) data from 2014 suggest that, of U.S. adults online, women are more active than men on consumer-oriented bookmarking sites such as Pinterest (42% vs 13%) and on Facebook (77% vs 66%). More women than men participate on Tumblr (7% vs 4%) (Pew Research Center, 2012). Women and men are using LinkedIn (27% vs 28%) and Twitter (21% vs 24%) at almost the same percentages (Pew, 2014). Race and ethnicity intersect with patterns in online activity; for instance, Blacks and Latina/os are more active than Whites on Twitter (27% vs. 25% vs. 21%) and Instagram (38% vs. 34% vs. 21%). In contrast, more Whites are on Pinterest compared to Blacks and Latina/os (32% vs. 12% vs. 21%) as Pew data show.[1] Women Instagram users outnumber men two to one; 90% of Instagram's 150 million users are under 35 years old (Smith, 2014) (Table 1).

BACKGROUND

Feminism is "an emancipatory, transformational movement aimed at undoing domination and oppression" (Steiner 2014, p. 359). Feminisms and feminist media are theorized as expressions that are explicitly political; take gender seriously; and view gender as socially constructed and as intersecting with other aspects of identity such as race, class, ability and nationality. Ultimately, although feminist theorizing is still striving to respond to emerging multiple feminisms, and to apply intersectionality more consistently in empirical studies, feminisms and feminist media are trying hard to address how power is distributed along gender lines and its intersections.

Although little feminist research has analyzed Pinterest, Instagram and Tumblr, scholars have been looking at individuals' uses of Facebook and feminist uses of blogs and Twitter. So-called hashtag activism does not lack for controversy.[2] Activism enacted through social media can help people organize;

Table 1. Facebook, Twitter, Instagram and Pinterest data from Pew Research Center (2014); Tumblr data from Pew Research Center (2012)

	Facebook	**Twitter**	**Tumblr**	**Pinterest**	**Instagram**
Women	77	21	56	42	29
Men	66	24	44	13	22
Black	67	27	NA	12	38
Latina/o	73	25	NA	21	34
White	71	21	NA	32	21
<30 yrs	87	37	11	34	53
High school or less	70	16	3	22	23
College+	74	30	5	32	24
Less than $30,000/yr	77	20	6	22	28
$30,000-$49,999	69	21	6	28	23
$50,000-$74,999	74	27	2	30	26
$75,000+	72	27	3	34	26
Urban	71	26	NA	25	28
Suburban	72	23	NA	29	26
Rural	69	17	NA	30	19

redefine themselves as having agency; fight exclusion; and highlight otherwise invisible structural problems. Regarding the anti-rape campaign SlutWalk, Mendes (2015) noted that mainstream news coverage was shallow, albeit highly supportive; in contrast, feminist blogs offered sophisticated, nuanced analyses of rape culture and rape myths. And new approaches to the intersection of feminisms and social media are emerging. Thrift (2014) described "feminist meme events" as hashtags that, by addressing specific issues, become events themselves. Meyer (2015) applied "culture jamming" to the project of "Vagenda," a U.K.-based online magazine: Twitter followers were encouraged to reword sexist tabloid headline without sexism.

But hashtags designed for activist purposes also have been ridiculed as a low stakes (perhaps no stakes) form that may be satisfying for the individual but "actually" accomplishes nothing (Risam, 2013). The derogatory concept of "slacktivism" implies that easily performed online political activities such as "liking" or retweeting make participants feel good but lack real impact on political outcomes (Morozov, 2009; Fuchs, 2014). Some argue that the affective pleasures of online participation may even derail important instrumental work, perhaps because when the novelty of online activism wears off people realize that their participation accomplished nothing and lose hope in all forms of activism (White, 2010). However, some studies expressing fears that online activities cannot achieve substantive political goals were published before social media took hold among new generations growing up with these formations.

Much of that research fails to consider the special circumstances and needs of complex alternative political movements such as feminisms. Even so, hashtag feminism has attracted equal amounts of celebration and vitriol. Tara Conley (2015) founded Hashtag Feminism (http://hashtagfeminism.com) to discuss and archive online feminisms and study the role of hashtags in feminist movements: "No matter the context—that is, grassroots, institutional, or corporate—hashtags compel us to act. They are political actors, and most importantly, hashtags represent evidence of women and people of color resisting authority, opting out of conforming to the status quo, and seeking liberation" (p. 1111). Conley found that texts, voices, images and videos posted to Twitter, YouTube and Instagram were highly important to the community that emerged on social media around the murder of a Detroit woman; social networking enabled comradery, kinship, counter-narratives and community organizing.

Apart from topical breadth the 2014-15 essays in *Feminist Media Studies* located many interconnected dimensions and functions in hashtags: searchability, collectability and archiveability; information sharing; visibility, especially of women of color and diversity; consciousness-raising and awareness of women's issues; mutual support and collaboration; critique of dominant narratives; dissemination of counter-narratives; direct address to journalists, companies, politicians and the public; calls for action; international outreach and pressure; creation of attention; and speed and convenience of use.

For all its benefits, however, hashtag feminism also presents pitfalls (Stache, 2015). Scholars critiqued how some hashtags go viral while other issues never circulate in hashtag form. Problems of access and digital literacy limit hashtag use. Underscoring the importance of situating hashtags in their specific national and historic contexts, researchers have highlighted the uneven visibility and inconsistent community of hashtags; intended and unintended distortions, misappropriations and dilution; the colonial/Western cooptation; the power of English-language hashtags; overexposure and intrusions of privacy via hashtags; the focus on hashtags to the detriment of offline political action; the uncertainty of (long-term) effects; and the use of humor to normalize violence against women.

But feminist scholars' research on social media are also marked by blind spots. Most studies focused on content (e.g. what furthers feminist agendas; misogyny; gendered expressions) and users (access issues; community; diversity in production; representation of voices) but rarely on software or technological issues that underlie users' interactions with social media and their interfaces (Bivens, 2015) or on political economy. Moreover, feminist scholars' own unreflexive use of social media for self-branding has been accused of feeding into the "self-interested, entrepreneurial, self-promoting, individualist" undercurrents of the neoliberal university (Banet-Weiser & Juhasz, 2011, p. 1768) rather than enacting feminist practices such as "public engagement in thinking out loud, honing a voice, self-naming, community-building, and stake-holding" (p. 1770). How can feminist values such as community building and public engagement benefit from social media, Banet-Weiser and Juhasz asked, when most feminist academics use social media for individualistic purposes?

In 2012, with the help of thousands of volunteers helping to translate the menu options, Twitter became available in Arabic, Farsi, Hebrew and Urdu; Twitter is now available in 33 languages. But most research has focused on the United States. When researchers have looked elsewhere, feminist claims about non-geographic affective communities have been criticized, especially with respect to Africa. #BringBackOurGirls helped bring attention to the abduction and persecution of Nigerian women and girls but was also accused of misrepresenting the political issues and of reproducing problematic and imperializing narratives of women. Objecting to the enthusiastic Western adoption of the rhetoric of "our girls," Loken (2014) criticized #BringBackOurGirls as infantilizing the Nigerian girls, even as it drew impassioned responses from far-away people who otherwise would have most likely remained apathetic. #BringBackOurGirls constituted "epistemic violence" (p. 347) against women and girls of the global south by enacting a liberal feminist salvation narrative based on a false equivalence between very different groups (Khoja-Moolji, 2015). Conceding that #JusticeForLiz drew attention to a gang rape in Kenya, Higgs (2015) asserted that Twitter's 140-character limitation over-simplified and decontextualized the problem. These abstractions and simplifications are especially concerning when African-originated campaigns cross national and cultural borders to engage Western audiences. In transnational interactions between African women's rights activists and Westerners, the White (feminist) savior complex threatens to undermine the project of cultivating solidarity. This failure underscores while transnational feminist practices involve "forms of alliance, subversion, and complicity within which asymmetries and inequalities can be critiqued … There IS NO SUCH THING as a feminism free of asymmetrical power relations" (Grewal & Kaplan, 2000, para 4, caps in original). Social media campaigns opposing misogyny in Africa can reinforce damaging stereotypes of African women, even as they simultaneously facilitate connections that can challenge and resist such representations.

Feminists in Asia and Europe have done better with social media. Indian feminists campaigned for mobility in public spaces and public transport with hashtags such as #BoardTheBus and #IndiaNeeds-Feminism (Eagle, 2015). In Iran, social media are illegal and provide the government with information on users; nonetheless, feminists tweeting #MyStealthyFreedom contested the stereotypes of obliging Iranian women and encouraged them to become more politically active (Novak, 2014). Eslen-Ziya (2013) concluded that the speed and international outreach of social media were crucial to the success of Turkish feminists in rolling back anti-abortion politics. In Europe, feminist individuals and organized groups of various backgrounds successfully use blogs, Facebook and Twitter to bring important issues into national consciousness and politics (Eckert, 2014). In the United Kingdom–similar to the United States–a plethora of feminist hashtags has emerged, addressing, among other issues, violence against women (#takebackthenight); street harassment (#everydaysexism, #ididnotreport); sexism in media (#thevagenda, #nomorepage3); victim blaming (#endvictimblaming); and consumerism (#bountymutiny). The highly viral Twitter hashtag #aufschrei [#outcry] exposed and protested everyday sexism in Germany (Carstensen, 2014; Eckert & Puschmann, 2013). German queer-feminist blogs reveal diverse portrayals of masculinity ranging from relational and situational masculinities that usefully intersect with other aspects of identity to "toxic masculinities" that need to be fought (Gerdes & Seidel, 2015, p. 324). Ganz (2013) called for incorporating feminist perspectives into the discourse in Germany regarding internet politics, specifically using the negative experiences of feminist bloggers to argue for more debate on communication cultures. Yet, in Switzerland, women's and feminists' blogs, Twitter and other social media are mostly confined to a discourse surrounding traditional motherhood as the desired norm (Eckert 2014); feminists pointed out that LGBTQ issues, women as working mothers, and other gender questions are discussed privately but rarely enter a larger debate online.

Instagram has gotten no attention from feminist scholars; and analyses of feminist content on Pinterest, Tumblr and Facebook remain rare. Moody-Ramirez (2014) found that 200 Pinterest users responded supportively and critically to the 50th anniversary of Betty Friedan's canonical *The Feminine Mystique* and the 2013 publication of Facebook COO Sheryl Sandberg's *Lean In*. Pins (as posts are called) on both books showed a pattern of links to YouTube, blogs and commercial sites to buy unrelated fashion, art and books. They also took seriously the controversies around the two books, identifying connections between them. Analogously, with respect to Wendy Davis, the first woman gubernatorial candidate in Texas, Tumblr, Pinterest, and Twitter users were discernibly different in how they framed Davis (Moody-Ramirez & Fissah, 2015).

A particularly useful attempt to theorize these efforts is Eckert's (2014) theory of fluid public clusters, which highlights the emergence of relatively "messy" constellations of people with shared interests. Eckert understands "publicness" as reflecting both conditions that Gitlin (1998) described as necessary for deliberation: having spaces with a similar degree of equivalent access, and interactions directed toward others and society. That is, contemporary activists strive to work together, not in isolation. Moreover, social media and participants are not fixed but develop over time; the landscape of social media changes over time, sometimes quickly. An analysis of the so-called "toxicity" among feminists on Twitter showed the dynamism of fluid public clusters: Twitter users can be part of feminist Twitter *and* #BlackTwitter *and* other clusters which represent different–and changing–aspects of feminists' and women's identities and concerns over time. Nonetheless, the emergence of a Black feminist Twitter also indicates a problem of feminism: despite vowing to counter *all* oppressions, women of color feel excluded or marginalized in feminism (Steiner & Eckert, in press). The bitter debate that has emerged online among feminists has rehearsed some of the same (valid) complaints that Black feminists have long expressed about how White feminists ignore or devalue the activism of women of color (Risam, 2015).

METHOD

This study used textual and visual analysis of Twitter,[3] Facebook, Tumblr, Pinterest and Instagram to investigate how feminists (with different backgrounds) use different but intersecting social media, thereby developing the approach of fluid public clusters. The sample included photos, graphics and texts from English-language users that use the keywords "feminism," "feminist" or variations thereof in their account and blog names. Search was limited to self-identified feminists to gauge the currency of these terms in social media.

Feminist critical discourse analysis (FCDA) was highly useful here, given its commitment to demystifying the complex ways in which hegemonic assumptions about gender and power are produced, sustained, negotiated and challenged. Lazar (2007) argued that FCDA unpacks otherwise naturalized assumptions about gender as comprising two "inherently contrastive yet complementary" (p. 147) sexes. FCDA critiques the otherwise taken-for-granted insistence on dichotomies. A third way that FCDA is relevant to this project is that it is "implicitly comparative rather than universalizing" (p. 149); it lends itself to looking at discourses from diverse places (geographically as well as online). That said, FCDA offers no methodological formulas; therefore, Hall's (1975) advice for grounding textual analysis in repeated detailed, close readings is followed here.

On Pinterest, founded in 2010, and as of April 2015 having 72.8 million users of which 85 percent were women (Smith, 2015a), users (pinners) combine images with texts to create pins, i.e. posts on their account. Pins belonging to one topic are arranged on one pin board. Pinners can populate their own "homepage" by following other pinners and boards. On Pinterest, a search with "feminism" resulted in 109 pinners, including names with the words "femin" and "femininity." After retaining results only with the word "feminism" and references to feminism (positive or negative), 24 were left. Of these, 18 contained at least one pin. A search with "feminist" yielded additional 48 users; only two of these did not contain a single pin. A total of 64 pinners were analyzed for content until pin board topics were saturated. Each pinner displays her/his pin boards, headlined by topics and visual images that "brand" the specific take on feminism and feminist issues. For each pinner the topics on their pin boards were analyzed.

On Tumblr, founded in 2007, and as of July 2015 hosting 243.3 million blogs, users can post texts, images, and videos; follow blogs; comment on posts; reblog posts; and use tags to help followers find posts or related pictures. On Tumblr, the search using "feminism" and "feminist" automatically was cross-referenced with the terms sexism, misogyny, equality, women and racism and yielded overlapping uncountable results. To stay within the realm of a manageable textual analysis, for each of the two search terms "feminist" or "feminism" the first 10 unique actively used blogs were analyzed that contained content. Each blog's homepage was analyzed.

Launched in 2010, Instagram (a portmanteau of "instant camera" and "telegram") had 75 million users as of December 2013 of which 49 percent were women (Smith, C., 2015b) Instagrammers can post texts, mobile pictures and 15-second long videos. The search terms "feminist" and "feminism" were used in the Instagram app embedded into the Google Chrome browser; profiles and home pages of 22 accounts thus located were analyzed. (Each search yielded a slightly different selection of blogs.)

Since its beginnings in 2004 Facebook has gained 1.44 billion users (Statista, 2015). For Facebook, the first 20 distinct (i.e., ignoring repeats) hits after entering "feminism" in the search bar for pages were used. Each one is marked by its avatar and is categorized by Facebook as "community" (for instance, lesbian, Black, African and several anti-feminist groups such as Women Against Feminism and Anti-feminism), "non-profit" (Feminism 2.0, Feminism=Equality, Go Feminist, Feminism + Equality Alliance) or "website" (Guerilla Feminism, Everyday Feminism). One could also search under feminist groups, some of which were closed; each attempt turned up different results.

Twitter was launched in 2006. Registered users can read and post tweets ("micro-blogs" of no more than 140 characters); unregistered users can only read them. In 2009, Twitter added a search bar and a sidebar listing "trending topics", i.e., the most common phrases appearing at the moment. By 2012 Twitter claimed that more than 100 million users posted 340 million tweets a day and that it handled 1.6 billion search queries per day (Twitter 2012). As of May 2015, Twitter has more than 500 million users, of which more than three-fifths are active.

RESULTS

Pinterest seems overwhelmingly consumerist and adamantly nonpolitical, with boards for gardening, cooking and fashion. Yet a search for feminist materials turns up a rich array of messages, usually terse and decidedly clever if not sassy. Photographs of people with feminist signs ("nobody asks what my rapist was wearing"); examples of everyday sexism and the objectification of women; and quotes from celebrities and ordinary people, abound; some of these getting as many as 6,000 "likes" and hundreds, if not thousands, of pins.

Pinterest results showed a strong emphasis on intersectionality among feminist organizations/groups and some individual users. The accounts for Guerilla Feminism, Intersectional Feminism and Everyday Feminism, among others, made this commitment explicit in their taglines. For instance, Intersectional Feminism asserted: "My feminism will be intersectional or it will be bullshit." These groups created pin boards for a range of critical topics including race and ethnicity, class, gender, sexuality, religion, critiques of ableism, heteronormativity, cissexism, classicism, faithism, xenophobia and racism. For instance, the site Feminist Apparel displayed boards with titles such as "Feminism for kids," "Body positivity," and "LGBTQA+." Their "Body positivity" board displayed encouraging images combined with slogans such as "fat fabulous," "Today I love my big curvy bum," and "Your body is wonderful. Any other message is a lie." The pin boards of Guerilla Feminism included titles such as "LGBTQAI," "Sex & Sexuality," and "Race & Ethnicity." On the latter, pins included criticism of "White Feminism" and White privileges. One pin showed a white woman surfing down a ski hill on the back of a black woman with the white women saying "Feminism is so empowering." Other pins included messages such as "The new racism is to deny that racism exists" and "A Brown woman's culture is not a white woman's accessory."

The individual pinners more often used "feminist" motivational quotes, graphics and products. Indeed "inspiration" was a category for many pinners. Individual pinners primarily addressed–from feminist perspectives–fashion, hair and makeup; crafts and DYI; food; travel; self-care; humor; popular culture; home making and gardening; birth, breast-feeding, children and parenting. Few dedicated pin boards to issues such as street harassment; politics/politicians (Hillary Clinton) and political representation; and violence against women. Overall, organizations' pin boards focused on larger issues of intersectionality while individual pinners addressed more the experiences, products and questions of everyday life.

Individual pinners did not explicitly defend the need for feminisms; instead they applied feminist ideas to all aspects of daily routines. Indeed, users showed the pervasive need for feminist principles, especially for body issues. Discussions of the importance of diverse feminisms implied that a post-feminist society has not yet been achieved but must be fought for incrementally, in daily individual practices. Pinboards enabled individual users to fashion personalized feminist worlds that relate to everyday experiences, while groups served as forums to discuss structural issues underlying identity.

On Tumblr, blogs displayed a combination of texts, links, images (photos, graphics, comics), videos and animated gifs (brief graphics that repeat a scene in a never-ending loop). Images and gifs frequently included visual material and quotes in favor of women's rights or gender equality. Among the 20 analyzed blogs, three contested feminism: Women Against Feminism, We Don't Need Feminism and Dear Feminist. Particularly We Don't Need Feminism can be read as reacting to the widespread project Who Needs Feminism, which has collected thousands of testimonials of women and men who took photos of themselves with posters and papers completing the sentence "I need feminism because...." Started as a class assignment by Duke University students in 2012, the project quickly grew beyond campus and is now present on a website, on Tumblr, Pinterest, Facebook and Twitter. Blogs contesting feminisms have imitated this format with women and men showing photos stating: "I don't need feminism because...." For instance, on Women Against Feminism the most recent posts included statements such as:

I don't need feminism because feminists made it possible for women to falsely accuse a man of rape without any proof. That man sent to prison was my husband. Feminism ruined my family. #veteran #army #sharpvictim

I don't need feminism because men and women are created for different purposes to help each other. They each have different things that they are good and praising one gender more than another isn't equality. Women in different countries who are abused every day for wanting their rights need feminism. They need the right to be equal and get to have the chance to work as a team with a man.

I don't need feminism because women are wired to be more emotional, motherly and sensitive than men. I like when men compliment my looks & body (even if they're strangers)! Promiscuity is **NOT** *okay!!! If I'm being harrassed [sic] by a man* OR A WOMAN, *I can defend* MYSELF! *I took responsibility for my own drunk actions and got* sober*!* ☺ *I love serving my man and letting him provide for and protect me! Being a woman is* Fun*!!! #notoppressed (caps and underlining in original)*

Thus, Tumblr accounts and posts that were anti-feminist or challenged feminism were primarily based on gender essentialism and/or a limited or misconstrued definition of feminism.

Tumblr accounts that self-identified as feminist often highlighted and celebrated their ideas of feminisms in reference to popular attacks on or misunderstandings of feminisms. For instance, Pita the Feminist Pug explained her site is about "social, political, and economic equality of the sexes." The Feminist Definition offered this self-description: "A feminist influenced blog, driven by youth perspectives on both modern and historical issues surrounding human rights, protection, liberation, and gender equality." It included a post with "80 reasons on why we need feminism." Others addressed sexism. For example, the motto of Feminism? Fuck Yeah! was "sexism sucks." Feminism. We Can Do It! asserted: "Feminism is really hated, but we just want equality, that's it. And a feminist is NOT a man hater." Some detailed their blog's intentions, for instance The Daily Feminist:

Any person who has opened their eyes to the realities of our world can see that our society is built on a system of inequalities against people. This is based on race, sexuality, class, gender, and a number of other human qualities. This blog is attempting to focus in on the way that women are treated in this society. This includes women of color, queer women, and literally everyone who identifies as a woman regardless of biology.

Thus, feminist blogs explained what they understand to be feminisms, that is, focusing on injustices that involve gender but also other aspects of identity.

Feminist Tumblr blogs addressed an enormous range of topics, including the portrayals of women in media (especially video games, often using the now well-known account of Anita Sarkeesian named Feminist Frequency); marriage equality and the 2015 U.S. Supreme Court decision constitutionally legalizing same-sex marriage; LGBTQ rights; ableism; sexism (especially in Hollywood); menstruation and celebrating the vagina; poverty and consumerism; what it means to be a woman and trans identities; body image and the right for women to show their naked chests as men are readily allowed to do; pornography; and other gender issues. Most blogs mixed visuals (photos, graphics) and texts, especially with inspirational quotes by women and/or feminists. For instance, Fempwr asserted: "When man gives opinion, he's a man. When woman gives opinion she's a bitch." Feminism. We Can Do It! published quotes on women's and LGBTQ issues from Taylor Swift, Cindy Lauper, Kristen Stewart, the Dalai Lama, St. Vincent, Jenny Lewis, Barack Obama and others.

In sum, feminist blogs on Tumblr addressed gender issues through a wide range of topics but also endeavored to justify feminisms, to explain why feminist movements and philosophies are still necessary. These blogs also explained how they define feminisms, pointing out manifest and subtle inequalities in their own way and highlighting the need for intersectional foci. Tumblr, in contrast to Pinterest, displayed more explicitly political messages.

Similar to Tumblr and Pinterest, almost all Instagrammers combined visuals (photos, graphics, comics, doodles, screen shots of chats and tweets) and brief texts. Most users posted quotes, usually superimposed on photos or images referring to the source or theme. Quotes usually were from famous men and women, including actors (Daniel Radcliffe, Taylor Schilling), musicians (Kanye West), athletes (Mia Hamm) but also political figures (Madeleine Albright), and generally inspirational personalities, such as Nobel Prize winner Malala Yousefzi. Quotes also came from fellow users or anonymous sources. Typical of quotes addressing gender equality was one posted by a Feminism from Patricia Arquette: "It's our time to have wage equality once and for all, and equal rights for women in the United States of America." Feminism.movement posted a quote from Emma Watson: "Both women and men should be free to feel sensitive. Both women and men should be free to feel strong." Other quotes were meant to inspire, encourage and motivate such as "You're looking gorgeous today" on Feministvoice or "She needed a hero and became one." Frequent topics included current issues and news coverage such as the U.S. Supreme Court decision to legalize gay marriage, police brutality in the United States, and sexist remarks by a Nobel Prize winning scientist. Users also addressed general gender-related issues such as LGBTQ rights; transgender identity; violence against women; body image and body diversity; and racism. The few that addressed U.S. party politics expressed support for Democratic presidential candidate Bernie Sanders and his advocacy for women's rights.

Several accounts included direct or indirect references to intersectionality in their bios. For example, the bio of Feminist etc. read: "Everyone Deserves Rights. Anti-war. Trans*rights. Sexuality acceptance. Body positivity. We all belong here. Intersectional feminism always." Likewise, Feministpride wrote: "Intersectional Feminist Anti war. Pro-Choice. SAGA advocate. Atheist. Apologists not welcome"; and Feminist.as.fuck wrote: "Either there is mutual respect or the conversation is over. Pronouns they/them/ their. Inclusive feminism." Posts on accounts also reflected intersectional intentions. For instance Feminism Is 4 Everyone posted: "A woman of color doesn't face racism and sexism separately. The sexism she faces is often racialized and the racism she faces is often sexualized" and the slogan "our liberation is intersectional, intergenerational, queer&transinclusive."

Instagram posts regularly addressed the need for feminism around the world. For instance, when someone tweeted that "women in other countries have it harder," an Instagrammer captured a screen shot of that tweet and commented, "there is plenty of feminism to go around bc it's a fucking concept, not a pizza." Others featured examples of gender issues in several countries; for instance, Feminism. as.fuck posted news about how in Austria traffic lights now display same-sex couples as green and red light symbols; the suicide rate of transwomen in Sweden; and marriage equality in Ireland.

Remarkably, across Pinterest, Tumblr and Instagram, many users displayed the iconic graphic of Rosie the Riveter as avatars, or a version of this image, for example, Rosie as Black or Asian. That popular Second World War image of the woman with her powerful arms was, for instance, the avatar representing Flowers_and_Feminism. It's unclear whether users chose that avatar knowing the image's history as a corporation's War Production Coordinating Committee poster encouraging women to work in shipyards and factories, often producing munitions and war supplies. In any case, Rosie the Riveter has come to symbolize feminists, or at least women with economic clout and political power. Another popular visual used as backgrounds for quotes within posts was the rainbow, used since 1978 to celebrate LGBT pride and a host of LGBTQ movements. The colors reflect the diversity of the LGBT community. Immediately after the U.S. Supreme Court ruling in favor of same-sex marriage, 26 million people used the feature created by Facebook to superimpose their profile pictures with semitransparent rainbow stripes (Dewey, 2015). This affirmation of support was used outside Facebook, too. For instance, the Instagrammers Feminism etc. and Feminist Pride superimposed rainbows on photographs of two young women, presumably the account users.

In sum, most Instagrammers posted about or from the position of intersectional feminism, addressing a range of issues and how they affect each other using short comments, quotes by other Instagrammers, Twitter users (via screen shots) and celebrities. Users mixed these critiques with encouraging quotes on self-care, especially loving one's body no matter which shape. For instance, Feminist Pride posted: "Sending love to all the girls out there trying to love themselves in a world that's constantly telling them not to." Compared to Tumblr, fewer accounts appeared to explicitly justify why feminism is needed; instead, activists demonstrated examples of feminisms' ongoing importance and value to individuals and society.

Regarding Twitter, scholars have devoted considerable efforts to examining feminist hashtags, especially hashtags originating in the United States, but also providing evidence that feminist hashtags are active in African, Asian and European countries. Hashtags across countries showed consistent themes: calling attention to violence against (trans)women (of color); the lack of and (mis)representation of women in media (ads, news, sports, video games); women's lack of or limitations of mobility in offline and online spaces due to gendered power; and the marginalization of women of color.

Attracting particular attention from pundits and scholars in the United States has been "Black Twitter," which Meredith Clark (cited in Ramsey, 2015) defined as a "temporarily linked group of connectors that share culture, language and interest in specific issues and talking about specific topics with a black frame of reference." Clark theorized that Blacks come together on Twitter in powerful and effective ways, at least if they possess a degree of Black cultural competency. Clark emphasized that Black Twitter does not represent just one shade of blackness: its users are also gay, trans, feminists–and people who do not identify as feminists. This makes Black Twitter a network for learning, teaching, exchanging information and protesting a wide range of issues, including harassment, sexual assault and violence (#YouOkSis; #IamJada; #BringBackOurGirls), police injustice (#BlackLivesMatter) and biased media coverage (#IfTheyGunnedMeDown; #DonLemonLogic). The focus on #BlackTwitter highlights the higher significance of social media for minority women and feminists to craft their own (counter)-narratives at the intersections of gender, race, geography and nationality.

Feminist magazines and organizations–nearly all of whom maintain their own distinct online presence and some of which are exclusively online–have Facebook pages. Facebook remains a popular way for organizations to communicate with followers. The format for the Facebook page is consistent—a section with data about subscribers, including numbers of followers; web address; summary of the pages' launch; brief mission statement; photo album; and a section with videos and links to events. In 2011, Facebook added a button potentially helpful for the kinds of sites analyzed here, since it enabled users to subscribe to or "follow" public postings without adding them as a friend. In 2013, Facebook introduced clickable hashtags to help follow trending discussions.

Analyzed here were the first 20 distinct (since there were repeats) hits in response to entering "feminism" in the search bar for pages. On what was essentially Facebook's directory, one could also find a "Like" button and how many people liked it, with names of people in one's own network who liked it. Pages linked to each other, for instance from Everyday Feminism one could get to A Perfect Feminist. This site described itself as "a webspace for angry feminists," a little known site highly committed to intersectionality as seen in their motto: "Intersectional feminism means that no matter which way we turn, there is additional work to do!" This was accompanied by a graphic of a street sign at the "intersection," as the signs read, of classism, racism, sexism, heterosexism, ableism and colonialism.

Also present on Facebook (and Tumblr and Twitter) was Feminist Frequency blogger Anita Sarkeesian's video series exploring gender representations, myths and messages in pop culture, particularly games. Her photo album featured posters and game characters but also many images of Sarkeesian in a gown and glamorous hairdo, and pictures of her at work. It presented some data, including that as of early July 2015 it had over 85,000 people who "liked" it. Feministing similarly has a Facebook page, and self-describes as young feminists blogging, organizing, "kicking ass" and "bringing you brainy, bad-ass feminist news."

The online magazine Everyday Feminism, founded in 2012, explains on its Facebook page that it wants to show people how to apply feminism to real life and heal from and stand up to everyday oppression. Unlike the self-consciously sassy approach of Feministing, Everyday Feminism writes that it strives to maintain a respectful, engaging and thoughtful community of feminists who are mutually supportive. Feminism In India described itself as a movement to learn, educate and develop a feminist consciousness among youth. It wants to unravel the "F-word" and demystify the negativity surrounding feminism. It offered links to events, other organizations and discussions of relevant issues, such as sexual harassment on Indian university campuses. As were the others, it was kept up to date.

In sum, feminist organizations on Facebook took an educational approach to (further) develop feminist consciousness; address and demonstrate intersectionality; and express mutual support. Feminist organizations' Facebook pages enjoyed high numbers of followers, speaking to the online community aspect that social media can create.

CONCLUSION

Sowards and Renegar (2006) mentioned the internet only in passing when describing third-wave feminist activists' distinct rhetorical strategies, that is, powerful yet personal and self-created strategies that apply to grassroots and everyday concerns. For example, contemporary feminists' principle of not dictating activism or judging other feminists for their perceived lack of activism projects flexibility. This highlights the importance of online platforms as effective, fulfilling sites for articulating feminist identities and oppositionality. Taken together, social media sites can function as a global platform for a new kind of consciousness-raising, albeit one particularly resonating with newly emerging generations of feminists.

What is clear is that social media allow more individuals, organizations, and communities to produce and distribute content for purposes of self-expression, information and conversion. Indeed, the fact that social media are used at all suggests that informing the world, if not converting the world, is a goal. But the huge numbers of sites and users and the uneven if not limited richness of the communication available in any single post on these sites, suggest that what is of paramount importance is "announcing" oneself or a group, declaring the existence of the position, the affiliation. These are ways of saying: "We exist. This is what we believe. Listen to us." While educating and raising consciousness, they also heavily self-brand with catchy names, mottos and images, cross-posting and working these online spaces to synchronize their contents to as many followers/likers/eyeballs as any of the sites can provide.

This analysis also shows that the fluidity of public clusters is expressed in many ways, including the shifting among different social media platforms and the flexibility in forms of expressions: still and moving images, audio and texts are perpetually recombined for new expressions. Some of the differences in content and focus among these platforms may reflect different corporate, organizational and cultural legacies, as well as the tastes and preferences of different generations of users. For example, Tumblr carries pornography and links to pornography; and its users skew young. Many celebrities have profiles on Instagram, sharing photos and videos of their personal and professional lives with fans, although some celebrities deleted their accounts after Instagram proposed selling images to advertisers without compensating users. (It immediately retracted the idea). Facebook, the oldest of these structures, is increasingly commercial and consumer oriented; its section on analytics includes sections on how to monetize apps with advertising, how to monetize by embedding ads from Facebook's two million advertisers, and how to "grow your app" and monetize your game across iOS, Android and the Web.

That said, 100 advocacy groups persuaded Facebook to change Facebook's policy on gender-based hate. Similarly responding to pressure from feminist activists, Twitter has improved its policies on reporting, banning and blocking harassment and trolls, and done more to address advertisements inserted into users' tweet streams. Thus, fluid public clusters are responding to evolving social media platforms' policies and practice. Activists must always play catch up and be eternally vigilant with respect to corporate agendas and attempts to infiltrate social media, but the evidence is that feminists are figuring out ways to use these tools. Like all media, social media have both centripetal (binding, uniting) and centrifugal (dividing, separating) dynamics. Jane Kramer's (2015) profile of Gloria Steinem described the effects of social media as paradoxical, "at once concentrating and diluting the political energy and solidarity of the women's movement, leaving young women free to confront new issues in necessarily new ways" (p. 55).

The brief tour of feminist uses of social media offered here is also strong evidence, if any doubt existed, that all kinds of feminists exist, with particular attention to race and ethnicity, global and economic positioning, sexuality and body issues. The proliferation of all issues feminist also shows that, however many different definitions and orientations to feminisms are proffered and however much feminisms are contested, including by feminists themselves, commitments to feminisms persist. Hence, the claims that feminisms are dead are vehemently refuted; only a handful of accounts proclaim that women, and men, do not need feminisms. So, in this sense, social media are mechanisms for keeping feminisms front and center, around the world, and especially for highlighting the intellectual strength and the political edge of intersectionality.

While several platforms did turn up uses targeting relatively young feminists, this study's sampling did not turn up places for old(er) feminists. Instagram seems to feature third-wave and millennial users, if the names of its feminist users are any indication. A specific search on Facebook for feminism for older women turned up only one small Canadian non-profit, the Older Women's Network. Indeed, age, among literacy and recourses, has been found to be a factor in willingness or resistance to use social media among feminist organizations and their participants (Fotopoulou, 2014). So, whether social media will sustain younger feminists as they age, that is, over the long haul remains an open question. A schism in communication tools may lead to a problematic divide among feminists by age and generation, making the sharing and transfer of knowledge and strategies more difficult.

Meanwhile, this research shows that social media users engage in selective exposure: at any one time, users elect to follow others in a relatively narrow cluster; thereby participating in fragmented interactions and forming divided groups. On the other hand, these clusters are fluid and dynamic; they endlessly shift. Fluid public clusters reach across different social media platforms. At the same time, repeating content may make a group's or individual's content more likely to be seen by different people with different backgrounds. For instance, user statistics show that more Blacks and Latina/os as a percentage of those adults online in the United States use Twitter and Instagram, while more Whites use Pinterest. More Latina/os and Whites are also on Facebook compared to Blacks. (Automatic) cross posting also serves as a back up to preserve content in case one site might be hacked, taken down (temporarily) or becomes less popular to use (by content producers and readers). Moreover, not all platforms are always and equally accessible in the same ways from laptops or mobile devices. Even feminisms highly conscious of and committed to intersectionality cannot eliminate these differences.

Instagram, Tumblr, Twitter and Facebook in particular are being used to advertise widely (in a literal sense) feminist groups, individuals, projects and campaigns, in case potential other converts might be browsing social media. The groups are trying to "brand" themselves. Yet, whether or how many people will find these platforms is unknown. Even with research, these platforms are difficult to find, so getting to them requires a combination of happenstance and personal networks. In some sense this is the reverse side of Louis Althusser (1972), who used the passive voice to describe interpellation: upon being hailed, individuals are made to recognize that they are being addressed, that they are being constituted by what Althusser called Ideological State Apparatuses. In contrast, social media are mechanisms through which feminists can actively hail.

Social media democratize access to message distribution tools that previously were restricted, costly or even off-limits to some groups, especially women of color, giving people the satisfaction of expressing their voices to potentially worldwide audiences. Of course, some activities are expensive for social media, at least at the level of individual users or groups. It was *New York* magazine that could afford to support journalists to spend six months interviewing and photographing 35 of the 46 women who have accused Bill Cosby of rape and sexual assault, sometimes after drugging them. The magazine could afford a compelling cover showing each of the 35 sitting in a chair, plus one empty chair. But the hashtag #TheEmptyChair, quickly set up to share personal stories and support for other sexual assault survivors, brought huge attention to the story, extended and amplified the conversation, and provided open-ended opportunities to comment, to report, and even to speculate on the meaning of the magazine cover image. Did the empty chair represent the women who were afraid to talk or were literally prohibited from discussing being abused by Cosby, or the men and women worldwide who had their own sexual abuse stories but before feared they would never be believed, or even the people who might still suffer such crimes in the future? Some thought the chair represented the silencing of rape victims and others interpreted it as an invitation to come forward. Within 24 hours, that hashtag was used nearly 13,000 times (Bever, 2015).

Here was a case when legacy and social media connected people across generations and confirms Guha (2015)'s point about "collaborative agenda setting" (p. 155): having found that in India hashtags need the power of mainstream media to reach their viral potential, Guha urged feminists to act in conjunction with both social media campaigns and mainstream media to reach broader publics. Indeed, when the magazine's own website was disabled for 12 hours shortly after "Cosby: The Women" was posted (the hacker did not, however, blame the Cosby story), the magazine announced on Twitter that it had moved the content to a Tumblr blog, although this cost them 500,000 unique visitors to its website (Lazzaro, 2015).

Feminisms are well and alive online, with diverse feminists using not only the mainstream spaces but also more niche social media to their advantage. Rather than giving up in the face of push back and harassment online, as well as commercial agendas, feminists have ignored or even exploited such problems, using sharp critique or gentle humor. They continue to experiment. And the point is not to count the number of converts but to signal commitment and mutual support to continue that long, slow, uneven road to political, cultural and economic transformation. This is especially significant for feminists of color and feminist sexual minorities, who have struggled even more than White and heterosexual feminists to produce news content and to be fairly represented in such content. The higher percentages of Blacks and Latinas using social media show this accumulated need to articulate previously ignored, marginalized, misunderstood, or misrepresented perspectives. The merging of online and offline efforts—these spaces are inseparable—is a major opportunity for all feminists to enact the often rhetorically proclaimed intersectionality, to listen to different feminisms and look out for potential new alliances. That is, by recognizing that feminists are part of fluid public clusters feminists can align with others according to situational needs and to engage with a variety of forms of feminisms to combat injustices. As long as social media (and other forms of digital communication still to be invented) are available to publics, they are also available for feminist purposes.

REFERENCES

Althusser, L. (1972). *Lenin and philosophy and other essays*. New York, NY: Monthly Review Press.

Augenbraun, E. (2011). Occupy Wall Street and the limits of spontaneous street protest. *The Guardian*. Retrieved July 27, 2015, from http://www.theguardian.com/commentisfree/cifamerica/2011/sep/29/occupy-wall-street-protest

Banet-Weiser, S., & Juhasz, A. (2011). Feminist labor in media studies/communication: Is self-branding feminist practice? *International Journal of Communication, 5*, 1768–1775.

BBC. (2013, Nov. 7). *Twitter shares jump 73% in market debut*. Retrieved July 28, 2015 from http://www.bbc.com/news/business-24851054

Bever, L. (2015). *#TheEmptyChair on NY magazine's Cosby cover takes on a life of its own*. Retrieved July 30, 2015 from http://www.washingtonpost.com/news/morning-mix/wp/2015/07/28/theemptychair-on-ny-magazines-cosby-takes-on-a-life-of-its-own/

Bivens, R. (2015). Under the hood: The software in your feminist approach. *Feminist Media Studies, 15*(4), 714-717. DOI:10.1080/14680777.2015.1053717.

Carstensen, T. (2014). Gender and social media: Sexism, empowerment, or the irrelevance of gender? In C. Carter, L. Steiner, & L. McLaughlin (Eds.), *The Routledge companion to media and gender* (pp. 483–493). New York, NY: Routledge.

Conley, T. L. (2014). From #RenishaMcBride to #RememberRenisha: Locating our stories and finding justice. *Feminist Media Studies, 14*(6), 1111–1113. doi:10.1080/14680777.2014.975474

Dewey, C. (2015). More than 26 million people have changed their Facebook picture to a rainbow flag. Here's why that matters. *Washington Post*. Retrieved July 27, 2015, from http://www.washingtonpost.com/news/the-intersect/wp/2015/06/29/more-than-26-million-people-have-changed-their-facebook-picture-to-a-rainbow-flag-heres-why-that-matters/

Eagle, R. B. (2015). Loitering, lingering, hashtagging: Women reclaiming public space via #BoardtheBus, #StopStreetHarassment, and the #EverdaySexismProject. *Feminist Media Studies, 15*(2), 350–353. doi:10.1080/14680777.2015.1008748

Eckert, S. (2014). *Digital rooms of their own: Women's voices online about the politics of women, family and maternity in four democracies*. (Unpublished doctoral dissertation). University of Maryland, College Park, MD.

Eckert, S., & Puschmann, C. (2013). *#Aufschrei/#outcry: Solidarity and aggression in a Twitter debate over sexual harassment*. Paper presented at the annual conference of the Association of Internet Researchers, Denver, CO.

Eslen-Ziya, H. (2013). Social media and Turkish feminism. New resources for social activism. *Feminist Media Studies, 13*(5), 860–870. doi:10.1080/14680777.2013.838369

Felski, R. (1989). *Beyond feminist aesthetics: Feminist literature and social change*. Cambridge, MA: Harvard University Press.

Fotopoulou, A. (2014). Digital and networked by default? Women's organizations and the social imaginary of networked feminism. *New Media & Society*. DOI: 10.1177/1461444814552264

Fuchs, C. (2014). *Social media: A critical introduction*. Thousand Oaks, CA: Sage. doi:10.4135/9781446270066.n2

Ganz, K. (2013). *Feministische Netzpolitik. Perspektiven und Handlungsfelder* [Feminist internet politics. Perspectives and relevant issues]. Gunda-Werner Institute. Retrieved July 27, 2015, from http://www.gwi-boell.de/de/2013/04/25/feministische-netzpolitik-perspektiven-und-handlungsfelder

Gerdes, G., & Seidel, A. (2015). Männlichkeiten in queer-feministischen Blogs. [Masculinities in queer-feminist blogs.] In A. Heilmann et al. (Eds.), *Männlichkeiten und Reproduktion* [Masculinities and reproduction] (pp. 309–328). Charn, Switzerland: Springer.

Gitlin, T. (1998). Public sphere or public sphericules? In T. Liebes & J. Curran (Eds.), *Media, ritual, identity* (pp. 168–175). London, UK: Routledge.

Grewal, I., & Kaplan, C. (2000). Postcolonial studies and transnational feminist practices. *Jouvert: A Journal of Postcolonial Studies, 5*(1). Retrieved July 27, 2015, from http://english.chass.ncsu.edu/jouvert/v5i1/grewal.htm

Guha, P. (2015). Hashtagging but not trending: The success and failure of the news media to engage with online feminist activism in India. *Feminist Media Studies, 15*(1), 155–157. doi:10.1080/14680777.2015.987424

Harp, D., Loke, J., & Bachmann, I. (2014). Spaces for feminist (re)articulations. The blogosphere and the sexual attack on journalist Lara Logan. *Feminist Media Studies, 14*(1), 5–21. doi:10.1080/14680777.2012.740059

Hauslohner, A. (2011). Is Egypt about to have a Facebook revolution? *Time*. Retrieved July 25, 2015 from http://content.time.com/time/world/article/0,8599,2044142,00.html

Higgs, E. T. (2015). #JusticeForLiz: Power and privilege in digital transnational women's rights activism. *Feminist Media Studies, 15*(2), 344–247. doi:10.1080/14680777.2015.1008746

Himelboim, I., Smith, M., & Shneiderman, B. (2013). Tweeting apart: Applying network analysis to detect selective exposure clusters in Twitter. *Communication Methods and Measures, 7*(3), 195–223. doi:10.1080/19312458.2013.813922

Irwin, D. (2013). Tweeting towards feminist revolution. *Clutch*. Retrieved July 27, 2015 from http://www.clutchmagonline.com/2013/12/tweeting-towards-feminist-revolution/

Khazan, O. (2015). The sexism of startup land. *The Atlantic*. Retrieved July 27, 2015 from http://www.theatlantic.com/business/archive/2015/03/the-sexism-of-startup-land/387184/

Khoja-Moolji, S. (2015). Becoming an "intimate publics": Exploring the affective intensities of hashtag feminism. *Feminist Media Studies, 15*(2), 347–350. doi:10.1080/14680777.2015.1008747

Kramer, J. (2015, October 19). Road Warrior. *The New Yorker*, 46-57.

Lazar, M. M. (2007). Feminist critical discourse analysis: Articulating a feminist discourse praxis. *Critical Discourse Studies*, *4*(2), 141–164. doi:10.1080/17405900701464816

Lazzaro, S. (2015). NY Mag Lost Over 500,000 Page Views on Cosby Cover Story During DDoS Attack. *The Observer*. Retrieved July 30, 2015 from http://observer.com/2015/07/ny-mag-lost-over-500000-page-views-on-cosby-cover-story-during-ddos-attack/#ixzz3hPiK9zhO

Lien, T. (2015). Why are women leaving the tech industry in droves? *Los Angeles Times*. Retrieved July 27, 2015 from http://www.latimes.com/business/la-fi-women-tech-20150222-story.html#page=1?ncid=newsltushpmg00000003

Loken, M. (2014). #BringBackOurGirls and the invisibility of imperialism. *Feminist Media Studies*, *14*(6), 1100–1102. doi:10.1080/14680777.2014.975442

Mendes, K. (2015). *SlutWalk: Feminism, activism and media*. New York: Palgrave Macmillan. doi:10.1057/9781137378910

Meyer, M. D. E. (2014). #TheVagenda war on headlines: Feminist activism in the information age. *Feminist Media Studies*, *14*(6), 1107–1108. doi:10.1080/14680777.2014.975451

Moody-Ramirez, M. (2014). *Representations of The Feminine Mystique and Lean In in user-generated content: A look at Pinterest pins*. Presented at AEJMC Midwinter Conference, Norman, OK.

Moody-Ramirez, M., & Fassih, L. (2015). *Citizen framing of Wendy Davis on Twitter, Tumblr and Pinterest*. Presented at AEJMC Midwinter Conference, Norman, OK.

Morozov, E. (2009). The brave new world of slacktivism. *Foreign Policy*. Retrieved July 27, 2015, from http://foreignpolicy.com/2009/05/19/the-brave-new-world-of-slacktivism/

Novak, A., & Khazraee, E. (2014). The stealthy protester: Risk and the female body in online social movements. *Feminist Media Studies*, *14*(6), 1094–1096. doi:10.1080/14680777.2014.975438

Pew Research Center. (2012). *Who uses tumblr*. Retrieved July 27, 2015 from http://www.pewinternet.org/2012/09/13/additional-material-and-demographics/

Pew Research Center. (2014). *Social media update 2014*. Retrieved July 27, 2015, from http://www.pewinternet.org/2015/01/09/demographics-of-key-social-networking-platforms-2/

Ramsey, D. X. (2015). The truth about Black Twitter. *The Atlantic*. Retrieved July 27, 2015, from http://www.theatlantic.com/technology/archive/2015/04/the-truth-about-black-twitter/390120/

Rentschler, C. (2015). #Safetytipsforladies: Feminist Twitter takedowns of victim blaming. *Feminist Media Studies*, *15*(2), 353–356. doi:10.1080/14680777.2015.1008749

Risam, R. (2015). Toxic femininity 4.0. *First Monday*. Retrieved July 7, 2015 from http://www.firstmonday.dk/ojs/index.php/fm/article/view/5896/4417

Smith, C. (2014). Here's why Instagram demographics are so attractive to brands. *Business Insider*. Retrieved July 27, 2015, from http://www.businessinsider.com.au/instagram-demographics-2013-12

Smith, C. (2015a). By the numbers: 90+ amazing Pinterest statistics (July 2015). *Expanded Ramblings*. Retrieved July 28, 2015 from http://expandedramblings.com/index.php/pinterest-stats/

Smith, C. (2015b). By the numbers: 150+ interesting Instagram statistics (July 2015). *Expanded Ramblings*. Retrieved July 28, 2015 from http://expandedramblings.com/index.php/important-instagram-stats/

Sowards, S. K., & Renegar, V. R. (2006). Reconceptualizing rhetorical activism in contemporary feminist contexts. *The Howard Journal of Communications*, *17*(1), 57–74. doi:10.1080/10646170500487996

Stache, L. C. (2015). Advocacy and political potential at the convergence of hashtag activism and commerce. *Feminist Media Studies*, *15*(1), 162–164. doi:10.1080/14680777.2015.987429

Statista. (2015). *Number of monthly active Facebook users worldwide as of 1st quarter 2015 (in millions)*. Retrieved July 28, 2015 from http://www.statista.com/statistics/264810/number-of-monthly-active-facebook-users-worldwide/

Steiner, L. (2014). Feminist media theory. In R. S. Fortner & M. Fackler (Eds.), *The Handbook of Media and Mass Communication Theory* (pp. 359–379). Hoboken, NJ: Wiley-Blackwell. doi:10.1002/9781118591178.ch20

Steiner, L., & Eckert, S. (in press). The potential of feminist Twitter. In R. Lind (Ed.), *Race and gender in electronic media: Challenges and opportunities*. New York, NY: Routledge.

Thrift, S. C. (2014). #YesAllWomen as feminist meme event. *Feminist Media Studies*, *14*(6), 1090–1092. doi:10.1080/14680777.2014.975421

Twitter. (2012). *Twitter turns six*. Retrieved July 28, 2015 from https://blog.twitter.com/2012/twitter-turns-six

Walby, S. (2011). *The future of feminism*. Malden, MA: Polity Press.

White, M. (2010). Clicktivism is ruining leftist activism. *The Guardian*. Retrieved July 27, 2015, from http://www.theguardian.com/commentisfree/2010/aug/12/clicktivism-ruining-leftist-activism

Williams, S. (2015). Digital defense: Black feminists resist violence with hashtag activism. *Feminist Media Studies*, *15*(2), 341–343. doi:10.1080/14680777.2015.1008744

Wingfield, N. (2014). Feminist critics of video games facing threats in 'GamerGate' campaign. *New York Times*. Retrieved October 8, 2015 from http://www.nytimes.com/2014/10/16/technology/gamergate-women-video-game-threats-anita-sarkeesian.html?_r=0

KEY TERMS AND DEFINITIONS

Facebook: This social media site allows users to post texts, links, hashtags, videos and images and to create pages and groups to interact with other users.

Feminisms: Expressions that are explicitly political; take gender seriously; and view gender as socially constructed and as intersecting with other aspects of identity such as race, class, ability and nationality.

Movements and individual practices that address, critique and seek transformation of oppressions and injustices of all kinds.

Fluid Public Clusters: Relatively "messy" emerging and shifting constellations of people with shared interests, especially on social media, based on the conditions of similar degree of equivalent access to (social) media and interactions directed toward others and society.

#Gamergate: A hashtag that attacked and threatened women who criticized sexism in video games as well as the gaming industry and culture, and thus provoked responses from feminists.

Hashtag: This is a keyword consisting of the pound sign (#) and a word or phrase on several social media platforms to make content better searchable.

Pinterest: This social media site allows users to create pin boards according to topics and to fill them with "pins," notes consisting of text, images and links.

Tumblr: This social media site combines the functions of a blog and of Twitter, allowing users to follow each other, posting texts, links, images, brief videos and hashtags.

Twitter: This social media site is a micro-blogging service allowing users to post brief "tweets" of 140 characters, including images, links and hashtags.

ENDNOTES

[1] Pew Research Center data do not distinguish black women vs. black men or white women vs. white men.

[2] Most people regard the Arab uprisings as the first large-scale social movement to rely on a hashtag to mobilize support; but Eric Augenbraun (2011) seems to have originated the term, in highlighting how the #ows hashtag mobilized Occupy Movement supporters around the world (Risam, 2015). Many journalists claimed that Facebook played a major role in the 2011 Egyptian revolution (e.g., Hauslohner, 2011).

[3] This study did not sample Twitter given that feminist studies of social media have extensively focused on Twitter; thus analysis was based on existing scholarship.

Chapter 14
Living Parallel–ly in Real and Virtual:
Internet as an Extension of Self

Jannatul Akmam
Chittagong Government Women's College, Bangladesh

Nafisa Huq
Eastern University, Bangladesh

ABSTRACT

With the marking of the digital age, all forms of digital technologies become a part of the existence of human life, thereby, an extension of self. The ever-increasing influence of the virtual world or Internet cultures demands to read its complex relationship with human existence in a digital world. Theory of psychoanalysis, specifically object-relation theory can be called forth to analyze this multifaceted relationship. Within the light of this theory, Internet cultures are acting as "objects" like games, memes, chat rooms, social net etc. and the virtual world can be interpreted as the "object world". The chapter is interested in reading the deep psychoanalytic experience of people (with a special focus on the youth) in reference to their relationship with the virtual arena. The experience can be associated with religion, spirituality, perception of beauty, sexuality, Identity formation and so on. Their behavior and responses to the virtual world will be framed within the psychoanalytic paradigm in the light of "object relation theory" in a digital age.

INTRODUCTION

According to Marvin Minsky, one of the founders of the MIT Artificial Intelligent Laboratory, human mind is "a meat machine" the assumption with which the Lab started working. With the increasingly developing digital technologies and their relationships with this "meat machine", the human psyche has come to be an ever vibrant landscape. This landscape can be best analogized with relevance to the discourse of psychoanalysis in a digital space.

With the marking of the digital age, all forms of digital technologies become a part of the existence of human life. The innumerable blessings in human life by the enormous technological advancement can never be denied. Ultimately, they become an extension of self. This field of extension can be best

DOI: 10.4018/978-1-5225-0212-8.ch014

understood by the extent to which the cyberspace has come to affect human life. The ever-increasing influence of the virtual world or Internet cultures demands to read its multifarious relationship with human existence in a digital world. So, in this particular context, a better comprehension of this emerging culture is important which includes how the cyberspace, reality, identity (formation and evolution), relationships and the self are experienced. These diverse internet cultures insist on an in depth analysis of human relationships with them.

Theory of psychoanalysis, specifically object-relation theory can be called forth in this regard to analyze this multifaceted relationship. Within the light of this theory, different forms of Internet cultures are acting as "objects" like games, memes, chat rooms, social net etc. and the virtual world can be interpreted as the "object world". These "objects" have both positive and negative facades depending on the way how they are dealt with by the subject. The "object world" works in the same way children idealizes their relationship with the parents or the primary care-giver and then internalizes certain ideals as a part of their own psychological building-up. This is very crucial in the learning process of the child to distinguish between the self and the other (object). Then, being specific in case of reading Internet cultures/virtual spaces psychoanalytically, people are using the void (virtual space) to fill up some void from the real life. At one point people start to project meaning to this empty space. In both the cases, setting boundaries and the process of separation (when and where to draw the separation or boundary lines) in their dealings with the virtual space is crucial in building up of the personality of people concerned. The influence is much greater in case of the youngsters. The paper is interested in reading the deep psychoanalytic experience of people (with a special focus on the youth) in reference to their relationship with the virtual arena. The experience can be associated with religion, spirituality, perception of beauty, sexuality, identity formation and so on. Their behavior and responses to the virtual world will be framed within the psychoanalytic paradigm in the light of "object relation theory" in a digital age.

The turn of the millennium marks the end of the Freudian century and we have turned to the digital age. Many people may have many different and contradictory ideas that psychoanalysis no longer needs to be talked about at such a time. In reality, the opposite is the demand of the age. The different objects in the new world of objects, i.e. Internet cultures need a psychoanalytic understanding to effectively meet our growing relationships head-on with them.

The potentials of getting involved emotionally with the artifacts arises some dramatic questions which the object-relation theory needs to address. One of the imposing questions is, "What is the appropriate relationship to have with cyberspace?" There are a wide range of positive activities involved in the cyberspace like, fund raising, blood donating, protesting against social and political causes. Yet the decisively sensitive and negative outcomes can never be ignored in any way.

In the end, the question is not just what kind of relationship it should be but whether cyberspace is challenging and imposing new meanings to the relationship itself, and ultimately putting new identities on the self. This paper considers the possibilities and questions regarding this by evaluating the extent of the relationship between human psyche and cyberspace.

"OBJECTS" DEFINED: EXPLAINING INTERNET CULTURES AS RELATIONAL ARTIFACTS

Initially, the designers of computational objects have focused on how these objects might extend and/ or perfect human cognitive powers. But computational objects do not simply do things *for* us; they do things *to* us as people, to our ways of being the world, to our ways of seeing ourselves and others (Turkle 2005[1984], 1995). Increasingly, technology also puts itself into a position to do things *with* us, particularly with the introduction of "relational artifacts", here defined as technologies that have "states of mind" (Turkle 2005a, 2005b). On the increasingly deeper level of understanding, they have come to be "explicitly designed to have emotive, affect-laden connections with people" (Turkle 2004). This understanding justifies the "relational artifacts" being described as "sociable machines" (Breazeal 2000).

Today, "relational artifacts" may include different digital creatures and robotic pets, specially designed and marketed for children, lonely elders etc. i.e. robot dogs and cats, robot infant dolls having baby sounds and facial expressions, crying inconsolably or even saying, "Hug me!" So, these baby dolls have baby "states of mind." As a result, Children approach a "Furby" or a "My Real Baby" and explore what it means to think of these creatures as "alive" or "sort of alive." Elders in a nursing play with the robot "Paro" and grapple with how to characterize this creature that presents itself as a baby seal (Taggart, W. et al. 2005; Shibata 1999, 2005). They move from inquiries such as "Does it swim?" and "Does it eat?" to "Is it alive?" and "Can it love?" Therefore, "projection of meaning" starts when the boundaries between the "self" and "other" blur, then "relational artifacts" take a decisive and active stand and in due course, become an extension of the self. In the same way (as this paper concerns itself), different forms of Internet cultures can be given a crucial interpretation as "relational artifacts." At this very point, the term "relational artifact" evokes the "object-relation" strand of psychoanalytic theory with its emphasis on the encounter between people and different internet cultures.

Internet culture involves a range of activities linked up with the Internet and other new forms of cyber communication, such as online communities, online gaming, social media, mobile apps, and such related issues as establishing identity in the absence of any physical interaction. Besides, there can be diverse activities, pursuits, places and metaphors, i.e. blogs, chat rooms, e-commerce, cybersex, internet memes, internet trolls, and different social networks. The online and the offline world are two separate ones, and there are marked differences in their mechanism and interactions with the self. Yet there are various "networked" human interactions in the cyberspace which go beyond the boundaries of virtual and real. The elements within the cyberspace ultimately act as "relational artifact." Here comes psychoanalytic theory.

Psychoanalytic object-relation theory talked about the objects in a dynamic inner landscape, according to the term by Minsky "a society of mind". With the increasing relationship between human beings and the development of different internet cultures, the "society of mind" has got newer dimensions.

This "object world" works in the same way children idealize their relationship with the parents or the primary care-giver and then internalize certain ideals as a part of their own psychological building-up, e.g. a child makes up a game to have its lost mother returned. Based on this initial approach by Sigmund Freud, later developments of the theory show that as a child grows up, it learns how to separate from the primary care-giver or parent image and become an independent human being. This is very crucial in the learning process of the child to distinguish between the self and the other (object). Then, being specific in case of reading Internet cultures/virtual spaces psychoanalytically, people are using the void (virtual space) to fill up some void from the real life. At one point people start to project meaning to this empty space. In both the cases, setting boundaries and the process of separation (when and where to draw the separation or boundary lines) in their dealings with the virtual space is crucial in building up of the personality of people.

Interacting with "objects" in cyberspace as relational companions challenge and change who we are. Different internet cultures as "relational artifacts" may perform as "companionate species." The ever-increasing popularity of cyberspace has become a great concern for critics because of the effects they generate on human behavior and relationships. There are numerous positive outcomes which can be derived from the use of cyber communication. People, at the same time, have to go through some negative experience. Thus, this renewed discourse of "relational artifacts" has generated theoretical debates and become the spotlight of psychoanalytic practitioners. These "rational artifacts" in cyberspace offer psychoanalysis an opportunity to inspect on how they can be read in the light of "object-relation" theory.

So, the question is how can we embrace these newer dimensions of internet cultures/ relational artifacts? We need to lead an ardent pursuit for the full understanding of the meanings of these "objects". The demand is far closer inspection of how these objects enter the process of development of the self and how the interaction between the self and these "objects" (who come to behave as "other" in construction of the self) is mediated. The object-relation strand of psychoanalysis provides us with the language and possible line of attack to talk about our ever mounting emotional interaction with the artifacts in cyberspace.

HISTORICAL PERSPECTIVE: PSYCHOANALYSIS, TECHNOLOGY, CYBERSPACE

The evolution of psychoanalytic practice can be briefly traced from its Freudian beginnings to current inter-subjective and relational theories. Freudian and early psychoanalytic theories posited that instinctual drives and the ego and superego's ability to cope with them determined the structure of the self and the extent of neuroticism or pathology (Freud, 1949). However, as early as the 1920s, American psychoanalysts began to look more closely at the interchange between a person, others, and the environment, in part due to the influence of Progressive Era ideologies about modernizing and improving the self, the political system, and society (Cushman 1995). Scientific interest in parent–child relationships and attachment also helped shape self psychology through explicating how individuals are influenced and formed by relationships and empathic attunement (Ainsworth et al. 1978; Bowlby, 1988; Winnicott, 1960).

In the 1960s, a cultural revolution began (spurred by feelings of discontent around civil rights and anti-war issues) that also influenced beliefs about relationships. As ''question authority'' became the dominant mantra of the young and a profound distaste for the powers and inequities that society engendered grew, interest in intimacy rocketed (Jamieson, 1998). Intimacy became associated with genuineness, mutuality, equality, and closeness that included deep and privileged knowledge and understanding of another and emotional connection (Hatfield & Rapson, 1993; Jamieson, 1998). By the end of the twentieth century, therapists tapped into postmodern and social constructivist philosophies that reflected a growing interest in the democratization of relationships and an increasing distrust of authoritative theories of knowledge. Relational and inter-subjective theories gained ground. According to those theories, knowledge, reality, and the self are relative and multiple and become co-created through various unique interactions (Curtis, 2012; Wachtel, 2008).

These newer ways of characterizing the self, relationships, and intimacy had already entered when cyber technology burst upon the cultural scene. In fact, social media arose within and perhaps best exemplify the ethos of less authoritative and more democratic and accessible relationships and the existence of multiply constructed selves. In this respect, the pertinent question is not whether or not technology erodes the self or close relationships, but how the self and relationships are expressed in a technological society and in what ways psychoanalysis can respond to the understanding of that cultural shift.

In fact, the psychoanalytic world has much to offer in this respect. In keeping with the orientations, the "object-relation" approach studies cyberspace primarily as a set of "relational artifacts" by asking how its use may affect or illuminate underlying conflicts, desires, relationships, or sense of self.

SELF(IE) CRAZE: NARCISSISM MANIFESTED IN CYBERSPACE

A British male teenager tried to commit suicide after he failed to take the perfect selfie. Danny Bowman became so obsessed with capturing the perfect shot that he spent 10 hours a day taking up to 200 selfies. The 19-year-old lost nearly 30 pounds, dropped out of school and did not leave the house for six months in his quest to get the right picture. He would take 10 pictures immediately after waking up. Frustrated at his attempts to take the one image he wanted, Bowman eventually tried to take his own life by overdosing, but was saved by his mom.

"I was constantly in search of taking the perfect selfie and when I realized I couldn't, I wanted to die. I lost my friends, my education, my health and almost my life," he told *The Mirror*.

Reported in an article "Scientists Link Selfies to Narcissism, Addiction & Mental Illness"[1], the case of Danny Bowman triggers such possibilities that selfie can cause narcissistic addiction and severe mental illness that can eventually lead to shattering penalty like suicide. Most likely, the idea that selfies might cause an array of physical and mental troubles has met with much attention from experts of diverse fields of knowledge with the news of Danny, who is believed to be the first selfie addict in UK.

Selfie, a name for a self-portrait photograph has become a buzzword of late. The huge advancement in digital technology has caused the rise of different cameras and smartphones which create an impulse to repetitively take and post selfies on different social networks like Facebook, Instagram, Twitter, and photo messaging applications such as Snapchat etc. Although photos in the "selfie genre" predate the extensive use of the word, according to *ABC Science blog*, the earliest usage of the word *selfie* can be traced as far back as 2002. It first appeared in Karl Kruszelnicki's "Dr Karl Self-Serve Science Forum", an Australian internet forum (ABC Online) on 13 September 2002.

Though initially trendy with young people, selfies gained wider esteem over a short period of time. But during and after 2010s, a few accidents regarding taking and posting selfie have drawn the attention of various scholars. Apart from the suicide attempt of Danny Bowman, there are other reports of minor to major physical and mental health hazards even death. Figure 1 and 2 are just two of many examples of how addictive selfie trend is affecting people's interaction with each other and disturbing health issues. This vital point can be an issue of discussion under the light of "object-relation"[2] strand of psychoanalytic theory.

People get addicted to the urge of posting selfies regardless of any thought to uninvited consequences. Selfies often trigger ideas of self-indulgence or attention-craving reliance. People are obsessed with looks and they intend to get "comments" and "like". This, in turn, questions the nature of responsibility with which to deal with social nets and the healthy or unhealthy behaviours and activities they bring on. Ultimately, online manifested narcissism can be a tactic to balance the sense of self-esteem. When people are appreciated and rewarded by others (through the count of likes and comments), they continue with their perpetual activities of crossing the boundaries of virtual and real. That's exactly what happened in case of Danny.

According to theorists later than Freud, including Melanie Klein, Margaret Mahler and Bernard Winnicott, to develop a separate sense of self, the self needs to learn to distinguish between self and other

Figure 1. Changed relationship patterns in digital age

Figure 2. Changing scenario: Health concerns

i.e. the "object." In case of people's interaction with any internet entity (in this context, selfie) this sense of separation is very crucial. Danny Bowman failed to develop the boundary line between him and the "object", and accordingly the process of acquiring autonomy and subjectivity was badly disrupted. Failure of such kinds leads to later problems evident in Danny and others injured from such cases. This effect has got the proper explanation by Michael Ryan, "… if separation fails, the self [child] might experience a narcissistic wound, a sense of a basic fault in existence that prevents the development of healthy relations … in one's world." (Ryan, 2004) If all that the self looks for is only "perfection" and the self's sense of confidence is determined by the count of likes and comments on the selfie, any disruption may lead to the destruction of the self itself.

Rachel Simmons in his article suggests that the appeal of selfies comes from how easy they are to create and share, and the control they give self-photographers over how they present themselves. Again, some feminists view selfies as a subversive form of self-expression that narrates one's own view of desirability. In this sense, selfies can be empowering and offer a way of actively asserting agency (Simmons, 2013). However, a 2013 study of Facebook users found that posting photos of oneself correlates with lower levels of social support from and intimacy with Facebook friends. The authors of the study suggest that "those who frequently post photographs on Facebook risk damaging real-life relationships." (Houghton et.al., 2013)

Writer Andrew Keen has pointed out that while selfies are often intended to give the photographer control over how their image is presented, posting images publicly or sharing them with others who do so may have the opposite effect— for instance, this can be considered dramatically so in the case of revenge porn[3], where ex-lovers post sexually explicit photographs or nude selfies to exact revenge or humiliate their former lovers (Murphy, 2013).

According to Rebecca Savastio, Bowman's parents, who are both mental health professionals, say that society has a "huge lack of understanding" about just how very dangerous electronic gadgets and social media can be to teens and adults alike. Experts say that while gadgets and social media cause addiction and other dangers, people are in extreme denial about the level of threat these types of communications pose, especially to impressionable teens. Bowman's parents recount how Bowman would spend many hours in his room taking selfies until his addiction culminated in not only a drastic weight loss, but also a terrifying suicide attempt. While Bowman's case may sound unique and extreme, experts in psychology as well as medical doctors say this problem is far more widespread than is generally understood (Rebecca, 2014).

"IT'S COMPLICATED": "NETWORKED" IDENTITY AND RELATIONSHIPS IN CYBERSPACE

"I'm not feeling well."

"I'm having a headache."

… … … … …

We often come across these words posted on Facebook wall as "status", the second line placed even with a selfie. These apparently uncomplicated words put on the social networking sites pose an alarming question: "Are they humans?" The question arises because of a sense of companionship shared by the words as if the persons involved are sharing their health conditions with someone close who can heal their pain and make them feel better.

In relating the adolescent experience of the cyberspace, Karen Zilberstein suggests a ratio of internet use by this particular group of people. The Internet and social media are increasingly used in daily life, changing, in some ways, how people communicate and relate. While Internet use remains high amongst many demographic groups, youth constitute the one most digitally connected. According to the Pew Research Center and The Berkman Center (2013), 78% of teens have a cell phone and 95% use the Internet. In contrast, 83% of young adults aged 18–29 use the internet, 77% of those aged 30–49, 52% of those aged 50–62, and only 32% of older adults (Pew Research Center, 2012; Zilberstein, 2013). In terms of the ensuing disputes and concerns, an abundance of cautionary books and articles now exist about these new media and the possible devolution of relationships through diminishing face-to-face contact, the impact of multitasking on attention and brain development, and the creation of false identities and relationships (Akhtar, 2011).

This is where the psychoanalytic studies are called for. Social Networking sites can act as "relational artifact" and they demand an intensive focus on our increasing relationships with them. They are not just a collection of words, images, hyperlinks; rather they are evocative "object" which can affect the way we "see ourselves and our world" (Turkle, 2004) and change one's sense of self.

A basic principle of object-relation theory is that we need form fitting relationships with other/object and failure in any forming successful early relationships leads to troubles later on. In a sensitive field like cyberspace, where relationships can be changed within a few clicks from "single" to "in a relationship", things get even more fluid.

A *New Yorker* cartoon captures the issue of psychoanalytic explorations of new technology: Paw on keyboard, one dog says to another, "On the internet, nobody knows you're a dog" (Steiner, 1993). Sherry Turkle gives an explanation of the interplay of Identity and Cyberspace: A rapidly expanding system of networks, collectively known as the Internet, links millions of people together in new spaces that are changing the way we think, the nature of our sexuality, the form of our communities, our very identities. A network of relationships on the Internet challenges what we have traditionally called "Identity" (Turkle, 1995).

Since the mid-1980s, with the development and widespread use of Internet, individuals can engage themselves in a wide variety of networked relationships. Eventually, " The Internet became a powerful evocative object for rethinking identity, one that encourages people to recast their sense of self in terms of multiple windows and parallel lives" (Turkle, 2004). The multiple windows on a computer screen can be a potential metaphor for several identities of the self and thus raise issues of redefining identity and the idea of Identity vs. Identity confusion. So, while using social networks, the self can be split and multiple facets can be experienced through the parallelism of virtual and real. Social networks can act as an inroad where the sense of self is shattered. If the tensile ground of separation from the "networked objects" is not dealt in a proper way, the self may have to suffer greater unintended consequences.

CONCLUSION

Walt Whitman (1855/1993) said, "There was a child went forth every day/ And the first object he looked upon, that object he became." We make technologies, and technologies make and shape us. We are not going to be the same people we are today, on the day we are faced with machines with which we feel in a relationship of mutual affection (Turkle, 2004). Cyberspace changes social bonds and conceptions of the self, both in a positive and negative way. It can also change "… the value placed on intimate relationships and people's willingness to pursue such affiliations…" (Zilberstein, 2013)

However, the final chapter on the interaction between human being and cyberspace is not yet written. Ideas, theories will continue to evolve and give this line of thought new and newer dimensions as Morawski (2001) states, "Theory entered practice, altered practice, and left needs for further theorizing."

REFERENCES

A brief history of the selfie. (n.d.). *ABC Science blog*. ABC Online.

Akhtar, S. (2011). *The electrified mind: Development, psychopathology, and treatment in the era of cell phones and the Internet*. Lanham, MD: Jason Aronson.

Breazeal, C. (2000). *Sociable Machines: Expressive Social Exchange between Humans and Robots*. (PhD Thesis). Massachusetts Institute of Technology, Cambridge, MA.

Houghton, D., Joinson, A., Caldwell, N., & Marder, B. (2013). *Tagger's delight? Disclosure and liking in Facebook: the effects of sharing photographs amongst multiple known social circles*. University of Birmingham.

Morawski, J. (2001). Gifts bestowed, gifts withheld: Assessing psychological theory with a Kochian attitude. *The American Psychologist*, *56*(5), 433–440. doi:10.1037/0003-066X.56.5.433 PMID:11355366

Murphy, M. (2013, April 3). Putting selfies under a feminist lens. *Georgia Straight*.

Ryan, M. (2004). *Literary Theory: A Practical Introduction*. Oxford, UK: Blackwell.

Savastio, R. (n.d.). *Selfies Cause Narcissism, Mental Illness, Addiction and Suicide?* Retrieved from http://guardianlv.com/2014/04/selfies-cause-narcissism-mental-illness-addiction-and-suicide/

Scientists Link Selfies to Narcissism, Addiction & Mental Illness. (n.d.). *Thinking Humanity*. Retrieved from http://www.thinkinghumanity.com/2014/06/scientists-link-selfies-to-narcissism-addiction-mental-illness.html

Simmons, R. (2013). *Selfies on Instagram and Facebook are tiny bursts of girl pride*. Retrieved from www.slate.com

Steiner, P. (1993). On the Internet, nobody knows you're a dog [cartoon]. *The New Yorker,69*(20), 61.

Taggard, W., Turkle, S., & Kidd, C. D. (2005). An Interactive Robot in a Nursing Home: Preliminary Remarks. In Proceedings of CogSci Wrokshop on Android Science. Academic Press.

Turkle, S. (1995). *Life on the Screen*. New York: Simon and Schuster.

Turkle, S. (2004). Whither Psychoanalysis in Computer Culture? *Psychoanalytic Psychology*, *21*(1), 16–30. doi:10.1037/0736-9735.21.1.16

Turkle, S. (2004). *Relational Artifacts* (NSF Grant SES-0115668). NSF.

Turkle, S. (2005). *The Second Self: Computers and the Human Spirit*. Cambridge, MA: MIT Press.

Turkle, S. (2005a). Relational Artifacts/Children/Elders: The Complexities of CyberCompanions. In *Proceedings of the CogSci Workshop on Android Science*. Academic Press.

Turkle, S. (2005b). *Caring Machines: Relational Artifacts for the Elderly*. Keynote AAAI Workshop "Caring Machines", Washington, DC.

Whitman, W. (1993). *Leaves of Grass*. New York: Random House.

Zilberstein, K. (2013). Technology, Relationships and Culture: Clinical and Theoretical Implications. *Clinical Social Work Journal, 41*(3).

ENDNOTES

[1]   Available at: http://www.thinkinghumanity.com/2014/06/scientists-link-selfies-to-narcissism-addiction-mental-illness.html.

[2]   One of the two major strands of psychoanalytic theory developed on the initial approach of Freud.

[3]   A pornographic image or film which is published, posted (e.g. on the internet), or otherwise circulated without the consent of one or more of the participants, usually with malicious and vindictive intent, such as following a break-up (http://www.collinsdictionary.com/dictionary/english/revenge-porn).

Chapter 15
The Self of the Camera:
Popular Practices of Photography and Self-Presentation in the New Social Media

Gilbert Ndi Shang
University of Bayreuth, Germany

ABSTRACT

This chapter examines the revolution in self-representation across the cyber-space engendered by the advent of new interactive social medias. It argues that in the attempt to face the challenges of self-imaging in everyday life and in an era where discourses of "identities in flux" have become the norm, photographic trends on Facebook usage seek to portray a sense of coherence of the self through popular media practices. In this dimension, the new media spaces have provided a propitious space of autobiographic self-showing-narrating through a mixture of photos/texts in a way that deconstructs the privileges of self-narration hitherto available only to a privileged class of people. The self (and primarily the face) has thus become subject to a dynamic of personal and amateurish artistic practices that represent, from an existentialist perspective, the daily practices of self-making, un-making and re-making in articulating one's (social) being.

INTRODUCTION

As a point of entry, let us pose the following questions with regard to the relationship between the camera, the cyberspace and the art of representation of reality: In recent times, can there be a life now without the camera pointed at the face, coercing it to surrender to the media? In recent media expansion, can "to be" now be anything less or other than "to be online"? What are the boundaries and horizons of a private life? Can there be any clean-cut distinction between private and public? Is there anything that is more real now than what is "virtually tangible"?

This chapter examines the poetics and tactics of self-invention, self-imagination and self-representation in the social media and how that has led to a new culture of the self in the everyday life. This article focuses specifically on the phenomenon of Facebook, one of the most popular of these media and one that arguably has the most revolutionary effect by its accessibility and capacity to make the face/self visible. On Facebook, the image culture of late capitalism is brought home to the self in a very literal

DOI: 10.4018/978-1-5225-0212-8.ch015

sense. The chapter thus seeks to probe into the mechanics of self-representation on Facebook and how this enhances new insights about self-creation and self-invention in the social mediascape.

We live in a visual age and what consumes one's visual energy is of ultimate importance. The social space has become a battleground of vision between different medias and mediating screens. What attracts visual attention in real life has come under virulent competition from omni-present screens offered by new communication technology and the tertiary industries of social media outlets. In the subway or in the buses, passengers are glued to their screens and their facial reactions/mental mechanisms are more influenced by the mediated world in which they are engrossed than by what actually takes place around them. The waiting rooms, the subway waiting stations constantly assail the visual subjects with enormous energy. Henceforth, the question of visual consciousness of one's presence and location in space cannot be examined without proper and due consideration of the virtual dimension of our being and existence.

At the individual level, the way one looks, what one shows to the world and what aspects of the highlighted self are actually consumed by others is of capital importance. There is an obsession with the art of "looking good" according to generalized and internalized social codes. Images, etiquettes and stereotypes promoted by the media through advertisement, popular talk shows, entertainment industry, etc. have become assimilated as part of mass culture. From Erving Goffman's *The Presentation of the Self in Everyday Life* (1959), much water has passed under the bridge and the "everyday life" has been pervasively influenced if not hijacked by virtual life. The "home" has virtually given way to the "homepage" and where the vocabularies of convivial co-habitation in "real life" has been overtaken by its virtual correlates of walls, windows, web, sites, key, etc., new social media have created a propitious space of self-staging and enhanced the desire for individual representation. To underline the growing use of the netscape in modern life, Nicholas Mirzoeff affirms that:

These forms of visualization are now being challenged by interactive visual media like the Internet and virtual reality applications. Twenty-three million Americans were online in 1998, with many more joining in daily. In this swirl of imagery, seeing is much more than believing. It is not just a part of everyday life, it is everyday life. (1999, p. 1)

Though access is far less than global, the Internet has reached hitherto enclaved corners of the world with tremendous speed. Sometimes Internet access conceals the dire economic sacrifices of its users, especially to those from the global South. Amongst the youth population all over the world, the social media now constitute the appropriate space for locating the *flâneur*, the stroller in the modern city. The functional modes of these spaces favor a strong tendency of cruising across the pages in a rather voyeuristic exploration of the vast landscape of desire. With the metronomic expansion of cybersphere, the camera, formerly a professional tool, an "arm" of the rich, or a rare family property, is now one of the most affordable gadgets of consumerist mass culture, asserting its power over almost every other asset due to its capacity to re-make and fix the self for socio-economic and even political exhibition. The very idea of the camera is built around a learning-on-the-job approach where amateurism is celebrated through a self-didactic apparatus, whose impact is always exponential. The camera holds the key to one's self-image. As Nicolas Mirzoeff puts it, "capital has commodified all aspects of everyday life, including the human body and even the process of looking itself" (1999, p. 27). Persons have used the camera invariably to recreate and project the image of the ideal or idealized self. Through the camera, the old and undesirable self is "shot" dead and smashed while a new image is minted and exhibited, with the edges of our body adequately trimmed in the process.

Popular practices of photography in social media are playing an important role in fixing and enhancing the self in a continuous process of self-presentation. This has led to concurrent and contradictory currents in popular photography which however collude in a frenzied re-invention of the self. Joanne Finkelstein asserts that notions of a fixed and identifiable self have been debunked in postmodernist discourses:

By the mid-twentieth century, the idea of a fixed personality based on a stable mentality became increasingly untenable and the counter idea, of identity or subjectivity being an asset to be groomed and presented to best effect, had gained acceptance. (2007, p. 3)

The idea of a stable self might be debunked in the academic spheres as essentialist and belonging to an outdated transcendental metaphysics that stresses the idea of core self. However, it is exactly this "stability of the self" that characterizes human interactions at every social level. Every human being, structure, entity or institution strives to represent itself as unified and inherently coherent even if that means silencing dissenting and contradictory components or voices within. In effect, every entity attempts to be a body, an organic system with internal system of coordination. In the same vein, nobody can bear portraying themselves as fragmentary in the social and public sphere.

My task in this chapter is thus to critically map out the process of self-construction in new social media by critically examining tactics of photography used by cyber subjects to present a sense of self-unity, self-coherence and the beauty of body-self. The process of self-invention in the social media is a constantly metamorphosing practice, functioning according to trends, a notion that seems more appropriate than fashion or vogue in social media parlance, since it has the advantage of both defining the dominant popular practices and underlining the viral/metronomic temporality within which such practices are inscribed.

The dominant motif of photography on Facebook is the presentation of the ideal body/self. This ideal body follows, but sometimes deconstructs, a repertoire of normalized social body etiquettes popularized by mainstream advertisement and showbiz cultures. One needs to be cautious not to construe popular practices as wholly influenced by dominant cultural images and trends. The reality is that new social media spaces, by virtue of the sheer diversity of users, have also contributed to the explosion of various perceptions of "beauty" and "photogenic body" that do not strictly follow the script of dominant clichés of generally Western parameters of beauty. In other words, we are also witnessing the valorization of the "beauty of unbeauty" and popular conceptions of the "photogenic" have been overly deconstructed to make room for everyone on the limitless and elastic borders of cyber world. Nevertheless, the idea of showcasing one's body as an innuendo of a stable and assertive self dominates social media. To underline the importance of the body, the outer shell in social interaction, Joanne Finkelstein affirms that:

There are certain ways of using the body to influence the opinions of others. The body is often the first visible sign we draw on to make judgments of one another. Its size and shape, facial expression and hand gestures are inscriptions of culture and history made into flesh. This explains in part the endurance (despite numerous refutations) of physiognomy as a system for reading one another. We learn about our self through the reactions of others. We learn that the controlled body is a passport to sociability. (2007, p. 31)

The body is the signpost of the self and in a very existential sense, the primal marker of the *thereness* of being and of social presence. Finkelstein adequately captures what can be described as the primordial importance of the body in the basic recognition of the other's presence and how it is registered in the subject's perception. The social acceptability of specific body practices is a matter of individual effort. If it is true that a certain group of people might share peculiar trends of self-presentation practices, the end result is the enhancement of the individual self and not necessarily the promotion of the image of the group. The new social media thus re-enforces the idea of the beautiful individual body as unique and distinct through the construction of unique self-images.

In her text, *Corporal Identity: When Self-Image Hurts,* Elena Faccio affirms that the feeling of being in the wrong body can result in a myriad disorders associated with low self-esteem and a longing for approval and appreciation from others (2013, p. 28). This opens the deep quest for proper appearance and the weight its absence or a feeling of inadequacy places on individual psyche. The "appearance of the self" or "the self of appearance" becomes a key quest of self-presentation in the social media space. In any case, this is not to create the impression of a generalized psychological crisis/pathology of the self for which the social media is a palliative or antidote. The point to drive home is that social media practices of photography constitute an interesting layer of self-identity representation as part of everyday life self-representation. The human self, to cope with the complexity of social realities and the social exigencies of social belonging, always needs a double, an invented identity, to suit the fluidity of life/ existence. With the proliferation of social mediascapes, this double has been normalized as the true image of the self in social interactions. The image of the self has to be doctored, literally and figuratively, to suit complex social circumstances and to grant a sense of being in control of one's body, identity and self-image. In this regard, Finkelstein states that:

The possibility of continual self-invention introduces an element of self-conscious playfulness into all sociability. At that moment when we begin to interact with another, a series of calculated decisions are made. These calculations take place in another dimension of the social moment, a separate back area where we estimate the degrees of fictionality that the immediate situation can sustain. (2003, p.13)

Through the social media, each one is offered the means to 'aggressively' but 'playfully' re-make the self and present it to the public in its most ideal form. Unbridled and systematic practices of self-making and self-presentation on a widely diffused mediascape, hitherto the preserve of the showbiz industry, has come right home, individualized and systematized by the masses in parts of the world that are otherwise considered politically, economically and socially marginal. Marketing the self through modern media has never been so evident on such a massive scale. What is interesting is the way self-imaging is done in a collaborative manner amongst social media users in a spirit of convivial co-existence. This interactive and convivial nature, a sense of an imagined cyber-community, cannot be afforded on TV or radio, media which to some extent, still carry the marks of official culture and whose constant users are still more or less aligned to a privileged class. The frenzy of self-representation takes place in a social space of mutual expression of convivial solidarity expressed through a flurry of "likes" ascribed to posted/ shared pictures and the numerous strings of compliments posted by both known and unknown "friends".

The new social media grant a sense of ownership of space and of self that is inconceivable in traditional media spaces. This space is managed with (putative) independence but users are nevertheless bound by codes of reciprocal appreciation of each other's physical look in a sense of community that transcends social categories of age, geographical location, race and other markers of social belonging. Whether this cyber-social confraternity can be coalesced into an ethical community; whether this can be converted and mobilized for political action; whether Facebook in general can be used to measure actual trends of social consumption, are various interrogations that necessitate ample investigations in their own right.

THE PRIMACY OF THE VISUAL

In a social media aimed at maximizing visibility, readability and audibility, the question of self-presentation meets its most appropriate medium. Visuality has an edge over other sensory apprehensions of the world when it comes to questions of social interaction and transaction of self-images. Reading and listening/hearing are functions that demand a measure of patience, presence of mind and cognitive attention, whereas the ocular/visible is capable of drawing attention by affect, thriving on the non-linear and non-toleological gradient of desire. A casual gaze is always a multifaceted, reflexive gesture, exercised with relative ease while at the same time constituting the most responsive mode of human desire/pleasure. Of all the human senses, it is sight that comes close to touch in the sphere of desire and obsessive possession. However, while touch, the ultimate sense of possession, might offer a sense of satisfaction to a longing, to touch with one's eyes constitutes the threshold of insatiable desire. As such, the social media is dominated by visuality, a situation that Nicholas Mirzoeff refers to as the "visual overload of everyday life"(1999, p. 8). Our impressions of others in social contexts are formed, however superficially and erroneously, through visual signals produced by our acts of seeing. These acts of seeing are in turn conditioned, though not limited by un/conscious acts of showing/concealing/simulating of others. The self desires, though not always successfully, to orient the sight of the other to aspects that enhance its integrity and social standing. To echo Freudian mechanisms, there are aspects of our visual self that are subtly projected while others are forever consigned to the backstage. In this way, there is a subtle battle of showing/concealing that is inscribed even in the most benign aspects of our everyday social experiences. This could be referred to as the "tact" that precedes and attempts to condition every human "act", "contact" or "encounter" with the other in a pacific war of day-to-day self-representation.

WHAT DO PICTURES DO?

While images have hitherto been considered as organized and professionally generated modes of representation, new social media offer an astounding production of photographs that profess their unprofessionalism while at the same time asserting their place in social interactions, desiring to be seen and accorded full recognition. Perhaps it is the unprofessional tint in these images that constitute their affect, the magic of judicious spontaneity and planned caprice that affect them. The field of visual culture itself has been forced to relax the horizons of what can be considered as visual cultural productions so as to cope with a variety and multiplicity of practices of mass self-iconography. This phenomenon has led to a critical re-evaluation of how images function in relation to self-invention and self-representation. In this regard, I pose a preliminary question here: What do pictures do?

To this seemingly benign question I affirm that images/pictures do three things: they assemble, they resemble and they dissemble. Photos assemble the disconnected pieces that constitute the self into a semblance of coherent unity. Thus, in the social media, pictures impress by creating a sense of unity out of f-r-a-g-m-e-n-t-e-d existence in the very present moment. Considered in certain religions, especially in Christianity, as an image of God though composed out of particles of dust, man thrives in the constructions of images of himself. The self in the image comes to be convinced that the image x-rays a self-quality, a resource, charisma yet to be discovered and exploited by its owner. The self that is imaged presents this other self, the finished self, as the real self that beckons for recognition. The imaged self is always an excess of the real self, revealing an excess potential that still lies to be exploited and mobilized.

Secondly, pictures attempt to resemble or depict the subject or individual. Out of many works of art, photography posits as the most mimetic in theory, purporting to replicate reality as it is. Unlike painting which, even when performed by a gifted hand, does not mechanically refer us to the subject/object depicted, photography intends to be a paper version of man in bones and flesh. The most basic thing expected of a photo is that of recognition, in the most prosaic denotation of the word. The capacity to point to the image of someone and say this is John and not Peter, Mary and not Susan. In the case of a group photo, we are expected to distinguish between John, Peter, Mary and Susan and to label them accordingly.

But would we be happy if a picture most faithfully reproduces us, the way we are (if there is ever such a thing), with all our physical features? Would we be happy if photos were to point their fingers at us, without any iota of doubt? I do not think so. For a photo to appeal to us, it has to dissemble us, to be a bit unlike us in a positive way, to act as an improved copy of the self. That is where dissemblance comes in. We like photos that are unlike us in some dimensions, photos that fill in the potholes in our body and our self (or personality); or that create them. With regard to the capacity of the photo to enhance the beauty of the depicted object, Sonntag asserts that a picture

Often sometimes looks, or is felt to look better in a photograph. Indeed, it is one of the functions of photography to improve the way things appear as we normally take them in. (Hence, we are always disappointed by a photograph that is not flattering; that is, that doesn't show us looking more attractive at its 'best'. After the tour of the new house, its proud owners might show the visitors an album of the photographs of it, and surely more than one mother has exclaimed to someone admiring her baby in the pram, 'you should see her photographs! (1977, p. 257)

The family photo album is considered as an improved representation of the beauty and coherence of the family in a way that the physical portrayal cannot. However, suffice it to say that even the time of the family album is drawing to an end and the online representation of the self and family have taken center stage. The family portrait now thrives online, either in the form of modern photos or scanned versions of long taken photos that are re-actualized and shared on Facebook for the view of friends and family.

The process of image-making has migrated unto the social media and amongst the masses, the only set of photos that ever make it in hard copy are passport photos used for official purposes. No one now seems to have patience for the hard photo anymore; it is more real when it is virtual. Though it is often taken in a contingent and worldly context and moment, a Facebook photo can be considered as a judicious exploitation of the nebulous space between occasionality and systematicity. That is, its power lies in the ability to stabilize the contingent, to anchor the fleeting moment into a *paysage* and to turn transience into tradition. In contemporary social media the picture does more. It locates the self within a culture of good life, not as a short-lived *joie de vivre* but rather as a permanent image of *jouissance* that is etched into the Facebook profile picture, or a cover picture. It seeks to make this permanent. A singular moment captured by the camera becomes the expression of a personal *zeitgeist*, the spirit of the time.

In the same way that the photo stabilizes the contingent, it can also contribute to the blurring of motifs, endowing the banal with a sense of majesty and nobility, creating a false auratic outlook. The camera has an immense capability to convert a yawn of disaffection and boredom into a sign of amazement and electrified surprise. It can turn an often lazy, hazy and benign gesture of sheer materiality into an iconic representation of sublime abstraction. In the frenzy of self-presentation on Facebook, there is an increasing trend of images showcasing users of this medium with celebrities. A picture with a diva is presented as a meeting between old time friends, concealing the tedious background negotiations and photo-diplomacy that culminated in the photographed scene. A picture with a loved one is inscribed as a Platonic/transcendental romance, concealing the probably difficult times that the portrayed couple may be experiencing in real life. Such a picture always needs to be read in its ample ambiguity. It stabilizes social relationships inasmuch as it moves or points unto a vision of a good life in the yet-to-come. It thus has kinetic properties, always in the moving-present. It is never meant to be a silence, but an ever-speaking image of a culture of happiness both of body and mind. As Elena Faccia asserts in her insightful study of the body and social representation,

There is a place where wrinkles and cellulite do not exist, joints and features are perfect, current standards of beauty adhered to, and where beauty is guaranteed. This place offering alternative bodies and identities, a different existence in a parallel world, is in cyberspace. It is called "Second Life"; it exists in virtual reality, yet because people believe and identify with it, is experienced in a very real way. (2003, p. v)

The cyber, as appropriated by the masses, has become a space for the staging of the ideal, desires and dreams and where intentions are represented as though they were lived in the present or might have been experienced as a past. In other words, the cyberspace has served the cause of a futuristic imagination of the self. Even if photos of the self serve in the narration of the subject's biography, as we shall witness below in relation to the use of black/white photos, it is a form of biography that appropriates hope in the form of an actualized ideal life.

ASSEMBLING THE FRAGMENTS

Since they play the same role as history albeit at the individual level, pictures seek to assemble the fragmented consciousness of any social event and re-present it in a holistic manner. Both history and photography seek to present the past as coherent, well ordered events that can be plotted on a logical sequence. However, in the social media, though there is a biographical dimension to pictures as representations of the past self, the frenzy to take stock of the "now" moment is equally overwhelming. The archiving of the self in the present moment through photography is an inalienable aspect of social media photographic landscape. In detail, the virtual visibility of the picture attempts to instill coherence, cohesion, and harmony around a "now" moment that might be underlined by a sense of doubt, indeterminacy and uncertainty in actual life. Some photos have gained stardom through the exquisite manner in which they present the fullness of the self in the present whereas the human beings behind them battle to make meaning out of the sutured fragments of the self. The camera is the most faithful ally of the self in its desire to stage this plenitude of existence.

It is becoming clear that with the advent of Facebook, the camera is a key player in our social life. Users of the Facebook medium can to some extent be described as camera-selves, not only in the sense of producing photos, but as selves produced by popular photographic practices. In some cases, the physical look of members of this space play a great role in the kind of friends that they receive and also how many friends (especially of the opposite sex) are willing to engage them in a friendly chat. Whether these photos are duplicates, controverts or amalgams of the self, it is difficult to generalize. Otherwise modest spaces that have hitherto passed unnoticed have been subjected to the intrusive and oppressive flashes of cameras of all fabrics. Give or lend a camera to anyone, you have given them an instrument of self-fashioning and self-multiplication. With the multiplicatory capacity of the camera and its mode of functioning through a sense of play, the self gains an unlimited capacity of re-imagining and re-staging itself.

The camera is the prime mediator of what reaches out to the world as representations of the self unto others and vice versa. It has produced the human face of modern technology. It is however left to everyone to answer the question as to if the camera is an article of ostentation or obfuscation. In other words, the camera might end up producing the chimera of the self. It seems that behind the infra-flashes of this magical instrument, to look for the real self (if ever it exists) will be a vain venture. But the camera is master at providing evidence, an emissary of the "there"-icity of social visibility of media(ted) selves. One thing is clear: in the ultra-modern world, it is not too much darkness but rather too much light that obscures reality. The bare reality of which the camera purports to bear witness is adulterated by the perspective of its author. Susan Sontag states that:

the photographic image, while a trace, can't be a transparency of something that did really happen. It is always the image that someone else chose; to photograph is to frame, and to frame is to exclude. For a long time, the fact that images were produced by a machine obscured the many senses in which photographs are as much 'made' by the person operating the camera as drawings and paintings are 'made' by an artist. (1977, p. 260)

In spite of its apparent mechanicity, every picture is authored and the result of a photographic exercise is not just the effect of the apparatus, but also the eye, the mind, the hand and the entire body behind it. What the eye brings into focus or highlights equally invites us to think about what is left out and banished from view. However, the Facebook photo's amateurish innocence lays claim to the there-icity of the subject. For some time, the tag "just me" has been a trendy caption for most Facebook photos, showcasing the humility and modesty of the photographed subject. The "just me" invites us to read the portrait as an honest testimony of the photographed body-self, with a tacit supposition of modesty and admission of self-imperfection. However, it can be noticed that, the image in the "just me" is rather in its best texture and posture of self-representation, making the "just me" sound more as a tacit tactic for the will to social power of the imaged self beyond its apparent humility.

BACK TO THE FUTURE OF BLACK/WHITE

By its diversity and appropriation by users from different parts of the world, Facebook brings together a broad array of photographic practices that respond to different and sometimes contradictory trends. This involves an incorporation of past practices as well as the most futuristic photographic trends in a bid to imagine the self creatively in the flow of various temporal conceptions. In this regard, even though Facebook has led to a boom in selfies, as we examine below, several users have used available image recast options to bring back to life the aesthetics of the black/ white picture. One is forced to think about the beauty of black/white photos taking us away from the glaze and glitz of modern color images. In fact, inscribing oneself in a black and white photo is to historicize the self, to tell one's story through other eyes and other times. In its attempt to historicize the present, to insinuate a temporal distance on a relatively recent footage of the self, the Black/white enables you to look at yourself through a self-made archive and to appreciate your own life much better from this temporal "distance". There is a certain pleasure in standing before your own image and being made to recognize or miscognize it. To make recourse to Walter Benjamin's idea of the aura, Black/white photos have an auratic presence given the half-lit backdrop in which they rest, leaving greater room for imagination and postulation:

The definition of the aura as the 'unique apparition of a distance, however near it may be', represents nothing more than a formulation of the cult value of the work of art in categories of spatio-temporal perception. Distance is the opposite of nearness. The essentially distant object is the unapproachable one. Inapproachability is, indeed, a primary quality of the cult image; true to its nature, the cult image remains 'distant, however close it may be'. (Diarmuid 2005, p. 173)

Black/white pictures rule over us from a distance even when they are archived in our family albums, scanned and posted online or carved out of a rather current photo through software on our smart phones or digital cameras. Even as we seek to possess them due to their appeal, they repel us with a *"Noli mi tangere*, touch me not, for I have not yet ascended to the father".[1] It is this inherent capacity to maintain distance its owner, to insinuate inaccessible curves, to deny absolute transparency to its beholder, that the black/white picture continues to emit an auratic presence.

One simple fact about pictures is: Pictures make us happy. Or let us say, pictures should make us happy. In our era of "selfies" where images are immediately hauled unto the social space without them tasting the aura of the archival album, the simulated black/white function on our gadgets seem to soothe the nostalgia for this type of image experience, reckoning the self away from an unaesthetic reality. The black/white picture affects its viewers through an exclamatory moment of recognition/mis-cognition. This exclamatory recognition/mis-cognition underlines the curtains between the self and the image, the forensic testimony of the passage of time and the evolution of the self. Black-and-white pictures seduce us with their beauty that is only earned through the passage of time. Who does not admire the strange familiarity of black/white pictures that reveal by concealing, attract by repelling and respond by inter-rogating? Drawing a black/white picture out of the family album/archive to view is an art in itself, a situational museum of casual re-telling that accords a sense of a family as an imagined unit of belonging.

Due to its temporal remove, the black/white presence on the user's profile accords it an autobiographi-cal dimension. In a judicious exploitation of relative qualities of black/white imaging and modern trends in popular photography, the Facebook page has become a space for the narration of autobiographies to those who might not otherwise have had access to any space of self-narration. In other words, popular appropriation of cyberspace has deconstructed the hierarchies that are implicitly inscribed in autobio-graphical writing and diffusion. Users' everyday practices on Facebook drive home the fact that every-one has a life story worth telling, that every life is a success story in its own way. The Facebook profile narrates the trajectories of the self through pictures and less through texts, for the relative advantage of the image that I earlier outlined above. There is no pure spectator, everyone is a key player. Facebook users take their images into their own hands and construct the reality and the fiction of the self, portray-ing their own philosophies of life, practices that are integral to mainstream autobiographical practices. They create their own images and sell to the world, enhanced by the elastic space of inscription that the cyber wall/world constitutes.

FACING THE CAMERA, FIXING THE SELF

One key aspect of photography in the new social media is the connection that subjects seek to draw between the appearance of the perfect body and the serenity of the self. The self assembles itself before the blitz of the camera. As a moment of summarizing the self for posterity, the frenzy of remembering one's self in the present, the pose, the composure, the posture, the style, the gaze. The outer shelf needs to bend to an ideal self within, that sense of unity that combines seriousness and equanimity, the face and the lens, the face and the self in a dialogue of the moment, fixing the body for the camera. And when there is overlap, we trim, we straighten. The photo dissects and splits the infinite "now" moment into pieces. It is by splitting our present-now-here (both as moment and as substance in space) re-building the nostalgic self, that the self belongs to us and to the splayed hands of time. We look at the photo and smile, smiling at our re-birth, but also our ephemerality - for sometimes, somewhere, other eyes shall look at us without us, thus the photo also archives the self for the others and for other times. The selfie rehearses the inevitability of the final moment. In the words of Susan Sontag,

Posing is like waiting for a moment, the shot, of which one knows nothing except that it must be the "right" moment. It's like a simple yet obscure emergency, the emergency of having to resemble oneself at a specific moment that will occur, which always occurs almost-now, always quite soon, always at risk of coming too early or too late. Having to resemble oneself soon becomes the requisitioning of a body ready, and thus readied, for the image. Posing consists of inventing a spare body for oneself, even against the will, inventing a proper site for the future remains of resemblance.[2] (1977)

Image-making is thus a temporal codification of self-invention par excellence. The act of resembling is thus necessarily tied to that of assembling, of pulling the self together for the camera in order that it should immortalize nothing but the most appropriate "now" moment. The moment where the self is at unity with the body is intended to correspond to a "now" of visual epiphany of the one taking the photo. The resultant photo should enhance the location of an ideal self on a perfectly disciplined body. If a photo were only a mundane reflection of surfaces, it would not infatuate or enthrall anyone the way it does. Photos 'know' more than that. A photo suggests a connection of the surface with the interior. The surface blitz, as transient as it is, posits as an innuendo that strips and teases the interior of the photographed being, exerting the exponential function of the photo - to convince us about the existence of a superlative interior beyond the positive surface. The ability of the photo to play with surfaces and suggest depths accounts for its appeal and evocative power. The pose and the gaze are removed from their casual and erratic enactments to suggest a sedimented way of being, of belief, of a locatable self, void of any peripheral attrition. Faced with such a photo, we almost inevitably desire to turn it around, to touch the nether side of something that is unfortunately inaccessible to human ability.

In conclusion, one can assert that through ludic practices and a sense of conviviality that characterize social media, a wide arsenal of strategies and tactics are employed by subjects to enhance self-image and self-esteem. In effect, an in-depth observation of the social media practices reveals the fact that the body, especially through its representative component the face is converted into an immense social text endowed with deeply symbolic codes. The body is constantly transversed by the camera lens to pose as an innuendo of something called "Self".

REFERENCES

Costello, D. (2005). Aura, Face, Photography: Re-Reading Benjamin Today. In A. Benjamin (Ed.), *Walter Benjamin and Art* (pp. 164–185). New York: Continuum.

Faccio, E. (2003). *The Corporeal Identity: When the Self-Image Hurts*. New York: Springer.

Finkelstein, J. (2007). *The Art of Self Invention: Image and Identity in Popular Visual Culture*. I.B.Tauris & Co Ltd.

Goffman, E. (1959). *The Presentation of the Self in Everyday Life*. Chicago: Anchor Books.

Mirzoeff, N. (1999). *An Introduction to Visual Culture*. London: Routledge.

Sontag, S. (1977). *On Photography*. New York: Farrar, Straus and Giroux.

ENDNOTES

[1]   Words spoken by Jesus Christ to May Magdalene when the latter recognised Him after resurrection. It is quoted in the Bible in John 20:17.

[2]   Elena Faccio expresses the now moment of the photographic shot in strikingly similar terms like Sontag. "Every single time a person has their photo taken they bring to life an image of themselves, perhaps even an imitation. Posing in front of the lens, in the moments before a photo is snapped, an individual, whilst pretending to be as natural as possible, has two things in mind: on the one hand she is trying to anticipate the finished image, and on the other, she assumes a manner and a posture she wishes to be identified from" (73).

Chapter 16
The Electric Soul:
Faith, Spirituality, and Ontology in a Digital Age

Benjamin J. Cline
Western New Mexico University, USA

ABSTRACT

This chapter will use media ecology, and rhetorical theories of ideology construction and social intervention to look at the ways that contemporary digital media interact with religious and spiritual practices in order to inform and create identities. This chapter will examine the ideology construction that occurs in the Crosswire.org applications, specifically PocketSword designed for the iPhone/iPad and AndBible designed for Android devices. This chapter will also look at the ideology construction and identity creation in the English language section of onislam.net, a website designed to help English-speaking Muslims live out their faith. Finally the chapter will consider Osel Shen Phen Ling, a website designed for "Practicing Buddhadharma in the Tibetan Gelugpa Tradition".

INTRODUCTION

The ontology that develops in a society shaped by new media is different than the ontology that might have been shaped without it. This chapter shows that through the electronic lifestyle that its media ecology has cultivated, the digital media age has given humans a different understanding of who we are. This ontological understanding develops within a framework which has been shaped by millennia of ontological discussion provided to us through the religious teaching and practices. Thus, the intersections where faith and spirituality meet with digital media are fruitful sites for the exploration of identity.

In addition to the concepts of identity provided by the religions informing the artifacts examined in this chapter, the chapter will use two important communication theoretical constructs as lenses whereby we can look at the phenomena of ontological construction in the media age: media ecology and the rhetoric of social intervention. The first theory is media ecology. "Media ecology is an intellectually vibrant, dynamic, and growing discipline within communication studies" (Forsberg, 2009, p. 137). It understands that media rea not merely parts of one's environments, rather media are environments (Postman N., 1970). These environments allow some ways of knowing, being, and valuing to develop easily while at the same time inhibiting others.

DOI: 10.4018/978-1-5225-0212-8.ch016

The rhetoric of social intervention (RSI) explains that communication messages act as interventions into ideologies as they are being socially constructed. In fact, RSI explains how ideology is socially constructed. RSI posits that interventions into society take place when communicators work to create "shifts" in one of three areas: on what society focuses its attention, in the perceptions of interpersonal needs, and finally in the social understanding of power structure (Brown, 1978; Opt & Gring, 2009). This chapter will show that the shift enacted by newer media in areas of spirituality are primarily shifts in attention. RSI contends that attention shifts come in three rhetorical forms, changes in the audience's epistemology, axiology or ontology (Brown, 1982; Huang, 1996; Gonzalez, 1989; Leroux, 1991; Opt & Gring, 2009; Stoner, 1989). The primary shift in spiritual communication when adjusting to new media is a shift in ontology.

This chapter will look at three specific spaces for interplay between faith and technology in order to explore the identity construction inherent in three spaces. Crosswire.org application, Onislam.net and Oshel Shen Phen Ling.

In order to study these sites, this chapter will have to lay some groundwork for the type of examination being done. First, the chapter will explain the role that media and faith each play separately in the process of identity construction. The chapter will thereby show that identity is not merely a construction of social messages. Rather, the media through which those messages are received and perceived also function in and of themselves to create identity. Our identity, then is at least partially constructed, not through what we are told, but by the medium that is used to tell us who we are.

The chapter will explain how religious practices function as media and thus how they can work into larger media ecology. In order to accomplish this, the chapter will refer to a broad range of spiritual activities as "faith-acts." Faith-acts can be understood as everything from communicating about one's faith or spiritual practice, creating or utilizing the mythology of one's faith or spiritual practice, to engaging in the actual rites and procedures of a particular practice. The chapter will show that inherent in that ideology is a rhetorical argument for a metaphysics that defines the identity of adherents.

By doing this, the chapter will have clearly shown that religious identity is more than simply checking a box in a demographic survey. Rather, the identity provided through religious and spiritual teaching is ontological and all encompassing. The faith-acts do more than tell a person who she or he is. They make a person who he or she is and who the other people around them are as well.

The chapter will then work to discuss the interplay between the two identity constructing agents. The chapter will show that the faith-based actions and artifacts which are enacted and created within the ecology inhabited by new media function as rhetorical interventions into the ideology which the medium is constructing. Following Brown (1978), the chapter will show that these interventions can be anomaly featuring, and thus can either counter the ideology inherent in the medium, or anomaly masking and thus can encourage the ideology in each of the media.

The first medium that will be analyzed will be the apps from Crosswire.org. The chapter will consider the ideology inherent in the way in which the apps work differently than reading an ink and paper Bible. The chapter will consider the ways in which the ideology of Bible-reading works for and against the ideology of on-screen delivery and the ways in which the apps create an argument in which anomalies are masked and identity is maintained.

The second medium considered is from the English Language portion of OnIslam.net. This chapter will look at the role of community constructions of the page. The chapter will consider the ways in which community can and cannot be constructed through an electronically mediated site and how those differences inherent in the media ecology of the internet might affect the identity of the adherents who use it.

Finally, the paper will look at the Osel Shen Phen Ling website. It will look at how the site works, succeeds, and fails to put the medium of the classic information-providing website in line with the faith's principles. We will look at how the site struggles with both its own identity and the identity of adherents in a media-saturated world.

Finally, this chapter will recommend other avenues for further research. The chapter will show how media ecology, the rhetoric of social intervention, and religious practice intertwine and have the potential to become a useful way of understanding and navigating identity.

BACKGROUND: FAITH, MEDIA ECOLOGY, AND RSI

Bringing the three concepts of faith, media ecology, and RSI together allows an understanding of how one derives one's ontological sense. Relationships between the three concepts of faith, media ecology, and the rhetoric of social intervention have been established separately. It will be in braiding these three together that will provide us with the means whereby we can see the establishment of ontological awareness and identity.

RSI is a body of theory which explains how ideology is rhetorically constructed and maintained. In this theory, ideology is seen as "that category of experience on which one is willing to bet the meaning of one's life" (Brown, 1978, p. 126). However, the fact such ideology holds such pertinence does not mean it holds permanence. Ideology is "a multidimensional fluctuating organic worldview wherein we have the possibility not only of processing information, but of incorporating that information in such a way that the entire ideology, remains stable and can undergo constant change due to the constant barrage of stimuli it encounters" (Cline, 2013, p. 111). A rhetor can change an audience's ideology by working in one of three ways: "the needs sub-cycle, the power sub-cycle and the input switching sub-cycle" (Brown, 1978 p. 135). Because all of these cycles are "simultaneously functioning sub-systems" (Stoner, 1989, p. 28), interventions have been tracked that have focused on the power sub-cycle (Brown, 1986; Snyder, 2009; Opt S., 2013) and on the needs needs sub-cycle (Opt S. K., 2012). However, this paper focuses on identity, which is an aspect of ontology.

Ontology tends to be primarily concerned with the "input-switching sub-cycle" which is often labeled as the "attention sub-cycle" (Brown, 1982; Gonzalez, 1989; Huang, 1996; Leroux, 1991; Stoner, 1989; Opt & Gring, 2009). In the attention sub-cycle, one can change between varying modes of epistemology, axiology and ontology (Brown, 1982, p. 22). One does this through "conceived-anomaly-masking and –anomaly-featuring" (p.22) wherein flaws in the ideological conception are either featured or masked to maintain or change the ideology. This is done by "shifting levels of interpretation, changing metaphors, and so on" (Stoner, 1989, p. 30). Opt and Gring explain that anomalies are recognized when "[l]ived experience fails to match the expectancies generated by our naming process." They go on to write: "Because we foreground some aspects of experience and background others to categorize symbolically, our names for experience are always *incomplete*. Our symbolic constructions always direct our attention *away* from parts of experience" (2009, p. 72) There are anomalies in every worldview that arise "when someone asserts that an accepted categorization of lived experience is 'inadequate' (Corley, 1983, p. 45) The end result is that a new system of accepting input either in epistemology, axiology, or ontology develops.

Cline established a relationship between the attention sub-cycle and media ecology (2012), explaining that media function as rhetorical interventions and that changes in media can, result in larger changes in ideology. That article focused on the role media play in epistemological construction. Because the sub-cycles are interconnected, media can logically play a role in one's ontology as well. When dealing with electronic means of understanding faith, the ecology of electronic media plays precisely such a role.

The relationship between faith and media ecology is a natural one. Forseberg (2009) has written about the link between faith and media ecology going as far as to comment on the minute difference between secular media ecologists and sectarian theologians. He positions one reason for this tie to the influence of the Jewish faith on Postman, one of the field's founders (Forseberg, 2005). While this tie is essential, the interplay between faith and media ecology is much greater.

Certainly, Postman's influence on the field of media ecology cannot be overlooked. The fact that Postman (1970) was the first to give the name, "media ecology," to the discipline adds to the fact that he did much to develop the field into what it is. His understanding of the way that media shape our politics (Postman N., Technopoly, 1992) and our society (Postman N., 1986) have allowed us to understand that media are not artifacts of our culture, nor the offspring of our culture, but progenitors of it. Nor can we overlook the influence of Postman's faith on his intellectual development. The fact that he referred to the narratives that allowed us to think within these ecologies as "idols" and "gods" (Postman N., The End of Education, 1996) shows that he was aware of the tie between the discipline he was creating and an understanding of the Divine.

The tie between media ecology and faith cannot be limited merely to Postman's Judaism. The faith-systems of other co-creators of the field of media ecology, especially the Catholicism of Walter Ong and the Christianity of Jaques Ellul, also had an impact on the field.

Both Ong and Ellul were explicit about the religious influence and both erase Forseberg's admittedly tenuous distinction between the media ecologist and the theologian. Ong and Ellul were both media ecologists and theologians drawing little distinction between the fields. Ong admitted that his study of communication was tied to his study of "the Word" in a liturgical and mystical sense:

[T]he Word was made flesh and dwelt, a Person, among us. . .[T]he word is here the proper name of a Person, the Son of God, himself God—eo verbum quo filius, runs the classic theological logion: 'He is Word by the fact that he is Son.' The designation Word thus belongs to the Son directly and immediately, just as the designation Son does. It is his divine name. (Ong, 1981, p. 15)

That study of the word cannot be separated from the media in which the word (or Word) is expressed:

[I]t would appear that the technological inventions of writings, print and electronic verbalization, in their historical effects are connected with and have helped bring about a certain kind of alienation within the human lifeworld. This is not to say that these inventions have been simply destructive, but rather they have restructured consciousness, affecting men's and women's presence to the world and to themselves in creating new interior distances within the psyche. (Ong, 1977, p. 17)

This change alters our sense not only of our language, but of everything: "Changes in the media of communication restructure man's sense of the universe in which he lives and his very sense of what his thought itself is" (Ong, 1967, p. 4). Media and faith, in Ong's germinal work in the study of media ecology, are, intimately intertwined.

For Ellul, faith was the primary components of reality: "[T]he presence of faith in Jesus Christ alters reality. . . It is not an illusion. On the contrary, it is reality itself" (Ellul J., 1981, p. 107). This reality was a necessary anchor in the midst of the transience and overwhelming effluvium of a mass mediated culture:

This claim may be shocking; but it is a fact that excessive data do not enlighten the reader or the listener; they drown him. He cannot remember them all, or coordinate them, or understand them; if he does not want to risk losing his mind, he will merely draw a general picture from them. And the more facts supplied, the more simplistic the image. (Ellul J., 1971, p. 87)

For Elull, the study of media ecology, was rooted in an attempt to understand the Divine and separate it from the excessive data in which he was drowning. Ellul explained this distinction while reflecting on the symbolism of Heaven, or New Jerusalem, and its possibility for spiritual clarity:

Jerusalem is surrounded with a wall, but this wall no longer has the meaning of a set of defenses, of a break between inside and outside. It is rather a sign of order, of harmony, of balance, of precision. That the holy city has for its foundations the twelve apostles obviously means that it is founded on the Word of God. It is not the apostles as persons who count, but the fact that they are bearers of the Word. This city is the opposite of the confusion of tongues, the opposite of Babel. In just this one fact we have the solution to the whole tragedy of our history. (Ellul, 1970, p. 197)

The belief that an understanding of both media, represented by Babel, and faith represented by Jerusalem could solve "the whole tragedy of our history" becomes an undergirding philosophy within media ecology.

RSI, media ecology, and faith have already been intertwined in the academic literature. A medium acts as a rhetor by altering the media ecology and thereby creating an ideological shift. Because ontology is one third of the input-switching sub-cycle, which is central to the concept of identity as a communication process, that ideological shift will certainly contain shifts in ontology, which includes visions of the self and identity. The ontological dimension of RSI, especially when considered from a media ecology perspective, becomes very much a spiritual dimension. It changes the view of the metaphysical self. So, identity is radically altered through one's mediated experience.

THE INTERPLAY OF MEDIA AND SPIRITUALITY

Issues, Controversies, Problems: The Faith Act as Media

The alteration of identity and ideology through mediated communication is complicated by the fact that religion and faith based practices are themselves media when considered from a media ecology perspective. Media ecology takes a broad definition of a medium as any means of producing or consuming communication, regardless of content. McLuhan explains that even a lightbulb can be seen as a medium because it allows an extension of sight into what would otherwise be a dark environment: "a light bulb creates an environment by its mere presence" (1965, p. 8). As a means of communicating, every religious rite can be seen not just as a single medium: "Rather it is an 'impure' genre. Like opera, which includes other genres, for example, singing, drama, and sometimes a little dancing—a ritual may include all of these and more" (Grimes, 1996/1990, p. 283). Faith-acts are multi-mediated activities often with multiple aims: "A fertility rite may not make crops grow. Nevertheless, it can succeed socially. Worship can lapse into civil ceremony and thus serve a vested political interest: thereby failing ethically. Meanwhile it can succeed in providing symbols that nourish or comfort individuals" (Grimes, 1996/1990, p. 283).

Furthermore, the acts done in faith are not always aimed at a human audience but are often done with a Divine auditor in mind. We cannot always argue that the human audience is the target of the media.

Whether or not the humans are primary audiences of the communication, there is certainly an effect that faith-acts have on the humans who experience them. Campbell said that these acts are three-fold. The first is "to reconcile waking consciousness to the *mysterium temendum et fascinans* of this universe *as it is*: the second being to render an interpretive total image of the same. . . it is the revelation to waking consciousness of the powers of its own sustaining source" (1968, p. 4). In RSI terms: to mask anomalies in the metaphysics of a community that are caused by the physics encountered by that community. This is accomplished by using metaphors that raise the level of abstraction. The third effect that Campbell said should come about from the faith act was "enforcement of moral order: the shaping of the individual to the requirements of his geographic and historically conditioned group" (1968, pp. 4-5). While the final function of a faith-act primarily functions in the power sub-cycle, the first two are inherently metaphysical arguments and ontological interventions into the input-switching sub-cycle of a given social group. Campbell summed up all three as giving "form to human life" (1972, p. 43). That form is certainly not a physical form, which humans have regardless of ideology, but rather a metaphysical form and thus an ontological argument.

According to Durkheim, that specific ontological argument divides reality into two "distinct terms which are translated well enough by the words *sacred* and *profane*" (1996/1915, p. 189). The sacred is holy, set apart from the profane but simultaneously the profane is an offshoot of the holy. Interestingly, the practitioners of a particular event must themselves be in a profane space that they must in some way make sacred. The media of the faith act is one of sanctification. Durkheim contrasts faith-acts with what he calls "magic" which he says "takes a sort of professional pleasure in profaning holy things." (Durkheim, 1996/1915, p. 191). Magic is the act of de-sanctification. It makes the otherworldly, worldly, rather than the converse. This definition is instructive in that magic is the opposite of what this chapter is referring to as a faith act. It is an act done in mockery of faith.

This provides an important tool when examining the faith-acts that will be analyzed later in this chapter. One can view the attempts to integrate the new media with the medium of a faith as either an act of faith or an act of magic. One can see it either as an act of sanctification, redeeming the worldly medium and making it holy or an attempt to profane the sacred by placing the sacred in the context of the worldly medium. Of course, this is not necessarily an either/or proposition. Durkheim admits to the ties between what he calls magic and what he calls religion: "magic is full of religion just as religion is full of magic" (Durkheim, 1996/1915, p. 191). Nonetheless he insists that a "line of demarcation can be traced between the two domains" (Durkheim, 1996/1915, p. 192). Acts of faith may be done side-by-side with acts of magic, but magic profanes while faith sanctifies.

Burke wrote extensively about the rhetorical process of sanctification. Acts of sanctification involve "transubstantiation, rituals of death and rebirth, whereby the individual identifies himself with a collective motive" (Burke, 1962, p. 38). In order to symbolically enter into a holy space, the individual must become holy. To do this, the individual "must seek to 'slay' within himself [or herself] whatever impulses run counter to the authoritative demands of sovereignty" (Burke, 1970, p. 406). Of course, one cannot literally slay a part of oneself. With apologies to *The Princess Bride,* one cannot be "mostly dead" (Reiner, 1987). The death must be accomplished "symbolically" by a group identifying themselves with a sort of vicar which "is profoundly consubstantial with those who, looking upon it as a chosen vessel would ritualistically cleanse themselves by loading the burden of their own iniquities on it" (Burke, 1962, p. 406), and putting it to death. The rhetoric of sanctification is tied to the natural human desire for perfection. To sanctify something is to move it toward perfection. This rhetorical ability to sanctify is not always a good thing in that it means putting to death the imperfect:

The principle of perfection . . . derives sustenance from other primary aspects of symbolicity. Thus, the principle of drama is implicit in the idea of action and the principle of victimage is implicit in the idea of drama. The negative helps radically to define the elements to be victimized. And inasmuch as substitution is a prime resource of symbol systems, the conditions are set for catharsis by scapegoat. (Burke, 1966, pp. 18-19)

Thus we see in some Christian rituals, the burial and rebirth of baptism a "putting to death" of a consubstantial "flesh" and in others, such as the Eucharist the transubstantial death of Jesus Christ bearing the sins of the adherents.

While the Christological parallels are explicit in Burke's work, Thames claims that Burke's notions of the negative as central the process of sanctification is a position which characteristic of Zen Buddhism rather than Christianity because the Nirvana of nothingness and oblivion is sought (Thames, 2007; Thames, 2012). Burke's notion of sanctification is a cultural universal without which, all cultures agree, we cannot enter into any holy place whether it be the pure nothingness of Nirvana or the purity of Heaven. The fact that Burke saw religion and sanctification as inherently tied to language, a fact which he referred to as "logology" (Burke, 1970), and given that all cultures have some sort of language, implies that Burke would not say his theory is limited to Christianity or Buddhism but can rather be seen as a "both/and." Indeed, Burke's germinal analysis of Hitler's work shows that the theory can even be applied, devastatingly, outside of any religious context (Burke, 1941).

This chapter examines the media ecology and ontological construction of the faith-acts originating in several faith communities. The faith-acts can be seen, as rhetorical interventions taking place within and defined by a media ecology. The chapter can then examine the ways in which that particular media ecology makes an ontological argument. The chapter will show that these faith-acts seek to sanctify certain mediated spaces and describe some of the scapegoating or anomaly masking that takes place to accomplish that goal.

Christianity and Crosswire: The Sanctification of Your Cell Phone

The ubiquity of the smart phone has radically changed the media ecology of the 21st century. Although every media function of the smart phone can find parallels in some previous medium, putting them all together in one place has radically changed human interaction: "it is the medium that shapes and controls the scale and form of human association and action. The content or uses of such media are as diverse as they are ineffectual in shaping the form of human association" (McLuhan, 1965, p. 9). Some of these associations seem almost seem reactionary when viewed across the history of human literacy. In 1981, Ong wrote: "The new age into which we have stepped entered has stepped up the oral and aural. Voice, muted by script and print, has come newly alive. For communications at a distance, written letters are supplemented and largely supplanted by telephone, radio and television" (p. 215). In many ways western society has reverted to textual communication. While people at one time primarily communicated with each other via voice and phones, now "18-24 year olds send or receive an average of 109.5 text messages per day—that works out to more than 3,200 messages per month" (Smith, 2011). While the book industry was dying out due to a greater interest in television, now "e-book sales as a percentage of overall revenue are skyrocketing" (Wasserman, 2012). The return to text-based communication over orality would logically give rise to a new placement of the Written Word of God.

That is exactly the attempt that Crosswire.org is making. On their "about" page, Crosswire says that their main purpose "is to distribute Scripture to as many people within a domain as possible" (The CrossWire Bible Society, n.d.). They do this is by providing "a place for engineers and others to come and collaborate on free, open-source projects aimed at furthering the Kingdom of our God" (The Cross-Wire Bible Society: Bringing the Gospel to a New Generation, n.d.).. For the apple family of mobile products including the iPhone, iPod touch, and iPad, they provide the PocketSword app (The CrossWire Bible Society, 2011). For android users, they provide the Android Bible App (Crosswire Bible Society, n.d.). They also provide applications for a number of other less popular operating systems (Crosswire Bible Society, n.d.).

Through these applications the user can download "modules" which include copies of the Bible in hundreds of translations into many languages. These modules, like the applications themselves are free of charge. Once downloaded, the "books" of the bible are placed in a navigable screen in their traditional order. The books can be navigated by book and chapter by tapping the appropriate part of the screen or by searching the text for words or phrases.

This makes navigation of the Bible different than navigating the print text. While searching for particular words would previously have taken at least two books, a Bible and a Concordance, searching for words now takes a single tap of the finger to call up the search box and a few clicks to type in the words. All conception of the size of books is gone. Psalms, which takes up more physical space than any two other books in a printed Bible now takes up a single small square, the same as the book of III John, which does not take up a single page in the printed text. The metaphor of the screen makes every book, and every chapter within a book, look the same. There are also differences in the way the applications can be used. A print version of the Bible is a powerful symbol to people who see the reader carrying around the hefty book. A Bible application can be read or carried with anonymity since there can be little difference to those around the reader as to whether it is the Bible or Facebook which is being accessed.

These differences in media result in a different experience with the text. According to Postman, media force us "to play certain roles" they "structure what we are seeing" and they "make us feel and act as we do" (Postman N., 1970, p. 161). The experiential change is powerful: "embedded in every tool is an ideological bias, a predisposition to construct the world as one thing rather than another, to value one thing over and other, to amplify once sense or skill or attitude more loudly than another" (Postman N., 1992, p. 13). The books of the Bible visually placed as equal, the ease of searching, the simplicity to which the application can be added to a device that is already present and then perused anonymously, all change the faith-act of Bible reading.

Every medium, according to Postman, "both rules out and insists upon certain kinds of content and inevitably, a certain kind of audience" (Postman N., 1986, p. 43). The question which must be considered in this chapter is whether the Bible application is sanctifying the cell phone user or if it is profaning the scripture reader: what is the ontological argument that is being made by this medium?

The question can be addressed by looking at the metaphors that the application itself. On the iPhone application, the icon is a backpack with a sword going through it. On the Android application, the icon is a small gold ichthys (the Christian fish symbol) on a black background. The release notes for the February 15th update explain that this icon replaced the cross on a black background because it was "safer for persecuted users" (CrossWire Bible Society, 2014). The cross is a well-recognized symbol of Christianity, and the ichthys is less well-known. The casual user who does not know much about Christian history would be able to look at the phone and not necessarily know that the user is engaging in a faith-act.

That fact alone means that the designers of the application are aware of the fact that anonymity is a feature of Bible reading in this medium. While this does put users in a position where they are less likely to have a witness forced on them, it does provide for a certain sanctification of a previously profane experience. The sanctification takes place in the mortification of the self. Jesus told his disciples:

And when thou prayest, thou shalt not be as the hypocrites are: for they love to pray standing in the synagogues and in the corners of the streets, that they may be seen of men. Verily I say unto you, they have their reward. But thou, when thou prayest, enter into thy closet, and when thou hast shut thy door, pray to thy Father which is in secret; and thy Father which seeth in secret shall reward thee openly. (Matt 6:5-6, King James Version)

The command is to create a secret, sacred space wherein the disciples could approach God. Christians who wanted to approach God had to find a separate physical space in which to do it. Christians who wish to approach God through the Bible application are able to do so anywhere and yet still find themselves in a sacred space, not one profaned.

The sacrifice made to sanctify the space may well be the "reward in full" to which Jesus referred. The person who prays in secret sacrifices the reward from his or her fellow adherents that they might have. The user of the crosswire family of applications does not get this reward. Rather, they are rewarded by an experience with the Divine.

This alters the ontology of the adherent. Rather than the confrontational self that a print copy of the Bible might create, the attention is shifted to an ontology of quiet communion with God. Living one's life for Christ does not need to mean living one's life as an attack on others. Rather it means living in a state where, through one's mobile device, there is always the possibility of apprehending God.

Islam and Onislam.net: A Far Flung Faith Community

Christianity is not the only faith-group which has entered begun to use 21st century technology in an attempt to adjust their faith-acts. Islam has embraced the internet as a means of creating community among far-flung adherents. A combination of factors including a high fertility rate have made Muslims the fastest growing religious group in the world (Lipka & Hackett, 2015). As a result of immigration, Islam is also the fastest growing population in areas not historically associated with the faith. For instance, Islam is the fastest growing religion in Europe (Koroma & Carlos, 2015). While it is not the fastest growing religion in North America, 60% of all refugees to the United States have been from Muslim-majority countries (US Refugee Program: Final FY2009 Admission Statistics, 2009). This means that there are an increasing number of Muslim people far from their traditional homes. For a religion which highly values community, or ummah, this can be difficult.

The concept of the ummah is an important part of Islam. It is a concept that there is one single community of Muslims, worldwide: "This ummah of yours is a single ummah, and I am your Lord, so worship me." (Surah al-Anbiya': 92). The purpose of this community is to allow people to come to a deeper understanding of their faith: "And surely this your nation is one nation and I am your Lord, therefore be careful (of your duty) to Me" (Surah Mu'minin 23:52). Many Muslim scholars believe that as the members of the Islamic faith grow in number and move worldwide, that Allah is returning people to a position of unity, as one people, all united in a single community: "But they were cut off from one another in the matter of their unity, and yet they will all return to Us." (Surah al-Anbiya': 93). Yet this unity can feel quite lonely to a Muslim person very far, physically, from the other members of the community and it can be hard for the Islamic community to instruct the individual Muslim who is far from them.

Bitzer has noted that situations create a rhetorical exigence which calls forth discourse (Bitzer, 1968). This exigence for community and instruction coupled with the actual construction of what McLuhan referred to as a "global village" (1965; 1962) through the internet has created a discourse which includes the medium of onislam.net (Onislam.net, 2015). Much of the site is simply a religious news outlet. Those wishing to know about the happenings of the Muslim faith and events in Muslim dominated countries can go there and learn about current events. A significant aspect of the site, however is dedicated to "counselling." Several links from the main English-Language portion of the page instruct the user to "Ask a Scholar," "Ask about Islam," "Ask about Parenting," "Ask about Hajj and Umra" and "ask the Counselor." These spaces allow the user to interact with other members of the Islamic community, in the English language they use every day, and receive instruction and deeper knowledge about his or her faith.

Of course the community online is different from face-to-face physical communities. There are consequences for breaking with the community's recommendations that are not necessarily realized in virtual space. For instance, under the category "common mistakes" in Onislam.net's ask a scholar category, an adherent named Timea asked whether or not was "permissible in Islam to use a cell phone while being in the bathroom." She explained that she knew that she wasn't allowed to talk, but she just wasn't sure about texting or using social media via a smart phone (Shihab & Timea, 2014). The answer was clearly given that people are not allowed to use social media while in the bathroom. One can imagine that in a more physical community, there would be customs and mores that would have instructed Timea in appropriate etiquette in these situations and she might not have asked at all. Furthermore, one wonders whether, now that she knows, whether Timea will alter her behavior and for how long she will do so. There is no physical community to reinforce her faith's dictates. The community is there to teach, but not to police.

Similarly, an adherent named Muslimah asked if it was okay to for men and women to dance together (Muslimah & Salamah, 2015). He was told that dancing is okay if a woman dances in front of her husband, but otherwise men should only dance in front of men and women in front of women. Whether or not Muslima took the advice or not was not something the community would be able to ascertain.

Assumedly, questions such as these are asked by adherents because of a legitimate desire to live out their faith in an authentic and pure way. There is every possibility that once they learned their community's standards, they made every effort to live their lives by them. On the other hand, one major difference between McLuhan's global village and an actual village is one of accountability. The lack of accountability comes from what Burke referred to as "recalcitrance." This is the main foil against a complete symbolic construction of reality. Statements can be made and interpreted but "the interpretations themselves must be altered as the universe displays various orders of recalcitrance to them" (Burke, 1954, p. 256). No matter how hard one tries to create a virtual community, one can simply turn one's computer off and go about one's private affairs to a much larger extent than one can turn off a face-to-face community.

There is, in Onislam.net an attempt to create something that is holy in Islam on the internet. Certainly, it is the purview of specific Islamic scholars, rather than scholars of communication, to decide whether or not this has succeeded or failed and the extent of that success or failure. However, from a

RSI standpoint, there is a strong question as to whether or not the media ecology of a website is really conducive to making the ontological shift of an actual community. According to Brown, an attention shift must be able to feature or mask anomalies by making a change in abstractions (Brown, 1982). The attempt is clearly made to sanctify a specific portion of the internet, but it seems that sanctification is at best a partial attempt.

Osel Shen Phen Ling: Electric Dharma

While McLuhan was excited about the potential for electronic communication to provide a means whereby the Global Village could come into being, and while community in some form or another is generally an aspect of most religions, not all attempts at ontological shift aim at community. A good example of a faith-based electronic site that is attempting another type of ontological shift is the Osel Shen Phen Ling (Foundation for the Preservation of the Mahayana Tradition, n.d.), a site for teaching the Mahayana Tradition of Buddhism.

The site makes little attempt at what has been called a web 2.0 environment, that is an environment that uses a great deal of user generated content (DiNucci, 1999). The site takes very little advantage of the possibilities of more recent versions of HTML or CSS. Visually, it is a site that would have been quite appropriate on the internet of 1998 and seems anachronistic on the contemporary web. Yet, the simplicity of the design seems to augment and reflect its purpose, and that purpose is the teaching of dharma, "he practice (*paṭipatti*) of . . . truth, and as its realization in stages (*paṭivedha*) up to nirvana, of which in this way dharma becomes a synonym" (Bowker, 1997) and the teachings of its manifestation, the Buddha.

The main part of the page involves the page's title across the top, a quote from a Buddhist writing in the center, surrounded on the left, bottom, and right with four links. Sometimes, if an important event is going on at their headquarters, there would be a link below about that. Finally, across the bottom is the physical and mailing address of the headquarters and the official seal of affiliation with the Foundation for the Preservation of the Mahayana Tradition.

Other than the links to the official page of the Foundation for the Preservation of the Mahayana Tradition, none of the links take the user to pages any more advanced than the home page. Many of the pages are textually heavy because they provide teachings and prayers without many hyper-links or pictures. This is not a site with which to fully interact. This is a site from which to learn by reading, and contemplation, a type of learning associated with Buddhist thought.

There would be a temptation to critique the rhetoric of the site. It does not make use of "all the available means of persuasion," in the Aristotelian sense (Aristotle, 2011), however, even Aristotle would not have advocated using all the available means, just knowing or finding them. After finding them it is wise to settle on the best one for the medium, the audience, and the message. From that point of view, a simplicity of the message reflected in the simplicity of the site provides precisely the type of site found here. Another critique that could be offered is that it does not take into account the best practices that develop from a web-based medium. That is, it resists the media ecology in which it finds itself.

That kind of resistance, however, has been the hallmark of Mahayana Buddhism since the Chinese took Tibet in 1951. Mahayana Buddhists set as their goal becoming Bodhisattvas by reaching six perfections: generosity, morality, tolerance, energy, meditation, and wisdom (Write, 2009). Thereafter, they are able to bring enlightenment to others by living in the world while resisting its pleasures. One teaching describes such a resistance to the environment:

In jungles of poisonous plants strut the peacocks,

Though medicine gardens of beauty lie near.

The masses of peacocks do not find gardens pleasant,

But thrive on the essence of poisonous plants.

In similar fashion, the brave Bodhisattvas

Remain in the jungle of worldly concern.

No matter how joyful this world's pleasure gardens,

These Brave Ones are never attracted to pleasures,

But thrive in the jungle of suffering and pain.

A more contemporary web design or a flashy page might be "pleasant" but it would, in many ways distract from the "suffering and pain" of these "Brave Ones." The simplicity of the page is not an act of violent resistance to the world in which it finds itself, but one of a more passive resistance.

Which is the ontological shift that the rhetoric of the site, as whole, is trying to make. The site is aimed at current adherents to Mahayana Buddhism. It is not asking them to rise violently against or in spite the world in which they find themselves. Rather, to rise in the world in which they find themselves without regard to that world. This resistance to the media ecology of the contemporary web mirrors the resistance in which the Bodhisattvas of Mahayana Buddhism aspire.

The website becomes a holy place, set apart, among the other tabs one may have opened on one's browser. It is a place where one quietly receives teaching rather than interactively moving a series of links or posting one's own thoughts. The pleasures of the contemporary web are sacrificed and the user undergoes what Burke refers to as a mortification, killing the pleasure of a media-rich website, as one gains teachings from the links. The use of the medium itself is an ontological attention shift. To receive these teachings is akin to the Bodhisattvas vows, allowing the one who is becoming enlightened to stand among the worldly pleasures of the internet, but simultaneously renounce their attraction. The identity as one who aspires to be a Bodhisattva is reinforced.

SOLUTIONS AND RECOMMENDATIONS

This chapter has used the communication theories of media ecology and RSI to assess the ontological shifts, the shifts in identity, which users of three different faith-based media experience. The chapter recognized and problematized the application of media ecology to faith-acts which were already forms of media themselves. To sort through these difficulties, this chapter has considered what faith-acts in general attempt to accomplish and found that all faith-acts work to sanctify the adherent so that he or she can then be brought into sacred space. That new sacred identity allows the adherent to gain access to the Divine despite being physically bound, in some ways, to the profane.

The chapter was able to begin to explore three very different ways that that the media of faith and electronic media converge to sanctify adherents. This chapter was even able to assess the effectiveness of this largely spiritual rhetoric by looking at the extent to which the media ecologies of the faith and the medium interacted.

The chapter found three very different approaches to the formation of the media ecologies. In Cross-Wire.org, the creation and alteration of the applications seems to have been a complete embrace of the medium's natural tendency toward anonymity. The applications are designed to allow the users to create a sacred space anywhere, to be sanctified and enter into the holy space while physically bound in the profane.

The second site, onislam.net used a very different approach. The attempt seems to be made to integrate the Islamic notion of community into the virtual community of the web 2.0 experience. The holy space is created by making the ummah into something like a cross between a social networking site and an advice column. This second strategy, integration, does not seem to work well in this case.

The third solution is that of resistance, in the case of Osel Shen Phen Ling. The site does not go in for the typical bells and whistles of a contemporary website. Instead, it resists the media ecology, finding a niche where it can exist less molested by the ecology of which it is a part. While this seems to work well in the specific ontological argument of Mahayana Buddhism, clearly it is a difficult path to follow.

Thus we arrive at three solutions for bringing together new media into the media of a faith: embrace, integration and resistance. All should be considered by those consciously considering the effect on the media ecology on their faith-acts. There may be a fourth choice as well, and that is rejection. Certain Mennonite factions, especially the Amish, are known for their rejection of new media into their faith-lives. Other groups such as the Reformed Presbyterian Church of North America and many independent Churches of Christ in the Restoration Movement have rejected even the notions of musical accompaniment to their worship because of fears closely related to media ecology (White, 1989). The complete and total rejection of particular media for sacramental purposes is certainly a sacrifice that could be used to make a space sacred.

FUTURE RESEARCH DIRECTIONS

Stanley Fish was asked by a reporter "what would succeed high theory and the triumvirate of race, gender, and class as the center of intellectual energy in the academy. [To which he] answered like a shot: religion" (Fish, 2005). Faith is one of the most powerful forces for shaping identity. It does not, however, do so in a vacuum. Faith shapes identity, but media create the ecology in which that faith develops and therefore, that ecology demands to be studied.

This chapter used RSI and media ecology as broad brushes with which to examine questions of how media create ontological shifts in one's faith. Further research might apply RSI and media ecology broadly to a number of faith-acts, practices and communities. However, both of these theories have more narrow applications which would also render unique insight into the way that a faith identity is developed. Both broad and narrow methodologies should be applied if scholars are to fully understand the interplay between faith, identity, and media.

The chapter identified four approaches of a faith community to a new medium: to embrace it, to integrate it, to resist it, or to reject it. However, the chapter only hinted at the variety of ways that this can be done. More sites need to be examined which do each of these and strategies for doing them well need to be described.

Furthermore, while this chapter chose sites for analysis that clearly analyze media which embrace, integrate, or resist the media ecology in which they are found, the fourth choice, rejection, does not lend itself to typical rhetorical or media studies analysis. The communication of a group rejecting a particular medium would not be found in the medium they are rejecting. A different type of analysis needs to be done looking at those trying to remain apart from a particular medium. Probably ethnographic or other anthropological techniques would be needed to investigate these sites.

Finally, because it is focused on the media ecology, this chapter virtually ignores the content that the sites are producing. McLuhan argued that the medium is the message, but that does not necessarily mean that the message should not be examined. More traditional textual analysis of mediated sites will almost certainly provide insight into the relationship they are creating between faith and identity.

CONCLUSION

This chapter has examined the relationship between media, faith, and identity. It explained theoretically and philosophically the relationship between the three. Using concepts of media ecology and RSI, the chapter proved that the medium in which a faith act occurs affects the ontology, and therefore identity, of the adherent. It has shown that the intersections where faith and spirituality meet with digital media are, fruitful sites for the exploration of identity. The specific sites investigated showed that a faith act can embrace, integrate, or resist the media ecology of a medium with consequences to the identity of this users by doing so. While the intersections of faith, media, and identity can probably never be fully mapped, this chapter has provided a sketch of how such a project can begin.

REFERENCES

Aristotle. (2011, September 27). *Aristotle's Rhetoric*. L. Honeycutt (Ed.). Retrieved 20 2012, February, from Aristotle's rhetoric: http://rhetoric.eserver.org/aristotle/index.html

Bitzer, L. (1968). The Rhetorical Situation. *Philosophy & Rhetoric, 1*(1), 1–14.

Bowker, J. (1997). *Dharma*. Retrieved July 3, 2015, from The Concise Osford Dictionary of World Religions: http://www.encyclopedia.com/doc/1O101-Dharma1.html

Brown, W. R. (1978). Ideology as communication process. *The Quarterly Journal of Speech, 64*(2), 123–180. doi:10.1080/00335637809383420

Brown, W. R. (1982). Attention and the rhetoric of social intervention. *The Quarterly Journal of Speech, 64*(1), 17–27. doi:10.1080/00335638209383588

Brown, W. R. (1982). Attention and the Rhetoric of Social Intervention. *The Quarterly Journal of Speech*, *68*(1), 17–27. doi:10.1080/00335638209383588

Brown, W. R. (1986). Power and the rhetoric of social intervention. *The Quarterly Journal of Speech*, *64*, 180–199.

Burke, K. (1941). *The Philosophy of Literary Form*. Baton Rouge, LA: Louisiana State University Press.

Burke, K. (1954). *Permanence and Change: An Anatomy of Purpose*. Los Angeles: University of California Press.

Burke, K. (1962). *A Grammer of Motives and A Rhetoric of Motives*. New York: The World Publishing Company.

Burke, K. (1966). *Language As Symbolic Action*. Berkeley, CA: Univeristy of California Press.

Burke, K. (1970). *The Rhetoric of Relgion: Studies in Logology*. Los Angeles, CA: Unviersity of California Press.

Campbell, J. (1968). *The Masks of God: Creative Mythology*. New York: The Viking Press.

Campbell, J. (1972). *Myths to live by: How we Re-Create Ancient Legends in Our Daily Loves to Release Human Potential*. New York: Bantam Books.

Cline, B. (2012). The Future of Reading/Thinking: Epistemological Construction in the Age of the Kindle. *Communication +1, 1*(1), Article 2.

Cline, B. (2013). Axiology and the FCC: Regulation as Ideological Process. In *E. Zack Stiegler, Regulating the Web: Network Neutrality and the Fate of the Open Internet* (pp. 109–120). Lexington, KY: Lexington Books.

Corley, J. R. (1983). A Communication study of Arthur F. Holmes as a worldview advocate (Doctoral Dissertation, The Ohio State University, 1983). *Dissertation Abstracts International*, *44*.

CrossWire Bible Society. (2014, February 15). *AndBible Release Notes*. Retrieved July 7, 2015, from AndBible: https://code.google.com/p/and-bible/wiki/ReleaseNotes

Crosswire Bible Society. (n.d.). *and-bible-- Bible App for Android*. Retrieved 07 05, 2015, from Google Codee: https://code.googlc.com/p/and-bible/

Crosswire Bible Society. (n.d.). *Mobile*. Retrieved July 6, 2015, from The CrossWire Bible Society: http://crosswire.org/applications/?section=Handhelds

Dharmarakshita. (n.d.). *The Wheel of Sharp Weapons Effectively Striking the Heart of the Foe*. Retrieved July 2, 2015, from Osel Shen Phen Ling: http://www.fpmt-osel.org/teachings/wheel.pdf

DiNucci, D. (1999). Framented Future. *Print*, *53*(4), 32–33.

Durkheim, E. (1996). Ritual, Magic, and the Sacred. In R. L. Grimes (Ed.), *Readings in Ritual Studies* (pp. 188–201). Upper Saddle River, NJ: Prentice Hall Inc.(Original work published 1915)

Ellul, J. (1970). *The meaning of the city* (D. Pardee, Trans.). Grand Rapids, MI: William B Eerdman's Publishing Company.

Ellul, J. (1971). *Propaganda: The formations of men's attitudes* (K. Kellen & J. Lerner, Trans.). New York: Alfred A. Knopf.

Ellul, J. (1981). *Perspectives on our age* (J. Neugroschel, Trans.). New York: Seasbury.

Ellul, J. (n.d.). *76 Reasonable Questions to ask about any technology*. Retrieved December 5, 2014, from T. David's Page: http://www.tdgordon.net/media_ecology/76_reasonable_questions.doc

Fish, S. (2005). One University, Under God?. *The Chronicle of Higher Education*, 18.

Forsberg, G. E. (2009). Media Ecology and Theology. *Journal of Communication and Religion*, *32*, 135–156.

Forseberg, G. F. (2005). Postman and the Judeo-Christian Worldview. *Journal of Communication and Religion*, *28*, 252–285.

Foundation for the Preservation of the Mahayana Tradition. (n.d.). Retrieved January 26, 2015, from Osel Shen Phen Ling: Land of Clear Light Benefitting Others: http://www.fpmt-osel.org/

Gonzalez, A. (1989). "Participation" at WMEX-FM: Interventional rhetoric of Ohio Mexican Americans. *Western Journal of Speech Communication*, *53*(4), 398–410. doi:10.1080/10570318909374317

Grimes, R. L. (1996). Ritual Criticism and Infelicitous Performances. In *Readings in Ritual Studies* (pp. 289–293). Upper Saddle River, NJ: Grimes, Ronald L.(Original work published 1990)

Huang, S. (1996). *To rebel is justified: a rhetorical study of China's cultural movement, 1966-1969*. Lanham, MD: University Press of America.

Koroma, S., & Carlos, M. H. (2015, January 16). *How Islam became the fastest growing religion in Europe*. Retrieved July 3, 2015, from Time.Com: http://time.com/3671514/islam-europe/

Leroux, N. (1991). Frederick Douglas and the Attention shift. *Rhetoric Society Quarterly*, *21*(2), 36–46. doi:10.1080/02773949109390915

Lipka, M., & Hackett, C. (2015, April 23). *Why Muslims are the world's fastest-growing religious group*. Retrieved from FactTank: The News In Numbers: http://www.pewresearch.org/fact-tank/2015/04/23/why-muslims-are-the-worlds-fastest-growing-religious-group/

McLuhan, M. (1962). *The Gutenberg Galaxy*. Toronto, Canada: Toronto University Press.

McLuhan, M. (1965). Understanding Media: The extensions of Man with a new introduction and bibliography by the author (Paperback ed.). New York: McGraw-Hill.

Muslimah, & Salamah, S. A. (2015, March 03). *Dancing: What Is Allowed and What Is Not?* Retrieved from Onislam.net: http://www.onislam.net/english/ask-the-scholar/arts-and-entertainment/singing-and-music/175634-dancing-what-is-allowed-and-what-is-not.html?Music=

Ong, W. J. (1967). *In The Human Grain: Further Explanations of Contemporary Culture*. New York: The Macmillan Company.

Ong, W. J. (1977). *Interfaces of the Word: Studies in the evolution of consiousness and culture.* Cornell University Press.

Ong, W. J. (1981). *The Presence of the Word: Some Prolegomena for cultural and religious history.* Minneapolis, MN: University of Minnesota Press.

Ong, W. J. (2002). Orality and Literacy: The Technologizing of the Word (2nd ed.). New York: Routledge.

Onislam.net. (2015). *On Islam.* Retrieved January 26, 2015, from Onislam.net: http://www.onislam. net/english/

Opt, S. (2013). Apology as Power Intervention: The Case of News of the World. *Western Journal of Communication, 77*(4), 424–443. doi:10.1080/10570314.2013.767471

Opt, S. K. (2012). Mammogram-Screening Policy as Need Intervention. *Journal of Applied Communication Research, 40*(1), 1–19. doi:10.1080/00909882.2011.636375

Opt, S. K., & Gring, M. A. (2009). *The Rhetoric of Social Intervention, An Introduction.* Thousand Oaks, CA: Sage.

Postman, N. (1970). The reformed English curriculum. In A. C. Eurich (Ed.), *High school 1980: The shape of the future in American secondary education* (pp. 160–168). New York: Pitman.

Postman, N. (1986). *Amusing Ourselves To Death, Public Discourse in the age of show business.* New York: Penguin Books Ltd.

Postman, N. (1990, October 11). *Informing Ourselves To Death.* Retrieved December 10, 2014, from Electronic Frontier Foundation: https://w2.eff.org/Net_culture/Criticisms/informing_ourselves_to_death. paper

Postman, N. (1992). *Technopoly.* New York: Alfred A. Knopf.

Postman, N. (1996). *The End of Education.* New York: Alfred A Knopf.

Postman, N. (2000, June 16). *The Humanism of Media Ecology.* Retrieved December 12, 2014, from Media Ecology Association: http://media-ecology.org/publications/MEA_proceedings/v1/humanism_of_media_ecology.html

Reiner, R. (Director). (1987). *The Princess Bride* [Motion Picture].

Shihab, W., & Timea. (2014, December 25). *Using Cell Phone in Bathroom: Allowed?* Retrieved July 3, 2015, from Onislam.net: http://www.onislam.net/english/ask-the-scholar/common-mistakes/481077-using-cell-phone-in-bathroom-allowed.html

Smith, A. (2011, September 19). *How Americans Use Text Messaging.* Retrieved from Pew Research Center: http://www.pewinternet.org/2011/09/19/how-americans-use-text-messaging/

Snyder, L. (2009). Born To Power: Influence in the rhetoric of the Posse Comitatus. In S. K. Opt & M. A. Gring (Eds.), *The Rhetoric of Social Intervention: An Introduction* (pp. 213–230). Los Angeles, CA: Sage. doi:10.4135/9781452274935.n11

Stoner, M. R. (1989). Understanding social movementL rhetoric of social intervention. *The Speech Communication Annual, 3*, 298–310.

Thames, R. H. (2007). The Gordian Not: Untangling the Motivorum. *K. B. Journal. The Journal of the Kenneth Burke Society, 3*(2). Retrieved from http://kbjournal.org/thames1

Thames, R. H. (2012). The Meaning of the Motivorum's Motto: "Ad bellum purificandum" to "Tendebantque manus ripae ulterioris amore". *K.B Journal: The Journal of the Kenneth Burke Society, 8*(1). Retrieved July 4, 2015, from http://kbjournal.org/thames_motivorum_motto

The CrossWire Bible Society. (2011, September 8). *PocketSword: an iPhone Bible Study app*. Retrieved July 5, 2015, from Crosswire.org: http://www.crosswire.org/pocketsword/PocketSword/PocketSword/PocketSword.html

The CrossWire Bible Society. (n.d.). *The CrossWire Bible Society*. Retrieved July 5, 2015, from About: http://crosswire.org/about/

The CrossWire Bible Society. (n.d.). Bringing the Gospel to a New Generation. *CrossWire*. Retrieved January 26, 2014, from CrossWire: http://www.crosswire.org/

US Refugee Program: Final FY2009 Admission Statistics. (2009, October). Retrieved April 16, 2011, from Cultural Orientation Resource Center: http://www.cal.org/co/refugee/statistics/final_FY2009.html

Wasserman, S. (2012). *The Amazon Effect*. Retrieved 6 2, 2012, from The Nation: http://www.thenation.com/article/168125/amazon-effect

White, J. F. (1989). *Protestant Worship*. Westminster, UK: John Knox Press.

Write, D. (2009). *The Six Perfections: Buddhism and the Cultivation of Character*. New York: Oxford University Press.

ADDITIONAL READING

Alexander, M. S. (2006). The Media Ecology Perspective. *The Review of Communication, 6*(4), 365–368. doi:10.1080/15358590601037225

Altheide, D. L. (1995). An Ecology of Communication: Cultural Formats of Control. New York: Berlin and Hawthorne.

Anton, C. (2012). McLuhan, Formal Cause and the Future of Technological Mediation. *The Review of Communication, 12*(4), 276–289. doi:10.1080/15358593.2012.687115

Barthes, R. (1981). *Camera Lucida* (R. Howard, Trans.). New York: Hill and Wang.

Bateson, G. (1972). *Steps to an ecology of mind*. New York: Harper & Row.

Blakesley, D. (2002). *The Elements of Dramatism*. New York: Longman.

Burke, K. (1968). *Counter-Statement*. Los Angeles: University of California Press.

Burke, K. (2007). *A Symbolic of Motives* (W. H. Rueckert, Ed.). West Lafayette, IN: Parlor Press.

Carey, J. W. (1989). *Communication as culture: Essays on media and scoiety*. Boston: Unwin Hyman.

Cavell, S. (1985). What photography calls thinking. *Raritan*, *4*, 1–21.

Crowley, D. J., & Heyer, P. (Eds.). (2011). *Communication in history: Technology, Culture and Society*. Boston: Allyn & Bacon/Pearson.

Ellul, J. (1970). *Prayer and the Modern Man* (C. E. Hopkin, Trans.). New York: Seabury Press.

Ellul, J. (1988). *Anarchy and Christianity* (G. Bromiley, Trans.). Grand Rapids, Michigan: William B. Eerdmans Publishing Company.

Gencarelli, T. F. (2000). The intellectual roots of media ecology on the thought and work of Neil Postman. *New Jersey Journal Communication*, *8*(1), 91–103. doi:10.1080/15456870009367381

Grimes, R. (1996). *Readings in Ritual Studies*. Upper Saddle River, NJ: Prentice Hall.

Landow, G. P. (1992). *Hypertext: The Convergence of Contemporary Critical Theory and Technology*. Baltimore: Johns Hopkins University Press.

Lull, J. (2000). *Media, Communication, Culture: A Global Approach* (2nd ed.). New York: Columbia University Press.

Lum, C. M. (2006). *Perspectives on Culture, Technology and Communication: The Media Ecology Tradition*. Cresskill, NJ: Hampton Press.

McLuhan, E. (1998). *Electirc Language: Understanding the Message*. Buzz Books.

McLuhan, M., & Fiore, Q. (1967). *The Medium is the Massage: An inventory of effects*. New York: Bantam Books.

Nevitt, B. (1982). *The Communication Ecology: Re-presentation vs. Replica*. Toronto: Butterworths.

Ong, W. (1971). *Rhetoric, Romance, and Technology*. Ithaca, NY: Cornell University Press.

Orr, D. (1992). *Ecological Literacty: education and the Transition to a Postmodern World*. Albany, NY: State University of New York.

Ross, S. M. (2009). Postman, Media Ecology, and Education: From Teaching as a Subversive Activity through Amusing Ourselves to Death to Technopoly. *The Review of Communication*, *9*(2), 146–156. doi:10.1080/15358590802326435

Sanderson, G., & Macdonald, F. (Eds.). (1989). *Marshall McLuhan: The Man and His Message*. Golden, CO: Fulcrum.

Strate, L. (2006). *Echoes and reflections: on media ecology as a field of study*. Cresskill, NJ: Hampton.

KEY TERMS AND DEFINITIONS

Anomalies: Holes in ideologies which develop when lived experience does not match up to one's ideology.

Faith Act: An act done as an expression of one's faith: everything from communicating about one's faith or spiritual practice, creating or utilizing the mythology of one's faith or spiritual practice, to engaging in the actual rites and procedures of a particular practice.

Input Switching Sub-Cycle (Attention Sub-Cycle): That part of our ideology that tells people what things to pay attention to.

Media Ecology: Understanding media as environments.

Medium (*plural, "Media"*)**:** Any means of producing or consuming communication, regardless of content.

Ontology: One's sense of being including metaphysics and identity.

Profane: Things which are not sacred.

Rhetor: Something or someone that is engaged in rhetoric.

Rhetoric of Social Intervention (RSI): A rhetorical theory that explains the ideology as a communication process.

Sacred: Something set apart for religious purposes.

Sanctification: Making something sacred.

Compilation of References

2015 Andrew T. Nadell Book Collectors Contest. (n.d.). Duke University Libraries. Accessed November 10, 2014. http://library.duke.edu/support/friends/book-collectors-contest

A brief history of the selfie. (n.d.). *ABC Science blog*. ABC Online.

Aarsand, P. A. (2007). Computer and video games in family life: The digital divide as a resource in intergenerational interactions. *Childhood*, *14*(2), 235–256. doi:10.1177/0907568207078330

Aberg, A. C., Sidenvall, B., Hepworth, M., O'Reily, K., & Lithell, H. (2004). Continuity of the self in later life: Perceptions of informal caregivers. *Qualitative Health Research*, *14*(6), 792–815. doi:10.1177/1049732304265854 PMID:15200801

About. (n.d.). Documenting the American South. Accessed November 11, 2014. Available: http://docsouth.unc.edu/support/about/

Adams, C. (2010). Cyberbullying: How to make it stop. *Instructor*, *120*(2), 44–49.

Admiral, G. (2014, September 17). 4Chan mods shutting down #GamerGate discussions. *Attack on Gaming*. Retrieved June 28, 2015, from http://attackongaming.com/gaming-talk/4chan-mods-shutting-down-gamergate-discussions/

Advertising Techniques. (n.d.). Retrieved March 1, 2013, Retrieved April 8, 2013 from http://www.foothilltech.org/rgeib/english/media_literacy/advertising_techniques.htm

Akbulut, Y., Sahin, T. L., & Eristi, B. (2010). Cyberbullying victimization among Turkish online social utility members. *Journal of Educational Technology & Society*, *13*, 192–201.

Akhtar, S. (2011). *The electrified mind: Development, psychopathology, and treatment in the era of cell phones and the Internet*. Lanham, MD: Jason Aronson.

Alberty, E. (2014, October 16). Anita Sarkeesian explains why she canceled USU lecture. *The Salt Lake Tribune*. Retrieved June 28, 2015, from http://www.sltrib.com/sltrib/news/58528113-78/sarkeesian-threats-threat-usu.html.csp

Albinsson, P. A., & Perera, B. Y. (2012). Consumer activism through social media: carrots versus sticks. In A. Close (Ed.), *Online consumer behavior: Theory and research in social media, advertising, and e-tail* (pp. 101–132). New York: Routledge.

Alexander, L. (2014, August 28). *'Gamers' don't have to be your audience. 'Gamers' are over*. Retrieved June 28, 2015, from http://gamasutra.com/view/news/224400/Gamers_dont_have_to_be_your_audience_Gamers_are_over.php

Allaway, J. (2014, October 13). #Gamergate trolls aren't ethics crusaders; they're a hate group. *Jezebel*. Retrieved June 28, 2015, from http://jezebel.com/gamergate-trolls-arent-ethics-crusaders-theyre-a-hate-1644984010

Althusser, L. (1972). *Lenin and philosophy and other essays*. New York, NY: Monthly Review Press.

Anderson, D., & Subramanyam, R. (2011, April 12). *The new digital American family: Understanding family dynamics, media and purchasing behavior trends.* Retrieved January 10, 2015, from Nielsen Media Research: http://www.nielsen.com/us/en/insights/reports/2011/new-digital-american-family.html

Anderson, N. (2009, January 22). Britannica opens up, aims the "literary canon" at Wikipedia. *Ars Technica.* Retrieved from http://arstechnica.com/business/2009/01/britannica-to-grind-wikipedia-beneath-its-heel-woth-small-moves-toward-openness/

Andrei Oghina. (n.d.). CrunchBase. Retrieved from https://www.crunchbase.com/person/andrei-oghina

Andriakaina, E. (2013). The Promise of the 1821 Revolution and the Suffering Body. Some thoughts on Modernisation and Anti- intellectualism. *Synthesis, 5,* 49-70.

Ang, R. P., Kit-Aun, T., & Mansor, A. T. (2010). Normative beliefs about aggression as a mediator of narcissistic exploitativeness and cyberbullying. *Journal of Interpersonal Violence, 26*(13), 2619–2634. doi:10.1177/0886260510388286 PMID:21156699

Anonymous. (2014, February 28). *Xi to lead CCP group on Internet safety and information.* Retrieved from Sina News: http://news.sina.com.cn/o/2014-02-28/042029584155.shtml

Aoyama, I., Utsumi, S., & Hasegawa, M. (2011). Cyberbullying in Japan: Cases, government reports, adolescent relational aggression and parental monitoring roles. In Q. Li, D. Cross, & P. K. Smith (Eds.), *Bullying in the global playground: Research from an international perspective.* Oxford, UK: Wiley-Blackwell.

Appcrawlr. (n.d.). *TasteKid.* Retrieved from http://appcrawlr.com/ios/tastekid

Aricak, T., Siyahhan, S., Uzunhasanoglu, A., Saribeyoglu, S., Ciplak, S., Yilmaz, N., & Memmedov, C. (2008). Cyberbullying among Turkish adolescents. *Cyberpsychology & Behavior, 11*(3), 253–261. doi:10.1089/cpb.2007.0016 PMID:18537493

Aristotle. (2011, September 27). *Aristotle's Rhetoric.* L. Honeycutt (Ed.). Retrieved 20 2012, February, from Aristotle's rhetoric: http://rhetoric.eserver.org/aristotle/index.html

Aroopala, C. (2012). 2011). Mobilizing collective identity: Frames & rational individuals. *Political Behavior, 34*(2), 193–224. doi:10.1007/s11109-010-9155-4

Arslan, S., Savaser, S., Hallett, V., & Balci, S. (2012). Cyberbullying among primary school students in Turkey: Self-reported prevalence and associations with home and school life. *Cyberpsychology, Behavior, and Social Networking, 15*(10), 527–533. doi:10.1089/cyber.2012.0207 PMID:23002988

Arthur, C. (2014, October 14). Goodbye, Ello? Searches for new social network collapse. *The Guardian.* Retrieved from http://www.theguardian.com/technology/2014/oct/14/goodbye-ello-google-seacrhes-social-network

Artisti Collection's Photos. (2011). Retrieved March 14, 2013 from http://www.facebook.com/photo.php?fbid=10150121738826259$set=pu.45324601258$type=1&theater%3Eweb

Artisti Collection's Photos. (2012). Retrieved February 4, 2013, from http://www.facebook.com/photo.php?fbid=10151141313996259&set=pb.45324601258.-2207520000.1364583379&type=3&theater

Arvanitakis, D. (2011). *Η Επανάσταση του 1821 και ο 'ΣΚΑΪ TV.* Retrieved April 6, 2013, from http://www.rizospastis.gr/story.do?id=6157921&publDate=20/3/2011

Asdrahas, S. (2003). Τουρκοκρατία – Λατινοκρατία. Οι γενικοί χαρακτήρες της ελληνικής ιστορίας, 1453-1770. In V. Panagiotopoulos (Ed.), Ιστορία του Νέου Ελληνισμού 1700-2000, (vol. 1, pp. 17-38). Athens: Ellinika Grammata.

Asdrahas, S. (2011, March 26). Προϋποθέσεις της Επανάστασης του 1821. *Enthemata-Avgi Newspaper*.

Augenbraun, E. (2011). Occupy Wall Street and the limits of spontaneous street protest. *The Guardian*. Retrieved July 27, 2015, from http://www.theguardian.com/commentisfree/cifamerica/2011/sep/29/occupy-wall-street-protest

Bahm, G. (2005). *The Daily Show:* Discursive Integration and the Reinvention of Political Journalism. *Political Communication, 22*(3), 259–276. doi:10.1080/10584600591006492

Baker, K. J. M. (2012). The Fight Against Misogyny in Gaming Enlists Some Big Names. *Jezebel*. Retrieved April 9, 2014, from http://jezebel.com/5922961/the-fight-against-misogynism-in-gaming-enlists-some-big-names

Baker, K. J. M. (2012, December 13). *Feminist Group Continues to Fuck With Victoria's Secret By Sneaking 'Consent Panties' Into Stores.* [Web log post]. Retrieved April 1, 2013 from http://jezebel.com/5968192/feminist-group-continues-to-fuck-with-victorias-secret-by-sneaking-consent-panties-into-stores

Ball, P. (2014, July 8). 'Wisdom of the crowd': They myths and realities". *BBC Future*. Available: http://www.bbc.com/future/story/20140708-when-crowd-wisdom-goes-wrong

Banet-Weiser, S., & Juhasz, A. (2011). Feminist labor in media studies/communication: Is self-branding feminist practice? *International Journal of Communication, 5*, 1768–1775.

Banet-Weiser, S., & Mukherjee, R. (2012). Introduction. In R. Mukherjee & S. Banet-Weiser (Eds.), *Commodity activism: Cultural resistance in neoliberal times* (pp. 1–17). New York: New York University Press.

Bangladesh, Tumbir. (2012a). Retrieved March 16, 2013, from http://fyeahbangladesh.tumblr.com/post/4620112214/asif-azim

Bangladesh, Tumbir. (2012b). Retrieved March 16, 2013, from http://fuckyeahethnicmen.tumblr.com/post/4283724312/asif-azim-is-a-top-ramp-model-of-bangladesh-and

Barlett, C. P., & Gentile, D. A. (2012). Long-term psychological predictors of cyber-bullying in late adolescence. *Psychology of Popular Media Culture, 2*, 123–135. doi:10.1037/a0028113

Barlett, C., & Coyne, S. M. (2014). A meta-analysis of sex differences in cyber-bullying behavior: The moderating role of age. *Aggressive Behavior, 40*(5), 474–488. doi:10.1002/ab.21555 PMID:25098968

Barmann, J. (2014, September 19). Zuckerberg has always believed that we're only entitled to one identity. *SFist*. Retrieved from http://sfist.com/2014/09/19/zuckerberg_has_always_believed_that.php

Barni, S., & Mondin, R. (1997). Sexual dysfunction in treated breast cancer patients. *Annals of Oncology, 8*(2), 149–153. doi:10.1023/A:1008298615272 PMID:9093723

Barrett, R. (1999). Indexing Polyphonous Identity in the Speech of African-American Drag Queens. In M. Bucholtz, A. C. Liang, & A. Sutton (Eds.), *Reinventing Identities: The Gendered Self in Discourse*. New York: Oxford University Press.

Barthes, R. (2013). *Mythologies: the Complete Edition, in a New Translation* (2nd ed.). (R. Howard & A. Lavers, Trans.). New York, NY: Hill and Wang.

Bauman, Z. (1987). *Legislators and Interpreters. In On Modernity, post-modernity and Intellectuals*. Polity Press.

Baumer, E., Sueyoshi, M., & Tomlinson, B. (2008). Exploring the role of the reader in the activity of blogging. In *Proceedings of the SIGCHI Conference on Human Factors in Computing Systems* (pp. 1111-1120). ACM. doi:10.1145/1357054.1357228

Baym, N. K. (2006). Finding the Quality in Qualitative Research. In D. Silver & A. Massanari (Eds.), *Critical Cyberculture Studies* (pp. 79–87). New York: New York University Press.

BBC. (2013, Nov. 7). *Twitter shares jump 73% in market debut.* Retrieved July 28, 2015 from http://www.bbc.com/news/business-24851054

Beaton, R. (2009). Introduction. In R. Beaton & D. Ricks (Eds.), *The Making of Modern Greece* (pp. 1–18). Ashgate.

Beck, L. (2012a, December 17). *Awesome Teenager Successfully Petitions Hasbro For Gender Neutral Easy-Bake Oven.* [Web log post]. Retrieved April 1, 2013, from http://jezebel.com/5969299/awesome-teenager-successfully-petitions-hasbro-for-gender-neutral-easy+bake-oven

Beck, L. (2012b, December 27). *Google Selling Ridiculous "Make Me Asian" and "Make Me Indian" Apps in Their Store* [Web log post]. Retrieved April 1, 2013 from http://jezebel.com/5971663/google-selling-ridiculous-make-me-asian-and-make-me-indian-apps-in-their-store

Bell, D. (1976). *The Cultural Contradictions of Capitalism.* New York: Perseus Books.

Bell-Jordan, K. (2008). Black, White and a Survivor of the Real World: Constructions of Race on Reality TV. *Critical Studies in Media Communication, 25*(4), 353–372. doi:10.1080/15295030802327725

Bello, D. C., Pitts, R. E., & Etze, M. J. (1983). The Communication Effects on Controversial Sexual Content in Television Programs and Commercials. *Journal of Advertising, 12*(3), 32–42. doi:10.1080/00913367.1983.10672846

Benjamin, W. (2005). The Work of Art in the Age of Mechanical Reproduction. (H. Zohn, Trans.). Random House. Accessed September 15, 2015. https://www.marxists.org/reference/subject/philosophy/works/ge/benjamin.htm

Benn, M. (2013). After post-Feminism: Pursuing material equality in a digital age. *Juncture, 20*(3), 223–227. doi:10.1111/j.2050-5876.2013.00757.x

Benoliel, J. Q. (1996). Grounded theory and nursing knowledge. *Qualitative Health Research, 6*(3), 406–428. doi:10.1177/104973239600600308

Benson, T. (2014, March 24). You are not a product: Ello wants to be the Anti-Facebook Social Network. *Motherboard.* Retrieved from http://motherboard.vice.com/read/you-are-not-a-product-ello-wants-to-be-the-anti-facebook-social-network

Beran, T., & Li, Q. (2005). Cyber-harassment: A new method for an old behavior. *Journal of Educational Computing Research, 32*(3), 265–277. doi:10.2190/8YQM-B04H-PG4D-BLLH

Bever, L. (2015). *#TheEmptyChair on NY magazine's Cosby cover takes on a life of its own.* Retrieved July 30, 2015 from http://www.washingtonpost.com/news/morning-mix/wp/2015/07/28/theemptychair-on-ny-magazines-cosby-takes-on-a-life-of-its-own/

Bhambra, G. (2014). Postcolonial and decolonial dialogues. *Postcolonial Studies, 17*(2), 115–121.

Billig, M. (1995). *Banal Nationalism.* London: Sage.

Bitzer, L. (1968). The Rhetorical Situation. *Philosophy & Rhetoric, 1*(1), 1–14.

Bivens, R. (2015). Under the hood: The software in your feminist approach. *Feminist Media Studies, 15*(4), 714-717. DOI:10.1080/14680777.2015.1053717.

Blumer, H. (1969). *Symbolic Interactionism: Perspective and Method.* Englewood Cliffs, NJ: Prentice-Hall.

Boellstorff, T. (2010). *Coming of Age in Second Life.* Princeton, NJ: Princeton University Press.

Bogado, A. (2015, February 9). *Native Americans say Facebook is accusing them of having fake names.* Retrieved from http://colorlines.com/archives/2015/02/native_americans_say_facebook_is_accusing_them_of_using_fake_names.html

Bogiatzis, V. (2009). Παναγιώτης Κονδύλης και ελληνική νεοτερικότητα. *Σημειώσεις, 69,* 7-55.

Bogiatzis, V. (2012). Μετέωρος Μοντερνισμός. Τεχνολογία, ιδεολογία της επιστήμης και πολιτική στην. *E (Norwalk, Conn.),* 1922–1940.

Bonilla-Silva. (2009). *Racism without Racists: Colorblind Racism and the Persistence of Racial Inequality in America* (3rd ed.). Lanham, MA: Roman and Littlefield.

Bordo, S. (2006). Beauty (Re)Discovers the Male Body. In R. K. Miller (Ed.), *Motives for Writing.* New York: McGraw-Hill.

Boskin, J., & Dorinson, J. (1985). Ethnic humor: Subversion and survival. *American Quarterly, 1,* 81-97.

Boulton, M., Lloyd, J., Down, J., & Marx, H. (2012). Predicting undergraduates' self-reported engagement in traditional and cyberbullying from attitudes. *Cyberpsychology, Behavior, and Social Networking, 15*(3), 141–147. doi:10.1089/cyber.2011.0369 PMID:22304402

Bourdieu, P. (1998, January 2). Dialogue entre Pierre Bourdieu et Toni Morrison. *Vacarme.* Retrieved from http://www.vacarme.org/article807.html

Bourdieu, P. (1984). *Distinction: A Social Critique of the Judgment of Taste* (R. Nice, Trans.). Cambridge, MA: Harvard University Press.

Bourdieu, P. (1986). The Forms of Capital. In *Handbook of Theory and Research for the Sociology of Education.* New York: Greenwood.

Bourdieu, P. (1990). *The Logic of Practice.* Polity Press.

Bowker, J. (1997). *Dharma.* Retrieved July 3, 2015, from The Concise Osford Dictionary of World Religions: http://www.encyclopedia.com/doc/1O101-Dharma1.html

boyd, d. & Crawford, K. (2012). Critical questions for big data: Provocations for a cultural, technological, and scholarly phenomenon. *Information, Communication & Society, 15*(5), 662–679.

boyd, d. (2010). Social Network Sites as Networked Publics: Affordances, Dynamics, and Implications. In *A networked self: Identity, community, and culture on social network sites.* New York: Routledge.

Brace, I. (2004). *Questionnaire Design: How to Plan, Structure and Write Survey Material for Effective Market Research.* London: Kogan Page Ltd.

Breazeal, C. (2000). *Sociable Machines: Expressive Social Exchange between Humans and Robots.* (PhD Thesis). Massachusetts Institute of Technology, Cambridge, MA.

Breslaw, A. (2012, November 10). *Factory Conditions at Zara Look To Have Improved Since Last Year (Kinda).* [Web log comment]. Retrieved April 1, 2013, from http://jezebel.com/5959456/factory-conditions-at-zara-look-to-have-improved-since-last-year-hopefully

Brogan, J. (2015, July 6). *What's In a Real Name?* Retrieved from http://www.slate.com/articles/technology/future_tense/2015/07/facebook_s_authentic_name_policy_ensnares_zo_cat_a_trans_woman_who_tried.html

Brooks, B. (2015, August 31). It's Not Just the Books, It's the Discussion. *The New York Times.* Retrieved from http://www.nytimes.com/roomfordebate/2015/08/31/what should-college-freshmen-read/its-not-just-the-books-its-the-discussion

Broom, D. (2001). Reading breast cancer: Reflections on a dangerous intersection. *Health, 5*(2), 249–268. doi:10.1177/136345930100500206

Brown, W. R. (1978). Ideology as communication process. *The Quarterly Journal of Speech, 64*(2), 123–180. doi:10.1080/00335637809383420

Brown, W. R. (1982). Attention and the rhetoric of social intervention. *The Quarterly Journal of Speech, 64*(1), 17–27. doi:10.1080/00335638209383588

Brown, W. R. (1986). Power and the rhetoric of social intervention. *The Quarterly Journal of Speech, 64*, 180–199.

Bryant, M. (2010, December 16). TasteKid now recommending movies, music and books to over 15,000 users. *TNW*. Accessed September 15, 2015, from http://thenextweb.com/eu/2010/12/16/tastekid-now-recommending-movies-music-and-books-to-over-15000-users/

Bucholtz, M. (2001). *White Kids: Language, Race and Styles of Youth Identity*. Oxford University Press.

Burchell, G. (1991). Peculiar Interests: Civil Society and 'Governing the System of Natural Liberty. In G. Burchell, C. Gordon & P. Miller (Eds.), The Foucault Effect: Studies in Governmentality (pp. 119-150). Chicago: University of Chicago Press.

Burgess, J., & Green, J. (2009). The entrepeneurial vlogger: Participatory culture beyond the professional-amateur divide. In P. Snickars, & P. Vonderau (Eds.), The YouTube reader (pp. 89-107). Stockholm: Kungliga biblioteket.

Burke, K. (1941). *The Philosophy of Literary Form*. Baton Rouge, LA: Louisiana State University Press.

Burke, K. (1954). *Permanence and Change: An Anatomy of Purpose*. Los Angeles: University of California Press.

Burke, K. (1962). *A Grammer of Motives and A Rhetoric of Motives*. New York: The World Publishing Company.

Burke, K. (1966). *Language As Symbolic Action*. Berkeley, CA: Univeristy of California Press.

Burke, K. (1970). *The Rhetoric of Relgion: Studies in Logology*. Los Angeles, CA: Unviersity of California Press.

Burke, N., Joseph, G., Pasick, R., & Barker, J. (2009). Theorizing social context: Rethinking behavior theory. *Health Education & Behavior, 36*(5 Suppl), 55S–70S. doi:10.1177/1090198109335338 PMID:19805791

Burton, K. A., Florell, D., & Wygant, D. B. (2013). The role of peer attachment and normative beliefs about aggression on traditional bullying and cyberbullying. *Psychology in the Schools, 50*(2), 103–114. doi:10.1002/pits.21663

Butler, J. (1990). *Gender Trouble*. London, UK: Routledge.

Butler, J. (1990). *Gender Trouble: Feminism and the Subversion of Identity*. Taylor and Francis Group.

Butler, J. (2000). Subjects of Sex/Gender/Desire. In S. During (Ed.), *The Cultural Studies Reader* (2nd ed.; pp. 340–353). New York: Routledge.

Butsch, R. (2000). *The making of American audiences: From stage to television, 1750-1990*. Cambridge, UK: Cambridge University Press. doi:10.1017/CBO9780511619717

Byers, M., & Crocker, D. (2012). Feminist cohorts and waves: Attitudes of junior female academics. *Women's Studies International Forum, 35*(1), 1–11. doi:10.1016/j.wsif.2011.09.003

Cairns, C. (2013). Air pollution, social media, and responsive authoritarianism in China. *UCLA Compass Conference*. Los Angeles, CA: UCLA.

Campbell, C. (2014, March 31). How 'Game Jam,' an indie game dev reality show, collapsed on its first day of filming. *Polygon*. Retrieved June 28, 2015, from http://www.polygon.com/2014/3/31/5568362/game-jam-reality-show-maker-studios

Campbell, J. (1968). *The Masks of God: Creative Mythology*. New York: The Viking Press.

Campbell, J. (1972). *Myths to live by: How we Re-Create Ancient Legends in Our Daily Loves to Release Human Potential*. New York: Bantam Books.

Canon. (n.d.). In *Glossary of Literary Theory*. Accessed November 10, 2014, from http://www.library.utoronto.ca/utel/glossary/Canon.html

Cappadocia, M. C., Craig, W. M., & Pepler, D. (2013). Cyberbullying: Prevalence, stability and risk factors during adolescence. *Canadian Journal of School Psychology*, *28*, 171–192.

Carlo, M. M. (2009). Advertising time expansion, compression, and cognitive processing influences on consumer acceptance of message and brand. *Journal of Business Research*, *62*(4), 420–431. doi:10.1016/j.jbusres.2008.01.019

Carpenter, J., Brockopp, D., & Andrykowski, M. (1999). Self-transformation as a factor in the self-esteem and well-being of breast cancer survivors. *Journal of Advanced Nursing*, *29*(6), 1402–1411. doi:10.1046/j.1365-2648.1999.01027.x PMID:10354235

Carstensen, T. (2014). Gender and social media: Sexism, empowerment, or the irrelevance of gender? In C. Carter, L. Steiner, & L. McLaughlin (Eds.), *The Routledge companion to media and gender* (pp. 483–493). New York, NY: Routledge.

Cassell, J., & Jenkins, H. (Eds.). (2000). *From Barbie to Mortal Kombat: Gender and Computer Games (Reprint edition)*. Cambridge, MA: The MIT Press.

Cassidy, W., Brown, K., & Jackson, M. (2012a). "Making kind cool": Parents' suggestions for preventing cyber bullying and fostering cyber kindness. *Journal of Educational Computing Research*, *46*(4), 415–436. doi:10.2190/EC.46.4.f

Cassidy, W., Brown, K., & Jackson, M. (2012b). "Under the radar": Educators and cyberbullying in schools. *School Psychology International*, *33*(5), 520–532. doi:10.1177/0143034312445245

Catterall, M., Maclaran, P., & Stevens, L. (2005). Postmodern paralysis: The critical impasse in feminist perspectives on consumers. *Journal of Marketing Management*, *21*(5-6), 489–504. doi:10.1362/0267257054307444

Center, P. R. (2014, August 27). *The 'Spiral of Silence' on Social Media*. Retrieved from http://www.pewinternet.org/2014/08/27/the-spiral-of-silence-on-social-media/

Chakrabarty, D. (2000). *Provincializing Europe. Postcolonial Thought and Historical Difference*. Princeton University Press.

Charmaz, K. (2006). *Constructing Grounded Theory: A Practical Guide Through Qualitative Analysis*. London: Sage.

Chatziioannou, M. C. (2010). Mediterranean pathways of Greek merchants to Victorian England. T*he Historical Revue. La Revue Historique*, *7*, 213–237.

Chen, W. (2014). *Taking stock, moving forward: The Internet, social network and civic engagement in Chinese societies*. Academic Press.

Chin, P. (2012, January 17*). Google: Remove the racist "Make Me Asian" & "Make Me Indian" apps from @GooglePlay*. Retrieved January 17, 2012, from https://www.change.org/p/google-remove-the-racist-make-me-asian-make-me-indian-apps-from-googleplay

Chisholm, J. F. (2006). Cyberspace violence against girls and adolescent females. *Annals of the New York Academy of Sciences*, *1087*(1), 74–89. doi:10.1196/annals.1385.022 PMID:17189499

Chiu, C., Ip, C., & Silverman, A. (2012, April). Understanding social media in China. *McKinsey Quarterly*. Retrieved from http://www.mckinsey.com/insights/marketing_sales/understanding_social_media_in_china

Chu, A. (2014, August 28). It's dangerous to go alone: why are gamers so angry? *The Daily Beast*. Retrieved June 28, 2015, from http://www.thedailybeast.com/articles/2014/08/28/it-s-dangerous-to-go-alone-why-are-gamers-so-angry.html

CinnamonSpice. (2012, December 18). *Please someone enlighten me*. [Web log comment]. Retrieved December 18, 2012, from http://jezebel.com/5969299/awesome-teenager-successfully-petitions-hasbro-for-gender-neutral-easy+bake-oven

Clare, A. (1998). *A Semiotic Analysis of Magazine Ads for Men's Fragrances*. Prifysgol Aberystwyth University. Retrieved March 5 2013, from http://www.aber.ac.uk/media/Students/awc9401.html

Cline, B. (2012). The Future of Reading/Thinking: Epistemological Construction in the Age of the Kindle. *Communication +1, 1*(1), Article 2.

Cline, B. (2013). Axiology and the FCC: Regulation as Ideological Process. In *E. Zack Stiegler, Regulating the Web: Network Neutrality and the Fate of the Open Internet* (pp. 109–120). Lexington, KY: Lexington Books.

Clogg, R. (2002). *A Concise History of Greece*. Cambridge, UK: Cambridge University Press.

CNNIC. (2012). *Statistics report of Chinese internet development*. Retrieved from China Internet Network Research Center: http://www1.cnnic.cn/

CNNIC. (2014). *Statistics report of Chinese internet development*. Retrieved from China Internet Network Research Center: http://www1.cnnic.cn/

Conley, T. L. (2014). From #RenishaMcBride to #RememberRenisha: Locating our stories and finding justice. *Feminist Media Studies, 14*(6), 1111–1113. doi:10.1080/14680777.2014.975474

Connell, R. W. (2005). Masculinities (2nd ed.). Berkeley, CA: University of California Press.

Connell, R. W. (2006).Understanding Men: Gender Sociology and the New International Research on Masculinities. In *The Sage Handbook of Gender and Education*. London: Sage Publication.

Consalvo, M. (2012). Confronting toxic gamer culture: A challenge for feminist game studies scholars. *Ada: A Journal of Gender, New Media, and Technology*, (1). Retrieved June 28, 2015 from http://adanewmedia.org/2012/11/issue1-consalvo/

Corcoran, L., Connolly, I., & O'Moore, M. (2012). Cyberbullying in Irish schools: An investigation of personality and self-concept. *The Irish Journal of Psychology, 33*(4), 153–165. doi:10.1080/03033910.2012.677995

Coreil, J., Wilke, J., & Pintado, I. (2004). Cultural models of illness and recovery in breast cancer support groups. *Qualitative Health Research, 14*(7), 905–923. doi:10.1177/1049732304266656 PMID:15296663

Corley, J. R. (1983). A Communication study of Arthur F. Holmes as a worldview advocate (Doctoral Dissertation, The Ohio State University, 1983). *Dissertation Abstracts International, 44*.

Correa, T. (2014). Bottom-up technology transmission within families: Exploring how youths influence their parents' digital media use with dyadic data. *Journal of Communication, 64*(1), 103–124. doi:10.1111/jcom.12067

Costello, D. (2005). Aura, Face, Photography: Re-Reading Benjamin Today. In A. Benjamin (Ed.), *Walter Benjamin and Art* (pp. 164–185). New York: Continuum.

Cote, A. C. (2015). 'I Can Defend Myself' Women's Strategies for Coping With Harassment While Gaming Online. *Games and Culture, 1555412015587603*. doi:10.1177/1555412015587603

Coyne, S. M., Nelson, D., A., & Underwood, M. K. (2010). Aggression in childhood. In P. K. Smith & C. H. Hart (Eds.), *The Wiley-Blackwell handbook of childhood social development* (pp. 491-509). Chichester, UK: Wiley-Blackwell.

Craib, I. (1992). *Anthony Giddens*. Routledge.

Craig, S. (1997). *Madison Avenue versus The Feminine Mystique: How the Advertising Industry Responded to the Onset of the Modern Women's Movement*. Paper presented at the Popular Culture Association conference, San Antonio, TX. Retrieved April 13, 2013 from http://www.rtvf.unt.edu/people/craig/madave.htm

Crenshaw, K. (1989). Demarginalizing the intersection of race and sex: A black feminist critique of antidiscrimination doctrine, feminist theory, and antiracist politics. *University of Chicago Legal Forum, 1989*, 139–167.

Crenshaw, K. (1989). Demarginalizing the Intersection of Race and Sex: A Black Feminist Critique of Antidiscrimination Doctrine. *University of Chicago Legal Forum, 1989*, 139–168.

Crenshaw, K. (1991). Mapping the Margins: Intersectionality, Identity, and Violence Against Women of Color. *Stanford Law Review, 43*(6), 1241–1300. doi:10.2307/1229039

Cronin, A. M. (2000). *Advertising and consumer citizenship: Gender, images, and rights*. London: Routledge.

Crooks, D. (2001a). The importance of symbolic interaction in grounded theory research on women's health. *Health Care for Women International, 22*(1-2), 11–27. doi:10.1080/073993301300003054 PMID:11813790

Crooks, D. (2001b). Older women with breast cancer: New understandings through grounded theory research. *Health Care for Women International, 22*(1-2), 99–114. doi:10.1080/073993301300003108 PMID:11813800

CrossWire Bible Society. (2014, February 15). *AndBible Release Notes*. Retrieved July 7, 2015, from AndBible: https://code.google.com/p/and-bible/wiki/ReleaseNotes

Crosswire Bible Society. (n.d.). *and-bible-- Bible App for Android*. Retrieved 07 05, 2015, from Google Codee: https://code.google.com/p/and-bible/

Crosswire Bible Society. (n.d.). *Mobile*. Retrieved July 6, 2015, from The CrossWire Bible Society: http://crosswire.org/applications/?section=Handhelds

Cullen, P., & Fischer, C. (2014). Conceptualising generational dynamics in Feminist movements: Political generations, waves and affective economies. *Social Compass, 8*(3), 282–293. doi:10.1111/soc4.12131

Daly, S. (2014, September 3). The Fine Young Capitalists' noble goals don't excuse them from scrutiny. *Gameranx*. Retrieved June 28, 2015, from http://www.gameranx.com/features/id/23968/article/the-fine-young-capitalists-seemingly-noble-goals-don-t-excuse-them-from-scrutiny

Danet, B. (1998). Text as Mask: Gender, Play, and Performance on the Internet. In *Cybersociety 2.0: Revisiting Computer-Mediated Communication and Community*. Los Angeles, CA: Sage.

Daniels, J. (2009). Rethinking Cyberfeminism(s): Race, Gender, and Embodiment. *Women's Studies Quarterly, 37*(1/2), 101-124.

Davis, D. (2011). Intergenerational digital storytelling: A sustainable community initiative with inner-city residents. *Visual Communication, 10*(4), 527–540. doi:10.1177/1470357211415781

Davis, K. (2008). Intersectionality as buzzword: A sociology of science perspective on what makes a Feminist theory successful. *Feminist Theory, 9*(1), 67–85. doi:10.1177/1464700108086364

De Ridder, S. (2015). Are digital media institutions shaping youth's intimate stories? Strategies and tactics in the social networking site netlog. *New Media & Society, 17*(3), 356–374. doi:10.1177/1461444813504273

Dehue, F., Bolman, C., & Vollink, T. (2008). Cyberbullying: Youngsters' experiences and parental perception. *CyberPscyhology & Behavior, 11*(2), 217–223. doi:10.1089/cpb.2007.0008 PMID:18422417

Dehue, F., Bolman, C., Vollink, T., & Pouwelse, M. (2012). Cyberbullying and traditional bullying in relation to adolescents' perceptions of parenting. *Journal of Cyber Therapy and Rehabilitation, 5*, 25–34.

Delalande, N. (2012). The Greek State: Its Past and Future. An interview with Anastassios Anastassiadis. *La Vie des idées*. Retrieved April 6, 2012, from http://www.booksandideas.net/The-Greek-State-Its-Past-and.html

deLara, E. W. (2012). Why adolescents don't disclose incidents of bullying and harassment. *Journal of School Violence, 11*(4), 288–305. doi:10.1080/15388220.2012.705931

del-Toso-Craviotto, M. (2008). Gender and sexual identity authentication in language use: The case of chat rooms. *Discourse Studies, 10*(1), 251–270. doi:10.1177/1461445607087011

Dertilis, B. G. (2010). *Ιστορία του Ελληνικού Κράτους 1830-1920, vol. Α΄- Β*. Athens: Estia.

Dettori, G. (2011). Adolescents' online literacies – Edited by Donna E Alvermann. British Journal of Educational Technology, 42(2). Doi:10.1111/j.1467-8535.2011.01173_1.x

Dewey, C. (2015). More than 26 million people have changed their Facebook picture to a rainbow flag. Here's why that matters. *Washington Post*. Retrieved July 27, 2015, from http://www.washingtonpost.com/news/the-intersect/wp/2015/06/29/more-than-26-million-people-have-changed-their-facebook-picture-to-a-rainbow-flag-heres-why-that-matters/

Dharmarakshita. (n.d.). *The Wheel of Sharp Weapons Effectively Striking the Heart of the Foe*. Retrieved July 2, 2015, from Osel Shen Phen Ling: http://www.fpmt-osel.org/teachings/wheel.pdf

Diamandouros, N. (1972). *Political Modernization, Social Conflict and Cultural Cleavage in the Formation of the Modern Greek State: 1821-1828*. (PhD dissertation). Columbia University, New York, NY.

Diamandouros, N. (2012). Politics, culture, and the state: Background to the Greek crisis. In O. Anastasakis & D. Singh (Ed.), Reforming Greece: Sisyphean Task or Herculean Challenge? (pp. 9-18). Oxford, UK: SEESOX.

Diamandouros, N. (2000). *Cultural Dualism and Political Change in Postauthoritarian Greece*. Madrid: CEACS. (Original work published 1994).

Diamanduros, T., & Downs, E. (2011). Creating a safe school environment: How to prevent cyberbullying at your school. *Library Media Connection, 30*(2), 36–38.

Didden, R., Scholte, R. H. J., Korzilius, H., de Moor, J. M. H., Vermeulen, A., & O'Reilly, M. et al. (2009). Cyberbullying among students with intellectual and developmental disability in special education settings. *Developmental Neurorehabilitation, 12*(3), 146–151. doi:10.1080/17518420902971356 PMID:19466622

Dietz, T. L. (1998). An Examination of Violence and Gender Role Portrayals in Video Games: Implications for Gender Socialization and Aggressive Behavior. *Sex Roles, 38*(5-6), 425–442. doi:10.1023/A:1018709905920

DiNucci, D. (1999). Framented Future. *Print, 53*(4), 32–33.

Donath, J. (1999). Identity and deception in the virtual community. In M. A. Smith & P. Kollock (Eds.), Communities in Cyberspace (pp. 29–59). New York: Routledge.

Downs, E., & Smith, S. (2010). Keeping Abreast of Hypersexuality: A Video Game Character Content Analysis. *Sex Roles*, *62*(11), 721–733. doi:10.1007/s11199-009-9637-1

Dragoumis, M. (2003). Review of J. Koliopoulos & Th. Veremis. (2002) Greece. The Modern Sequel: From 1821 to the Present. In Ιστορικά Κριτικά. Βιβλιοκριτικές των έργων του Θάνου Βερέμη (pp. 113-118). Athens: Kastaniotis.

Dragoumis, M. (2009). *Μεταρρυθμιστές όλων των κομμάτων αλληλοϋποστηριχθείτε.* Retrieved November 2, 2011, from http://e-rooster.gr/10/2009/1681

Dragoumis, N. (1973). *Ιστορικαί Α.* Athens: Ermis. (Original work published 1879)

Drushel, B. (2013) Performing Race, Class, and Gender: The Tangled History of Drag. *Reconstruction: Studies in Contemporary Culture*, *13*(2).

Duncan, D. R. (2004). The impact of family relationships on school bullies and victims. In D. L. Espelage & S. M. Swearer (Eds.), *Bullying in American schools* (pp. 277-244). London: Lawrence Erlbaum Associates.

During, S. (1999). *The Cultural Studies Reader* (2nd ed.). New York: Routledge.

Durkheim, E. (1996). Ritual, Magic, and the Sacred. In R. L. Grimes (Ed.), *Readings in Ritual Studies* (pp. 188–201). Upper Saddle River, NJ: Prentice Hall Inc.(Original work published 1915)

Eagle, R. B. (2015). Loitering, lingering, hashtagging: Women reclaiming public space via #BoardtheBus, #StopStreetHarassment, and the #EverdaySexismProject. *Feminist Media Studies*, *15*(2), 350–353. doi:10.1080/14680777.2015.1008748

Eagleton, T. (1985). Subject of Literature. *Cultural Critique*, (2). Available: http://www.jstor.org/stable/1354202

Eckert, S. (2014). *Digital rooms of their own: Women's voices online about the politics of women, family and maternity in four democracies.* (Unpublished doctoral dissertation). University of Maryland, College Park, MD.

Eckert, S., & Puschmann, C. (2013). *#Aufschrei/#outcry: Solidarity and aggression in a Twitter debate over sexual harassment.* Paper presented at the annual conference of the Association of Internet Researchers, Denver, CO.

Economist. (2013, April 6). China's internet: A giant cage. *Economist.* Retrieved from economist.com

Eden, S., Heiman, T., & Olenik-Shemesh, D. (2013). Teachers' perceptions, beliefs and concerns about cyberbullying. *British Journal of Educational Technology*, *44*(6), 1036–1052. doi:10.1111/j.1467-8535.2012.01363.x

Efthymiou, M. (2007). Instead of Introduction: The Communities of the Greek Peninsula Under Ottoman Rule. An Attempt of Schematic Classification, According to their internal economic and political function. *Eoa and Esperia*, *7*, 239–245.

Ehlers, N., & Krupar, S. (2012). Introduction: The body in breast cancer. *Social Semiotics*, *22*(1), 1–11. doi:10.1080/10350330.2012.640060

Ehrenreich, B. (2009). *Bright-Sided: How Positive Thinking is Undermining America.* New York: Picador.

Elledge, L. C., Williford, A., Boulton, A. J., DePaolis, K. J., Little, T. D., & Salmivalli, C. (2013). Individual and contextual predictors of cyberbullying: The influence of children's provictim attitudes and teachers' ability to intervene. *Journal of Youth and Adolescence*, *42*(5), 698–710. doi:10.1007/s10964-013-9920-x PMID:23371005

Ellison, N., Steinfield, C., & Lampe, C. (2007). The Benefits of Facebook "Friends": Social Capital and College Students' Use of Online Social Network Sites. *Journal of Computer-Mediated Communication*, *12*(4), 1143–1168. doi:10.1111/j.1083-6101.2007.00367.x

Ellison, N., Steinfield, C., & Lampe, C. (2011). Connection Strategies: Social Capital Implications of Facebook-enabled Communication Practices. *New Media & Society*, *13*(6), 873–892. doi:10.1177/1461444810385389

Ellul, J. (n.d.). *76 Reasonable Questions to ask about any technology*. Retrieved December 5, 2014, from T. David's Page: http://www.tdgordon.net/media_ecology/76_reasonable_questions.doc

Ellul, J. (1970). *The meaning of the city* (D. Pardee, Trans.). Grand Rapids, MI: William B Eerdman's Publishing Company.

Ellul, J. (1971). *Propaganda: The formations of men's attitudes* (K. Kellen & J. Lerner, Trans.). New York: Alfred A. Knopf.

Ellul, J. (1981). *Perspectives on our age* (J. Neugroschel, Trans.). New York: Seasbury.

Entertainment Software Association. (2014). *Essential Facts about the Computer and Video Game Industry: 2014 Sales, Demographic and Usage Data*. Retrieved June 28, 2015, from http://www.theesa.com/wp-content/uploads/2014/10/ESA_EF_2014.pdf

Erdur-Baker, O. (2010). Cyberbullying and its correlation to traditional bullying, gender and frequent and risky usage of internet-mediated communication tools. *New Media & Society, 12*(1), 109–125. doi:10.1177/1461444809341260

Esarey, A., & Qiang, X. (2011). Digital communication and political change in China. *International Journal of Communication, 5*, 298–319.

Eslen-Ziya, H. (2013). Social media and Turkish feminism. New resources for social activism. *Feminist Media Studies, 13*(5), 860–870. doi:10.1080/14680777.2013.838369

Evans, M. (2011). *Feminist waves, Feminist generations*. Basingstoke, UK: Palgrave MacMillan LTD; doi:10.1057/fr.2010.41

Faccio, E. (2003). *The Corporeal Identity: When the Self-Image Hurts*. New York: Springer.

Fanti, K. A., Demetriou, A. G., & Hawa, V. V. (2012). A longitudinal study of cyberbullying: Examining risk and protective factors. *European Journal of Developmental Psychology, 8*(2), 168–181. doi:10.1080/17405629.2011.643169

Fat, Ugly or Slutty. (2014). *Fat, Ugly or Slutty*. Retrieved April 9, 2014, from http://fatuglyorslutty.com/

Felski, R. (1989). *Beyond feminist aesthetics: Feminist literature and social change*. Cambridge, MA: Harvard University Press.

Ferdon, C. D., & Hertz, M. F. (2007). Electronic media, violence, and adolescents. An emerging public health problem. *The Journal of Adolescent Health, 41*(6), 1–5. doi:10.1016/j.jadohealth.2007.08.020 PMID:17577527

Festl, R., Schwarkow, M., & Quandt, T. (2013). Peer influence, internet use and cyberbullying: A comparison of different context effects among German adolescents. *Journal of Children and Media, 7*(4), 446–462. doi:10.1080/17482798.2013.781514

Filias, V. (2012). *Ποιοί πλαστογραφούν την αληθινή Ιστορία του 1821*. Retrieved April 2, 2013, from http://www.antibaro.gr/article/4250

Finch, J. (2008). Naming Names: Kinship, Individuality, and Personal Names. *Sociology, 42*(4), 709–725. doi:10.1177/0038038508091624

Fine Young Capitalists. (2014, September 3). *On apologizing for getting punched in the face*. Retrieved June 28, 2014, from http://thefineyoungcapitalists.tumblr.com/post/96578864050/on-apologizing-for-getting-punched-in-the-face

Finkelstein, J. (2007). *The Art of Self Invention: Image and Identity in Popular Visual Culture*. I.B.Tauris & Co Ltd.

Fink, M., & Miller, Q. (2014). 2013). Trans-media moments: Tumblr, 2011–2013. *Television & New Media, 15*(7), 611–626. doi:10.1177/1527476413505002

Finlay, G. (2014). *History of the Greek Revolution* (Vol. 2). Campridge University Press. (Original work published 1861)

Fish, S. (2005). One University, Under God?. *The Chronicle of Higher Education*, 18.

Fletcher, J. (2012). *Sexual harassment in the world of video gaming.* Retrieved April 9, 2014, from http://www.bbc.co.uk/news/magazine-18280000

Flottemesch, K. (2013). Learning through narratives: The impact of digital storytelling on intergenerational relationships. *Academy of Educational Leadership Journal, 17*(2), 53.

Forsberg, G. E. (2009). Media Ecology and Theology. *Journal of Communication and Religion, 32*, 135–156.

Forseberg, G. F. (2005). Postman and the Judeo-Christian Worldview. *Journal of Communication and Religion, 28*, 252–285.

Fotopoulou, A. (2014). Digital and networked by default? Women's organisations and the social imaginary of networked Feminism. *New Media & Society.* doi:10.1177/1461444814552264

Foucault, M. (1969). *What Is An Author?* Lecture to Societé Francais de philosophie. Available: https://wiki.brown.edu/confluence/download/attachments/74858352/FoucaultWhatIsAnAuthor.pdf

Foucault, M. (1972). *The Archaeology of Knowledge.* Routledge. Retrieved from http://www.marxists.org/reference/subject/philosophy/works/fr/foucault.htm

Foundation for the Preservation of the Mahayana Tradition. (n.d.). Retrieved January 26, 2015, from Osel Shen Phen Ling: Land of Clear Light Benefitting Others: http://www.fpmt-osel.org/

Fredrick, K. (2010). Mean girls (and boys): Cyberbullying and what can be done about it. *School Library Media Activities Monthly, 25*(8), 44–45.

Fuchs, C. (2014). *Social media: A critical introduction.* Thousand Oaks, CA: Sage. doi:10.4135/9781446270066.n2

Futrelle, D. (2014, September 8). Zoe Quinn's screenshots of 4chan's dirty tricks were just the appetizer. Here's the first course of the dinner, directly from the IRC log. *We Hunted the Mammoth.* Retrieved June 28, 2015, from http://wehuntedthemammoth.com/2014/09/08/zoe-quinns-screenshots-of-4chans-dirty-tricks-were-just-the-appetizer-heres-the-first-course-of-the-dinner-directly-from-the-irc-log/

Galani, K. (2010). The Napoleonic wars and the disruption of Mediterranean shipping and trade: British, Greek and American merchants in Livorno. *La Revue Historique, 7*, 179–198.

Gallagher, C. A. (2003). Color-Blind Privilege: The Social and Political Functions of Erasing the Color Line in Post-Race America. *Race, Gender, & Class, 10*(4), 22–37.

Gall, T. L., Charbonneau, C., & Florack, P. (2011). The relationship between religious/spiritual factors and perceived growth following diagnosis of breast cancer. *Psychology & Health, 26*(3), 287–305. doi:10.1080/08870440903411013 PMID:20309779

GamerGate Wiki. (2015). *Timeline.* Retrieved June 28, 2015, from http://wiki.gamergate.me/index.php?title=Timeline

Ganz, K. (2013). *Feministische Netzpolitik. Perspektiven und Handlungsfelder* [Feminist internet politics. Perspectives and relevant issues]. Gunda-Werner Institute. Retrieved July 27, 2015, from http://www.gwi-boell.de/de/2013/04/25/feministische-netzpolitik-perspektiven-und-handlungsfelder

Gellner, E. (1983). *Nations and Nationalism.* Oxford, UK: Blackwell.

Gerdes, G., & Seidel, A. (2015). Männlichkeiten in queer-feministischen Blogs. [Masculinities in queer-feminist blogs.] In A. Heilmann et al. (Eds.), *Männlichkeiten und Reproduktion* [Masculinities and reproduction] (pp. 309–328). Charn, Switzerland: Springer.

Gibson, J. (1979). *The Ecological Approach to Visual Perception*. New York: Psychology Press.

Giddens, A. (1997). Living in a Post-Traditional Society. In Reflexive Modernization. Politics, Tradition and Aesthetics in the Modern Social Order (pp. 56-109). Cambridge, MA: Polity Press.

Giddens, A. (1984). *The Constitution of Society: Outline of the Theory of Structuration*. Cambridge, MA: Polity Press.

Giddens, A. (1991). *Modernity and Self-Identity*. Stanford, CA: Stanford University Press.

Giddens, A. (2001). *Modernity and Self-identity: Self and Society in the Late Modern Age*. Polity Press.

Gilbert, D. (2014, October 31). Hacker, hoaxer, whistleblower, spy: the many faces of Anonymous – review. *The International Business Times*. Retrieved June 28, 2015, from http://www.ibtimes.co.uk/hacker-hoaxer-whistleblower-spy-many-faces-anonymous-review-1472581

Gill, R. (2009, Dec.). *Rethinking Masculinity: Men and Their Bodies*. Seminar, The London School of Economics and Political Science. Retrieved February 20, 2013 from, http://fathom.lse.ac.uk/Seminars/21701720/21701720_session2.html

Gillespie, T. (2012). Can an algorithm be wrong? *Limn, 1*(2).

Gillespie, A. A. (2006). Cyber-bullying and harassment of teenagers: The legal response. *Journal of Social Welfare and Family Law, 28*(2), 123–136. doi:10.1080/09649060600973772

Gill, R. (2011). Supersexualize Me! In G. Dines & J. Humez (Eds.), *Gender, Race, and Class in Media: A Critical Reader* (pp. 278–284). Thousand Oaks, CA: Sage Publications.

Gitlin, T. (1998). Public sphere or public sphericules? In T. Liebes & J. Curran (Eds.), *Media, ritual, identity* (pp. 168–175). London, UK: Routledge.

Gjoni, E. (2014, August 16). TL;DR. *The Zoe Post*. Retrieved June 28, 2015, from https://thezoepost.wordpress.com/2014/08/16/tldr/

GLAAD. (2014). *2014 GLAAD TV reports*. Retrieved June 10, 2015, from http://www.glaad.org/files/GLAAD-2014-WWAT.pdf

Glaser, B., & Strauss, A. (1967). *The Discovery of Grounded Theory: Strategies for Qualitative Research*. New Brunswick, NJ: Transaction.

Goebert, D., Else, I., Matsu, C., Chung-Do, J., & Chang, J. Y. (2011). The impact of cyberbullying on substance use and mental health in a multiethnic sample. *Maternal and Child Health Journal, 15*(8), 1282–1286. doi:10.1007/s10995-010-0672-x PMID:20824318

Goffman, E. (1959). *The Presentation of the Self in Everyday Life*. Chicago: Anchor Books.

Goldberg, D. (2008). *The Threat of Race: Reflections on Racial Neoliberalism*. Malden, MA: Wiley-Blackwell. doi:10.1002/9781444304695

Gonzalez, A. (1989). "Participation" at WMEX-FM: Interventional rhetoric of Ohio Mexican Americans. *Western Journal of Speech Communication, 53*(4), 398–410. doi:10.1080/10570318909374317

Google Ad Planner. (2012). *Google Display Network*. Retrieved from https://www.google.com/adplanner/#siteSearch?uid=Jezebel.com&geo=US&lp=false

Gorzig, A., & Frumkin, L. A. (2013). Cyberbullying experiences on-the-go: When social media can become distressing. *Cyberpsychology: Journal of Psychosocial Research on Cyberspace, 7*(1), article 1. doi: 10.5817/CP2013-1-4

Gouldner, A. (1971). *The Coming Crisis of Western Sociology*. London: Heinemann Educational Books Ltd.

Gourgouris, St. (1996). *Dream Nation. Enlightenment, Colonization, and the Istitution of Modern Greece*. Stanford University Press.

Gray, K. (2013). Collective Organizing, Individual Resistance, or Asshole Griefers? An Ethnographic Analysis of Women of Color in Xbox Live. *Ada: A Journal of Gender, New Media, and Technology*. Retrieved June 28, 2015, from http://adanewmedia.org/2013/06/issue2-gray/

Gray, R., Sinding, C., & Fitch, M. (2001). Navigating the social context of metastatic breast cancer: Reflections on a project linking research to drama. *Health, 5*(2), 233–248. doi:10.1177/136345930100500205

Grayson, N. (2014a, January 8). Admission quest: Valve Greenlights 50 more games. *Rock, Paper, Shotgun*. Retrieved June 28, 2015, from http://www.rockpapershotgun.com/2014/01/08/admission-quest-valve-greenlights-50-more-games

Grayson, N. (2014b, March 31). The indie game reality TV show that went to hell. *Kotaku*. Retrieved June 28, 2015, from http://tmi.kotaku.com/the-indie-game-reality-tv-show-that-went-to-hell-1555599284

Grewal, I., & Kaplan, C. (2000). Postcolonial studies and transnational feminist practices. *Jouvert: A Journal of Postcolonial Studies, 5*(1). Retrieved July 27, 2015, from http://english.chass.ncsu.edu/jouvert/v5i1/grewal.htm

Grigg, D. W. (2010). Cyber-aggression: Definition and concept of cyberbullying. *Australian Journal of Guidance & Counselling, 20*(02), 143–156. doi:10.1375/ajgc.20.2.143

Grigg, D. W. (2012). Definitional constructs of cyberbullying and cyber aggression from a triagnulatory overview: A preliminary study into elements. *Journal of Aggression, Conflict and Peace Research, 4*(4), 202–215. doi:10.1108/17596591211270699

Grimes, R. L. (1996). Ritual Criticism and Infelicitous Performances. In *Readings in Ritual Studies* (pp. 289–293). Upper Saddle River, NJ: Grimes, Ronald L.(Original work published 1990)

Gu, Q. (2014). Sina Weibo: A mutual communication apparatus between the Chinese government and Chinese citizens. *China Media Research, 10*(2).

Guardian. (2015, April 10). *Chinese broadcaster apologizes for Mao Zedong insults*. Retrieved from The Guardian: http://www.theguardian.com/world/2015/apr/10/chinese-broadcaster-apologises-mao-zedong-insults-bi-fujian

Guariguata, L. (2000, October 3). Morrison Lectures on Digitization of Literature. *The Cornell Daily Sun*. Accessed September 15, 2015, from http://cornellsun.com/blog/2000/10/03/morrison-lectures-on-digitization-of literature/

Guha, P. (2015). Hashtagging but not trending: The success and failure of the news media to engage with online feminist activism in India. *Feminist Media Studies, 15*(1), 155–157. doi:10.1080/14680777.2015.987424

Guillory, J. (1993). *Cultural Capital: The Problem of Literary Canon Formation*. University of Chicago Press.

Guo, L., & Harlow, S. (2014). User-generated racism: An analysis of stereotypes of African Americans, Latinos, and Asians in YouTube videos. *The Howard Journal of Communications, 25*(3), 281–302. doi:10.1080/10646175.2014.925413

Guo, L., & Lee, L. (2013). The critique of YouTube-based vernacular discourse: A case study of YouTube's Asian community. *Critical Studies in Media Communication, 30*(5), 391–406. doi:10.1080/15295036.2012.755048

Gustafson, D. H., McTavish, F. M., Stengle, W., Ballard, D., Hawkins, R., Shaw, B. R., & Landucci, G. et al. (2005). Use and impact of eHealth system by low-income women with breast cancer. *Journal of Health Communication*, *10*(sup1), 195–218. doi:10.1080/10810730500263257 PMID:16377608

Gustafson, D., Hawkins, R., McTavish, F., Pingree, S., Chen, W. C., Volrathongchai, K., & Serlin, R. et al. (2008). Internet based interactive support for cancer patients: Are integrated systems better? *Journal of Communication*, *58*(2), 238–257. doi:10.1111/j.1460-2466.2008.00383.x PMID:21804645

Hall, S. (1997). *Representation: Cultural representations and signifying practices*. London: Sage Publications Ltd.

Haniver, J. (2014). *Not in the Kitchen Anymore*. Retrieved April 9, 2014, from http://www.notinthekitchenanymore.com/about/

Han, J., Shah, D., Kim, E., Namkoong, K., Lee, S.-Y., Moon, T. J., & Gustafson, D. et al. (2011). Empathic exchanges in online cancer support groups: Distinguishing message expression and reception effects. *Health Communication*, *26*(2), 185–197. doi:10.1080/10410236.2010.544283 PMID:21318917

Han, J., Shaw, B., Hawkins, R., Pingree, S., Mctavish, F., & Gustafson, D. (2008). Expressing positive emotions within online support groups by women with breast cancer. *Journal of Health Psychology*, *13*(8), 1002–1007. doi:10.1177/1359105308097963 PMID:18987072

Hardy, J. (2015). Mapping Commerical Intertextuality: HBO's True Blood. In Gender, Race, and Class in Media: A Critical Reader. Thousand Oaks, CA: Sage Publications.

Harold, C. (2004). Pranking rhetoric: "Culture jamming" as media activism. *Critical Studies in Media Communication*, *21*(3), 189–211. doi:10.1080/0739318042000212693

Harp, D., Loke, J., & Bachmann, I. (2014). Spaces for feminist (re)articulations. The blogosphere and the sexual attack on journalist Lara Logan. *Feminist Media Studies*, *14*(1), 5–21. doi:10.1080/14680777.2012.740059

Harris, A. (2004). *Future Girl: Young Women in the Twenty-first Century*. New York: Routledge.

Hathaway, J. (2014, October 10). What is Gamergate and why? An explainer for non-Geeks. *Gawker*. Retrieved June 28, 2015, from http://gawker.com/what-is-gamergate-and-why-an-explainer-for-non-geeks-1642909080

Hatmaker, T. (2014, October 3). The single vigilante behind Facebook's 'real name' crackdown. *The Daily Dot*. Retrieved from http://www.dailydot.com/technology/realnamepolice-facebook-real-names-policy/

Hatton, C. (2015, February 24). *Is Weibo on the way out?* Retrieved from BBC News: http://www.bbc.com/news/blogs-china-blog-31598865

Hatzopoulos, M. (2009). From resurrection to insurrection: 'sacred' myths, motifs, and symbolsin the Greek War of Independence. In R. Beaton & D. Ricks (Eds.), *The Making of Modern Greece* (pp. 81–94). Ashgate.

Hauslohner, A. (2011). Is Egypt about to have a Facebook revolution? *Time*. Retrieved July 25, 2015 from http://content.time.com/time/world/article/0,8599,2044142,00.html

Hawkins, R. A. (2010). Boycotts, buycotts and consumer activism in a global context: An overview. *Management & Organizational History*, *5*(2), 123–143. doi:10.1177/1744935910361644

Hawkins, R., Han, J., Pingree, S., Shaw, B., Baker, T., & Roberts, L. (2010). Interactivity and presence of three eHealth interventions. *Computers in Human Behavior*, *26*(5), 1081–1088. doi:10.1016/j.chb.2010.03.011 PMID:20617154

Hebdige, D. (1979). *Subculture: The Meaning of Style*. London, UK: Routledge.

Hegde, R. S. (2001). Global makeovers and maneuvers: Barbie's presence in India. *Feminist Media Studies*, *1*(1), 129–133. doi:10.1080/14680770120042918

Heirman, W., Angelopoulos, Weege, D., Vandebosch, H., Eggermont, S., & Walrave, M. (2015). Cyberbullying-entrenched or cyberbully-free classrooms? A class network and class composition approach. *Journal of Computer-Mediated Communication, 20,* 260-277.

Heirman, W., & Walrave, M. (2012). Predicting adolescent perpetration in cyberbullying: An application of the theory of planned behavior. *Psicothema*, *24*, 614–620. PMID:23079360

Hennen, P. (2004). Fae Spirits and Gender Trouble: Resistance and Compliance among the Radical Faeries. *Journal of Contemporary Ethnography*, *33*(5), 499–533. doi:10.1177/0891241604266986

Henriksen, N., & Hansen, H. P. (2009). Marked bodies and selves: A literary-semiotic perspective on breast cancer and identity. *Communication & Medicine*, *6*, 143–152. doi:10.1558/cam.v6i2.143 PMID:20635551

Hern, A. (2014, October 15). Feminist games critic cancels talk after terror threat. *The Guardian*. Retrieved June 28, 2015, from http://www.theguardian.com/technology/2014/oct/15/anita-sarkeesian-feminist-games-critic-cancels-talk

Hess, A. (2009). Resistance up in smoke: Analyzing the limitations of deliberation on YouTube. *Critical Studies in Media Communication*, *26*(5), 411–434. doi:10.1080/15295030903325347

Hickey, A. M. (2001). Understanding Men: Gender Sociology and the New International Research on Masculinities. *Social Thought & Research*, *24*(12), 33–35.

Higgs, E. T. (2015). #JusticeForLiz: Power and privilege in digital transnational women's rights activism. *Feminist Media Studies*, *15*(2), 344–247. doi:10.1080/14680777.2015.1008746

Hill, P., & Butter, E. (1995). The role of religion in promoting physical health. *Journal of Psychology and Christianity*, *14*, 141–155.

Himelboim, I., Smith, M., & Shneiderman, B. (2013). Tweeting apart: Applying network analysis to detect selective exposure clusters in Twitter. *Communication Methods and Measures*, *7*(3), 195–223. doi:10.1080/19312458.2013.813922

Hinduja, S., & Patchin, J. W. (2007). Offline consequences of online victimization. *Journal of School Violence*, *6*(3), 89–112. doi:10.1300/J202v06n03_06

Hinduja, S., & Patchin, J. W. (2012). Cyberbullying: Neither and epidemic nor a rarity. *European Journal of Developmental Psychology*, *9*(5), 539–543. doi:10.1080/17405629.2012.706448

Hinduja, S., & Patchin, J. W. (2013). Social influences on cyberbullying behaviors among middle and high school students. *Journal of Youth and Adolescence*, *42*(5), 711–722. doi:10.1007/s10964-012-9902-4 PMID:23296318

Holevas, K. (2014). *Από την κότα του Καποδίστρια στις μίζες του σήμερα*. Retrieved April 20, 2012, from http://www.antibaro.gr/article/9890

Holloway, K. F. C. (1992). *Mooring and Metaphors: Figures of Culture and Gender in Black Women's Literature*. New Brunswick, NJ: Rutgers University Press.

Holpuch, A. (2014, September 13). Facebook under fire from drag queens over 'real-name' rule. *The Guardian*. Retrieved from http://www.theguardian.com/technology/2014/sep/13/facebook-under-fire-drag-queens-real-name-rule

Honan, W. H. (1996, April 2). Georgetown University Fills Shakespeare Gap. *The New York Times: Campus Journal*. Accessed September 16, 2015, from http://www.nytimes.com/1997/04/02/us/georgetown-university-fills-shakespeare-gap.html

Hong, K. (2013, July 3). *Tencent's WeChat chalks up 70 million users outside of China thanks to aggressive global marketing*. Retrieved from http://thenextweb.com/asia/2013/07/03/tencents-wechat-chalks-up-70-million-users-outside-of-china-thanks-to-agg

Hooks, B. (2004, July). *Understanding Patriarchy*. Louisville Anarchist Federation.

Hopkins, R. (2012, November 12). *Victoria's Secret's Racist Garbage Is Just Asking for a Boycott*. [Web log post]. Retrieved April 1, 2013, from http://jezebel.com/victoria.s-secret-fashion-show/

Hossain, M. S. and Hossain, T.T. (2011). From Nabab to Kebab: the re-gazing of masculinity in Bangladeshi haute couture visual discourse. *Harvest, 26*.

Hossain, M. S. (2011). Ecstatic Dance! Artistic Bang!!: Economics of metrosexual masculinity in Bangladeshi haute coutre visual discourse. *Nrivijnana Patrika, 16*, 1–16.

Houghton, D., Joinson, A., Caldwell, N., & Marder, B. (2013). *Tagger's delight? Disclosure and liking in Facebook: the effects of sharing photographs amongst multiple known social circles*. University of Birmingham.

Hroch, M. (1985). *Social Preconditions of National Revival in Europe: A Comparative Analysis of the Social Composition of Patriotic Groups among Smaller European Nations*. Cambridge, UK: Cambridge University Press.

Huang, J., Su, S., Zhou, L., & Liu, X. (2013). Attitude Toward the Viral Ad: Expanding Traditional Advertising Models to Interactive Advertising. *Journal of Interactive Marketing, 27*(1), 36–46. doi:10.1016/j.intmar.2012.06.001

Huang, S. (1996). *To rebel is justified: a rhetorical study of China's cultural movement, 1966-1969*. Lanham, MD: University Press of America.

Huang, Y., & Chou, C. (2010). An analysis of multiple factors of cyberbullying among junior high school students in Taiwan. *Computers in Human Behavior, 26*(6), 1581–1590. doi:10.1016/j.chb.2010.06.005

Hunt, D., & Ramón, A.-C. (2015, February 25). *2015 Hollywood diversity report: Flipping the script*. Retrieved June 10, 2015, from http://www.bunchecenter.ucla.edu/wp-content/uploads/2015/02/2015-Hollywood-Diversity-Report-2-25-15.pdf

Irwin, D. (2013). Tweeting towards feminist revolution. *Clutch*. Retrieved July 27, 2015 from http://www.clutchmagonline.com/2013/12/tweeting-towards-feminist-revolution/

Janus, K. K. (2013). Finding common Feminist ground: The role of the next generation in shaping Feminist legal theory. *Duke Journal of Gender Law & Policy, 20*(2), 255.

Jelavich, B. (1983). *History of the Balkans* (Vol. 1). Cambridge University Press.

Jenkins, R., & Pargament, K. (1995). Religion and spirituality as resources for coping with cancer. *Journal of Psychosocial Oncology, 13*(1-2), 51–74. doi:10.1300/J077V13N01_04

Jenson, J., & de Castell, S. (2010). Gender, Simulation, and Gaming: Research Review and Redirections. *Simulation & Gaming, 41*(1), 51–71. doi:10.1177/1046878109353473

Jeon, Y.-H. (2004). The application of grounded theory and symbolic interactionism. *Scandinavian Journal of Caring Sciences, 18*(3), 249–256. doi:10.1111/j.1471-6712.2004.00287.x PMID:15355518

Joas, H., & Knobl, W. (2004). *Social Theory*. Cambridge, UK: Cambridge University Press.

Johnston, C. (2014, September 9). Chat logs show how 4Chan users created #GamerGate controversy. *Ars Technica*. Retrieved June 28, 2015, from http://arstechnica.com/gaming/2014/09/new-chat-logs-show-how-4chan-users-pushed-gamergate-into-the-national-spotlight/

Joinson, A. (1998). Causes and implications of behavior on the Internet. In J. Gackenbach (Ed.), *Psychology and the Internet: Intrapersonal, interpersonal, and transpersonal implications* (pp. 43-60). San Diego, CA: Academic Press.

Jones, J. (2014, January 28). Harold Bloom Creates a Massive List of Works in The 'Western Canon': Read Many of the Books Free Online. *Open Culture*. Accessed September 15, 2015, from http://www.openculture.com/2014/01/harold-bloom-creates-a-massive-list-of-works-in-the-western-canon.html

Josi, H. (2015, June 6). Toni Morrison added to Literature Humanities. *Columbia Spectator*. Retrieved from http://columbiaspectator.com/spectrum/2015/06/06/toni-morrisonadded-lit-hum-becomes-first-black-author-syllabus

Jubas, K. (2008). Adding Human Rights to the Shopping List: British Women's Abolitionist Boycotts as Radical Learning and Practice. *Convergence, 41*(1), 77.

Juni, S., & Katz, B. (2001). Self-effacing wit as a response to oppression: Dynamics in ethnic humor. *The Journal of General Psychology, 128*(2), 119–142. doi:10.1080/00221300109598903 PMID:11506044

Jurgenson, N. (2012). When atoms meet bits: Social media, the mobile web and augmented revolution. *Future Internet, 4*(1), 83–91. doi:10.3390/fi4010083

JustKiddingFilms. (2012, January 15). *Shit Asian dads say*. Retrieved from https://www.youtube.com/watch?v=o5MJbZ4l4J8

JustKiddingFilms. (n.d.). *About*. Retrieved from http://www.justkiddingfilms.net/about/

JustTheTippiHedren. (2012, December 18). *The vast majority of folks will never pursue a career as a chef*. [Web log comment]. Retrieved April 1, 2013, from http://jezebel.com/5969299/awesome-teenager-successfully-petitions-hasbro-for-gender-neutral-easy+bake-oven

Kain, E. (2014, October 9). #GamerGate Is Not A Hate Group, It's A Consumer Movement. *Forbes*. Retrieved June 28, 2015, from http://www.forbes.com/sites/erikkain/2014/10/09/gamergate-is-not-a-hate-group-its-a-consumer-movement/

Kang, J. (2012). A Volatile Public: The 2009 Whole Foods Boycott on Facebook. *Journal of Broadcasting & Electronic Media, 56*(4), 562–577. doi:10.1080/08838151.2012.732142

Karpf, D. (2010). Online Political Mobilization from the Advocacy Group's Perspective: Looking Beyond Clicktivism. *Policy & Internet, 2*(4), 7–41. doi:10.2202/1944-2866.1098

Keller, J. M. (2012). Virtual feminisms: Girls' blogging communities, feminist activism, and participatory politics. *Information Communication and Society, 15*(3), 429–447. doi:10.1080/1369118X.2011.642890

Kendall, D. E. (2011). *Framing class: Media representations of wealth and poverty in America*. Lanham, MD: Rowman & Littlefield.

Kendall, L. (2000). 'OH NO! I'M A NERD!' Hegemonic Masculinity on an Online Forum. *Gender & Society, 14*(2), 256–274. doi:10.1177/089124300014002003

Kenne Sarenmalm, E. K., Thoren-Jonsson, A.-L., Gaston-Johnsson, F., & Ohlen, K. (2009). Making sense of living under the shadow of death: Adjusting to a recurrent breast cancer illness. *Qualitative Health Research, 19*(8), 1116–1130. doi:10.1177/1049732309341728 PMID:19638604

Khazan, O. (2015). The sexism of startup land. *The Atlantic*. Retrieved July 27, 2015 from http://www.theatlantic.com/business/archive/2015/03/the-sexism-of-startup-land/387184/

Khoja-Moolji, S. (2015). Becoming an "intimate publics": Exploring the affective intensities of hashtag feminism. *Feminist Media Studies, 15*(2), 347–350. doi:10.1080/14680777.2015.1008747

Kim, E., Han, J. Y., Shah, D., Shaw, B., McTavish, F., Gustafson, D. H., & Fan, D. (2011). Predictors of supportive message expression and reception in an interactive cancer communication system. *Journal of Health Communication, 16*(10), 1106–1121. doi:10.1080/10810730.2011.571337 PMID:22070449

King, G., Pan, J., & Roberts, M. (2013). How Censorship in China Allows Government Criticism but Silences collective expression. *The American Political Science Review, 107*(2), 326–343. doi:10.1017/S0003055413000014

Kirby, A. (2009). *Digimodernism: How new technologies dismantle the postmodern and reconfigure our culture.* New York: Continuum.

Kirsch, M. H. (2000). *Queer Theory and Social Change.* London, UK: Routledge.

Kitromilides, P. (1999). *Νεοελληνικός Διαφωτισμός. Ο.* Athens: MIET.

Kitromilides, P. (2010). Adamantios Korais and the dilemmas of liberal nationalism. In P. Kitromilides (Ed.), *Adamantios Korais and the European Enlightenment* (pp. 213–223). Oxford UK: Voltaire Foundation.

Klein, N. (2002). Farewell to the 'End of History': Organisation and Vision in Anti-Corporate Movements. *Socialist Register, 38*(38).

Kleinmann, A. (1988). *The Illness Narrative. Suffering, Healing and the Human Condition.* New York: Basic Books.

Kochenderfer-Ladd, B., & Pelletier, M. (2008). Teachers' views and beliefs about bullying: Influences on classroom management strategies and students' coping with peer victimization. *Journal of School Psychology, 46*(4), 431–453. doi:10.1016/j.jsp.2007.07.005 PMID:19083367

Kokkinos, G., & Gatsotis, P. (2010). Το σχολείο απέναντι στο επίμαχο ιστορικό γεγονός και το τραύμα. In G. Kokkinos, D. K. Mavroskoufis, P. Gatsotis & E. Lemonidou (Eds.), Τα συγκρουσιακά θέματα στη διδασκαλία της Ιστορίας (pp. 13-120). Athens: noogramma.

Koliopoulos, J., & Veremis, T. (2010). *Modern Greece. A Historiy since 1821.* Wiley-Blackwell.

Kordatos, Y. (1976). *Η Κοινωνική σημασία της Ελληνικής Επαναστάσεως του 1821.* Αθήνα: Εκδόσεις Διεθνούς Επικαιρότητας.

Koroma, S., & Carlos, M. H. (2015, January 16). *How Islam became the fastest growing religion in Europe.* Retrieved July 3, 2015, from Time.Com: http://time.com/3671514/islam-europe/

Kotzer, Z. (2014, January 23). Female game designers are being threatened with rape. *Vice.* Retrieved June 28, 2015, from http://www.vice.com/en_ca/read/female-game-designers-are-being-threatened-with-rape

Koulouri, C., & Loukos, C. (2012). *Τα πρόσωπα του Καποδίστρια. Ο πρώτος Κυβερνήτης της Ελλάδας και η νεοελληνική ιδεολογία (1831-1996).* Athens: Poreia.

Kowalski, R. M., & Limber, S. P. (2007). Electronic bullying among middle school students. *The Journal of Adolescent Health, 41*(6), 22–30. doi:10.1016/j.jadohealth.2007.08.017 PMID:18047942

Kramer, J. (2015, October 19). Road Warrior. *The New Yorker,* 46-57.

Kubik, E. (2012). Masters of Technology: Defining and Theorizing the Hardcore/Casual Dichotomy in Video Game Culture. In *Cyberfeminism 2.0* (pp. 135–152). New York, NY: Peter Lang Pub.

Kuznekoff, J. H., & Rose, L. M. (2013). Communication in multiplayer gaming: Examining player responses to gender cues. *New Media & Society*, *15*(4), 541–556. doi:10.1177/1461444812458271

LaCapra, D. (1980). Rethinking intellectual history and reading texts. *History and Theory*, *19*(3), 245–276.

Landow, G. P. (n.d.). *The Literary Canon*. Available: http://www.victorianweb.org/gender/canon/litcan.html

Lazar, M. M. (2007). Feminist critical discourse analysis: Articulating a feminist discourse praxis. *Critical Discourse Studies*, *4*(2), 141–164. doi:10.1080/17405900701464816

Lazuras, L., Barkoukis, V., Ourda, D., & Tsorbatzoudis, H. (2013). A process model of cyberbullying in adolescence. *Computers in Human Behavior*, *29*(3), 881–887. doi:10.1016/j.chb.2012.12.015

Lazzaro, S. (2015). NY Mag Lost Over 500,000 Page Views on Cosby Cover Story During DDoS Attack. *The Observer*. Retrieved July 30, 2015 from http://observer.com/2015/07/ny-mag-lost-over-500000-page-views-on-cosby-cover-story-during-ddos-attack/#ixzz3hPiK9zhO

Le Reve wear your dream's photos. (2012). Retrieved March 15, 2013 from http://www.facebook.com/photo.php?fbid=414238065301562&set=pb.134736613251710.-2207520000.1364582065&type=3&theater

Le Reve wear your dream's photos. (2013). Retrieved March 20 2013, from http://www.facebook.com/photo.php?fbid=513198755405492&set=pb.134736613251710.-2207520000.1364581878&type=3&src=http%3A%2F%2Fsphotos-c.ak.fbcdn.net%2Fhphotos-ak-prn1%2F28170_513198755405492_1277405004_n.jpg&size=533%2C800

Lee, D. (2014, October 29). Zoe Quinn: GamerGate must be condemned. *BBC*. Retrieved June 28, 2015, from http://www.bbc.com/news/technology-29821050

Leibold, J. (2011, November). Blogging alone: China, the internet, and the democratic illusion? *The Journal of Asian Studies*, *70*(4), 1023–1041. doi:10.1017/S0021911811001550

Lekakis, E. J. (2012). Will the fair trade revolution be marketised? Commodification, decommodification and the political intensity of consumer politics. *Culture and Organization*, *18*(5), 345–358. doi:10.1080/14759551.2012.728392

Lekkas, P. (1997, July 6). Οι Αντιδράσεις του Ορθολογισμού. *To Vima Newspaper*.

Lekkas, P. (1992). *Η εθνικιστική ιδεολογία. Πέντε υποθέσεις εργασίας στην Ιστορική Κ*. Athens: EMNE-Mninon.

Lekkas, P. (2005). The Greek War of Independence from the Perspective of Historical Sociology. *La Revue Historique*, *2*, 161–183.

Lekkas, P. (2012). *Abstraction and Experience: Toward a Formalist Theory of Ideology*. Athens: Topos.

Leroux, N. (1991). Frederick Douglas and the Attention shift. *Rhetoric Society Quarterly*, *21*(2), 36–46. doi:10.1080/02773949109390915

Li, J. (2014, April 14). *'Twitter' and 'Facebook' of China are best frenemies*. Retrieved from Market Watch: http://www.marketwatch.com/story/twitter-and-facebook-

Li. (2015, January 14). *China to force social media users to declare their real names*. Retrieved from South China Morning Post: http://www.scmp.com/news/china/article/1679072/china-beefs-social-media-rules-forcing-people-use-real-name-registration?page=all

Liakos, A. (2000). Encounters with Modernity: Greek Historiography Since 1974. *Cercles: revista d'història cultural*, *3*,108-118.

Liakos, A. (2008). Hellenism and the Making of Modern Greece: Time, Language, Space. In K. Zacharia (Ed.), *Hellenisms. Culture, Identity, and Ethnicity from Antiquity to Modernity* (pp. 201–236). Aldershot, UK: Ashgate.

Liata, E. (2004). Οι Ελληνικές Κοινότητες (17ος - 19ος Αι.). Από την ιστορία των θεσμών στην ιστορία των τοπικών κοινωνιών και οικονομιών. In P. Kitromilides & T. Sklavenitis (Eds.), Ιστοριογραφία της νεότερης και σύγχρονης Ελλάδας 1833-2002, (vol. B, pp. 533-549). Athens: Κέντρο Νεοελληνικών Ερευνών-ΕΙΕ.

Lien, T. (2015). Why are women leaving the tech industry in droves? *Los Angeles Times.* Retrieved July 27, 2015 from http://www.latimes.com/business/la-fi-women-tech-20150222-story.html#page=1?ncid=newsltushpmg00000003

Lipka, M., & Hackett, C. (2015, April 23). *Why Muslims are the world's fastest-growing religious group.* Retrieved from FactTank: The News In Numbers: http://www.pewresearch.org/fact-tank/2015/04/23/why-muslims-are-the-worlds-fastest-growing-religious-group/

Li, Q. (2007). Bullying in the new playground: Research into cyberbullying and cybervictimization. *Australasian Journal of Educational Technology, 23,* 435–454.

Livingston, J. (1990). *Paris is Burning.* Miramax Films.

Lloyd, A. W. (2005). Defining the Human: Are Transgender People Strangers to the Law? *Berkeley Journal of Gender, Law & Justice, 150.*

Loken, M. (2014). #BringBackOurGirls and the invisibility of imperialism. *Feminist Media Studies, 14*(6), 1100–1102. doi:10.1080/14680777.2014.975442

Loukos, C. (2003). Ο Κυβερνήτης Καποδίστριας. Πολιτικό έργο, συναίνεση και αντιδράσεις. In V. Panagiotopoulos (Ed.), Ιστορία του Νέου Ελληνισμού 1700-2000, (vol. 3, pp. 185-216). Athens: Ellinika Grammata.

Lövheim, M. (2011). Young women's blogs as ethical spaces. *Information Communication and Society, 14*(3), 338–354. doi:10.1080/1369118X.2010.542822

Low, S., & Espelage, D. (2013). Differentiating cyber bullying perpetration from non-physical bullying: Commonalities across race, individual, and family predictors. *Psychology of Violence, 3*(1), 39–52. doi:10.1037/a0030308

Luckman, S. (1999). (En)Gendering the digital body: Feminism and the internet. *Hecate, 25*(2), 36–47.

Luo, Y. (2014). The Internet and agenda setting in China: The influence of online public opinion on media coverage and government policy. *International Journal of Communication, 8,* 1289–1312.

Lynch, A. (2015, February 4). *China demanding real names be used on social media.* Retrieved from Lighthouse News Daily: http://www.lighthousenewsdaily.com/china-

MacKenzie, G., & Marcel, M. (2009). Media coverage of the murder of U.S. transwomen of color. In L. Cuklanz & S. Moorti (Eds.), *Local violence, global media: Feminist analyses of gendered representations.* New York: Peter Lang.

Macridge, P. (2012). The heritages of the modern Greeks. *British Academy Review, 19,* 33–41.

Madden, M., Lenhart, A., Duggan, M., Cortesi, S., & Gasser, U. (2013). *Teens and technology 2013.* Retrieved from: http://www.pewinternet.org/2013/03/13/teens-and-technology-2013/

Maeckelberghe, E. (2000). Across the generations in Feminist theology: From second to third wave Feminisms. *Feminist Theology, 8*(23), 63–69. doi:10.1177/096673500000002312

Mailer, N. (1966). *Cannibals and Christians.* New York: Dial Press.

Manesis, A. (2009). Η πολιτική ιδεολογία του P. In P. Kitromilides (Ed.), *Ρήγας Βελεστινλής. Ιδρυτές της Νεότερης Ελλάδας* (pp. 144–150). Athens: TA NEA-Istoriki Vivliothiki.

Marcum, C. D., Higgins, G. E., Freiburger, T. L., & Ricketts, M. L. (2012). Battle of the sexes: An examination of male and female cyber bullying. *International Journal of Cyber Criminology, 6*(1), 904–911.

Marwick & boyd. (2011). To See and Be Seen: Celebrity Practice on Twitter. *Convergence, 17*(2), 139-158.

Marwick, A., & boyd, . (2011). I tweet honestly, I tweet passionately: Twitter users, context collapse, and the imagined audience. *New Media & Society, 13*(1), 114–133. doi:10.1177/1461444810365313

Marwick, A., & boyd, . (2014). Networked privacy: How teenagers negotiate context in social media. *New Media & Society, 16*(7), 1051–1067. doi:10.1177/1461444814543995

Mason, K. (2008). Cyberbullying: A preliminary assessment for school personnel. *Psychology in the Schools, 45*(4), 323–348. doi:10.1002/pits.20301

Mathieson, C., & Stam, H. (1995). Renegotiating identity: Cancer narratives. *Sociology of Health & Illness, 17*(3), 283–306. doi:10.1111/1467-9566.ep10933316

McCombs, M. (2005). A look at agenda-setting: Past, present and future. *Journalism Studies, 6*(4), 543–557. doi:10.1080/14616700500250438

McDonald, I. R., & Lawrence, R. G. (2004). Filling the 24× 7 News Hole Television News Coverage Following September 11. *The American Behavioral Scientist, 48*(3), 327–340. doi:10.1177/0002764204268989

McGee, M. (2008, October 21). 7 Search Tools You May Not Know… But Should. *Search Engine Land.* Accessed September 15, 2015, from http://searchengineland.com/7-search-tools-you-may-not-know-but-should-15198

McGrew, W. (1976). The land issue in the Greek War of Independence. In N. Diamandouros, J. P. Anton, & J. Petropoulos (Eds.), *Hellenism and the First Greek War of Liberation, 1821-1830* (pp. 111–130). Thessaloniki: Institute for Balkan Studies.

McIntyre, K. (2004). *The Limits of Political Theory. Oakeshott's Philosophy of Civil Association.* Imprint Academic.

McLuhan, M. (1965). Understanding Media: The extensions of Man with a new introduction and bibliography by the author (Paperback ed.). New York: McGraw-Hill.

McLuhan, M. (1962). *The Gutenberg Galaxy.* Toronto, Canada: Toronto University Press.

McNally, V. (2014, August 28). A disheartening account of the harassment going on in gaming right now (and how Adam Baldwin is involved). *The Mary Sue.* Retrieved June 28, 2015, from http://www.themarysue.com/video-game-harassment-zoe-quinn-anita-sarkeesian/

McNeil, M. (2010). Post-Millennial Feminist theory: Encounters with humanism, materialism, critique, nature, biology and darwin. *Journal for Cultural Research, 14*(4), 427–437. doi:10.1080/14797581003765382

McRobbie, A. (2009). *The aftermath of feminism: gender, culture and social change.* Los Angeles, CA: SAGE.

Mendes, K. (2015). *SlutWalk: Feminism, activism and media.* New York: Palgrave Macmillan. doi:10.1057/9781137378910

Mesch, G. S. (2009). Parental mediation, online activities, and cyberbullying. *Cyberpsychology & Behavior, 12*(4), 387–393. doi:10.1089/cpb.2009.0068 PMID:19630583

Metcalf, A., & Humphries, M. (1985). *Sexuality of Men.* London: Pluto Press.

Meyer, R. (2014, June 28). *Everything We Know About Facebook's Secret Mood Manipulation Experiment*. Retrieved from http://www.theatlantic.com/technology/ archive/2014/06/everything-we-know-about-facebooks-secret-mood-manipulation-experiment/373648/

Meyer, M. D. E. (2014). #TheVagenda war on headlines: Feminist activism in the information age. *Feminist Media Studies, 14*(6), 1107–1108. doi:10.1080/14680777.2014.975451

Miliori, M. (2002). Ambiguous partisanships. Philhellenism, turkophilia and balkanology in 19th century Britain. *Balkanologie, 6*(1-2), 127–153.

Millios, Y. (1988). *Ο Ελληνικός K*. Athens: Exandas.

Millward, S. (2012, May 30). *The rise of social media in China with all new user numbers*. Retrieved from Tech in Asia: http://www.techinasia.com/rise-of-china-socialmedia-infographic-2012/

Mirzoeff, N. (1999). *An Introduction to Visual Culture*. London: Routledge.

Mitchell, K. J., Ybarra, M., & Finkelhor, D. (2007). The relative importance of online victimization in understanding depression, delinquency, and substance use. *Child Maltreatment, 12*(4), 314–324. doi:10.1177/1077559507305996 PMID:17954938

Mitsi, Ef, & Muse A. (2013). Some Thoughts on the Trails and Travails of Hellenism and Orientalism: An Interview with Gonda Van Steen. *Synthesis, 5*, 159–178.

Moody-Ramirez, M. (2014). *Representations of The Feminine Mystique and Lean In in user-generated content: A look at Pinterest pins*. Presented at AEJMC Midwinter Conference, Norman, OK.

Moody-Ramirez, M., & Fassih, L. (2015). *Citizen framing of Wendy Davis on Twitter, Tumblr and Pinterest*. Presented at AEJMC Midwinter Conference, Norman, OK.

Moore, M. J., Nakano, T. N., Enomoto, A., & Suda, T. (2012). Anonymity and roles associated with aggressive posts in an online forum. *Computers in Human Behavior, 28*(3), 861–867. doi:10.1016/j.chb.2011.12.005

Morawski, J. (2001). Gifts bestowed, gifts withheld: Assessing psychological theory with a Kochian attitude. *The American Psychologist, 56*(5), 433–440. doi:10.1037/0003-066X.56.5.433 PMID:11355366

Morley, J. (2014, August 26). Autobótika's Lola Barreto Discusses The Fine Young Capitalists. *Cliqist*. Retrieved June 28, 2015, from http://cliqist.com/2014/08/26/autobotikas-lola-barreto-discusses-the-fine-young-capitalists/

Morozov, E. (2009). The brave new world of slacktivism. *Foreign Policy*. Retrieved July 27, 2015, from http://foreignpolicy.com/2009/05/19/the-brave-new-world-of-slacktivism/

Morozov, E. (2009, May 19). The brave new world of slacktivism. *Foreign Policy*. Retrieved July 10, 2015, from http://www.foreignpolicy.com

Mouttapa, M., Valente, T., Gallagher, P., Rohrbach, L. A., & Unger, J. B. (2004). Social network predictor of bullying and victimization. *Adolescence, 39*, 315–335. PMID:15563041

Mouzelis, N. (1996). The Concept of Modernization: Its Relevance for Greece. *Journal of Modern Greek Studies, 14*(2), 215–227.

Mouzelis, N. (2008). *Modern and Postmodern Social Theorizing: Bridging the Divide*. Cambridge University Press.

Mowles, J. M. (2008). Framing Issues, Fomenting Change, 'Feministing': A Contemporary Feminist Blog in the Landscape of Online Political Activism. *International Reports on Socio-Informatics, 29*.

MsLovelace. (2011, July 31). 1 Answer. "how to categorize "tastekid" and "clerkdogs" recommender system." *Stack-Exchange*. Retrieved from http://stackoverflow.com/questions/5026269/how-to-categorize-tastekid-and-clerkdogs-recommender-system

Mudhar, R. (2011, December 13). "Shit Girls Say" video a viral hit for Toronto duo. *The Toronto Star*. Retrieved from http://www.thestar.com

Mukherjee, R. (2012). Diamonds (are from Sierra Leone): Bling and the promise of consumer citizenship. In R. Mukherjee & S. Banet-Weiser (Eds.), *Commodity Activism: Cultural Resistance in Neoliberal Times* (pp. 114–133). New York: New York University Press.

Mulvey, L. (2004). Visual Pleasure and Narrative Cinema. In L. Braudy & M. Cohen (Eds.), *Film Theory and Criticism*. Oxford, UK: Oxford U P.

Murphy, M. (2013, April 3). Putting selfies under a feminist lens. *Georgia Straight*.

Muslimah, & Salamah, S. A. (2015, March 03). *Dancing: What Is Allowed and What Is Not?* Retrieved from Onislam. net: http://www.onislam.net/english/ask-the-scholar/arts-and-entertainment/singing-and-music/175634-dancing-what-is-allowed-and-what-is-not.html?Music=

Nakamura, L. (2002). *Cybertypes: Race, Ethnicity and Identity on the Internet*. New York, NY: Routledge.

Nakamura, L. (2008). *Digitizing Race: Visual Cultures of the Internet*. Minneapolis, MN: University of Minnesota Press.

Namkoong, K., DuBenske, L., Shaw, B., Gustafson, D., Hawkins, R., Shah, D., & Cleary, J. et al. (2012). Creating a bond between caregivers online: Impact on caregivers' coping strategies. *Journal of Health Communication*, *17*(2), 125–140. doi:10.1080/10810730.2011.585687 PMID:22004055

Namkoong, K., Shah, D., Han, J., Kim, S. J., Yoo, W., Fan, D., & Gustafson, D. et al. (2010). Expression and reception of treatment information in breast cancer support groups: How health self-efficacy moderates effects on emotional well-being. *Patient Education and Counseling*, *81*, S41–S47. doi:10.1016/j.pec.2010.09.009 PMID:21044825

Nardin, T. (2015). Oakeshott on theory and practice. *Global Discourse*, *5*(2), 310–322.

National Cancer Institute. (2012). *Coping with cancer: Managing physical effects*. Retrieved from http://www.cancer.gov/cancertopics/coping/physicaleffects/

Nava, M. (1992). *Changing cultures: Feminism, youth and consumerism*. London: Sage Publications.

Navarro, R., Serna, C., Martinez, V., & Ruiz-Oliva, R. (2013). The role of Internet use and parental mediation on cyberbullying victimization among Spanish children from rural public schools. *European Journal of Psychology of Education*, *28*(3), 725–745. doi:10.1007/s10212-012-0137-2

Nip, J. Y. M. (2004). The relationship between online and offline communities: The case of the Queer Sisters. *Media Culture & Society*, *26*(3), 409–428. doi:10.1177/0163443704042262

Nixon, S. (1997). *Exhibiting Masculinity. Cultural Representation and Signifying Practices. Stuart Hall* (pp. 291–336). London: Sage Publication.

Nocentini, A., Calmaestra, J., Schultze-Krumbholz, A., Scheithauer, H., Ortega, R., & Menesini, E. (2010). Cyberbullying: Labels, behaviours and definition in three European countries. *Australian Journal of Guidance & Counselling*, *20*(02), 129–142. doi:10.1375/ajgc.20.2.129

Novak, A., & Khazraee, E. (2014). The stealthy protester: Risk and the female body in online social movements. *Feminist Media Studies*, *14*(6), 1094–1096. doi:10.1080/14680777.2014.975438

O'Neill, B., & Dinh, T. (2013). *Cyberbullying among 9-16 year olds in Ireland.* London, UK: EU Kids Online.

Olweus, D. (1999). Sweden. In P. K. Smith, Y. Morita, J. Junger-Tas, D. Olweus, R. Catalano, & P. Slee (Eds.), *The nature of school bullying: A cross-national perspective* (pp. 7-27). New York, NY: Routledge.

Olympitou, E. (2003). Τεχνικές και Επαγγέλματα. Μια εθνολογική προσέγγιση. In V. Panagiotopoulos (Ed.), Ιστορία του Νέου Ελληνισμού 1700-2000, (vol. 1, pp. 305-316). Athens: Ellinika Grammata.

Ong, W. J. (2002). Orality and Literacy: The Technologizing of the Word (2nd ed.). New York: Routledge.

Ong, W. J. (1967). *In The Human Grain: Further Explanations of Contemporary Culture.* New York: The Macmillan Company.

Ong, W. J. (1977). *Interfaces of the Word: Studies in the evolution of consiousness and culture.* Cornell University Press.

Ong, W. J. (1981). *The Presence of the Word: Some Prolegomena for cultural and religious history.* Minneapolis, MN: University of Minnesota Press.

Onislam.net. (2015). *On Islam.* Retrieved January 26, 2015, from Onislam.net: http://www.onislam.net/english/

Ono, K. A., & Pham, V. N. (2009). *Asian Americans and the media.* Malden, MA: Polity Press.

Oprah's Book Club List. (n.d.). Retrieved from http://oprahbookclublist.com/tag/toni-morrison/

Opt, S. (2013). Apology as Power Intervention: The Case of News of the World. *Western Journal of Communication,* *77*(4), 424–443. doi:10.1080/10570314.2013.767471

Opt, S. K. (2012). Mammogram-Screening Policy as Need Intervention. *Journal of Applied Communication Research,* *40*(1), 1–19. doi:10.1080/00909882.2011.636375

Opt, S. K., & Gring, M. A. (2009). *The Rhetoric of Social Intervention, An Introduction.* Thousand Oaks, CA: Sage.

Ortega, R., Elipe, P., Mora-Merchán, J. A., Genta, M. L., Brighi, A., & Guarini, A. et al. (2012). The Emotional Impact of Bullying and Cyberbullying on Victims: A European Cross-National Study. *Aggressive Behavior,* *38*(5), 342–356. doi:10.1002/ab.21440 PMID:22782434

Orth, U. R., & Denisa, H. (2004). Men's and women's responses to sex role portrayals in advertisements. *International Journal of Research in Marketing,* *21*(1), 77–88. doi:10.1016/j.ijresmar.2003.05.003

Oster, I., Astrom, S., Linda, J., & Magnusson, E. (2009). Women with breast cancer and gendered limits and boundaries: Art therapy as a 'safe place' for enacting alternative subject positions. *The Arts in Psychotherapy,* *36*(1), 29–38. doi:10.1016/j.aip.2008.10.001

Palmer, L. (2003). *The next generation: Third wave Feminist psychotherapy.* Malden, MA: Blackwell Publishers.

Palsson, G. (2014). Personal Names: Embodiment, Differentiation, Exclusion, and Belonging. *Science, Technology & Human Values,* *39*(4), 618–630. doi:10.1177/0162243913516808

Pan, Z. (2010). *Articulation and Re-articulation: Agenda for understanding media and communication in China.* Academic Press.

Panagiotopoulos, V. (2004). Η αριστερή ιστοριογραφία για την Ελληνική Επανάσταση. In P. Kitromilides & T. Sklavenitis (Eds.), Ιστοριογραφία της νεότερης και σύγχρονης Ελλάδας 1833-2002, (vol. A, pp. 567-577). Athens: Κέντρο Νεοελληνικών Ερευνών-ΕΙΕ.

Panagiotopoulos, V. (2007, June 17). Ποιός θα διορθώσει ποιόν. *To Vima Newspaper,* 17- 06-2007.

Panagiotopoulos, V. (2011). *Εθνική Ιστορία ή μήπως εθνική μυθολογία*. Retrieved April 17, 2012, from http://political-reviewgr.blogspot.gr/2011/03/blog-post_25.html

Papacharissi, Z. (2002). The virtual sphere: The internet as a public sphere. *New Media & Society, 4*(9), 9–27.

Papaderos, A. (2010). *Μετακένωσις. Ελλάδα –Ορθοδοξία –Διαφωτισμός κατά τον Κοραή και τον Ο*. Athens: Akritas.

Parker, G. (1999). The role of the consumer-citizen in environmental protest in the 1990s. *Space and Polity, 3*(1), 67–83. doi:10.1080/13562579908721785

Parks, M. (2010). Social Network Sites as Virtual Communities. In Z. Papacharissi (Ed.), *A networked self: Identity, community, and culture on social network sites*. New York: Routledge.

Passey, D. (2014). Editorial on intergenerational learning and digital technologies: New perspectives from research. *Education and Information Technologies, 19*(3), 469–471. doi:10.1007/s10639-014-9339-3

Passonen, S. (2011). Revisiting Cyberfeminism. *Communications, 36*, 335–352.

Patchin, J. W., & Hinduja, S. (2006). Bullies move beyond the schoolyard: A preliminary look at cyberbullying. *Youth Violence and Juvenile Justice, 4*(2), 148–169. doi:10.1177/1541204006286288

Paul, O., & Vezina, R. (1997). Provocation in Advertising: A conceptualization and assessment. *International Journal of Research in Marketing, 14*(2), 177–192. doi:10.1016/S0167-8116(97)00002-5

PBS Newshour. (2015, February 14). *Will 'Fresh off the Boat' turn the tide for Asian Americans on TV?* Retrieved June 10, 2015, from http://www.pbs.org/newshour/bb/will-fresh-boat-turn-tide-asian-americans-tv/

Pearl, M. (2014, August 29). This guy's embarrassing relationship drama is killing the 'gamer' identity. *Vice*. Retrieved June 28, 2015, from http://www.vice.com/read/this-guys-embarrassing-relationship-drama-is-killing-the-gamer-identity-828

Pell, C. (1995). Civil Discourse is Crucial for Democracy to Work. *Insight (American Society of Ophthalmic Registered Nurses), 11*(37), 13.

Pels, D. (2000). *The Intellectual as Stranger. Studies in spokespersonship*. London: Routledge.

Peltola, P., Milkie, M. A., & Presser, S. (2004). The "Feminist" mystique: Feminist identity in three generations of women. *Gender & Society, 18*(1), 122–144. doi:10.1177/0891243203259921

Pelusi, J. (2006). Sexuality and body image. *American Journal of Nursing, 106*, 32–38. doi:00002820-200603002-00013

Petmezas, S. (1990). Patterns of Protoidustrulization in the Ottoman Empire. The case of Eastern Thessaly, ca. 1750-1860. *The Journal of European Economic History, 19*(3), 574–603.

Pew Research Center. (2012). *Who uses tumblr*. Retrieved July 27, 2015 from http://www.pewinternet.org/2012/09/13/additional-material-and-demographics/

Pew Research Center. (2014). *Social media update 2014*. Retrieved July 27, 2015, from http://www.pewinternet.org/2015/01/09/demographics-of-key-social-networking-platforms-2/

Pham, M. H. T. (2011). Blog ambition: Fashion, feelings, and the political economy of the digital raced body. *Camera Obscura, 26*(76), 1-37.

Pina-Cabral, J. (2010). The Truth about Personal Names. *Journal of the Royal Anthropological Institute, 16*(2), 297–312. doi:10.1111/j.1467-9655.2010.01626.x

Pinto, J. (2009). *Feminist waves, Feminist generations: Life stories from the academy*. Thousand Oaks, CA: Sage Publications INC.

Pissis, N. (2011). Αποκαλυπτικός λόγος και συλλογικές ταυτότητες (17ος-18ος αι.). In A. Dimadis (Ed.), *Ταυτότητες στον ελληνικό κόσμο (από το 1204 έως σήμερα)* (Vol. 5, pp. 687–696). Athens: European Society of Modern Greek Studies.

Pitts, V. (2004). Illness and Internet empowerment: Writing and reading breast cancer in cyberspace. *Health, 8*(1), 33–59. doi:10.1177/1363459304038794 PMID:15018717

Pizanias, P. (1987). Η εφαρμογή της θεωρίας για τις σχέσεις του 'καπιταλιστικού κέντρου' και της 'υπανάπτυκτης περιφέρειας' στην Ελληνική ιστοριογραφία. Ν. Ψυρούκης-Κ. Τσουκαλάς. *Mnimon, 11*, 255–286.

Plunkett, L. (2014, August 28). We might be witnessing the 'death of an identity'. *Kotaku*. Retrieved June 28, 2015, from http://kotaku.com/we-might-be-witnessing-the-death-of-an-identity-1628203079?utm_

PMS Clan. (2011). *Our Mission*. Retrieved June 28, 2015, from http://www.pmsclan.com/

Politis, A. (2007). *Το μυθολογικό κενό. Δοκίμια και σχόλια για την ιστορία, τη φιλολογία, την ανθρωπολογία και άλλα*. Athens: Polis.

Pollay, R. W. (1986). The Distorted Mirror: Reflections on the Unintended Consequences of Advertising. *Journal of Marketing, 50*(2), 18–36. doi:10.2307/1251597

Pope, M. (2012, December 19). *Hasbro: Feature boys in the packaging of the Easy-Bake Oven*. Retrieved December 19, 2012 from https://www.change.org/p/hasbro-feature-boys-in-the-packaging-of-the-easy-bake-oven

Pornari, C. D., & Wood, J. (2010). Peer and cyber aggression in secondary school students: The role of moral disengagement, hostile attribution bias, and outcome expectancies. *Aggressive Behavior, 36*(2), 81–94. doi:10.1002/ab.20336 PMID:20035548

Poster, M. (1995). *The second media age*. Cambridge, MA: Polity Press.

Postman, N. (1990, October 11). *Informing Ourselves To Death*. Retrieved December 10, 2014, from Electronic Frontier Foundation: https://w2.eff.org/Net_culture/Criticisms/informing_ourselves_to_death.paper

Postman, N. (2000, June 16). *The Humanism of Media Ecology*. Retrieved December 12, 2014, from Media Ecology Association: http://media-ecology.org/publications/MEA_proceedings/v1/humanism_of_media_ecology.html

Postman, N. (1970). The reformed English curriculum. In A. C. Eurich (Ed.), *High school 1980: The shape of the future in American secondary education* (pp. 160–168). New York: Pitman.

Postman, N. (1986). *Amusing Ourselves To Death, Public Discourse in the age of show business*. New York: Penguin Books Ltd.

Postman, N. (1992). *Technopoly*. New York: Alfred A. Knopf.

Postman, N. (1996). *The End of Education*. New York: Alfred A Knopf.

Pozner, J. (2010). *Reality Bites Back: The Troubling Truth about Guilty Pleasure T.V*. New York, NY: Seal Press.

Prieto, R. R. (2015). From margin to center: Applying the theoretical framework of postcolonial Feminism to human rights. *Athenea Digital (Ed. Impresa), 15*(2), 81–110. doi:10.5565/rev/athenea.1363

Pullen, C. (2009). *Gay Identity, New Storytelling and the Media*. Basingstoke, UK: Palgrave Macmillan. doi:10.1057/9780230236646

Puranik, A. (2012). *Meaning, Definition, Objective and Functions of Advertising*. Retrieved March 8, 2013, from http://www.publishyourarticles.org/knowledge-hub/business-studies/advertising.html

Quinn, Z. (2014, March 31). Unreality: my takeaways after being on and subsequently walking off a reality show about game jams. *Dispatches from the Quinnspiracy*. Retrieved June 28, 2015, from http://ohdeargodbees.tumblr.com/post/81317416962/unreality-my-takeaways-after-being-on-and

Rainie, L. (2011, January 6). *Asian-Americans and technology*. Retrieved November 11, 2014, from http://www.pewinternet.org/2011/01/06/asian-americans-and-technology/

Rains, S. A., & Young, V. (2009). A meta analysis of research on formal computer mediated support groups: Examining group characteristics and health outcomes. *Human Communication Research*, *35*(3), 309–336. doi:10.1111/j.1468-2958.2009.01353.x

Ralph Retort. (2014, November 29). *The Ralph's exit interview with Internet Aristocrat*. Retrieved June 28, 2015, from http://theralphretort.com/theralph-s-interview-with-internet-aristocrat/

Ramsey, D. X. (2015). The truth about Black Twitter. *The Atlantic*. Retrieved July 27, 2015, from http://www.theatlantic.com/technology/archive/2015/04/the-truth-about-black-twitter/390120/

Raskauskas, J. (2010). Text-bullying: Associations with traditional bullying and depression among New Zealand adolescents. *Journal of School Violence*, *9*(1), 74–97. doi:10.1080/15388220903185605

Re-channeling the myth of masculinity: the emergence of androgyny in the Bangladesh media. (n.d.). Retrieved on 22 February, From http://www.lawyersnjurists.com/articles-reports-journals/others-articles-reports-journals/re-channeling-myth-masculinity-emergence-androgyny-bangladeshi-media/

Recitatif. (2001, August 9). *Literature, Arts, and Medicine Database*. New York University. Retrieved from http://litmed.med.nyu.edu/Annotation?action=view&annid=11854

Reiner, R. (Director). (1987). *The Princess Bride* [Motion Picture].

Rentschler, C. (2015). #Safetytipsforladies: Feminist Twitter takedowns of victim blaming. *Feminist Media Studies*, *15*(2), 353–356. doi:10.1080/14680777.2015.1008749

Revenson, T., & Pranikoff, J. (2005). A contextual approach to treatment decision making among breast cancer survivors. *Health Psychology*, *24*(4, Suppl), S93–S98. doi:10.1037/0278-6133.24.4.S93 PMID:16045426

Rhagavan, R. (2009, July 22). *Digital activism on YouTube*. Retrieved February 12, 2015, from http://googleblog.blogspot.com/2009/07/digital-activism-on-youtube.html

Rideout, V. J., Roberts, D. F., & Foehr, U. G. (2005). *Generation M: Media in the lives of 8-18-year-olds: Executive summary*. Menlo Park, CA: Henry J. Kaiser Family Foundation.

Risam, R. (2015). Toxic femininity 4.0. *First Monday*. Retrieved July 7, 2015 from http://www.firstmonday.dk/ojs/index.php/fm/article/view/5896/4417

Robson, C., & Witenberg, R. T. (2013). The influence of moral disengagement, morally based self-esteem, age, and gender on traditional bullying and cyberbullying. *Journal of School Violence*, *12*(2), 211–231. doi:10.1080/15388220.2012.762921

Rodgers, B. (2006). Becoming Radical Faerie: Queering the Spirit of the Circle. *Popular Spiritualities: The Politics of Contemporary Enchantment*, 117.

Rodino, M. (1997). Breaking out of Binaries: Reconceptualizing Gender and its Relationship to Language in Computer-Mediated Communication. *Journal of Computer-Mediated Communication*, 3.

Rogers, K. (2014, December 18). The FBI is investigating #GamerGate. *Motherboard*. Retrieved June 28, 2015, from http://motherboard.vice.com/read/the-fbi-is-investigating-gamergate

Rogers, M. F. (1999). *Barbie culture*. London: SAGE Publications.

Romano, A. (2014, August 20). The sexist crusade to destroy game developer Zoe Quinn. *The Daily Dot*. Retrieved June 28, 2015, from http://www.dailydot.com/geek/zoe-quinn-depression-quest-gaming-sex-scandal/

Rose, G. (2001). *Visual Methodologies*. London: Sage Publication.

Rose, N. (1999). *Powers of Freedom. Reframing Political Thought*. Cambridge University Press.

Rosenberg, S. (2010). *Say everything: How blogging began, what it's becoming, and why it matters*. New York: Crown.

Rossing, J. (2012). Deconstructing Postracialism: Humor as a Critical Cultural Project. *The Journal of Communication Inquiry*, *30*(1), 44–61. doi:10.1177/0196859911430753

Roynon, T. (2007). Toni Morrison and Classical Tradition. *Literature Compass*, *4*(6), 1514–1537. DOI: 10.1111/j.1741-4113.2007.00496.x

Rozenzweig, R. (2011). *Clio Wired. The Future of the Past in the Digital Age*. New York: Columbia University Press.

Rustow, D. (1968). Modernization and Comparative Politics. *Comparative Politics*, *1*(1), 37–51.

Rutten, K., & Vandermeersche, G. (2013). Introduction to literacy and society, culture, media and education. *CLCWeb: Comparative Literature and Culture*.

Ryan, E. G. (2012, November 2). *The Least Practical Items From Oprah's $18,000 Favorite Things List, Measured in Gwyneth Paltrows*. [Web log post]. Retrieved April 1, 2013, from http://updates.jezebel.com/post/34842276933/the-least-practical-items-from-oprahs-18-000-favorite

Ryan, M. (2004). *Literary Theory: A Practical Introduction*. Oxford, UK: Blackwell.

Sahin, M. (2010). Teachers' perceptions of bullying in high schools: A Turkish study. *Social Behavior and Personality*, *38*(1), 127–142. doi:10.2224/sbp.2010.38.1.127

Sakellariou, M. (2012). *Η Πελλοπόνησος κατά την Δευτέραν Τουρκοκρατίαν, 1715-1821*. Athens: Herodotus. (Original work published 1939)

Sandaunet, A.-G. (2008). A space for suffering? Communicating breast cancer in an online self-help context. *Qualitative Health Research*, *18*(12), 1631–1641. doi:10.1177/1049732308327076 PMID:18955462

Sarid, E. (2014). *Don't Be a Drag, Just Be a Queen – How Drag Queens Protect Their Intellectual Property Without Law*. Retrieved from http://ssrn.com/abstract=2511477

Sariyannis, M. (2011). *Παίζοντας με την κονσόλα της Ιστορίας*. Retrieved April 20, 2012, from http://enthemata.wordpress.com/2011/03/26/marinos/

Sauers, G. (2011, August 19). *Zara Says It Really Had No Idea Its Clothes Were Being Manufactured In "Slave-Like Conditions"*. [Web log post]. Retrieved April 1, 2013, from http://jezebel.com/5832541/zara-says-it-really-had-no-idea-its-clothes-were-being-manufactured-in-slave+like-conditions

Savastio, R. (n.d.). *Selfies Cause Narcissism, Mental Illness, Addiction and Suicide?* Retrieved from http://guardianlv. com/2014/04/selfies-cause-narcissism-mental-illness-addiction-and-suicide/

Scammell, M. (2000). The internet and civic engagement: The age of the citizen-consumer. *Political Communication, 17*(4), 351–355. doi:10.1080/10584600050178951

Schiappa, E., Gregg, P., & Hewes, D. (2006). Can One TV Show Make a Difference? Will & Grace and the Parasocial Contact Hypothesis. *Journal of Homosexuality, 51*(4), 15–37. doi:10.1300/J082v51n04_02 PMID:17135126

Scholastic. (2009). *Classroom Library (Grade 7-12): Monster; Twilight Series; Chosen Series; the House On Mango Street; to Kill a Mockingbird; Their Eyes Were Watching God; My Brother Sister & I; Othello; the Bluest Eye" on Books*. Accessed November 23, 2014, from http://www.amazon.com/Classroom-Library-Grade-7-12-Mockingbird/ dp/1500256935/ref=sr_1_1?s=books&ie=UTF8&qid=1416722871&sr=1-1&keywords=toni+morrison

Schreier, J. (2014, November 13). The Anita Sarkeesian hater that everyone hates. *Kotaku*. Retrieved June 28, 2015, from http://kotaku.com/the-anita-sarkeesian-hater-that-everyone-hates-1658494441

Scientists Link Selfies to Narcissism, Addiction & Mental Illness. (n.d.). *Thinking Humanity*. Retrieved from http://www. thinkinghumanity.com/2014/06/scientists-link-selfies-to-narcissism-addiction-mental-illness.html

Scimeca, D. (2014, October 13). *Indie developer mocks GamerGate, chased from home with rape and death threats*. Retrieved June 28, 2015, from http://www.dailydot.com/geek/brianna-we-gamergate-threats/

Seraphita, N. (2014, September 9). Truth in gaming: an interview with The Fine Young Capitalists. *APG Nation*. Retrieved June 28, 2015, from http://apgnation.com/articles/2014/09/09/6977/truth-gaming-interview-fine-young-capitalists

Sevcikova, A., Machackova, H., Wright, M. F., Dedkova, L., & Cerna, A. (2015). Social support seeking in relation to parental attachment and peer relationships among victims of cyberbullying. *Australian Journal of Guidance & Counselling, 15*, 1–13. doi:10.1017/jgc.2015.1

Sevcikova, A., & Smahel, D. (2009). Online harassment and cyberbullying in the Czech Republic: Comparison across age groups. *The Journal of Psychology, 217*(4), 227–229.

Severn, J., Belch, G. E., & Belch, M. A. (1990). The Effects of Sexual and Nonsexual Advertising Appeals and Information Level on Cognitive Processing and Communication Effectiveness. *Journal of Advertising, 19*(1), 14–22. doi:10.1 080/00913367.1990.10673176

Shapka, J. D., & Law, D. M. (2013). Does one size fit all? Ethnic differences in parenting behaviors and motivations for adolescent engagement in cyberbullying. *Journal of Youth and Adolescence, 42*(5), 723–738. doi:10.1007/s10964-013-9928-2 PMID:23479327

Shariff, S., & Hoff, D. L. (2007). Cyber bullying: Clarifying legal boundaries for school supervision in cyberspace. *International Journal of Cyber Criminology, 1*, 76–118.

Shaw, A. (2013). On Not Becoming Gamers: Moving Beyond the Constructed Audience. *Ada: A Journal of Gender, New Media, and Technology*, (2). Retrieved June 28, 2015, from http://adanewmedia.org/2013/06/issue2-shaw/

Shaw, A. (2011). Do you identify as a gamer? Gender, race, sexuality, and gamer identity. *New Media & Society, 14*(1), 28–44. doi:10.1177/1461444811410394

Shaw, B. R., McTavish, F. M., Hawkins, R. P., Gustafson, D. H., & Pingree, S. (2000). Experiences of women with breast cancer: Exchanging social support over the CHESS computer network. *Journal of Health Communication, 5*(2), 135–159. doi:10.1080/108107300406866 PMID:11010346

Shaw, B., Han, J., Kim, E., Gustafson, D., Hawkins, R., Cleary, J., & Lumpkins, C. et al. (2007). Effects of prayer and religious expression within computer support groups on women with breast cancer. *Psycho-Oncology, 16*(7), 676–687. doi:10.1002/pon.1129 PMID:17131348

Shaw, B., Hawkins, R., McTavish, F., Pingree, S., & Gustafson, D. (2006). Effects of insightful disclosure within computer mediated support groups on women with breast cancer. *Health Communication, 19*(2), 133–142. doi:10.1207/s15327027hc1902_5 PMID:16548704

Sheets, C. A. (2012, March 29). What does TLDR mean? AMA? TIL? Glossary of Reddit terms and abbreviations. *The International Business Times*. Retrieved June 28, 2015, from http://www.ibtimes.com/what-does-tldr-mean-ama-til-glossary-reddit-terms-abbreviations-431704

Shihab, W., & Timea. (2014, December 25). *Using Cell Phone in Bathroom: Allowed?* Retrieved July 3, 2015, from Onislam.net: http://www.onislam.net/english/ask-the-scholar/common-mistakes/481077-using-cell-phone-in-bathroom-allowed.html

Simcott, R. (2014, February 27). *Social media fast facts: China. Social Media Today.* Retrieved from Social Media Today: http://www.socialmediatoday.com/content/social-media-fast-facts-china

Simmons, R. (2013). *Selfies on Instagram and Facebook are tiny bursts of girl pride.* Retrieved from www.slate.com

Simpson, M. (2003). *Metrosexual? That rings a bell...* Retrieved from http://www.marksimpson.com/pages/journalism/metrosexual_ios.html

Skai. (2009). *Μεγάλοι Έλληνες-Kapodistrias.* Retrieved April 20, 2012, from https://www.youtube.com/watch?v=7M0QyS7_Ml4

Sloan, A. (2014, March 19). *China's suprise freedom of speech crackdown on WeChat.* Retrieved from https://www.indexoncensorship.org/2014/03/chinas-suprise-freedom-speech-crackdown-wechat/

Slonje, R., & Smith, P. K. (2008). Cyberbullying another main type of bullying? *Scandinavian Journal of Psychology, 49*(2), 147–154. doi:10.1111/j.1467-9450.2007.00611.x PMID:18352984

Smith, A. (2011, September 19). *How Americans Use Text Messaging.* Retrieved from Pew Research Center: http://www.pewinternet.org/2011/09/19/how-americans-use-text-messaging/

Smith, A. D. (1995). *The 1995 Warwick Debates on Nationalism.* Retrieved from http://gellnerpage.tripod.com/Warwick.html

Smith, B. R. (1997). Teaching the Resonances. *Shakespeare Quarterly, 48*(4). Available: http://www.jstor.org/stable/2871255

Smith, C. (2014). Here's why Instagram demographics are so attractive to brands. *Business Insider*. Retrieved July 27, 2015, from http://www.businessinsider.com.au/instagram-demographics-2013-12

Smith, C. (2015a). By the numbers: 90+ amazing Pinterest statistics (July 2015). *Expanded Ramblings*. Retrieved July 28, 2015 from http://expandedramblings.com/index.php/pinterest-stats/

Smith, C. (2015b). By the numbers: 150+ interesting Instagram statistics (July 2015). *Expanded Ramblings*. Retrieved July 28, 2015 from http://expandedramblings.com/index.php/important-instagram-stats/

Smith, I. V. J. (2014, September 25). Ello's traffic deluge almost caused a total new user freeze-out, crisis averted. *The Observer*. Retrieved from http://observer.com/2014/09/ellos-traffic-deluge-almost-caused-a-total-new-user-freeze-out-crisis-averted/

Smith, S., Choueiti, M., & Pieper, K. (2013). *Previous research.* Retrieved June 10, 2015, from http://annenberg.usc. edu/pages/~/media/MDSCI/Racial%20Inequality%20in%20Film%202007-2013%20Final.ashx

Smith, A. D. (2001). Perennialism and Modernism. In A. Leoussi (Ed.), *Encyclopedia of Nationalism* (pp. 242–244). London: Transaction Publishers.

Smith, P. K., Mahdavi, J., Carvalho, M., Fisher, S., Russell, S., & Tippett, N. (2008). Cyberbullying: Its nature and impact in secondary school pupils. *Journal of Child Psychology and Psychiatry, and Allied Disciplines, 49*(4), 376–385. doi:10.1111/j.1469-7610.2007.01846.x PMID:18363945

Snyder, L. (2009). Born To Power: Influence in the rhetoric of the Posse Comitatus. In S. K. Opt & M. A. Gring (Eds.), *The Rhetoric of Social Intervention: An Introduction* (pp. 213–230). Los Angeles, CA: Sage. doi:10.4135/9781452274935.n11

Sontag, S. (1977). *On Photography.* New York: Farrar, Straus and Giroux.

Sowards, S. K., & Renegar, V. R. (2006). Reconceptualizing rhetorical activism in contemporary feminist contexts. *The Howard Journal of Communications, 17*(1), 57–74. doi:10.1080/10646170500487996

Stache, L. C. (2015). Advocacy and political potential at the convergence of hashtag activism and commerce. *Feminist Media Studies, 15*(1), 162–164. doi:10.1080/14680777.2015.987429

Stathakopoulos, D. (2011). *Τα Ημαρτημένα.* Retrieved April 20, 2012, from http://www.antibaro.gr/article/4025

Stathis, P. (2011). *Στα όρια επιστήμης και πολιτικής: το 1821 στον Σκάϊ.* Retrieved April 18, 2012, from http://enthemata. wordpress.com/2011/03/13/stathis/

Statista. (2015). *Number of monthly active Facebook users worldwide as of 1st quarter 2015 (in millions).* Retrieved July 28, 2015 from http://www.statista.com/statistics/264810/number-of-monthly-active-facebook-users-worldwide/

Stavrositu, C., & Sundar, S. S. (2012). Does Blogging Empower Women? Exploring the Role of Agency and Community. *Journal of Computer-Mediated Communication, 17*(4), 369–386. doi:10.1111/j.1083-6101.2012.01587.x

Steffgen, G., Konig, A., Pfetsch, J., & Melzer, A. (2011). Are cyberbullies less empathic? Adolescents' cyberbullying behavior and empathic responsiveness. *Cyberpsychology, Behavior, and Social Networking, 14*(11), 643–648. doi:10.1089/ cyber.2010.0445 PMID:21554126

Steiner, P. (1993). On the Internet, nobody knows you're a dog [cartoon]. *The New Yorker,69*(20), 61.

Steiner, L. (2014). Feminist media theory. In R. S. Fortner & M. Fackler (Eds.), *The Handbook of Media and Mass Communication Theory* (pp. 359–379). Hoboken, NJ: Wiley-Blackwell. doi:10.1002/9781118591178.ch20

Steiner, L., & Eckert, S. (in press). The potential of feminist Twitter. In R. Lind (Ed.), *Race and gender in electronic media: Challenges and opportunities.* New York, NY: Routledge.

Stockmann, D. (2014). *Media commercialization and authoritarian rule in China.* Cambridge University Press.

Stockmann, D., & Gallagher, M. (2011). Remote control: How the media sustains authoritarian rule in China. *Comparative Political Studies, 44*(4), 436–467. doi:10.1177/0010414010394773

Stoner, M. R. (1989). Understanding social movementL rhetoric of social intervention. *The Speech Communication Annual, 3*, 298–310.

Strauss, A., & Corbin, J. (1990). *Basics of Qualitative Research: Grounded Theory Procedures and Techniques.* Newbury Park, CA: Sage.

Stuart, K. (2014, December 3). Zoe Quinn: All gamergate has done is ruin people's lives. *The Guardian*. Retrieved June 28, 2015, from http://www.theguardian.com/technology/2014/dec/03/zoe-quinn-gamergate-interview

Sullivan, G. (2014, August 22). Study: More women than teenage boys are gamers. *The Washington Post*. Retrieved June 28, 2015, from http://www.washingtonpost.com/news/morning-mix/wp/2014/08/22/adult-women-gamers-outnumber-teenage-boys/

Sullivan, G. (2014, September 25). *Social network Ello gets boost after Facebook boots drag queens*. Retrieved from http://www.washingtonpost.com/news/morning-mix/wp/2014/09/25/social-network-ello-gets-boost-after-facebook-boots-drag-queens/

Sullivan, J. (2012). A tale of two microblogs in China. *Media Culture & Society*, 774–783.

Szabla, C. (2007). *George Finlay's Greece: Between East and West*. (Senior Thesis). Department of History, Columbia University, New York, NY.

Taggard, W., Turkle, S., & Kidd, C. D. (2005). An Interactive Robot in a Nursing Home: Preliminary Remarks. In Proceedings of CogSci Wrokshop on Android Science. Academic Press.

Takaki, R. (2008). *A Different Mirror: A History of Multicultural America*. Little, Brown, and Company.

Tambaki, A. (2004). Η ιστοριογραφική οπτική του μεταφραστικού εγχειρήματος: από τη 'μετακένωση' στη διαπολιτισμικότητα; In Ιστοριογραφία της νεότερης και σύγχρονης Ελλάδας 1833-2002, (vol. A, pp. 419-431). Athens: Κέντρο Νεοελληνικών Ερευνών-ΕΙΕ.

Tangen, D., & Campbell, M. (2010). Cyberbullying prevention: One primary school's approach. *Australian Journal of Guidance & Counselling*, 20(02), 225–234. doi:10.1375/ajgc.20.2.225

Thames, R. H. (2012). The Meaning of the Motivorum's Motto: "Ad bellum purificandum" to "Tendebantque manus ripae ulterioris amore". *K.B Journal: The Journal of the Kenneth Burke Society, 8*(1). Retrieved July 4, 2015, from http://kbjournal.org/thames_motivorum_motto

Thames, R. H. (2007). The Gordian Not: Untangling the Motivorum. *K. B. Journal. The Journal of the Kenneth Burke Society, 3*(2). Retrieved from http://kbjournal.org/thames1

The Comedy Central Roast of Justin Bieber. (2015). Comedy Central.

The CrossWire Bible Society. (2011, September 8). *PocketSword: an iPhone Bible Study app*. Retrieved July 5, 2015, from Crosswire.org: http://www.crosswire.org/pocketsword/PocketSword/PocketSword/PocketSword.html

The CrossWire Bible Society. (n.d.). Bringing the Gospel to a New Generation. *CrossWire*. Retrieved January 26, 2014, from CrossWire: http://www.crosswire.org/

The CrossWire Bible Society. (n.d.). *The CrossWire Bible Society*. Retrieved July 5, 2015, from About: http://crosswire.org/about/

Theotokas, N., & Kotaridis, N. (2006). *Η Οικονομία της Βίας. Παραδοσιακές και Νεωτερικές Εξουσίες στην Ελλάδα του 19*. Athens: Vivliorama.

Thrift, S. C. (2014). #YesAllWomen as feminist meme event. *Feminist Media Studies*, 14(6), 1090–1092. doi:10.1080/14680777.2014.975421

Tiidenberg, K. (2015). Boundaries and conflict in a NSFW community on Tumblr: The meanings and uses of selfies. *New Media & Society*. doi:10.1177/1461444814567984

Toni Morrison. (n.d.). In *TasteKid*. Available: http://www.tastekid.com/like/Toni+Morrison

Topcu, C., Erdur-Baker, O., & Capa, A. Y. (2008). Examination of cyber-bullying experiences among Turkish students from different school types. *Cyberpsychology & Behavior, 11*(6), 644–648. doi:10.1089/cpb.2007.0161 PMID:18783345

Tosh, J. (2008). *Why History Matters*. Palgrave-MacMillan.

Totilo, S. (2014, August 20). From the EIC. *Kotaku*. Retrieved June 28, 2015, from http://kotaku.com/in-recent-days-ive-been-asked-several-times-about-a-pos-1624707346

Totura, C. M. W., MacKinnon-Lewis, C., Gesten, E. L., Gadd, R., Divine, K. P., Dunham, S., & Kamboukos, D. (2009). Bullying and victimization among boys and girls in middle school: The influence of perceived family and school contexts. *The Journal of Early Adolescence, 29*(4), 571–609. doi:10.1177/0272431608324190

Triandafyllidou, A., Gropas, R., & Kouki, H. (2013). *The Greek Crisis and European Modernity*. Palgrave-MacMillan.

Tsukayama, H. (2012, April 23). In online video, minorities find an audience. *The Washington Post*. Retrieved November 11, 2014, from http://www.washingtonpost.com/blogs/faster-forward/post/in-online-video-minorities-find-an-audience/2012/04/23/gIQAQneobT_blog.html

Tuan, M. (1998). *Forever foreigners or honorary whites?: The Asian ethnic experience*. New Brunswick, NJ: Rutgers University Press.

Turkle, S. (2004). *Relational Artifacts* (NSF Grant SES-0115668). NSF.

Turkle, S. (2005a). Relational Artifacts/Children/Elders: The Complexities of CyberCompanions. In *Proceedings of the CogSci Workshop on Android Science*. Academic Press.

Turkle, S. (2005b). *Caring Machines: Relational Artifacts for the Elderly*. Keynote AAAI Workshop "Caring Machines", Washington, DC.

Turkle, S. (1995). *Life on the Screen*. New York: Simon & Schuster.

Turkle, S. (2004). Whither Psychoanalysis in Computer Culture? *Psychoanalytic Psychology, 21*(1), 16–30. doi:10.1037/0736-9735.21.1.16

Turkle, S. (2005). *The Second Self: Computers and the Human Spirit*. Cambridge, MA: MIT Press.

Turner, G. (2010). Approaching celebrity studies. *Celebrity Studies, 1*(1), 11-20.

Twitter. (2012). *Twitter turns six*. Retrieved July 28, 2015 from https://blog.twitter.com/2012/twitter-turns-six

Tziovas, D. (2001). Beyond the Acropolis: Rethinking Neohellenism. *Journal of Modern Greek Studies, 19*(2), 189–220.

US Refugee Program: Final FY2009 Admission Statistics. (2009, October). Retrieved April 16, 2011, from Cultural Orientation Resource Center: http://www.cal.org/co/refugee/statistics/final_FY2009.html

Usher, W. (2014, September 10). TFYC discuss #GamerGate, recovering from hacks, 4chan support. *Cinema Blend*. Retrieved June 28, 2015, from http://www.cinemablend.com/games/TFYC-Discuss-GamerGate-Recovering-From-Hacks-4chan-Support-67239.html

van der Goot, J. (2014, September 24). *Ello: A Design Disaster*. Retrieved from https://medium.com/@jvdgoot/ello-a-design-disaster-d53022ab3a62

Van der Tuin, I. (2009). Jumping generations: On second- and third-wave Feminist epistemology. *Australian Feminist Studies, 24*(59), 17–31. doi:10.1080/08164640802645166 van Dijck, J. (2009). Users like you? Theorizing agency in user-generated content. *Media Culture & Society, 31*(1), 41–58. doi:10.1177/0163443708098245

van Dijck, J. (2013). *The Culture of Connectivity*. New York: Oxford University Press. doi:10.1093/acprof:o so/9780199970773.001.0001

Van Uden-Kraan, C., Drossaert, C., Taal, E., Shaw, B., Seydel, E., & van de Laar, M. (2008). Empowering processes and outcomes of participation in online support groups for patients with breast cancer, arthritis, or fibromyalgia. *Qualitative Health Research, 18*(3), 405–417. doi:10.1177/1049732307313429 PMID:18235163

Vandebosch, H., & van Cleemput, K. (2008). Defining cyberbullying: A qualitative research into the perceptions of youngsters. *Cyberpsychology & Behavior, 11*(4), 499–503. doi:10.1089/cpb.2007.0042 PMID:18721100

Vanderhoef, J. (2013). Casual Threats: The Feminization of Casual Video Games. *Ada: A Journal of Gender, New Media, and Technology*. Retrieved June 28, 2015, from http://adanewmedia.org/2013/06/issue2-vanderhoef/

Veremis, T. (2011a, February 6). Περί Εθνικισμού. *I Kathimerini Newspaper*.

Veremis, T. (2011b, February 13). Τα μηνύματα που μας διαφεύγουν. *I Kathimerini Newspaper*.

Veremis, Th. (1982). Κράτος και Έθνος στην Ελλάδα: 1821-1912. In D. Tsaousis (Ed.), *Ελληνισμός και Ελληνικότητα. Ιδεολογικοί και Βιωματικοί Άξονες της Νεοελληνικής Κοινωνίας* (pp. 59–67). Athens: Estia.

Vivienne, S., & Burgess, J. (2012). The Digital Storyteller's Stage: Queer Everyday Activists Negotiating Privacy and Publicness. *Journal of Broadcasting & Electronic Media, 56*(3), 362–377. doi:10.1080/08838151.2012.705194

Wade, L. (2012, November 20). *The Gender Politics of Doll House*. [Web log post]. Retrieved April 1, 2013, from http://jezebel.com/5962277/the-gender-politics-of-the-dollhouse

Wade, A., & Beran, T. (2011). Cyberbullying: The new era of bullying. *Canadian Journal of School Psychology, 26*(1), 44–61. doi:10.1177/0829573510396318

Wagner, P. (1994). *A Sociology of Modernity. Liberty and Discipline*. London: Routledge.

Walby, S. (2011). *The future of feminism*. Malden, MA: Polity Press.

Walker, D., & Myrick, F. (2006). Grounded theory: An exploration of process and procedure. *Qualitative Health Research, 16*(4), 547–559. doi:10.1177/1049732305285972 PMID:16513996

Wang, K. Y., Atkin, D. J., & Lau, T. (2014). Media versus individual frames and horizontal knowledge gaps: A study of the 2010 healthcare reform debate online. *Electronic News, 8*(1), 30–48.

Wang, W. Y. (2013). Weibo, framing, and media practices in China. *Journal of Chinese Political Science, 18*(4), 375–388. doi:10.1007/s11366-013-9261-3

Wasserman, S. (2012). *The Amazon Effect*. Retrieved 6 2, 2012, from The Nation: http://www.thenation.com/article/168125/amazon-effect

Wazny, K. M. (2010). Feminist Communities Online: What it means to be a Jezebel. *B Sides, 8*. Retrieved from http://ir.uiowa.edu/cgi/viewcontent.cgi?article=1012&context=bsides

Wellman, B. (1997). An electronic group is virtually a social network. In S. Kiesler (Ed.), Culture of the Internet (pp. 179–205). Mahwah, NJ: Erlbaum.

West, L. (2012). *What the Hell is Black Friday for?"* [Web log post]. Retrieved April 1, 2013, from http://jezebel.com/5961936/in-which-i-try-to-figure-out-what-the-fuck-black-friday-is-for

Weymans, W. (2004). Michael de Certeau and the Limits of Historical Representation. *History and Theory, 43*(2), 161–178.

White, M. (2010). Clicktivism is ruining leftist activism. *The Guardian.* Retrieved July 27, 2015, from http://www.theguardian.com/commentisfree/2010/aug/12/clicktivism-ruining-leftist-activism

White, J. F. (1989). *Protestant Worship.* Westminster, UK: John Knox Press.

Whitman, W. (1993). *Leaves of Grass.* New York: Random House.

Wikipedia. (2015a). *Jewish Internet Defense Force.* Retrieved June 28, 2015, from http://en.wikipedia.org/wiki/Jewish_Internet_Defense_Force

Wikipedia. (2015b). *The Fine Young Capitalists.* Retrieved June 28, 2015, from http://en.wikipedia.org/wiki/The_Fine_Young_Capitalists

Wilkinson, S. (2001). Breast cancer: Feminism, representations and resistance—a commentary on Dorthy Broom's 'Reading breast cancer.'. *Health, 5*(2), 269–277. doi:10.1177/136345930100500207

Williams, D. (2006). A brief social history of game play. In P. Vorderer & J. Bryant (Eds.), *Playing video games* (pp. 197–212). Mahwah, NJ: Erlbaum. Retrieved June 28, 2015, from http://is.muni.cz/el/1421/podzim2013/IM082/um/WilliamsSocHist.pdf

Williams, D. (2003). The Video Game Lightning Rod. *Information Communication and Society, 6*(4), 523–550. doi:10.1080/1369118032000163240

Williams, K. R., & Guerra, N. G. (2007). Prevalence and predictors of Internet bullying. *The Journal of Adolescent Health, 41*(6), s14–s21. doi:10.1016/j.jadohealth.2007.08.018 PMID:18047941

Williams, S. (2015). Digital defense: Black feminists resist violence with hashtag activism. *Feminist Media Studies, 15*(2), 341–343. doi:10.1080/14680777.2015.1008744

Wilson, D. (2014, August 28). A guide to ending 'gamers'. *Gamasutra.* Retrieved June 28, 2015, from http://gamasutra.com/blogs/DevinWilson/20140828/224450/A_Guide_to_Ending_quotGamersquot.php

Wingfield, N. (2014). Feminist critics of video games facing threats in 'GamerGate' campaign. *New York Times.* Retrieved October 8, 2015 from http://www.nytimes.com/2014/10/16/technology/gamergate-women-video-game-threats-anita-sarkeesian.html?_r=0

Winograd, M., & Hais, M. (2011). *Millenial Momentum: How a New Generation Is Remaking America.* Rutgers University Press.

Woodruffe-Burton, H. (1998). Private desires, public display: Consumption, postmodernism and fashion's "new man". *International Journal of Retail & Distribution Management, 26*(8), 301–310. doi:10.1108/09590559810231760

Wright, M. F. (2015a). Cyber victimization and adjustment difficulties: The mediation of Chinese and American adolescents' digital technology usage. *CyberPsychology: Journal of Psychosocial Research in Cyberspace, 1*(1), article 1. Retrieved from: http://cyberpsychology.eu/view.php?cisloclanku=2015051102&article=1

Wright, K. B. (1997). Shared ideology in Alcoholics Anonymous: A grounded theory approach. *Journal of Health Communication, 2*(2), 83–99. doi:10.1080/108107397127806 PMID:10977242

Wright, M. F. (2014a). Cyber victimization and perceived stress: Linkages to late adolescents' cyber aggression and psychological functioning. *Youth & Society.*

Wright, M. F. (2014b). Predictors of anonymous cyber aggression: The role of adolescents' beliefs about anonymity, aggression, and the permanency of digital content. *Cyberpsychology, Behavior, and Social Networking, 17*(7), 431–438. doi:10.1089/cyber.2013.0457 PMID:24724731

Wright, M. F. (2014c). Longitudinal investigation of the associations between adolescents' popularity and cyber social behaviors. *Journal of School Violence, 13*(3), 291–314. doi:10.1080/15388220.2013.849201

Wright, M. F. (2015b). The role of the media and the cyber context in adolescents' popularity. In P. Lorentz, D. Smahel, M. Metykova, & M. F. Wright (Eds.), *Living in the Digital Age: Self-Presentation, Networking, Playing, and Participation in Politics*. Brno: Muni Press.

Wright, M. F. (in press). Adolescents' cyber aggression perpetration and cyber victimization: The longitudinal associations with school functioning. *Social Psychology of Education*.

Wright, M. F. (in press). Understanding gender differences in cyber aggression: The role of technology, behaviors, masculinity, and femininity. *Sex Roles*.

Wright, M. F., Kamble, S., Lei, K., Li, Z., Aoyama, I., & Shruti, S. (2015). Peer attachment and cyberbullying involvement among Chinese, Indian, and Japanese adolescents. *Societies, 5*(2), 339–353. doi:10.3390/soc5020339

Wright, M. F., & Li, Y. (2012). Kicking the digital dog: A longitudinal investigation of young adults' victimization and cyber-displaced aggression. *Cyberpsychology, Behavior, and Social Networking, 15*(9), 448–454. doi:10.1089/cyber.2012.0061 PMID:22974350

Wright, M. F., & Li, Y. (2013a). Normative beliefs about aggression and cyber aggression among young adults: A longitudinal investigation. *Aggressive Behavior, 39*(3), 161–170. doi:10.1002/ab.21470 PMID:23440595

Wright, M. F., & Li, Y. (2013b). The association between cyber victimization and subsequent cyber aggression: The moderating effect of peer rejection. *Journal of Youth and Adolescence, 42*(5), 662–674. doi:10.1007/s10964-012-9903-3 PMID:23299177

Write, D. (2009). *The Six Perfections: Buddhism and the Cultivation of Character*. New York: Oxford University Press.

Writers Guild of America. (2015, March 3). *News and events*. Retrieved June 10, 2015, from http://www.wga.org/uploadedFiles/who_we_are/tvstaffingbrief2015.pdf

Wu, B. (2015, February 11). I'm Brianna Wu, And I'm Risking My Life Standing Up To Gamergate. *Bustle*. Retrieved June 28, 2015, from http://www.bustle.com/articles/63466-im-brianna-wu-and-im-risking-my-life-standing-up-to-gamergate

Xenakis, S. (2013). Normative Hybridity in Contemporary Greece: Beyond "Modernizers" and "Underdogs" in Socio-Political Discourse and Practice. *Journal of Modern Greek Studies, 31*(2), 171–192.

Xu, Y. (2012). Understanding netizen discourse in China: Formation, genres, and values. *China Media Research, 8*(1).

Yang, H. (2014). Young people's friendship and love relationships and technology: New practices of intimacy and rethinking Feminism. *Asian Journal of Women's Studies, 20*(1), 93–124. doi:10.1080/12259276.2014.11666174

Ybarra, M. L., Diener-West, M., & Leaf, P. (2007). Examining the overlap in internet harassment and school bullying: Implications for school intervention. *The Journal of Adolescent Health, 1*(6), 42–50. doi:10.1016/j.jadohealth.2007.09.004 PMID:18047944

Ybarra, M. L., & Mitchell, K. J. (2004). Online aggressor/targets, aggressors, and targets: A comparison of associated youth characteristics. *Journal of Child Psychology and Psychiatry, and Allied Disciplines, 45*(7), 1308–1316. doi:10.1111/j.1469-7610.2004.00328.x PMID:15335350

Yiannopoulos, M. (2014, September 1). Feminist bullies tearing the video game industry apart. *Breitbart*. Retrieved June 28, 2015, from http://www.breitbart.com/london/2014/09/01/lying-greedy-promiscuous-feminist-bullies-are-tearing-the-video-game-industry-apart/

Yin, R. K. (1984). *Case Study Research: Design and Methods*. Beverly Hill, CA: Sage Publication.

Yoo, W., Chih, M.-Y., Kown, M.-W., Yang, J., Cho, E., McLaughlin, B., & Gustafson, D. et al. (2012). Predictors of the change in the expression of emotional support within an online breast cancer support group: A longitudinal study. *Patient Education and Counseling*, *90*(1), 88–95. doi:10.1016/j.pec.2012.10.001 PMID:23122429

York, J. C. (2015, March 6). What to Facebook may be a 'fake name' may be the expression of your authentic self. *The Guardian*. Retrieved from http://www.theguardian.com/technology/2015/mar/06/facebook-internet-fake-name-authentic-self

Young, A. A. (2010). New life for an old concept: Frame analysis and the reinvigoration of studies in culture and poverty. *The Annals of the American Academy of Political and Social Science*, *629*(1), 53–74. doi:10.1177/0002716209357145 PMID:24489382

Your life your rules . (2011). Retrieved February 22, 2013, from http://www.youtube.com/watch?v=egseZdgVo0k

Yuval-Davis, N. (2006). Intersectionality and Feminist politics. *European Journal of Women's Studies*, *13*(3), 193–209. doi:10.1177/1350506806065752

Zee. (2008, October 28). TasteKid Lets You Find Stuff Similar to Stuff You Like. *TNW*. Retrieved from http://thenextweb.com/2008/10/28/tastekid-lets-you-find-stuff-similar-to-stuff-you-like/

Zhao, Y. (2013, September 23). *Anti-graft watchdog told to convey results*. Retrieved from China Daily: http://www.chinadaily.com.cn/china/2013-

Zilberstein, K. (2013). Technology, Relationships and Culture: Clinical and Theoretical Implications. *Clinical Social Work Journal*, *41*(3).

Zoo, N. (2014). *Introduction to the Chinese games markets*. Retrieved from New Zoo: http://www.proelios.com/wp-content/uploads/2014/03/China-Games-Market-Newzoo-Report-2014.pdf

About the Contributors

Alison N. Novak is an Assistant Professor of Public Relations and Advertising at Rowan University. She is a graduate of Drexel University's program in Communication, Culture, and Media. Her work looks at the journalistic treatment of age, gender, and engagement.

Imaani Jamillah El-Burki is a media scholar whose work investigates intersectionality. Her research examines the ways in which media representations of various social groups become visual, textual and linguistic expressions of both dominant and peripheral definitions of difference. She further investigates the relationship between media representation, media framing and individual and collective identity; social policy; and existing social hierarchies.

* * *

Jannatul Akmam is a former student of the Department of English, Jahangirnagar University, Dhaka, Bangladesh. On completion of her BA (Honors) in English Literature and Language, and MA in English Literature, she joined Jamea Ahmadia Sunnia Mohila Madrasah. She is also guest-lecturing at Chittagong Government Women's College under National University of Bangladesh. Her area of interest involves Gender Studies, Cultural Studies and Media Studies.

Eleni Andriakaina has taught at the Aristoteleion University of Thessaloniki and the University of Crete, and since 2012 she has been teaching as Assistant Professor at Panteion University. Her latest book is Beyond Positivism and Postmodernism. Essays in Historical Sociology (Opportuna, Patras 2009/ in Greek). Her recent publications include the article "The Promise of the 1821 Revolution and the Suffering Body. Some thoughts on Modernisation and Anti-intellectualism", Synthesis 6 (2013). Her research interests lie in three areas: The Postmodernist Challenge to History; Memory, Nationalism & Greek Revolution; Sociology of Intellectuals.

Benjamin J. Cline's research focuses on viewing contemporary communication situations through a classical, humanities-based, lens. He has taught in several different institutions throughout the United States and now serves as Assistant Professor of Speech and Communication at Western New Mexico University in Silver City, NM. He lives in Silver City with his wife, daughter, two dogs, and a cat.

Stine Eckert is an Assistant Professor in the Department of Communication at Wayne State University and Vice-Chair of the Feminist Scholarship Division of the International Communication Association. Her Ph.D. is from the University of Maryland.

David H. Gustafson (PhD, University of Michigan) is a Research Professor of Industrial and Systems Engineering, and Director of the Center for Health Enhancement Systems Studies, at the University of Wisconsin-Madison.

Helen K. Ho received her Ph.D. in Communication Studies from the University of Michigan and is currently an Assistant Professor of Communication Studies at Saint Mary's College in Notre Dame, IN. She has teaching and scholarly interests in race/ethnicity, gender, and popular culture.

Nafisa Huq is an English major student, completed graduation in 2010 and post graduation in 2011 from Jahangirnagar University, Dhaka, Bangladesh. She was a grantee of Erasmus Mundus Scholarship in 2012 and did her 2nd Masters in Aristotle University of Thessaloniki, Greece. She is currently working in Eastern University, a pioneer private university of Bangladesh. Her area of interest involves Gender Studies, English Literature, and Modern Drama.

Shawnika Hull (PhD, University of Pennsylvania) is an Assistant Professor in the Department of Prevention and Community Health, Milken Institute School of Public Health, at George Washington University.

Md. Shafiqul Islam is a Lecturer in English at United International University, Dhaka, Bangladesh. He has completed his MA in Literatures in English and Cultural Studies and BA (Honors) in English with distinction from the Department of English, Jahangirnagar University. His areas of research interest include postmodernism, women and gender, cultural studies, ecocriticism and science fiction literature. He can be reached through email at sabuj.si@gmail.com and through his blog at www.shafiqul-islam.com.

Dustin Kidd is Associate Professor of Sociology at Temple University and the author of Legislating Creativity (Routledge 2010) and Pop Culture Freaks (Westview 2014).

Bryan McLaughlin (Ph.D University of Wisconsin, Madison) is an Assistant Professor in the Department of Advertising, College of Media and Communication, at Texas Tech University.

Nusrat Zahan Mou has completed her M.A in Literature in English and Cultural Studies. She is currently working as a Lecturer at IUBAT. Her research interest includes Gender Studies, Cultural Studies, Postcolonial Literature and others.

Kang Namkoong (PhD, University of Wisconsin, Madison) is an Assistant Professor in the Department of Community and Leadership Development at the University of Kentucky.

Greg Niedt is a Ph.D. candidate at Drexel University in the Communication, Culture, and Media program, with a background in Sociolinguistics (M.A., Georgetown University). His research interests include critically examining intercultural communication in urban neighborhoods, and how media allow for the performance of radical identity through text.

Veronika Novoselova is a PhD Candidate in Gender, Feminist and Women's Studies at York University in Toronto. Her doctoral research project explores the problem of online harassment on participatory media platforms. Her research interests include gender studies, digital media and online interactional dynamics.

Rachel R. Reynolds is an Associate Professor in the Department of Anthropology. She specializes in semiotics and critical discourse analysis, language and globalization, and African migration.

Julia C. Richmond is a Ph.D. candidate at Drexel University in the Communication, Culture, and Media program. She received her B.A. from Temple University in Sociology. Her work explores the mediated intersection of humor and politics.

Dhavan Shah (PhD, University of Minnesota) is Maier-Bascom professor in the School of Journalism and Mass Communication at the University of Wisconsin.

Gilbert Ndi Shang is a former DAAD scholar and a literary critic from Cameroon. He completed his doctoral studies in Comparative Literature from the Bayreuth International Graduate School of African Studies (BIGSAS), University of Bayreuth, Germany. He has published several articles in international literary journals. The geographical scope of his research covers parts of Africa and Latin America. His research interests include: literature and politics, politics/poetics of the body, violence in literature and visual culture. Presently he is a Post-doc fellow in the University of Bayreuth.

Linda Steiner is Professor of Journalism at the University of Maryland, and editor of Journalism & Mass Communication Monographs. Her Ph.D. is from the University of Illinois at Urbana-Champaign.

Amanda Turner is a doctoral student in Sociology at Temple University. She received her AA from Edmonds Community College in 2006, her BA in Sociology from Western Washington University in 2008, and her MA in Sociology from Temple University in 2013. She has taught Popular Culture, Gender in America, as well as Statistics and Research Methods labs. Her research areas are culture and gender in the context of video game play. Her past work has included connecting textual analyses of video game content to interviews and focus groups with players of The Sims 2, Halo: Reach, and Assassin's Creed: Brotherhood in order to understand player experience and meaning making. Her dissertation work will continue this research while expanding to include analyses of video game production and the social world. She has recently published on the relationship between adolescent video game play and STEM major choice in Emerald Studies in Media and Communication: Communication and Information Technologies Annual Doing and Being Digital: Mediated Childhoods.

Jacqueline Wigfall writes about literature, culture, and identity. She holds a Ph.D. in English from Stanford University and an M.A.T. from Duke University.

Michelle F. Wright is a postdoctoral research fellow at Masaryk University. Her research interests include the contextual factors, such as familial and cultural, which influence children's and adolescents' aggression and victimization as well as their pursuit, maintenance, and achievement of peer status. She also has an interest in peer rejection and unpopularity and how such statuses relate to insecurity with one's peer standing, aggression, and victimization.

Yu Zhang teaches at New York Institute of Technology (China Program).

Index

Information Resources Management Association

Become an IRMA Member

Members of the **Information Resources Management Association (IRMA)** understand the importance of community within their field of study. The Information Resources Management Association is an ideal venue through which professionals, students, and academicians can convene and share the latest industry innovations and scholarly research that is changing the field of information science and technology. Become a member today and enjoy the benefits of membership as well as the opportunity to collaborate and network with fellow experts in the field.

IRMA Membership Benefits:

- **One FREE Journal Subscription**
- **30% Off Additional Journal Subscriptions**
- **20% Off Book Purchases**
- Updates on the latest events and research on Information Resources Management through the IRMA-L listserv.
- Updates on new open access and downloadable content added to Research IRM.
- A copy of the Information Technology Management Newsletter twice a year.
- A certificate of membership.

IRMA Membership $195

Scan code to visit irma-international.org and begin by selecting your free journal subscription.

Membership is good for one full year.

Printed in the United States
By Bookmasters